A HISTORY
OF
READING
IN THE WEST

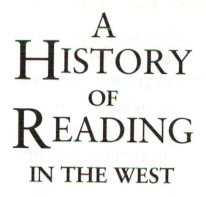

A HISTORY OF READING

IN THE WEST

EDITED BY
GUGLIELMO CAVALLO AND
ROGER CHARTIER

Translated by
Lydia G. Cochrane

UNIVERSITY OF
MASSACHUSETTS PRESS
AMHERST

First published in France as *Histoire de la lecture dans le monde occidental*, edited by Guglielmo Cavallo and Roger Chartier, © Giuseppe Laterza & Figli Spa, Rome-Bari, 1995, and Éditions du Seuil, Paris, March 1997.

English-language edition © 1999 by Polity Press. First published in 1999 by Polity Press in association with Blackwell Publishers Ltd.

First published in the United States of America in 1999 by the University of Massachusetts Press, Box 429, Amherst, MA 01004.

Library of Congress Cataloging-in-Publication Data

Storia della lettura nel mondo occidentale. English
   A history of reading in the West/edited by Guglielmo Cavallo and Roger Chartier; translated by Lydia G. Cochrane.
      p.   cm. – (Studies in print culture and the history of the book)
   Includes bibliographical reference (p.   ) and index.
   ISBN 1-55849-213-5 (alk. paper)
   1. Books and reading–Europe–History.   2. Written communication–Europe–History.   I. Cavallo, Guglielmo.   II. Chartier, Roger, 1945–   .
III. Cochrane, Lydia G.   IV. Title.   V. Series.
Z1003.3.E85S7613   1999
028'.9'094–dc21   99-22447
                                                               CIP

This book is published with the support and cooperation of the University of Massachusetts Boston.

Contents

Contents   vii

Publisher's Note

The introduction and chapters 1, 2, 4, 6, 8, 9, 10, 13 and the bibliography were translated from the Italian by Lydia G. Cochrane. Chapter 11 was translated by Andrew Winnard. Chapters 3, 5, 7 and 12 were supplied in English by their authors.

The publishers wish to thank the Cultural Service of the French Embassy in London for their support.

Introduction

❧

Guglielmo Cavallo and Roger Chartier

> Far from being writers – founders of their own place, heirs of the peasants of earlier ages now working on the soil of language, diggers of wells and builders of houses, readers are travellers; they move across lands belonging to someone else, like nomads poaching their way across fields they did not write, despoiling the wealth of Egypt to enjoy it themselves. Writing accumulates, stocks up, resists time by the establishment of a place and multiplies its production through the expansionism of reproduction. Reading takes no measure against the erosion of time (one forgets oneself *and* also forgets), it does not keep what it acquires, or it does so poorly, and each of the places through which it passes is a repetition of the lost paradise.[1]

In this passage Michel de Certeau establishes a fundamental distinction between a written mark – something fixed, lasting, preserving – and its readings, which are always of the order of the ephemeral, plurality and invention. In doing so he also defines the basic aim of the present book, which has been written by several hands, and is based on two essential ideas. The first is that reading is not already inscribed in the text; that it is not true that there is no imaginable gap between the meaning assigned to it (by the author of the text or its editor, by criticism, by tradition, etc.) and the use or interpretation that readers may make of it. The second recognizes that a text exists only because a reader gives it meaning.

> Whether it is a question of newspapers or Proust, the text has a meaning only through its readers; it changes along with them; it is ordered in accord with codes of perception that it does not control. It becomes a text only in

its relation to the exteriority of the reader, by an interplay of implications and ruses between two sorts of 'expectation' in combination: the expectation that organizes a *readable* space (a literality), and one that organizes a procedure necessary for the *actualization* of the work (a reading).[2]

The task of the historians who have contributed to this volume has thus been to reconstruct, in their differences and their singularities, the various ways of reading that have been characteristic of Western societies since classical antiquity.

Such a venture requires paying close attention to how the encounter between the 'world of the text' and the 'world of the reader' (as Paul Ricoeur calls them) operates.[3] If we are to reconstruct that process in its historical dimensions, we have to begin by considering how the meanings of texts depend on the forms and the circumstances through which they are received and appropriated by their readers or listeners. Readers are never faced with an abstract, ideal text detached from everything material: they manipulate objects; they listen to words whose modalities govern the way they read or listen, but in the process also govern ways of comprehending the text. In contrast to a purely semantic definition of the text – which has permeated not only all the variants of structuralist criticism, but also the sorts of literary theory keenest on reconstructing the reception of works – we need to hold that forms produce meanings, and that a text is invested with a new meaning and a different status with every change in the support that makes it available to reading. Any history of the practices of reading is thus necessarily a history of both written objects and the testimonies left by their readers.

We also have to accept the notion that reading is a practice that is always realized in specific acts, places and habits. Unlike the phenomenological approach that considers reading as an anthropological invariant and ignores its concrete modalities, we must identify the specific distinctive traits of communities of readers, reading traditions and ways of reading.

This approach requires that we recognize the existence of several sorts of contrasts. The first of these is among degrees of reading competence. The basic but oversimplified gap between the literate and the illiterate does not exhaust differences in people's relation to the written word. All those who can read texts do not read them in the same manner, and in every age there is an enormous difference between the most virtuosic and the least skilled readers. There is just as much difference, from one community of readers to another, among the norms and conventions of reading that define the legitimate uses of the book, manners of reading, instruments and interpretive procedures. Finally, there is a great disparity in the very different sets of expectations and interests that different groups of readers invest in the practice of reading. Questions of practice such as these determine how texts can be read, and read differently, by readers who use different intellectual methods, whose relation to writing is not the same, or who attribute different meanings or values to the seemingly identical act of reading a text.

A comprehensive history of reading and readers must thus consider the historicity of ways of using, comprehending and appropriating texts. It must consider the 'world of the text' as a world of objects, forms and rituals whose conventions and devices bear meaning but also constrain its construction. It must also consider that the 'world of the reader' is made up of what Stanley Fish calls the 'interpretive communities' to which individual readers belong.[4] In its relation to writing, each of these communities displays a shared set of competencies, customs, codes and interests. This means that throughout this book we will be looking at both the physical aspects of texts and their readers' practices.

'New readers ... make new texts, and ... their new meanings are a function of their new forms.'[5] In this statement Donald F. McKenzie neatly defines the two sets of variables – variations in the written forms and in the reading public – that any history intent on reconstructing the shifting and multiple meaning of texts needs to take into consideration. In the present book we have taken McKenzie's lesson to heart in several ways: by identifying the chief contrasts among manners of reading through the long time span; by describing differences in reading practices among various communities of readers within the same society; by focusing on transformations of the forms and codes that affect both the status of text genres and the public for them.

Although our common perspective is firmly inscribed within the tradition of the history of the book, we none the less intend to suggest changes in the traditional questions and methods. For some time now, history of the book has concentrated on measuring book ownership among the various groups that make up a given society. That aim has led – necessarily so – to constructing indexes of cultural difference in order to ascertain, for example, inequalities in book ownership in a given place and at a specific time, to establish a hierarchy among libraries according to the number of books they contain, or to provide a thematic description of collections based on an estimate of how various bibliographical categories are represented in them. In this view of the history of the book, describing reading styles is above all a matter of building series, establishing thresholds and constructing sets of statistics. What it comes down to is noting how social differences translate into cultural terms.

This approach has accumulated information without which it would have been unthinkable to raise further questions or produce the present book. Still, it is insufficient to a history of the practices of reading. First, by implication, that approach postulates that cultural cleavages are necessarily organized according to previously established social differences. Hence it describes differences in reading practice in terms of a priori social contrasts, either on a macroscopic scale of differentiation (the dominant versus the dominated, the élites versus the people) or on a smaller scale (for example, setting up a hierarchy among social groups defined by status, occupation or economic level).

The problem is that cultural differentiation is not necessarily organized according to the one grid of social status as the controlling factor in an unequal distribution of objects or variations in practices. We must reverse this way of looking at the question and begin by noting milieus or communities that share a relation with writing. When we start from the circulation of objects and similarities in practice, rather than from classes or groups, we can recognize the many principles of differentiation that explain cultural variety, such as belonging to a common sort or generation or sharing a religious affiliation, community solidarities or educational or corporative traditions.

Each of the 'communities of interpretation' that we identify in this manner has a relationship to writing established through particular techniques, acts and ways of being. Reading is not a solely abstract intellectual operation; it involves the body, is inscribed within a space, and implies a relationship to oneself or to others. This is why the authors of this book have paid particular attention to ways of reading that have either disappeared in the contemporary world or become marginal. One of these is reading aloud, in its dual function of communicating the written word to those who are unable to decipher writing and reinforcing the interlocking forms of sociability – within the family circle, in convivial social intercourse or in literary discussion among like-minded persons – that make up private life. A history of reading must not be limited to the genealogy of how we now read, in silence and using the eyes alone. Its task is also, perhaps above all, to retrace forgotten gestures and bygone habits. This is an important task: not only does it reveal the remoteness and strangeness of practices that were once common; it also depicts the first, specific status of texts composed for reading styles that are not habitual among today's readers. In the ancient world, in the Middle Ages and as late as the sixteenth and seventeenth centuries, the sort of reading implicit in many texts was oralized (as was their actual reading). The 'readers' of those texts were listeners attentive to a reading voice. The text, addressed to the ear as much as to the eye, played on forms and formulas that adapted writing to the demands of oral performance.

'Whatever they may do, authors do *not* write books. Books are not written at all. They are manufactured by scribes and other artisans, by mechanics and other engineers, and by printing presses and other machines.'[6] Rejecting the notion that the text exists in itself, separate from any material manifestation (an idea elaborated by literature itself that the more quantitatively inclined histories of the book have taken over), we should keep in mind that no text exists outside of the physical support that offers it for reading (or hearing) or outside of the circumstance in which it is read (or heard). Authors do not write books: they write texts that become written objects – manuscripts, inscriptions, print matter or, today, material in a computer file. All these objects are handled, in various ways, by flesh and blood readers whose reading habits vary with time, place and milieu.

That process is all too often forgotten. We have placed it at the centre of a book that seeks to describe, within each of the chronological segments we have chosen, the fundamental changes that transformed reading practices in the Western world and that reached beyond those practices to transform relations with writing. This aim has dictated the organization, both chronological and thematic, of our volume as its thirteen chapters move from the invention of silent reading in ancient Greece to the new practices made possible (or imposed) by the current electronic revolution.

The Greek and Hellenistic World: Diversity in Practice

'Every word [*logos*], when once it is written, is bandied about [lit., rolls; *kulindeitai*], alike among those who understand it and those who have no interest in it, and it knows not to whom to speak or not to speak.'[7] This thought, which Plato puts in the mouth of Socrates in the *Phaedrus*, plays on the verb *kulindein*, 'to roll', which stands for the roll book, metaphorically 'rolling' in all directions as it makes its way to its readers. Its 'speech' (*legein*) can only refer to oral reading, to reading aloud or, more properly, to vocalized reading. Plato continues: 'When ill-treated (*plemmeloumenos*) or unjustly reviled it [the *logos*] always needs its father to help it; for it has no power to protect or help itself.'[8] Here the use of the verb *plemmelein*, literally, 'to play music off key', refers to a reading in which an 'off-key' vocal interpretation – that is, one not consonant with the author's intentions – can distort the meaning, thus offending the written discourse.

This passage from Plato raises (directly or indirectly) other questions basic to the history of reading in the ancient Greek world. Above all, we should think of relations among systems of communication not only in terms of orality/writing but also within orality, which varies according to whether it reflects simple spoken discourse or is a vocalized version of writing, oralized by a reader. Spoken discourse – what Plato called the 'discourse of truth' and thought useful for the cognitive process – chooses its interlocutors and can study their reactions, respond to their questions, and resist their attacks. Written discourse, on the other hand, is like a painting: if asked a question, it cannot respond; the best it can do is repeat itself *ad infinitum*. Writing, inert and circulated by means of a material support, has no idea whom it should address (that is, it does not know whether a given person is capable of understanding it) and whom it should not address (because that person is incapable of receiving it). In short, because writing is circulated without controls, it has no idea who will provide the instrument of a voice or whose reading will bring out a meaning. Every act of reading thus constitutes a different interpretation of the text directly conditioned by the reader. The positive aspect of this (despite Plato's reservations) is that the book enjoys the freedom to 'roll' in all directions; it lends itself to free reading, interpretation and use.

The novelty of a book that bears a written *logos* destined to be read has other implications as well. In Greece from the sixth to the late fifth century BC, the gap was narrowing between a relative scarcity of books and a fairly wide diffusion of literacy and familiarity with reading (at least of official or private inscriptions), perhaps even among the lower levels of urban society. On a more fundamental level though, that disparity affected the very function of the writing of the period. The production of written matter to be exposed for public reading, and especially the typologies of such writings and the forms in which their content was exposed, are part of what defined Athenian democracy from its inception (508/507 BC).

If, as Jesper Svenbro tells us in chapter 1, writing 'may have been put to the service of oral culture ... to further the production of sound, effective words and resounding glory', that function regards written composition in the 'aural' phase (that is, the phase of oral delivery) of Greek text production. This was particularly true of the epic and, more generally, of works in verse, although inscriptions and microtexts inscribed on objects might be put in the same category. Writing (in particular, writing a book) had the quite different function of preserving a text. Ancient Greeks were acutely aware that writing had been 'invented' to give texts a fixed form, thus making it possible to recall them to memory – in practice, to preserve them. We have ancient testimony to poetic, scientific and philosophical works produced for the temples and preserved in them; there is also evidence of the use of an author's *sphregis* or seal to guarantee the textual authenticity of the work. Such seals can be explained only if a book's function is to preserve the written text, rather than simply facilitate reading it aloud (although the existence of seals does not preclude having someone, perhaps the author himself, read the text aloud in public).

The late fifth century BC seems to offer a threshold between a time when the book was almost totally dedicated to fixing and preserving a text and a time when the book was designed to be read.[9] Scenes on Attic vases of the period document the shift from scenes of books being used as school texts, hence used for educational purposes on a fairly high cultural level, to scenes of genuine reading that first present male readers alone but soon show female readers as well. These are not isolated figures; rather, they appear in contexts of entertainment and conversation, a sign that the practice of reading was understood above all as an opportunity for social gatherings. Although purely individual reading was not unknown, it was rare, at least to judge from the few (in fact, very few) remaining iconographic or literary instances.

Another question concerns the modalities of reading aloud, which was the form of reading most widespread throughout antiquity. It has been pointed out that reading aloud derived from a need to make sense out of *scriptio continua*, or writing with no breaks between words, which remained ambiguous and inert unless it was vocalized. There is evidence that silent reading was practised as well, even from extremely ancient times.[10] We shall have to ask, first, to what point the two practices differed if reading *scriptio continua* was its aim and, second, whether the two practices were not always simultaneously present rather than dependent on reading situations alone.

The earliest testimony to silent reading in Euripides and Aristophanes goes back to the late fifth century BC and concerns objects other than the book: a message on a tablet and an oracular response. This evidence is reliable. Still, we might well wonder whether silent book reading was not perhaps practised in particular circumstances. In Aristophanes' *The Frogs*, Dionysus begins a sentence with 'There as, on deck, I'm reading to myself the *Andromeda* (of Euripides, performed in 413)';[11] the protagonist of the *Phaon*, a comedy written by the playwright Plato, a near contemporary of Aristophanes, states 'I want to read (*dielthein*) this book for myself in solitude' (fr. 173, 1–5 Kock). When he is interrupted by another character who asks what he is doing, Dionysus begins to read his book (a treatise on the art of cookery) aloud. We cannot exclude the possibility that the phrase 'for myself' (*pros emauton*) refers to a reading that is both individual and silent, hence to an internal reading voice with which Dionysus addresses himself alone.

Another sort of reading – reading while travelling – was clearly not unknown in ancient Greece. This was in some sense reading for entertainment, so it cannot be counted as reading out of professional obligation, even if in the example above we see Dionysus, a god closely connected to the theatre, both travelling and involved in reading something that relates to his 'profession'. The question is more general, however, since it involves the problem of variation among readers and extended reading practices, a problem that arose when books first circulated. The written *logoi* mentioned in Platonic dialogues are usually philosophical texts that circulated in the milieu of the Academy.[12] Indeed, the first collections of books that we know of (even the first private collections) are professional in nature, as were those of Euripides and Aristotle.

During the same period, however, another model of private book collecting arose. When Socrates asks Euthydemus why he owns so many books, he suggests several possible professional orientations as a reason, the last of which is, 'perhaps a rhapsodist, then?' Socrates adds, 'They tell me you have a complete copy of Homer.'[13] This is, of course, not the case, but Socrates' question has highly significant implications. It is clear from the dialogue (as reported by Xenophon) that Socrates takes it for granted that possession of certain writings (*grammata*) is linked to the exercise of a discipline or profession, be it medicine, astrology, architecture, geometry or the writing and recitation of poetry. Euthydemus rejects that obligatory connection. His only desire is to procure and read as many books as possible – that is, he wants to acquire a library that is not purely professional. Other texts present evidence that seems to go even further. In Euripides' *Erechtheus* the lines 'the lance laid down . . . and the Thracian shield hung up . . . I can unleash the voice of the tablets from which the wise draw fame' (fr. 60 Austin) necessarily refer to reading (aloud) that has no professional implications, although here reading from a tablet is implied, not from a roll. What is more, the book on the culinary art that the playwright Plato mentions tells us that as early as the beginning of the fourth century BC there were some works for general consumption in circulation.

That same fragment from the *Phaon* indicates specific manners of reading.[14] The infinitive of the aorist *dielthein* that Plato uses here indicates reading with utter attention, scrutinizing the text in every detail. It is employed here to comic effect, in contrast to the banality of the modest cookbook the character is reading. The variety of verbs that the Greeks used to indicate reading implies distinct meanings or nuances of meaning, at least in the first phase of their semantic definition. Verbs such as *nemein* or its compounds (*ananemein, epinemein*) indicate reading in the most common sense of 'distributing' the content of the written matter, thus implying vocal reading; *anagignoskein* focuses on reading as the moment of 'recognizing' or 'deciphering' letters and their sequence in syllables, words and phrases. Adverbs and adverbial phrases serve to discriminate between the various levels of that 'recognition': *tacheos* (rapidly), *bradeos* (with difficulty), *ortos* (correctly), *kata syllaben* (one syllable after another). Verbs that use spatial metaphors – *dierchomai* and *diexeimi* – refer to a text that is 'covered' or attentively 'gone through from beginning to end', hence studied in depth.

It seems to be the case that from their beginning in ancient times, reading practices moved from a style of reading as 'distribution of a text', performed by the few who were literate for the many who were illiterate, towards a more widespread reading as direct 'recognition' of letters (on a variety of levels), to arrive (between the fifth and fourth centuries BC) at a reading style capable of reading 'through' a text and permitting attentive consideration, examination and probing of what was being read. Isocrates bears clear witness to the semantic difference between *anagignoskein* and *diexeimi* when he speaks of 'those who read superficially' and 'those who instead read ... through very attentively'. In that same context we see the first appearance of an intermediate form of reading with the verb *patein*, which presents an image of the book continually 'frequented' (or, literally, trampled on), hence read and reread. Was this a form of intensive reading?

If we can judge from the carefully articulated range of expressive possibilities documented in the language, all these considerations show that a variety of reading practices existed in ancient Greece, correlated with different functions and levels of competence. In later times, however, certain verb meanings that had originally been distinct from one another came to be used interchangeably, or else they took on shades of meaning that can be hard to discern.

It is difficult to say whether or not the new, broader uses of written culture in the Hellenistic age (demonstrated above all by the production and utilization of large numbers of documents) contributed not only to more widespread instruction (hence to increased schoolteaching as well), but also to a broader range of reading practices. The documents of some government functionaries (Callimachus, Posidippus) show traces of cultivated reading, but the significance of that fact should not be exaggerated.

What should be stressed, however, is that in the Hellenistic age, although oral forms of reading persisted, the book began to play a highly important role. By then, literature was dependent on writing and the book, which served for the composition, circulation and preservation of works. When Alexandrian philology turned its attention to attributions and to editing, transcribing and commenting on texts, it put into book form (admittedly, books destined for scholarly solitary reading) an entire earlier literature not originally created for book form.[15] In short, Alexandrian philology imposed the concept that a text was a written text, and that access to it was to be had through 'readings' preserved thanks to the book. The library at Alexandria, the archetype of the great Hellenistic libraries,[16] was both 'universal' and 'rational'. It was universal because it was dedicated to the preservation of books of all ages and from the entire known world; it was rational because the books it contained were to be reduced to order and to a system of classification (as demonstrated by the *Pinakes* of Callimachus) that enabled them to be arranged according to author, work and content. That universality and rationality, however, were directly dependent on writings that could be evaluated critically, copied, put into a book, categorized and placed with other books.

If such purposes were to be fulfilled, a more clearly structured support for all texts, both old and new, was needed, and it was provided by rolls, or *volumina*. The external characteristics of the *volumen* meant that it offered standard sizes, and limits were soon established as to the height of the roll and the length of the text. A roll normally contained one 'book' of a multi-book work or one autonomous text, the exact length of which was determined by the literary genre to which it belonged and its structure. Exceptions to this rule were very long texts, which might be subdivided into two or more rolls or 'volumes', and very short texts, which might be grouped together on one roll. Reading was facilitated by arranging the written text in columns, by systems of titles and subtitles, and by a number of devices (*paragraphos, coronis*) that divided one text from another or indicated divisions between the sections of a given text. The reorganization of literary production and the development of book technology served the dual purpose of furthering the creation of great libraries and renewing reading practices.

The great Hellenistic libraries were not reading libraries. They were manifestations of the greatness of the ruling dynasty (the Ptolemies, the Attalids); they were also work-places and professional instruments for a circle of scholars and men of letters. In short, although from a technical point of view the books were arranged for reading, they were accumulated rather than actually read. The model for the Hellenistic libraries remained the book collections of the scientific and philosophical schools, which were reserved to a very small number of masters, pupils and disciples.

Aside from the great libraries whose fame has come down to us through the historical documents, we know little about public libraries in the Hellenistic age. Although doubts have been raised as to whether libraries in gymnasia occupied a specific, designated space,[17] it is clear from archaeological evidence of various sorts that libraries were established in a number of cities of the Hellenistic world. We might well ask, however, what their function was. How many people really had access to them? It seems that the limited public capable of reading did so in private. To judge from the remaining fragments, large and small, of Greco-Egyptian rolls, the repertory of texts seems to have been the traditional one, works of the classical age for the most part. Technical manuals, philological texts and works of literary criticism, for example, also flourished in the Hellenistic age, as did purely practical treatises on such topics as military tactics and agriculture. The latter were perhaps professional references rather than texts offered to the general public. Monumental and sepulchral sculpture shows increasing numbers of figures engaged in reading, and unlike the sculpture of the classical age, these are almost always individual readers, thus giving the impression that a more intimate, private relationship with the book had been established. Reading as an occasion for associating with others in a way unique to the *polis* had shifted to being a way of turning back into oneself in an internal search – a shift that in fact reflects cultural attitudes and currents of thought in Hellenistic civilization.

Still, there are indications that reading was more widespread than it had been in the previous age. Outside the sphere of scholarly institutions, the new role of the book was reflected in a vogue for dedicatory epigrams or sponsors' presentations either addressed to the book or 'spoken' by the book. Just as in the late archaic period the custom of reading aloud had 'animated' inscribed materials (funereal stelae or objects for personal use), so it 'animated' the book, thus indicating a more widespread reception of writing in books. In any event, the book came to have a personality of its own, and it entered into reciprocal relations with its readers, whom it addressed and to whom it lent a voice. In the imperial age, when reading attained its broadest diffusion in the ancient world, the theme of the 'animate' book became popular among Latin authors.[18]

Also in the Hellenic age the author established a closer relation between the book and the reader by facilitating access to the text, particularly when the work was complex and was spread over a number of books. Polybius, for instance, wrote a prologue to Book XI of his *Histories*, because a word from the author 'fixes the attention of those who wish to read the work and stimulates and encourages readers. . . . By this means any matter that we are in search of can be easily found.'[19] Historians usually used a heading to each part of their works to offer a summary of what followed, thus facilitating reading and consultation. This practice continued in later ages, and can even be found in Latin authors such as Ovid, who places cross-references in his works to related topics and to the various phases of publication. In his *Natural History*, Pliny follows his dedicatory letter to Emperor Titus with a summary of the thirty-six books of that work, numbered by book and accompanied by a list of his sources (or 'authorities').

It was hardly a coincidence that a genuine theory of reading came to be established in the Hellenistic age. Thanks in particular to Dionysius Thrax (and following the Sophists and Aristotle), there were manuals of rhetoric and grammatical treatises that imparted theory and provided highly detailed lists of precepts for organizing the expressive qualities of the voice in the act of reading.[20] Without the art of vocal reading, writing was fated to remain a series of incomprehensible marks on papyrus. Every *anagnosis*, or reading, whether individual or in the presence of an audience, must be a *hypokrisis*, an interpretation using voice and gesture to give the best possible rendering in keeping with the literary genre and the author's intentions. Otherwise, the reader risked being thought ridiculous. This theory of reading was in fact derived from the *actio* of oratory, which in turn was connected with theatrical practice. This connection explains why ancient writers searched for a hermeneutic methodology for grasping indications inherent in the text to guide correct reading.

Reading in Rome: New Texts and New Books

Beginning at least with the age of the Scipios (third century BC), and in particular in the later second century BC, Rome took over from the Greek world both the physical characteristics of the literary *volumen* and certain reading practices. In the Roman world before that time the customs of written culture were by and large exclusive to the priestly caste and the nobility. This makes it difficult to imagine that there could have been books other than the *annales maximi* (chronicles compiled by the *pontifex maximus*), the *commentari augurum* (books for the interpretation of augury) and the *libri Sybillini*, or Sybilline books (collections of prophecies), kept in a safe place along with a few other *libri reconditi*. The nobility accumulated archival documents rather than books: accounts of the posts they had filled, for example, or eulogies. This means that we can hardly speak of a practice of reading that went beyond reading inscriptions or expository documents. As society changed in the third to second centuries BC, however, the uses of the book began to spread and expand. Most books were Greek. Comic playwrights, for instance, used Greek works as a source of inspiration for plots and gags, thus for professional purposes. The rise of Latin literature was tied to Greek models, therefore to Greek books.

At first book reading was a practice that was completely private and exclusive to the upper classes. In the second and first centuries BC Greek books arrived in Italy as war booty. In 168 Aemilius Paulus brought back books from Macedonia; in 86 Sulla brought back books from Athens; in 71–70 Lucullus brought books from Pontus. Such books, housed in the dwelling of the conqueror, formed the nucleus of private reading libraries and served as a focus and meeting place for small social groups. Polybius evokes his long-standing friendship with Scipio Aemilianus and Aemilius Paulus when he speaks of books lent and conversations that arose out of such loans; later Cicero drew on the library of Faustus Sulla, the dictator's son, and Cato Uticensis plunged into reading the Stoics in the library that the younger Lucullus had inherited from his father. Following the Hellenistic model, the Roman library was built with a portico and a connecting garden; originally an exclusive and private space, it moved toward becoming a space for living.

During the Empire reading practices took a new turn, thanks in large part to increased literacy. Written culture had a vast circulation in the Greco-Roman world, although it is important to distinguish between one period and another, between Rome and the provinces, among regions, and even within one region, between rural areas and urban centres or among cities. Aside from a broad variety of inscriptions, ranging from official epigraphs to graffiti, there were massive amounts of written matter in circulation. Signs were carried in processions, used as *ex votos*, or brandished in celebration of military victories; polemical or defamatory pamphlets and handbills, some in verse, some in prose, were distributed in public places; there were medals bearing written legends, writings on cloth, calendars, proclamations of grievances, letters and messages, and more. There were also the documents of civil administration, the military and the courts. Written production was immense, but only an extremely limited proportion of it is attested, either directly or indirectly.

A more widespread ability to read and a broader circulation of written matter led to an increased demand for books and a greater use of reading. That demand was met on three levels. Public libraries were created, and private ones enlarged, a move that elicited a flurry of treatises to guide the reader in choosing and acquiring books; new or newly edited texts appeared for the benefit of new groups of readers; a new form of book, the codex, came to be produced and distributed. It not only served the needs of new groups of readers; it also changed reading practices.

We have little information on the function of public libraries as spaces for reading. It is clear that Roman libraries, unlike their Hellenistic counterparts, were not reserved to restricted circles of readers. They were still 'scholarly libraries', however, in the sense that although they were open to anyone, in reality they were frequented by a reading public from the middle-to-high levels of society – that is, roughly the same persons who had access to private libraries. For this reason the increased numbers of public libraries cannot be taken as a clear indication of an increased demand for reading. When such libraries were founded by the *princeps*, they tended to be celebratory monuments designed to preserve his historical memory (indeed, they functioned as archives) and to select and codify the literary patrimony. Some public libraries were even built by private patronage as urban places for cultural entertainment.

The works selected for public libraries might on occasion reflect the censorship of texts that had displeased the power structure. This is what happened to Ovid's works, but their circulation among his contemporaries and their transmission to later generations prove that the public libraries were far from orienting or conditioning readers' choices. Even if certain works were not preserved in public libraries, readers were free to acquire them, have transcriptions made of them, and read them or have them read in private – all activities that encouraged the multiplication of copies of such works, thus enhancing their chances of survival.[21]

The increased number of private libraries undoubtedly reflects an expanded desire to read, and even when libraries were superficial in their culture because they were founded out of personal vanity or with a desire to display the owner's economic power (the collections of uneducated parvenus like Petronius's Trimalchio or Lucian's ignorant book collector spring to mind), they demonstrate that within the sphere of representations of the Greco-Roman world, books and reading were among the pleasures and pursuits of a life of ease. Even Trimalchio opens a *librum* and reads a phrase or two, and Lucian's ignoramus was always to be seen with a book in hand and could read with facility, even if he understood little of what he read. There are treatises of the imperial age, now lost but mentioned in the literature (among others, the *On Knowing Books* of Telephus of Pergamus, *The Choice and Acquisition of Books* of Herennius Byblius and *The Bibliophile* of Damophilos of Bithynia) that were obviously intended to guide the choice of books for putting together a collection. The presence of such works suggests either that book production was sizeable and so much more diversified than in the past that book buyers became confused or that the reading public was not made up exclusively of the élite, but also included less experienced, indecisive readers.

New texts emerged in response to an increased demand for reading matter. This was a complex operation. Again, Ovid offers an example. Thanks to his acute sensitivity to the variety, demands and humours of his readers, Ovid added a third book aimed at women readers to the original first and second books of his *Ars amatoria*. The emancipation of women had made progress in the imperial age, and at least some women had gained entry into the world of the written word, and were able to read the *libellus* that Ovid dedicated to them. The figure of the female reader, vaguely hinted at in Greece of the classical age, truly emerged in imperial Rome. Ovid also refers to books on relatively frivolous topics, such as the rules of social games or hints on entertaining. Although such books circulated among people of a discrete level of instruction and even culture, others were created or published with a broader and less select audience in mind that even included people of very little education or intellectual preparation.

A final response to a wider demand for reading matter was the codex. This new book form slowly replaced the roll, beginning in the second century AD. It became the preferred form for Christian writings, hence for Christian readers. In the early third century, a broader demand for reading (including texts for growing numbers of Christians) brought book production techniques to a turning point. The mechanisms for producing and distributing books that had served the traditional culture of the roll were still linked to servile manpower or fairly costly craft copy shops and to a physical support, papyrus, that was imported from Egypt. A number of factors contributed to the success of the codex, the book 'with pages'. First, the per copy price was less, because a page could be used on both sides; second, it could use parchment (outside Egypt), which could be produced anywhere; third, its more practical format was better adapted to non-professional manufacture, to distribution through new channels, to a reading style freer in its physical movements, and to a form of reading reliant on references and requiring intellectual concentration (Christian reading, juridical reading) that gradually became predominant in late antiquity.

Transformations in the book and transformations in reading practices necessarily went hand in hand.

The Middle Ages: From Monastic Writing to Scholastic Reading

The codex provides the link between reading practices in the ancient world and in the Middle Ages, with one difference, however: despite the fact that the Latin West and the Greek East shared a book typology, the fracture between old and new practices was much sharper in the West. The book continued to occupy a place of central importance in the Byzantine world. 'Tell me, I beg of you, how and when will the end of this world come?' Epiphanius asks his master, St Andrew the Mad. He continues: 'By what signs will the proof come that time is accomplished, and how will our city, the new Jerusalem, pass away? What will happen . . . to the books?' (*PG* III, 854a). This is a clear statement that the book was of primary importance as an instrument of Byzantine civilization. Throughout the Middle Ages, schools – public and private, elementary and advanced – continued to function in the East. Literacy, aided by a continuity in both the central and peripheral bureaucracies, never flagged in lay society; indeed, many who entered religious communities had already learned to read and write outside those institutions. Private reading circles and private libraries persisted. The book was still a commercial commodity produced by craftsman-copyists, but it might also be produced by monks or by individuals who copied books out of love for them. The roll was still widely used, at least for liturgical purposes, although with changes in the ways written matter was disposed on it. It is significant that in the Byzantine world the model for reading that had been formulated many centuries earlier by Dionysius Thrax and had been repeated by his Byzantine commentators persisted unchanged. It stated that whatever the book, the reader's attention should focus on the title of the work, its author, intent, unity, structure and result. This implied a certain order for reading and a meditative probing of its meanings.[22] Byzantium also retained the ancient (later, the Greco-Roman) custom of reading aloud, which brought written discourse closer to spoken, preached and proclaimed discourse, rather than adopting the murmured or silent reading of the Latin medieval West. The ancient, continued heritage of a language of culture and of rhetorical structure (a language that had by that time become rigid, solidified into what has been called the 'cultural archaeology' of Byzantium[23]) provides only a partial explanation of why traditional reading practices persisted in the East. The history of Byzantine reading is a chapter still to be written, and it offers a challenge to historians of written culture.

In the Latin West the break with the past was profound. The reading in literary *otium* of the ancient world, much of which had taken place in gardens and under their surrounding porticos (although city squares and streets also provided places for exposing writings and opportunities to read), was replaced in the early Middle Ages by reading practices that took the confined spaces of churches, monks' cells, refectories, cloisters, religious schools and, on occasion, courts as their setting. Moreover, reading matter was usually limited to Holy Scripture and texts of spiritual edification. Only within ecclesiastical and monastic walls could poems (*carmina*) celebrating books, reading and libraries flourish, which means that such works give us a fair notion of the ways in which reading was represented in the early Middle Ages. Tombstones found a place within those same spaces, and although their formulaic 'O you who read this . . .' perpetuated the ancient, highly codified tradition of the 'appeal to the reader' of a bygone world of high literacy, their inscriptions reached only a limited number of readers.

Another change that occurred in Europe during the early Middle Ages was a shift from reading aloud to silent or murmured reading. A number of things contributed to this change: books were now read above all to gain knowledge of God and to improve the soul's chances of salvation; hence texts were to be comprehended, meditated upon, even memorized. The codex, with its pages that facilitated breaking up the text into sections, made it easier to reread or compare passages, thus aiding meditative reading. Community life in the religious circles in which the act of reading often took place required readers to lower their voices. Both the significance and the function of the book had changed. Although many books were written, thanks to the fact that the labour of transcription was itself considered a form of prayer, 'carried on not with the mouth but with the hands' (Peter the Venerable, *Epist.* 1.20), few books were read. The book was not always made to be read: it served not only to provide a form of pious labour and an instrument of salvation but also to increase patrimonial wealth, and in its most hieratic, precious and monumental forms it became a sign of the sacred and of the holy mysteries.

There were not many persons of high culture like Ratherius, the bishop of Verona who had 'his nose always ... in a book' (*Qualitatis coniectura*, 2). Few books were read, and those few were read only on certain occasions or seasons of the year (in monastic circles, during Lent), which meant that lack of practice hindered the rapid, sure scansion of words and phrases required for vocal reading. All these considerations dictated a silent reading or, at best, a murmured reading like the buzzing of bees. The change in reading style had several direct consequences: words came to be separated on the page as an aid to a reading style that could no longer rely on rhetorical phrase rhythms; graphic conventions, or *litterae notabiliores*, came into use – distinctive writing styles that guided the eye from one portion of the text to another – along with punctuation practices and ways of marking the text designed to aid comprehension (or a particular comprehension) of the text rather than for rhetorical declamation. Malcolm Parkes gives a full description of this entire process in chapter 3.

Just as the ancient world provides instances of silent reading, so the Middle Ages offer examples of vocal reading. Liturgical texts and works of edification were commonly read out loud in church, in the refectories of religious communities, for school exercises and perhaps also in certain forms of individual monastic *lectio*. On occasion even some historical narratives seem to have been destined for reading aloud in public. Although each of the two modes of reading predominated at one time or another, we cannot draw too neat a dichotomy. Moreover, intermediate forms of whispered or murmured reading were always practised, as evidenced by the 'pretty whisper' (*lepido susurro*) with which Apuleius invites his reader to read his *Metamorphoses*, or by the *ruminatio* of monks muttering the words as they read.

The years between the end of the eleventh century and the fourteenth century signal a new direction in the history of reading. Cities were reborn and with them schools, the seat of books. In Europe one can see steadily increasing literacy, a growth of writing at all levels, and greater diversity in the ways and purposes of using books. Writing practices and reading practices, which in the early Middle Ages had remained to some extent separate, now joined forces to function together as an organic and indivisible whole. People read in order to write – notably, in the *compilatio*, the method of composition characteristic of scholasticism. And they wrote to be read.

People read much and in different ways. Reading was no longer aimed at simple comprehension of the literal meaning (*littera*) of writing; that sort of comprehension was only a beginning, after which a reader must pass on to the meaning (*sensus*) of the text, in order to reach the proposition (*sententia*), or doctrine, in its full profundity.[24] Books and reading must be governed by *ratio*: Reason, who debates the uses of books with Joy in Petrarch's *De librorum copia*, castigates the mania for a vain accumulation of volumes, and outlines a theory (and also a history) of reading as a practice that should 'lock' books 'in your mind', not 'in your bookcase'.[25] These were the basic principles of the *lectio* practised by the scholastics and in the universities, a reading model that penetrated writing profoundly, permitted the creation of commentary, and bolstered the allocation of authority.

The book – better, the written page – which had been made for reading, study, commentary and prayer, was adapted to the functions that those activities required. Writing came to be thick with abbreviations to aid more rapid reading; the page was divided into two fairly narrow columns, a move that made each line easier to grasp at a single glance; the text was subdivided into sections to facilitate consultation and understanding. In short, the book was recast as an instrument of intellectual work, as Jacqueline Hamesse tells us in chapter 4. By that time the book was an object to be used: it was a source from which to draw knowledge (or specific bits of knowledge), rather than a depository for things to ruminate (*ruminare*) or simply an object to be kept. When the page was broken up by a complex series of devices, reading could concentrate on particular sections rather than involve the entire text. What had formerly been total, intensive and repetitive reading of a limited number of books gave way to scattered reading of many books.

Moreover, this occurred in an age – the age of scholasticism – characterized by an immense increase in the number of written texts and by a demand for a broad but fragmentary knowledge.

Beginning with the modest devices for subdividing a text or separating one text from another that were known in the early Middle Ages (devices that relied less on specific signs than on ornament and on the chromatic prominence given to initials, distinctive writing styles and borders), we thus move to a genuine system of techniques to aid the reading and consultation of books. These techniques were chiefly aimed at rapid identification of the passage that the reader sought: rubrication, paragraph separation and paragraph signs, chapter titles, an organic but correlated separation of text and commentary, summaries, concordances of terms, indexes and alphabetical analytical tables.

At the same time books began to be organized in new ways. The rise of the mendicant Orders in the thirteenth century brought a new model for a library focused on reading rather than the accumulation and conservation of a patrimony of books. System came to be imposed on the library, centring on a catalogue. No longer a simple inventory, the catalogue became an aid to consultation that noted where books could be found in a given library or even in a given geographical area. Another invention was the *memoriale* to note that a work was on loan. Architecturally, the new library was an oblong hall with benches and reading desks lined up on either side of a central aisle. The volumes available for reading and study were chained to the reading desks. The basic layout of the library resembled that of the Gothic church, a similarity that went beyond architecture to reflect a shared mind-set basic to Gothic civilization. The library emerged from its monastic isolation or from the limited space that a bishop could command in the Romanesque cathedrals to become both urban and spacious. Like the church, which offered images, pointed arches and colours for the benefit of the faithful, the library provided a setting that exposed the book to view and made it available to readers. The defining characteristic of the new library was silence: books were consulted in a silence disturbed only by the clinking of the chains that attached them to the reading desks; silence accompanied the search for an author or a title, which could now be found, arranged in orderly fashion, in a catalogue that could be consulted with no need to ask questions; reading was now silent, because it was completely visual, practised individually in a setting shared with others.

In chapter 5 Paul Saenger outlines the eventual consequences of that sort of individual, visual reading removed from all interferences, and he traces how it influenced ways to use a book, led to the formation of a critical awareness of the written text, and left its mark on the elaboration of thought, devotional practices, dissent and even eroticism. We have reached the threshold of the modern age. Still, the spread of literacy among the laity from the thirteenth to the fourteenth centuries introduced other models for reading besides the scholastic model of the universities. The book in the vernacular was born at that time, and on occasion books were written by reader-consumers themselves.[26] Although readers who were representatives of official culture certainly read the vernacular book, it circulated above all in the hands of a lay 'bourgeoisie' of merchants and craftsmen whose level of literacy varied and who knew little if any Latin.

Courtly reading, as practised among the scholarly and sometimes highly cultured aristocracies of Europe, provides yet another model of reading. Courtly books were, for the most part, conceived as entertainment or used for devotional purposes, but their function transcended simple reading. Books were ornaments. They were a sign of courtliness, civility and refined living; wealth, even opulence, was displayed in their rich illustrations and their bindings made of rare leathers, fine stuffs and precious metals. They were objects that recalled, restored and celebrated the splendour of the ruler and his court. Books commissioned from bookseller-experts, received as gifts, or inherited in various ways were gathered together to make up lordly libraries that differed in many ways from the religious libraries. Aristocratic collections included vernacular works that sang of arms and of love, recounted more or less fantastic stories, and 'popularized' the great texts of the classical tradition. Their Latin works were devotional books, Bibles, books of hours and breviaries. In the fifteenth century humanism invaded courtly libraries in the form of books by Greek and Latin classical authors, sharing shelf space with books by contemporary authors, books of entertainment and devotional works. Court life provided free time for reading, which was carried on not so much in the library itself as in the rooms of the aristocratic residence devoted to social gatherings, relaxation and repose.

The Modern Age: Geographical Variations in Reading

Between the sixteenth century and the nineteenth century, the geography of reading practices in the Western world depended primarily on the vicissitudes of history. In each region relations with written culture were inscribed within a specific combination of circumstances involving literacy rates, religious preferences and the area's degree of industrialization. The resulting differences created well-established, durable frontiers. One of these separated a Europe that had achieved a high rate of literacy early on from a Europe that only later became literate; another lay between lands that remained Catholic and lands that became Protestant; still another divided areas of early economic development from regions that long retained a traditional economy.

These differences were reflected in variations in censorship, in publishing activity, in the book trade and in the market for books. Contrasts of the sort are typical of 'revolutions' in reading. One such moment of transition came between the Middle Ages and the early modern age, when silent reading, using the eyes alone, became internalized as a rule and a common practice; another occurred between the eighteenth and nineteenth centuries, when readers became familiar with a vastly increased and more accessible print production that encouraged new publishing formulas.

Geographical differences in the history of reading are reflected in the available documents. One sort of serial document that can be found nearly everywhere is the estate inventory of personal possessions that has enabled scholars to evaluate how many books different sorts of people owned and to reconstruct the contents of private libraries. Booksellers' catalogues and catalogues of libraries sold at auction show what sorts of books were available. Other sources of information are the rules and regulations and the catalogues of institutions that, beginning in the eighteenth century, enabled people to read books without having to acquire them, institutions such as lending libraries (known variously as circulating libraries, *cabinets littéraires*, *Leihbibliotheken*) and reading societies (book clubs and subscription libraries, *chambres de lecture*, *Lesegesellschaften*). The subscription lists of such institutions provide information about their declared patrons and about potential readers for any given book.

Archival sources provide sizeable sets of serial data, but the chances of arriving at a more accurate estimate of book circulation or reading practices vary enormously from one country to another. In Mediterranean lands and their colonial possessions the records of interrogations conducted by the Inquisition include statements by the accused of what works they had read, how they had acquired such works, and (more important for our purposes) how they had understood them. In northern European lands and England's American colonies, we need to seek elsewhere to find out what people read, notably in the spiritual autobiographies encouraged by Puritan or Pietist Protestantism; in life stories written by people who ranged from the humble and unschooled to representatives of the educated élite; in account books, journals and memoirs that, thanks to advances in literacy, were no longer the exclusive prerogative of the prominent and the lettered; finally (although these were exceptional cases), in the letters that readers sent to authors or publishers.

In every national, linguistic and cultural area, reading practices lay within an essential historical process. In Italy, Spain and Portugal (and in France, but without the Inquisition), readers learned to fear or to circumvent a church and state censorship that was determined to hinder the diffusion of ideas that were considered a threat to the authority of the Catholic Church and the power of absolute sovereigns. In Germany in the latter half of the eighteenth century a new way of reading characterized as a *Leserevolution* sprang from a widespread penetration of the *Aufklärung* (the Enlightenment) and a new public space. In England the Industrial Revolution uprooted traditional practices, eventually creating new categories of readers and a new market for print. On each of these occasions the history of ways to read permits new and original insights into traits that make up national history and identity. Among these are the weight of the prohibitions imposed by the Catholic Counter-Reformation, the specific forms that the Enlightenment took in German lands, and the construction of relationships between the classes (and between the sexes) in the Protestant societies of England and North America.

Revolutions

The first transformation to affect reading practices in the modern age was technological: in the mid-fifteenth century, the ways in which texts were reproduced and books were made changed radically. With movable print and the printing press, copying a manuscript was no longer the only way to reproduce and circulate a text. Johannes Gutenberg's invention permitted the circulation of texts on a scale hitherto impossible. For one thing, printing drastically reduced the per copy cost of making a book by spreading that cost over the entire press run. For another, it shortened the time needed to produce a book, which was long for a manuscript, even after the invention of the *pecia* system in which works were assigned to students one quire at a time so that several segments of a work could be copied simultaneously. With printing, every individual reader could have access to a greater number of books, and every book could reach more readers. Moreover, printing made it possible to reproduce texts in a large number of identical copies (or nearly identical, if we consider corrections made during printing), thus transforming the very conditions for the transmission and reception of books.

Does this mean that the invention and spread of printing alone were responsible for bringing about a fundamental revolution in reading? Perhaps not, and for several reasons. First, it is clear that the new technique did not revolutionize the basic structures of the book. At least until the beginning of the sixteenth century, the printed book remained dependent on the manuscript, imitating its page layout, its writing hands and its general appearance. As with the manuscript, many people contributed to making a printed book: the illuminator painted ornamental or illustrative miniatures and initials; the corrector, or *emendator*, added punctuation marks, rubrics and titles; the reader placed his own marks, comments and marginal notes on its pages.

Even beyond its immediate derivation from the manuscript, the book – both before and after Gutenberg – and the manuscript were similar objects composed of sheets folded and gathered into quires and assembled within one binding or cover. It is thus hardly surprising that all the systems of reference that have somewhat hastily been credited to printing existed well before its invention. One of these was the use of signatures and catchwords to help assemble the pages in the right order. Other signalling devices aided reading: folios, columns or lines might be numbered; the page could be divided up more visibly by the use of devices such as ornamented initials, rubrics and marginal letters; an analytical (rather than a simple spatial) relationship between the text and its glosses could be set up; different characters or different colours of ink could be used to distinguish between text and commentary. Thanks to its organization in quires and to its clear divisions, the codex, whether manuscript or printed, was easy to index. Concordances, alphabetical tables and systematic indexes were common practice even in the age of the manuscript, and it was in monastic scriptoria and stationers' workshops that these modes for the organization of written material were invented. Printers picked them up later.

Finally, it was also during the last centuries of the hand-copied book that a lasting hierarchy among book formats was established. The large in-folio volume, or 'bench book', that needed a firm surface to rest on and that was the book of the university and of scholarship stood apart from both the more easily handled, middle-sized humanist book used for classical texts and new texts and the *libellus*, the portable book small enough to slip into a pocket or leave by a bedside, whose uses were multiple and whose readers were many but less wealthy. The printed book inherited from the manuscript a differentiation based on a combination of format, text genre, and the time and manner of reading.

There is yet another reason for stressing continuity from 'scribal culture' to 'print culture'. The invention of printing had little decisive influence on the long process in which increasing numbers of readers moved from a necessarily oralized reading style in which vocalization was indispensable for the comprehension of meaning to a silent, purely visual reading style. Although both ways of reading had coexisted in

Greek and Roman antiquity, it was during the long centuries of the Middle Ages, as Paul Saenger demonstrates, that the ability to read silently, a style at first restricted to the circles of the monastic scribes, reached the universities and eventually, during the fourteenth and fifteenth centuries, became common practice among lay aristocrats and men of letters. This trend continued after Gutenberg until even the humblest readers had acquired a reading style that no longer implied oralization. We can see a proof, *a contrario*, of this evolution in some Western societies today, where people are considered illiterate not only if they cannot read at all, but also if they can understand a text only when they read it aloud.

The first 'revolution in reading' of the early modern age was thus in the main independent of the technological revolution in book production of the fifteenth century. If we are interested in seeking the roots of the revolution in reading, we need to look to changes in the very function of writing that took place in the twelfth and thirteenth centuries, when the monastic model, which assigned to writing a task of preservation and memory that was in great part dissociated from reading, was replaced by the scholastic model of reading, which made the book both the object and the instrument of intellectual labour. Whatever its origins, the opposition between a necessarily oralized reading and a possibly silent reading marks a break of capital importance. Silent reading initiated a commerce with writing that was potentially freer, more secretive and wholly internal. It permitted a rapid, skilled reading that could not be baffled by either the organizational complexity of the page or the multiple relationships set up between the discourse and its glosses, references and commentaries, texts and indexes. It also permitted variety in the uses of any given book, which might be read aloud for others or with others when sociability or ritual so demanded or read in silence for oneself alone in the privacy of the study, the library or the oratory. The revolution in reading thus preceded the revolution of the book, because the opportunity for silent reading arose (at least for cultivated readers, both clerical and lay), well before the mid-fifteenth century. Hence we should not be too quick to impute the new ways of considering and handling writing uniquely to the technical innovation of the invention of printing.

The same is quite obviously true of the second 'revolution in reading' of the early modern age, when printing became industrialized. According to the traditional thesis, during the second half of the eighteenth century, an 'intensive' reading gave way to another sort of reading, called 'extensive'. The 'intensive' reader had access to a limited, closed corpus of books, which were read and reread, memorized and recited, deeply understood and possessed, and transmitted from one generation to another. Religious texts (in Protestant lands, primarily the Bible) were privileged objects of a reading style profoundly imbued with sacrality and authority. The 'extensive' reader, the reader stricken by the *Lesewut* (rage to read) that gripped Germany in Goethe's day, devoured a large number and a wide variety of ephemeral print materials. These new readers read rapidly and avidly, subjecting what they read to a critical regard that spared no domain from methodical doubt. A communal and respectful relationship to written matter made of reverence and obedience gave way to a free, more detached and irreverent sort of reading.

This highly disputable thesis has in fact been disputed. In reality, there were many 'extensive' readers in the periods of 'intensive' reading. We need only think of the literary humanists. The two objects that symbolize their manner of reading are the book wheel, which permitted one reader to keep several books open for consultation at any given time, and the commonplace book, in which the reader might use a variety of headings to note quotations and bits of information that he had encountered and observations that he had made or collected. Both devices imply a learned practice based on accumulated reading and reliant on making extracts, moving materials from one context to another, and comparing the items selected. The most learned of these readers were led into philological criticism.

What is more, the most 'intensive' sort of reading developed at the very moment of the 'revolution in reading', thanks to authors such as Rousseau, Bernardin de Saint-Pierre, Goethe and Richardson. In their works the novel takes hold of its readers, absorbing them into a reading process that it governs just as firmly as the religious text had done. Older reading habits were shifted to a new literary form with *Pamela*, *La Nouvelle Héloïse*, *Paul et Virginie* and *The Sufferings of Young Werther*. The novel was read and reread, memorized, cited and recited. Readers were invaded by a text; they inhabited the text, identified with its characters, and applied the vicissitudes of its plot to real life. Their entire sensibility was engaged in this new sort of 'intensive' reading. Readers (who were often female) were unable to hold back their emotions and their tears, and often they took up their pens to express their own sentiments or to write to the author as a director of conscience and guide for living.

Furthermore, readers of novels were not the only 'intensive' readers of the age of the 'revolution in reading'. The reading habits of the most numerous and humblest sorts of readers, whose reading matter was pedlars' books, were still guided by the old ways. Chapbooks, the publications of the *Bibliothèque bleue*, and the *literatura de cordel* show lasting signs of a reading style in which reading was an unaccustomed practice, a difficult task highly reliant on listening and memorization. The texts that made up the chapmen's stock lent themselves to an appropriation based on recognition (of genres, works and themes) more than on a discovery of novelty. They had little appeal for the hurried, insatiable or sceptical reader.

These considerations challenge any simplistic contrast between two reading styles. Still, as Reinhard Wittmann tells us in chapter 11, they do not invalidate an analysis situating one of the revolutions in reading in the latter half of the eighteenth century. Support for such an idea can be found in England, in Germany and in France, and it includes such elements as a growth in book production, which tripled or quadrupled between the beginning of the century and the 1780s, the rapid multiplication of newspapers, the triumph of small book formats, lower book prices brought about by pirated editions and the proliferation of institutions (reading societies and lending libraries) that made it possible to read books and periodicals without having to buy them. The picture so often presented by the painters and the writers of the late eighteenth century of the extended peasant family gathered together in the evening to listen to the patriarch read the Bible aloud speaks to a nostalgia for a bygone form of reading. In that ideal representation of peasant life so dear to the lettered élite, reading in community stood for a world where the book was revered and authority was respected. By implication, that mythic representation was a denunciation of the habits of a contrary sort of reading that was urban, superficial and detached. All contemporary observers were struck by the rage for reading, whether they described it as a danger to political order and a 'narcotic' (as Fichte said) that turned people away from true enlightenment, or whether they considered it a derangement of the imagination and the senses. Insatiable reading undoubtedly played an essential role (throughout Europe, but especially in France) in detaching subjects from their rulers and Christians from their churches.

In our own time, the electronic transmission of texts and the reading styles that it imposes have brought on the third revolution in reading since the Middle Ages. Reading a monitor screen is not the same as reading a codex. The new representation of writing changes many things. First, it alters our notion of context by replacing the physical contiguity among the texts present in one object (a book, a journal, a newspaper) with their position and their distribution in the logical architectures that govern data bases, electronic files and the retrieval systems and key words that make it possible to access information. It also redefines the 'material' nature of works by shattering the physical connection that used to exist between the print (or manuscript) object and the text or texts it bore and by giving readers (rather than the author or the publisher) control over the organization and the appearance of the text that they bring up on the screen. Thus the entire system for identifying and handling texts has been radically refashioned. When today's readers (even more, tomorrow's readers) scroll through a computerized text, they resemble readers of antiquity reading a *volumen* or roll. There is an enormous difference, however: the text on the monitor screen scrolls vertically, and it makes use of all the retrieval devices proper to the codex: pagination, indexing, tables of contents, etc. The combination of the two forms of logic that were operative in the earlier writing supports, manuscript and printed, *volumen* and codex, implies a wholly original, totally new relationship to the text.

That new relationship is part of a complete reorganization of the 'economy of writing'. By making the production, transmission and reading of a given text simultaneous, and by uniting in one individual operator the tasks, until now distinct, of writing, publishing and distributing, the electronic representation of texts annuls the old distinctions between intellectual roles and social functions. At the same time it makes it imperative to redefine all the categories that pertained until now in readers' expectations and perceptions. These include the juridical concepts that define the status of writing (copyright, literary property, author's rights, etc.), aesthetic categories that have been used since the eighteenth century to describe works (integrity, stability, originality), administrative notions (legal deposit, national libraries) and technical notions proper to library science (cataloguing, classification, bibliographic description), all of which were invented for another mode of production, preservation and communication of writing.

The world of electronic texts removes two constraints that have always been considered unavoidable. The first is a strict limitation on the reader's ability to intervene in the book. Since the sixteenth century – that is, since the time when printers took on responsibility for the signs, marks and titles that in the age of the incunables the corrector or the owner of the book had added to the printed page by hand – the reader's own writing could be entered only in the blank spaces in a book. The print object imposed its form, structure and spaces on the reader, and no material physical participation on the reader's part was supposed. If the reader none the less wanted to inscribe his presence in the object, he could do so only surreptitiously, by occupying the spaces not occupied by type in the end sheets, blank pages and page margins.

All this changes with the electronic text. Not only can readers subject texts to a number of operations (they can be indexed, annotated, copied, shifted from one place to another, recomposed); they can become co-authors. The distinction between writing and reading and between the author of the text and the reader of the book, which had been immediately discernible in the printed book, now gives way to a new reality: the reader seated before a monitor screen becomes one of the authors of a multi-author text; at the very least, he or she can 'cut and paste' to make up a new text on the basis of fragments freely extracted from elsewhere. Like the owner of many manuscripts who could assemble works of a very different nature into one collective work – one *libro-zibaldone* – readers of the electronic age can construct original texts at will whose existence, organization and appearance depend only on themselves. Moreover, they have the power to intervene at any moment to modify a text, rewrite it, or appropriate it. All this has profoundly changed our entire relationship with writing.

Electronic texts have abolished another constraint for the first time in history. Since classical antiquity Western Europeans have been haunted by the contrast between a dream of a universal library that would bring together all the texts ever written and all the books ever published, on the one hand, and, on the other, real libraries, which, no matter how big they are, necessarily fall short of that mark, providing only a partial, incomplete and mutilated image of universal knowledge. The libraries of Alexandria and Babel have furnished the West with mythical examples of that yearning for an impossible and ardently desired exhaustiveness. Electronic techniques for communicating texts over a distance annul the distinction, until now ineradicable, between the place of the text and the place of the reader. They make the ancient dream thinkable; indeed, they promise it. The text in its electronic representation, detached from all material characteristics and from its old localization, can (in theory) reach any reader anywhere. If we could suppose that all existing texts, manuscript or printed, were converted into electronic form, universal access to the entire patrimony of writing would become possible. Any reader with a computer connection to a network that distributes texts could consult, read and study any text, whatever its original form and location.

As Armando Petrucci demonstrates in chapter 13, traditional reading has had stiff competition from the image in our contemporary world, and reading risks losing repertories, codes and ways of behaving once inculcated by educational or social norms. A second 'crisis' brings another threat, albeit a lesser one and one whose presence is less felt in some countries than in others. A change in the physical support for writing forces the reader to perform new gestures and learn new intellectual practices. The move from the codex to the screen is just as great a change as the shift from the roll to the codex. It challenges the entire order of books familiar to the men and women of Western Europe since the earliest centuries of the Christian era. It establishes (in fact, dictates) new ways of reading that we cannot yet completely describe, but that will quite surely bring new and unprecedented reading practices.

Typology

As the history of reading moved through the three revolutions that transformed reading practices from the Middle Ages to the twentieth century, several major models have succeeded one another. The first of these, analysed by Anthony Grafton in chapter 7, was 'humanist' reading. This characteristic model of the learned reading of the Renaissance was based on the specific intellectual technique of collecting 'commonplaces'.

Two objects provided both a physical support and a symbol for this style of reading. The first is the reading wheel. Its existence pre-dates the Renaissance, but that was when advances in mechanics enabled engineers to perfect it. The reading wheel, a vertical wheel turned with the help of a system of gears, permitted readers to keep a dozen or so books, placed on individual shelves, open before them at one time. This meant that the sort of reading the wheel made possible was simultaneous perusal of a certain number of books. The ideal user of a contraption of this sort was a reader who wanted to place texts side by side in order to compare and collate passages; a reader who read books in order to extract quotations and examples from them, then note down the more striking passages for easy retrieval or indexing.

The commonplace book, the second object emblematic of humanist reading, was both a pedagogical instrument that every schoolchild or university student was expected to keep and an indispensable accompaniment to scholarly reading. The reader, apprentice or expert, copied into notebooks organized by topics or rubrics fragments of texts that he had read that struck him for their grammatical interest, their factual content, or their usefulness as demonstrative examples. Commonplace books composed on the basis of readings substituted for the classical techniques of the arts of memory, and they might in turn serve as a resource for the production of new texts. The abundance of the material they contained, which embraced both extracts from texts and notations on things seen, events observed and works read, nourished the rhetorical ideal of the *copia verborum ac rerum* necessary for all argumentation. In the sixteenth century the commonplace book, always a product of cultivated reading, became a genuine publishing genre when not only prestigious authors (Erasmus, Melanchthon) but bookseller-publishers composed them for widespread general use, producing versions in such fields as law, pedagogy and theology.[27]

There were readers who specialized in the reading style characteristic of the technique of the commonplace book. These were the 'professional' readers employed by aristocratic families to supervise their sons' studies or serve the father in the multiple role of secretary, reader aloud and 'facilitator' (a term reported by Lisa Jardine and Anthony Grafton[28]). Their job description included compiling epitomes and abridgements, collections of citations and extracts designed to help their patrons and aristocratic protectors in the reading of the classics that was necessary to their rank or post. Beyond these 'professionals', who were often university graduates or former university professors, all lettered people read by the commonplace method. Jean Bodin provides an excellent example of this. On the one hand, Bodin recommends that anyone wishing to know the history of reading compile three notebooks devoted to human affairs, natural events and things divine. Bodin seems to have practised that technique himself, given that his *Universae Naturae Theatrum* (1596) is organized on the basis of an accumulation of quotations, observations and information, divided under various headings in the same manner as a commonplace book. In any event, that was the way the book was read, as we can see from marginal notes found in book copies noting passages that the note-taker wanted to remember and assigning them to the various rubrics of a typical commonplace book.[29]

There were not many readers during the Renaissance who strayed from that dominant model, but Montaigne was one of them. His behaviour as a reader contrasts, step by step, with that of scholarly readers. He kept no commonplace book as he read, and he refused to copy or compile; he did not note the books he read in order to retrieve extracts or quotations, but rather entered his own opinion at the end of the book itself. Finally, he did not use the available commonplace books as he wrote his *Essays*, but rather composed freely, without bothering about what he had gleaned from his reading and without interrupting his train of thought to give scholarly references. Montaigne was a singular reader who rejected the rules and postures of studious reading. He never read at night, and he never read while seated; he read without method, and his library, far from being an open, usable resource like the typical humanist collection, was instead a privileged place of retirement from the world. Nothing shows better the strangeness of Montaigne's practice and, *a contrario*, the dominant strength of the model it opposed than the efforts that others made to submit the oddity of the *Essays* to a division by *loci communes* and to a thematic reorganization that would facilitate the sort of reading that underlay the selection of extracts and examples. We can appreciate Montaigne's originality better by comparing his methods to the conventions and the habits governing scholarly reading in the Renaissance.

The religious reforms of the sixteenth and seventeenth centuries set up a second great model of reading in Western Europe in the early modern period. As Jean-François Gilmont shows in chapter 8 and Dominique Julia in chapter 9, the widespread dissemination of a new corpus of Christian texts profoundly changed the relation of the faithful to written culture. New divisions were established that bear little resemblance to traditional historiography's division between Protestantism and Catholicism. The contrast between Protestantism as a religion of the written word, founded on a personal reading of the Bible, and Catholicism as a religion of speech and listening, therefore of clerical mediation, although often reiterated, is no longer tenable.

For one thing, we see the same techniques of proscription and prescription on both sides of the confessional divide, as rival versions of Christianity attempted to lead the faithful toward their authorized texts. To be sure, prohibitions varied in rigour from one geographical area to another, and the power to back them up varied as well, as we can see from the role played in the Roman Catholic Church by the Index of Prohibited Books and the condemnations of the Inquisitorial courts. All churches, however, attempted to transform Christians into readers, and they all worked to support the new comportment required by religious reform by producing a large number of instructional manuals, books of devotion and liturgical works. Where spirituality and worship were concerned, reading came to be entirely determined by the relationship with God. Reading was not an end in itself; rather, it was to nourish the Christian life of the faithful, who would be led beyond the book by means of the book – by means of texts deciphered, commented on, and meditated upon – to a singular, unmediated experience of holiness.

The greatest contrast in Christian reading styles lay between Lutheranism and Catholicism, on the one hand, and Calvinist and Pietist Protestantism, on the other. Lutheranism was no more a religion centred on individual reading of the Bible than Roman Catholicism was, at least until the late seventeenth century. In Lutheran Germany (but also in northern Europe in general) the Bible was a parish book; it was a book for pastors or pastors in training that was to be kept out of the hands of those who might be tempted to read it in heterodox or dangerous ways. This explains the essential role played by the pastoral word in both Lutheran and Catholic lands and the many books designed to teach the correct interpretation of Scripture. Prime examples of this mediated reading are catechisms, psalteries and books of Bible stories (which rewrite the biblical text) that much resembled each other on both sides of the confessional divide.

In Calvinist and Puritan lands familiarity with the Bible on both the personal and the family level led to quite different reading practices.

A direct, unmediated relationship between the faithful and the sacred Word made knowledge of the Bible a fundamental spiritual experience, and it raised Bible reading to the level of a model for all other possible forms of reading. Whether the Bible was read silently by individuals, read aloud to the assembled family in the privacy of the home, or read in church, Bible reading was present at every moment of existence. It defined a relationship with writing that was invested with an extraordinary intensity. In the Calvinist and Puritan communities Bible reading, the prime model for all reading (and the perfect form of 'intensive' reading) dominated all other forms of reading, both religious and secular. After the second Reformation in the last decades of the seventeenth century, this was true of the Pietists as well.

The history of reading practices thus enables us to emend the conventional, oversimplified contrast between Protestantism and Catholicism thanks to a new appreciation of similarities (long unperceived) between the Roman Catholic Church and Lutheranism and of lasting differences within the world of the Reformation. The history of reading practices also enables us to inscribe within the context of Western societies other forms of reading practice that provide a counterpoint to the dominant Christian models. The practices of the Jewish communities that Robert Bonfil analyses in chapter 6 provide one example of such forms. Beyond obvious differences in its relation to writing, what we gain from that minority reading style, which was often forbidden and even punished (in Spain, for example), is a circuitous appropriation of texts that used fragments from Christian works condemning heretical propositions with the aim of reconstituting a tradition and a religion.[30] Even outside Jewish communities, reading *en creux* in that manner – that is, deciphering texts to find in them precisely what has supposedly been censored or obliterated – was a defensive tactic used by all readers when a dominant order attempted to keep them from reading prohibited works. This was the case with Protestants in the territories of the Counter-Reformation, Catholics in Protestant lands, and rebel spirits in absolutist regimes.

In the nineteenth century increased literacy throughout Europe heralded the introduction to written print culture of such new classes of readers as women, children and workers. It also brought a diversification of print production and a broad variety of new models for reading, as Martyn Lyons demonstrates in chapter 12. Educational norms, imposed everywhere, tended to define one sole, controlled and codified ideal of legitimate reading, but those norms contrasted strongly with an extreme diversity of practice among various communities of readers, both those long familiar with writing and newcomers to print. Admittedly, all readers under the various old regimes in the West did not read in the same fashion, and the range of skills between the virtuosos of reading, who were readers by inheritance, profession or habit, and the least skilled readers of the chapmen's books must have been enormous. Still, behind the appearance of a common culture in the almost universal reading literacy that acculturation to writing, both in and out of the schools, had brought to the more developed regions of Europe in the nineteenth century, there lay an extreme diversity in both reading practices and markets for the book (or the newspaper). The typology of the various dominant models of the relationship to writing that succeeded one another from the Middle Ages on (moving from the monastic model of writing to the scholastic model of reading; from the humanist technique of commonplaces to the spiritual and religious reading styles of Reformed Christianity; from popular reading styles to the 'revolution in reading' of the Enlightenment) gives way in contemporary societies to a scattering of customs related to reading that reflects the broad diversity of the social world. With the nineteenth century, the history of reading enters the age of the sociology of differences.

Reading between Constraint and Invention

The history of reading has long been divided into two sorts of approach. The first aims at overthrowing or improving upon traditional literary history; the second begins from a social history of the uses of writing. The aesthetic of reception of German scholars, the 'reader-response theory' of American literary criticism, and studies based on Russian and Czech formalism (all of which are critical stances more historically oriented than French or American structuralism) were attempts to separate reading from the work and to understand reading as an interpretation of a text not completely determined by linguistic and discursive techniques and devices. The history of reading has also found powerful support in the history of literacy and schooling, in the history of cultural norms and competencies, and in the history of the diffusion and the uses of print. It has seemed a possible, even necessary, continuation of classic studies that describe, for different localities in Europe, the combined effects of publishing production, the sociology of book owners and booksellers' customers and literary associations and reading societies.

English and American scholars have used bibliographic analysis to propose a possible connection between these two overall approaches. First, they show how book formats and page layouts influence the construction of the meaning of the text. Second, they are interested in collecting traces of a book's circulation from the book itself (in marks of

ownership, *ex libris* labels, notations of purchase, gift, or loan, etc.),
as well as traces of reading (underlinings, marginal notes, personal
indexes, manuscript texts appended, etc.). They remind us that texts are
always communicated to their readers in forms (manuscript or print,
written or oral) that constrain them but do not destroy their freedom.

The history of reading that we propose collectively in this book
attempts to combine these various approaches, although our interests
are admittedly more historical than literary. Our objective is dual: to
recognize the constraints that limit the frequenting of books and the
production of meaning and to inventory the resources that can be mobil-
ized by the reader's liberty – a liberty that remains in many ways
dependent but is capable of ignoring, shifting about, or subverting the
techniques and devices designed to limit it.

The first of these limiting devices were instituted by law. Readers
were restrained by censorship and by self-censorship, but also by laws
stipulating the authors' rights and those of their heirs. Readers were
deprived when the majority of them were denied prohibited works
available only to a more privileged or more daring minority who
bought from sellers of clandestine books. They suffered from excessive
zeal when expurgated texts, cut and refashioned by the censors' decree
or the insistence of the executors of an author's will, bore little
resemblance to the works' original form or their author's intentions.

Publishing strategies hemmed in reading practices as well. It is true
that when the publishers invented new text genres and new publishing
formulas and when they made inexpensive print products available to a
less affluent public (first, the books of the *Bibliothèque bleue*, chapbooks and *pliegos sueltos*; later, newspapers and popular collections),
they offered the public an increasingly broad and diversified range of
reading matter. None the less, the readers' freedom to choose could be
exercised only within a range of choices that had already been made on
the basis of interests or preferences that were not necessarily theirs. Even
if such preferences were not all, or at all times, purely commercial, they
were the ones that governed editorial policies and determined what
reading matter would be offered. Control over reading matter at the
source, by editorial decision, was a lasting trait of *ancien régime* societies,
although it was relaxed in the age of the industrialization of print.

Within the territory available to them, readers took command of
books (and other print objects), gave them meaning, and invested them
with their own expectations. That appropriation was not without its
own rules and limitations. Some of these arose out of strategies inherent
in the text itself, which was intended to produce certain effects, dictate
a posture, and condition the reader. The snares laid for readers, and
into which they fell without even realizing it, were as clever as the rebel

inventiveness they are supposed to have possessed. The image contained equally constraining and equally subversive reading codes. Often used to accompany a printed text, images set up a protocol for reading that was intended either to present the same message as the one formulated in the written text, using a different sign language but an identical grammar, or else to present, in a language specific to the image, what logical discourse was powerless to express. In either case (and the two indicate quite different functional relationships between the text and the image), when illustrations were given the task of guiding interpretation, they might instead bear an 'other' reading, detached from the letter of the text and capable of creating a space of its own.

This dialectic of constraint and invention implies a meeting place between a history of the conventions that regulate the hierarchy of genres and define the modalities and levels of discourse, on the one hand, and, on the other, a history of the schemes of perception and judgement inherent in each community of readers. One of the major objectives of the history of reading thus necessarily resides in identifying the fault lines that, over the long term, separate the readers or readings imagined, designated or targeted in specific works from the plural and successive publics those works actually had.

A gap of that sort seems to have been produced by the way the text of certain works was presented. That *mise en texte* varies according to the author's desires, the publisher's decisions and the typographer's (or the copyist's) personal preferences. It is significant in two ways. First, the form of a publication transmits how the person who created that text or that book perceived the readers' abilities; second, that same form dictates a way of reading the text and of creating comprehension and controlling interpretation. Formal and material differences on several levels exist in both manuscript and print texts. The first is the line, where in the early Middle Ages, the appearance of word separation made silent reading possible. The next is the page, which underwent two transformations: in the fourteenth and fifteenth centuries, marginal texts (rubrics, glosses, commentaries) disappeared; in the sixteenth and seventeenth centuries, divisions into paragraphs and paragraph indentations appeared. The last difference is on the level of the book itself, and it first occurred when printing gave the book an identity, clearly defined on the title page, and a new ease of manipulation, thanks to the widespread and durable customs of pagination and indexing.

The history of reading practices that is proposed in this book hopes to make use of all these various approaches and different ways of understanding the encounter between texts and their readers. One idea underlies them all: to bring to a study of the transformation in ways of reading a fresh perspective on the major changes – cultural, religious and political – that Western societies encountered as they evolved from classical antiquity to today. As early as the ancient Greek world, those were societies of the written word, the text and the book. Thus they were societies of reading. But reading is not an anthropological invariant removed from history. The men and women of Western Europe have not always read in the same fashion. Several models have governed their practices, and several 'revolutions in reading' have changed their actions and their habits. This volume hopes to survey those models and those revolutions, and make them more comprehensible.

1

Archaic and Classical Greece: The Invention of Silent Reading

Jesper Svenbro

When alphabetic writing swept into Greek culture around the eighth century BC, it arrived in a world that had a long oral tradition. If the spoken word was present 'in the beginning', as the familiar phrase goes, it also wielded power. In archaic Greece the spoken word reigned uncontested, in particular as *kleos* (renown) that the Homeric bards conferred on the epic heroes. *Kleos* was a primordial value, even a genuine obsession. If the Homeric hero accepted dying combat, it was because he hoped to win 'imperishable renown', and it is significant that the root meaning of *kleos* – 'renown', but also 'glory' – is 'sound' (as shown by etymologically related words in the Germanic languages – *Laut*, for example). The glory of Achilles was thus a glory for the ear, a sounded, acoustic glory. Indeed, Homer uses *kleos* in the plural as a technical term to speak of his own epic poetry. The sonority of the spoken word was effective; it was what gave the hero existence.

We can also trace the valorization of sound in the changes that the Greeks made in the consonant alphabet they borrowed from the Semites, when they redefined a certain number of signs to note vowel sounds. If we want to understand why and in what perspective the Greeks appropriated Phoenician writing, we would do well to keep that valorization in mind. This might seem paradoxical: what purpose could 'mute writing' serve in a culture whose oral tradition was thought capable of perpetuating itself with no other support than memory and the human voice? The simplest answer may lie, precisely, in the production of even greater *kleos* – for example, in funerary inscriptions that guaranteed a new form of posterity to the deceased. Thus writing may have been put to the service of oral culture and its aims, not to safeguard the epic tradition (although in the end it did just that), but to further the production of sound, effective words and resounding glory.

This explanation is in reality a hypothesis regarding the nature of reading in archaic Greece. It seems unavoidable that the first Greek readers read aloud, given that in a culture that valued the spoken word as highly as the Greeks did, writing held little interest except as vocalized reading. This hypothesis by no means reverses long-standing ideas about ancient reading. Although it is formulated on the basis of cultural information, it echoes another generally admitted hypothesis reached by extrapolating from the evidence of later ages: if the Greeks of the classical age read aloud, we must assume that their ancestors did the same. When there are no documents, it seems logical to conclude that reading aloud was the primordial form of reading.

The Vocabulary of Reading in Greek

If at first sight there seems to be a total lack of evidence regarding archaic Greek reading (providing that we take 'evidence' to mean descriptions of the act of reading or of reactions to that act), the situation changes the minute we turn to the vocabulary that was forged, from the archaic era on, to express the idea of reading. The Greek language possesses more than a dozen verbs signifying 'to read', attested from around 500 BC. Such a large number may seem surprising. It is probably due to the linguistic diversity of Greek dialects and to the fact that the 'trial period' for the circulation of such terms (after which only some remained) had not yet ended when they began to appear in inscriptions and texts. These verbs constitute our principal means of access to the logic of archaic reading: the basic meaning of the various verbs used to indicate 'reading' shows us how the act was thought of when each specialized use of it appeared, and perhaps later as well. Such indications are all the more precious because they are situated on the level of shared acquisitions and language; thus they go beyond individual or occasional use. This means that we must examine specific instances of vocabulary and grammar in order to corroborate the hypothesis that archaic reading was vocal in nature. This approach emphasizes the otherness of reading in a culture profoundly different from our own, but it also reminds us that ancient Greek culture was close enough to our own to permit profitable comparison.

In 1950 Pierre Chantraine wrote a ground-breaking article on Greek verbs that signify 'to read'.[1] The article is useful, even though it is limited to the study of four words. There is one verb that Chantraine neglected to mention, however, that seems to me of particular importance, the verb *nemein* (literally, 'to distribute'). It will serve us as a point of departure. To judge by the written documents, this verb was used only infrequently in the sense of 'to read', and its very rarity may in fact explain why Chantraine did not include it in his study. Aside from three entries in the Alexandrian lexicographer Hesychius (fifth century AD), it is attested only once in a simple form: Sophocles (496–406 BC) uses it in a brief fragment preserved precisely because of its use of the verb that concerns us. As the Greek chiefs gathered before departing for Troy, they reviewed their troops: 'You who are seated on the throne and hold the tablets of writing in your hand, read [*neme*] the list so we can see if any of those who swore the oath are absent!'[2] Earlier, when Tyndaros had had to pick a husband for his daughter Helen from among the many suitors who had come to Sparta, he made them all swear to defend the rights of the man whom he would choose. This was why Menelaus could count on having a large contingent of heroes to come to his aid when Paris made off with Helen. The reader mentioned in this fragment holds in his hand the list of names of the men who had pledged their aid. His reading (literally, his 'distribution') was aimed at finding out who was absent. He was reading aloud before an assembled group, orally 'distributing' the contents of the written tablet.

Thus the verb *nemein*, whose root meaning is 'to distribute', might take on the sense of 'to read' or, more precisely, 'to read aloud'. It seems, however, that the compound forms of this verb were more likely to be used in this specialized sense, beginning with *ananemein*, a term that the poet Theocritus tells us was current 'in the Dorian dialect'.[3] This bit of information is confirmed by two very ancient attestations. The first is in the poet Epicharmus (*c*.530–440 BC), a Sicilian, hence of Dorian dialect;[4] the second is from a vase with a Dorian inscription found in Sicily and dating from the early decades of the fifth century.[5] Hesychius also gives this verb in the sense of 'to read', as does an ancient scholiast, commenting on Pindar.[6] We must thus agree with Theocritus that *ananemein* was the Dorian verb for 'to read'. Although the active form, *ananemein*, is found in the Dorian dialect (that is, in Sparta and in Sicily), we find instead the middle form *ananemesthai* in an inscription in the Ionian dialect from Euboea dating from the first half of the fifth century BC. It is on the funerary stela of a certain Mnesitheos, whose epitaph begins, 'Salutation, O passers-by! I rest, dead, under here. You who draw near, read out [verb *ananemesthai*] who is the man buried here: a stranger from Aegina, Mnesitheos by name.'[7]

In the Dorian dialect the active form *ananemein* makes the reader an instrument in the service of writing: the question did not arise in Sparta as to whether or not the reader himself had received the message that he 'distributed' to others. The same observation holds for both the simple form *nemein* and the compound *epinemein*, which is attested in Hesychius in the sense of 'to read'. The middle form of the same verb, used in Mnesitheos's epitaph, has a meaning subtler than 'to distribute', since it means 'to distribute while including oneself in the distribution'.[8] Thus the reader invoked in the epigraph from Euboea 'distributes' the content of the inscription not only to the 'passers-by' indicated in the text, but also to himself. The words that the reader pronounces are addressed to other auditors as well as to himself. In the end, such a reader might 'distribute' the content of the writing without having any auditors: he 'distributes' it to himself, becoming his own auditor. It is as if he needed to vocalize the letters for his ear, which was capable of grasping their sense, in order to understand the graphic sequence. His own voice becomes the instrument.

If we think about this reader who 'distributes' writing to himself and, by reading, does what seems to us a sonic detour in order to grasp its meaning, we cannot escape the strong impression that he deciphers writing slowly and with difficulty. His reading seems to require considerable effort, an effort that may perhaps be expressed in the prefix *ana-*, as Chantraine suggests.[9] We can look at this laborious process in two ways, from the viewpoint of the reader's competence and from that of the material presentation of writing. Concerning the reader's competence, we know from Plutarch that in Sparta instruction in letters was reduced to the strictly necessary,[10] and it is highly probable that the situation was not very different in Euboea. It is likely that even the competence of someone who read an inscription to passers-by, who, for their part, simply listened, was highly relative. As for its material presentation, Mnesitheos's inscription would have been written in *scriptio continua* – that is, with the letters following one another with practically no spaces between the words, a style (as anyone who has tried his hand at deciphering it can attest) that makes reading slow and hesitant and irresistibly calls for using the voice.

Thus the verb *nemein* stands at the centre of a lexical family whose members all signify 'to read'. One might even wonder whether *nomos*, the active noun formed from *nemein*, might not have the basic meaning of 'reading'. From the formal point of view, there is no obstacle to such a hypothesis. It is true that the dictionaries contain no hint of such a meaning for *nomos*, which is ordinarily translated as 'law'. Nothing, that is, except for the *nomoi* of the birds in Alcman, a poet of the seventh century BC.[11] At first sight the 'melodies' of the birds (the proper translation here) do not seem to have much in common with the laws of the archaic legislators. They do, however. The *nomoi* of Charondas, one of the major legislators of archaic Greece, 'were chanted', according to one ancient author.[12] The dissemination of the law thus might take a vocalized form, and birds and *nomoidoi* – 'law-chanters'[13] – might be involved in perfectly analogous forms of 'distribution'. The law had a vocal distribution, based at first on memory, later on writing. This notion is in conformity with the dual sense of *nemein* and *ana-nemesthai*, because those two verbs can refer to a vocal distribution backed by memory, whether someone 'cites' a maxim (verb *nemein*), as in Simonides, or 'recites' genealogies, as in Herodotus (verb *ana-nemesthai*).[14] As we have seen, these verbs can also refer to a vocal distribution based on writing, as with reading a list or an inscription. In the seventh century BC, the kings of Boetia described by Hesiod 'distributed' (verb *nemein*) justice, which, as Hesiod himself tells us, was a justice to be listened to, a justice distributed orally.[15] When that justice had a written support for its 'distribution', it became reading.

The oral distribution to which *nemein* and *nomos* refer can thus be a distribution backed up by memory as well as by writing; hence it can be a recitation from memory just as easily as a reading aloud. The *nomos* adapts to an oral situation or a written one. This is not the case with the word used in Sparta for 'law', *rhetra*. We know from Plutarch that it was forbidden in Sparta to set down the law in writing.[16] Thus it is logical that the word that meant 'law' in Sparta was derived from the verb *eirein*, 'to speak'. In Rome, to the contrary, 'law' seems to have presupposed writing: *lex* is the active noun of *legere*, 'to read';[17] hence its basic meaning was 'reading' (without the ambiguity we find in *nomos*). This can be represented schematically as follows:

Orality	*eirein*, 'to say'	*rhetra*
Orality/writing	*nemein*, 'to recite/read'	*nomos*
Writing	*legere*, 'to read'	*lex*

Why did the Romans choose the word *legere* ('to pick, gather, collect') for the verb 'to read'? To answer that question, we should probably take into account the fact that although dictionaries do not give the sense, the Greek *legein* could mean 'to read'. We see proof in a phrase from Plato's *Theaetetus*: 'Well, slave, take the book and read (*lege*)!'[18] Another indication is the phrase, *lege ton nomon*, 'read out the law', frequent among fourth-century BC orators.[19] Furthermore, if *lego* signifies 'I read', we have a right to assume that the Romans understood this Greek word when they borrowed the Greek alphabet. What could be more natural than to use the Latin homonym, *lego*, the imperative of which, *lege*, was also perfectly consonant with the Greek, as a technical term for 'to read'? Thus the sense of 'to pick' is not fundamental to the semantics of the Latin *legere*, 'to read', even though it played a role in the later development of that word.

Legein, then, could signify 'to read' just as well as *nemein* could. Again, it is in particular the compounds of the simple verb that we meet in the sense of 'to read', beginning with *analegein*, attested in an inscription from Teos dating from 470–460,[20] and *analegesthai*, attestations for which are of a later date.[21] What we have seen regarding the prefix *ana-* and the difference between the active form *ananemein* and the middle *ananemesthai* of course applies to these two verbs as well, in a parallel that confirms the sense of 'to distribute orally' and 'to read' for *nemein*. In fact, *nemein* and *legein* each form the nucleus of a lexical family, whose members all signify 'to read', but with different nuances.

The family of *legein*, 'to read', is incomplete, however, without an important member, *epilegesthai*, a verb frequent in Herodotus, who wrote in the Ionian dialect of the fifth century BC. It, too, means 'to read', and it is attested only in the middle (whereas its parallel in the other group, *epinemein*, 'to read', is attested only in the active),[22] a form that can be explained in the same way as the middle forms *ananemesthai* and *analegesthai*, 'to distribute, including oneself in the distribution' and 'to read, including oneself in the reading'. The middle form implies that the reader is reading aloud, possibly for auditors, but also for himself. As to the meaning of *epilegesthai*, its literal meaning is 'to add something said to' something. The reader adds his voice to the writing, which is incomplete in itself. Writing is supposed to need the *legein* or the *logos* that the reader adds; without the reader, writing would remain a dead letter. Reading is thus added to writing as an 'epi-logue'.

In this manner, we obtain the following strikingly symmetrical schema:

epinemein	*ananemein*	*nemein*	*legein*	*analegein*
	ananemesthai		*analegesthai*	*epilegesthai*

The verb that first comes to mind for how the Greeks expressed 'to read', however, is probably *anagignoskein*, the earliest attestation of which is in a poem of Pindar dating probably from 474 BC.[23] If *ananemein* was the principal verb in Dorian and *epilegesthai* was frequent in Ionian, *anagignoskein* was the verb used for 'to read' in Athens. In the Attic dialect reading was thus literally 'recognizing', the root sense of *anagignoskein*. Chantraine writes, 'This verb was highly appropriate for signifying reading, that is, for recognizing characters and deciphering them.'[24] In my opinion this interpretation (which is essentially shared by the Liddell–Scott–Jones *Lexicon*) is unsatisfactory. The recognition to which this verb refers is not a recognition of the individual alphabetic sign designated in Greek by the word *gramma*. Reading cannot be reduced to identification of the letters of the alphabet alone; one can 'know his letters' – *ta grammata epistasthai*[25] – without being able to read. A modern example can serve to illustrate how I believe 'recognition' in reading should be understood.

The first word on the first page of Raymond Queneau's *Zazie dans le métro* is 'Doukipudonktan'. This presents the reader with several challenges to normal reading habits. First, the phrase is written in *scriptio continua* (as was Greek writing); second, it is not written etymologically, the normal fashion in French, but phonetically (the norm in Greek); third, the syntax of the phrase is that of the spoken language (the case in Greek before a written idiom noticeably different from the spoken language arose). For these three reasons, French readers are startled when they encounter the phrase 'doukipudonktan' for the first time. Their situation is much like that of a reader in archaic Greece: only by using the voice can the reader 'recognize' what is not clear at first sight. The French eye (and here the analogy with Greece ends) would of course have preferred the 'normal' version of the phrase, which is '[C'est] d'où qu'ils puent donc tant?' (roughly: 'So how come they smell so bad?' or, literally, 'From where [is it] that they stink so much, then?'). In short, what comes into play here is not recognition of a graphic sequence, nor of individual letters. More accurately, it is a recognition that the graphic sequence is language.

French readers who pronounce the sequence *doukipudonktan* for the first time recognize it as language, thanks to their ear, perhaps adding to themselves, 'Aha! So that's what it means!' Even before this oral and aural recognition, they may have identified the letters and noted the odd presence of two k's, but that first summary identification is not yet reading. The decisive moment, the moment of recognition, comes when the letters, whose meaning was at first unclear, like letters chosen by chance, turn out to bear meaning thanks to the reading voice. This is the moment when, to return to the Greek perspective, alphabetical signs are transformed into *stoicheia*, 'elements constituting language', or, more accurately, 'letters forming a sequence'.[26] By pronouncing the letters, the reader recognizes whether or not they form an intelligible sequence.

It is true that ancient Greek had other verbs signifying 'to read', whose signification is not obviously related to oralized reading. After the archaic age, the act of reading could be expressed by verbs whose literal meaning was 'to unroll' (*anelissein*),[27] implying a scroll book; 'to go through' (*diexienai*);[28] or 'to have an interchange with,' even 'have sexual relations with' (*entynchanein* and *syngignesthai*).[29] Most Greek verbs signifying 'to read' insist on the practice of oralized reading, however, probably because people normally read little and haltingly, but also and above all because of the enormous value given to the sounded *logos*, a 'prince', as the Sophist Gorgias was to say,[30] in a culture in which the *nomos* (which was also sounded) was 'king'.[31]

The Triple Lesson of Verbs Signifying 'To Read'

Our examination of Greek verbs that express 'to read' has presented at least three traits typical of reading in ancient Greece. All three are important. The first is the instrumental nature of the reader or the reading voice, something that we have seen in connection with *nemein* and its compounds. The second is the incompleteness of writing, which is supposed to require being translated into sound, as demonstrated by the verb *epilegesthai*. The third logically follows from the first two: if the reader's voice is the instrument for the full realization of writing, this means that the people to whom the writing is addressed are not 'readers' in the strict sense of the term, but rather 'auditors', as in fact the Greeks called them. The 'auditors' of the text – *akouontes* or *akroatai* – are not its readers, as the dictionaries tell us. Apart from the reader, 'who includes himself in the reading' and hears his own voice, Greeks read absolutely nothing. They simply listened to reading, just like the passers-by in Mnesitheos's epitaph.

But why did the Greeks think writing incomplete? If a text must be read in order for it to be complete, it follows logically that reading is an integral part of the text. Michel Charles begins his *Rhétorique de la lecture* with a similar notion: 'I will confine myself to the essential fact that reading is part of the text; it is inscribed in it.'[32] How does that concept relate to ancient Greece? How was that sounded act a part of what for us is a mute event? How was the one included in the other? A first response lies in the physical nature of written matter in Greece because, as we have seen, *scriptio continua* made vocalization practically unavoidable. The absence of spaces and the lack of standardized spelling made every reading a sounded experience. In the sense that such absences negatively programmed oral reading, we can say that such a reading was inscribed in the text. We will have to go further, however. Playing on the etymology of the word 'text' (from the Latin *textus*, 'woven cloth'), I might say that it is as if the text were made of a warp of writing and a vocal woof that weave together in reading and unravel afterwards. On this view, which I believe is faithful to the ancient experience of reading, the text is not a static object but the name given to a dynamic relationship between writing and voice and between the person writing and the reader. The text thus becomes the sounded realization of writing, and without the reader's voice, writing would have no way of being distributed or expressed.

Still, if writing is incomplete without the voice, that means that it must take on a voice in order to be fully realized. As we have seen, the writer counts on the arrival of a reader prepared to put his voice at the service of the writing, so that its contents can be distributed to the passers-by, the 'auditors' of the text. He counts on having a reader who will respect the constraints imposed by the letters. Reading is thus putting one's own voice at the disposition of the writing (and behind it, at the writer's disposition); it is lending one's voice for the duration of the reading, a process in which the writing appropriates the voice, which means that while the reader is reading, his voice is not his own. He has relinquished it. His voice submits to the writing, and unites with it. The process of being read consequently exerts a power over the reader's body, even when great distances and long time spans are involved. The writer who succeeds in being read acts upon someone else's vocal capacities; even after his own death, he uses those capacities as an *instrumentum vocale*, much as he would a slave or a person or thing in his service.

In a culture in which the absence of constraints was a defining trait of citizenship, such a conception of reading was obviously fated to become problematic. In order to participate in the life of the city, the citizen had to be *eleutheros* – free, without constraints. Indeed, an Athenian who prostituted himself, thereby selling his autonomy, could not address the Council or the Assembly; if he did so, he would be condemned to death, the orator Aeschines tells us.[33] As Michel Foucault has shown, this concept of the citizen was in basic contradiction to the practice of pederasty, in the sense that pederasty defined the two lovers in terms of domination and submission: the younger man and future citizen submits to the pleasure of the adult partner.[34] This submission threatens to disqualify him morally unless he shows restraint by not becoming identified with his role. If the boy cedes to the lover, he must do so not for his own pleasure, but for the pleasure of his partner. He must not identify with his role as instrument. In his relation to the pederast, he is just as instrumental as the reader is in relation to the writer. The Greeks themselves thought of written communication in terms of the pederastic relation, as can be seen in the Dorian inscription from Sicily that we have already encountered.[35] That inscription attempts nothing less than a definition (one of the earliest known) of the nature of reading: 'The writer of the inscription will "bugger" (*pygixei*) the reader.' Reading here implies taking on the role of the scorned passive partner, whereas the writer identifies with the dominant, admired active partner.

The scorn of the reader illustrated in this metaphor, which is not an isolated case, perhaps explains why reading was a task often left to a slave, given that the function of slaves was precisely to serve and submit. Here the slave is an instrument, an 'instrument gifted with a voice'. In Plato's *Theaetetus* it is Eucleides' slave who reads the *logos* that his master has put into writing. Terpsion and Eucleides himself are the two presumed auditors of the *logos* read by the slave. The tendency to disparage the reader's task also explains a relative resistance to reading that we also see in Sparta's limitation of instruction in letters to the 'strictly necessary'; but this was probably true in other places as well. Reading was thus not entirely incompatible with the role of citizen, but we have the impression that it should be practised with a certain moderation, so as not to become a vice. Someone who reads must take care not to identify too much with the role of reader if he wants to remain free, or at least free of constraints imposed by others. It is better to be *ta grammata phaulos*, 'poor at reading', to use Socrates' expression[36] – that is, able to read, but barely.

The 'I' and the Voice

The problem merits closer scrutiny. If, in order to speak truly, a person has to speak *en idiois logois*, or 'with his own words' (another expression of Socrates[37]), what are we to think of the archaic reader who deciphers aloud an inscription of the type, 'I am the tomb of Glaukos'[38] to a group of auditors? The later comic poets were sensitive to the ambiguity inherent in the situation of possible confusion between a statement read and a statement spoken by the reader himself. In all probability, that ambiguity appeared with the first inscriptions that designated the inscribed object as 'I', hence with the very earliest Greek inscriptions in the eighth century BC. The reader of that inscription speaks an 'I' that is not himself. Because the 'I' is inflexible, it cannot be modified by saying 'This claims to be the tomb of Glaukos'. That would not be reading. The inscription has to be pronounced as it is written. When the reader does so, he puts himself at the service of the written text, to which he has lent his body, his vocal apparatus and his voice. He belongs to it. Consequently, there is no contradiction, because, according to the reasoning I am proposing, the voice that says 'I' belongs to the writing; it is part and parcel of it, and is united with it for the time needed to read it. There is no contradiction, but there is undeniably a degree of violence done to logic, against which the only defence is to refuse to read.

In reality, the use of the first person singular to designate the inscribed object is so surprising, and at the same time so frequent in Greek inscriptions, that it demands deeper reflection. Although it marks the reader's subservience to the writing, that relation does not exhaust its significance. It reveals a singular way of thinking, shared by an entire culture, about the relation of the writer, the inscribed object and the reader. To summarize: the inscribed object designates itself in the first person singular, whereas the writer designates himself in the third person. It is in fact only after 550 BC that we begin to see objects that explicitly refer to themselves in the third person, as if to mask the genuine violence suggested by the 'I'. A sixth-century amphora provides an example: 'Kleimachos made me and I am his (*ekeinou eimi*).'[39] At the moment of reading, Kleimachos would no longer be there: he would be absent, as the demonstrative pronoun *ekeinos* clearly states (*ekei-nos* is the third person demonstrative, indicating that the person is not 'here' but 'over there', even 'far away' (*ekei*)). The amphora will be there, however, and no one has a better claim to the 'I' of the inscription than it. Kleimachos cannot make that claim. He writes on his amphora because he knows that he will not be there in the future (otherwise there would be no sense in writing). He designates himself as absent by the very fact that he has written the inscription. Everything else takes place between the inscribed amphora and the reader, face to face as 'I' and 'you'.

Because of their first person inscriptions, Glaukos's tomb and Kleimachos's amphora belong to a category of objects that have long been referred to as 'speaking objects'. Mario Burzachechi, the author of a ground-breaking article (in 1962) about such objects, attempted to explain the astonishing choice of the first person to designate the inscribed object.[40] His explanation is animist in that, according to Burzachechi, the fact of attributing a soul and a voice to objects is typical of primitive civilizations, and only in the second half of the sixth century BC can one 'begin to note a certain rationalization of the statue, which lost its former halo of magic'. In reality, however, categorization began on another level, in the relation established between the voice and the first person designating the inscribed object (the only criterion of selection in this corpus). By designating themselves with an 'I' (at times, with a 'we'), such objects are supposed to 'speak'. The object is taken to be gifted with speech, for the sole reason that it designates itself as 'I'.

It is true that a connection between the first person and the voice might seem self-evident, but if the voice were what constituted the first person, a mute could not claim an 'I'. This is totally absurd, and it forces us to break that connection unless we want to remain prisoners

of a metaphysics of the voice. The first person is no more endowed with
a voice – or with an inner being – than the third. In itself it has no voice
at all. What the first person does do is situate its referent, whether that
referent is a human being or an object. The choice of the first person to
designate the inscribed object, instead of being a sign of animism,
derives from an original staging of that object, which is present ('I')
before the reader ('you') in the absence of the writer ('he' or 'she'). At
the same time (but this is another story) it testifies to a psychological
density that the archaic Greeks attributed to the 'I'.

Although for all these reasons we would do well to avoid the current
definition of the term 'speaking object', it applies perfectly to the
inscribed object that appropriates the reader's voice. In a culture that
practises oralized reading, any inscribed object is necessarily a 'speaking
object', independent of its structure as an utterance (on the condition,
obviously, that it finds a reader). Used thus, the term would probably be
easy to justify if the other expression, 'inscribed object', did not already
occupy the terrain. It seems wiser, then, to reserve the term 'speaking
object' for objects that use the metaphor of the voice for their own purposes, such as the inscription (to which we will soon return): 'To
whoever asks me, I answer the same thing, namely, that Andron, son of
Antiphanes, dedicated me as a tithe.'[41] The archaic statuette that bears
this inscription is a 'speaking object', not because of its use of the first
person 'I', but because it uses a verb meaning 'to answer' – orally, of
course. It raises its 'voice', its metaphorical voice, that is.

This metaphor is extremely rare in the archaic period, and the inscription cited, which dates from the late sixth century, is in fact our first
undisputed example of it. As long as such an inscription is classified as a
'speaking object' in Burzachechi's sense, its exceptionality may easily go
unremarked, because what could the metaphor of the voice add to an
object that is already supposed to be talking? Let us attempt here to give
the metaphor its full weight; it is so remarkable that it invites both global
and detailed study. The logic that it sets up seems to run counter to all
that has been said so far about reading in ancient Greece. More precisely, in a culture in which the reader lends his voice to writing so that
such writing can attain its complete, sounded realization, the metaphor
of the voice, referring to the inscribed object that uses the metaphor,
seems strangely superfluous, unless it renders the reader's voice superfluous. Even before any sounded realization, the 'speaking' object possesses
a 'voice', its own metaphoric voice which distinguishes it from other
inscribed objects. This means that the 'speaking' object possesses a
'voice' without ever being read aloud by the reader. Everything happens,
in fact, as if the inscription of Andron, son of Antiphanes, could raise its
own metaphorical voice and do without the voice of the reader.

This is why I have insisted on the notion of 'speaking object' and on giving it a new definition. The object that uses the metaphor of the voice to designate its own written utterance ('I answer') enables us to suggest, as a hypothesis, the existence of a new form of reading, opposed to the one we have been considering thus far. The logic of Andron's inscription seems not to conform to traditional reading. Thanks to what has been said so far, we can sense the almost shocking nature of a non-oralized sort of reading – of silent reading. Silent reading was an incongruous idea, both in relation to oralized reading, which was beyond doubt the dominant form in antiquity, and in relation to modern research, which has generally remained deeply sceptical of the notion that the ancient Greeks might have practised non-oralized reading.[42] If for the Greeks the aim of alphabetic writing was, as stated above, the production of sound, of effective words and resounding glory, how did they get the idea of silent reading? Why would anyone read silently in a culture that makes silence a synonym of oblivion? This presents a formidable obstacle. We will have to look elsewhere – in particular, in the culture of the age in question – for a plausible basis for the hypothesis of silent reading. We can find elements of that basis in the law, justice and the *nomos*, a domain that, as we have seen, is related to reading, and one that displayed a remarkable internalization of the voice in the fifth century BC.

In an extremely dramatic scene toward the middle of Plato's *Crito*, the *Nomoi* (Laws) personified speak, and they continue to hold the floor throughout much of the rest of the dialogue. They back up the arguments of Socrates and Crito to explain at some length why Socrates should not escape from prison. Socrates, who directs the debate, remarks, 'Be well assured, my dear friend, Crito, that this is what I seem to hear, as the frenzied devotees of Cybele seem to hear the pipe; and this sound of these words re-echoes within me and prevents my hearing any other words. And be assured that, so far as I now believe, if you argue against these words, you will speak in vain!'[43] Obviously, despite its 'sound', the voice of the *Nomoi* is not an actual, external voice. Socrates hears the *Nomoi* that he evokes within himself, without any external acoustic stimulus. Normally, Socrates' internal dialogue, the 'soul's dialogue with itself', has no need of a voice, as stated in the *Sophist* and in the *Theaetetus*,[44] where Socrates' thoughts are produced in silence. Here that is no longer the case. The voice of the *Nomoi* is so strong that Socrates cannot 'hear any other words', let alone other voices. He will heed the words of the *Nomoi* that reverberate within him. He will not heed Crito, his old friend. External voices no longer count. Socrates hears nothing but the internal voice telling him what he must not do.

Socrates' inner voice also strongly recalls the 'daemonic' voice evoked in the *Theages*, the *Phaedrus* and, above all, the *Apology*, where Socrates says: 'I have had this from my childhood; it is a sort of voice that comes to me, and when it comes it always holds me back from what I am thinking of doing, but never urges me forward.'[45] The same passage informs us that Socrates often spoke to his fellow citizens about that inner voice; the accusation that led him to his death seems to allude to it as well. What we might call the 'voice of conscience' seems to have been a new, even shocking idea. For the majority of Socrates' contemporaries, the voice of the *nomos* was probably always an external voice, not an internal, individual one. For them, the *nomos* was distributed publicly. They had difficulty imagining Socrates' 'little distributor', the *daimonion*, whose strictly personal and internal discourse others could not hear.[46]

. As we have seen, the *nomos* could be understood as a vocal distribution, a recitation, or a reading aloud. In all these instances it was a sounded, acoustic phenomenon: the distribution of justice – of the *dike* – was an external operation whose instrument was the voice. Consequently, the *dike* itself was an external justice, publicly disseminated, for example, by the Hesiodic kings alluded to previously in connection with the meaning of *nemein*. As Eric Havelock has shown, however, it was only in the age of Herodotus and Protagoras, who were contemporaries of Socrates, that the *dike* was internalized, as in the word *dikaiosune*, or 'sense of justice'.[47] Evidence on the lexical level thus verifies the internalization of the *nomos* as Socrates' 'voice of conscience' in Plato's dialogues. In reality, what we see here is part of a broader trend toward internalization that took place in the fifth century, the century that also furnishes the first direct evidence of silent reading, or the internalization of the voice of the reader, henceforth able to 'read in his head'.

Silent Reading

In his article 'Silent reading in antiquity' (1968), Bernard Knox cites two fifth-century BC texts that seem to prove that the Greeks (more precisely, certain Greeks) practised silent reading, and that at the time of the Peloponnesian War, dramatists could count on their audience's familiarity with the habit.[48] The first of these texts is a passage from Euripides' *Hippolytus*, performed in 428 BC. Theseus notices a writing tablet hanging from the hand of the dead Phaedra, and he wonders aloud what it might tell him. He breaks the seal. The chorus expresses anxiety, but Theseus breaks in: 'O woe! What second pain on top of pain is this, pain unendurable, unspeakable! What misery is mine!'[49] At the request of the chorus he reveals the contents of the tablet, not by reading it aloud but by summarizing its contents. He has clearly read silently while the chorus was singing.

The second text that Knox cites is a passage from Aristophanes' *The Knights* (424 BC). In it Nicias has managed to steal from Paphlagon some written prophecies given by an oracle. 'I'll read it; hand it over,' Demosthenes tells Nicias, who fills a goblet of wine for him. Nicias asks: 'What do they say?' At that point, Demosthenes, absorbed in reading the prophecies, says: 'Fill me another cup.' Nicias, thinking Demosthenes is reading aloud, replies, '*Fill me another*? Is that really there?' The gag is repeated and developed in the lines that follow, until Demosthenes finally says: 'O villainous Paphlagon! . . . Herein is written how himself shall perish,' upon which he summarizes what the oracle had said.[50] Demosthenes does not read the prophecies; he has already done so silently. This passage thus shows us a reader accustomed to reading in his head (as demonstrated by the fact that he is able to interrupt his reading and ask for more wine), along with a listener who does not seem at all familiar with the practice, since he takes what the reader says to be taken from the text, which of course is not the case.

The scene from *The Knights* is particularly instructive, at least at first sight, because it indicates that the practice of silent reading was not familiar to everyone in 424 BC (Plato was five years old at the time), even though the author assumes that the theatre audience was familiar with it. Silent reading was probably practised by only a limited number of readers and was unfamiliar to a good many Greeks, especially to illiterates who knew about writing only 'from the outside'. The two documents that Knox cites come from Athens, and in other places (Sparta, for example, where school instruction in letters was limited to 'strict necessity') silent reading would have been even less likely to have been known, let alone practised. The reader who read little and only sporadically, slowly and with difficulty deciphering writing, was unlikely to need to internalize the voice, precisely because the voice was the instrument by means of which the graphic sequence was recognized as language. As we have seen, the sonorization of writing was negatively programmed by the absence of spaces between words, and since sonorization was valued as a good in itself, why should anyone feel the need to abandon the *scriptio continua* that was a technical impediment to the development of silent reading?

The absence of breaks in the written line was indeed a hindrance to silent reading, and it remained so. It was not an insurmountable obstacle, however, as we can surmise from the medieval experience. According to Paul Saenger, in the Middle Ages word division was a necessary condition for the dissemination of the practice of silent reading, developed by monks who copied texts under a rule of silence.[51] As we have seen, the Greeks seem to have been able to read in silence, even while retaining their *scriptio continua*. Knox suggests that frequenting a large number of texts opened the way to silent, hence rapid, reading in antiquity. In the fifth century Herodotus may easily have abandoned reading aloud in the course of his work as a historian, and in the later sixth century those who worked in Athens under Peisistratus and his successors to pursue a near-philological investigation of the Homeric text (the poet Simonides, for instance) probably had occasion to develop the technique of silent reading. It was of course a skill reserved to a minority, but an important minority that certainly included the dramatists.

The introduction of word division was not enough, by itself, to disseminate silent reading in the Middle Ages. It took more than a technical innovation introduced as early as the seventh century AD to do that. Only with scholasticism could the advantages of silent reading (rapidity and intelligibility) be rediscovered and exploited on a large scale. Silent reading took hold only within scholasticism, what is more; it remained nearly unknown in the rest of medieval society.[52] Similarly, in my opinion frequenting great numbers of texts was not in itself enough to make silent reading take hold in certain milieus of fifth-century BC Greece. It seems to me that extensive reading was the result of a qualitative innovation, a change in readers' attitudes toward writing. It sprang from an entirely new mental framework powerful enough to restructure the categories of traditional reading. Silent reading cannot have been structured by quantity alone: indeed, Knox himself cites post-classical authors (for example, the highly learned Didymus of Alexandria, the author of several thousand books) only when he speaks of the vast reading of ancient scholars. Silent reading might, on the other hand, have emerged out of theatrical experience.

The Theatrical Model

What traits typical of theatrical representation are sharply enough defined and original enough to have lent structure to the new practice of silent reading? The first thing that comes to mind is the marked separation between the stage and the public. That distance set apart the fictional events taking place on the stage; to a certain extent, it is what is original about drama. The audience cannot intervene as the story is played out. It cannot communicate to characters on-stage what it already knows about the fate that awaits them. It cannot stop the action to tell the characters what they should do. In tragedy, it can only 'contemplate' (*theasthai*) them as they advance toward their own destruction. The tension that this situation creates makes the stage action all the more fascinating: the theatrical spectacle takes place with an autonomy that the audience must not disturb, as Thespis declared in the rules of the 'game' (*paidia*) laid down in the mid-sixth century, defending his new art in the face of Solon's indignant criticisms.[53]

The audience (and this was true as early as Thespis's days) must look and listen passively. It was not up to the spectators either to take part in the stage action or to read the text that, absent from the stage, none the less commanded the action. The text, memorized by the actors, was not visible at the moment it was spoken;[54] the actors had replaced it, translating it into 'vocal writing' (an expression discussed below) rather than into reading aloud. The actors did not read the text; they produced a vocal copy of it. In that, they differed from the ordinary reader, who lent his voice to the written matter before him. We cannot view the ordinary reader as producing another (vocal) writing when he read, for the simple reason that his voice was perceived as the 'natural' continuation of that writing or as its completion or necessary supplement. Nor can the reader's voice be considered a copy of a written text. Reading aloud took place in the presence of the written text, and anyone hearing the reading could not mistake the connection between writing and voice. Unlike the words pronounced by an actor, the words of a reader are not learned by heart, although any reader is free to memorize what he reads.

The dramatic text, on the other hand, seems to have been sufficiently separated from its dissemination by the actors to enable us, provisionally at least, to call it 'vocal writing'. The actors may have read the text in order to memorize it, but during the performance their voices substituted for the written text. The spectators listened to their 'vocal writing'. And although the actor is not to be confused with the reader, listening to such vocal writing does not make the spectators into readers in the traditional sense. As spectators, theatre audiences had no need to activate or reactivate writing by the intervention of their own voices, for the writing was speaking to them autonomously. They listened – passively – to a vocal writing.

The separation between the stage, where that vocal writing was delivered, and the audience, which listened, is probably clear enough to have suggested to the Greeks an analogous separation between writing and the reader, or, more precisely, to have opened up to them the possibility of a new attitude towards writing. The traditional reader, who needed to use his voice in order to 'recognize' the graphic sequence, engaged in a notably active relation with writing on the level of sonorization (even

though his role was that of a 'passive partner' of the writer, whose programme he executed). He had to make a mental and physical effort to
accomplish his instrumental function, or the letters would continue to
bear no meaning. Someone who is able to read in silence has a seemingly passive relation to writing; he is no longer the instrument of
writing, which 'speaks' to him unaided. It is the reader's task to listen
passively.

Put differently, the activity of the person who reads in silence is not
experienced as an effort to decipher. It is an activity unaware of itself as
an activity, just as the interpretive activity of the 'ear' listening to a
sound sequence that bears meaning is unaware that it is engaged in
something active, rather than passive reception. Its 'recognition' of
meaning is immediate, not preceded by a moment of meaninglessness.
Readers who read in their heads do not need to activate or reactivate
writing by the intervention of the voice. Writing seems to them simply
equivalent to speaking. They listen attentively to writing, just as spectators in a theatre listen to the vocal writing of the actors. Writing that
is 'recognized' visually seems to possess the same autonomy as theatrical performance. The letters read (or rather, speak) themselves. The
'silent' reader does not need to act on the stage of writing: the letters are
capable of 'speaking', and they can do so without the intervention of
the reader's voice. They already have a voice of their own. The reader's
task is to 'listen' to that voice within himself. The reading voice has
become internalized.

If the reader's 'passivity' is inherited from the passivity of the theatre-
goer, how far back in time can we hope to trace it? George Thomson's
analysis of the verb form *hypokrinomai* (or *hypokrinesthai*), 'to play a
role', may help to pinpoint the decisive moment when that passivity was
established.[55] As Thomson remarks, *hypokrinomai* has two distinct
meanings in Homeric poetry, 'to answer' and 'to interpret' (a dream or
omen). Unlike other scholars, who attempted to choose between these
two meanings to explain the origin of the noun *hypokrites*, 'actor',
Thomson wonders why the same word served for both meanings. He
cites a passage from the *Odyssey* in which Peisistratos asks Menelaus,
'Is this omen intended for you or for us?' Menelaus then wonders 'how
he should *interpret* it (or *answer*) aright'.[56] The key to the problem,
Thomson states, is given in a passage from Plato's *Timaeus* defining the
word *prophetes*. Thomson says, paraphrasing Plato, 'Some people ...
speak of *prophêtai* as though they were the same as *mánteis*,
"prophets" [seers who give their statements in the grip of ecstasy], but
this usage is incorrect: the *prophêtai* are not prophets, but interpreters
(*hypokritaí*) of enigmatical utterances and appearances.'[57] If such
a person is the leader of a chorus that is performing a rite whose

significance is not understood by the audience, the *hypokrites* can 'respond' to questions by 'interpreting' what is happening. For example, he can state, 'I am Dionysus, and these are the daughters of Eleuther, whom I have driven mad.'[58] Later, when the leader of the chorus began to give 'responses/interpretations' without being asked for them, he was, by that token, no longer a *hypokrites* in the traditional sense, but had become an actor. The separation between the stage space, become autonomous, and the spectators, now passive, had been established.

As it happens, that very verb, *hypokrinesthai*, appears in the inscription of Andron, son of Antiphanes, which we have already seen. This metrical inscription in Attic dialect found in Athens belonged to a bronze statuette, now lost, of the late sixth century BC. It states:

pasin	*is'*	*anthropois hypokrinomai hostis eratai*	
to any	man		who asks
		I answer	
	in identical fashion		

----

hos	*m' anethek'*	*Andron*	*Antiphanous*	*dekaten*
that		Andron	son of Antiphanes	
	dedicates me			as a tithe

The transcription and its translation call for several remarks. By the end of the sixth century BC, the theatre already existed in an institutionalized form. Tragedy competitions began in 534, and performances (before Aeschylus, with one actor and a chorus) probably date from some thirty years earlier.[59] When Andron's statuette was inscribed, the tragic poet Thespis (the inventor of the actor) was already at the height of his career. The verb *hypokrinomai* thus inevitably has a richer meaning than the translation 'I answer', given above, would indicate. In Attic dialect 'to answer' was not in fact *hypo-krinesthai*, as it was in Ionian. In Athens people used *apo-krinesthai* in that sense. If the author of the inscription had wanted to write 'I answer', he would have used *apokrinomai*, the metrical equivalent of *hypokrinomai*. He did not do so. We are thus led to think that the verb was chosen to express more than the simple idea of a response.

When the inscribed statuette uses the term *hypokrinomai*, it raises its 'voice'; it 'speaks'. By force of circumstance, its speech is as much theatrical as vocal: in its metaphorical voice, the inscription answers a question that is not asked of it at the moment but one that it anticipates with full autonomy of action. The inscription operates like the *hypokrites* on the stage who gives his 'response' without being asked for it. But if *hypokrinomai* also indicates that the statuette interprets what is presented as an enigma (that is, what meaning should be given to the inscribed statuette), it gives its own interpretation of itself. It deciphers itself before the eyes of the spectator-reader, who need make no effort to vocalize the writing, because here the writing 'vocalizes' itself. The statuette, as both actor and reader, offers us a representation of the voice. This was new. Before the invention of silent reading, writing aimed at the production of a voice, not at a representation of it. Until writing was turned into sounds it represented no more than random letters.

When the inscription addressed a spectator-reader who had no need to make his own voice heard, it could deliver its meaning directly to the eye. Why read aloud, if the inscription can 'speak' in silence? The meaning of the object arrives at the reader's eyes like a sort of irradiation or 'effluvium'. The object radiates its meaning to the reader. The meaning of the object is no longer laboriously activated by the reader's voice. Its writing is autonomous; it 'speaks'. This is what seems to me to be the logic of this inscription, which testifies indirectly (not directly, as in the passages from *Hippolytus* and *The Knights*) to the practice of silent reading in late-sixth-century Athens and, by the same token, testifies to the internalization of theatrical space into written space. Henceforth, written space might be a stage.

This new form of reading, in which the reader was made a passive spectator of an active writing that radiated its meaning, reflected a concept also found in the theories of visual perception elaborated in the fifth century by Empedocles, Leucippus and Democritus. At the start, with Empedocles, the situation seems confused. According to Aristotle, 'Empedocles seems sometimes to imagine that one sees because light issues from the eye.'[60] This means that Empedocles' position contradicted the theory implied in silent reading, where the writing emitted meaning in the direction of the eye. Aristotle adds, however, 'At times [Empedocles] explains vision in this way, but at times he accounts for it by emanations (*aporrhoiai*) from objects seen.'[61] Empedocles' successors preferred the latter position. The atomists, beginning with Leucippus, saw vision as the result of an emanation or effluvium (*aporrhoe*) from the objects seen that travelled toward the eye. One third-century AD philosopher summarized their theory thus: 'They attribute to vision certain images that, having the same form as the object, flow [the verb *aporrhein*] ceaselessly from the objects seen to arrive at the eye. This was the position of the schools of Leucippus and Democritus.'[62] The atomists thus thought vision could be explained by a continuous emission of particles coming from the object seen and passing (in somewhat complex ways, given constraints inherent in atomistic theory) to the receiving eye. Empedocles' position probably owes its ambiguity to the fact that he had to abandon a widely accepted theory in an attempt to elaborate another new, more satisfactory one. The atomists who inherited that new theory were more decisive, at least about what interests us here. The eye does not emit a ray in order to see; it receives an effluvium from the objects seen. Vision moves from object to eye.

The analogous relation between visual perception and silent reading, with the eye passively receiving the irradiation of writing, cannot be understood fully unless it is connected with a fundamental fact in atomistic theory. The various combinations of elements in the physical world can be explained, the atomists stated, by reference to the model of the alphabet, whose twenty-four letters combine to form words. In Greek *stoicheia* in fact means both 'letters' and 'elements'.[63] 'Tragedy and comedy are written with the same letters,' Leucippus declared.[64] Similarly, in the physical world a limited number of elements combine and recombine to change things. As Heinz Wissmann has pointed out, we can accurately speak of the 'ontography' of the atomists. In atomist theory visual perception nearly becomes a silent reading of the world.

If in the sixth century BC the statuette that Andron dedicated is an isolated case of a 'speaking' object (in the sense defined above), by the fifth century that metaphor had become more and more frequent, not in the domain of inscriptions but among authors with a less laconic style who, for that reason, were open to changing their reading habits. My first example is Aeschylus, whose leadership in this domain is significant. In *Seven Against Thebes* three heroes' shields, those of Capaneus, Eteocles and Polynices, suggest to Aeschylus the metaphor of the speech of writing.[65] 'For blazon', the Messenger tells Eteocles, Capaneus 'hath a man, a fire-bearer, armourless, save that in his hands for weapon a torch blazes; and in letters of gold he saith (*phonei*) "I will fire the town" '. In the context of drama, where one can encounter such remarkably synesthetic expressions as 'I see the noise', it seems logical for objects to talk and for the figure on a shield to 'vociferate' as this one does, or 'shout' (*boai*), as the figure on Eteocles' shield does, according to the alphabetical letters placed around it. On Polynices' shield, finally, we see Justice personified, identified not by her traditional attributes, but by a legend. The scout reports: 'Justice, it seemeth, she declares herself, as the legend runs (*legei*).'

My second example comes from Herodotus. In his works, too, the letters of the alphabet begin to talk (*legein*), and effusively. Written oracles speak. and stelae and tripods raise their 'voices', as does a stone statue of the king of Egypt, Sethos (Seti), which 'pronounces' its own inscription.[66] For a historian who wrote extensively and read even more, silent reading, which theatrical experience made possible (and we might recall that Herodotus was a friend of Sophocles), was a natural choice. Herodotus needed to read fast, if only in order to work out his own written works. Moreover, at a certain point, increased reading speed necessarily implies internalization of the reading voice, which removes the physical voice from reading and shifts reading to the head.

Staged Writing and Writing in the Soul

The inscription of Andron, son of Antiphanes, marks a decisive moment in the Greeks' relations with written space. It is no accident that Plato's *Phaedrus* echoes it, more than a century later, in a passage concerning the essence of writing.[67] Socrates compares writing to painting, and he reproaches writing with 'always say[ing] only one and the same thing', which was precisely what Andron's inscription had boasted of doing. Socrates might of course have reproached actors for always repeating the same words, given that their voices were only the instruments of an immutable text, rather than the voice of someone who possesses knowledge (*episteme*). He does in fact do just that elsewhere. The two situations are comparable because, as we have seen, writing and the actor are analogous and interchangeable. The actor replaces writing on the stage; writing substitutes for the actor in Andron's inscription. When the actor produces what I call 'vocal writing', he opens the way for a new attitude toward writing, and creates the possibility for reading to be silent. In reality, the inscribed statuette dedicated by Andron defines itself as an 'actor' (*hypokrites*), which presupposes this new attitude. By giving the reader the role of spectator, written space borrows its logic from the theatre to become a 'stage'. It internalizes theatre.

This conclusion is justified both by Andron's inscription and by the passage from Euripides' *Hippolytus* that we have already looked at, where the writing tablet of the dead Phaedra 'cries aloud, it cries aloud of horror! (*boai boai deltos alasta*)'. As Euripides stages the scene, writing not only 'speaks' during the act of silent reading; it 'cries aloud'. It is even capable of singing: several lines later, Theseus continues, 'Such is the song I in my wretchedness have seen whose tune sounds in the writing! (*hoion hoion eidon en graphais melos phthengomenon*).'[68] The actor who sings the role of Theseus (this is a lyric passage) thus sings a sounded *melos* (a song for the eye) that emerges out of writing.

On the stage we have a singing actor; on the writing tablet (which is read in silence, thus internalizing theatrical space) we have 'singing' letters. It is hard to imagine a scene that would tell us more about silent reading than this one. First, it places the figurative song of the written text within the context of a song actually sung on the stage, thus emphasizing the analogy between theatrical space and writing read in silence. Next, it establishes a clear correlation between the 'speaking' object and silent reading, where the 'voice' heard in the head during silent reading corresponds perfectly to the 'speaking' object. Thus the *Hippolytus* offers more than external fact, which would not allow us to make an indisputable distinction between silent reading and reading that is merely inaudible to others. It also presents an internal aspect that confirms Bernard Knox's interpretation by adding facts regarding the mental architecture of genuinely silent reading.

If the theatre was internalized in the book, the book was in turn internalized in the mental space variously designated as *phren*, at times as *psyche*. This occurred well before Plato, who compares ordinary writing with 'writing in the soul' in the *Phaedrus*.[69] The first to use the metaphor of 'the book of the soul' was in fact Pindar, who exclaims in a poem (which we have already seen above in relation to the verb *anagignoskein*), 'Read me the name of the Olympian victor! ... Tell me where it is written [verb *graphein*] in my heart [*phren*]!'[70] It is with the tragedians, however, that the metaphor was most used before Plato picked it up. And for good reason: the dramatic poets, who produced texts that the actors learned by heart, had had experience with the process of inscribing the text in the actors' minds. From the dramatist's point of view, the actor received an inscription just as much as a stone or a sheet of writing did. Within the actor there was a scripted space; the dramatic text was 'inscribed' in the mind of the person who was to speak it on the stage. This is what justifies the expression 'vocal writing' that I have used throughout these pages. We can understand why Aeschylus (the second actor was introduced in his plays[71]) 'writes' on his actors' memory, whereas Homer (if indeed he was capable of writing) cannot be considered to have written on the memory of the rhapsodes, who were too remote from him in time and space for that metaphor to have had any meaning.

The works of Aeschylus provide good examples of the metaphor, although Sophocles and Euripides, the two other great tragic dramatists, used it as well. In *Prometheus Bound* the protagonist declares: 'First, to thee, Io, will I declare thy much-vexed wandering, and do thou engrave it on the recording tablets of thy mind (*phrenes*).'[72] The figure of Prometheus is linked to the origins of writing. According to one tradition, Danaüs has similar connections. He tells his daughters: 'And now that I have taken forethought also as to what may befall us here ashore, I charge you, record my injunctions on the tablets of your minds and give them good heed.' In the *Eumenides*, the chorus compares Hades' memory to a writing tablet: 'For the Lord of Death is mighty in holding mortals to account beneath the earth; and he surveyeth all things with his recording mind (*phren*).' In a last example from

Aeschylus, Electra says to Orestes: 'Hear my tale and grave it on thy heart (*phrenes*).' The poet might have said the same to one of his actors.

Athens: The Alphabet on Stage

The relationship between the theatre and the book and between the book and the mind thus came to be internalized. This dual inward trend – from the theatre to writing and from writing to the mind – was reflected in a dual outward movement. Mental space found a natural externalization in the book. Although we cannot document it, we can even postulate that silent writing existed. Indeed, written *hypomnema* might substitute for a weak memory.[73] This might constitute an external, objective memory something like a personal notebook, not to be confused with the living memory of a person. Plato made use of this objectivized memory (although he was aware of its limitations). So did the dramatic poets, whose texts constituted a *hypomnema* that was not written with a view to readers in later ages, but for the single, immediate performance, which was probably its indispensable condition.

If mental space could be externalized in written space, that written space could in turn be externalized in theatrical space. This first occurred quite naturally when the dramatic text was staged, in a movement basic to the system of interdependent representations, because it produced what I have called 'vocal writing'. In ancient Greece that externalization was put on the stage quite literally and in a singular fashion in the *Grammatical Play*, or *Alphabet Show* (in Greek, *Grammatike theoria*), of the Athenian poet Callias.[74] The play's date of composition poses a thorny problem, as does its musical and metrical relation to Euripides' *Medea* (431 BC) and Sophocles' *Oedipus Rex* (soon after 430). Did Callias's play inspire the other two plays, or was it a parody of them? Without entering into this debate here, let us simply date this work to the latter half of the fifth century BC. All the proposed dates fall within that period, and it will do for our purposes.

What did the *Alphabet Show* offer for the contemplation (*theoria*) of its spectators (*theatai*)? Nothing less than a chorus of twenty-four women who represented the Ionian alphabet. They introduce themselves in the Prologue:

> Say alpha, beta, gamma, delta, and then
> The God's [Apollo's] epsilon, zeta, eta, theta,
> With iota, kappa, lambda, mu and nu,
> Xei and omicron, pei, rho, sigma, tau,
> Upsilon, phei, chei, psei, to omega.

Next, the chorus, ranged in pairs, presents a typical elementary school exercise:

Beta alpha ba
Beta epsilon be
Beta eta be
Beta iota bi
Beta omicron bo
Beta upsilon bu
Beta omega bo.

In the antistrophe they sing, 'Gamma alpha ga; gamma epsilon ge', and so on, through 'gamma eta' to 'gamma omega', in all, seventeen strophes sung to the same melody.

After this 'syllabic chorus' (which modern language learning specialists would find appalling) comes a dialogue between the choragus, playing the role of a schoolmaster, and two women of the chorus:

Woman: Alpha alone, dears, I must say, and then
            Epsilon alone.
Choragus: And third alone you'll say –
Woman: Eta.
Choragus: And fourth alone –
Woman: Iota.
Choragus: And fifth –
Woman: Omicron.
Choragus: Sixth alone upsilon say.
Woman: Upsilon.
Choragus: And the last of the seven vowels
            In seven lines alone, I give you omega,
            And when you've said that say all to yourself.

In the following fragment Callias amuses himself by describing two letters in detail without saying their names but making quite clear what they are. Euripides does the same thing in his *Theseus*, where an illiterate shepherd describes the letters of the name 'Theseus' without himself knowing what the letters spell.[75] In Callias's play, the device is obviously not based on ignorance of the letters. One woman (who may personify the art of writing) announces:

Dears, I'm with child. So help me Modesty,
I'll spell you the baby's name – a long upright
With short up-slanting strokes on either side,
And then a circle on two little feet.[76]

These are clearly the letters Ψ and Ω, two signs from the Ionian alphabet, hence illegitimate in an Athenian context. It is precisely those two letters, what is more, that should have ended the seventeenth strophe of the 'syllabic chorus'. Unfortunately, we do not know the precise significance of *psi*, though it is undoubtedly obscene. In any event, *psi* must refer to something that the woman is ashamed to say. Moreover, the joke is delivered on the stage, and those two particular letters have a pictographic value that lends itself to obscene pleasantries. After all, Sophocles used an actor dancing the form of the letters in his satiric play *Amphiaraos*.[77]

Be that as it may, during the latter half of the fifth century BC, the Ionian alphabet appeared on the stage in the theatre of Dionysus in Athens, a noteworthy event. In the same period, letters begin to 'speak' repeatedly in the works of Herodotus, a friend of Sophocles, thus providing indirect evidence of the practice of silent reading (and, I might add, of silent writing). In a movement exactly counter to Andron's inscription (which preceded it by about a century), the *Alphabet Show* made writing, which was normally concealed in the theatre, visible. Writing, the 'great absentee', finally appeared on-stage. The title of Callias's play insists on this visibility: the word *theoria*, a word derived (as was *theatron*) from *theaomai* ('I see, I contemplate'), the literal meaning of which is a spectacle for the eyes. Thus the audience could see the letters in the theatre, not simply hear the 'vocal writing' of the actors. The letters of the alphabet were displayed to view, not just inscribed in the actors' memory. The stage as a whole was clearly a 'scripted' space capable of 'responding', that is, of speaking itself, reading itself, and interpreting itself aloud.

The idea of a dramatic representation of this sort could have been born in the mind only of someone for whom letters were already autonomous and for whom their vocalization was not a necessary condition for comprehension. In other words, it must have come from the mind of someone for whom the letters had become 'pure' representations of a voice (a real voice transcribed or a fictional voice, as in the case of silent writing), and for whom their primordial aim of producing *kleos* (resounding fame) was no longer their only purpose – in short, in the mind of someone intimately familiar with silent reading.

This conclusion is still inadequate, however, to the extent that it suggests that silent reading eventually triumphed in the Greek world. In reality, silent reading remained a marginal phenomenon, practised by professionals of the written word – people plunged into such vast amounts of reading as to encourage the internalization of the reading voice. For the average reader the normal manner of reading continued to be reading aloud, as if the original reason for Greek writing, which was to produce sound, not to represent it, could not be eliminated. The voice never abdicated in ancient Greece. For cultural reasons, its reign was not even seriously threatened. This means that silent reading never developed a vocabulary of its own; instead, it took over existent terms such as *anagignoskein*, which eventually came to refer not only to an acoustic recognition of writing read aloud, but also to a visual recognition of the graphic sequence as it 'speaks' directly to the eye. Innovative though it was, silent reading among the Greeks remained profoundly determined by reading aloud, whose irrepressible internal echo it retained.

2

Between *Volumen* and Codex: Reading in the Roman World

Guglielmo Cavallo

What is the earliest date at which we can speak of the presence of genuine books in Rome or of the rise of reading practices? It is clear that in the early centuries of Rome the use of writing was limited to the priests and to aristocratic groups who were the depositories of the city's fundamental stores of knowledge, both sacred and juridical, in areas such as measuring time and chronicling events. Those stores of knowledge were very probably contained in *lintei* books (books made of linen cloth used mostly to note religious matters) or written on wooden tablets or *tabulae*. The earliest forms of literature in Rome remained tied to the small circle of the governing class and to particular needs in community life. Thus we find oratorical prose in a sober style, eulogies (*mortuorum laudationes*), records of magistracies and chronicles of the city written with no attempt at rhetorical ornament. Cato the Censor (234–149 BC) read his orations from tablets;[1] he also composed a 'History of Rome' that he wrote out 'in large characters' (to make the text easier to read) so that his son could profit from the experience of the past as he learned the rudiments of reading.[2] We are still far from genuine books and real reading practices, but the age of Cato was a turning point.

In 181 BC came the discovery of the so-called books of Numa, papyrus rolls wrapped in sheets of cedar bark. The sources (which disagree in some particulars) tell us that some of these rolls, written in Greek, were philosophical and doctrinal in content. These were burned, perhaps because they ran counter to institutionalized religion. Others were written in Latin, and were about priestly law (*de jure pontificum*).[3] The rolls were forgeries (Livy states that they were 'of very recent aspect'[4]), but they tell us that at that time the *volumen*, the book roll made of papyrus that had been in circulation in the Hellenistic world for some time, was known in Rome. They also tell us that papyrus was being imported into Rome, which means that it could be used for books. In the same period we find the first reliable attestations in the Roman world (in Ennius and, some decades later, in Lucilius) of the use of papyrus as a writing material, hence the first evidence of the roll as a support for literary texts.[5]

The rise of the roll can be linked with two events of capital import- ance that were highly characteristic of Roman culture between the end of the third and the beginning of the first century BC: the birth of a Latin literature invigorated by Greek models and the arrival of entire Hel- lenistic libraries in Rome as war booty. These two events occurred in an age when Greek influence was increasing and a passion for collecting objects of Greek manufacture was on the rise, which means that imported Greek books were models for the Latin book at its birth. Works such as Livius Andronicus's *Odyssia* and Naevius's *Bellum Poenicum* were indeed written in papyrus *volumina*, but it does not appear that they were intentionally subdivided into an ordered series of books that followed a conscious plan.[6] None the less, the fact that Ennius's *Annales* was divided into eighteen books from the start,[7] and that the grammarian Ottavius Lampadio later divided Naevius's *Bellum Poenicum* into seven books (after its composition) indicates that Romans were responsive to the growing presence of Greek books, and were gradually becoming aware of the relation between text and book. This was a matter not only of transposing *exemplaria Graeca* into a dif- ferent cultural context, but also of taking inspiration from those models to acquire an overall discipline of how to structure a book, organizing and disposing the text so as to facilitate reading.

The Birth of a Reading Public

The story goes that before he took his life, Cato Uticensis retired to his chamber, took up the *Phaedo*, Plato's dialogue on the soul, and read a good part of it. Realizing that his sword was not hanging in its usual place, he called a servant, and asked him who had removed it. Receiv- ing no answer, he went back to his reading, interrupting it after a while to tell the servant to fetch the sword. When he had finished the book, and still no one had brought back the sword, he raised his voice, demanding to be obeyed. When the sword was brought to him, he returned to Plato's text, rereading it perhaps twice. He then slept for a while, but early the next morning he took his life by thrusting the sword into his breast.[8]

Aside from the quite particular psychological circumstances in which Cato appears here as a reader, we see a man reading in the privacy of his own chambers, interrupting his reading to give orders to the servants and take a quick nap. At the end of the Republic the rise of domestic reading in solitude and the rise of 'privacy' seem to have gone hand in hand in Rome. It is not surprising that our reader, Cato, should be engrossed in a Platonic dialogue: in the first century BC reading works of high culture, especially those by Greek authors, had become a widespread practice among the governing class in Rome. According to Cicero, the younger Cato often arrived at the Senate with a book in his hand, or could be seen immersed in reading the Stoic philosophers in the villa in Tusculum of the younger Lucullus,[9] who had inherited a library that his father had brought to Rome from the East as *Pontica praeda* after defeating Mithradates.

The first private libraries in Rome were the spoils of conquest.[10] Even before Lucullus, Aemilius Paulus had brought back to Italy the books of Perseus, the king of Macedonia, and the dictator Sulla had sacked Athens, transferring to his villa at Pozzuoli the *volumina* of Apellicon of Teos, the bibliophile and peripatetic philosopher whose enviable collection of books even included volumes that had belonged to Aristotle and Theophrastus. These libraries, structured on the Hellenistic-Alexandrian model, inspired new private and wholly Roman libraries that served a growing number, but still an élite group, of readers. A new model for the library slowly took form in Rome, as we can see from Cicero's letters. He divided his libraries, in Rome and in his villas at Formia and Tusculum, into two collections, Greek and Latin, thus representing Rome's joining of the two cultures. The library of his brother Quintus was similarly arranged.

The formation of these new libraries (those of Cato and of Cicero and his brother Quintus, but also those of Atticus and Varro) was impeded by current conditions for the production of Latin books, which were far from coming up to the standards of quality of Greek books:[11] 'As for the Latin books, I don't know which way to turn; they are copied out and sold so full of mistakes,' Cicero wrote to Quintus, who already had a Greek library but wanted to create a Latin collection.[12] Cicero himself had difficulty finding Latin works that he had read and admired as an adolescent,[13] and in order to add to his 'Latin library' he did not hesitate to have transcriptions made of books sent to him by Vibius, a mediocre poet.[14] When Lucius Papirius Paetus gave Cicero the library he had inherited from his brother, Cicero thanked him particularly warmly for the Latin books, which he may have enjoyed more than the Greek ones.[15]

When we find Cato immersed in reading the Stoics in Lucullus's library, or when we see Cicero not only using his own books to good advantage but also dipping into the collections of Faustus Sulla, Lucullus and his friend Atticus,[16] it shows us that behind these libraries lay the idea of a noble residence or villa that provided an opportunity for tranquillity and *otium* amid books and friends. Such villas, which were furnished not only with libraries but also with porticoes, spaces for relaxation, art galleries, gardens and spaces whose designations – *academia*, *gymnasium*, *lyceum* or *palaestra* – were intended to evoke Hellenistic institutions, were places of sociability. They provided a background for the private reading of the cultivated classes.[17] Similarly, the fact that outsiders (also of the limited 'closed caste') could consult books in private libraries shows that such collections fulfilled a need for reading (for both study and recreation) that was broader than it had been in the past. None the less, individual libraries could not satisfy that need, largely because book production was still small in scale, disorganized and technically backward. This may explain why an author (Cicero, for example) might turn to expert *librarii* or to friends when he wanted to 'publish' a large number of books. Still, the first notice we have of the activity of bookshops is in Catullus and Cicero,[18] who were also the first to distinguish between certain categories of readers. On the booksellers' benches one could find *volumina* (perhaps roughly produced) of *pessimi poetae*, works that connoisseurs with refined tastes may have disdained, but that always had their circle of readers. Cicero speaks of a *multitudo* who were impressed by the inviting but *perfacilis* doctrine of the Epicurean Caius Amaphinius and his followers, whose writings were invading *Italiam totam*.[19] Cicero also states, however, that those who dabbled in undistinguished philosophical doctrines found few readers besides themselves and their immediate circles.[20] Cicero's reference to people of modest social standing (craftsmen and old people) who were fond of 'history' calls for comment: Cicero stresses that such people read (or listened to) historical works for pleasure (*voluptas*), not for the *utilitas* to be drawn from reading that was the aim of the better-educated reader.[21] Cicero hypothesized that the differences in reading style that he noted were linked to types of readers, and he thought it likely that writings in a somewhat simple style (a decade or so later, the biographies of Cornelius Nepos, or the deeds of Caesar as recounted by his generals) might also appeal to less educated readers.[22] In short, both Catullus and Cicero (the latter more explicitly) refer polemically to cultural contexts and circles of readers who were less skilled than the élites that they themselves represented, but at that time these were circles whose interests were as limited as their size.

What the library (either 'professional' or 'for reading') was like in the first private Roman collections can be judged from the only example to have survived, the library of the 'Villa of the Papyri' at Herculaneum. The Greek section, which is made up in very large part of Epicurean works, some imported from the East to Herculaneum and some brought together in the villa by Philodemus of Gadara, is, practically speaking, a philosophical library for professional use. The Latin section, as far as we can judge from the very few fragments of contemporary works, among them a work about the war between Octavian (Augustus) and Mark Antony, *Carmen de bello Actiaco*,[23] was instead intended to provide texts for various sorts of reading. This Latin library takes us into the Empire, however, when the scenario of reading in Rome was changing.

The same period saw the diffusion of the *novus liber*, which Cicero sought and Catullus described.[24] This was the Latin literary *volumen*, a high-quality product aimed at cultivated readers. These *volumina* inspired by Greek models had existed for centuries in the Hellenic world, but they were also produced in Italy in the late Republic and the Principate, as we can see from the Greek rolls at Herculaneum. A high grade of new papyrus was used for such works; the writing was carefully laid out on the page; the graphic forms used were accurate and at times even elegant; the texts were correct; distinctive initials highlighted section heads; and the name of the author and the title of the work were given in a special writing style at the end of each 'book' on the roll. Cylindrical sticks glued to the beginning and end of the text made it possible to roll and unroll the *volumen*. Presumably, the extant fragments of the imperial age in both verse (Cornelius Gallus)[25] and prose (Sallust)[26] came from Latin rolls of this sort.

This new interest in book production and layout paralleled the development in Rome of a new high-level literature that was much influenced by Greek culture (we need only think, once again, of Catullus and the neoteric poets). In contrast, the presence of another public, indifferent to the quality of the physical book and to the technical devices it employed, who read only for *voluptas* rather than *utilitas*, shows that reading was gradually broadening its scope. Eventually a genuine reading public grew up, made of readers who could no longer be classified as coming from the predictable circles, but who instead were anonymous and unknown to the authors. There were many authors of the imperial age who, unlike Cicero, eventually took such readers into account in their strategies for reaching an audience. In the age of Augustus the new reading public, although sizeable, was limited to the

Italian peninsula; but by the end of the Julian–Claudian age it had become much bigger and more varied, and was scattered throughout the Empire. This trend grew even stronger as Italy's sociopolitical and cultural hegemony over the provinces weakened, when authors and readers alike took advantage of an increased ethnic and social mobility to emerge out of the middle classes and move away from the provincial cities. The men of letters of the time enthusiastically imagined their writings being distributed, thanks to books, to the very extremities of the world. The reading public was still a minority, however: 'Not millions, not even hundreds of thousands, perhaps at the height of Roman civilization no more than a few tens of thousands.'[27] None the less, that minority was capable of supporting both literary production and book-making production that reflected a variety of cultural levels. There is no way that we can measure the exact number of readers, the number of copies in any one 'press run', the number of books that were actually read, or which books were read the most.

The first segment of that reading public included the same leisured and cultivated aristocratic circles for whom reading had always been part of *otium*. Next, and closely connected with the first group, came the ranks of grammarians and rhetoricians, some of whom might even be slaves or freedmen, and only some of whom were fond of reading the 'classics'. Finally, there was a public of new readers distinct from both the highly educated circles of literati and teachers and from the uncultivated masses, a mid-range public that even included some members of the lower classes.

The spread of reading practices in the imperial age was directly related to increased literacy. Paul Veyne responds to the question of whether literacy was a privilege of the Roman upper class by stating: 'From Egyptian papyruses we can be sure of three things: there were illiterates who employed others to write for them; some people of the lower orders knew how to write; literary texts, classics, could be found in the smallest towns. . . . Beyond this we have only hints.'[28] In a more strictly Roman context, written traces of this complex literate public, which ranged from the humblest members of society to people with some education and, at times, even to highly cultivated people, can be found on the walls and in the houses of Pompeii in the form of graffiti that offer obscenities, scurrilous jokes, a line or two from a well-known author and elegant poetic compositions.

Reading, like study, was an 'ornament' of the traditional cultivated classes in Rome, who were imitated by the newly literate and social parvenus. An increase in reading in the Roman world (more precisely, the Greco-Roman world) between the first and the third centuries AD is an accepted fact. It is demonstrated (among other ways) by the use of scenes of reading in frescoes, mosaics and sculpted reliefs with a frequency too high to be attributed to an iconographic stereotype alone.

It is not always clear, however, just how the public had access to reading. Only up to a point can the increase in the number of public libraries in Rome and in the Roman world be related to an increased demand for reading.[29] Such libraries were created either as acts of public-spirited patronage or, when founded by the emperor, in an attempt on the part of the power structure to concentrate and appropriate written culture. In Rome at least the most important libraries – the library of Apollo on the Palatine founded by Augustus, for example, or the Ulpian library in Trajan's forum – were created with the aim of selecting and preserving either a specific literary patrimony or the written civil and religious records of Rome. We have no iconographic sources that show scenes of reading inside a public library; moreover, the usual practice of reading aloud, often standing, and using gestures and body movements to accompany delivery, would have been inappropriate for a space shared with many other people. Libraries were instead places in which to seek out old or rare works, to verify a fact, or to skim a passage or two; they were also spaces for urban living, places to meet with other people. They were, in substance, erudite libraries, originally conceived as places accessible to all, but in reality frequented by a limited public of the learned and the professional literati. The larger baths may have had minor libraries associated with them that contained works of a different sort (probably escapist literature),[30] but the works they contained were probably not read within the *exedrae* for books but elsewhere, along the major streets, inside the basilica, or in the halls of other buildings connected with the baths. The public libraries' potential readers were in large part the same people who could afford (or who did in fact have) a private library. Their numbers increased around the turn of the first century BC to the first century AD, when a private library even became an obligatory part of an opulent residence, even when the wealthy owner had little education or could not read fluently. By that time the book and reading had become solidly established in the repertory of artefacts that distinguished people of a certain social prominence.

Even if we do not know precisely how books were distributed in that period, it is a traditionally accepted notion that they were produced within aristocratic residences, not only for the proprietor's use, but also for that of his circle of friends and clients. We also have evidence of increasing numbers of bookshops, *tabernae librariae* run by entrepreneurs of modest social origins, freedmen in general. Some of the booksellers of imperial Rome made a name for themselves, the Sosii brothers, Dorus and Triphonius, to name a few. Atrectus had a bookshop that had shelves inside and inscriptions outside advertising his books, while in the provinces there were bookshops in Gaul (in Lyons and Vienne) and in Britannia.[31] Bookshops might also be places where one could meet people and participate in learned conversations. Gellius remembers having attended a heated discussion about how Sallust's *Histories* should be read when, as a very young man (around the beginning of the second century), he was in a bookshop in the Sandalmakers' Street.[32] In sixth-century Constantinople, several centuries later, bookshops seem to have continued to be places for cultivated sociability, even for gatherings of 'pseudo-intellectuals'.

Ways to Read

Reading a literary text demanded a high level of technical skill and a broad culture. For other purposes a lesser degree of literacy would suffice. For instance, reading public announcements, documents or messages was facilitated by the repetition of certain formulas.[33] Until the second or third century AD 'reading a book' normally implied reading a roll. The reader grasped the upper portion of the roll in the right hand, unrolling it as he went with the left hand, which held the part he had already read. When he finished reading, the roll would be completely rolled up in the left hand. These phases of the reading process, along with certain complementary gestures and movements, are reflected in scores of figurative representations, above all on funerary monuments.[34] Such depictions show a variety of poses. At times the roll is shown held in the right hand with an open portion sticking out to the left as if the reader were just beginning to read; at other times the reader holds the cylinders of the roll in his two hands, displaying a section of the text, of varying length, that he is in the process of reading. In depictions of 'interrupted reading' one hand holds both cylinders of an open roll, leaving the other hand free. On occasion the roll is shown held open to the final portion and held to the right side, indicating that the reader has almost come to the end. Finally, the roll can be shown completely rolled up, held in the left hand. Both iconographic and literary sources also testify to the use of a wooden reading stand to hold the roll that is being read; this device is shown resting on the lap of a seated reader or placed on a low supporting column. By using a stand to read a roll the portion of the text available for reading could be varied, making one column of writing visible or as many as five or six columns at one time, to judge by the amount of the roll that has been left open in certain depictions. When a roll was opened to show several columns at once, the reader could glance from time to time at the column he was reading and move easily from one passage to another. If the roll had illustrations, the eye could 'read' a sequence of images almost simultaneously, letting the mind fill in the temporal and spatial distances between the scenes represented in the pictures.[35]

Iconography also shows more general reading situations. We can see the reader alone with his book or reading in the presence of listeners, a schoolmaster reading to his pupils, an orator declaiming his discourse from a written text, a traveller reading in his cart, a guest lying on a banqueting couch glancing at the lines of a roll he holds in his hands, and a young girl reading intently, standing or seated under a portico. From literary sources we also know that Romans read when they went hunting as they waited for the game to be driven into nets or at night when they suffered from insomnia. In short, just as in the modern age, reading seems to have been very free, not only in its circumstances but also in its physiology.

The conditions for learning to read were different from one age to another, and they also varied according to social level and circumstances. In general, people learned to read within the family circle, with a private reading teacher, or in the public schools. The different phases and levels of learning varied as well, but all Romans probably began by learning to read the letters, capitals first. Reading skills might be limited to learning the indispensable rudiments, with the reader capable of reading only the 'box capitals', like Petronius's Ermerotus.[36] Through advanced training with grammar and rhetoric teachers, a reader might hone his skills to reach the advanced levels, even complete mastery. Before learning how to read, however, everyone learned to write. Children of school age (and since the age of first schooling varied from one period to another, between Rome and peripheral areas, and from one social group to another, the precise moment when they started school is hard to ascertain[37]) first had to learn the 'appearance and names' of the letters in strict alphabetical order, perhaps with the aid of ivory letters or other similar objects. Then they learned to write, following on a wooden board letters that the teacher had inscribed and eventually tracing them independently. In the final stages of this initial learning process pupils moved on to syllables, entire words and finally sentences.[38]

Reading was taught not only separately from writing, but also after writing, which means that some individuals whose schooling stopped after the early years could write but not read. Learning to read followed the same pattern as learning to write: the first reading exercises concentrated on recognizing the individual letters, later moving on to syllabic combinations and whole words. For quite some time reading speed continued to be very slow in these exercises, only gradually reaching a respectable rate of reading without error – an *emendata velocitas*. The student read aloud, and he learned to fix his eyes on the words that followed the words he was reading, an exercise that Quintilian (from whom we have all this information) considered very difficult, because it required divided attention (*dividenda intentio animi*). In sure and rapid reading the eye ran ahead of the mouth, thus reading was simultaneously visual and vocal. When Petronius says admiringly of a young slave who served him as a lector, 'he can ... read books at sight' (*librum ab oculo legit*), he is referring to the skill of an expert eye instantaneously deciphering writing. It is unclear, however, whether Petronius was talking about purely visual (hence silent) reading or vocalized reading.[39]

As Quintilian tells us in other passages and various other sources confirm, the most common way to read was thus reading aloud (at all levels and for all functions).[40] A text might be read directly or with a reader intervening between the book and the listener or listeners. The structure of certain poetic texts suggests that multiple readers might be involved. All these practices illustrate the close interaction between literary works and reading: the literary writing style was dominated by rhetoric, and its categories were adopted by other literary forms such as poetry, historiography and philosophical and scientific tracts. This means that such texts (especially when read aloud before an audience) required an expressive reading style, in which the reader's tone of voice and cadences were adjusted to the specific nature of the text and its typical stylistic effects. Not surprisingly, the verb used for poetic reading is often *cantare*, with the adjective *canora* referring to the voice that interprets poetry. In short, reading a literary text could be compared to performing from a musical score.[41] Even in school, a child who was learning to read had to learn 'when [he] should take breath, at what point he should introduce a pause into the line, where the sense ends or begins, when the voice should be raised or lowered, what modulation should be given to each phrase, and when he should increase or slacken speed, or speak with greater or less energy'.[42] When students did this sort of exercise, they began with passages from Homer and Virgil, then went on to the lyric, tragic and comic poets (some of the lyric poets – Horace, for example – in excerpts that avoided the licentious parts), and certain archaic poets and prose writers. Finally, students in the rhetoric schools read the orators and historians, either listening in silence, following the text as the master read, or taking turns to read aloud. One aim of such lessons was to locate possible formal defects in the text used. Reading a complex author in depth meant not stopping at the 'outer skin', but penetrating to the 'very blood and marrow of his words'.[43]

We have evidence of how much effort readers put into reading aloud from works on medicine that place reading among forms of physical exercise good for one's health,[44] which makes sense if we recall that reading was usually accompanied by fairly accentuated movements of the head, chest and arms. This custom may explain the iconographic motif of 'interrupted reading' encountered fairly frequently in depictions of reading a roll. The reader might do so to comment on a passage, make or exchange a remark with someone, or mark a pause; but he might also want to free one hand in order to emphasize a point with a strong gesture. Voice and gesture made reading a performance.

Expressive reading in turn conditioned literary writing, which was shaped to the practices and styles of oral delivery precisely because it was usually read aloud.[45] This means that the dividing line between the book and speech was far from clear. Methods for composing a text, with the author murmuring as he set it down or speaking as he dictated it to a scribe or read it to friends (a practice frequently attested), contributed to a written style so dependent on hearing that any infringement of the rigid rules of rhetoric was immediately apparent. The voice thus accompanied the written text in every phase of its journey from author to audience. Quintilian states that while memorizing 'the mind should be kept alert by the sound of the voice'. Reading aloud varied in its sonic qualities, however, according to the occasion and the nature of the text.[46]

Except when it was done by an expert or professional reader, reading was a slow operation. The writing hand presented a first difficulty: it might be a calligraphic 'book' hand (called in fact *libraria*), or it might be semi-cursive or cursive and full of ligatures that distorted the letters. Not everyone familiar with one form of writing could read another easily (or at all). Moreover, parsing the text aloud slowed down visual reading speed, and the clearer the reading, the surer and better the reader's articulated rendering, the slower it was. Other things hindered rapid reading as well. Until the first century AD the Romans used *interpuncta*, mid-level dots that indicated word division; but as early as the end of the first century even Latin texts began to be written in the *scriptio continua* that was common practice in the Greek world.[47] Writing had very few internal distinguishing features, and its series of continuous letters made it difficult for an unpractised eye to discern the limits of individual words and grasp their meaning. This means that vocal articulation was a great help to understanding the meaning of a text: once the graphic structure of the written text had been deciphered, hearing served better than sight for grasping how words followed one another, what each phrase meant, and when the reader should pause. Interpunction and other signs were not only aids to grasping the logical progression of a text, but also a help in clarifying its 'rhetorical' structure by signalling where to pause to take a breath and where to break up the rhythm of reading aloud. A further complication was that punctuation was not used systematically; nor did the various signs have any fixed function.

Scriptio continua had certain advantages. It offered the reader a neutral text on which to mark what he wanted to emphasize and where he planned to pause, according to the inherent difficulty of the text, but also (and above all) to his own level of comprehension and his reading skill. In all cases, because the author provided no firm indication of how the text should be read and none was inherent in the way the written text was presented, a good reading demanded not only cognitive skills and experience, but also an adequate preparation of the written text to plan where and how words would be subdivided, pauses signalled, discriminations drawn between assertions, and questions and metric structures communicated.

Henri-Jean Martin has called the practice of public readings 'one of the Romans' great institutions'.[48] Literary works were 'launched' in collective ceremonies known as *recitationes*,[49] and in fact in Latin the verb *recitare* does not imply reciting from memory, but 'the dual operation of the eye and the voice' of reading from a written text before an audience.[50] *Recitationes* were held in public places such as *auditoria*, *stationes* and *theatra*. The length of these reading sessions was usually determined by the length of the roll, which means that they varied within the technical limits of conventions governing the book roll itself, special cases aside. It should be stressed that public readings of this sort were social gatherings, times for worldly exchange among people of intellectual habits. Moreover, precisely because they were literary and social 'rites', public readings were attended not only by cultured individuals who might have a special interest in the text, but also by less highly skilled readers more accustomed to listening than reading, and even by inattentive or bored listeners. By means of such readings, however, a public larger than true readers alone participated in the launching and circulation of certain works.

Individual, intimate reading was practised in private, but so was reading by a lector, slave or freedman. There is ample evidence of this figure in the households of wealthy Romans. Augustus himself had readers in his service, and we can assume that many who were capable of reading for themselves also had books read aloud to them. Private readings are also attested, in which a lector read at convivial social gatherings, and even of readings of extracts from a recent work that an author might offer a few close friends.[51] Readings like these served to cement friendships, make new social contacts, and perpetuate (or, for the emerging classes, imitate) the habits of the cultured élite.

Silent reading, although admittedly much less frequent, was not a total anomaly.[52] It may have been practised above all for letters, documents, messages and the like, but it is attested (from Horace to St Augustine) for literary texts as well.[53] In imperial Rome in particular, ways to read, like the positions and sites for reading, were quite free. In the early modern age silent reading was considered the final stage in a learning process that began with reading aloud and progressed to murmured reading, which means that in a given society the difference between vocal and visual modes of reading can be taken as an indication of sociocultural difference.[54] In antiquity, however, silent reading was not considered to require a more advanced level of technical skill than expert reading aloud; from the evidence we have, it seems that readers chose between the two modes according to circumstances or their mood. Silent reading was practised by individuals who read aloud. Nor was a murmured reading unknown, but it too depended on the circumstances of reading or the nature of the text, rather than on an individual's reading skills.

Strongly 'expressive' forms of reading occurred above all with a certain type of literature dominated by rhetoric and its artifices; it required highly cultivated readers or listeners who possessed the necessary preparation in rhetoric. There were other forms of reading, however, that met the needs of a highly stratified public in the early centuries of the Roman Empire. When Apuleius says in the introduction to the *Metamorphoses* that he wants to caress his readers' ears with a 'pretty whisper' (*lepido susurro*),[55] he is addressing his novel to both that greater public and to an individual, murmured reading. Works of pure entertainment, a genre less appropriate for reading aloud in public, were undoubtedly read with a murmur or silently.

New Spaces for Reading

The new reader of the early centuries of the Empire was a reader no longer (or not exclusively) obliged to read by his functions as an author-writer, a professional technician, a civil official or military officer, a schoolmaster, or even a student. He was instead a 'free' reader who read for pleasure, out of habit, or because of the prestige attached to reading. In short, people took up reading beyond any practical or instrumental need to read; some literate, even educated, people read even though they had no connection with professions linked to the book and to written culture.

Lucian, an author of violent satires, traced the portrait of a second-century reader, or rather, of a certain category of readers who

accumulated books in their houses, perhaps reading many of them, but
who could grasp little in the texts their books contained because they
were unable 'to know the merits and defects of each passage', to 'understand what every sentence means', or know 'how to construe words'.
Lucian calls his reader 'a silly ignorant fellow', but he admits that such
readers none the less always had a book in their hands, 'read all the
time', and could even read 'some of them aloud with great fluency'.
Like another 'ignorant fellow' from Corinth who read Euripides'
Bacchae, a work the satirist judged to be beyond the man's modest level
of instruction, Lucian's book collector was a reader who 'disgraced' the
book, 'warping its meaning', and who confused authors, works and literary genres. Although the man was unaware of the proper styles for
reciting poetry or prose, and could never pose as someone who had
'had an education', even Lucian had to admit that he nevertheless read
books (or had books read to him).[56]

Readings of poetry or of 'high' and sometimes 'difficult' prose,
ancient and contemporary, must necessarily have been limited to a cultivated public that, although larger than in earlier periods, was hardly
vast. The ludicrous lovers of books and libraries who imitated them,
but lacked the necessary competence, offended prominent authors and
invited ridicule, just as Lucian's ignorant reader did. Still, bibliophiles
and other readers who lacked the finest intellectual preparation were
none the less able to comprehend less challenging reading matter. They
joined the new world of readers whom authors called *vulgus*, *plebs*,
media plebs or *plebeiae manus*. This was not a homogeneous cultural
group, but rather a stratified public differing in both social extraction
and education, whose interests (hence whose choices in reading matter)
varied widely. It was also an anonymous public. In Pliny's or Tacitus's
day it could be found in the forum or at the circus.[57] In general, this
'average' reading public was made up of a middle social stratum of
people with some schooling (some might even be very well educated)
that included technicians, government functionaries, high-ranking
military men, merchants, relatively cultivated craftspeople and agri-
culturists, wealthy parvenus, well-off women and *faciles puellae*.

The imperial age signalled women's broader access to the world of
the written word. Even in republican Rome, there had of course been
matronae and *puellae doctae* who could read (Cornelia, the mother of
the Gracchi, is one example that springs to mind; another is Sempronia,
who read both Greek and Latin authors). Such figures were fairly rare,
however. The female reader came into being no earlier than the Augustan
age. Moreover, it was roughly then that women in reading poses began
to join male readers in the paintings at Pompeii and on sarcophagi.
Women paid a price for their entry into the world of writing, however:

certain segments of Roman society and some authors saw an educated woman as intolerable, and thought a man well-advised, in his choice of a wife, to make sure that 'there should be something in her reading which she does not understand'.[58]

Ovid, one author who was highly sensitive to his age's increased demand for reading matter, was the first to include women among the *media plebs* of his readers, which makes him a key figure for comprehending and describing the new relation between women and written culture. Byblis, tormented by an incestuous love for her brother, tries to express her tumultuous and insane emotions in words she inscribes on a waxed tablet, rubs out, and rewrites;[59] Philomela, her tongue cut to the root, weaves into a cloth the *miserabile carmen* that recounts her rape, thus enabling her sister Procne to 'read' her story;[60] *heroides* such as Briseis write letters, even autograph letters spattered with tears as they are written or reread.[61] Ovid dedicated the third book of his *Ars amatoria* to women,[62] and women were by definition the main readers of his *Medicamina faciei*, a brief treatise on the preparation of cosmetics and the art of women's make-up. His *Remedia amoris* speaks of women (not all of them *juvenes*) tormented by love. Once women had gained access to the world of the written word, they could be depicted in the act of writing or reading something that narrated or reflected women's experiences and emotions.

Reactions to an increased demand for reading matter varied with the author function and with the sociocultural stratification of the reading public. We can see this diversified response above all in the literary motif of the personified book that speaks for the author.[63] Horace represents the book as a young man eager to leave his family home (a sign that Horace's work had a potential circulation outside limited social and literary circles) who has to face contact with an anonymous *vulgus* of uncertain cultural identity, hence risk encountering improper ways of being read. Ovid prefers to have the book ask the reader to lend it a hand. For him the book is an intermediary between his text and a 'reader-friend' who is none other than the new, anonymous reader from the very *plebs* for whom he writes. In the age of Martial that *plebs* grew even larger and became even more varied, including even readers of average to low educational levels.

One consequence of a broader range of readers was the rise, under the Empire, of a 'consumer' literature of works of entertainment that had not been among the traditional genres: escapist poetry, paraphrastic epic, history in the reduced form of biographies or abridged in compendia, little manuals on cooking or sports, brief works on games and pastimes, erotica, horoscopes, texts on magic or the interpretations of dreams, and, above all, fictional narratives spun out of typical situations, stereotyped descriptions and schematic psychological situations featuring complicated plots and unexpected turns of events against a background of love and adventure. Another new genre aimed at a wide circulation was the 'pamphleteering literature' of the *Acta Alexandrinorum* restored from Greco-Egyptian fragments.[64] This 'subversive' and perhaps clandestine literature relates the condemnation and torture of the pagan martyrs of Alexandria who rebelled against Roman domination. At least some of the escapist and entertaining texts appealed to both readers of average (for certain texts, lower) educational levels and the cultivated reader. They were aimed at the new reader, accustomed to read with no other idea in mind than the pleasure inherent in the text. Cultural divisions among readers did not always imply different reading choices. Different groups might read the same texts; what differed were the ways in which they read, comprehended and appropriated a written text. This sort of reading matter thus had a 'transversal' circulation.

To return to Ovid, he also mentions another sort of text: literary works of a didactic nature giving advice on leisure activities.[65] A 'library' of treatises and brief pieces of that sort would provide 'a practical guide for the use of free time' that readers might find especially useful during the Saturnalia. They could derive pleasure as well as find rules and information, cast in literary form, for various sorts of social games.[66] In Ovid's day, books of this sort also cemented social relationships, and were often offered as gifts among cultivated friends and men of letters broadminded enough not to scorn such minor literary works. Even Ovid wrote works of pure entertainment; his volumes of erotic poetry in particular were produced 'one after the other, probably in response to a growing public demand'.[67] Some decades later this entire genre of light literature was offered (perhaps in a simplified, more insipid form) to a wider, more undifferentiated audience of modest intellectual accomplishments. Martial, who aimed at a reading public broader than Ovid's, considered the publication of a new book in the weeks before the Saturnalia as 'an opportunity that he willingly grasped to show readers that his poetry could be a lively and active part of pleasurable entertainment, offered for reading precisely when the market for entertainment and distraction was greatest and most intense in Roman society, and when book production worked to satisfy demands for amusement and distraction'.[68]

Perhaps more than any other genre, erotic literature in various forms and adaptations was aimed at readers whose reading skills varied but who shared a desire to be amused. There were readers for Ovid's elaborate erotic works; there were soldiers who read Aristides' infamously obscene *Milesakia*; we even have evidence of manuals of eroticism

illustrated by *obscenae tabellae* such as the *molles libelli* of Elephanti-
des, a genre popular in the first and second centuries (even the emperor
Tiberius owned such a work). To end the list, there were booksellers
who 'peddled' roll books containing nothing but pornographic *figurae
Veneris*.[69]

Fiction occupied an important place in all this 'transversal' reading
matter. Above all, certain Greek romances connected with the Second
Sophistic Movement – Achilles Tatius's *Leucippe and Cleitophon*,
Longus the Sophist's *Daphnis and Chloe* and Heliodorus's *Ethiopica* –
satisfied the demands of readers accustomed to texts of a high literary
level, but were also aimed at a different level of reception, where they
delighted readers, male and female, who were fully literate but might
not have enjoyed (or understood?) the great authors of ancient literature. Longus calls his romance a 'delightful possession' for the comfort
and pleasure that could be derived from it.[70] What appealed to the
vulgus who read these novels were situations that unravelled around a
couple of lovers in a fast-paced narrative involving changing events and
a plot full of twists and turns in which the lovers were separated, found
each other again, betrayed each other, and were eventually reunited, as
the narrative shifted its tone from tragic to merry, gloomy to brilliant,
religious to sensual.[71]

The educated women among this reading public must have been
particularly given to this sort of sentimental, fantastic literature whose
plots featured stories about women (perhaps precisely to attract female
readers). Antonius Diogenes, a writer of romances whose work is
known only through fragments and mentions, dedicated his *Marvels
beyond Thule* to his sister Isidora.[72] Whether she was real or fictional,
the dedication to Isidora indicates that there were forms of literature,
romance for one, that were intended (perhaps especially) for female
consumption. Women lived far removed from the preoccupations of
public life, and if a woman had some education, she could create her
own private space as a reader of works (probably escapist texts) that
reflected her.[73] The reading of works of this sort would have been silent
or, at most murmured, and must have been quite different from the
rhetorical reading aloud that was ultimately 'male' reading. The settings
for female reading that we see in late Hellenistic images from Pompeii is
the private house, where the woman is usually shown reading alone,
absorbed in reading a book roll. There is some evidence of a woman
reading in a public place, however: 'She had in her hands a roll with
both of its ends rolled up, and she seemed to be reading one part and to
have already read the other; and as she walked along she conversed
with one of her companions.'[74] In his description of this woman who
reads as she walks and interrupts her reading now and then to speak

with someone in her entourage Lucian presents a vivid portrait of female reading.

Still within the general context of fiction, the Latin novel – Petronius's *Satyricon*, for example, or Apuleius's *Metamorphoses* – shows how diverse the various levels of reading could be. Cultivated readers found the stories of rascals, pederasts, pandering priestesses and gross *nouveaux riches* in Petronius's novel just as much to their taste as did readers of average (or scant) culture, among them some of the same sort of parvenus of Greco-Roman society who people the novel. More cultivated readers could also find in the work a deeper level of tormented soul searching not apparent in a superficial reading for entertainment, and they might have enjoyed the author's skill at portraying different levels of style.[75] That was perhaps what Apuleius had in mind in his *Metamorphoses* when he addressed the 'careful reader'(*lector scrupulosus*).[76] As Apuleius represents his readers, they were capable of grasping all the shades of meaning in his work and all its implications if they paid close attention to every detail (*inspicere*) as they read the roll of Egyptian papyrus (*papyrum Aegyptiam*) that bore his text.[77] In short, the fictional book seems to have arisen as entertainment, but cultivated entertainment.

There was, however, a broader reading public who inscribed the fictional text – the book – within a different cultural matrix from the one the author had intended. This means that texts gradually came to be enjoyed by a public of less intellectual refinement whose reading was approximate and who read for the basic situations of love, adventure and fantastic events in the text with only a relative interest in its coherence. In this case, the reader's lack of education made him fall short of being a *lector scrupulosus*. When the same reader struggled to reach the threshold of an average level of schooling, lower-level texts were available that reduced a fantastic plot to its essence or provided sensual thrills. These works included texts such as the *Phoinikika* of Lollianos,[78] fragments of which have been preserved, or the *Rhodiaka* of Philippus of Amphipolis, a work now lost that one learned source placed among 'utterly lewd' texts.[79] At times lighter fictional works were provided with the sort of 'aids for inexperienced readers' one encounters in school books.[80] One fragment of a narrative of this sort, the so-called Greek Satyricon, has a page layout that also helps to guide reading.[81] We can surmise that such devices were used to facilitate comprehension of the text, even for less skilled readers who had learned to read only in the style of school exercises.

Gellius tells us that in the port city of Brindisi he bought some Greek books for a modest price, and that he 'ran through all of them hastily' in the next two nights.[82] These books contained, among other things, tales of extraordinary, legendary and incredible events; they could be no other than an escapist literature all the more appropriate as shipboard reading for travellers of varying levels of education and even for seamen. We also have evidence of a sort of pedlar who took his wares from door to door in search of readers for the most part of the *plebs*, but able to read simply structured literary books, especially when reading aids were provided.[83]

The fragments found in Egypt of Greek illustrated books of the early imperial age are also instructive. Some of these were texts adapted from high literature (Homeric poetry, for instance), typically with a text that had been abridged, cut, and simplified. Others were new texts of pure entertainment with illustrations. Whether these texts were produced in poor, rough books or finely made ones, they were not aimed at literary cognoscenti. Given their mixture of the obvious and the banal, they must have been conceived for a public of fairly modest cultural expectations or for the newly rich, who surrounded themselves with the appurtenances of written culture but, like Petronius's Trimalchio (who owned three libraries), could only read books with a simplified text or with illustrations to make them more attractive and comprehensible.[84] Such works were a degraded form of the original model of the literary *volumen* as it spread, in more popular form, to lower social and cultural strata.

Certain fragments that date from between the second and third centuries make one think that the 'literary field' was principally occupied by the image and that the text, reduced to its essence, came to resemble captions. Examples of this trend include one scene recalling the tale of Cupid and Psyche,[85] an illustration of the *Iliad* showing the abduction of Briseis,[86] and a sort of Homeric omnium gatherum featuring the ghost of Patrocles appearing to Achilles.[87] There were also illustrated books of an abysmally low literary and linguistic level, such as one *volumen* recalling the comic strip of the labours of Hercules in which the characters are simply caricatures.[88]

The Roman Empire, in short, saw the dissemination of a 'literature for literates' different from the more traditional 'literature for the learned'. There was no lack of learned reading matter, but it was reserved to a scholarly élite that might (and often did) also have access to the humbler forms of reading matter. The world of readers was complex, and it covered a wide range. Authors gradually came to be aware of that complexity, responding to the reading public's expectations in more ways than providing enthralling stories. Beginning with the age of Ovid, in fact, we can see authors attempting to attract potential users to a book by facilitating access to reading. This aim, which had existed in the Hellenistic age, became the norm in imperial Rome.

Ovid, an author who was always attuned to his anonymous public (especially in his erotic works, which presumably were the most widely distributed), continually remarks on the place of a book with respect to his others, points out where a second edition varies from the first, or refers to another of his works on some particular topic.[89] Pliny provides a detailed summary, subdivided by books, in introduction to his formidable *Natural History*, to render it more accessible to the *vulgus* – farmers, craftsmen or anyone with a desire to read and know the work. Introductions to technical and scientific works of the age reflect a similar intent.

Experimentation with book forms other than the roll was another way to bring the book closer to the reader and to meet the reader halfway. This brings us to the rise of the codex, the book 'with pages'. Books in codex format were easier to make, thus shortening the production process and encouraging book circulation. Because the page could be written on both sides rather than on one side alone, putting out a given text in codex form represented a notable saving of space, thus lowering per copy costs in comparison to the *volumen*. The codex, which could be held in one hand, left the other one free, freeing the reading process as well. Martial, writing toward the end of the first century, encouraged readers to acquire his works by noting information in them on the shops and booksellers who sold them;[90] he was also the first literary author to recognize the new opportunities offered by the codex.[91] Although Martial was also read by highly cultured people, he wrote with one eye on the more numerous, less wealthy readers – the centurion, the *puellae*, the *plebs* of the *ludi Florales*, and all people on all levels of reception skills who took pleasure in reading his verse in easily handled booklets.

Volumen *and Codex: From Recreational Reading to Normative Reading*

As a book with literary content, the codex was a Roman invention. Beginning in the second century AD the book in the form of a roll, which Hellenistic works had introduced to Rome centuries before, began to lose ground and eventually lose out completely to the codex. When? The picture we have of the Greek world, as amply documented in Greco-Egyptian archaeology, shows the moment of the definitive affirmation of the codex to have been the early fifth century. In the Roman West it may have predominated earlier, however, though the available evidence is too scanty to be definitive. In any event, Martial (late first century) tells us that the codex of literary content (containing

works of Homer, Virgil, Cicero, Livy, Horace or his own *Epigrams*)
was produced by bookshops, hence in a certain number of copies.
Admittedly, he speaks of this as something new. The last Latin books
still produced as rolls can be assigned, at the latest, to somewhere
between the end of the third and the beginning of the fourth century.
One of the oldest extant codices, datable to the first or second centuries,
is a fragment of a Latin work, the so-called *De bellis Macedonicis*.[92] All
this suggests that the codex won a permanent place among the book
practices of the Roman West no later than the end of the third century,
thus at a decidedly earlier date than the early fifth century, as was the
case in the Greek world.

Throughout the Mediterranean world of Greek and Latin culture,
Christians rapidly adopted the codex, to the point that from the start,
nearly all Christian books were in codex format. This does not mean
that Christians originated the codex: from earliest times, tablets, notebooks and notepads with pages had been known in the Roman world.
Moreover, early Christianity was a religion founded on speech, on
preaching and on the 'living voice', which was also the basis for formal
rhetoric, school lessons and training in the technical disciplines in the
Hellenistic-Roman tradition, although the book might also function as
a teaching aid or a guide. Still, Christianity operated at a time and in a
society where individuals had widespread access to written culture, and
when it wanted to spread its message, it opted to use the book in codex
format.

There has been much debate about the reasons for that choice.[93] We
should perhaps begin by acknowledging that as a model for a 'container
for a text' different from the book roll, the codex was linked with the
traditional literary culture of the dominant classes. When Christianity
became a written religion of universal appeal, it directed its proselytiz-
ing efforts toward literate groups of various social and cultural levels
made up of people of middling or low education, rather than relying
primarily or exclusively on the traditional reading public for book rolls.
Even when these less-educated readers were familiar with rolls containing somewhat simple texts or a literature of popular entertainment,
their acquaintance with written culture was more in the form of school
readings or technical manuals. This meant that they had known books
in codex format as school notebooks, notepads and professional
manuals. The Christian choice of the codex thus coincided with the
format for written products most familiar to that sort of reading public.
It was also less expensive. The codex's pagination and its greater capacity also contributed to its success: together these permitted much greater
amounts of text than a roll could contain, and they also gave a unified
aspect to the canonical texts of the new religion and facilitated

cross-references and the retrieval of particular sections and passages. All these considerations explain Christianity's choice of the codex, but the format was used almost exclusively only for Holy Scripture. In many cases, Christians themselves, both as authors and as readers of works of literature (classical and secular, but also patristic) continued to use the roll for some time to come. A gradual preference for parchment over papyrus as a writing material paralleled the substitution of the codex for the roll. The Christian option (or at least the Christian preference) for parchment seems to have contributed to this process.

In any event, in late antiquity in both the East and the West, the codex came into general use for all forms of writing, sacred and secular, and among all levels of the reading public.

The popularity of the codex did not immediately change overall reading strategies. Even Christians, who had massively adopted the codex book format, persisted in the traditional ways: the faithful wrote and exchanged books; reading was individual or, in community gatherings, mediated by the voice of a lector; Christian texts were composed for, and circulated among, a public of new readers of average or lower culture that emerged in the imperial age and provided Christianity with many of its converts. The 'dense, almost impenetrable vegetation' that was early Christian literature was probably read as narrative[94] – that is, as a series of stories expressing and reflecting the social and spiritual anxieties of the time. It was only later that certain texts became canonical, while others, considered apocryphal, were rejected and condemned, and that the canonical texts were promoted as the foundation of doctrine and obligatory reading matter for all good (literate) Christians.

Moreover, there was an entire body of texts – canonical and apocryphal (the apocryphal ones complementing the canonical ones, filling in the gaps about persons, events and details and catering to an appetite for narrative), apocalyptic works and mystery writings, acts of the martyrs, saints' lives, *exempla* and tales of Christian inspiration – that were simple transpositions of pagan literature of entertainment, the romance in particular. These texts emphasized emotion in their treatment of characters and events, and they relied heavily on the reiterated *topoi* of the atrocious sufferings of martyrdom, unassailable convictions and *amor mortis*, not to mention borrowings from tales of voyages, adventures and miraculous happenings like those in the romances. Once again, we see a literature that lent itself to a 'transversal' circulation, in that it was aimed at readers with a solid education, able to grasp certain rhetorical schemes or doctrinal references, and others of an average or lower educational level, whose reception of texts was usually limited to the plot and a rudimentary comprehension of Christian morality.

In the third and fourth centuries, while the codex was gradually spreading and becoming the most current format for the book, profound transformations were taking place in society and culture. In particular, the literacy rate declined, which meant that there were fewer readers, pagan or Christian. Illiteracy was widespread among women. In the fourth century St Cyril of Jerusalem exhorted men and women to keep a book in their hands during liturgical services, but he adds that while some of the men were listening to someone read, the women might instead sing.[95] St Augustine's ideal of a 'lettered' woman was, at best, one whose literacy was no better than basic.[96] In late antiquity only the great Christian ladies shone for their erudition, and when they did, they demonstrated a knowledge not only of Greek and Latin, but also of Hebrew, all languages necessary to the study and comprehension of the sacred texts. Melania, a great lady who became a saint, spent several hours a day reading Holy Scripture or sermon collections; after these texts she found the Lives of the Fathers, with their narrative structure, almost escapist literature. Melania was not only a book lover; she also acquired as many books as possible, purchasing them, borrowing them, and spending time every day copying them.[97] Still, like other Christian ladies of the age (Blesilla, Paula and Eustochium), Melania belonged to a small élite that was, incidentally, soon to disappear. In the fifth and sixth centuries, reading became rarer, even among the church hierarchy.

Although the codex had been circulated in response to a broader demand for reading in a society in which illiteracy, already widespread in the fourth century, became even more so in the fifth and sixth centuries, it gradually became a book format for a privileged few. It echoed current reading practices and ways of reading, but it also transformed them profoundly. First of all, the codex changed the very notion of what a 'book' was. With the roll, what constituted a book had been a fairly stable concept linked to definite conventions of manufacture and content. The physical object was immediately linked to a work, whether that work was contained in one book roll or distributed over more than one. A work spread over more than one roll might contain textual units or 'books' that could be read singly, or only some of which could be read. In any event, the roll did not always coincide with an entire work (in fact, it rarely did so). This means that the notion of total reading might encompass a single roll or two or three short segments contained on one roll, even when the entire work had many 'books'. The codex, by contrast, brought together in one container, a single volume, a series of organic textual units (one or more works by the same author; a miscellany of homogeneous writings), or disparate units (different works, which might even make up what has been called a 'library without a library'[98]). This means that the codex brought about a profound change in both the notion of a book and the notion of total reading. The notion of a book, which was no longer immediately connected to a work, came to coincide with an object that might contain writings of a quality and a quantity that were no longer controlled by definite conventions; the notion of total reading came to imply a reading that, in order to be total, had to be extended to cover the content of an entire codex, even if that book, as was usually the case, contained more than one work.

It was precisely the custom of bringing together in one codex the various books of a single work or several works, perhaps very different ones, that determined the formation (or the reinforcement), between the fourth and the sixth century, of 'editorial' devices to mark internal divisions in a single written work or clearly separate different texts, a separation that was all the more necessary when the texts were heterogeneous. Such devices had not been necessary in the *volumen*, where each textual unit was distinguished, even delimited, by the autonomous book that contained it. The need for distinguishing divides in the codex led to special writing styles, different in size and shape from the style used for the text and often decorated or enhanced by touches of colour, that were used for initial titles or to signal the end of a text. The separation between texts was also marked by a system of ornamentation, often used in combination with distinctive lettering styles. Finally, one text was clearly detached from another by the use of the *implicit* to signal the start of a text or a portion of text and the *explicit* to mark its end. Despite these distinguishing devices, however, the reader 'inevitably ended up considering the individual texts contained in the book that he had in his hands as a unified whole'.[99] Moreover, he used books in that manner, which strongly influenced study practices.

Because the codex was not bound to fixed conventions of manufacture and make-up, but could instead take on different formats and sizes ranging from a handy pocket size to a weighty tome, it changed the way the book was correlated to the physiology of reading. The physical structure of certain books dictated, hindered or at least suggested certain postures, gestures and ways of reading. Although when the codex first circulated, it permitted a more agile mode of reading than the *volumen*, freeing the reader's movements because it took only one hand to support the book, even in late antiquity – a time of social and spiritual unrest when some were intent on organizing and preserving the heritage of both pagan and Christian culture – its capacity was often used to the maximum, giving rise to books of imposing dimensions. Volumes containing all the books of the Bible with commentaries, legislative and jurisprudential *corpora*, or canonical classical texts (either for school use or condensed in various ways) were all of a size and weight that made them difficult to read. As a result, they were used less for reading than for consultation and citation, operations that were facilitated by page numbering and by the various distinctive devices used within the text.

Freeing one hand from the task of holding the book enabled the reader to use it to write, hence to make annotations in the margins of the pages of the codex. The practice of writing in a book as one read arose with the codex. Authors of late antiquity such as Cassiodorus (fourth century) theorized on how to make and where to place reading notes.[100] The codex provided readers with other spaces to write on: entirely or partially blank pages, endpapers and the inside surfaces of bindings could be used for notations of all sorts, even 'anarchical' ones. Textual exegesis by more than one hand often accumulated in the page margins; entire commentaries had to be transferred to separate books. Thus the codex imposed a simultaneous and co-ordinated reading that moved back and forth between the principal text and its accessories. When this was the case, reading became extremely demanding, and interpretation was conditioned by the commentary. This was a reading style reserved for the few.

Above all, the codex dictated a totally different way of reading a text. In the roll the columns that followed one another in the portion of the text held open by the reader made possible what has been called 'the panoramic aspect' of reading, because the eye could pass immediately and without interruption from one column to the next.[101] In the codex, to the contrary, the portion of the written text displayed before the reader's eyes was predetermined by the size of the page, thus denying the reader a continuous view of the whole. This layout favoured a fragmented style of reading, page by page, hence one segment of text after another that was often (particularly with Holy Scripture) fragmented even further by subdivision into short sections (*cola* and *commata*) visually distinguished by means of such devices as enlarged initial letters, initial letters placed outside the body of the text, segments of the text placed out of line or in line, etc. The result was a piecemeal style of reading shorter or longer bits. This style had certain advantages: it made 'the meaning clearer to the reader',[102] and it aided retrieval and memorization, thanks to a style reliant on aphorisms and to a number of devices that permitted the reader to return to passages already read. Interpunction (*codices distincti*) became the norm. Interpunction was one among many devices that guided reception of the text, and led readers away from individual interpretations toward a regulated interpretation based on acknowledged *auctoritates*. For Cassiodorus the *distinctiones* – interpunction and diacritical marks – were paths to meaning that, almost like an illuminating commentary, gave readers the clearest possible instruction.[103]

In the case of the illustrated book, the series of scenes that the reader's eye could grasp on the roll and connect to an ongoing narrative was replaced by a repertory of isolated figures, each framed on a page. Illustrations were no longer integrated into the context; they were instead increasingly autonomous, leading to a separation between the written discourse and the iconographic discourse.[104] Once again, Cassiodorus stresses the power of the picture as an instrument of knowledge.[105]

Reading as a form of literary *otium*, which moved from column to column through a book in an uninterrupted sequence and at the pace of a reading voice, gave way to a concentrated and attentive reading that was carried on at lower and lower voice levels, that imposed meaning through the use of textual devices, that aimed at an authoritative reception of the text, and that was conceived as a means for strongly conditioning modes of thinking and acting. From a free, recreational reading we pass to a firmly oriented, normative reading; the 'pleasure of the text' gave way to a slow labour of interpretation and meditation. Melania reading in her cell, concentrating on Scripture, neither speaking to the mother superior nor even looking at her for fear she might miss even a single 'expression' or 'concept' in what she was reading, testifies to a manner of reading remote (even very remote) from that of Lucian's Roman woman several centuries earlier, who read her roll (in all probability an escapist tale) in a teeming urban milieu, interrupting her reading now and then to give her companions a word or a glance.

Melania read the Old and the New Testaments three or four times a year, and she recited the psalms from memory. That fact merits reflection. The codex had gradually become (exceptions aside) the instrument of a shift from an 'extensive' reading of many texts (in the varied and stratified public of the early centuries of the Roman Empire) to an 'intensive' reading of few texts, above all the Bible and the law, read, reread, repeated in the form of citations and maxims, committed to memory and recited. In the world of late antiquity all authority was founded on those written texts, hence on the book and on reading. This was true at the summits of power, among the church hierarchy, in lay society and within the nucleus of the family. Only the codex could represent that authority.

3

Reading, Copying and Interpreting a Text in the Early Middle Ages

M. B. Parkes

The early Middle Ages inherited from antiquity a tradition of reading which embraced the four functions of grammatical studies (*grammaticae officia*): *lectio, emendatio, enarratio* and *iudicium*.[1] *Lectio* was the process whereby a reader had to work out the text (*discretio*) by identifying its elements of letters, syllables, words and sentences, in order to read it aloud (*pronuntiatio*) according to the accentuation required by the sense. *Emendatio*, a process entailed by the realities of manuscript transmission, required a reader (or his teacher) to correct the text in his copy, and sometimes tempted him to 'improve' it.[2] *Enarratio* was the process of recognizing (or commenting upon) features of vocabulary, rhetorical and literary form, and above all of interpreting the subject matter of the text (*explanatio*). *Iudicium* was the process of exercising judgement of the aesthetic qualities or the moral and philosophical value of the text (*bene dictorum conprobatio*).

To help him the reader had also inherited a corpus of grammatical teaching from late antiquity which served more to facilitate the process of reading than to promote an interest in language itself. The narrowness of this approach to language was preserved for a long time in this period by the belief that man should concern himself with the language of the Word of God, and by the tendency to accept the existence of different language systems as an inevitable consequence of the Tower of Babel.[3] The traditional grammars were based upon the recognition of the word as an isolable linguistic phenomenon, and employed morphological criteria to establish a set of word classes (called 'parts of speech'). They presented and discussed paradigms of associated forms ('declensions and conjugations') and the surface syntactical relations between words in the construction of sentences ('concord').[4] In this way the grammars gave substantial help and practice for a reader when analysing a text, and for identifying the elements of the Latin language which presents a great deal of morphological information by means of thematic and inflected elements. Such help was especially invaluable during the early part of this period, when manuscripts were still being copied in *scriptio continua* – that is, without separation of words or indication of any pauses within a paragraph of text.

Reading for the Salvation of One's Soul

Christian teachers and writers had applied this tradition of grammatical scholarship to the interpretation of the Scriptures, and, as a result, religious education and literary instruction were closely associated at all levels.[5] This situation was different from that in pagan antiquity, where the highest culture had been reserved for a social élite.[6] In these changed circumstances all Christians who could read were exhorted to do so, but 'all those who wished to claim the name of monk could not be permitted to remain ignorant of their letters'.[7] As Dhuoda was to point out later, in a treatise written for her son, one learns about God from reading books.[8] The motive for reading was now the salvation of one's soul, and this compelling motive was reflected in the texts that were read. The elementary reader, and the child's copy-book, became the Psalter (knowledge of which was the basic test of literacy for many centuries).[9] For those who learned more readily from examples than precepts, there were saints' lives which characterized the Christian ideals. For others a new programme of texts led to the *libros catholicos*, the study of divinity, which helped a reader to formulate the correct interpretation of the Word of God itself for the nourishment of his or her soul. 'In commentaries on Scripture one recognizes how virtue should be acquired and retained, in stories of miracles we see how that which has been acquired and retained is made manifest.'[10] Grammatical studies and other texts were subordinated to this purpose, and were employed to improve a reader's knowledge of Latinity. Isidore observed that 'the teaching of grammarians can even be profitable for our life, provided one draws nourishment from them to apply to better uses'.[11]

Reading Aloud and Silent Reading

Another new development was a change in attitude to the act of reading itself. In antiquity the emphasis had been on the oral delivery of a text – reading aloud with proper articulation of the sense and rhythms – an emphasis that reflected the ideal of the orator which had dominated ancient culture.[12] The purpose of silent reading had been to study the text beforehand in order to comprehend it adequately.[13] The ancient art of reading aloud survived in the liturgy. In the seventh century Isidore of Seville laid down the qualifications required of those who were to hold the office of Lector in the church:

> Whosoever is to be promoted to a rank of this kind shall be deeply versed in doctrine and books, and thoroughly adorned with the knowledge of meanings and words, so that in the analysis of *sententiae* he may understand where the grammatical boundaries occur: where the utterance continues, where the sentence concludes. In this way he will control the technique of oral delivery (*vim pronuntiationis*) without impediment, in order that he may move the minds and feelings (*sensus*) of all to understand, by distinguishing between the kinds of delivery, and by expressing the feelings (*affectus*) of the *sententia*: now by the tone of one expounding, now in the manner of one who is suffering, now in the manner of one who is chiding, now in the manner of one who is exhorting, or by those according to the kinds of appropriate delivery.[14]

A beginner also had to read aloud to enable a teacher to assess the pupil's progress. Beyond the elementary stage reading skills and fluency in Latin could be stimulated and assessed by means of reading aloud in a group. The comedies of Terence were copied frequently in the ninth and tenth centuries, and, since these texts had been used in antiquity to give students practice in delivery and to improve their eloquence, they would have been equally suitable for this purpose in the Middle Ages.[15] In the tenth century Hrotsvit of Gandersheim wrote plays for her fellow nuns as a Christian and feminist alternative to the pagan Terence.[16] Interest in such texts represented perhaps not so much enthusiasm for the drama as a literary form itself, but a way of promoting fluency in the language of the spiritual life. Reading aloud, or at least *sotto voce*, was also practised during the monastic *lectio* to instil into the reader an aural and muscular memory of the words as a basis for *meditatio*. The term employed in the various rules for this kind of reading was *meditari litteras* or *meditari psalmos*.[17]

However, from the sixth century onwards we find more attention given to the role of silent reading. In the Rule of St Benedict we find references to private reading, and to the need to read to oneself so as not to disturb others. Since such reading was to be supervised, to ensure that it was not an excuse for slackness or that the reader's attention did not wander, the implication is that silent reading was not uncommon in such circumstances.[18] Although Isidore had laid down the requirements for reading aloud in church, he also saw the preparation for the office of Lector as an elementary stage in clerical education.[19] He himself preferred silent reading which ensured better comprehension of the text, since (he said) the understanding of the reader is instructed more fully when the voice is silent. In this way one could read without physical effort, and by reflecting upon those things which one had read, they escaped from the memory less easily.[20]

The Written Word as Visible Language

This attitude to silent reading, although determined by practical considerations, is also to be associated with a much more fundamental shift in attitude towards the nature of the written word. The development of the perception of the written medium as a different manifestation of language, with its own 'substance', and with a status equivalent to, but independent of, its spoken opposite number, was a long process.[21] Nevertheless, we may see the beginnings of this development in this period.[22] The written word had played a crucial role in preserving the orthodox traditions of the Church, in transmitting that heritage, and in fostering those traditions among new generations. The more it was perceived as the medium which transmitted the authorities of the past (and in the Middle Ages these texts held a greater authority for many more people than before), the less it was perceived merely as a record of the spoken word. Whereas in the fourth century Augustine had regarded letters as signs of sounds, and the sounds themselves as signs of the things we think, by the seventh century Isidore regarded letters as signs without sounds which have the power to convey to us silently (*sine voce*) the sayings of those who are absent. The letters themselves are the signs of things.[23] Writing is a visible language which can signal directly to the mind through the eye.

The practice of making children read verses they had copied from the psalms aloud to their teachers, without necessarily learning the order of the letters in the alphabetical series first (the ancient practice), was also significant.[24] It not only helped them to identify the functions of letters and words in the text but was intended to help them to make the transition from an oral culture to the apprehension of the graphic conventions of that written culture by which the Christian tradition had been handed down.

However, the readers who came to perceive most readily the written medium as an autonomous manifestation of language were those on the fringes (or outside) the area of *lingua romana* or *lingua mixta* of the old Roman Empire. These were the speakers of Celtic and Germanic languages for whom Latin was an alien linguistic system. In spite of the help they received from their grammatical studies, some readers continued to experience difficulties when analysing elements of a Latin text. The nature of these difficulties may be determined from the evidence of vernacular glosses to the text, many of which were personal glosses made at the moment of reading and scratched on the page with a stylus so that they might be unobtrusive, hence illegible or invisible to other readers.[25]

Some glosses reflect misreadings of letters, and hence failure to identify words correctly. An Irish scribe glossed *eversione* instead of *aversione*, and *coinquinare* instead of *concinnare*; an Anglo-Saxon scribe glossed *occasio* instead of *occassu*.[26] Other glosses reflect failure to identify words correctly because of faulty word separation. An Irish scribe glossed *innumero* instead of *in numero*, whereas an Anglo-Saxon scribe glossed *in occiduas* instead of *inocciduas*.[27] Some glosses reveal problems in construing the syntax. When an Irish scribe glossed *gratum tibi esse officium est obtimum*, he took *optimum* with *gratum* and produced *ambudech forrcimen* 'the best grateful'; *a seruo quippe uinctus* has been glossed *conarracht assa mugsini* 'who had been bound out of his servitude'.[28] Other glosses reflect the difficulties of distinguishing between different pronouns or between pronouns and adverbs: *quo* (which can be an adverb, or ablative singular masculine of the interrogative pronoun *quis*) has been glossed by a German scribe with *thara* (adverb 'thence, whence'), *thiu* (instrumental of *ther*, demonstrative pronoun) and *in thiu*; *quam* (which can be an adverb, or accusative singular feminine of *qui* or *quis*) is glossed only when it appears as an adverb *denni* ('as, then', 'so as'). Anglo-Saxon scribes often gloss the pronoun by repeating the antecedent noun.[29] Some glosses assist a reader to construe the Latin by indicating the case of a word, either by means of the relevant preposition in the vernacular, or by indicating the equivalent of the Latin inflection, but not the meaning. Thus an Anglo-Saxon scribe glossed *mentis* with (-)*des* (probably the genitive ending of *modes*) and *reverenter* with (-)*ce* (an adverbial inflection).[30]

Another practice introduced by insular scribes is the use of construe marks to elucidate the syntax of texts, especially verse, in which word order was constrained by artifice or style. The earliest surviving examples appear in Irish and Welsh manuscripts produced in the ninth century.[31] There were two systems. The first consists of patterns of dots and marks which indicate grammatical concord (adjective and its noun); or regimen (subject and verb), and those which connect modifiers (adverb to verb) not affected by concord or regimen. The second, apparently later, system consists of marks or letters which indicate the order or series in which words should be read.[32]

By contrast, until the late tenth century speakers of a romance language reading a Latin text encountered a written form which approximated to their spoken language, but was recorded according to an ancient tradition which excluded a large number of features in their speech as unacceptable in that written form.[33] Hence their glosses in *lingua romana* sometimes introduce contemporary or colloquial forms to interpret what were regarded as archaic, obsolescent or unfamiliar words. For example, the interpretations found in the ninth-century Reichenau glosses include forms which subsequently passed into Old French: *compellere* and *cogere* have been glossed by *anetsare* (Old French *anesser*), *nocere* by *hostare* (Old French *oster*), *arenam* by *sabulo* (Old French *sablon*) and *emit* by *comparavit* (Old French *comperer*).[34] The earliest romance glosses which reflect problems with syntax are the 'Glosas Emilianenses' in an eleventh-century manuscript from the monastery of San Millan de la Cogolla in La Rioja.[35]

Alongside grammatical treatises which helped a reader to identify the elements of a text were other treatises which dealt with rhetorical figures, and not only enabled a reader to recognize them but assisted him or her during the process of reading to construe the unfamiliar word order which they created in a text. One of the most widely used was Bede's *De schematibus et tropis* which drew its examples from the Bible, and offered explanations of figures of expression and thought, skilfully selected with emphasis on those which produce an order of words alien to spoken idiom.[36] These include *prolepsis* (where those things which ought to follow have been placed before) and *syllepsis* (where nouns in different cases are brought together in a single significance: for example, 'Adtendite populus meus legam meam inclinate aurem vestram', where the vocative and the second group of accusatives have the same referent). Among the tropes are *hysteronproteron*, where the order of words is changed, and *parenthesis*, which, until the end of the fourteenth century when parenthesis marks were first introduced, must have caused readers some difficulty. The ability to recognize such figures must have facilitated the process of *discretio*.

Another technique adopted in the process of *discretio* was to apply the rhetoricians' analysis of the attributes of a specific argument involving named persons and particular occasions, to explicate the content of a passage, or to introduce a work (*accessus*). These attributes were known as the seven circumstances of human actions (*circumstantiae rerum*): person, action, time, place, cause, method and instrument.[37]

They were frequently applied in the form of questions: *quis* (who), *quid* (what), *quando* (when), *ubi* (where), *quare uel cur* (why), *quomodo* (how), *quibus amminiculis* (by what means or instrument). There are commentaries and a short treatise, which show how these questions can be used to identify the positions of subject (*quis*), verb and object (*quid*) and various adverbial adjuncts (*quando, ubi, quomodo*), thus helping the reader at a more basic level. Thus the sentence 'Cicero Rome diu mire disputat propter communem utilitatem magna excellentia ingenii' may be analysed as follows: *quis?*, 'Cicero'; *quid?*, 'disputat'; *quando?*, 'diu'; *ubi?*, 'rome'; *quare?*, 'propter communem utilitatem'; *quomodo?*, 'mire'; *quibus amminiculis?*, 'magna excellentia ingenii'.[38] In some commentaries they are referred to as *circumstantiae sententiarum*.[39]

New Developments in the Presentation of Texts

The need for these readers to have more convenient access to texts stimulated major developments in the techniques of presenting texts on the page. Insular scribes who regarded writing first and foremost as a means of recording information on the page, and Latin as a 'visible language', began to develop certain new graphic conventions – features of representation and display – to facilitate access to the information transmitted in this visible medium.[40] These conventions were based on applications of principles which they derived from the grammarians. I propose to discuss these developments in the order of the stages of the reading process, rather than in the chronological order of their first appearance.

The ancient grammarians regarded each letter as the minimum phonological as well as the minimum graphic unit. Each letter had three properties: its shape (*figura*), its name (*nomen*) and its phonemic referent (*potestas*).[41] The cursive scripts of the late Roman Empire, which had largely replaced the Uncial and Half-uncial scripts in books, contained many ligatures in which individual letters took several different variant forms. Anglo-Saxon scribes were the first to seek to restrict the number of variant forms of the same letter, and to produce *litterae absolutae* (or invariable letters) in minuscule script, letters in which each form has a single shape, thus improving the legibility of a text.[42] Subsequently, on the Continent, this graphic convention was accompanied by greater emphasis on those minimum distinctive features required to differentiate between different letter forms. The result was a minuscule script which was used throughout the West for several centuries, and eventually became the basis of modern type-faces (where each letter has its own shape, and the ampersand – originally an *et* ligature – is perceived as a form in its own right).

When Irish scribes copied Latin texts, they abandoned the *scriptio continua* of their exemplars, and adopted as the basis for their scribal practices the morphological criteria they had found in the analyses of the grammarians: they set out the words by introducing spaces between the parts of speech. By contrast, when copying texts in their native language, they copied as a single unit those words which are grouped round a single chief stress and which have a close syntactical connection with each other (*isaireasber* : *is aire as ber*, 'Cambrai Homily').[43]

Irish scribes sought to isolate not only the parts of speech but also the grammatical constituents within a Latin sentence. They clarified punctuation by substituting new marks in which the number of marks increases according to the importance of the pause. They also developed the *littera notabilior* (or 'more noticeable letter') to give more visual emphasis to the beginning of a text or section. Later, on the Continent, scribes adopted this principle by incorporating individual letters from ancient book scripts for tertiary 'display' purposes – that is, to be used as *litterae notabiliores* at the beginnings of new *sententiae*, the rest of which were copied in minuscule script. Where a scribe has used Rustic Capitals or Square Capitals for this purpose, we may speak literally of 'capital letters' as an element of punctuation for the first time.

Anglo-Saxon scribes integrated ancient scripts with minuscule scripts in new page designs. The Scriptures, works by the Fathers, rules of monastic life, and the documents which conveyed the authority of the Roman Church in ecclesiastical affairs had been transmitted to the Anglo-Saxons originally in copies written in Uncial and Rustic Capitals. Anglo-Saxon scribes had come to regard these ancient scripts as peculiarly appropriate for such authoritative texts, and began to employ these scripts to distinguish the extracts from such authorities, which were incorporated into texts or commentaries copied in minuscule.[44] They thus consolidated the convention that extracts from sources embedded in a text should be distinguished from the text itself, making them much easier for a reader to identify.

The practices of insular scribes were developed in response to the needs of readers for whom Latin was a second language, and represented increasing recognition of written Latin as an autonomous substance of manifestation of that language. They established the rudiments of the grammar of legibility in relation to new scripts as well as old, and their practices must have been of considerable benefit to their readers.

By contrast, when we examine the way in which a ninth-century Reims scribe analysed the language of his sixth-century Italian exemplar in *scriptio continua*, the results are quite different.[45] Word separation is so inconsistent that we must assume that it was not a major criterion, and that his analysis must have been based on principles different from those adopted by insular scribes and their followers. If we assume that the Reims scribe's own personal language system was rooted in a *lingua romana*, and that he could perceive some relationship between it and the Latin he was copying (however remote that relationship might have been), we can recognize features which seem to reflect such a situation.

Already in antiquity the spoken language had diverged considerably from that represented by contemporary written systems. The grammarian Velius Longus observed that although one always wrote *illum* and *omnium*, when speaking one never pronounced the final nasal before a following vowel, as in the collocations *illu(m) ego* and *omniu(m) optimum*.[46] When we examine this ninth-century copy of Hilary, we often observe that in such collocations **m** has been indicated by a mark of abbreviation: *ad ipsu(m) extra suu(m) inquo*, and *legendu(m) est*. A most likely explanation is that the scribe's spoken language may have encouraged the use of a suspension in such a context, but did not dictate it; the practice is not consistent, and the marks are therefore still marks of abbreviation, not a form of diacritic. Similarly, a written form like *c̄locaret* leaves open the question as to whether or not the form *conlocaret* or a form with assimilation – *collocaret* – was intended.

Although the grouping of words on the page must always reflect the amount of text which a scribe could retain in his mind's eye, when transferring his attention from the page of his exemplar to the page of his copy, nevertheless the grouping also presupposes an analysis of the language of that exemplar by the scribe as reader, and not merely a series composed of a random quantity of letters. What we find in the copy by the Reims scribe are examples of groupings like *sermodomini*, *&cumnecessesit, aequesemper* (when talking of the Trinity), *nonconsequatur, aliquodrebus, inintelligibleest* and *possibileest*. Such examples might reflect what might be termed 'conceptual units', or a possible relationship between the words in a situation governed by conditions of syntactic stress in the scribe's spoken language.

In such an analysis based on a scribe's own personal language system the analysis will not be consistent, because it will reflect the variations in the degree of the relationship which he can perceive at the time between the two systems – that of the Latin he is copying and that of the language he speaks.[47] The less familiar the language of the text he is copying, the greater the likelihood that his analysis of it will be arbitrary. In one Carolingian manuscript of Pliny copied from another surviving Carolingian manuscript, the word separation in the copy is different from that in the exemplar, and also varies on different pages of the copy itself. For example, whereas the exemplar has *auulpibus quiiocur animaliseius aridum ederint*, the copy has *a uulpibus quiiocuranimalis eius aridum ederint* (for *a uulpibus qui iocur animalis eius aridum ederint*). This discrepancy probably reflects the scribes' difficulty in understanding Pliny's text at this point (that chickens are not attacked by foxes if they have eaten dried fox liver) and hence their inability to recognize immediately the Latin terms he used.[48] Nevertheless, we may suspect that the reading habits of speakers of *lingua romana* and the problems they encountered are likely to have differed from those of speakers with Celtic and Germanic language systems.

Eventually, sometime in the second half of the tenth century, most Western scribes based their practices on the analyses of the grammarians or on those found in more recent exemplars, and adopted word separation. But it was not until the twelfth century that word separation became consistent. Scribes persisted in confusing free and bound morphemes, because some ancient grammarians had confused the negative prefix *in-* with the prefixal use of the preposition *in* when citing words like *indoctus* and *infelix* in a discussion of inseparable prepositions (*praepositiones loquelares*).[49]

Christian Exegesis and the Interpretation of Texts

The preliminary stages of reading led to the exercise of Christian hermeneutics (corresponding to the processes of *enarratio* and *iudicium* of pagan texts) to produce personal readings or exegeses of the text. Gregory the Great argued that the processes of reading ought to be a dialogue with the text – particularly the text of the Bible. Just as we recognize the faces of those whom we scarcely know, but understand their thinking only when we engage with them in conversation, so a reader only begins to apprehend the thinking that lies behind the biblical text when he engages with it as if in conversation.[50] In the late eighth century, Beatus, in a treatise *adversum Elipandum*, likened the body of grammar to the body of man. But this is not enough for man's needs: just as man consists of body and soul and spirit, so a book has to be understood historically, morally and mystically.[51]

The most influential treatise on hermeneutics in this period was Augustine's *De doctrina christiana*, which began to circulate more widely from the ninth century onwards. Augustine regarded allegory as a gift of the Holy Spirit to stimulate our understanding. The process of puzzling out the significance of a text led to a better comprehension of truth, and was intrinsic to the monastic *lectio*.[52] Bede exploited the grammatical tradition in his *De schematibus et tropis* to provide a handbook of exegesis for Christian readers: much of the section on tropes was devoted to the various figures of *allegoria*, including *enigma*, illustrated by examples from the Bible. It was widely used, but, as Boniface remarked, the treatises of the Fathers are the best guides for those who studied the sacred page.[53] From the seventh to the eleventh centuries the works of the Fathers were tracked down and copied. The search was based on earlier works which were treated as authoritative bibliographies: Jerome-Gennadius, *De viris inlustribus* supplemented by Isidore (where an author's works were listed among the biographical details); the first book of Cassiodorus's *Institutiones* (which recommended books by subject in the course of discussion); and the lists produced by authors themselves, most notably Augustine's *Retractationes* (which refers to his works in chronological order, by their proper titles, with brief summaries of the content and the opening words).[54] Up to the end of the eleventh century those who wished to read or discuss the Scriptures followed the patristic tradition with the utmost fidelity. If discrepancies were to be found in the teachings of the Fathers, then a ninth-century scholar of the calibre of John the Scot could attribute such discrepancies to the multiplicity of the senses of Scripture, all of which were in agreement with the faith.[55]

In the ninth century Rabanus Maurus wrote a training manual for clerks, called *De clericorum institutione*. In the third book he explains how all those things which are written in books of divinity are to be investigated and taught, together with those useful things in the studies and arts of the pagans (*gentilium*) which ought to be examined by a man of the Church.[56] His principal arguments are taken directly from Augustine's *De doctrina christiana*, but given further emphasis through compression. First, anything in the Bible which does not immediately relate to either honesty of morals or truth of the faith must be interpreted figuratively.[57] Secondly, in such interpretations one must observe strictly the rule that all interpretations must be consonant with the true faith.[58] In short, each word or phrase contains nourishment for the soul. The tradition of allegorical and tropological interpretation was not confined to biblical texts.[59] One of the works adopted for study in the schools in the second half of the ninth century was the *De nuptiis Philologiae et Mercurii* of Martianus Capella, an allegory of the seven liberal arts. Those studying classical texts drew on the allegorical interpretations of pagan myths in the *Mithologiae* of Fulgentius Planciades, a fifth-century Christian scholar, and towards the end of the ninth century a new handbook was produced by an anonymous compiler known to modern scholars as 'Mythographus II'.[60]

The Development of Punctuation

As the number of readers increased, this concern with that meaning or significance of a text which lies behind the interpretation offered at the outset by the syntactical structures led to developments in the application of punctuation. The following passage is taken from a ninth-century copy of Book XVI, 1–2 of Augustine's *De civitate Dei*. The modern semi-colon mark is used here to represent the *punctus versus* which indicated the end of a *sententia*, and the point indicates pauses within it. The punctuation has been supplemented by a corrector.

> ; sicut ipsa eiusdem noe . & uinee plantatio & ex eius fructu inebriatio. & dormientis nudatio. & que ibi cetera facta atque conscripta sunt propheticis [s]unt grauidata sensibus . & uelata tegminibus. sed nunc rerum effectu iam [in] posteris consecuto que operta fuerant satis aperta sunt;[61]

> So too the planting of the vine by Noah himself and his drunkenness through its fruit . and his nakedness while he slept . and the other things which were done at that time and written down are all pregnant with prophetic meanings . and veiled with mysterious coverings . but now by the bringing about of actual events which has subsequently followed those things which had been concealed are sufficiently revealed;

When one contrasts and compares the punctuation of this copy with that in other copies,[62] it emerges that here the punctuation after *inebriatio* (and after 'fruit' in the English version) separates the planting of the vine and Noah's drunkenness from the events of his nakedness. The punctuation after *sensibus* ('meanings') distinguishes between prophecy and mystery, identifying them as two different concepts. The short pause after *tegminibus* ('coverings') relates all these events, particular and general, to the revelation of their prophetic and mysterious significance in the unfolding of subsequent events. The emphasis in this interpretation indicates that the various events, and the process by which their significance has been revealed, belong to a single continuum of time, or eternity.

However, improvements in the notation of punctuation in the ninth century enabled a contemporary corrector of the manuscript to respond to form as well as content. His sophisticated reading exploits the punctuation of the original scribe, and by adding a few further marks draws attention to that contribution to the message of the text made by the rhetorical structure of Augustine's prose. Punctuation emphasizes the rhymes *inebriatio/nudatio, sensibus/tegminibus*; and the reading of the passage as a single *sententia* enables correspondences to emerge between the ideas of fruit/effect/meanings/prophecy, and contrasts to be drawn between those in the parallel group of nakedness/veiled/concealed/revealed. A mind conversant with Augustine, and accustomed to allegorical readings, may be expected to have perceived the ambiguity of *fructus* in the two senses of 'fruit' and 'effect', and that that which is to be uncovered is a fruit just as the nakedness is the effect of the vine. The corrector has drawn upon a wide range of experience which embraced both theological and literary matters, and has drawn on this experience in his assessment and interpretation of the message of the text. The application of punctuation marks has brought hermeneutic analysis on to the page, to be apprehended by a reader as part of the process of reading itself.

The Presentation of Vernacular Texts

The earliest surviving copies of vernacular texts in the West also belong to this period. A scribe who copied a vernacular text could rely on a reader's familiarity with his own native language, and the writing of the vernacular reflected the phenomena of spoken language more than the copying of Latin did: diversity of spellings can reflect diversity of sounds in different dialects. In the earliest surviving Irish texts, the eighth-century copy of the 'Cambrai Homily', and the oldest glosses, words were grouped in units which reflected a consciousness of syntactical stress. In romance languages the eighth-century 'Verona Riddle' was copied in *scriptio continua* when it was entered vertically in the margin of a Latin text; in the ninth-century Strasbourg Oaths most words were separated, but some groupings reflect sentence stress. However, the practice of glossing Latin words taught scribes how to recognize word boundaries in the vernacular. In the eighth-century copies of the Old English 'Caedmon's Hymn' and the ninth-century copy of the Old High German *Hildebrandslied*, words and the elements of compounds were frequently separated, but there is confusion in the treatment of prepositions and proclitics analogous to that in the treatment of *praepositiones loquelares* in copies of Latin texts. Gradually scribes adopted the practice of word separation, the use of *litterae notabiliores* and punctuation found in Latin texts, although the rhythmic structure of vernacular verse was not at first indicated by stichic layout, as it was in copies of Latin verse.[63]

Nowhere does history repeat itself as it does in the history of reading, when each new generation of readers goes through the same stages of learning and experience of the process as its predecessors. But some generations produce readers with their own particular pressing needs which stimulate new developments reflected on the pages of the new texts they read. Perhaps the most obvious characteristics of the period I have been discussing are: first, the impact of a new motive for reading, and the consequent demand by readers, for whom Latin was an alien language, for easier access to the information contained in texts; secondly, the influence of principles found in the works of the ancient grammarians on attempts to evolve a pattern of conventions to meet this demand – the evolution of the rudiments of what I have called a 'grammar of legibility'.[64]

4

The Scholastic Model of Reading

Jacqueline Hamesse

Profound changes took place in reading in the age of scholasticism.[1] Reading first became a school exercise, then a university exercise governed by its own rules. Hence it was primarily in the schools, then in the universities, that reading took place. Whereas during the early Middle Ages reading had gone on above all within the framework of the monasteries (collective reading during offices, reading during meals or during spiritual exercises, or individual reading in times for study or meditation), the scholastic age brought a radical renewal of the very concept of the act of reading. Is it by chance that the title of the first treatise on the art of reading, Hugh of Saint Victor's *Didascalicon*, was written in the twelfth century and stresses the fundamental role of reading in the school curriculum?[2]

The age clearly brought a new awareness of the act of reading. Henceforth reading could no longer be conceived of without implying a certain organization. Although such notions were never explicit, we can find early versions of the ideas of utility and profit, which became fundamental to reading beginning in the thirteenth century. Books could no longer be approached freely: reading a text required an understanding of the proper method of approach. One of Hugh of Saint Victor's contemporaries clearly expressed concern in a letter to Hugh that he subtitled 'On the manner and the order to be followed in reading Holy Scripture'.[3]

The new organization of reading created new needs. The reader had to be able to find what he was looking for with ease, without having to leaf through pages. Texts responded to that need: divisions began to be established, paragraphs were marked, the various chapters were given titles, and concordances were drawn up, along with tables of contents and alphabetical indexes that made rapid consultation of a work easier and helped to locate the necessary documentation. The new scholastic reading was totally different from the monastic model, which had been focused on a slow, rigorous comprehension of all of Holy Writ.

From ruminatio *to* lectura

During the early Middle Ages *Sacra Scriptura* was the book *par excellence*. Scripture was read at all times, and monastic spirituality was based on it. Was it by chance that authors spoke of 'rumination' (*ruminatio*) in connection with the exercise of assimilation of the Bible and meditation on it? Reading was truly the spiritual nourishment of monks. Marcel Jousse called it 'mastication of the Word'.[4] It was a slow, regular reading in depth. Readers who had dedicated their lives to God learned some passages by heart, and they meditated incessantly on certain phrases. Reading aloud was frequent. The habit of articulating the syllables as one read was so widespread that even when reading individually for oneself alone the words were sounded out in a low voice.[5] Reading aloud encouraged reading at a very slow pace, and it aided assimilation of the content of works: the three exercises assigned to monks were reading (*legere*), meditation (*meditari*) and contemplation (*contemplari*).

Armando Petrucci notes that three types of reading existed at the time: silent reading (*in silentio*); reading in a low voice, called 'murmured reading' or 'rumination' (used to encourage meditation and help in memorization); and reading aloud, which required a particular technique, as it had in classical antiquity, and was quite similar to liturgical recitation or chanting.[6]

In that world orality predominated over writing.[7] Oral reading even affected writing: in the medieval scriptorium, texts that were copied – classical works or works of the Church Fathers – were dictated. Later, when works were no longer copied by having one reader dictate to a number of copiers, the method that an individual used for writing was still closely linked to reading, with sight replacing hearing for grasping and comprehending the words to be reproduced. A good many scribes continued to read silently the phrases they were copying, inwardly pronouncing the words they saw.

The greatest change that scholasticism brought to reading lay in the importance of reading in the context of teaching. As Father Marie-Dominique Chenu states: 'The entire medieval pedagogy was based on the reading of texts, and in the universities, scholasticism gave this type of work institutional form and enlarged upon it.[8] Unlike in classical antiquity, when a reader might make it possible for a large audience to become acquainted with an author's recent work, we cannot speak in terms of public reading in medieval teaching. What we have in the age of scholasticism is a person reading, explaining and commenting on a work that was an integral part of a programme of studies. This technique was not new. In the early Middle Ages, school lessons had been based on the explanation of and commentary on classical texts, as we have seen in the preceding chapters. What was new was rather the development of that exercise and its subjection to rules: henceforth it took place at determined times and places and in pre-established ways.

It goes without saying that the new manner of collective reading, organized within teaching programmes, neither eliminated nor supplanted intellectuals' direct contact with an author's text. The acquisition of a personal culture continued to flourish along with pedagogical formation. Still, as time wore on, private reading began to change as well. The conditions under which books were produced evolved, book circulation increased, and the reader's relationship to the text was profoundly altered. An abundant literary production encouraged a new approach to the works available to be read. For all these reasons, one can truly speak of a scholastic reading style different from all the ways of reading we have seen thus far.

One interesting fact deserves mention: in classical Latin, the term *legere* is ambiguous, because it designates both the act of 'teaching' and the act of 'reading'. John of Salisbury remarked on this in his *Metalogicon* as early as the twelfth century:

> The word 'reading' (*legendi*) is equivocal. It may refer either to the activity of teaching and being taught, or to the occupation of studying written things by oneself. Consequently, the former, the intercommunication between teacher and learner, may be termed (to use Quintilian's word) the 'lecture' (*praelectio*); the latter, or the scrutiny by the student, the 'reading' (*lectio*), simply so called.[9]

To do away with a linguistic ambiguity, John of Salisbury proposes reserving the term *praelectio* for the teaching process and using *lectio* for individual reading. It is interesting that at least some people were aware of the dual function of reading as early as the twelfth century. A study of the vocabulary used in the city schools of the time shows, however, that *legere* was seldom used in the teaching sense, and in fact was not widely used until the rise of the universities.[10] Similarly, in the scholastic age *lectio*, which for John of Salisbury represented direct reading of a text, became the most general term for designating a university course. These differences in meaning reveal profound changes in the habits of people of the Middle Ages, but they also reflect equally profound changes brought about by new institutions and by the trials and hesitations typical of a period of flux.

The Latin syntax of many texts makes the various meanings of the verb *legere* clearer by constructing the phrase differently according to whether the author intended the teaching of the master, the instruction of the student, or private, individual reading. Thus *legere librum illi* indicates explaining a book to someone; *legere librum ab illo*, learning from a book with the aid of someone; *legere librum*, reading a book. Linguistic analysis is always interesting, particularly when its results run counter to what at first might seem obvious. For example, unlike *lectio* and *legere*, which belong to the vocabulary of classical Latin, *lectura* is a medieval creation that dates from the rise of the universities, when it appears in the context of teaching to designate a specific procedure of textual analysis.

The term *lectura* first arose in the schools of law to refer to a method for the explication of a text that consisted in glosses written in the margins of a manuscript of a 'required' text with the aim of elucidating difficult passages.[11] It was only during the thirteenth century that the term came to be used in the technical sense of the contents of a course or a 'reading' of a text with commentary and explication.[12] In French the words *leçon* (lesson) and *lecture* (reading) mean two different things, and it is curious to note that the noun *lectura* did not appear in the Latin language until the latter half of the twelfth century.

The various religious Orders also played an important role in the circulation and utilization of the book in the age of scholasticism. Their involvement affected the book both on the level of the overall transmission of written culture and on that of the selection of works to be read.[13] They encouraged the dissemination of certain texts, while the ecclesiastical authorities considered others dangerous and not to be placed in all hands. As early as the thirteenth century, the very concept of reading underwent a fundamental evolution that requires rigorous analysis and definition.

Reference *to* Auctoritates

Since literary production increased incessantly from the twelfth century on, other, more rapid reading methods had to be found if intellectuals were to become familiar with a large number of works. Those methods were soon quite diverse. A visual approach to the text replaced hearing;

henceforth readers needed not only to be able to read fast, but also to have convenient ways to find the passages they wanted to use and know what arguments were indispensable in a given domain. Medieval men always referred to authorities (*auctoritates*) in their literary compositions. These came in the form of phrases, citations or entire passages from the Bible, the Fathers of the Church, or the authors of classical antiquity, which they used to lend more weight to their own line of argumentation. Florilegia facilitated the search for such extracts; anthologies of texts were also used as an aid to memorization or a guide to finding the passage a reader sought. Other sorts of reading aids appeared with the florilegia in the twelfth century, which helped readers to find their way in a manuscript or to locate certain passages without having to read the entire text. An uninterrupted reading of an entire work, one that took time and permitted assimilation of the whole (or at least the whole gist), was gradually replaced by a more fragmented, piecemeal reading style that had the advantage of providing a quick grasp of selections but no longer encouraged any deep contact with the text or any genuine assimilation of the doctrine it contained. Utility outstripped knowledge.

Beginning in the early Middle Ages, collections of extracts were compiled in many domains: there were exegetical florilegia, theological, patristic and ascetic ones, and anthologies of classical authors, to name only the main types. These were working aids that responded to a variety of needs. They made accessible the essence of works that an intellectual might not be able to acquire for his own personal use, given the small number of copies available and the high cost of manuscripts, and a working method that encouraged recourse to the *auctoritates* in teaching, literary production and preaching.[14] Such volumes gave what was essential in a work or a topic, and they often presented the texts in short, easily memorized sentences, which was just what their users wanted.[15] It must be admitted, however, that in spite of the large number of these works in the libraries, they served purely as reservoirs of texts, inspiring little creativity. Consulting works of this sort never encouraged the elaboration of new theories or launched an original methodology, either for exegesis or a personal commentary.[16] As we shall see, the florilegia – given the personality of their compilers – offered the advantage of containing no passages that could be suspected of heresy, an argument that very probably contributed to their success.

A number of texts by medieval authors furnished interesting information on both the methods and the terminology of such works. Chief among these are Robert of Melun's prologue to his *Sententiae*, the prologue to Abelard's *Sic et Non*, Hugh of Saint Victor's *Didascalicon* and John of Salisbury's *Metalogicon*. There were many others, both in the twelfth century and in the following centuries. Such texts provide direct testimony to the way in which medieval authors conceived of teaching, reading and argumentation. They also tell us the meaning of technical terms referring to reading. This is an important help, because in this period most of those terms, which had been inherited from classical antiquity, began to change meaning in response to both the new requirements of teaching and a demand for greater precision.

As early as the thirteenth century, in fact, following the new developments that the creation of the universities brought about in all domains and as a result of the need for strict definitions to designate new practices, vocabulary became noticeably more technical. The twelfth century was a time of transition, and it is precisely this flux that makes the texts of that age so interesting. At times the words they use retain their old meanings, but we can see new meanings creeping in, thus enabling us to grasp the beginnings of an evolution visible on all levels at a later date.

In the prologue to his *Sententiae* Robert of Melun, writing in the twelfth century, alludes to professional readers (*recitatores*) who gave oral readings of texts that they did not necessarily fully understand.[17] Robert distinguishes between someone who simply reads aloud a text written by someone else (the *recitator*) and the more usual sort of reader (*lector*) who tries to understand a text while he reads it. There is in fact a rubric next to this passage in a manuscript of this work preserved in Bruges: 'Concerning those who apply themselves to the exercises of reading and citations of authorities and do not understand them.' Such passages clearly show how the well-trained memories of men of the Middle Ages enabled them to remember a large number of texts without necessarily fully understanding them.[18] In the fourteenth century, for all the progress that had been made in teaching and in spite of new scientific demands, the situation had hardly changed (at least in certain circles), given that a passage in a work incorrectly attributed to William of Ockham denounces parroting from memory as a bad habit.[19]

Intellectual Working Tools

The literary explosion in the twelfth century made access to books more complicated. Texts had become so numerous that no one person could read them all. It became difficult, even impossible, to memorize the larger number of works available, and just as impossible to be fully informed about any topic, given the lack of inventories, indexes and résumés to help gather the indispensable documentation. The authors of the time were aware of these difficulties, and they relied heavily on summaries composed to resolve just such problems. Among those works were the *Glossa ordinaria*, an irreplaceable working tool for understanding the Bible; Gratian's *Decretum*, which gave jurists the materials indispensable to their discipline; and, for the theologians, Peter Lombard's *Libri sententiarum*. In the preface to that work, Peter Lombard explains the intentions typical of the twelfth-century author: he 'gathers together in one short volume the opinions of the Fathers ... so that the seeker need not consult an abundance of books [because] the brevity of the extracts assembled offers, effortlessly, what he is looking for'.[20]

Authors of the age constantly used the Bible, the *Glossa ordinaria*, Gratian's *Decretals* and Peter Lombard's *Sentences*. Such works were their prime nourishment; but has enough attention been paid to other working tools that medieval authors made use of just as frequently? These included the *Summa aurea* (Golden Compendium) of William of Auxerre, the *Summa quaestionorum theologicarum* of Philippe le Chancelier, and the *Summa* of Prepositino di Cremona, to cite only the best-known works of the sort.

In spite of such attempts to offer intellectuals working tools that would condense the essence of what they should know in a given domain, there was yet another problem to be solved. How could any one person keep abreast of all the books produced and become informed about everything that was being published? The question worried intellectuals. A first solution was to compile encyclopedias in an attempt to assemble essential knowledge in the various domains. Among the many ambitious enterprises that appeared were Alexander Neckam's *De naturis rerum* (*c.*1195), Arnold of Saxony's *De finibus rerum* (*c.*1220), the *De proprietatibus rerum* of Bartholomaeus Anglicus (*c.*1240), the *De natura rerum* of Thomas de Cantimpré (*c.*1245) and the *Speculum majus* of Vincent of Beauvais (*c.*1245–60). Certain religious Orders played a fundamental role in this endeavour: Bartholomaeus Anglicus was a Franciscan; Thomas de Cantimpré and Vincent of Beauvais were Dominicans.

A large number of glossaries and lexicons accompanied these encyclopedic works, and they too were an invaluable aid to the correct interpretation of certain terms used in the Latin texts. Papias's *Elementarium*, an eleventh-century work, figures as a precursor here: in his prologue to this anthology, Papias gives, for the first time, rules for a systematic alphabetical classification. Unfortunately, the system he advocated did not take hold in his own day, and more than a century passed before his principles of classification re-emerged. I might add that the scientific rigour he demonstrated in his prologue was not always applied systematically.

Although members of the mendicant Orders figure among the compilers of encyclopedias, the Dominicans and the Franciscans were not the first to elaborate similar working tools. They were preceded in the twelfth century by the Cistercians, true master-builders when it came to organizing documentation. Knowledge became the prime goal of reading. The reader's first priority was no longer wisdom, as it had been with the monks and their spiritual readings, and obtaining knowledge required a certain number of keys for rapid retrieval of the passages one wanted to use.

Richard H. Rouse has written several works that are fundamental to a grasp of the Cistercians' efforts to divide the text, organize it into sections, and highlight the passages they considered the most important.[21] Here we enter into a new world that suggests modern reading habits. After the pioneering labours of the Cistercians to organize the content of a manuscript, other aids appeared and flourished: the table of contents, the concept index, concordances of terms, alphabetically arranged analytical tables, summaries and abridgements. Even the great twelfth-century *summae* were abridged: they were admittedly easier to handle when reduced to a single volume. The abridgements were a pale reflection of the originals, however.

The rise of this new literary genre inevitably meant that reading was no longer direct: now a compiler served as an intermediary, and reading was filtered by selection. Reference to the book changed. Its contents were no longer studied for themselves with the aim of acquiring a certain wisdom, as Hugh of Saint Victor had recommended.[22] Henceforth knowledge was primary, and it took precedence over everything else, even when it was fragmentary. Meditation gave way to utility in a profound shift of emphasis that completely changed the impact of reading.

Certain scholars are quite aware of the important role of these working tools for learning in the Middle Ages,[23] but others have failed to grasp their influence among intellectuals. As any fourteenth-century inventory will show, florilegia, concordances and tables abounded, not only in the libraries of the religious Orders, but also in college and university libraries. Such compilations often replaced consultation and, *a fortiori*, direct reading of authors' works, and even though they constitute a second-tier literature, their sizeable role in the intellectual preparation of medieval men cannot be denied. Today we have such different methods for acquiring culture that it is difficult for us to comprehend that even the great writers of the age of scholasticism made use of these handy tools for easy access to documentation that was indispensable to their work. The large number of manuscripts that have come down to us bear witness to the use and dissemination of such compilations.

Working tools like these provided a ready source of documentation that could be used whenever a large number of texts was needed to shore up a thesis or an argument; all scholars in search of *auctoritates*, following the working methods outlined above, had easy access to them in such works. Moreover, by summarizing doctrines that were at times difficult to grasp and putting them in short, easily memorized sentences, such works often provided a simple introduction to a work, thus serving as an initiation into the author's thought.

Compilations offered so many advantages that individual book reading tended to disappear, replaced in many cases exclusively by consultation of extracts. It is understandable that the young students of the Faculty of Arts should have prized these anthologies so highly when they first came to the university and encountered doctrines that were obscure to them.[24] In the fourteenth century some of these collections were even used as course textbooks, especially in the Faculty of Arts, first in the German universities, then in those of other European lands.[25] Thus the use of such compilations evolved. At first their aim was documentary, but it was so easy to gain a general idea of a text through them that many people no longer sought out the original work to read it in its entirety. Students were content to use them as an introduction to a work, and eventually professors began to base their courses on them instead of the original texts. One result was a genuine impoverishment in knowledge of the works that served as obligatory texts 'read' and explicated in the various required courses of study in the universities.

Why Florilegia and Abridgements were so Successful

Much work remains to be done regarding the textbooks that were the basis of teaching in the various university faculties. One reason why we know so little about them is because many anthologies remain unpublished, hence scholars have not been able to exploit them. It is also true, however, that there are some historians of ideas who think that second-tier literature of this sort is uninteresting and not worth studying. The fact remains that it was through such humble textbooks that medieval men received their introduction to the required curriculum and their first contact with the thought of their predecessors.[26]

The teaching methods of the early universities encouraged the reading of texts,[27] but what they had in mind was not the same sort of reading that had been practised in the monastic age. In the universities explication and commentary (*lectio*) took up a preponderant share of class time. The university was organized to provide other teaching methods as well: discussion (*disputatio*) and preaching (*praedicatio*). The three stages of monastic culture – reading, meditation and contemplation – were replaced in the age of scholasticism by three different approaches to a text: explication and commentary (*legere*), the art of discussion (*disputare*) and consideration of the spiritual dimension (*praedicare*). It is clear, however, that discussion soon became preponderant, eventually absorbing the roles formerly played by the other two practices. In the thirteenth century Aristotelian philosophy made an overwhelming impact, the teaching of dialectics intensified, and the art of reasoned argumentation reigned supreme. By the fourteenth century logic dominated all fields of study, and argumentation was cultivated as a technique, to the detriment of the contents of the texts. Over-organization and an exaggerated specialization destroyed the balance of the university's original teaching programme, and reading, discussion and preaching were no longer considered equally valuable. All these reasons worked to encourage a search for working tools in all domains, rather than simply reading the Bible, the text that had provided the foundation for all of culture. No one in the fourteenth century was interested in biblical commentary, not even in a Faculty of Theology. A change of perspective created a different mind-set. People moved on to a different sort of reading.

There were other reasons for the change. Students were extremely young when they arrived at the university to begin their studies. The Faculty of Arts, which (everywhere but in Bologna) provided an obligatory basic instruction before students could choose an area of specialization, was more or less equivalent to secondary education today. The instruction that university students had received before they arrived at the university did not even remotely prepare them for in-depth comprehension of complete works, read and commented upon during class sessions. Public readings of the required texts had to be organized in such a way that all students could gain some comprehension of those works. The teaching method that the universities had inherited from the twelfth century divided comprehension into three levels: a 'grammatical', word-for-word explanation (the *littera*); a literal commentary or paraphrase aimed at providing a grasp of both the general meaning and the nuances of each phrase (the *sensus*); and, finally, a deeper, personal explication of the passage as interpreted by the professor (the *sententia*). That technique normally enabled every student to achieve a firm comprehension of the work.

For example, students received no previous initiation in the works of Aristotle, on which all university teaching in philosophy was based. In spite of the literal explications that the teachers were obliged to give, in spite of their commentaries, and in spite of the exercises held outside the course schedule to familiarize beginners with a doctrine new to them, many students quite obviously failed to reach any deep understanding of Aristotle's thought. Aristotelian florilegia were thus one way of facilitating access to a philosophy that can at times be obscure and whose meaning even specialists can find hard to grasp. Most students made no effort to read the author's actual text, and were instead satisfied with extracts and with the commentaries on those extracts made by the professors during their lectures.

Many teachers, what is more, did not consult the original text of the author they were supposed to explain and comment upon. The inherent difficulty of the text proved a real stumbling block for some of them, but for many others economic constraints entered into the picture as well. Two things limited access to the complete works that teachers may have wanted to know or use: the first was the high cost of parchment (someone has calculated that it would take the skins of an entire flock of sheep to make one Bible) that made a book a sizeable capital outlay; the second was the labour involved in writing or copying, long considered a servile task.[28] Until the thirteenth century most intellectuals kept secretaries or had their writing work done by qualified copyists, also at notable expense. Even in the age of the universities, when the act of writing became a necessary part of the intellectuals' habits, certain mendicant religious Orders forbade the brothers to spend their time copying texts.[29] Study time was too precious; one could not waste it recopying other people's works. The economic factor, combined with the low esteem in which writing was held, explains why scholars solved the problem of an increasing need for texts by the use of working tools that made the essence of a work accessible in one volume of representative extracts or a summary.

In the age of the universities certain libraries lent books to readers, but the number of books in circulation made it impossible for libraries to satisfy the intellectuals' growing demands. As one way to resolve the problem, universities launched the system for reproducing texts by *exemplar* and *pecia*.[30] The university authorities exercised a tight quality control over the texts circulated in this manner, in order to avoid the dissemination of incorrect versions.[31] In spite of their efforts, however, many students took the easier way and were content to use florilegia and summaries to learn about a text, never bothering to read the original.

In spite of the universities' many prohibitions and regulations, the tendency to simplification increased, especially in the Faculty of Arts. It was easier to give students brief, easily memorized summaries than to linger over a detailed explication of the difficult line of thought encountered in some of the works on the programme of studies.

The university curriculum was impoverished for other reasons as well. The university population changed after the Black Death and its ravages, which hit cities particularly hard. Students came increasingly from rural areas, and their level of culture seems to have been lower than their predecessors. The various aids for the study of texts were well suited to their need for an introduction to the courses of study. Students were tempted by facility as well, and the large number of exercises they were expected to attend encouraged them to memorize extensively. Their writing skills were often less than excellent, and at times they found it hard to take full, accurate notes during lectures. Thus they turned to the many summaries that circulated in the form of tables, abridgements, concordances, indexes and florilegia.

One of the greatest problems connected with these working tools was selection. The importance of the extracts chosen and the quality of the passages transmitted depended entirely on the judgement and intelligence of the compiler. When today's scholars consider such compilations, they raise basic and obligatory questions concerning the method used by the person who chose the extracts and the goal he had in mind. These questions are not always easy to answer. First, many florilegia are anonymous; second, most of them have no preface. When there is a prologue stating the compiler's intentions, we need to ask whether it is original, or rather (as is often the case at this period) a model borrowed from a previous anthology. When that problem has been solved, the next question is to what extent the intentions expressed were in fact realized. This too is not always easy to evaluate.

Useful as they were, such compilations were a poor substitute for consulting the works themselves. If at first they were conceived as a stopgap measure when a text was inaccessible or direct consultation was difficult, we can see from the broad use that was made of them that very soon students used florilegia because they facilitated study and dispensed them from reading an entire work. This was true of all sorts of florilegia. In general, the literature of compilations, extracts and abridgements had the unfortunate effect of turning medieval students away from direct consultation of authors' works. An interesting echo of this can be found in the introduction to the third volume of the *Chartularium Universitatis Parisiensis*, in which the authors of that work impute the lack of interest in theological studies and the success of nominalism in the fourteenth century to an excessive consultation of collections of extracts as a source for thought:

> For a long time, the theologians, a few exceptions aside, had neglected the [most] remarkable source of theology, which is the study of the Fathers of the Church. Indeed, the catalogues of manuscripts from that troubled age

contain no apographa of the works of the holy Fathers with the exception of brief treatises, usually treating spiritual life. If they still showed some knowledge of the Fathers, they drew it from earlier works of theology or from collections arranged by alphabetical order that gathered together the thoughts of the Fathers. That scholastic method came from the customs of antiquity. That is how theology has become sterile and is even more sterile than ever, while nominalism reigns in philosophy.[32]

This negative judgement shows how greatly the literature of extracts limited creativity, and how it necessarily guided studies in the direction of sterility when such collections of quotations were no longer considered as working tools but became an end in themselves. When the original presentation of an author's thought was reduced to a series of quotations, more or less well-chosen and always taken out of context, a number of doctrines were distorted, and readers had no contact with the wealth of certain works. Moreover, because the choice of selections was left to the arbitrary judgement of the compiler, whole portions of works thought unworthy of inclusion were cast into oblivion. Finally, the compilation process often distorted the author's original thought. Drastic abridgement almost always implies an excessive simplification and, above all, a lack of nuance.

Moreover, the custom of highlighting the more important passages of a text (*notabilia*) was a teaching technique in both the Faculty of Arts and the *studia* of the religious Orders. It is hardly surprising that this custom produced even more compilations, this time of *notabilia* extracted from professors' textbooks. They provided a ready-to-use documentation. Working tools that gave rapid, easy access to the texts had been widely circulated in all milieus, and their high point came in the age of the universities. The need for texts had in fact grown along with the regulations in the university statutes. In almost all the universities the students were expected to possess the texts read in class sessions so that they could follow the professor's explanations.[33] The many university exercises demanded from students a culture sufficient to permit them to take part in discussions carried on by exchanging citations of *auctoritates*. They had to have read a good many texts if they were to train their minds and arrive at the point where they could express personal opinions. This was why many summaries, concordances and florilegia were composed.

The Role of the Religious Orders

At the same time the various religious Orders encouraged the composition and distribution of compilations for other reasons as well, chief

among them to avoid errors of philosophical interpretation that might
lead some religions to profess theories that contradicted Christian doctrine. It was thus to the advantage of the Order to have compilations
made that contained only clear, easily understood selections that
avoided ambiguous problems. Soon after the formation of the Dominican order, for example, the *Constitutions* of Jordan of Saxony forbade
the young brothers to read philosophical works unless a Dominican
master was available to explain and comment on the texts,[34] but they
might have free access to theological works. Humbert de Romans's
opinion was less categorical: he divided the friars into three categories
according to their intellectual capacities, setting rules for each group.[35]

It is important to note that the extracts contained in these florilegia,
summaries and concordances were all selected by someone, which
means that the compiler could deliberately exclude any passage that
might lead to a dubious interpretation not in conformity with the teachings of Christian doctrine. In their desire to avoid heretical discussions,
the various religious Orders encouraged the composition and circulation of working tools over which they could exercise control. Such
works even arrived (by various paths) at the papal court in Avignon,
where they were used by the popes, in certain cases sparing even them
from having to read complete works that they had neither the time nor
the inclination to read.

Pope John XXII (1316–34), for example, was very fond of abridgements.[36] Even if he used such collections extensively, however, John was
personally acquainted with the complete work of most of the authors
he cited. In one of his sermons, he even criticizes his detractors for
basing their arguments uniquely on abridgements or extracts.[37] Several
popes who did not have time to read entire works, either to pursue a
personal interest or to form an opinion on a text that had been
denounced as heretical, called upon regular clergy to draw up collections of extracts for them.[38] There are many florilegia in the inventories
of the papal library in Avignon. King Robert of Anjou owned similar
volumes, as did other prominent figures. Federigo da Montefeltro, duke
of Urbino (fifteenth century), ordered a florilegium of Aristotle from a
Dominican, Jordanis de Bergomo.[39] One of the reasons for the commission given in the dedicatory letter in the manuscript is the difficulty
of understanding Aristotelian philosophy,[40] which was also among
the basic arguments for creating Aristotelian florilegia for teaching
purposes.

How much influence did the compilations of the religious Orders
have? How well prepared were the brothers to take on that sort of
work? Did they, either deliberately or involuntarily, put their own mark
on the working tools they created? Their goals, the requirements of

their sponsors, their own motivations and the results they obtained all deserve more painstaking investigation than they have as yet received.

Humanistic Compilations

Can we speak of progress between the Middle Ages and the Renaissance where university compilations are concerned? Father Charles H. Lohr has recently remarked that evolution was slight, and that university courses at the end of the sixteenth century required many of the same basic textbooks that had been used since the thirteenth century, in philosophy at least. Was that true of all the faculties? Even if there had been a certain continuity in the transmission of basic textbooks, the atmosphere in the universities had changed. Intellectuals reacted differently towards *auctoritates*. The teaching of logic and the art of reasoning had done its job through the centuries, and *ratio* tended to gain ground over *auctoritas* in all domains, in spite of all the theologians' efforts. Change occurred in people's approach to the texts and in how they discussed them, rather than on the level of the compilations of texts themselves.

In certain cases working methods changed as well. The humanists restored individual reading to a place of honour, and recommended direct contact with original works. Compilations of extracts were still made, even in large numbers, but many of them were florilegia compiled for personal use and thus reflected one humanist's or one scholar's notes on his reading. In this period the boundary between a florilegium and a collection of texts is often hard to draw.[41] The aims of a collection of personal notes differed greatly from those of the medieval compilers, making some of these works more like anthologies than florilegia. On this level, as on others, a precise definition of terms is useful.[42] Most collections made for private use had only a limited circulation, and in some cases no circulation.

During the Renaissance the mendicant Orders continued to play an important role in providing working tools for philosophical study. We need only think of such names as Paul of Venice, an Augustinian; Antonio Trombetta, a Franciscan; or Thomas de Vio, a Dominican; to see that this tradition lasted well beyond the Middle Ages.[43]

Florilegia by no means disappeared with the coming of humanism. In certain cases the genre evolved, but it did not die. Production diversified: compilations were used by men of letters, preachers and teachers as practical, easily accessible collections of documents, and they continued to be used as classroom teaching aids.[44] In the sixteenth century the Jesuits encouraged their use.[45] This is hardly surprising, given that the florilegia presented expurgated texts that did not risk contaminating young minds or leading young people down dangerous paths. During the same age, many Latin compilations that had been made during the Middle Ages were translated into the vernacular.

The Decline of the Scholastic Model

After the twelfth century, reading styles evolved in ways that enable us to distinguish scholastic reading from the sorts of reading that had been practised earlier. In the age of scholasticism, acquisition of knowledge became more important than the spiritual dimension of reading. The linguistic evolution analysed above shows the direction taken by the reading of texts. Teaching and the fastest possible acquisition of culture replaced a deep knowledge of works. Henceforth people read diagonally: meditation on Holy Scripture gave way to an examination (often superficial) of other texts that were part of the curriculum. Most of the time academics no longer read for pleasure, but rather with the one aim of acquiring the indispensable elements of a utilitarian culture.

In the twelfth century Peter Lombard, Peter the Chanter, Maurice de Sully and Robert de Courçon worked to make knowledge more accessible, rather than still strictly individual and restricted to the monastic milieu, but their generous efforts were in vain. Organized technical reading won out over spiritual reading. On all levels the encyclopedic point of view replaced reading and meditation. Logic, which had been used formerly as a means for sharpening the mind, seduced the intellectuals and invaded university circles. The art of debate came to be prized over a deep knowledge of texts.[46] The well-developed memory of men of the Middle Ages helped them to make do without consulting the original works, relying instead uniquely on extracts selected by others. Working methods changed. In many cases individual creativity gave way to a highly structured mode of composition that was locked into a strict framework and reliant on typical scholastic phraseology. That highly technical language contributed to the inevitable decline of the scholastic method. The fourteenth century marked a decisive turning point in spite of a few figures of brilliant intelligence.

Although university procedures profoundly influenced reading practices, other ways to gain access to texts were practised by certain cultured intellectuals and bibliophiles who had retained a love of books: Richard de Bury provides a good example.[47] According to Richard Fitzralph, bishop of Armagh (fourteenth century), the mendicant Orders bought enormous numbers of books for their community libraries, in order to provide their friars with the intellectual baggage they thought indispensable. Fitzralph tells us:

At Oxford it is no longer possible to buy even one book of philosophy or theology, and in medicine and canon law opportunities are rare because the mendicant Orders, which have founded communities everywhere, grab everything for their friaries. The first thing one encounters there is a large, fine common library; furthermore, each individual student is copiously furnished with books. The penury of working tools produced in the market by these purchases of the mendicant Orders had even obliged three or four clerics sent to Oxford by the archbishop to give up their studies.[48]

This report confirms the thinking of the religious Orders when they prohibited their friars from wasting their time copying texts.

The problem of the scarcity of books and working tools indispensable to studies on all levels found a natural solution of sorts in the late fourteenth century, after the Black Death decimated Europe. Cities were hit particularly hard. Since that was where intellectuals had gathered for reasons of study, a massive decline in the numbers of both professors and students left a disproportionate quantity of books available, radically changing the acquisition and circulation of texts. Books were again accessible, and university people, who had to some extent lost a taste for reading during the preceding century in their pursuit of a more utilitarian contact with knowledge, rediscovered reading.

Humanists in Italy began to search out texts from classical antiquity and put them back into circulation. The new atmosphere that resulted, along with the introduction of printing and a love of *belles lettres*, changed the reader's relationship to the book yet again. Movements such as the *Devotio moderna* attempted to revive the sort of reading that had been practised in the monastic age.[49] Henceforth, the development of cities and the democratization of teaching worked to diversify the interests of readers, who were as likely to be burghers or merchants as intellectuals.

5

Reading in the Later Middle Ages

Paul Saenger

The Twelfth Century

In northern Europe, the twelfth century has been widely recognized as a crucial period for innovation in law, theology, philosophy and art. However, for the history of reading, it was primarily a time of continuity and consolidation of the text format of separated script which in the eleventh century had become the medium of reading not only in the British Isles, where it had existed since the seventh century, but in France, Germany and Lorraine as well. The canonical separation of words that placed clearly perceptible units of space between each and every word of the sentence, including monosyllabic prepositions, minimized the need for oralization in the reading process. This new text format was complemented by an equally significant linguistic change: the evolution in Latin of conventions for word order, or at least the grouping of grammatically linked words within linearly arranged sentences. Together, word separation and word order were conductive to the precise expression of ideas in the clear and unambiguous manner so essential for communicating the subtle distinctions of scholastic philosophy.[1] They were also prerequisites for the development of syntactic punctuation and rapid silent reading which depended on the swift visual recognition of word shape and the perception of larger graphic contours of the page: the clause, the sentence and the paragraph.

One of the most striking examples of the new medium of word-separated communication can be found in the works of Guibert of Nogent (d. *c.*1125). Born in Normandy in the mid-eleventh century, he studied under Anselm of Bec, whose works were disseminated only in separated script. Guibert epitomized the study and scribal habits of the eleventh century. His own script and that of his secretaries, preserved in Paris, Bibliothèque Nationale lat. 2500, 2502 and 2900, from the library of the abbey of Nogent-sous-Coucy, near Soissons, were canonically separated, with terminal forms including the capital *S*, used to accentuate the image of the word.[2] The clear distinction of words was also enhanced by monolexic abbreviations in which short words, especially function or linking words, were represented by a single unambiguous sign, of which the ampersand standing for the conjunction *et* and the Tironian sign used for the verb *est* are examples. Both Guibert and his secretaries employed the *trait d'union*.

The new medium of canonically separated script was also that of Hugh of Saint Victor (d.1141). The oldest manuscripts of Hugh's works from the Augustinian abbey of Saint Victor in Paris were separated with the terminal signs for *us*, *tur*, *m* and *orum*, and the terminal round *s* all enhancing Bouma shape, the term of modern psychologists for word shape. *Traits d'union* were provided by the scribe. Paris, Bibliothèque nationale lat. 15009, the earliest copy of his *De tribus maximis circumstantiis gestorum*, included among monolexic abbreviations the Tironian sign for the conjunction *et*, and among terminal forms the crossed capital *S* for *orum*, the capital *NS* ligature and the capital *R*. Bonn, Universitätsbibliothek S 292/1, containing the *De sacramentis Christianae fidei*, was written in 1155 – that is, within fourteen years of Hugh's death, for the Cistercian abbey of Altenburg.[3] Like most Cistercian manuscripts, this codex was canonically separated with inter-word space twice the unity of space; that is, the quantity of space contained between the minim strokes of the letter *n*. The use of initial capitals to indicate proper nouns was common to these and other early codices of Hugh's works.

The pages of Hugh's early manuscripts took full advantage of coloured initials to give to each opening a quasi-distinct image to aid memorization.[4] In his grammatical and historical works, he used page format to simplify the presentation of information. In Hugh's hands, graphic display of information with the aid of coloured initials and architectural motifs perfected by eleventh-century scribes at abbeys like Fécamp and Saint-Germain-des-Prés became a conscious pedagogical tool. In the *De tribus maximis circumstantiis gestorum*, he counselled schoolboys to fix their gaze on the book and to remember its colour patterns and letter forms as cues to the page position of specific information within the text.[5] For Hugh, the visual interaction between reader and book was an integral part of study, and in the *Didascalicon*, he explicitly set forth three modes of reading: reading to another, listening to another read and reading to oneself by gazing (*inspicere*) – that is, silent private reading.[6]

Hugh's application of the verb *inspicere* with its visual connotations to the activity of reading harks back to Anselm's use of the term and earlier insular and subsequent eleventh-century continental use of *videre* as a synonym for reading. According to Hugh, the reader first mastered the grammatical construction (facilitated by the grouping of related words upon the page), then the literal sense, and finally proceeded to the more profound meaning in a procedure free of the ancient emphasis on oral articulation with correct accentuation.[7] It was precisely these largely visual processes that the eleventh-century restructuring of written language had facilitated. Hugh described the signs, or *notae*, of the ancient grammarians, including punctuation, as marks normally present in books. They were to be inserted by the scribe to aid the reader in comprehending the text. In ancient times, it had been the reader rather than the scribe who had added signs to aid parsing. Hugh's assumption that it was the scribe's responsibility to prepare the text for the reader exemplified the transformed mentality that the previous century had wrought. In his *De grammatica*, Hugh included an extensive vocabulary for critical notes, and he was the first medieval grammarian to enumerate tie notes among the signs that scribes were to provide for the reader.[8] These notes, which presupposed the ocular gestures of silent consultation, had become increasingly abundant from the late tenth century onward.

Hugh's contemporary, Hugh of Fouilloi, whose works in subsequent centuries would often erroneously be ascribed to Hugh of Saint Victor, composed the *Liber rotae verae religionis*, of which the schematic illustrations represented an advanced form of the infusion of script into image that had accompanied the word separation in so many eleventh-century codices from the British Isles and northern France.[9] For the reader of *Liber rotae verae religionis* and Hugh of Fouilloi's other works, the *Liber avium* and the *De pastoribus et ovibus*, the roles of viewer of image and reader of text fully merged. The text of the *Liber rotae verae religionis* referred to the miniature containing within it canonically separated text. In Brussels, BR II, 1076, a codex of the late twelfth century, the legends incorporated in the miniatures contained numerous terminal forms, including the terminal capital *S*, the sign that had become the hallmark of eleventh-century, proto-scholastic writing. In these drawings, the 'good abbot' was shown motionless in study, staring at an open book. This iconography of silent reading had its antecedents in eleventh-century book illuminations copied at the abbeys of Fécamp and Luxeuil.

The school of Chartres provided an important bridge, transmitting the proto-scholastic graphic innovations of the eleventh century to the twelfth centuries. Writing at Chartres had been separated since the time of Fulbert, who had studied with Gerbert. Ivo of Chartres' (d.1116) *Decretum* and the *Panamia* were diffused north of the Alps exclusively in separated script, as was the *Decretum* of Gratian, which supplanted them. Abelard and John of Salisbury, both of whom studied at Chartres, composed and disseminated their works only in word-separated codices. John of Salisbury, like Hugh of Saint Victor, distinguished in his vocabulary between the reading aloud of a master to a student (*praelectio*) and private, silent, visual reading (*lectio*).[10] Like the late eleventh-century masters of the *ars lectoria*, John viewed grammar as including the art of correct writing, and he regarded punctuation as paratextual signs for communicating between author and reader analogous to the neumes used for the notation of music.[11] Also in keeping with the tradition of monastic emendation as it had evolved in the previous century, John showed a keen awareness of the importance of correct word separation for maintaining the acute parafoveal vision necessary for the private scrutiny of manuscript texts.[12] Elsewhere in France, the pattern was the same. Gilbert of Poitiers affixed his emblematic critical notes, inspired by eleventh-century models, to manuscripts such as Troyes, BM 988, which were written in canonically separated script.

As in Italy, the Cistercian order in the north became an important conduit for spreading canonical separation, the most advanced form of the new text format. The manuscripts produced at the abbey of Notre-Dame of Signy, founded in 1135, are typical of the Cistercian page.[13] Charleville, BM 187, a collection of *Logica vetus* texts, including Boethius's monographs, was written in canonically separated script with inter-word space equivalent to twice the unity of space on lines ruled in pencil rather than Carolingian dry point better to guide the reader's eye. Terminal forms were the usual signs for *us*, *tur* and *bus*, the elevated round *s* and the capital *S*. Monolexic abbreviations included the insular sign for *est*, the Tironian sign for the conjunction *et* and numerous superscript forms. *Traits d'union* were present, and the scribe employed acute accents to denote monosyllables and the double *ii*. Charleville, BM 196c, Jerome's *Commentarii in Prophetas minores*, was written in canonically separated script with inter-word space equivalent to twice the unity of space and with the terminal elevated *s* and suspended ligatures.[14] A contemporary emendator added alphabetical construction notes, *traits d'union* and the successor note to the *diastole*. Red and green alternating initials generated a quasi-unique image to each leaf. The scribe who wrote Augustine's *opuscula*, Charleville, BM 202, wrote in a similar canonically separated script. Notre-Dame of

Signy scribes who worked for William of Saint Thierry in Charleville, BM 49 and 114, used canonically separated script.[15] The abbey also provides examples of twelfth-century foliation.

The Cistercian abbey of Beaupré, near Beauvais, established in 1135, produced in the twelfth and early thirteenth centuries the first large quantity of canonically separated manuscripts replete with a panoply of *prosodiae*, or diacritical marks, enhancing the visual images of words. Many of these codices were contemporaneously foliated. Paris, BN lat. 1777, John Chrysostom's *Homiliae in Matthaeum*, was written in the second half of the twelfth century, with inter-word space varying from 1.66 to twice the unity of space. The manuscript was contemporaneously foliated. Paris, BN lat. 2243 (I–II), Gregory the Great's *Homiliae in Ezechielem*, was written in canonically separated script with frequent accenting of the double *ii* and the tonic syllable. This foliated codex contained a table providing reference to its foliation. At least twenty-two other early Beaupré manuscripts bear contemporary foliation, making this scriptorium one of the first in the Latin West to add foliation systematically to its books.[16]

The earliest manuscripts of Cistercian authors were always separated. While no autograph or authorial manuscripts of Bernard of Clairvaux (d.1153) are known, Geoffroy of Auxerre's (d. after 1188) autograph corrections to his *Vita prima sancti Bernardi*, Paris, BN lat. 7561, were written in script separated by twice the unity of space and employing the *trait d'union*.[17] The text that Geoffroy corrected had been written by a secretary who had denoted proper names with capitals and employed the elevated round *s* as a terminal form and the Tironian symbol for the conjunction *et*. The earliest twelfth-century manuscripts of Bernard of Clairvaux's *opera* were all separated. In Munich, Stb Clm. 7950, from the Cistercian abbey of Kaisheim, Bernard was represented in a miniature that exemplifies the complete fusion of image with *nomina personae*, inscriptions and *banderolles*.[18] Bernard's intimate associate, William of Saint Thierry, retired to the abbey of Notre-Dame of Signy, and left a copy there with autograph revisions of his *Epistola ad fratres Montis Dei*, Charleville, BM 114, fos 1–45 and 102–213.[19] His writing was canonically separated, and incorporated the standard eleventh-century terminal forms. Monolexic abbreviations included the Tironian sign for *et* and superscript forms, and he made regular use of *traits d'union*. Like Geoffroy of Auxerre, William employed emblematic punctuation as an intrinsic part of his textual composition. Chicago, Newberry Library, 21.1, a copy of the *Anticlaudianus* of Alain of Lisle (d.1201), was written not long after his death in canonically separated script, with *prosodiae* including the *traits d'union* and prominent inter-word ligatures. Emblematic punctuation was placed at the end of each line in columns reserved for this purpose, a format presupposing an extended field of vision that only separated writing afforded.

The tendency for Cistercian abbeys' textual traditions to be advanced in word separation and the diagrammatic intermixture of text and image was paralleled in the Cistercian innovative attitude towards punctuation. Cistercian scribes even employed marks to indicate a presumed negative or positive response to questions, in order to complement graphically the interrogative particles of the ancients.[20] The diple, and eventually underlining, were used in Cistercian manuscripts as consistent inter-textual marks of quotation.

The new silent reading habits already evinced by Guibert of Nogent, Hugh of Saint Victor and John of Salisbury were explicitly noted by the Cistercian Richalm, prior of Schöntal (1216–19). In his *Liber revelationum de insidiis et versutiis daemonum adversus homines*, Richalm described the contrast between silent and oral reading much as we know it when he recounted how demons disrupted his silent *lectio* by forcing him to read aloud, and thereby deprived him of inward understanding and spirituality.[21] Richalm's preference for silent reading was totally consonant with Cistercian spiritual psychology as articulated by Bernard of Clairvaux, Isaac of Stella, William of Saint Thierry and Aelred of Rievaulx (d.1167).[22] These Cistercian monks regarded the heart as the seat of the mind, and considered reading to be a principal tool for influencing the *affectus cordis*. Individual reading was inextricably linked to, and indeed a prerequisite for, meditation. Aelred maintained that the presence of books was essential to the pursuit of the *via meditativa*. This ideal, first enunciated in the eleventh century by John of Fécamp and Anselm of Canterbury, was pervasive in the Cistercian Order. William of Saint Thierry, in his *Epistola ad fratres Montis Dei*, considered *lectio* closely bound to *meditatio*.[23] The anonymous and probably Cistercian author of the *De interiori domo* described meditation through the metaphor of internal reading.[24] An indication of the exceptionally advanced character of the visual reading habits of the Cistercians was their introduction, in the first half of the thirteenth century, of books of *distinctiones* supplemented by sophisticated indices based on foliation and alphabetically designated locations on the page.[25]

The new techniques of reference consultation and silent reading were also well developed by certain twelfth-century Benedictines. Bernard Itier, monk of Saint Martial who died in 1225, used foliation in Paris, BN lat. 1338, as a means of organizing the preliminary notes for his *Chronicon*, placing, for example, the notes for the year 1112 on folio 112.[26] Peter of Celles, author of the *De disciplina claustrali*, who considered reading in silence as a prerequisite for meditation, used the term *videre*, like insular authors of earlier centuries, as a synonym for reading.[27] Peter referred to the private reading in the cloister that gave rise to meditation as being chained to silence. The *Liber de disciplina claustrali* survives only in canonically separated script.[28] A copy of Peter's *Sermones*, transcribed at Clairvaux within a generation of his death, Troyes, BM 253, was canonically separated with monolexic abbreviations, including the Tironian sign for *et*, suprascript forms and emblematic punctuation.[29] Oderic Vital, the English-born monk of Saint Evroul whose *Historia ecclesiastica* ranks among the principal Norman historical compilations of the first half of the twelfth century, was a paradigm of the scribal productivity which he described in his chronicle.[30] His own writing was separated by more than twice the unity of space, and he used capital letters both to denote proper names and as terminal forms.

Authorship

The intimacy which regular word separation created between the reader and his book also occurred between the author and his manuscript. Quintilian, who lived when script was separated by interpuncts, had recommended that authors write their own works.[31] However, in late antiquity, authors had generally dictated their compositions, in large measure because of the difficulty of manipulating the *scriptura continua* that from the end of the second century AD was the normal form of writing. The adoption of separated writing sparked an interest in auto-graph composition. With the renewed desire of authors to write their own works, certain authors such as Othlon of Saint Emmeran in the eleventh century and Guibert of Nogent in the twelfth century expressed intimate sentiments hitherto not set down on parchment because of the absence of privacy when composition depended upon dictation to a secretary. Guibert's mastery of the medium of separated script penetrated his own consciousness as an author. In his *De vita sua sive Monodiarum libri tres*, he described a sense of privacy that would become characteristic of late medieval literate culture. Guibert secretly composed in written form erotic poems modelled on those of antiquity, which he then hid from his confrères.[32] He also secretly composed a commentary on Genesis which he concealed from his master Anselm of Bec. Like Anselm, he consciously divided his works into chapters to facilitate their private consultation.[33] In his final years, blindness forced Guibert to cease writing his own compositions and to dictate to a sec-retary. In his *Tropologiae in Osse, Amos ac Lamentationes Jeremiae*, he complained bitterly that his loss of vision obliged him to compose 'sola memoria, sola voce, sine manu, sine oculis'. He resented the interfering presence of a secretary, and regretted that he could no longer look at his own written text to revise its style and emend his choice of words.[34] The ocular gestures of silent reading and composition, sorely missed by the sightless Guibert, clearly presupposed the medium of word separation that, in the region of Soissons, was less than a century old at the time of Guibert's death in 1124.

Guibert, like other twelfth-century authors, had, before his blindness, emended his compositions with interlinear additions, a mode of textual amplification that flourished in close association with word separation. The new authorial manuscripts, identifiable by their erasures, corrections and interlinear additions, formed a new genre of literary evidence, documenting a dimension to intellectual life that did not exist before the late tenth century.[35] Guibert of Nogent, like his eleventh-century predecessor Othlon of Saint Emmeran, felt secure enough to set down in this medium intimate details of his dreams. Guibert was particularly fascinated by the relationship between outer written expression and interior feeling, repenting of his erotic poetry by accepting it as a written record of feelings he no longer possessed.[36] Eschewing secretaries, he wrote his works in private to keep them secret. Odon of Orléans, who also wrote erotic verse, as abbot restored the abbey of Saint-Martin of Tournay (1105–13), and established a new scriptorium that produced canonically separated books.[37]

The composition of twelfth-century *erotica* exploited a new intimacy between author, writer and reader which had already been implicit in the devotional works of John of Fécamp and Anselm, Guibert's childhood master. In the twelfth century, the equation of author-writer became increasingly evident both in practice and in the Latinity of lettered men. The Cistercian statutes of 1144 implicitly looked upon composition as a private written act subject to juristic control.[38] Even Bernard of Clairvaux, who dictated a large portion of his corpus, wrote some drafts in his own hand.[39]

The desire of authors to compose in written form, rather than by oral dictation, spurred on by the new aids to facilitate reading, was frustrated by the difficulty of writing in formal book scripts that necessitated a slow, measured pace. As a consequence, most authorial manuscripts of the eleventh and twelfth centuries were books like those of Berengar of Tours, Geoffroy of Auxerre and William of Saint Thierry, in which the author as scribe and corrector was only one participant in preparing a codex written by several hands; the author's assistants worked from an authorial text written on wax tablets or scraps of parchment. Manuscripts written entirely or predominantly by the author, like Cambridge, Corpus Christi College 371, containing

Eadmer's autograph of the *Vita Anselmi* and other of his compositions, were typically set down over extended periods of time.[40] William of Saint Thierry, who rapidly produced large quantities of prose, was obliged to use secretaries as adjuncts to the process of composition. However, the desire of the writer to have a personal, direct control over his work, explicit in the case of Guibert of Nogent, was implicitly expressed in the erasures and marginal and interlinear additions of word-separated authorial manuscripts.

The first miniatures showing scribes as authors, as opposed to scribes taking dictation, date from the eleventh century.[41] The poet Notker Balbulus was depicted in three eleventh-century codices as a writer cogitating in the isolation of his cell.[42] The earliest images of Bernard of Clairvaux as author, dating from the thirteenth century, show him as an author-scribe.[43] Such representations were to become explicit in the thirteenth century, when Alexander of Buxtehude was depicted writing under the legend 'hic scribat et dictat' in the presence of the *Agnus Dei* with a *banderolle* stating, 'Rorant e celo tibi que scribenda revelo'.[44] In the twelfth century the verb *dictare* had lost its obligatory oral connotation, and was used for written composition and visual copying.[45]

These changes did not mean, however, that the iconographic conventions that had originated in late antiquity and the early Middle Ages disappeared. Authors of the eleventh and twelfth centuries were shown frequently as dictators or as scribes writing from dictation, and the evangelists were normally depicted in this manner.[46] The apostle Paul was regularly shown as the dictator of his epistles or as a scribe taking dictation.[47] In Paris, BN lat. 11624, fol. 94^v, an eleventh-century codex originating from Saint Bénigne of Dijon, Ambrose was shown dictating over the shoulder of a scribe. A similar scene appears in an eleventh-century manuscript from Tours, Tours BM 291, fol. 132. In a twelfth-century codex, Admont, Stiftbibliothek 34, written in about 1175 in separated script, Abbot Irimbert was depicted dictating his *Expositio in libros Josue, Judicum et Ruth* to a scribe writing on wax tablets, and Saint Jerome in a miniature in the same codex was also shown dictating to a scribe with stylus and tablets.[48]

Book Production

Just as word separation stimulated the change from oral to written modes of composition, so it encouraged the continued transition from oral to visual modes of book production that had transpired in the previous century.[49] The process of visual copying was in evidence in the scriptorium of Guibert of Nogent. The twelfth-century scribe who visually copied Jerome's *Commentarii in Habacuc* in Canterbury, Cathedral X.1.lla, using a Canterbury copy dating from the time of Lanfranc (now Cambridge, Trinity College B.3.5 (84)), carefully reproduced the punctuation, *prosodiae* and many terminal forms of his exemplar.[50] When in the early twelfth century, Hermanus, in his *Liber de restauratione sancti Martini Tornacensis*, described the copying of manuscripts in the scriptorium set up by Odon of Orléans, he specifically noted that the scribes worked *in silentio* on special carefully constructed tables.[51] Some eleventh- and twelfth-century miniatures show scribes copying a codex placed upon their knees from an exemplar positioned on a table. In 1173, Gregory of Narek was depicted in this position, as was Gregory of Nazianzus.[52] Other miniatures show scribes using a book stand for the exemplar and a table for the book. Specialized furniture for copying designed to minimize the degree of ocular displacement between the exemplar and the copy was described by John of Garland, and such furniture was abundantly depicted in miniatures of the late Middle Ages, especially in vernacular texts intended for the laity.

The new furnishings of the scriptorium of which crude antecedents were first in evidence in the thirteenth century, allowed the scribe to replicate a page as a set of visual images in a routine mechanical manner and thus to dispense with oralization as an essential aid to short-term memory.[53] Miniatures and woodcuts depicting late medieval scriptoria showed scribes with sealed lips, seated at special tables equipped with book stands, employing a variety of new mechanically controlled line-markers to guide their eyes in following the text of the exemplar.[54] In the thirteenth century, the exemplars of university stationers, codices used exclusively for copying, provided a slightly larger ratio of inter-word space, no doubt as a special aid to the scribes who were expected to copy mechanically from them.[55] At the end of the Middle Ages, Petrach used the term *pictor* (painter) for a scribe who copied texts without understanding them.[56] The iconography of fifteenth-century books of hours assimilated the iconography of scribes and painters, particularly in scenes depicting the apostle Luke, the patron saint of painters, writing his Gospel.[57] In place of dictation, many depictions of the four evangelists showed them copying from an exemplar held by angels. The cognitive skills of the late medieval copyist increasingly resembled those of a typist, whose mechanical reading process differs from that of the normal reader.[58] The painter-scribe, like a typist, read with an invariable eye–hand span while mindlessly replicating the black-on-white images of his exemplar. Imposition, perfected in the fifteenth century, was predicated on this kind of mechanical visual copying. The intricate manipulations of the sheet that this process required would have been incompatible with dictation.[59]

Canonical Word Separation and Changes in Scholastic Grammatical Theory

Languages without traditions of literacy do not have a word for 'word'.[60] Scholastic grammarians, for whom canonical separation was normal, articulated with great precision the distinction implicit in the scribal practice of rigorously differentiating monosyllabic prepositions and bound syllables on the basis of function, regardless of pronunciation.[61] These grammarians also refined the definitions of different kinds of words. The Dominican Johannes de Balbis, in his *Catholicon* completed in 1286, enumerated adjective and noun as virtually independent parts of speech.[62] While some of the changes in medieval Latin, such as the distinguishing of prepositions and other short words by the insertion of inter-word space or the addition of signs of interrogation to complement interrogative particles, were purely graphic, and therefore imperceptible when a text was pronounced aloud, other changes that transformed the appearance of the continental book between the late tenth and the early thirteenth century were equally in evidence whether a text was viewed or recited. Medieval Latin of the twelfth and thirteenth centuries, quite apart from its text format, was inherently less ambiguous. The scribal innovation of placing a space after unaccented function words was made all the more prominent by the greatly augmented use of these words at the expense of parataxis. Other linguistic innovations, like the placing of the adjective before the noun and the adverb before the verb, as well as the use of subject–verb–object word order, had been anticipated by insular sequential construction notes. Scholastic grammarians postulated the subject–verb–object order of the vernacular as the natural one for Latin.[63] Guido Favo, in his *Summa dictaminis*, regarded it as the natural arrangement, appropriate for the clear exposition of an idea expressed in the artificial word order of ancient authors.[64] In the context of Latinity governed by conventions of word order, the symbols formerly used as construction notes became scribal note of revision.[65]

The tendency of ancient authors to compose periodic sentences in which clauses were intertwined within each other and verbs and adjectives were distant from the nouns they governed waned as Latin became an analytical language consciously moulded to serve as an unambiguous vehicle for expressing logical distinctions, In the mid-thirteenth century, Roger Bacon, who set down principles for syntactic punctuation, recognized word order and word proximity as important semiotic aspects of language.[66] In 1348, Jean Bolant used this simplified word order and word grouping to explicate the intricate constructions of Ovid's

Metamorphoses.[67] The late Middle Ages began to produce an increasingly larger proportion of prose texts formed by the accretion of syntactic distinctions. Increased use of graphic punctuation signs naturally accompanied Latin prose that was incorporated in a structure of compact discrete distinctions of words with close grammatical relations.

The combination of the new analytic character of scholastic Latin and the new text format of separated script accompanied by emblematic punctuation facilitated the extraction of meaning from text, and reduced the reliance upon aural memory as a component of reading. In place of the oral reading of antiquity, the late Middle Ages relied on a visual process dependent on texts which, in their syntax and graphic expression, were simple and analytic. Word separation, word order, emblematic punctuation, discrete clauses, the ordering of both words and clauses within complex sentences, and the use of conjunctions and adverbial conjunctions for the construction of compound and complex sentences all facilitated sequential understanding of meaning successively within the boundaries of clause and sentence. Whereas the ancient reader relied on aural memory to retain an ambiguous series of sounds as a preliminary stage in extracting meaning, the scholastic reader swiftly converted signs to words and groups of words to meaning, after which both specific words and their order might quickly be forgotten. Memory was employed primarily to retain a general sense of the clause, the sentence and the paragraph.[68] Albertus Magnus, Thomas Aquinas, Roger Bacon, Duns Scotus and William of Ockham, despite their divergent national origins, all wrote a similar simple and direct scholastic Latin, remarkable for a clarity and precision of expression achieved at the sacrifice of classical rhythm, meter and mellifluous sonority.

Written Culture in the Thirteenth, Fourteenth and Fifteenth Centuries

The effects of this dual transformation of the written Latin language on the culture of the central and late Middle Ages was profound. Thirteenth-century scholars increasingly endeavoured to synthesize and impose systematic order on the new ideas that had emerged in the twelfth century. In this task, authors such as Duns Scotus and William of Ockham found they could no longer formulate and organize their complex thoughts within the limited space of wax tablets. The task of composing works of synthesis of great length ultimately led to the development of the author's autograph manuscript, written in fully separated Gothic cursive script. Composition in the medium of Gothic cursive on quires and sheets of parchment meant that authors could revise and rearrange their texts while composing them. This capacity aided thirteenth-century scholastic writers in preparing texts rich in cross-references, which presupposed that the reader, like the author, could flip from folio to folio in order to relate arguments to their logical antecedents and to compare comments on related but disparate passages of Scripture. The medium of the tablet inhibited the development of a flowing, looped cursive script much as it had in ancient Rome. Thirteenth-century authors, writing in the margins of parchment codices to compose marginal notes and commentaries, modified the letter forms of *glossularis*, and created a separated script that was fast and easy to write on either parchment or paper. At first, it was idiosyncratic and often difficult even for contemporaries to read, but by the year 1400, it had become fluid, standardized and often highly legible.[69]

Before the fourteenth century, writing on parchment had been an arduous task. The writing hand was poised so that only the point of the pen touched the support. In early illuminations, scribes were drawn writing with a pen in one hand and a knife in the other. In addition to aiding erasure and cutting the pen, the knife served to balance the raised hand holding the pen and anchored the parchment support used for formal books; for writing the bold strokes of Gothic textual script required pressure that changed in direction with the frequent liftings of the pen.[70] Writing in informal Gothic cursive on casually assembled quires and sheets made the physical act of writing less laborious and more compatible with intellectual activity. In fourteenth-century miniatures, authors composing in the new cursive script were depicted in more relaxed positions. The support, whether parchment or paper, easier to write on than membrane, was usually held in place by the hand in the modern fashion.[71] The author, depicted in miniatures, alone in his study or on occasion in an idyllic pastoral setting, using Gothic cursive, was at once freed from the labour of writing and the reliance on scribes. The new ease in writing enhanced the author's sense of intimacy and privacy in his work. In solitude, he was personally able to manipulate drafts on separate quires and sheets. He could see his manuscript as a whole, and by means of cross-references develop internal relationships and eliminate redundancies common to the dictated literature of the twelfth century. He could also at his leisure easily add supplements and revisions to his text at any point before forwarding it to a scriptorium for publication. Initially, composition in written form had been used for Latin texts, but by the mid-fourteenth century, vernacular forms of cursive scripts enabled authors of vernacular texts also to write their works.

The new and more intimate way in which authors silently composed their texts, in turn, affected their expectation of the way people would read them. In antiquity and the early Middle Ages, when texts were composed orally, authors expected them to be read aloud. In the fourteenth century, when texts were composed in silent isolation in cursive script, authors expected them to be read silently. Nicolas of Lyra, the great Franciscan biblical commentator of the fourteenth century, addressed himself to the reader, not to the listener.[72] Jean Gerson advised that the reader of Scripture place himself in the affective state of the writer.[73] Fourteenth-century scholastic texts composed in cursive script were marked by a new visual vocabulary indicating that both the author and the reader were expected to have the codex before them.

While private silent reading was pervasive in the fourteenth and fifteenth centuries, public lectures continued to play an important role in medieval university life. However, because of the complexity of the subject matter, visual reading was essential for its comprehension. While the professor read aloud from his autograph commentary, the students followed the text silently from their own books. This was a change from the *lectio divina* of late antiquity and the early Middle Ages, where one monk had read aloud to others, who listened without the aid of a written text. In 1259, the Dominican house of the University of Paris required that students, if possible, bring to class a copy of the text expounded upon in the public lectures. Humbert of Romans (*c.*1194–1277) held that collective prayer could be enriched by individuals gazing on the text of a written prayer as it was collectively pronounced.[74] Regulations requiring students to bring books to class also existed in Paris at the College of Harcourt and at the universities of Vienna and Ingolstadt.[75] In 1309, Pierre Dubois, the most celebrated of the legists in the service of Philip the Fair, observed that students who did not have a copy of the text before them could profit little from university lectures.[76] Students too poor to purchase their own copies could borrow them from libraries like that of the cathedral of Notre-Dame in Paris, which received bequests especially for this purpose.[77] The statutes of the Sorbonne provided for lending books against security deposits.[78] In the final years of the fifteenth century, the printing press provided the copies needed for classroom use.[79]

Additional changes in the format of thirteenth- and fourteenth-century manuscripts occurred with the spread of silent reading in private and in the classroom. Oral reading had usually consisted of a continuous reading of a text or a substantial section of it from beginning to end. Many Caroline codices, like ancient scrolls, had not been divided into sections shorter than the chapter.[80] From the thirteenth to the fifteenth century, subdivisions were introduced into classical and early medieval texts.[81] In some cases, works which had already been subdivided into chapters in late antiquity were further, and more rationally, subdivided by university scholars.[82] This new mode of presenting old texts became an integral aspect of the newly composed texts which were conceived in terms of chapters and *distinctiones*. Using the points of reference established by the new divisions, tables of chapter headings, alphabetical tables by subject and running heads became standard features of the scholastic codex.[83] Illuminated capitals were employed in the fourteenth century to help clarify the new sequential argumentation in the fashion *ad primum, ad secundum* and so on. A new form of punctuation, the coloured paragraph mark, came into common use from the early thirteenth century onward to isolate units of intellectual content.[84] The system of sequential marginal notes using letters of the alphabet to denote location, which had first appeared in the books of Benedictine abbeys of northern France in the late tenth century, was adapted for juristic texts.[85] At the end of the fourteenth century, it was also employed to gloss literary texts. In the fifteenth century, we find alphabetical tie notes used for attaching the glosses of Nicholas of Lyra in incunable editions.[86] The intricate schematic diagrams accompanying scholastic texts, the origins of which were the diagrams accompanying proto-scholastic works when they had first been diffused in separated script at Reims and Fleury, were understandable only to the single reader who held the codex in his own hands.[87] These diagrams continued to be an important accoutrement of the page in the new humanist translations of Aristotle, and even after the invention of printing, scribes added them to incunables as part of the printed codex's final stage of confection.[88] The complex structure of the written page of a fourteenth-century scholastic text presupposed a reader who read only with his eyes, going swiftly from objection to response, from table of contents to the text, from diagram to text, and from the text to the gloss and its corrections.[89]

Scribes of the late Middle Ages continued the practice of copying texts visually, and the oft reported thesis that scholastic books were written by students transcribing professorial dictation during professional lectures is unsubstantiated by contemporary descriptions of the medieval classroom. Iconographic evidence supports the conclusion of visual copying. A fifteenth-century miniature suggests that the *Flores Augustini de civitate Dei* of François of Mayronnes was analogous to the notes made by a secretary during a lecture.[90] While certain early modern engravings may appear to show classroom dictation of textbooks, fourteenth- and fifteenth-century miniature illuminations depict no classroom scenes of students taking down verbatim transcriptions of professorial lectures. Indeed, medieval writing did not possess a shorthand system that could have permitted precise copies to be made.[91] Instead, the illuminations typically show the professor lecturing from his text to students who, with the occasional exception of the recording scribe, either had no pens or books or, more usually, were holding already written books.[92]

In medieval education, dictation was primarily a pedagogical device for instructing the young in writing and orthography, and it was in this form that it was represented in medieval miniatures. When dictation was used for university book production, the books were produced separately from, and prior to, the professional lecture on the text. Thus, at the new university of Louvain (established in 1425), when the stock of school-books was still inadequate and libraries to lend them were wanting, professors arranged special dictation sessions so that students could come to class with the required books.[93] At Paris in 1355, the university recognized that the artificially slow pace of lecturing in order to facilitate extensive class notes of copies interfered with the student's need to focus his attention on the text in order to comprehend the subtleties of the master's lecture.[94] Other, more efficient means for the dissemination of written texts existed outside the classroom. In the thirteenth and fourteenth centuries, the professional scribes of the *pecia* system at the University of Paris provided highly legible standardized copies of the basic texts of the university curriculum.[95] In the fifteenth century, scribes at the University of Angers were capable of producing copies of professorial lectures in a month's time at relatively low cost. These manuscripts may even have been circulated before the lectures, so that the student could silently read along with the professor to grasp more easily the subtle arguments.[96]

If access to books was important for comprehending the complexities of public lectures, it was even more necessary for private study, which increasingly was a part of university life. Illuminations of the fourteenth and fifteenth centuries in vernacular books intended for laymen showed motionless scholars reading in chained libraries, both in groups and in isolation, with their lips sealed, an unmistakable iconographic statement of silence.[97] Inexpensive Latin and vernacular compendia of large treatises became popular, to serve the growing student need for private study.[98] Pierre Dubois recommended their production as fundamental to his scheme of educational reform.[99] Nicolas of Lyra, in the prologue to his *Tractatus de differentia,* declared that he had written this epitome of his lengthy *Postillae* so that poor students could afford to purchase copies for their own study.[100]

Changes in reading also effected changes in libraries. The cloister libraries of the twelfth century had been suited to a culture where oral and silent reading had cohabited.[101] The spacious cloister and carrels,

divided by stone walls, had allowed monks to read aloud or in a
muffled voice to themselves or to compose by quietly dictating to a secretary without disturbing the contemplation of silent reading of their
confrères. Because monastic authors had retained large amounts of
Sacred Scripture by rote oral memorization, formal collections of reference books were not always essential. At the end of the thirteenth
century, library architecture and furnishings began to change dramatically. In thirteenth- and fourteenth-century Oxford and Cambridge colleges and at the Sorbonne and other Paris colleges, libraries were
installed in central halls, and were furnished with desks, lecterns and
benches where readers sat next to one another.[102] Important reference
books were chained to lecterns so that they could always be consulted
in the library. The first such reference collection was established at
Merton College, Oxford, in 1289.[103] A similar one was created at the
Sorbonne in 1290.[104] In the mid-fifteenth century, the arts faculty of the
University of Louvain created a wide-ranging scholastic reference
library.[105] Chained reference books typically included alphabetical
dictionaries and concordances, the *Summa*s of Thomas Aquinas, the
biblical commentaries of Hugh of Saint Cher and Nicolas of Lyra, and
other lengthy works frequently cited by scholars. The statutes governing
chained libraries emphasized that chained books were provided for the
common good, so that all could consult them.[106] The library was henceforth clearly regarded as a place where professors and students could go
to read, write and study.[107] It was just such a library that Charles V
installed in the Louvre and stocked with specially commissioned French
translations of classical and scholastic authors.

It was in the chained libraries of the late thirteenth century that the
reader's need for silence was first made explicit. In the late antique
library and early medieval monastery, where readers had read aloud,
each reader's own voice had acted as a physiological screen blocking
out the sounds of the adjacent readers.[108] When readers began to read
visually, noise became a source of potential distraction. Even quiet oral
reading at the crowded desks of the chained reference collection in the
medieval library would have made study difficult. Humbert of Romans,
in the *De instructione officialium*, demanded that each Dominican
house establish a common reading room in a silent location within the
friary.[109] At Oxford, the regulations of 1412 recognized the library as a
place of quiet.[110] The statutes of the library of the University of Angers
of 1431 forbade conversation and even murmuring.[111] The statutes of
the Sorbonne library, written down in the late fifteenth century, but
reflecting practices established at an earlier date, proclaimed the chained
library of the college to be an august, sacred place where silence
should prevail.[112] A similar rule existed in the library of the popes,

re-established in Rome after the great Schism.[113] Reference tools intended for rapid visual perusal within the library included aids to the use of the library itself, such as catalogues with alphabetical author indexes and special union catalogues representing the holdings of libraries in a city or region.[114] The supervised emendation of previously written manuscripts by the addition of *prosodiae*, punctuation and textual variants had been since the eleventh century a regular practice of scribes and rubricators of monastic communities.[115] However, visual reading encouraged private readers to use books as instruments of study by noting passages in the margin with brief phrases, symbols and doodles enhancing subsequent visual recall. In the highly individualistic world of the late medieval university, rules were necessary to limit these activities, in order to ensure the preservation of collections intended for common use.[116]

The transition to silent reading and composition, by providing a new dimension of privacy, had even more profound ramifications for both the lay and the scholastic culture of the Middle Ages. Psychologically, silent reading emboldened the reader, because it placed the source of his curiosity completely under personal control. In the still largely oral world of the ninth century, if one's intellectual speculations were heretical, they were subject to peer correction and control at every moment, from their formulation and publication to their reception by the reader. Dictation and public *lectio*, in effect, buttressed theological and philosophical orthodoxy. In the eleventh century, heresy began to be linked to solitary intellectual curiosity and speculation. Berengar of Tours, who belonged to the second generation to write in separated script, lapsed into heterodoxy by applying the logical techniques of Aristotle and Boethius to the Eucharist.[117] Reading with the eyes alone and written composition removed the individual's thoughts from the sanctions of the group, and fostered the milieu in which the new university and lay heresies of the thirteenth and fourteenth centuries developed. These heresies were spread by the privately read *tractatus* as vehicle of intellectual expression.[118] Alone in his study, the author, whether a well-known professor or an obscure student, could compose or read heterodox ideas without being overheard. In the classroom, the student, reading silently to himself, could listen to the orthodox opinions of his professor and visually compare them with the views of those who rejected established ecclesiastical authority.[119] Even during the performance of public liturgy, a forbidden text could be read. Private visual reading and composition thus encouraged individual critical thinking, and contributed ultimately to the development of scepticism and intellectual heresy. In England, the mere possession of Lollard writings was legal grounds for formal charges of heresy.[120]

University professors of the late Middle Ages were aware that they were addressing visual readers other than those who attended their lectures, and the anxiety created by the silent diffusion of ideas outside the lecture hall was reflected in contemporary university regulations. In the thirteenth century, university statutes forbade attendance at the public readings of forbidden books.[121] In the fourteenth century, the forbidden writings themselves were ferreted out and destroyed, as in 1323, when the general chapter of the Dominican Order decreed that all privately held writings on the prohibited art of alchemy be burned.[122] In 1346, the University of Paris declared that the writings of Nicolas of Autrecourt were to be incinerated.[123] However, some copies of heretical works were necessary, if only for the theologians who wrote to refute them. The medieval rules of the library of the Sorbonne presupposed that heretical writings in the library should be used only by professors of theology for composing refutations of error.[124] But how were individual scholars to be supervised when they read silently? In 1473, Louis XI offered a response when he ordered not only that nominalist doctrines not to be taught, but that all nominalist books in the libraries of the University of Paris be chained shut.[125] The king realized that to forbid the teaching of nominalist doctrines was meaningless if nominalist writings could be easily read in numerous manuscripts in the libraries of the university.

The transformation from an early medieval oral monastic culture to a visual scholastic one had at first only a limited effect on the reading habits of lay society, particularly in northern Europe, where oral reading and dictation of vernacular texts were commonly practised until at least the thirteenth century. Until the mid-fourteenth century, French kings and noblemen rarely read themselves, but were read to from manuscript books prepared especially for this purpose. When princes such as Saint Louis could read, they frequently read aloud in small groups.[126] In addition to liturgical texts, the literature read to princes consisted of chronicles, *chansons de geste*, romances and the poetry of troubadours and trouvères. Most of these works were in verse, and were intended for oral performances. Thirteenth-century prose compilations, such as the *Roman du Lancelot* and the *Histoire ancienne jusqu'à César*, were also composed to be read aloud. The nobleman was expected to listen to the feats of his predecessors or ancient worthies.[127] However, the illustrations, which from the twelfth century onward were more common in vernacular books prepared for the laity than in Latin books meant for scholars, suggest that vernacular codices were also intended for private visual reading.

In the early Middle Ages, the written vernacular had developed in northern Europe as a complement to word separation to facilitate

reading. Perhaps the fact that vernacular texts were meant for the listener, and not just for the reader, helps to explain why the practice of
composing by dictation seems to have persisted longer for them than for
Latin scholastic works.[128] Joinville dictated his *Histoire de Saint Louis*,
and the author of the *Roman du Lancelot* was depicted dictating.[129] The
tardy development of vernacular proto-cursive and cursive scripts both
reflected and encouraged the widespread practice of dictating vernacular texts. Much medieval vernacular poetry and prose was composed,
memorized and performed orally, and only later set down in writing.[130]
In the thirteenth century, when Latin writers were beginning to write
their thoughts themselves on unbound sheets and quires and to develop
cursive handwriting for this purpose, vernacular texts were still written
down in *textualis* after having been composed orally. Word separation,
which was canonical in thirteenth-century Latin texts, was still often
imperfect in early thirteenth-century vernacular manuscripts, and
remained far less rigorous than for Latin, especially in Italy, until the
end of the Middle Ages. Scribes who knew that a proper Latin text had
word separation as late as 1300 often hesitated to insert the spaces
necessary for establishing which groups of syllables or morphemes constituted correctly written vernacular words.[131] Separation of function
words, normal for Latin, was still not realized in 1500 for the Romance
vernacular tongues. The article was one part of speech possessed by
ancient Greek that had been wanting in Boethius's translations of the
Logica vetus.[132] Precisely because the vernacular was easier to understand than Latin, scribes were less pressed to aid the reader by inserting
inter-word space for the demarcation of boundaries that were imperceptible to the ear. As a consequence, the graphic definition of the vernacular word, particularly of prepositions and articles, remained more
ambiguous than in Latin, where the article, borrowed from French, had
in northern Europe always been treated by university scribes as a separate graphic entity. The lack of orthographic uniformity within copies of
the same vernacular text in the twelfth and thirteenth centuries confirms
that the letters within words were the principal signs of a decoding
process that remained profoundly oral.[133]

Nevertheless, after word separation had been established definitively
in Latin texts, it had profound effects on vernacular text format,
grammar and orthography. The separation and diverse conventions for
word order that increasingly came to characterize the written vernacular after 1200 discouraged the retention of inflection which in ancient
Latin had aided the reader in properly recognizing and accenting words.
Word separation clearly permitted vernacular spelling, particularly in
Middle French and English, to be less phonetic than that of Latin, for
once vernacular words were established as distinct visible units of

letters, spelling often remained the same even when gradual changes in pronunciation rendered certain letters silent.[134] In the late Middle Ages, university-trained scribes, without intending to alter the pronunciation, often inserted silent consonants into vernacular words in order to make them visually closer to the Latin from which they were derived, giving to words a purely visible etymology equivalent to that occurring with Chinese characters but totally lacking in ancient Latin.[135] Mid-thirteenth-century scribes copying vernacular texts preferred to use well-separated exemplars replete with terminal forms including the terminal round *s*, punctuation and *prosodiae*. These exemplars were analogous to those used by the professional scribes of the *pecia* system.[136] From the thirteenth century onwards, certain vernacular texts were copied visually, with uniform page and text format similar to the editions of standard scholastic texts produced by university stationers. The copies of Guillaume Fillastre's *Thoison d'Or*, produced in the 1460s for the Burgundian Order of the Golden Fleece, were marked by the same striking similitudes in text and page format first evident in the eleventh century.[137] Vasque de Lucène's French translation of Quintus Curtius's *History of Alexander*[138] and Henri Romain's *Compendium historial* were other examples of texts reproduced in this manner for the Burgundian and French courts.[139]

In the early fourteenth century, when Latin cursive was fully developed, authors began to employ it in conjunction with standardized word separation to compose vernacular documents and, at a slightly later date, literary texts. At the royal court of France, the task of administering the realm had become too complex to be mastered by illiterate princes who depended solely on the services of readers and scribes. Royal secretaries began to use cursive vernacular scripts to prepare drafts for the king's perusal; Charles V corrected drafts of his letters in his own hand, and signed the originals.[140] A century later, certain royal letters were expected to be written in the king's hand, and many others were expected to bear his autograph signature.[141] Unlike the earlier Latin charters composed by dictation and written in a rhythmical prose to be read aloud, the new royal documents were written in prose as arhythmical as scholastic Latin and decorated with miniatures to be placed before the eyes of the sovereign.[142]

In the mid-fourteenth century, the French nobility began to accept the same practice of silent reading and composition for vernacular literary texts which had become established for the Latin literature of the universities during the previous century. The reign of John II marked the beginning of a major effort to translate Latin literature into French.[143] Because the syntax of the scholastic texts closely resembled that of the vernacular, and thus eliminated the excessive burdening of short-term memory, these translations tended to be far more successful than those of the periodic sentences of ancient Latin authors that late medieval readers found difficult to understand.[144] After John's death in exile, Charles V continued the royal patronage of translations, and he was the first king to assemble a true royal library, located in a tower of the Louvre. The king equipped the library with furnishings modelled on those used in contemporary university libraries.[145] In a miniature, he was painted seated in his library, his hands motionless, reading with sealed lips in silent and tranquil isolation. Manuscripts also depicted the king attending lectures, visually following a copy of the text in university fashion as he listened to the lecture.[146] New portable private books of prayer specifically intended to be brought to Mass contained vernacular texts to be read silently during the public recitation of the apposite Latin texts.[147] While theologians held that liturgical texts of the canonical hours had to be read aloud, even if not understood, devotional texts read silently had to be read with comprehension. Because the monastic term *in silentio* often referred to quiet muffled oralization in *submissa* or *suppressa vox*, fifteenth-century vernacular authors employed a new vocabulary for reading, describing mental devotion from a written text as reading with the heart as opposed to the mouth.[148] In the fifteenth century, the verb *veoir* and the phrase *lire au coeur* were used in aristocratic texts to refer to private silent reading, much as in the eleventh and twelfth centuries *videre* and *inspicere* had been used as alternatives to *legere*.[149] Authors close to the French royal house, including Jean Froissart and Christine de Pisan, were shown as writers in the illuminations decorating their manuscripts.[150] Even princes of the blood were depicted writing their own compositions. Charles V's grandnephew, René d'Anjou, a prolific author, was shown writing out his own texts in the manner of contemporary authors of Latin works.[151] In the fifteenth century, the word *écrire* became, like *scribere*, synonymous with composition.[152]

Silent private reading by the king and great princes of the realm, such as Jean de Berry, Philip the Bold and René d'Anjou, had a dramatic effect on the number and kinds of books prepared for royal and aristocratic courts. Just as fourteenth- and fifteenth-century university libraries far surpassed the size of earlier monastic collections, so royal and aristocratic libraries after 1350 grew to be far larger than their predecessors. Like the contemporary schoolmen whose appetite for books increased in quantity because they had adopted the habit of silent reading, laymen also required a greater quantity of reading material, particularly books of hours and vernacular works. The new vernacular texts composed for princes were almost exclusively in prose, in contrast to an earlier preference for literature in verse. The new aristocratic books were replete with the tables of contents, alphabetical glossaries, subject indexes, running heads and the intellectual complexities characteristic of fourteenth- and fifteenth-century scholastic codices. Glosses with intricate cross-references accompanied the new French translations of the Bible, Saint Augustine, Aristotle and Valerius Maximus, forming awkward compound texts that would have been difficult for a professional reader to read aloud but which were highly suited to visual perusal and study. These were the texts that Jean Gerson specifically recommended for the education of Charles VI.[153] In the codices containing these works, orthography became increasingly standardized, enabling the reader to recognize words by their global image as in Latin, rather than having to decode them phonetically by *ad hoc* synthetic combination of phonemes. In the first half of the fifteenth century, French authors composed new reference books for the nobility, including alphabetical dictionaries of saints and gazetteers.[154] The number of illustrations increased in vernacular aristocratic books as miniatures evolved to play a more direct role in the comprehension of the text, serving a didactic function analogous to that of the diagrams accompanying scholastic literature.[155] In the form of *banderolles*, written text permeated the miniatures of vernacular texts much as it did Latin works. As in Latin books, vernacular *banderolles* presupposed the reader's ability to decode text and image simultaneously.[156]

The growing practice of silent reading among the aristocracy stimulated important changes in the script of books copied for lay patrons. Before 1300, when princes were read to, vernacular books could be written in the same *textualis* as in Latin texts because those who read to princes had normally had a university training. The absence of most monolexic abbreviations other than the Tironian sign for *et*, used as an ideograph to represent *et* in French and *and* in English, and the inconsistent use of phonetic spelling reflected the oral character of these translations. When in the fourteenth century noble laymen began to read to themselves, they found Gothic *textualis* difficult to read. A major source of difficulty was the confusion in recognizing the letters *m*, *n*, *i* and *u* composed of the identical minim strokes that had troubled earlier readers of Latin. To eliminate ambiguity in the representation of these letters more effectively than by the use of acute accent marks, the scribes preparing books for the aristocratic market in the last two decades of the fourteenth century began to employ a form of *cursiva formata* which closely resembled that used by the Royal Chancery for the preparation of vernacular documents.[157] A new vocabulary, *lettre de note*, *lettre de court* and *lettre courante*, was created to denote this new cursive book script.[158]

In the first half of the fifteenth century, *cursiva formata* evolved into a new unlooped form for which no equivalent documentary script existed. Contemporaries called this script *lettre bâtarde* to indicate that it was part cursive and part *textualis*.[159] Modern paleographers who often refer to the Latin equivalent of this script as *hybrida* have not been able to determine the exact date and place of its invention. One variety was used at an early date by the Brothers of the Common Life, who copied many books of devotion for sale to the Dutch laity. Another variety was used primarily for the French-speaking nobility.[160] Unlike Gothic cursive, *lettre bâtarde*, or *hybrida*, appeared almost simultaneously in vernacular and Latin texts.[161] This fact marks a singular change in the relationship between the written vernacular and Latin, for the former was no longer written in scripts that had evolved for the transcription of the latter. Rather, the vernacular played an active role in the evolution of the new handwriting. This is particularly true of the most legible form of *bâtarde*, the *lettre bourguignonne*, exemplified by the handwriting of David Aubert.[162] In France, *lettre bâtarde* became the standard script for both vernacular and Latin books copied for secular patrons in the latter portion of Charles VII's reign. At a slightly later date, it was frequently used in place of *textualis* for the vernacular pious treatises produced in large numbers for laymen and members of religious Orders. In the mid-fifteenth century in aristocratic circles, the use of the less legible Gothic *textualis* was gradually restricted to Latin Bibles, books of hours and some liturgical books, all of which contained intensively read texts habitually read aloud.[163] Many laymen who could only read Latin liturgical texts aloud phonetically, without understanding their content, read vernacular texts silently with full comprehension. In vernacular *lettre bâtarde* texts, punctuation was borrowed from Latin university books, and was calculated to guide the eye of the private reader, rather than to regulate the voice of a professional reader.[164] Aristocratic books of the fifteenth century regularly used paragraph signs, underlining and capitalization to divide texts into intellectual rather than rhetorical units.

Although the text format of Italian Latin manuscripts had been retarded in its development from the tenth to the twelfth century, and had continued to lag behind that of the north even in the fourteenth century, the habit of private reading among laymen seems to have begun at least a half century earlier in Italy than in northern Europe. The earliest manuscripts of Dante's *Inferno* and *Paradiso* were intended to be held under the eyes of the reader.[165] The scribes who copied these texts for the libraries of aristocrats and great urban families used a new variety of highly legible Italian *cursiva formata*, which seems to have been developed especially for the transcription of lay literature.[166] In the second half of the fourteenth century, the burgeoning lay readership stimulated experimentation with hybrid scripts to achieve greater legibility in vernacular codices transcribed for lay patrons.[167] Experimental Italian *hybrida* scripts travelling northward via the Rhine valley may have inspired the northern *hybrida* and *lettre bâtarde*, but *hybrida* was not generally adopted in Italy for texts intended for laymen in the early fifteenth century, because under the influence of humanism, scribes and authors turned to Caroline *textualis* as an alternative method of achieving superior legibility. A relatively large number of fifteenth-century lay Italian readers were literate in Latin, which even at the end of the Middle Ages was easier for Italians to understand.

Although Italian scribes deviated from canonical separation in Italian, and even in Latin, far more frequently than those of the north, Italian humanists never questioned the desirability of word separation, even though they knew quite well that their beloved ancients had written in *scriptura continua*.[168] To the scholars of the Renaissance, the advantage of word separation for maintaining textual integrity was indisputable.[169] The introduction of word separation into texts contained in ancient manuscripts was a normal part of editing, and the use of medieval signs of punctuation was in integral part of humanistic authorship.[170] Only on rare occasions did fifteenth-century scribes ever emulate ancient *scriptura continua*, and then only for display scripts.[171] Humanistic script was created by taking the writing found in twelfth-century, rather than ninth- and tenth-century, codices as a model. Among those elements that humanists emulated were the *et* ligature and the protruding vertical stroke of the letter *t*, both of which served to enhance Bouma shape and thus augment the rapidity of reading. The use of terminal capitals and capitals to denote proper names was also emulated. So too was the use of *prosodiae*, especially the acute accent, frequently for monosyllables, the *trait d'union* and the suspended *ct* ligature, an alternative mode of signalling the continuation of a word divided at line ending. The use of foliation, particularly foliation using very un-roman arabic numerals, was common in Italian humanist books.

Ancient scribes, at least after separation by interpuncts had been abandoned, had used no punctuation marks, and when they read Cicero, it had been the reader's responsibility to articulate the metrical *clausulae*, the Roman aural equivalent of punctuation.[172] The punctuation of humanist texts was more influenced by the visual achievements of the separated northern European Caroline texts of the eleventh and twelfth centuries than that of Italian Gothic script. Humanist scribes invented modern quotation marks by borrowing the angular marks used to separate text from commentary in twelfth-century manuscripts and systematically employing them as a substitute for Gothic red underlining.[173] Building on twelfth-century late medieval and perhaps

Byzantine, precedents, humanist scribes employed full syntactical sentence punctuation with the characteristically modern usage of the comma and full stop.[174] They integrated these punctuation marks with the syntactical patterns of late Gothic capitalization in order to achieve optimal conditions for silent reading. The humanist scribes' most original contribution was the use of the parenthesis, a mark specifically employed to give graphic representation to the aside, a device of ancient oratorical eloquence.[175] The parenthesis in fifteenth-century humanist texts permitted the private silent reader to re-create vicariously an oral experience. Chiefly via printed books, the graphic parenthesis spread throughout Italy, and at the end of the fifteenth century it was one of the humanistic innovations in graphic language that was most readily received in northern Europe.[176] Parentheses were enumerated for the first time as graphic signs in a French grammatical treatise of the end of the fifteenth century.[177] Used in Latin scholastic texts, parentheses developed nuances which had no direct equivalent in oral rhetoric. They were written in a rejuvenated *littera antiqua* highly suitable for private silent reading.[178]

The spread of *lettre de court*, *lettre bâtarde* and the humanistic *textualis* in the late fourteenth and fifteenth centuries both reflected and encouraged a dramatic change in the reading habits of the aristocracy and the urban élite of the cities of Italy and the lower Rhine valley. Saint Louis had read aloud surrounded by an entourage. Charles V, Louis XI, Lorenzo de Medici and Flemish merchants in the paintings of Memling and Van Eyck read to themselves in inner solitude. Vernacular authors of the late fourteenth century began to assume that their audience was composed of readers rather than listeners. Froissart, in the 1370s, expected that young noblemen would *look into* and read his *Chroniques*.[179] Between 1388 and 1392, Phillippe de Mezières anticipated that the young king Charles VI would personally read the *Songe du vieil pèlerin*, including the special table designed to guide the secular reader through the complex long histories told in parables and symbols.[180]

The visual mode for lay reading led authors to enrich vernacular texts with scholastic complexities that had hitherto been the restricted province of Latin literature. Just as separated written Latin had facilitated the birth of scholasticism, so separated vernacular writing allowed for the transference of the subtleties of fully developed scholastic thought to a new lay audience. In northern Europe, the penetration of vernacular literature by Latin scholasticism became prevalent in the fourteenth and fifteenth centuries. Questions pertaining to the quarrel between nominalism and realism were discussed in the vernacular glosses accompanying Nicolas Orseme's translation of Aristotle and in the extensive corpus of treatises prepared for the Burgundian court.[181] The polemical tracts generated in the dispute between Philip the Fair and Boniface VIII were translated for the edification of Charles V and Charles VII.[182] Complex arguments such as that over the nature of the Holy Blood of Christ were presented in vernacular treatises composed by university masters for aristocratic patrons close to Louis XI.[183] Vernacular meditations inspired by the Latin genre invented in the eleventh century by John of Fécamp and Anselm of Canterbury were composed for lay aristocratic readers.[184] The new corpus of vernacular literature and the silent mode of reading it imbued the aristocracy with a sense of private piety, and made possible individual intellectual judgements on scholastic positions similar to those made by university scholars. In the numerous debates composed for great princes, it was the lay reader who was forced to decide between two or more subtly defined positions.[185]

The privacy afforded by silent reading and writing may also have increased displays of irony and cynicism. The chronicles of France in the royal copy of the *Rozier de guerre*, which presented itself as the work of Louis XI, was marginally annotated with sarcasms which kings, two centuries before, reading orally with a group would never have permitted themselves to express.[186] Even more important, private reading provided a medium for expressing subversive political thoughts. Charles of France, the rebellious brother of Louis XI, left a copy of Cicero's *De officiis* with underlined passages justifying rebellion and the assassination of tyrants.[187] Guillaume Fillastre, in the epoch of the War of the Public Good, used arguments modelled on those of the conciliarists to justify the deposition of tyrannical kings. In the second half of the fifteenth century, the privately read aristocratic manuscript book became the principal medium for disseminating ideas justifying resistance to royal authority, much as the Latin *tractati* of the fourteenth century had provided a medium for those advocating resistance to papal authority.[188]

The new privacy afforded by silent reading also had dramatic and not entirely positive effects on lay spirituality. Private reading stimulated a revival of the antique genre of erotic art. In ancient Greece and Rome, material that today might be termed pornographic was read orally and displayed openly in a tolerant pagan society. Before the thirteenth century, erotic decorations in books were usually oblique and suggested the repressed illicit desires of the chaste rather than artfully crafted graphic fantasies intended to excite the reader.[189] In fifteenth-century France, where pornography was forbidden, private reading encouraged the production of illustrated salacious writings intended for the laity that were tolerated precisely because they could be disseminated in secret. Miniatures of French and Flemish vernacular texts depicted bordello scenes of carnal lust with explicit and seductive realism.[190] Inspired by Boccaccio's *Decameron,* an anonymous Burgundian author prepared for Duke Philip the Good the *Cent Nouvelles Nouvelles,* an illustrated *summa* of sexual escapades which attributed licentious acts to the same reformed monks and friars who championed poverty and chastity. The author of the *Cent Nouvelles Nouvelles* anticipated that the prince would read it privately as an 'exercise de lecture et d'estude'.[191] Like scholastic texts, the *Cent Nouvelles Nouvelles* was preceded by a table that gave in abbreviated form the high points of each adventure so as to help the reader browse and choose the story he preferred. This illustrated text was circulated in modest format, so that it could be discreetly passed from reader to reader, much as the forbidden texts of William of Ockham and Marsilio of Padua had been surreptitiously disseminated among university scholars a hundred years earlier.[192] By the end of the fifteenth century, the intimacy of silent reading permitted explicit graphic representations of human sexuality to permeate religious literature. In books of hours, enticing miniatures depicting David spying upon Bathsheba in her bath accompanied the Penitential Psalms. Other miniatures illustrating the calendar showed embracing naked male and female figures representing the month of May and suggestive scenes of fondling.[193] Illuminated borders displayed both heterosexual and homosexual encounters. In analogous fashion, the new habit of silent autograph composition allowed laymen to breach matters of erotic intimacy in handwritten notes and letters. Philip the Good, writing in his own hand to his companion John of Cleves, discussed sexual escapades in frank and earthy language.[194]

The freedom of expression that private silent reading gave to hitherto suppressed sexual fantasies also paradoxically intensified the depth of lay religious experience. Private silent reading in the vernacular gave laymen the means of pursuing the individual relationship to God which had been the aspiration of erudite Christians since Saint Augustine. The *De imitatione Christi,* written by Thomas à Kempis for his fellow monks, was soon after its composition translated into French and circulated at the Burgundian court.[195] Scores of other religious texts, including translations and original compositions, stressed the importance of reading, vision and silence in achieving spiritual solace. In the prologue to his *Vie de Christ,* Jean Mansel declared that the spoken word was fleeting, while the written word endured, and he called upon knights and princes disposed to devotion for the profit of their souls to *see* the content of his book.[196] Proceeding from the reading of the life of Christ, each person ought to meditate using the 'eyes of his contemplation'.[197] The vernacular life of Peter of Luxembourg described the scion of an aristocratic family who spent his silent nocturnal hours reading sermons, saints' lives and patristic texts.[198] In the vernacular literature intended for laymen, separation from the group for the purpose of private reading and prayer was emphasized repeatedly. Peter of Luxembourg himself stressed the need for private prayer and silent study.[199] Ludolf of Saxony's *Life of Christ*, translated for Louis of Bruges, advocated the solitary reading of Scripture as a principal element of the contemplative life.[200] Through the translation, the author now advised pious laymen to place before their eyes the deeds and words of Christ.[201] Books of hours, produced in increasing numbers for laymen, were tailored to serve the need for individualized spiritual experience.[202] Both vernacular and Latin devotional books intended for the laity incorporated the paratextual aids to reading that had been introduced into continental Latin books in the eleventh century, including punctuation, capitalization, *traits d'union* and the successor to the *diastole* to aid in the distinction of words in Gothic *textualis*.[203]

Isolated private reading and prayer as the pathway to salvation, in turn, may have fostered insecurities about the worthiness of each individual's faith and devotion, thereby stimulating zeal for religious reform. The reformed mendicant Orders of the fifteenth century found their strongest supporters among the urban merchant families and the aristocratic families who silently read vernacular religious manuscript books. Three generations later, many scions of these same families would become supporters of John Calvin. On the eve of the Protestant Reformation, the mode of dissemination of ideas had been so revolutionized that laymen, like university schoolmen, could formulate dissenting views in private and communicate them in secret. The inconography of motionless silent reading in Gerard Dou's portrait of Rembrandt's mother had its antecedent in the iconography of silent devotional reading of the Virgin at the moment of the Annunciation. The printing press would play an important role in the ultimate triumph of Protestantism, but the formulation of reformist religious and political ideas and the receptivity of Europe's élite to making private judgements on matters of conscience owed much to a long evolution that began in the late tenth century and culminated in the fifteenth century in the manner in which men read and wrote.

6

Reading in the Jewish Communities of Western Europe in the Middle Ages

Robert Bonfil

For Jews and Christians alike, the practice of reading posed a political problem for the élites who exercised (or aspired to exercise) authority and power, because they perceived it as their duty to impose control over the dissemination of ideas. Exercising authority always implies asking what significance should be attributed to the antagonistic relationship between those who control and those who are controlled. In the case of reading, that opposition always results in a set of repressive statements, but also in another set of positive, at times didactic, statements that form a genuine indoctrination for the purpose of prohibiting the harmful and promoting the useful.

In this context there is no difference between the ways in which the mental baggage of the Jews and the Christians was constituted. Still, the Jewish experience was different in a number of ways. Because throughout the Middle Ages Jews in Europe were unable to exercise power independently,[1] they were subject to a unique redoubling of normative authority, on the one hand, from whoever held actual power (non-Jews, who were by definition outside the Jewish sociocultural sphere), but on the other hand from the Jewish leadership, which, because it held no true power, was constrained to rely on the power of others or else use more or less effective surrogates for power. The Jewish leadership was always dually conditioned by outside forces: it had to submit to laws imposed by others that were often contrary to the norms it would have liked to impose; it was forced to mould its own norms so as to avoid conflict with the power structure, which would always prevail in any event. This means that even in the pre-modern age the leadership of the Jewish diaspora found itself in a situation in many ways analogous to that of the Roman Catholic Church in the age of the triumph of secularism.[2] Because the Jewish leadership was forced to define control in terms of lobbying those who held actual power, to deal with those over whom it claimed control by preaching and persuasion rather than by menacing them with genuine repression, and to proffer threats of heavenly ire and excommunication rather than actually burning books, it was also forced into a style of discourse that was relatively less rigid, more open and more secular than that of Christian leaders. As we shall see, this was a particular aspect of a more general characteristic of medieval Jewish society: a clearly secular component was introduced into an overwhelmingly religious general picture, in striking contrast to the modern age, where that relationship has been reversed. Viewed from this perspective, it seems to me that the specific nature of the Jewish experience will be clearer if we observe it against the background of the gradual 'opening' of the book to a larger and larger potential public during the Middle Ages, and if we view that process in terms of a more general transformation in the mental baggage of both Jews and Christians regarding the relation between the sacred and the profane as both communities dealt with questions of the book and reading.

The Book and Reading in the Domain of the Sacred

Throughout the early Middle Ages the Jews of the Christian West seem to have sacralized the book in much the same way as contemporary Christian society. For Jews as well as Christians the book was a religious object with magical properties, rather than an instrument for communication through reading. Its supernatural charge made it a relic for pious and contemplative adoration, rather than a reservoir of contents that could be drawn upon freely. In short, the book was doubly closed to direct exploitation: it was closed within its binding, and it was closed within the ark, to which ordinary people did not have access. This view was in clear contrast to the idea of the 'open' book (in both senses) that began to circulate after the year 1000.[3] One clear example of this view of the book can be seen in the so-called *Chronicle of Aḥima‘az*, an epic genealogical work composed in southern Italy in 1054 on the basis of oral traditions dating back to the second half of the ninth century.[4] It recounts the story of a woman who brought down the wrath of God on her family, causing the death of several relatives, because one Friday she lit a candle before a sacred book while she was menstruating. The details of the story are somewhat murky; nor is the function of the light (or the contents of the book) at all clear. What seems beyond doubt, however, is the custom of keeping a light before the *Book of the Chariot*, an ancient Hebrew mystical text. The woman's act is supposed to have contaminated the holiness of the book, here treated as a genuine relic.[5]

Further passages in the *Chronicle of Aḥima'az* and other works amply confirm the sociopolitical structure underlying the attitudes implicit in this story[6] – that is, the structure of a society that entrusts tightly closed élite groups with the transmission of the contents of its culture, and that sees that function as a mediation between sacred space, which is dominated by those groups as the custodians and legitimate interpreters of books, and the 'secular' space of ordinary people, who receive an oral explanation of the contents of books.[7] The early Middle Ages was a time (also among non-Jews, both Christian and Muslim) when the exercise of authority was perceived in terms of hierarchical sacrality associated with a legitimate interpretation of traditional texts and, consequently, with the publication of laws that derived from those texts. In the geopolitical context of the Christian West the Jews perceived the distance between the overwhelming majority of people and the legitimate readers and interpreters of those texts even more concretely than did Jews in the Muslim East. In the West the sacred texts reached Jews through a double mediation, once by the local leadership but also, and above all, by an ecumenical leadership (from the ninth century on, nearly exclusively Babylonian) that was situated outside their geographical area.[8] In short, although we tend to comprehend the act of reading as the installation of a complex relation between the written text and its targeted user – that is, as a relation that transcends the simple communication of words – it is clear that in the context of that particular society a distinction had been set up in the area of public activity between those who were endowed with sacred authority and were authorized to expound the meaning of the writings that belonged within the sacred space and those who were not so authorized, thus associating the idea of hermeneutic *lectura* with the idea of the *lex*.[9] The mental structure implied by this viewpoint was one of an orality profoundly respectful of rhetoric, the medieval Hebrew equivalent of which was derived from the biblical *meliz* (Genesis 42:23), and which signified 'intermediary', or 'mediator'. This attitude was totally consistent with a respect for static conservatism rather than dynamic innovation, and in the final analysis it was consistent with a defence of the essentially closed sociopolitical structure discussed above.[10]

This explains why not one recorded instance of censorship has come down to us from a time when, both inside the specifically Jewish sphere and outside it, reading was the privilege of a very small élite of 'the elect to whom all reading matter is permitted'. Since reading was an activity considered by definition dubious if not dangerous, it is logical to figure that it was carried on, for the most part, elsewhere than in the spaces common to the greater society to which those élites belonged, in more or less hermetically closed places, and even without being openly acknowledged.

The Jewish experience was also unique in having texts that were 'imported' from the non-Jewish cultural sphere and 'Hebraicized' – that is, filtered and manipulated. Two early medieval examples of this phenomenon are the *Book of Yossippon*[11] and Shabbetai Donnolo's Commentary on the *Book of Creation*,[12] both of which have obvious roots in the Christian literary tradition. The *Book of Yossippon* even transfers into the Jewish cultural domain materials almost exclusively drawn from texts that later Hebraic sensitivity would doubtless have considered highly dangerous, apocrypha that were canonical texts in the Christian Bible but 'external' to the Hebraic canon and Hegesippus' Christianized version of Flavius Josephus. One constant over the very long time span that was typical of early medieval Jewish culture, and that can occasionally be found in our own day in certain 'orthodox' circles, was to show a convergence between what was perceived to be positive from a religious viewpoint (thus what could legitimately be situated within an ideal cultural space) and what was situated outside that same space. In this, Jewish culture followed Islam even more than Christianity. In all such cases, the cultural space of the group had to be restructured without corroding the basic idea of necessary limits controlled by those who, in virtue of their own intellectual superiority, arrogated to themselves an exclusive right to abolish those limits. For both Jews and Christians, however, that logic was more and more severely tested by the greater practical opportunities to read that were brought by the various 'renascences'. With regard to reading, the minoritarian condition of the Jews, who were constantly subjected to urgent confrontation with the majority culture, transformed a mirror perception of the Other into a relatively greater tendency toward openness of the sacred space of reading, hence into something homologous to the subordination of Jewish authority to Christian authority, concerning the hermetic closing of that space. That trend became even more marked in the following age.

The Book and Reading in the Urban Setting

The process of rapid urbanization of the Jews in Western Europe after the year 1000[13] set off an equally rapid transformation in the socio-cultural profile of Jewish society.[14] For one thing, the strata of Jewish peasant society, which are clearly mentioned in early medieval sources, disappear. For another, an increasingly urban Jewish society becomes known for a relatively high level of literacy. Without forcing the documentation too much, I think we can assert that between the twelfth and thirteenth centuries the figure of the Jew (the male Jew, of course) as totally illiterate, unable to read even a prayer text, becomes increasingly rare. The writer (perhaps the glossator) of the *Sefer Ḥasidim*, foreseeing that the reader might not believe him when he gives an *exemplum* of a minister of God who, not knowing how to read, bursts into spontaneous prayer, feels he has to specify, 'He was a Jew'.[15] Similarly, one can easily discern a note of astonishment in the account of a learned man from the Rhine valley, as reported in the *Sefer Ra'avià*: 'I have seen in a collection of responses that in Spain and in Babylonia it is the custom *still in our own day* for the celebrant to do the *Seder* [the Passover ceremony] in the synagogue because the common people are not accustomed to reciting the *Haggadah* [the traditional Passover story].'[16]

However one might interpret the persistence of this custom in Spain (where it is documented at least until the beginning of the thirteenth century), there seems to be little doubt that, as with similar instances of the norms registered in the Mishnah, the custom originated at a time when illiteracy was so widespread that illiterates could not be ignored when it came to establishing rules for ritual.[17] Spain might also have been unique, because there and in Provence flight from rural areas was less drastic and less rapid than in other regions of Europe, to the point that Jews engaged in agriculture can be documented in those regions as late as the first half of the fifteenth century. In any event it is clear from the way that such mentions of illiteracy are expressed that they were exceptions.

The problem of control appears (one might even say 'naturally') to be closely connected with the progress of literacy and the growth of book circulation. In all cases – the controversy that centred on Maimonides' *Guide for the Perplexed*,[18] the ban that Rabbi Solomon ben Adret and his followers pronounced in 1305 against persons under twenty-five years of age (because they were considered insufficiently versed in Talmudic studies) who wanted to study 'external' sciences[19] and other less-studied and less well-known events[20] – a firm guiding hand had to be kept on society by exercising control over literature, which was always seen as a potential threat to social equilibrium. In the Jewish minoritarian community all such initiatives, in the age preceding the invention of printing, seem to have prolonged and institutionalized the tendency, typical of the early Middle Ages, to concentrate on the activities implied by reading and on individuals, not on books. That is to say, the authorities attempted to define the sphere of such activities more rigorously and to specify the criteria for admitting people to them; they also attempted to defend the connection between the sacred and the perilous, which meant defending (among other things) the existent socio-cultural structure that gave control of knowledge to leaders who were absolute masters in that domain. This perspective resolves the apparent contradiction (which scholars have often stressed) between the anathemas hurled at intellectual activity dependent on 'external' readings and the incontrovertible fact that the authors of those same condemnations invariably turned out to be imbued with the very reading matter that they anathematized.[21] This characteristic deserves to be emphasized, because it ran counter to the viewpoint of the Christian powers, who, as early as the thirteenth century, were intolerant of 'dangerous' books. When that attitude was applied to the Hebrew book, it produced the first public burning of the Talmud in Paris in 1241.[22]

Did the structural weakness of Jewish self-government encourage the persistence of the *via antiqua* in the Jewish camp? Two things seem to point in this direction: first, during the controversy over Maimonides' work, some Jews attempted to involve the Christian powers in order to resolve the question once and for all, even among Jews, with a book burning. It is beside the point in the context that concerns us here whether or not the Jews asked Christians to intervene or whether this is an example of propagandistic 'disinformation' about which we still know too little to judge.[23] Be that as it may, the idea of a repressive policy regarding books was immediately connected with the idea of an effective exercise of power; moreover, that effectiveness required concrete proof, preferably through the ritual of exorcism and purification by fire. Later developments confirm this interpretation: for Jews and Christians alike the moment when debate about reading became most acute was during printing's first great 'boom', when those who considered themselves responsible for society's behaviour viewed having too many books available as that many potential dangers.

Jews seem to have used the weapon of excommunication (their almost exclusive effective means of exercising power) against any and all persons who read certain books even earlier than Christians did. The first to have used it seems to have been Leone di Vitale, called Messer Leon (d. *c.*1490). Leone pronounced a formal ban on anyone who dared to read the biblical commentary of Gersonides, whom he found guilty of rejecting belief in creation *ex nihilo* (a move that should probably be connected with the preparation of the *editio princeps* of Leone's work by the Mantua bookseller Abraham Conat in 1475).[24] Messer Leon was able to combine the exercise of rabbinical authority with an effective exercise of power thanks to an extraordinary combination of circumstances (for which space does not allow a detailed explanation here[25]) that gave ordained rabbis the exclusive prerogative of pronouncing excommunications. Messer Leon was one of these. Moreover, his title of 'doctor' had been granted by the emperor, a signal honour that probably gave him an inflated idea of his authority, or so his detractors insinuated. This means that, *mutatis mutandis*, in Messer Leon's opinion the exercise of authority among the Jews converged with the exercise of authority among those who held real power.

Recourse to repression of the book was constantly associated with the belief that the rabbinical prerogative of excommunication could be translated into an effective exercise of power in a situation of a keenly perceived danger that control over what people read might be lost. In the final analysis, however, the weapon of excommunication was less potent in the hands of the Jewish leaders than in those of the Christian power structure. For one thing, because there was no supreme rabbinical authority, the targeted person could always pronounce a counter-excommunication. Although excommunication was seen as a terrifying move by the popular religious imagination, it could not only be turned back against the person who pronounced it, but (and this is more important for our purposes) it was powerless to set in motion any clearly irreversible process, such as burning at the stake. Moreover, excommunication was often subject to authorization by the Christian courts, once again making the exercise of Jewish authority dependent on Christian power. In any event, the exercise of control over reading was necessarily less effective among Jews than among Christians. Not only did Messer Leon's initiative fail; as we shall soon see, even later attempts to apply a policy of repression of the book were only relatively effective. The combination of repression and the exercise of authority proved a good deal more fragile in the Jewish camp than on the Christian side. None the less, that combination did exist among the Jews.

Crisis of Authority and Repressive Policies

Although it is true that as time went by the Jews failed to obtain a greater measure of self-government (in fact, they lost ground on that score), delay in transforming the idea of control over reading into a policy of repressing books seems to indicate that their attempt to institute such a policy coincided with a critical moment when a crisis of authority and power led to an effective loss of control. As is always the case, the more acute the sense of crisis became, the more desperate the demonstrations of force, as the Christian world of the thirteenth and fourteenth centuries amply demonstrates. The Jews, who lived in a permanent climate of crisis of power, eventually transformed a congenital weakness into a force of habit, thus limiting their need to change course to exceptionally difficult circumstances. In that sense, the sixteenth century presented the Jews with a much more critical context than did the thirteenth century. In later times the Jews had to deal not only with the restructuring of knowledge that resulted from the introduction of printing, but also with tragic expulsions, beginning with the expulsion of the Jews from Spain in 1492, which forced them to restructure their entire existence. When (exceptionally) the leaders of the Jewish communities adopted a radically repressive policy regarding books, we can undoubtedly interpret that move as an acute symptom of extreme weakness and a momentary loss of faith in their ability to exercise control over reading.[26] But if the repression of books effectively reduces opportunities to read, it also (albeit indirectly) strikes at the sociocultural and political culture that decides who are the controlling authorities and who the controlled subjects.[27] The unavoidable conclusion is that if such events were exceptional, it was more because of the revolutionary radicalism that informed them. They can be called revolutionary because, even though their effect was transversal, they undermined the authoritarian structure of a society built on a binary opposition between an élite culture and a popular culture in which a few held a paternalistic authority over a populace conceived of *sub specie infantis*. In this perspective, shoring up authority and power always necessarily meant restoring a modified version of the *status quo ante*. The means to that end were the definition of divisions in knowledge, control of production, preventive censorship, the creation of *indices librorum prohibitorum* (which created a virtual destruction of books and a real restructuring of the situations in which forbidden readings became permissible) and, finally, a control over the texts of books.[28]

It is significant that the first ordinance regarding books put out by a Jewish community comes from Italy in the Tridentine epoch. Delegates from the Italian Jewish communities met in Ferrara in 1554 soon after (and probably as a direct result of) the promulgation of the papal bull of September 1553 decreeing that all copies of the Talmud be seized and burned. The delegates in Ferrara decreed:

Printers shall not be permitted to print any hitherto unpublished book except with permission of three duly ordained Rabbis, and the consent of the heads of one of the communities nearest the place of printing, if the city in which the book is printed is a small one. If it is a large city, the agreement of the heads of that Community shall suffice provided the consent of three ordained Rabbis is obtained as said above. The names of the Rabbis and the heads of the Communities sponsoring the book shall be printed at the beginning of the volume. Otherwise no one shall be permitted to buy the book under penalty of a fine of twenty-five *scuti*. The fine shall be given to the charity fund of the city of the transgressor.[29]

As far as we know, this ordinance failed miserably. Because the leaders of the Jewish communities did not have the backing of the Christian power structure, they were continually forced to take into account Christian cultural and religious tendencies, and they had to assert their authority by using persuasion rather than repression. Even among Christians book burning rapidly gave way to preventive censorship and *indices librorum prohibitorum*, thus reinforcing in a number of ways (that this is not the place to recall) the link between power and knowledge, between authority and the pen.[30]

One highly significant case in point was the opposition to a book written by 'Azariah (Bonaiuto) de Rossi (*c.*1511–78), *Meor 'Enáyim* (The Light of the Eyes), in which several rabbis and Italian community leaders detected subversive ideas.[31] While authorities from outside Italy (in particular from Safed and Prague) thundered their condemnation, and threatened to excommunicate anyone who read the book, authorities in Italy limited themselves to prohibiting reading of the book to people insufficiently prepared to face the danger of the adventure, but they expressly authorized others to do so. In other words, excommunication was deemed ineffective in a geographical location near where the book had been published (where the problem was resolved exactly as it had been centuries before), but it was also, *mutatis mutandis*, considered ineffective in a Tridentine climate that worked to bring an author's intentions into line with the demands of a censorious establishment. The outcome of this case was highly significant: rather than suffer the consequences of refusing to compromise with the representatives of authority, the author agreed to make changes, censoring his own text. Without entering into details, the episode was symptomatic of the weakness of both the author and the establishment, but it also shows their respective strengths, given that they reached a compromise. This case seems to show that the best way to resolve a problem effectively within the Jewish community – that is, without recourse to the Christian power structure, which obviously took a great interest in the dissemination of a book subversive of Hebrew culture – was to restore the close connection between the exercise of authority and the production of texts offered to the public, in this instance by encouraging the inclusion (even if only *sui generis*) of the author within the sphere of authority. From the perspective of the powerless Jewish minority, this incident seems to reflect the same sort of difficulties regarding effective exercise of censorship that Christian censors encountered in the Tridentine period.[32] Moreover, it seems to anticipate analogous manifestations of weakness within the Christian majority such as the Roman Catholic Church's struggle with secularism.[33]

The case of 'Azariah de Rossi, and in a broader sense the situation of the Jewish minority, can thus be seen as a particular example of a more generalized restoration of the old connection between authors and authority, set within the framework of the restructuring brought on by a sharpened awareness (thanks to the introduction of printing) of their respective weaknesses. I might recall in passing that the establishment's loss of control over authors, as Europe entered the early modern age, paralleled authors' loss of control over their own works, which henceforth anyone might purchase and read. Thus preventive censorship in effect paralleled authors' proprietary rights to their work,[34] achieved through pressure from a culture increasingly shaped by consumers' desires – a situation exactly opposite to that of the age of the manuscript.[35] A highly significant case in point in this respect is the strict relationship between an early form of copyright[36] and the history of the repression of Hebrew books, as exemplified in the chronicle of the vicissitudes of Venetian printing in the sixteenth century.[37] Although the particulars of the affair are not totally clear (and space does not permit a full recapitulation here), the papal bull of 1553 calling for the burning of the Talmud and the opposition to that ruling had much to do with the history of the rivalry between the Bomberg and the Giustiniani printing firms, an affair that involved what we would call 'industrial spying' and secret accusations.[38] The interests of authors and printers coincided with those of the power structure, but they also clashed with them, with sociocultural and political results that are all too familiar.[39] A final observation taken from the history of the Jewish minority, where that ambiguous convergence sometimes had unique and to some extent curious aspects, will show it to have been much stronger than it seemed at first sight.[40] Without entering into the details, it is easy to show that in certain cases the exercise of Christian censorship effectively modified the content of texts in circulation among the Jews, shaping those texts to Christian tastes and ultimately helping to narrow the gap between Jewish culture and Christian culture.[41] With hindsight the phenomenon might seem to have been positive, but it was none the less a form of exercise of repressive power over a powerless minority.

The link between texts and power is a good deal more complex than some critics have shown it to be.

From the viewpoint of the difficulties involved in instituting control over reading, the transformation of the sociocultural profile of Jewish society (which was accelerated by the rapid urbanization of the Jews in the West) reveals several analogies with the corresponding phenomenon in Christian society. It also shows differences, however. We have already seen one of these in a comparison between the Jewish and the Christian communities at times when the latter's control over reading matter was observably weak, notably at the time of the Roman Catholic Church's struggle with secularism. In virtue of the Jews' weakness, the relation between the sacred and the secular (expressed in categories such as useful/harmful, permitted/forbidden, etc.) was a good deal less rigidly polarized among them, and less apt to be transformed into an actual policy of repression than in the Christian society that surrounded them.

Reading and Society: Toward the Open Book

We have already seen how deeply rooted the idea of a need for an authoritative mediation between the sacred text and the individual might be, even among the Jews of the Middle Ages, and I have offered several reasons for this. One result, among both Jews and Christians, was that orally transmitted literature predominated over written texts.[42] Both forms of access to texts were strictly regulated: 'It is not permitted to transmit orally what should be written, nor is it permitted to put in writing what must be transmitted orally' (T. B. Ghittin 60b).

Throughout the early Middle Ages, which coincided with the age of the 'closing of the book' in the Christian West, the intellectual leaders of the Babylonian ecumenical hegemony elaborated on that idea. In their eyes the successive stages in the formation of the corpus of written literature that makes up traditional Hebrew learning were as many phases of decadence.

In the work known as the *Epistle of Rav Sherirà Gaon*, which met with extraordinary success during the Middle Ages,[43] the tenth-century author reduces that interpretation of the contrast between written and oral literature to a system. In doing so, however, he unequivocally defined those 'phases of decadence' as moments in the reconstruction of the areas of orality and of writing in which texts that had previously been closed to the vast public were 'opened up' to it, thus enlarging the field of reading for that public. However Rav Sherirà might have understood them, those phases had already occurred by his day. By defining

an enlargement of the field of writing and reading in terms of decadence, he obviously intended to reinforce the authority of his peers, the
leaders, who considered themselves the sole authoritative and authorized mediators between the sacred and the secular and the exclusive representatives of God on Earth, *vicarii Dei* similar to the *vicarii Christi*
who sat on the throne of Peter in Rome. As with the Church of Rome,
however, the limits to that authority had to be established in terms of
an actual ability to translate authority into social and political power.
As a consequence, what happened to the Church of Rome beginning
roughly in the fourteenth century also happened to the ecumenical spiritual leadership of the Jews around the year 1000, when, for a number
of reasons, the sacred hierarchical structure set up in the age of the
Abbasid Caliphate collapsed. In the Christian West the Jews relegated
to the realm of the imaginary the idea of the predominance of the Word
and any implied decadence in a gradual broadening of the range of texts
accessible to all. In the new reality, the unique sociopolitical conditions
of the diaspora forced the Jews to make a virtue of necessity, so that the
idea of decadence encouraged a perception of access to the sacred texts
in terms of 'diminished sacrality', but it also provided a justification for
having that same access.[44] In other words, one might logically expect
that because of the Jews' lesser ability to exercise power, the medieval
'closing' of books would be less effective among them than among
Christians, that it might require less effort for Jews to 'open' a book to
a growing public, and that the length of time needed for that to happen
would be shorter than for Christians – consequently, that Jews of the
Middle Ages would display a greater secularization in their reading
practice than Christians.

In reality, however, the texts that Jews considered 'closed', and that
were for the most part transmitted orally in hermetically closed milieus,
were restricted in the early Middle Ages to mystical or magical texts.
The *Chronicle of Aḥima'az* specifically refers to such a text. As I have
shown elsewhere,[45] the prohibition against reading mystical books
should probably be related to the process of diffusion in the West,
beginning in the ninth century, of the Babylonian Talmud as a substitute for the substratum of Palestinian culture to which many such books
have rightly been assigned. In my opinion, however, there is an effective
parameter for measuring the difference between Jewish and Christian
society in that period. Although we are still rather poorly informed
regarding the extent of public access to books in the early Middle Ages,
it is almost certain that not even then did Jewish society experience anything like the typically Christian phenomenon of the production and
preservation of books in monastic milieus. No matter how generously
we might evaluate lay presence in such environments, the very fact that

the great monastic foundations generally reflected a strict blending of political power and religious power was quite naturally translated into hindering (or at least limiting) access to books, in conformity with the will of the powerful.[46] As far as we know, nothing of the sort occurred among Jews in the Christian West.

Study as Religious Ritual

One basic and critically important difference between Judaism and Christianity in the realm that interests us here involves study, a practice at the time almost impossible to distinguish from reading.[47] Several factors contributed to the shaping of the idea of study in Western medieval Jewish thought. Chief among these were an emphasis, as early as the first century, after the destruction of the Temple, on academic activity as a substitute for ritual; the decline of the Eastern ecumenical hegemony, which occurred precisely as the Jewish communities were forming throughout most of the West;[48] the eminently urban character of those communities;[49] the pre-eminence of commerce in money among the Jews' economic activities; the tradition, already well established during the age of the Eastern ecumenical hegemonies, of a close connection between knowledge (understood mostly in terms of sacrality), and the exercise of authority and power. The political component of that connection was necessarily limited, but it was none the less understood in terms of sovereignty, the semantics of which the rabbis took over.[50] More than anything else, however, it was the Jewish perception of study as religious ritual that differentiated the Jews' cultural identity from the Christians'. The two groups' contrasting views probably originated in their awareness of the antithetical constructs of the Word–Christ–Logos (for Christians) and the Torah–Writing–Nomos (for Jews). That opposition, which was all too clear in the Christians' long centuries of polemics with Jews, is expressed with equal clarity in Jewish sources of the early centuries of the Common Era – for example, in the definition of the Torah as the 'divine pedagogue' (Midrash *Genesis Rabbah*, 1.1[51]), in contrast to the idea of the human 'paedogogos' that Christian writers, beginning with St Paul (Galatians 3:24; Romans 10:4), wanted to eliminate in the religion of Christ.[52] These contrasting views produced a long-lasting difference between Jewish and Christian ways of thinking. The tension between one camp and the other regarding writing and the spoken word could be strong enough to seem like a total opposition. We should recall that until the early modern period the Jews did not limit access to writing in favour of the spoken word anywhere near as much as did Christians, who relaxed their efforts to restrict writing only with the advent of the Reformation. For a people who modelled their religious identity on the 'Text of the Laws' rather than on the 'Word of the Son of God' – that is, who punctiliously observed rules contained in that text rather than operating with a less precisely defined faith; who followed the letter of the law (the *littera*), as Christian accusations were fond of reiterating – it was natural that studying the Text should be of primary importance.

A tradition that by then had lasted for centuries in fact dictated that Jewish men had the duty – the religious duty – to devote themselves to systematic study. In theory at least, in the aim of fulfilling his duty to study, any Jewish male had to have free access to all texts that were, by general consensus, not considered dangerous. The traditional justification for excluding women from studies was based on the idea of the risk they would run if peradventure they entered into an enterprise inappropriate to the lightweight female mind (see T. B. Sabbath 33b; Kiddushin 80b). Jews found a clear formulation of the ethos of individual reading in the synagogue in the opening pages of the Talmud:

> Returning from the fields in the evening, may he enter the synagogue [before going home]; may he who is able to read [the Bible], read; may he who is able to study *mishnah* study mishnah; may he then recite the *Shemà* [Deut. 6:4–9, 11:13–21; Num. 15:37–41, which religious practice dictated must be recited in the morning and the evening] and the evening prayer, and then may he go to eat. (T. B. Berakhoth 4b)

The next codification of the law simply repeated and developed this ancient norm.

The Synagogue as Public Library

If we can use historical developments in the Christian camp to establish a correlation between the relaxation of prohibitions concerning access to texts and the advance of secularization, and if we can read differences between Jews and Christians in this regard from a similar viewpoint, we can now return to the more general topic of reading. From the moment of the earliest discernible movement from orality toward writing around the year 1000, the practice of individual reading in the synagogues of the medieval West seems strikingly modern in comparison to Christian practice. The medieval synagogue was nothing like the Christian church. I have written elsewhere about synagogues in Italy, where I indicated typical characteristics that, in my opinion, are universally valid (*mutatis mutandis*, of course) for all groups that stood apart from the majority in the realm of religion.[53] Although the age was imbued with the religious, secular elements are clearly perceptible. In the Middle Ages the synagogue functioned not only as a place of prayer, but also as a genuine 'social centre' for Jews. This means that, among other things, it functioned as a public library. We find collections of books stored within the confines of the synagogue for the purpose of cultivating an ethos rooted in some of the most basic, most persistent elements of Jewish cultural ideology. These included the responsibility of group members for one another, the organization of the community as a corporate institution based on a juridical vision of society,[54] and, of course, the idea of study as a religious obligation for both the individual and the group. Admittedly, these notions are still nothing like modern ideas about public reading as a way to influence society and the state, about the institutional definition of the state's or society's responsibility to administer libraries available to the public, about the library understood as public property and so on.[55] None the less, we have already arrived at a point where private management of a collection of books merged with the public institutions of society, which means that the idea of the public library emerged among the Jews long before it arose among Christians. Given the Jews' limited ability to wield public power, we can probably interpret access to collections of books as a particular instance of a more general enlargement of the scope of private initiative and as an example of the Jewish community's conception of itself as a corporate society, in the sense that it worked to neutralize status (a basic force in medieval society) in favour of the more typically modern idea of contractuality.[56] The ideology of collective (even tribal) responsibility lay behind the notion that privately owned books should be put at the disposition of others in order to encourage the practice of individual study, which was primarily the practice of reading.

In the area of Mediterranean culture at the turn of the eleventh century, for example, a *responsum* of Rabbi Gershom, known as 'Light of the Exile' (*Me'or Ha-Golah*; 960–*c*.1028), states axiomatically: 'Books are not made to be stored away, but rather to be lent.' The question that elicited this response concerned the case of books left as security for a loan that were found to be worn when the loan was repaid and the books were returned. The borrower demanded an indemnity, but the lender claimed that use of the books was implied in the transaction. He states, in fact, 'On that condition I agreed to the loan with those books as a pledge – on the condition of being able to study and teach with them and even to lend them to others.'[57]

Among the rules of the pietists of the Rhine area pertaining to religious morality (*Hassidey Ashkenaz*, twelfth–thirteenth centuries), there is an entire section of some sixty paragraphs that discusses books: how to keep them 'in a fine and decorous ark', how to avoid damaging them, and so forth. These precepts reflect an evolution in sensitivity regarding the book. It is of course still seen as an object to be treated with great respect because it contains the divine message, but by now there is the added argument that it is an extremely costly object not within everyone's means. At the same time, however, these precepts reflect the awareness of a need to remedy that difficulty and open up access to books to everyone. They even include *exempla* of pious people who make their own books available to others.[58] Some documents (admittedly, very few, and those few still await prosopographic and sociological studies) tell us that individuals not only bequeathed their own books to the synagogues,[59] but also left them there on deposit as a permanent loan – that is, they made them available to the public, but retained ownership of them. In this manner, for example, one Italian Jew listed on a blank page of a manuscript bearing the date 1433 the books that his uncle, Isaac of Tivoli, owned and had left on deposit at the local synagogue.[60] Isaiah Sonne, in a study of an inventory of the books of the heirs of a certain Leon ben Joab (redacted in Cesena in 1445), was the first to see this sort of book collection as a 'public library in Renaissance style'. Sonne compares this collection to the one that Domenico Malatesta founded not long after (in 1452) in imitation of Cosimo de' Medici's collection (1441), the one that is generally acknowledged as being the first of its kind.[61] The singularity of this particular model of books not given to the synagogue but simply deposited there can perhaps be explained by the great instability of Jewish settlements and their consequent mobility. Book owners saw books as one form of investment,[62] and they evidently wanted to make sure that their act of generosity would not prevent them from profiting from their own books should they move elsewhere. It may have entered into their calculations that books were excluded from taxable wealth, as several sources attest.[63]

As is obvious, all these practices were reflections of a paternalistic conception of both society and education: it was the wealthiest, hence the most powerful, people who decided what would be made available for public use. In their capacity as the financial backers of the community, the powerful were *magna pars* in the formation of the collective mentality of the synagogue, which was the institution that best spoke for the establishment. They were not its absolute masters, however. Fairly early on, the Jewish communities set up a quite special system of mixed taxation in which the poor were exempt from having to contribute to the payment of public expenses, but unless they were dependent on charity, they participated in the administration of the synagogue. This meant that the synagogue was much more democratic than other public institutions. Private initiative was channelled into the public institution in an atmosphere of almost democratic (albeit *sui generis*) consensus. Hence the wealthy members of the synagogue who deposited their books there were not absolute masters of the field of reading, in the sense that they could not promote dissent from the general consensus in the same way that well-funded persons or groups who want to encourage sociocultural or political opposition can do today. Given that the collections of books in the synagogues represented consensus, we can regard them as representative of collective attitudes towards preferred reading matter. Studied in this light, such collections undoubtedly would reflect differences among the various cultural areas – as, for example, between Jews who lived in German lands (Ashkenazim) and Jews of the Spanish or Italian tradition (Sephardim).[64]

A systematic serial study of medieval inventories of Hebrew books has yet to be made, but some interesting general characteristics emerge from the work that has been done so far.[65] On the list of the books that Leon ben Joab of Cesena left to the synagogue, for example, we might be surprised to find a copy of *The King's Son and the Monk*, a work of secular (though moralizing) literature, which was bound with a treatise of the *Mishnah*, *Avoth*, with a commentary by Maimonides. Moreover, along with the doctrinal texts (normative, ethical and exegetic works for the most part) that take up most space in the inventory, we also find grammar textbooks. In other words, this synagogue collection had a decidedly secular component. The very small number of documents containing inventories of this sort makes it impossible to draw any conclusions as to typical contents. I might add, however, that our impression of a mix of the sacred and the secular is stronger in the listings of private collections, which are clearly in the majority. The range of books in the Jewish community cannot have differed greatly from Christian book collections, which have been studied in a number of histories of *mentalités* and in Philippe Ariès's analyses of the customs of the most Christian King Francis I and Marguérite de Navarre.[66] The same mix is amply confirmed in the literary production of the age.[67] The fact that private collections seem singularly similar to public ones that we know of suggests that we might venture the cautious hypothesis (as yet unconfirmed) that on the whole the contents of the Hebrew book collections made available to readers reflected a more general trend toward secularization. Be that as it may, we can learn something much more important from an examination of the works on such lists: in the Jewish collections, both public and private, the dividing line between the sacred and the profane is linguistic, rather than based on content. The works in Hebrew include a broad range of works, some of them downright 'scandalous' if viewed from a puritan standpoint or in relation to their context, but there are almost no texts in Latin or in the vernacular in this sampling of what the Jews read.

Holy Language, Vernacular Languages

Ascertaining the literacy of Jews in the Middle Ages is not a matter of determining how many people could take a written text and transform it into oral spoken expression, or of asking how many people could write the letters of the alphabet. At least from the eleventh century on, Judaic society can be considered to have been highly literate in the strict sense. Even Jewish women were able to read a prayer formulary and to follow the written text of the liturgy and the Bible readings in the synagogue. Reading mechanically is one thing, however, and comprehending the meaning of what one reads is quite another. Given that the Hebrew in which most of the 'internal' texts were written was not the language of the Jews' daily speech, it is highly likely that degrees of literacy in Jewish society operated differently from among Christians. With the increased circulation of works in the vernacular, especially in the print age, a rising literacy rate among Christians reduced the distance between texts and society. Among the Jews the opposite was true: Hebrew literacy made no revolutionary strides, but the situation was radically different regarding vernacular languages. Although analysis of this phenomenon is in its infancy, its broad lines seem clear. I have made a beginning in this direction with a study of Italy in the baroque age.[68]

For a more complete grasp of the significance of the changes initiated by the Jews in the sixteenth century, we should recall that the exclusive use of Hebrew as the language of literary production among the Jews of the Christian West was in striking contrast to Muslim areas, where Arabic, often written in Hebrew characters and enriched with Judaic terms and idioms, was universally adopted as a legitimate means of literary expression, even for doctrinal or religious works.[69] The almost total absence of works in the Latin language in Western Hebraic book production can probably be attributed to the fact that in the Middle Ages Latin was the language used almost exclusively for intellectual communication among lettered Christians, the majority of whom were churchmen.[70] One might logically conclude that from the Jewish point of view Latin had a greater negative charge than Arabic, which could even seem neutral in comparison. If this is true, then the language of literary expression functioned as a genuine cultural barrier between Jews and Christians in Christian lands. Moreover, in the period in which Latin was the privileged language of literary expression, the vernacular was generally thought to be inferior to it. Jews and Christians were in complete agreement on that point. Both groups relegated the vernacular to the realm of 'inferior' activities. The vernacular was the language of daily, hence secular, discourse; it was the language of communication with non-Jews and was considered culturally inferior because it was Christian; it was the language of women, whose gender defined them as inferior. Even at this late date, women were only extremely rarely capable of understanding anything but a very elementary text in Hebrew, and when their comprehension was greater, they were considered extraordinary. It is telling that until a relatively late date Jewish books destined for female readers were in the vernacular,[71] but were written in Hebrew characters,[72] a clear reminder of the distinction between literacy and genuine (not mechanical, not ritual) reading. It is probable that as the vernacular came to bear a less negative charge, reading (and later production) in the vernacular tended to be seen as more legitimate among both Jews and Christians; at the same time Jews tended to do without the mediation of Hebrew. That process was probably accelerated by a more general change in people's attitudes toward writing (from the sixteenth century on where print was concerned) and by the gradual transformation of Latin into an increasingly neutral lingua franca of science. Increasing numbers of Jews felt authorized to read in both the vernacular and in Latin, even when the contents of a work might pose problems from the viewpoint of religious belief. In short, the changed attitude toward Hebrew can be interpreted in terms of a weaker perception of language as a social and religious barrier, which was in turn part of a more general process of secularization following the spread of printing and the rise of nationalism. From the standpoint of reading, that process was undeniably an 'opening' to non-Hebrew texts. Henceforth, Hebrew became an esoteric language, accessible to the few 'elect', most of whom were 'adepts' of religious culture, rabbis and teachers of Judaism. Hebrew was increasingly a 'holy language' or, more accurately, a 'sacred' language. At the same time, thanks to a more widespread literacy, the vernacular became the true language of access to knowledge in general. It was the language of social and cultural communication with both Jews and non-Jews, a language common to both men and women (or at least to literate women), and the language of secularism.

Mutatis mutandis, this was true throughout the Christian West, in much of which the Jewish population was slowly growing, thanks in part to *conversos* returned to Judaism and eager to learn more about their heritage by reading texts in both the vernacular and Latin.[73]

Something similar occurred in Eastern Europe, but for different reasons. Without going into excessive detail, we can state that the region's particular socio-economic situation played an important role, given that a large number of Jews 'returned to the land', forming a peasant society in which the literacy rate was noticeably lower.[74] Where the Jews of Eastern Europe are concerned, we can attribute the medieval 'closing' of texts to that shrinkage. A radical improvement in the ability of the Jewish general public of that region to read texts in the vernacular came only in very recent times (a topic that exceeds the limits of the present study). This means that while a radical separation was being set up between Jewish and non-Jewish culture in Eastern Europe, the gap (analogous to the one that occurred in Western Europe for different reasons) between the text in Hebrew and the majority of readers broadened. This trend was accompanied by another gap (also reflected in Western Europe) between ordinary readers and the few who were capable of mastering Hebrew texts. Hence the most noteworthy difference between manifestations of Jewish and Christian mentalities as the Middle Ages moved into early modern times was the marked presence of a conservative 'medieval' component within Jewish cultural space, which strongly contrasted with the various forms of modernizing 'openings' (however these occurred or were understood) in the Christian sphere.

Reading as Religious Ritual: Persistence of Medieval Modes

The persistence of a medieval component in Jewish thought had a variety of outcomes, some of which are as yet imperfectly known. The more notable of these none the less deserve mention. First, Jews were strongly encouraged to practice reading as a religious ritual. This has an obvious parallel in a similar phenomenon in all medieval societies characterized by high rates of illiteracy and in which texts were assigned an almost magical value, with the difference, however, that in the transition to the early modern age 'illiteracy' among Jews was restricted to Hebrew, the dominant language of the realm of the sacred. Practices of the sort included the custom of reading texts of 'traditional wisdom' ritualistically without attaching any great importance to comprehending their contents, and in fact demonstrating a preference for somewhat incomprehensible, esoteric texts, the *Zohar* in particular. Recent anthropological studies of similar activities, systematically observed within contemporary 'Eastern' communities, help to elucidate the major traits of such practices.[75] In such communities the reader usually reads aloud text units defined without reference to their content, often chanting them in singsong. One nearly universal custom, for example, is to read passages from the *Mishnah* for the intention of the souls of the dead whose only connection is that the first letter of the paragraphs that are read form an acrostic of the names of the deceased. An even more telling custom applies to ritual readings of the *Zohar*, for which booklets of the various readings are often printed with each passage ending or beginning abruptly in the middle of a sentence. This is an extreme case of the magical nature of both the ritual and the book used specifically for ritual purposes. Some who participated in rites of the sort in fact attributed metaphysical qualities to the *Zohar*, which was thought to cure illnesses, offer help in delicate sentimental situations, make barren women fertile, and even hasten Messianic redemption. Customs of ritual reading of the sort are attested as early as the twelfth century,[76] but they became truly widespread only in the second half of the sixteenth century, thanks in particular to the many confraternities dedicated to promoting various socio-religious activities. The magical quality of these readings made them appropriate for use especially (but not exclusively) on occasions connected with rites of passage, as prayers for the souls of the dead, during vigils preceding circumcisions, and on at least three of the feasts connected with the changing seasons: 15 Shebat, Shabuoth (the night of the Jewish Pentecost) and the night of Hosha'ana rabbah (the last day of the Feast of Tabernacles).

The persistence of medieval methods of teaching and study in the Talmudic academies, the *yeshivot*, was another noteworthy trait of reading in the Jewish communities. Space does not permit a detailed discussion of these methods, but they included an emphasis on memorizing the text of the Talmud, the practice of having two students work together in oral dialogue, and on a ritualized, musical style of reading following the ancient Talmudic tradition,[77] all of which merit an anthropological study of their own and testify to an extraordinary persistence of orality in the sphere of Jewish culture.

One special aspect of the persistence of orality is probably the Jews' refusal to use print in the specific realm of normative ritual, a refusal that goes along with an extraordinary lag in their adoption of print for all documents involving social relations that have a ritual connotation. As a general rule, the stronger the ritual component in any particular practice, the greater the resistance to the introduction of print in place of writing by hand. The use of print for acts of divorce is considered unthinkable to this day: such documents must be written not only by hand, but with a pedantic respect for detailed rules that has often been ridiculed in literature. The same might be said of the *Meghilloth* (the plural of *Meghillah*) used for the ritual reading of the Book of Esther on the Feast of Purim. I might add that although these writings still conform to medieval practice, the *Meghilloth* (one might say, paradoxically) can be illustrated with miniatures, something that is absolutely forbidden in the scrolls used for ritual reading of the Torah. The only known attempt to use print for such documents comes from sixteenth-century Italy; it proved a miserable failure.[78] Indeed, in today's synagogues the custom of reading from parchment scrolls has spread to ritual reading of the other four books. The use of parchment is not prescribed, but from time immemorial it has been customary on the three principal feasts and the fast of 9 Av commemorating the destruction of the first and second Temples (the readings are the Song of Songs at Passover, the Book of Ruth at Pentecost, Ecclesiastes on Succoth, and the Lamentations of Jeremiah on 9 Av). On the same order of ideas is the use (until recent times) of manuscript texts, often richly illustrated, of the Passover *Haggadoth*. It is interesting that only in the nineteenth century was printing used for *ketubboth* (the plural of *ketubbah*, a marriage contract listing the husband's duties toward his wife), and that the Eastern communities, which were cut off from Western Christendom, had printed *ketubboth* long before the European communities. It is even more interesting that the *ketubbah*, like the analogous marriage certificates of seventeenth- and eighteenth-century France, was the *locus naturalis* for early print pieces.[79] The Jews' negative attitude toward print is confirmed by the connection, established in recent times, between the culture of the manuscript and a perception of Jewish otherness, a view perfectly in tune with the persistence of medieval traits in Jewish culture.

Individual Reading: The Organization of Graphic Space

Did Jews read differently from Christians? And if so, how was their reading 'different', and to what degree? Investigations of reading in the Christian world suggest several paths to follow.

First, the book should be studied as a 'constellation of signs' capable of eliciting a specific response from the reader. In other words, we need to study the various uses of graphic space (and, after the introduction of printing, typographical space) in order to identify the various invitations that those signs and images extended to potential readers.[80] A first superficial glance seems to reinforce the general impression that in Jewish book production, the distribution of graphic space and the graphic and ornamental elements that were used reflect a mental baggage much like that of the Jews' Christian neighbours. One fairly recent study of writing has convincingly shown that this similarity was not unique to the West, but was a constant everywhere over the long term, beginning in antiquity. To remain in the field of reading and writing, there was an extraordinary visual similarity between medieval Hebrew writing and some forms of Christian writing – Gothic script, for instance; between the ways both groups laid out and decorated the page and used initial letters, and in how they used micrography in ways combining ornamentation and content,[81] between the round cursive hand typical of the Italian Renaissance and the Hebrew cursive of the same age; between the ways Christians and Jews handled the page layout of incunables and sixteenth-century print books, and in many other details that it would be superfluous to recall. If we investigate further along these lines, we can see among the Jews a gradual separation of the visual aspects of the message from its contents that is homologous to the increasingly radical distance between orality and writing in the Christian camp. That trend is evident, for example, in the gradual abandonment of micrography as an ornamental element in printing. Whereas before the age of print micrography was a standard procedure in the *Massorah*, in the *editio princeps* of the Bible with *Massorah* printed by the Bomberg firm in Venice (1517–22), the latter's text in a small typeface is still printed surrounding the biblical text, but there is no other graphic decoration. This represents a transitional stage between the medieval practice of decorative micrography arranged in fanciful shapes and the later practice of giving the *Massorah* that accompanied the text at the foot of the page like any normal critical and exegetical apparatus. A similar separation gradually came to be made between the reading matter, which was structured as a monolithic whole on the 'sacred page', using the page layout to emphasize its central importance, and an authoritative exegesis given in a few privileged comments. In the early sixteenth century, in fact, biblical commentaries began to be printed separately – that is, without giving the corresponding biblical text at the centre of the page.

Jewish practice regarding typographical space reflects the duality that we have seen on the linguistic level. One aspect of Jewish otherness was an unwavering persistence of medieval models pointing towards a reversal of the structure that had been typical of a preceding age marked, as we have seen, by a precocious 'modernity'. To put it differently, Jewish otherness is reflected in the persistence of the medieval model concerning the relationship between the page layout and the importance of the text. Not only did the first printers structure the page in certain classic works of Jewish culture in ways that returned to models current in medieval practice, but also (and this is more important) that same structure was, as it were, frozen from that time on. The model of the *editiones principes* of the Bible, the Talmud, and the Codes of Maimonides and Jacob ben Asher (*Turim*) with commentaries remained fixed in Jewish typographical practice from that day to our own. Moreover, the small-format pocket-book in the vernacular that proved so highly successful elsewhere for literature of entertainment was less popular in the Jewish camp.[82] Book production continued to be dominated by folio and quarto formats, books to be read at a lectern, preferably with the reader standing as a mark of deference toward the authority inherent in the text and as symbolic of the act of *lectura* as a transmission of knowledge from the lector to the listeners. The most common medieval model for a lectern (which functioned not only to support a book for reading but also to house a small number of books, often all the household possessed) persists as a typical item of furniture in today's *yeshivot* and in the houses of Orthodox old-fashioned scholars and their modern imitators. It is called a 'stander', a term vaguely reminiscent of the custom of standing for *lectura*. The custom was not universal, however, even in the Middle Ages and even less in the age of humanism, at least to judge from the many miniatures that show readers seated before a reading stand.[83]

The Iconography of Reading

The mention of miniatures invites us to look further at the practice of reading as it is represented in art and in literature, in pictures and illustrations of all sorts, in autobiographies, memoirs and collections of folklore and in various kinds of indirect evidence.[84] Even without taking into account the problems of interpretation involved in this sort of documentation,[85] there is very little of it. Few Jews wrote autobiographies or memoirs in the periods we are examining;[86] pictorial documentation is practically non-existent; and what little illustrative documentation there is (miniatures, illustrations in printed books) is very limited in scope. None the less, something can be gleaned. As with the book as an object, readers' descriptions give an idea, faint though it may be, of evolving attitudes that can be correlated with the socio-economic changes taking place as Western Europe moved from the Middle Ages into the early modern period. As time passed, for example, we can sense a gradual increase in book circulation, especially among women, that corresponded to an increased emphasis on the individual as medieval society shifted in the direction of the more 'bourgeois' society that followed.

We might cite as iconographic evidence of the custom in Spain of reading the Passover *Haggadah* in the synagogue an image in an illuminated Spanish codex of the fourteenth century.[87] This miniature shows some of the stereotypical motifs of the medieval concept of the social significance of 'literacy': for example, it translates the 'high to low' relationship of the officiant/reader to the listeners, who are incapable of reading the text of the ritual, into a 'high/low' spiritual relationship. The implications of this should be obvious.[88] We must admit, however, that no matter how seductive that interpretation of this image might be, or how seemingly universal its acceptance, it presents some difficulties. For one thing, the phrase that accompanies the image does not refer to a synagogue, or to a congregation listening to an officiating rabbi, but rather to a home, where a *pater familias* reads to the members of his household. For another, two of the listeners hold a book in their hands, implying that they are able to read. One of these is clearly a man, given that he is pictured with a long beard. The other seems to be a child: he is much shorter than all the other participants; his clothing is bright red, whereas none of the adults wear that colour; he is clearly placed between the spaces occupied by men and women, none of whom is holding a book. The fact that no woman is pictured with a book may perhaps permit us to compare this miniature with others of the same type and discern a certain progress in the presence of the book, hence in the reading capacity of the public at large, without distinction of gender. This may indicate the feeble beginning of a substitution, on the level of literature, of the opposition literate/illiterate for the opposition men/women. Indeed, in one Spanish miniature datable to around 1350–60,[89] only some of the participants in the *Haggadah* ritual have a book before them, but it is impossible to draw a distinction between men and women as potential readers. What is clear here, however, is a differentiation of the space of those with a book and those without, among them one man with a long beard. The same might be said of a miniature from mid-fifteenth-century Germany.[90] In this example as well, only some of the participants in the *Haggadah* ritual have a book before them, and there is no discernible difference between men and women as readers. Here, however, no distinction is made between the space of the literate and that of the illiterate. On the other hand, in one view of the inside of an Italian synagogue (*c.*1460–70)[91] all the people at prayer have a prayer formulary open before them.[92] Finally, two images of the *Haggadah* ritual from the Rhine region, dating from the second quarter of the fifteenth century,[93] show all those in attendance holding a formulary in their hands.

The Spaces of Reading

The diffusion of the vernacular and the transformation of Hebrew into a sacred language are in part confirmed by the inventories of books owned by private individuals. Italy offers a particularly good opportunity to examine such lists, thanks to exceptionally good documentation. In the case of Mantua, lists are even available of all the books owned by the members of one entire community at the turn of the seventeenth century.[94] These lists were submitted to the Inquisition as proof that their owners possessed no forbidden books. Although we obviously cannot draw any conclusions regarding books that do not figure on these lists, especially if they were likely to have been considered suspect, we can probably take some of the data derived from this singular documentation to be reliable. Two things seem particularly telling: first, nearly all the titles still fall under the category of 'religious' literature (Bibles, biblical commentaries, works on the law, prayer books and so forth). These texts are in Hebrew; thus by their very nature they were circumscribed for use within the community. Second, works of 'secular' literature are present only in very limited quantities, generally in Hebrew translation. There are very few titles in Italian, but what is more significant is that at this date, there are those few, which is a visible sign that a radical transformation was at work. As we have seen, and as I have tried to show elsewhere,[95] that transformation was completed in only a few generations. In my opinion, serial analysis of the inventories of the books owned by Mantuan Jews reflects a tendency to transform an opposition between languages (Latin and the vernacular) into an opposition between the sacred and the profane – that is, to replace a distinction between internal and external space with a separation between the secular and the religious that assigns the internal space to Judaic religious practice.

If I am right, this trend should be seen as complementary to the early stages of the nascent replacement, within the closed space of the Jewish community and on the plane of reading, of the men/women opposition with a contrast between the literate and the illiterate. That process should in turn be correlated with the analogous revival of a distinction between secular and religious space in Christian practices in the preceding century, thus suggesting that the relation between female and male space be reassessed accordingly.[96] What we know to date provides us with disconnected impressions and suggestions for future research, rather than solid results based on study. Still, it seems to have been a relatively modern development, concentrated above all in the West,[97] to associate an internal, sacred and profoundly Hebraic space with an idealized image of the Jewish woman, mistress of that internal space and priestess of the home,[98] and to connect a lay, secular, external space with the equally idealized image of the Jewish man, who alone was exposed to the dangers of contact with the outside world. Once again, the Jews' mental baggage proves to have resembled that of both churchmen and Christians in general during this acute phase of secularization in the early modern world. The differences between men and women in representations of reading among Christians in the early modern age should, in my opinion, be seen in similar terms.[99] There is an important difference, however: the relationship between the ideas of strength and weakness, which are immediately associated with gender difference, takes on a particular and much more ambivalent nuance among Jews, because to assign defence of the values of religion and morality to the 'weak' woman, enclosed within the defended space of the house, meant entrusting her with the defence of Jewish otherness! In other words, once again two 'weaknesses' (that of the Jew and that of the woman) combined to become a strength and a power of resistance.

From the standpoint of reading, that dual role signifies, in the final analysis, a fundamental association between medieval qualities and internal space that provides a concrete symptom of a more general connection between medievalness and specifically Jewish culture in the early modern age.[100] This characteristic also connects Judaism in Western and Eastern Europe (where medieval traits strongly persisted) in a framework of a continuity determined by the socio-economic and cultural evolution of the region.

Orality and Writing: The Need for Mediation

The impression of a *sui generis* medievalness in the Jewish communities of Western Europe is not only confirmed but reinforced north of the Alps. A recent study of print editions of the Bible in Yiddish has clearly demonstrated the persistence, well into the nineteenth century, of methods of elementary education founded on mechanical reading of the Bible in Hebrew, accompanied by Yiddish versions that were in fact paraphrastic and exegetical works mingling edification with legend and folklore. We can even identify several successive stages in the gradual abandonment of orality and the consignment of its complex of traditions and translations to writing (that is, to print) by referring to the dissemination of vernacular 'calque' translations nearly impossible to comprehend without continual reference to the Hebrew text they gloss. We can also sense that scholars became increasingly dissatisfied with such works, a dissatisfaction that eventually led to permanently abandoning the genre and to the 'revolutionary' work of Moses Mendelssohn and his group.[101] The various phases of the 'conquest' of mediation between the obscure biblical text and the current system of cultural references (*teitch, hibber, zusatz*) bring to mind the conquest of biblical exegesis by both Christian and Jewish scholars in the twelfth century (*sensus, littera, sententia*).[102] In reality, within the milieu roughly defined by the use of Yiddish a sense of the persistence of medievalness is a good deal more strongly marked than it might seem from this fortuitous phenomenological analogy. It is clearly reflected in the memoirs of Glückel of Hameln (1646–1724), a document that seems more unique than rare.[103]

Glückel was a 'literate' woman, in the sense that she knew how to read and write. However, close analysis of her journal shows beyond a shadow of a doubt that she read only Yiddish, for the most part moralizing and edifying literature. She did not read the Bible in the Hebrew text, because she was obviously unable to do so, which means that she knew the Bible stories only indirectly, through a mix of 'oral' literature (for example, from sermons preached in the synagogue) and the sorts of literature she could read. In her case mediation took place without any direct contact with a vernacular Pentateuch of the sort discussed above. Because she was a woman, Glückel had not received an elementary formal education of the sort imparted to males, who were the prime audience for those vernacular versions. Nor did she read the vernacular 'calque' translations of the Bible, which means that every time she speaks of a Bible story she makes mistakes typical of oral transmission (times are contracted, persons with like names are confused, etc.). On occasion she grafts on to biblical or Talmudic stories anecdotes that she has picked up somewhere: we can plausibly conjecture that she memorized them, copied them letter by letter from a book open before her as she wrote, or noted them down as someone translated them for her from Hebrew. In her case orality and writing are so intertwined that it is difficult to separate them. The moralizing literature that made up the better part of the corpus of Glückel's reading matter is constantly reflected in her choice of words, her style, and the stereotyped and highly artificial phrases that she affects. She is well aware that she 'talks like a printed book', something that at times displeases her and for which she makes excuses. In Glückel's case the usual differences between the male world and the female world are quite muted: in spite of the obviously large cultural gap separating her from literate men, and in spite of the equally obvious gap in the cultural potential granted to men but denied to women, in practice there is little difference between her skills and those of a great many men; in fact, she is even culturally superior to many of them.[104] As a cultural phenomenon, Glückel and women like her display several traits characteristic of the persistence of medieval modes: memorization as one of the basic mechanisms for acquiring knowledge, a stereotyped repertory of expressions, and a complex dialectic between writing and orality.[105]

The Doubling of Fields of Reading

For questions such as whether readers read silently or aloud as Western Europe moved into the early modern period, whether they read alone or in company around the hearth,[106] and whether they went from a reverential, intensive form of reading to more extensive, nonchalant modes[107] the situation is a good deal more complex among the Jews than among their Christian neighbours. Where reading is concerned, that greater complexity reflects contradictory trends implicit in a growing differentiation between the public sphere and the private one, which split reading into two fields. A secular sort of reading among the Jews cannot be assigned to the private sphere; nor can we trace in it a corresponding tendency among reading practices to turn inward narcissistically (a trend in which one scholar even sees implications of play[108]). We see no echo of the growth of a middle-class mentality in society, or the diffusion, typical of the West, of the concept of reading as an end in itself, of a search for simple pleasure rather than spiritual edification, or even of reading for purposes of study, devotion and prayer. The generically medieval component of the internal space that defined Jewish otherness slowed – even annulled – tendencies typical of the reading practices of society at large in the early modern age. In other words, a duality in the field of reading seems to have been a basic, structural characteristic of the Jewish community.

Hence texts of classical literature, history and geography were not a part of that internal space, and in fact did not appear in Hebrew until the fourteenth century. With even greater reason, nor were romances, entertainment literature, works of practical information, or newspapers and periodicals centred on current affairs. None of these appeared in Hebrew before that time. All such 'amenities' (what we might call 'real' reading matter, similar in every way to what Christians read) were part of external space, secular space. Even today, some more 'orthodox' milieus consider them ritually forbidden. The proliferation of books, with its attendant desacralization, had no place in the internal space of the Jews.[109] In a certain sense this definition of internal space contradicts the female qualities generally associated with pleasurable introspection. It seems to me, however, that the same contradiction existed in the Christian camp, where there was also a sacred space within the home associated with the woman and a secular space that was associated with the man.[110] The function of the woman as mediator between these two spaces probably deserves investigation: it is a function confirmed by a number of indications, but as yet it has not been studied in depth.[111] A study of the sort would probably throw light on the radical difference between the ways in which female mediation was manifested in Western and Eastern Europe, where, as we have seen, the persistence of medieval traits was continuous and organic.

'Modern medievalness' thus isolated the 'sacred' internal space from the external world even more than it had in the actual Middle Ages. It also maintained a public component within that internal space, translating every instance of reading into an act of ritual study. The text of the Talmud was read in singsong, even in solitude; the Bible and the traditional commentaries on Holy Scripture were read within the family, in particular within the framework of ritual meals; texts of religious edification were read in public in the synagogue – yet another means for emphasizing oral mediation between the authoritative, but often inaccessible, Hebrew text and readers. Above all, a fairly limited number of revered texts were read repeatedly, with the result that large portions of them were committed to memory. One text emblematic of these attitudes toward reading is the so-called *Hok-le-Israel* (law, but also daily ration, for Israel), an immensely popular pot-pourri of traditional commentaries and selected passages from the Mishnah, the Talmud and post-Talmudic literature. This work was organized around commentary on the weekly readings from the Pentateuch, and the week was conveniently divided into seven sections, one for each day, thus fulfilling the religious duty of daily 'study' in the home.[112] Perhaps just as emblematic was the extraordinary success (which continued to a fairly late date, especially in Yiddish culture) of manuals on the art of memory such as the *Lev Arie* of Leon Modena (first edition, Venice 1612, second edition, Vilna 1886).[113] All this was the result of a clearer separation – indeed, a genuine divorce – between the sacred and the secular in the early modern age. Those two areas, which in the preceding age had been perceived as contiguous and in part complementary, were henceforth seen as opposed. That opposition was at times freighted with overtones of alienation, the alienation typical of the Jew in modern times.

7

The Humanist as Reader

Anthony Grafton

On 10 December 1513 Niccolò Machiavelli wrote a letter to his friend Francesco Vettori. In the previous year, when Piero Soderini's government fell and the Medici regained control of Florence, he had lost everything he valued most. He had tried to build a citizen army; it collapsed. He had prized his position in the government; he was sacked. Suspected of conspiracy, he was imprisoned, tortured and ended up on his farm outside Florence. Here he yearned for any sort of political occupation, quarrelled and gossiped with his neighbours – and read. He described the life of his mind to Vettori in unforgettably vivid detail:

> Partitomi del bosco, io me ne vo a una fonte, e di quivi in un mio uccellare. Ho un libro sotto, o Dante á Petrarca, o un di questi poeti minori, come Tibullo, Ovvidio e simili: leggo quelle loro amorose passioni e quelli loro amori, ricordomi de' mia, godomi un pezzo in questo pensiero. Transferiscomi poi in su la strada nell'osteria, parlo con quelli che passono, dimando delle nuove de' paesi loro, intendo varie cose, e noto varii gusti e diverse fantasie d'uomini ... Venuta la sera, mi ritorno in casa, et entro nel mio scrittoio; et in su l'uscio me spoglio quella veste cotidiana, piena di fango e di loto, e mi metto panni reali e curiali; e rivestito condecentemente entro nelle antique corti degli antiqui uomini, dove, da loro ricevuto amorevolmente, mi pasco di quel cibo, che solum è mio, e che io nacqui per lui; dove io non mi vergogno parlare con loro, e domandarli della ragione delle loro azioni; e quelli per loro umanità mi rispondono; e non sento per 4 ore di tempo alcuna noia, sdimentico ogni affanno, non temo la povertà, non mi sbigottisce la morte: tutto mi trasferisco in loro.[1]

Leaving the wood, I go to a spring, and from there to my bird-snare. I have a book with me, either Dante or Petrarca or one of the lesser poets like Tibullus, Ovid, and the like: I read about their amorous passions and about their loves, I remember my own, and I revel for a moment in this thought. I then move on up the road to the inn, I speak with those who pass, and I ask them for news of their area; I learn many things and note the different and diverse tastes and ways of thinking of men. When evening comes, I return to my home, and I go into my study; and on the threshold, I take off my everyday clothes, which are covered with mud and mire, and I put on regal and curial robes; and dressed in a more appropriate manner I enter into the ancient courts of ancient men and am welcomed by them kindly, and there I taste the food that alone is mine, and for which I was born; and there I am not ashamed to speak to them, to ask them the reasons for their actions; and they, in their humanity, answer me; and for four hours I feel no boredom, I dismiss every affliction, I no longer fear poverty nor do I tremble at the thought of death: I become completely part of them.

Books for the Beach and for the Battlefield

Historians have often quoted this letter, because it moves on to describe the composition of Machiavelli's most notorious piece of writing: *Il principe*. But they have not often used it as a document in the history of reading. That seems a pity; for it reveals as graphically as any other the historical and physical diversity of the books that Renaissance humanists read and the emotional diversity of the forms of attention they brought to the act of reading.

Machiavelli describes himself as reading two sorts of book. The first he characterizes so precisely as to leave no doubt at all about its textual or physical character. They are the pocket-sized octavo editions of the classics – classics both of Latin and of the *volgare* – which Aldo Manuzio had begun to issue in the previous decade. These books, printed in an italic type which made it possible to cram whole texts into a few hundred pages in small format, had filled Aldo's customers with enthusiasm, and inspired his trade rivals in Lyons and elsewhere to pay him the ultimate homage of plagiarism.[2] They contained texts with prefaces and sometimes a few illustrations, but offered no commentary. And evidently Machiavelli used them in the simplest of ways, much as we would use the less classical – but equally handy – books that we take to the ocean in the summer: as a portable means of escape from problems of all sorts. They served as a stimulus not for thought but for revery – as entertainments in which the reader could lose himself.

The other sort of book and style of reading Machiavelli describes allegorically. He personifies his authors (and their characters) as great men who deign to speak to him in his study, but does not descend to such small details as their names. From the body of the *Prince* and from other texts, however, we can identify them as the works of Greek and Roman statesmen and generals, whose actions Machiavelli saw as the principal sources and models of practical wisdom for his own time. The authors in question included philosophers like Cicero and perhaps others, but above all the historians: Plutarch, Livy, Tacitus. Their texts Machiavelli read, evidently, not in the handy pocket size in which Aldo printed some of them, but in the larger folios and quartos which filled the shelves of Renaissance scholars' studies. He approached them – as his allegory makes clear – in a spirit entirely different from that in which he read his love poets by the spring. He asked of them not distraction but instruction. He raised specific questions and tried to evoke sharp answers. And he did so with a formality and lucidity, an interest not in ethereal erotic dreams but in practical political action, that his allegory of reading as formal discussion at court vividly evokes.

Two sets of ancient texts, two ways of reading: of the latter, one seems instantly recognizable, the other curiously remote. We find it easy to imagine reading ancient books for relief from present difficulties and stimulation of erotic feeling; harder, presumably, to imagine reading for lessons which can guide a government in its final crisis or explain the failure of an army and a polity. But Machiavelli practised both sorts of reading with no apparent sense of strain or difficulty, and clearly felt able to choose his mode of interpretation as easily as the text he meant to apply it to. Our task is simple to state, if difficult to execute. We must try to place Machiavelli's experience in its wider setting. What other possibilities flanked his on the spectrum of ways of reading that the humanists used? How typical were his choices of texts and methods?

'The unmediated text'

From the 1930s to the 1970s, great European scholars – above all Erwin Panofsky, Hans Baron and Eugenio Garin – taught that the humanists transformed the experience of reading in one uniform and powerful way.[3] Medieval scholars, they explained, had read a canonical set of authorities – Aristotle and his commentators, the legal, medical and theological authorities, the Vulgate Bible, Ovid's *Metamorphoses* and Boethius's *Consolatio philosophiae* – in a uniform way. For all their differences of origin and substance, medieval readers considered these texts the components of a single system. Official interpreters made all of them serve as the basis for the system of argument and instruction

known as scholasticism. They did so, quite simply, by treating the texts
not as the work of individuals who had lived in a particular time and
place but as impersonal bodies of propositions. By decades of hard
work with hammer and chisel, they fashioned a complex Gothic set of
walls and buttresses which preceded, surrounded and supported the
texts: headings, commentaries, separate treatises. This apparatus succeeded in imposing a medieval outlook on the most disparate ancient
texts. From a humanist point of view, however, it embodied and rested
on a systematic error. The commentators had set out not to explain the
text for what it was, but to bring its content up to date. If the *Corpus
Iuris* mentioned *sacerdotes* and *pontifices*, for example, the commentator Accursius assumed that it referred to the presbyters and bishops of
the Christian church he knew, and found in the ancient text the charter
for modern practices.[4] The texts, in short, remained popular, not
because they depicted an ancient world, but because they served the
needs of a modern one. And the very packaging that ensured their
utility also distorted their content. A tight network of assumptions and
instructions, given material form in the system of glosses, bound them
to the existing scholastic system of instruction, rather than to their
historical place and time.

From the start, the humanists set out to rescue the classics from the
crenellated *hortus conculsus* in which the medieval commentaries
imprisoned them. They claimed that the glossators had consistently distorted the original intent of the texts. Petrarch, for example, refused to
go on studying Roman law because he found that his teachers failed
to see or convey the 'history' in the law.[5] He and other humanists tried
to read the original directly. They normally claimed that they ignored
the medieval commentaries, except to make fun of their errors. The
need to penetrate the screen that the old apparatus interposed between
reader and text would remain a commonplace of humanist polemic
down to the sixteenth century. Mutianus Rufus ridiculed the standard
commentary on Boethius's *Consolatio*, then ascribed to Aquinas, for
thinking that Alcibiades must have been a woman. Erasmus lampooned
the even wilder guesses that he found in medieval commentaries on the
Bible: 'they turn trees into four-legged beasts and jewels into fish.'[6]

Once the stone wall of misreading was torn down, Petrarch and his
followers explained, the reader could meet the ancients as they really
were: not atemporal and ahistorical *auctoritates* fitted out for the fifteenth century, but people who had lived in a specific time and place. In
the naked text the ancients came back to life in all their colours and
dimensions, dressed in ancient clothing and inhabiting classical settings,
for all the world like the heroes depicted in a Mantegna fresco. Historians have long taken this rhetoric at face value. They have described the

humanists as reading the classics 'directly', 'as they really were'; as innovators who treated books not as ingredients from which to construct a modern system of ideas, but as a window through which they could converse with the honoured dead. Petrarch, after all, actually wrote letters to the ancients, describing to Virgil his respect for the Latin poet's near-Christian virtue and to Cicero his shock at the great orator's involvement in the sweat and noise of politics. And one corresponds, surely, only with people, not with books.

In fact, however, as Machiavelli's case suggests, the humanists read classical texts in many different ways. One who wished to treat ancient poetry as a pastime could do as Machiavelli did, taking a pocket Ovid out into the country to read about love. But one who wished to treat ancient poetry as the highest branch of philosophy could do that as well, reading a folio Virgil in his study and conversing, mentally, not only with the poet, but also with ten or eleven allegorical and moral and historical commentators, ancient and modern. Hieronymus Muenzer relaxed by reading – of all texts – the *Corpus Hermeticum*: 'I read and reread', he wrote in his copy, 'and refreshed myself with that sweetest of readings.' Isaac Casaubon found the same text infuriating; the book not only did not relax him, but provoked him to a sort of philological assault and battery. He worked through his copy phrase by phrase to show that it could not be authentic.[7] In each case the reader, like Machiavelli, would adopt a particular physical stance and mental attitude, as well as a particular text to apply them too. Any history of this complex and protean enterprise must eschew grand theses and rapid transitions and accept the possibility of paradox and contradiction.

Classicism and the Classics: The Text and its Frame

Machiavelli, as we also saw, described himself not only as interpreting texts, but also as handling books: particular physical objects, which followed specific conventions of format and typography, and which he used in well-defined circumstances. From the 1960s on, scholars have devoted an increasing amount of attention to the physical and aesthetic development of books in early modern Europe. And they have shown that the humanists demanded, produced and consumed new kinds of book, as well as a new canon of texts. For the humanists objected not only philologically to the content of the medieval scholarly book, but also aesthetically to its form.

The *auctoritates* of the medieval scholarly world were produced by the specialized, efficient stationers of the university towns. They divided model copies of the standard texts into *peciae*, segments which scribes could rent one by one and reproduce rapidly and uniformly. The texts thus produced were laid out in two columns and written in a spiky, formal Gothic script. They occupied a relatively small space in the centre of a large page. And they were surrounded, on that page, by a thick hedge of official commentary written in a still smaller, still less inviting script. This was, of course, the very mass of medieval glosses which the humanists so disliked on principle. Such books naturally repelled Renaissance scholars, to whom they seemed a visual as well as an intellectual distortion of their own content.[8]

From the start, the humanists saw Gothic script as the outward and visible sign of Gothic ignorance: ugly, stupid, impenetrable. Petrarch hated 'the tiny and compressed characters' that the scribe himself 'would be unable to decipher, while the reader ends up buying not a book, but blindness along with it'.[9] His disciples and successors set out deliberately to replace the standard forms of writing with more appropriate ones. In the early fifteenth century Coluccio Salutati and Poggio Bracciolini devised a new, rounded, elegant minuscule, which they considered more classical than the Gothic of their own day. Scholars and artists – notably Alberti and Mantegna – learned from Roman inscriptions to draw capital letters in a convincingly symmetrical and grandiose style. Others – above all the scholar Niccolò Niccoli and the scribe Bartolomeo Sanvito – invented an elegant cursive. This could be used for less formal purposes, like the compilation of notebooks, and fitted more text into less space than the standard, straightforward humanist script. These new scripts were gradually taught to other scholars and, with difficulty, to professional scribes (who seemed to Poggio *faex mundi*, 'the excrement of the universe').[10] Eventually they reached canonical form in writing-books and were adopted across Europe.

Humanist manuscripts were produced to fit every need. Vast presentation folios, splendidly illuminated, offered the results of philological research to patrons (the latter were often shown receiving the author's or editor's homage and his book in the first, illuminated initial or on an independent title page with an architectural border). Smaller, less formal books, in which the text covered the whole page, with no commentary to interfere between *auctor* and *lector*, became the core elements in humanist collections. Some private manuscript collections swelled to include several hundred texts in the new style.[11]

Private and public libraries – from the *Studiolo* of Federigo da Montefeltro at Urbino to the Vatican Library, which took its original shape under Nicholas V and Sixtus IV – changed as dramatically as the books themselves. Large, open rooms and small, classical jewel boxes, designed to facilitate study and conversation, lighted by windows, replaced the dark rooms and chained books of the older type. Two of the grandest and most coherent buildings programmes of the sixteenth century – the Piazzetta of Serlio in Venice and the rebuilt Vatican Library of Sixtus V – had public collections of books, splendidly housed, as their centre-pieces.[12] Just as glamorous, if less permanent, was the Florentine garden where the Rucellai circle discussed ancient history and rhetoric, with its busts of ancient writers and its collection of flowers mentioned in classical texts.

Sometimes the encounters between new readers and the newly available texts burst the formal boundaries of traditional learning. Humanist reading took place in settings even more unexpected than Machiavelli's spring. Petrarch never seems more modern than in the celebrated letter on his ascent of Mt Ventoux, in which he described how he carried his pocket-sized copy of Augustine's *Confessions* to the top of Mt Ventoux and consulted it there. The princes of the fifteenth century loved to emphasize the prominent place that books and reading held in their lives. Alfonso of Aragon invited the humanists at his court to hold *ore del libro* – public literary duels in which they competed to explicate and emend the hard passages in the text of Livy.[13] Federigo da Montefeltro like to have himself painted text in hand. In one portrait, attributed to Justus of Ghent, he appears with his son, holding a splendid folio. In another, attributed to Fra' Carnevale, which appears in a fine manuscript of Landino's *Disputationes Camaldulenses*, he looks down at a courtier while grasping a small, portable book. In each case the engagement with literature seems as characteristic of the man as his formidable, beaky profile.[14] Federigo could be swept away by his interest in a specific new book. He confessed to Donato Acciaiuoli that he had kept Acciaiuoli's messenger longer than he should in order to be able to read Acciaiuoli's new commentary on Aristotle's *Politics* immediately.[15] Reading the right books, evidently, was as much a part of the new style of the Renaissance court as hiring the right architects or wearing the right clothing,

As printed books gradually replaced manuscripts, moreover, the new forms of books and new experiences of reading pervaded the world of European learning. The type-faces of learned printers reproduced the scripts of scribes and artists, sometimes detail by detail. The earliest classical texts produced by Sweynheym and Pannartz at Subiaco and Rome and by Koberger in Nuremberg already used a humanistic type-face.[16] The Aldine octavos, at their first appearance in 1501, reproduced a humanist cursive – sometimes identified as that of Sanvito – feature by feature.[17] It became second nature, as E.P. Goldschmidt showed, to assume that classical texts deserved a classical presentation. And even those printers and illustrators whose training did not fully equip them to provide historically accurate illustrations and lettering did their best. The young Dürer, for example, tried to represent a Roman theatre for a Strassburg edition of Terence, only to go wrong and make the actors far too large and the seats far too small because he worked from a sketch which did not indicate the scale of the original.[18]

Perhaps more important, the printed book could infiltrate a still wider range of settings and activities than the manuscript it emulated. One of Aldo Manuzio's early customers, Sigismund Thurzo, wrote from Budapest in 1501 that the new Aldine pocket-books had given him a new lease, if not on life, at least on literature:

> For since my various activities leave me no spare time to spend on the poets and orators in my house, your books – which are so handy that I can use them while walking and even so to speak, while playing the courtier, whenever I find a chance – have become a special delight to me.[19]

The new book, austere and elegant, practical and portable, had become the norm. And Machiavelli's range of contracts, in informal and formal settings, with small and large books, seems typical of his milieu. It was only a step from his experience of reading love poetry in the country to that of the young gallants described by the whores in Aretino's *Ragionamenti*, clustered in the street below a young woman's window, their copies of Petrarch in their hands. To some extent, then, the history of the book suggests that Renaissance humanists really did encounter the classics in a new and dramatically more direct way.

Yet the historians of the book have also qualified the optimism of the historians of ideas in one vital respect. They have shown that the forms in which the humanists took their classics, whether small or large, love poetry or Roman history, manuscript or printed, were anything but classical. In the first place, even the purest humanistic manuscripts and printed books were not the revival of something old, but the invention of something new. Their components included genuinely classical elements applied to new ends, like the epigraphic capitals that came to define titles, headings and lists of contents. But scribes and authors also revived some medieval devices that had gone out of use in recent times. Their formal book hand imitated not an ancient script, since there was no classical minuscule for them to imitate, but the minuscule script of Carolingian manuscripts, as chaste in form as it was unclassical in origin. Modern forms and fashions like italic script and the floral illumination of many first pages made Renaissance books still more attractive. To be sure, the scribes and printers produced texts that *looked* classical to their readers. But, like all classicisms, theirs incorporated the aesthetic assumptions of their own day as well as genuinely antique models and methods. In its final form the humanist's book emerged from complex and difficult negotiations among many parties. *Cartolai*, scribes, artists and scholars all had their say, and the medieval models that remained in partial use exerted their own subtle attraction, pulling scribes' and scholars' pens into what now seem clearly unclassical patterns of punctuation and abbreviation.

In the second place, humanists continued to use many books that were not physically set out in new, chaste form. Petrarch loved his copy of Virgil, now in the Ambrosian Library; he confided to it both his sorrow at Laura's death and the date of their first meeting. But that vast manuscript, as Petrucci has pointed out, was in fact a 'modern' – that is, a medieval – manuscript, with anachronistic illustrations by Simone Martini.[20] And this second medieval form of classical text – literary rather than technical texts in Gothic script, often equipped with illustrations in which the characters wear modern dress, meant for courtly rather than learned readers – had a powerful afterlife in the Renaissance, even as the *auctoritates* of the university were discarded. Some of the purist humanists of Florence disapproved of illustrations; but the courtly readers of Milan and other northern states liked their eloquent Latin ancient histories, classical though the texts were, bedecked with the great illuminated initials of the medieval romance. In the famous example of a north Italian Plutarch now in the British Library, Antony wears the armour of a knight, Sertorius is murdered before a tapestry at a medieval feast, and Pyrrhus meets his death amid the walls and towers of an Italian city.[21]

Even in the heartlands of Renaissance classicism, then, medieval and Renaissance conventions, the desire to bring the ancient world up to date, and the desire to reconstruct it as it was, coexisted. In 1481, Petrucci shows, classical style and classical content met in a copy of Aesop executed for the Aragonese court by Cristoforo Maiorana: 'per lo principio', says the treasury record, 'ha facto con spiritello, animalii et altri lavuri antichi et in la lictera grande sta un homo anticho' – no doubt Aesop himself, dressed *all'antica*.[22] The reader of this Aesop would know from the start that he had made contact with an ancient writer. But the reader of Gherardo di Giovanni's Florentine Aesop of the same period, now in the Spencer Collection of the New York Public Library, would have learned exactly the reverse. He would have seen Aesop portrayed as a modern (and a well-fed one, to boot). And he would have seen Aesop's human and animal characters depicted in the most up-to-date terms, settings and clothing. They moved through a Tuscan landscape, inhabiting Florentine shops and bedrooms, hunting outside the walls of a city dominated by the Duomo. Even a wart-hog sharpens his tusks on a modern rotary grindstone. Only the gods seem ancient – naked, white and equipped with the proper attributes. And even they mingle and speak with Tuscan men and women. The result, as visually satisfying as it is anachronistic, is a spectacularly alluring evocation of an ancient world that hovers near the present and is hardly classical.[23] No wonder, then, that classical schemes of decoration did not always replace medieval ones in specific textual traditions.[24]

Even the most humanistic books now remind us less of antique than of Renaissance canons of taste and elegance. Many Italian bookmen deliberately combined classical and contemporary, humanist and chivalric conventions. And in the many non-Italian environments from Dijon to Cracow where medieval and Renaissance, vernacular and Latin traditions converged like currents of different temperatures in an ocean, all sorts of whirlpools formed. New mixtures of classical and modern, cosmopolitan and vernacular features appeared in the margin of the script or print alike. The magnificent experiments in publication carried out for Maximilian I by Dürer and others – his hieroglyphic *Ehrenpforte*, the *Weisskunig*, the *Theuerdank* and the unfinished *Prayerbook* – offer a spectacular series of cases in point.[25]

Like the interpreters, in short, the bookmen did not experience or present the ancient world as it really was. They re-created it in images that they found coherent and pleasing. No one would claim that their work was insignificant; it amounted, indeed, to an aesthetic revolution in the processing and presentation of literary texts.[26] But it also amounted as much to an imaginative construction of a lost paradise as to a historical re-creation of a lost society. And Machiavelli's two ways of meeting his classics, as little octavo love poets and as grand, austere folio statesmen, in the dreamy peace of the countryside and in the engaged intellectual activity of the *studiolo*, both reflect the economics and aesthetics of Renaissance publishing.

How, then, do we move from the varieties and vagaries of individual experience to the normal conditions of humanist reading? How can we identify what really changed and what remained stable in the world of the book? Only a wide range of complementary investigations can yield the information we seek. We must study the tastes and follow the activities of the middlemen who chose the texts and defined the physical forms of the humanist books that would become most popular.[27] We must enter the schoolroom and listen to the weary chanting of master and schoolboys as they grind their way through set texts. Only thus can we identify the particular hard-won skills with which humanists were trained to approach any classical or classicizing book. Finally, we must follow some individual humanists into their studies and watch them actually using their books. Only thus, in the end, will we come to understand either the physical form in which the humanists embodied the texts that meant most to them or the intellectual tools by which they extracted meanings from them – not to mention the interaction among these. Though we must pay a high price of entry to these scenes from a lost past, we may hope for rich rewards. We may even gain a new understanding of the forces that shaped reading in the last age when European intellectuals saw books as the principal source of facts and ideas.

Meeting the Middlemen: Cartolai, Printers and Readers

Books are not the result of parthenogenesis. Entrepreneurs and merchants hired and instructed the scribes, typesetters and illuminators who produced them. And those who dominated the economics of publishing also had much to do with the identity and physical form of the books that the humanist public read. This simple set of facts – which obviously holds true for the age of printed books – also holds for the age of manuscripts that preceded it. On the other hand, customers also shaped the products they bought – both in the normal sense that the bookmen tried to provide what they wanted and, as we shall see, in a more thoroughgoing sense as well.

Historians have tended to model the transformation of the world of books by printing on the later history of the Industrial Revolution. A craft system of production, in which each book is designed and executed for a single customer, is replaced by an industrial system. Wholesale supersedes retail; uniform mass production replaces the artisanal techniques of the scribes. The book thus becomes the first of many works of art to be altered fundamentally by mechanical reproduction. Its reader now confronts not a warmly personal object whose script, illuminations and binding he has chosen, but a coldly impersonal one whose physical form has been determined in advance by others. The emotional charge the book carries as an object comes from its place in the owner's personal experience, from the memories that it calls up, more than from its own physical character.[28] Some contemporaries, like the *cartolaio* Vespasiano da Bisticci, deplored these developments. He denounced the ugly, short-lived products of the press, which seemed to him unworthy of places in a really great library. Others, like Erasmus, delighted in them. Even Ptolemy Philadelphus, he wrote, could not match the services to learning rendered by Aldo Manuzio. Where the great king had built a single library that was eventually destroyed, Aldo was building a 'library without walls' which could reach any reader and survive any cataclysm. Both sides agreed that printing fundamentally transformed reading; or so, at least, historians have often told us.[29]

This long-accepted story omits a good many vital facts. The stationers, or *cartolai*, of Renaissance Italy, as R. H. Rouse and M. Rouse
have now shown, stood as squarely as the printers would between
ancient authors and modern readers. They shaped the experience of
texts for the vast majority of the reading public.[30] The *cartolai* dominated the production and sale of manuscript books in the early fifteenth
century; after 1450 they often collaborated with, and sometimes
became, printers. Like other late medieval and Renaissance entrepreneurs, they worked on a grand scale. They bought up large supplies of
paper or vellum – normally the most expensive item in book production. They hired scribes and illuminators, and chose the texts the craftsmen worked on. And they often produced multiple copies of individual
works, not because customers had requested them, but in order to stock
their shops for retail sales. True, the *cartolai* did not anticipate the book
fairs of the age of print. In other respects, however, they laid down the
paths that printers would follow. They created books in large quantity
and on speculation. They advertised their wares systematically, and
fought off competition from unregulated outsiders, just as the printers
would.[31] Above all, they worked with their employees and their customers to create a canon of the books that most deserved readers and a
vision of the physical forms these should take.

The Rouses show that the *cartolai* not only chose which texts to
reproduce, but also arranged for many of the illuminations which gave
them their stamp of classicism. The most splendid of these they provided on commission for individuals who had requested them. The
grand architectural frontispieces of the great Renaissance manuscripts
in Urbino and elsewhere, in which authors, scholars and patrons, carefully posed in classical settings, introduce the texts, were specially
ordered. Some of the most creative painters in Italy, like Botticelli, illuminated manuscripts. Other forms of decoration, however, were produced wholesale. The *cartolai* provided dozens of their products with a
'mass-produced, almost assembly-line sort of frontispiece ... *bianchi
girari* frontispieces, comprised of a two-, three- or four-quarter frame
made of intricately interwoven white vinestem, usually with two putti at
the bottom supporting a wreath left blank for a heraldic device'.[32] The
fact that the wreaths or roundels remained blank shows that the decorations were as ready-made as the texts they preceded. The individual
owner would have his arms inserted in these highlighted spaces when he
bought the book. But the general presentation of the book – and the
general appropriateness of the characteristic Renaissance decoration *all'
antica* to high classical texts – were determined by the businessmen who
paid for them, not the readers who consumed them. Obviously, then,
the printers who left space for similar vine-stem decorations in their

mass-produced products – or emulated the *cartolai* by leaving initials to be filled in for each owner by the illuminator – merely made their own the practices of the entrepreneurs of the age of manuscripts – just as they hired the same scribes to decorate the printed books who had once performed that service for manuscripts.[33]

Rich evidence shows that the *cartolai* made conscious choices in these questions of taste. No text reveals more about the attitudes of bookmen than Vespasiano's memoirs, that vivid collection of biographical sketches which helped to inspire Burckhardt's *Civilization of the Renaissance in Italy*. Vespasiano usually figures in histories of the book as a die-hard reactionary, a lover of fine individual books and hater of print. He recalled with pride that Federigo of Montefeltro's library at Urbino consisted entirely of manuscripts: 'In quella libraria i libri tutti sono belli in superlativo grado, tutti iscritti a penna, e non v'è ignuno a stampa, a che se ne sarebbe vergognato.'[34] And he appears as an entrepreneur only in one famous case: that of the library of Cosimo de' Medici, which he produced regardless of expense in only twenty-two months, hiring forty-five scribes to do the work. He seems a nostalgic character, obsessed like a Renaissance Chesterton or Belloc with an imagined past – a clean city made noisy only by the songs of happy artisans doing good work for the love of God.

In fact, however, these versions of Vespasiano rest on a very limited selection of his statements about the world of the book. He painted a picture with much harder edges, a collective portrait of sharp characters operating in a competitive, profit-minded literary market-place, where frequent bulletins identified the level of each writer's stock on the exchange of reputations. He also insisted, still more significantly, that he (and other *cartolai*) could spot a potential bestseller – and that their intervention could be crucial in the career of book and author. Of Sozomeno of Pistoia's reworking of the Chronicle of Eusebius and Jerome, for example, he remarks that after producing a really excellent piece of work, Sozomeno 'non si curava darne copia'. Fortunately, Vespasiano intervened: 'Sollecitato e confortato da me, la dette; e fu di tanta riputazione, che la mandò per tutta Italia, e in Catalogna, e in Spagna, in Francia, in Inghilterra, e in corte di Roma.'[35] Even in the manuscript book trade, it took an intermediary with flair to perform the quintessential act of the gifted publisher: to identify the 'exciting' book whose potential the author or editor himself could not see.

Producing a successful book, moreover, did not only mean choosing a valuable text. Then as now, a book needed a proper apparatus and design to bring out its full potential. Vespasiano mentioned, for example, that the Florentine Francesco di Lapacino had seen the possible interest of a very rich but very difficult text: the *Geography* of Ptolemy, which had been translated into Latin at the beginning of the fifteenth century, but had thereafter been ignored, since 'fu fatto il testo senza la pittura'. The Greek manuscripts, by contrast, were in a spectacular large format, with massive collections of splendid maps. Francesco took care 'di fare la pittura di sua mano', and to give the Latin equivalents of the Greek place names. He thus imposed on Ptolemy's great atlas what became its immensely popular canonical form: 'dal qual ordine sono usciti infiniti volumi che si sono di poi fatti, e ne sono andati infino in Turchia'.[36] Vespasiano knew, in short, that the format and splendour of the maps – rather than the Latin version of the text – gave Ptolemy's text its cachet. This was considerable; Vespasiano's atelier and others made it the chief coffee-table book of the Italian renaissance, as the many surviving luxury manuscripts of it – all quite useless from a scholarly standpoint – show. When Federigo of Montefeltro's young son Guido demonstrated his command of the *Geography*, showing that he could find any two places on the maps and recite the distance between them, he followed a cultural fashion that had begun in a *cartolaio*'s shop.[37] No wonder that the printers soon followed Vespasiano's example, producing edition after edition that matched the manuscripts in size and elaboration – and that still depended, in the famous case of the Ulm editions of 1482 and 1486, on illustrators to colour each map by hand.[38]

The intermediaries, then, helped to shape the experience of reading for all Renaissance intellectuals. And the intermediaries had pronounced preferences. They liked rich materials: Vespasiano showed the Florentines' characteristic expert eye for textures as he lingered over the gold brocade and scarlet cloth bindings of Federigo's books. He even spoke with enthusiasm of the fine 'lettera antica', 'carta di cavretto', illuminations and binding that Matteo Palmieri used for the unique copy of his heretical *Città di Vita*, which he had locked away until his death – a work which was – rightly, so Vespasiano thought – not published in the Renaissance.[39] The editors and printers imitated the *cartolai*; they put out limited editions printed on vellum for connoisseurs, as well as larger ones on paper for the ordinary market, and they hired the most skilled illuminators for special customers. Koberger must have been one of the first to have his own binder, who covered the boards of many copies of the *Nuremberg Chronicle* in vellum. In the mid-seventeenth century, Joan Blaeu offered 'the most expensive book that money could buy', his *Atlas maior*, with plates coloured or uncoloured, and in standard vellum with gilt tooling or a variety of special bindings in purple velvet and other precious fabrics.[40] The owners – who included a Barbary pirate, Admiral Michiel de Ruyter and the Sultan of Turkey – clearly appreciated this bibliographic treasure, as is clear from the splendid cabinets in which some of them housed their copies.

The intermediaries thus conditioned the customers whom they took most seriously to treat books in a certain way. On the one hand, they made clear that the external appearance of a book told a story about its content and its intended public. Just as an intellectual in 1991 brought one set of expectations to the stark white products of Gallimard and another to the elegantly lurid creations of Zone Books, so an intellectual in 1491 or 1511 brought different expectations to a book in humanistic or Gothic script, with or without commentary, in folio or octavo, splendidly illuminated or austerely printed, produced by Vespasiano or by Aldo. Individual writers knew perfectly well that a particular physical form could ensure a market and prepare a reader for what they had written. Erasmus wrote to Aldo, as early as 1507, that an Aldine edition of his translations for Euripides would make him immortal, 'especially if printed in those little characters of yours, which are the most elegant in the world' – 'tuis excusae formulis . . . maxime minutioribus illis omnium nitidissimis'.[41] A century and a half later, Nicolas Heinsius would plead with his printers, the Elzeviers, not to crowd his edition of Ovid into their favourite, and unreadably small, format.[42] Both agreed, heartily, that format and typography mattered.

On the other hand, the *cartolai* and the printers who followed them also supported another range of practices – one far more alien to us than the previous set. They suggested that the properly educated reader would not simply buy a ready-made book and consume it *tel quel*. He would personalize it. In the first place, the educated buyer would normally have his own books bound. As we have seen, splendid or durable binding materials were the covering of choice for good books, and a well-educated reader knew that he must pay for these. Fine binding became a speciality – even an obsession – for Renaissance bookmen. The great collectors, from Federigo of Urbino to de Thou, encouraged the development of new styles of ornament and new methods for stamping these on leather and vellum. They employed famous artists to design intricate traceries for the leather-covered boards that protected their books. Patterns from ancient coins and medals often gave these a classical patina, and the owner's name or initials or motto, which often figured amid the classicizing ornament, identified the patron whose tastes were on display. The great man's book could certainly be told by its cover. And even plain men, paid scholars, considered it tasteless to keep a book in paper wrappers. 'I can't stand to read books unless they're bound' – so Joseph Scaliger commented as he made a rare exception to read a polemic against him and a friend by the Jesuit Serarius. The catalogue of his library, made for its sale by auction on 11 March 1609, confirms his statement. Of the almost 250 books designated as containing his marginal notes, not a single one figures in the section of 'libri incompacti'.[43] The book was thus defined, from its entry into a public or an individual library, as both a precious object and a personal possession – the point at which a cultural and an individual style should intersect.[44]

The cultivated reader, moreover, learned from those who produced his books to adorn their bodies as well as their carapaces. As we have seen, *cartolai* and printers alike assumed that a customer of standing would have his arms inserted in the front of a book. They also assumed that he would wish at least the opening pages of his text to illustrate its content in an appropriate way: with a framework of classical element or vine-leaves, with characters from history, myth or modern times that illuminated its content. The most discerning customers lavished resources on the production of an appropriate visual setting for their texts. When Cardinal Francesco Gonzaga had a Greek and Latin text of the *Iliad* written for him in 1477, the scribe inserted the first page of the Latin into a huge and splendid architectural frame. The top of this, divided into three parts, contained three scenes from the poem separated by pilasters – and thus gave the reader a more vivid foretaste of the pleasures to come than the summary of Book I that also preceded the text could.[45] Sixtus IV's copy of Aristotle's *Historia animalium*, translated into Latin by Theodore Gaza, advertised its contents even more spectacularly. Aristotle, wearing a rich robe and a splendid tall hat, appears at the start of the text. He sits writing at a desk, in front of a curved wall flanked by columns. Before him appear the animals he will describe in the text – including a nude man and woman and a stately unicorn.[46] Even the oldest of manuscripts might need illumination to make them seem really antique. When the canons of the chapter of S. Pietro gave the unique (and famous) ninth-century Orsini manuscript of Plautus to Leo X, they took care to embed the opening of the text in rich classicalizing decorations, which were executed on strips of parchment that were then glued to the first two leaves.[47]

Evidently the patrons learned their lessons well. And the vision of antiquity which they liked to enter – like that of the *cartolai* – had nothing in common with the austere world of white sculptures and noble simplicity that the neo-classicists of a later century would admire. Where antiquity was concerned, too much decoration was barely enough. Rich colours and elaborate textures defined the harmonious cities and Arcadian landscapes that the remainder of the text would evoke by its content. This taste for elaborate opening illustrations – like that for rich bindings – not only survived, but flourished wildly in the age of printing. The printed title page could, of course, offer as elaborate a pictorial stage setting for the text as a drawn one. Drawn or printed book markers – Dürer produced these for his friend Pirckheimer

– could make a book as personal a possession as a coat of arms in the first initial. And sometimes individual readers went still further to impose personal stamp on the start of an ancient book. Thus Willibald Pirckheimer had Dürer illuminate the opening page of his Aldine Theocritus with a spectacular illustration of pastoral life, keyed detail by detail to the text.[48] Patron and artist – like *cartolaio* and craftsman – could shape the impression a text made by designing these elaborate gateways.

Sometime the collaborations between writer, reader and artist became more systematic and intricate. One famous case is Sebastian Brant's edition of Virgil, in which a sequence of illustrations served as the most striking commentary on the text. This seems familiar enough; we still produce and consume illustrated editions of the classics. But other cases have a period flavour. Holbein, for example, adorned an annotated edition of Erasmus's *Praise of Folly* with a series of comic sketches, some literally keyed to the text, others more imaginative. Myconius showed these to Erasmus, and recorded the author's responses to the artist's responses to the text.[49] The book, as Sandra Hindman has shown, thus became not the model for an illustrated edition, but the deposit of a unique effort to capture all the implications, explicit and implicit, literal and unintended, of a notoriously polyphonic text. And other efforts to combine text and pictures, narrative and commentary, also seem to reflect the effort to produce not a model for multiple copies to be sold, but a treasure to be shared with a few particularly discerning friends.[50]

Finally, the *cartolai* and their customers developed what has ever since been the dominant attitude of the rare book trade, but has been forgotten by the retailers of ordinary new books. Sellers and buyers agreed that the transfer of books is a terribly important and valuable activity, a dramatic transaction, cultural as well as financial, which requires almost the same level of taste and knowledge as writing them.[51] Certainly Renaissance readers took the occasions when they acquired their books very seriously. They often recorded in the books the places, dates and circumstances of acquisition. And they expanded these originally short, limited entries into what amounted to partial diaries, writing themselves into the margins and endpapers of the books they had chosen so carefully. Petrarch drew up a list of the books that meant most to him ('libri mei peculiares'); he used many of them as the parts of a diary in which he could vent not only his love for Laura but also more mundane matters, like his irritation at his peasants.[52] The Nuremberg scholar Hieronymus Muenzer, to take a less celebrated case, noted that he had imported one of his medical books from Venice in 1478, another from Bologna in 1490; still another he had bought during his own

Italian journey while studying in Pavia in 1477. Muenzer too moved outside the realm of acquisition into that of unrelated anecdote, as when he recorded in a manuscript that he had met the man who wrote it for the first time 'after 32 years', with great pleasure, on 26 April 1501.[53] The book, bought with such care, dressed with such meticulous attention to detail, became far more than a mere text. It served as a record of one's life, a chart of one's network of literary connections, and a confidant for one's feelings.

The book that a humanist read, whether manuscript or printed, was something both familiar and alien to us. It usually originated in mass production; but it then underwent a metamorphosis and took on individual form, as the owner fused his own vision with that of the entrepreneur who produced it. In the shop, it usually sold for a modest amount, and stood next to other copies of the same work that resembled it closely in content and layout.[54] But in the owner's hands even a printed book often became as rich, strange and valuable as any manuscript. The humanist approached his book, in the first instance, as the Californian teenager of the 1950s approached a car made in Detroit. He bought a product with a specific, vivid look, something that experts had designed to appeal to his tastes and desires. But he redesigned the product as he used it, changing the very look he appreciated, adding unique decorations, customizing the result of mass production. An active, even an artistic form of collaboration between consumer and producer was the norm. This relation between owner and book would persist, in the upper orders of European society, for centuries. It lasted longer, indeed, than has our present relationship, in which we passively accept books in the form imposed on them by the factory. And it was created by extravagantly gifted entrepreneurs, whose names we often forget, as well as by the sympathetic collectors whose calf- and vellum-bound collections still line the shelves of our libraries and museums.

Meeting the Intermediaries:
The Schoolmaster and the Reader

In 1435 Ambrogio Traversari visited Vittorino da Feltre's school near Mantua. He heard the young Gonzaga prince, then fifteen years old, recite 200 Latin verses on the emperor's entrance to Mantua, so well that Traversari 'found it hard to believe that Virgil pronounced book 6 of the *Aeneid* more gracefully before Augustus'.[55] Around the same time, Guarino of Verona wrote a famous letter to his pupil Leonello d'Este: 'Whatever you read,' it begins, have ready a notebook ... in which you can write down whatever you choose and list the materials you have assembled. Then when you decide to review the passages that struck you, you won't have to leaf through a large number of pages. For the notebook will be at hand like a diligent and attentive servant to provide what you need ... Now you may find it too boring or too much of an interruption to copy everything down in such a notebook. If so, some suitable and well-educated boy – many such can be found – should be assigned this task.[56]

These two texts reveal some of the élite learning and professional teaching strategies of the Renaissance – a set of varied and sometimes curious techniques that left a stamp on every educated reader.

Vittorino's young prince recited his text. The humanist had trained him to see ancient literature on the page as the script for an oral performance, one that required a trained memory and enunciation. Throughout the fifteenth and sixteenth centuries, the aural qualities of written texts would continue to be central to the ways that students encountered and adults appreciated them. Young boys like Piero de' Medici boasted of the large quantity of lines they had memorized and could recite.[57] A rarer bird, the educated young woman Alessandra Scala, won warm praise for her ability to recite the lines of Euripides' Electra with what seemed to her audience native Attic charm.[58] And as late as the end of the sixteenth century, great scholars like Justus Lipsius and Joseph Scaliger won astonished praise for their ability to produce classical texts, impeccably pronounced, from memory. Lipsius offered to recite the entire text of Tacitus while a dagger was held to his throat, to be plunged in if he went wrong; Scaliger translated a whole book of Martial into Greek, working from memory, as he lay in bed. The humanist read a text in the first instance, then, for the formal qualities that made its wording memorable. Metre, alliteration, particularly striking combinations of sounds, became the landmarks of a text mapped out aurally rather than visually. The humanist met the text most intimately not as he interpreted the words on paper or vellum, but as he rolled their sounds sensuously between his lips. Petrarch started something important when he fell in love with the sound of Latin as written by Cicero and Virgil.

But the sense of the text also, obviously, had a vital place in its interpretation. To this the student gained access by staged exercises. In the first instance, the teacher would paraphrase the classical document in question, line by line. Prose and verse, philosophy and history, all were ground up and repackaged as dry, if correct, Latin narrative. Only then would the teacher go through the same passages for a second time, more slowly. On this trip he would identify historical individuals and facts, explain myths and doctrines, and reveal the logic of tropes, using the many problems that came up as the pretexts for digression into every imaginable subject. The student thus learned that each text was not only a straightforward story but a complex puzzle, the deeper logic of which the teacher had to unlock with a whole pocketful of skeleton keys.

Classical texts printed for colleges in sixteenth-century France and elsewhere make clear the sequence and relation of these processes. The printers put a metal bar between each two lines of type, producing a thick white space between the printed lines. Here the student could enter the teacher's running Latin summary. The printers also left wide margins, and in these – especially in the earlier portions of their texts – students would record the more detailed, technical comments, usually in a hand so neat as to reveal that they were making fair copies of earlier notes in rougher form. These routines long persisted. When P. D. Huet prepared his series of Latin texts for the dauphin after 1670, he equipped them with both a running paraphrase, or *ordo verborum*, and a more detailed variorum commentary.[59]

The range of practices that the printers codified was hardly new. Neither was the belief which underpinned them – that a text had to be broken up for schoolboys into hundreds of smaller segments, each to be discussed independently. One can find both general precedents and specific sources for the methods of the humanist commentator in the schools of late antique Rome, of Byzantium and of the twelfth-century Latin Renaissance.[60] The basic mental skills that one learned to apply to a classical literary text thus remained basically similar over a period that is almost too long to be called *la longue durée*.

The young reader amassed a great deal of history, mythology and geography as he picked his way across the curriculum texts, twenty lines a day. More important, he developed an attitude, and mastered a set of tools. Michael Baxandall has argued that by identifying perceptual skills that had to be learned with great effort, we can reconstruct a period eye – the way in which identifiable individuals were trained by their culture to see works of art.[61] Similarly, and more directly, we can use the practices of the humanist school to re-create a period style in reading. Hundreds of commentaries converge on certain basic interests and techniques. The young reader learned to understand writers' choices of words and images as instances of the rules of formal rhetoric. He learned to search for allusions, to treat any major text as an echo chamber in which the words before him interfered with and altered the subtexts that the writer had expected to share with his similarly educated readers. All humanist writers expected their readers to be masters of this art of decoding. When Dirck Volckertzoon Coornhert attacked Justus Lipsius for recommending that governments execute contumacious heretics, Lipsius felt deeply injured. To be sure, he had urged the authorities to burn and cut, 'Ure et seca'. But, he pointed out, he had expected his readers to recognize that he was using a phrase from Cicero's *Philippics*, which referred not specifically to the stake, but generally to the need to use serious remedies, like surgery, for serious ills.[62] What made these practices novel, in the Renaissance, was not their content but their audience. The humanists insisted on teaching young laymen to apply them, and claimed that such an education was more appropriate than a scholastic one for young ecclesiastics as well. But these changes have to do with the social history of readers – and education – rather than the history of reading as a cultural form. The actual formal skills with which a schoolboy learned to dissect a text, laying bare its muscles, nerves and bones, were classical ones; and to that extent the methods of humanism were as much a classical revival as the canon of texts they were applied to.

The main technical innovation we can identify came when the student passed from construal and interpretation to the higher task of application – putting the text to use. Guarino's young aristocrat, like those at Vittorino's school, read the classics. But Guarino told him to do far more than pronounce his syllables clearly. He should find another young man, one who was a scholar by necessity rather than by choice, and ask him to digest and process the classical material for re-use. Reading thus became a social rather than a private activity – a game rather like cricket, carried out by collaboration between a gentleman and a player. Often teachers – like Guarino himself – eliminated the intermediaries and provided their own predigested introductions to the classics, which naturally became the core of Renaissance pedagogy.[63]

The young prince, nobleman or cleric did not encounter the ancients by plunging unaided into their books, to sink or swim. Rather, a humanist expert packaged the ancients for him, processing them and transforming them from jagged, unmanageable, sometimes dangerous texts into uniform, easily retrievable, reproducible bits of utterance and information. This form of instruction rendered the ancient texts reliably useful; it also gave the young reader a model he could imitate if he set out to do the same job of processing in later years, when reading on his own. It took place in classrooms across Europe; and by the early sixteenth century some of the most innovative teachers were providing the same sort of guidance in print, creating an imaginary classroom far larger than an individual class could really be. At this point the separate histories of ideas, of the book and of reading converge suggestively.

Consider the *Adages* of Erasmus, that vast collection of proverbs and commentary which reached its canonical, though not its final, form in the Aldine edition of 1508. This book grew from an original short collection of 800-odd Latin sayings, printed in Paris in 1500, to a vast heap of almost 4,000 essays, some long enough to be printed independently, on Greek and Latin aphorisms of the most diverse origins and nature, drawn from the whole range of Greek literature and lexicography. Despite its formidable size, the *Adages* became one of the best-sellers of the northern Renaissance, as the records of publishers and the library lists of the many students who died in sixteenth-century Cambridge both show. Its neatly potted morals taught the learned young many sound lessons in morality and Latinity, all packaged in a compressed and effective form. Readers of the *Adages* could urge a friend who tended to irritate his elders and betters *ne ignem gladio fodias*, 'not to pole the fire with a sword'; they could encourage a friend dissatisfied with his lot to believe that *Spartam nactus es, hanc orna*, 'You've got your job, now make the best of it'; they could warn a friend unable to finish a dissertation that every scholar and artist must learn to take *manum de tabula*, 'his hand from the picture'; and they could warn belligerent young kids that *dulce bellum inexpertis*, 'war is great fun to those who haven't tried it'.[64]

So much is well known. What is less well known, however, is that the *Adages* were designed to serve not only as an aid to the production of good Latin prose, but also as a manual of techniques for reading – and a collection of predigested texts to apply them to. Erasmus not only compiled lapidary sayings; he identified their sources in the classics, tracing the alterations they had undergone in the course of Greek and Latin literary history. And he embedded them in a framework as elegant and effective as the drawn and painted frameworks of the humanist manuscript: an exposition that ensured their utility for modern, Christian readers.

One exemplary tag, by Erasmus's own account, is *Festina lente*, 'Hasten slowly', which he discussed at length. This adage began, he explained, as an oxymoronic twist on a normal Greek phrase found in Aristophanes' *Knights*: *speude tacheos*, 'hasten quickly', that is 'hurry up'. Though clearly compressed, it contained a wealth of meaning. It taught a lesson that princes above all needed to learn: that haste and wilfulness caused more harm than good. Erasmus used this simple lesson in the generally Stoic ethics of humanism as the peg on which to hang an extraordinary range of classical materials. He showed its application to a properly moral reading of a basic poetic text: the beginning of Book I of the *Iliad*. Here Agamemnon, deprived of his female slave Chryseis, takes Achilles' female slave Briseis in return:

> Homer appears to have portrayed Agamemnon with a too great slackness and supineness of mind, the *bradeos* ['slowly'] part of the proverb, so that

no high deed or show of spirit is recorded of him except that he flew into
a rage over the removal of Chryseis, and stole Briseis from Achilles. To
Achilles, on the other hand, he attributes undisciplined impulses, that is
the *speude* ['hasten'] part; unless it is an example of both ['hasten slowly']
when he draws his sword in council to fall upon the king, and is persuaded by Pallas to limit his indignation to violent abuse.[65]

From mortality in literature Erasmus passed, with no evident strain, to
morality in history. Fabius Maximus, he pointed out, was one of the
few historical heroes who had won immortal fame by hastening slowly.
And those two model emperors, Augustus and Vespasian, had made
this proverb one of their favourites, Vespasian had even stamped it, in
hieroglyphic form, on his coins: these showed an anchor with a dolphin
wrapped around it, expressing the same oxymoronic notion of speed
and slowness combined as the original phrase.

From adage to hieroglyph, from the crystallized verbal pith of morality to its physical embodiment, was never a long journey in the Renaissance. Erasmus made it with lightning speed, finding in this single
hieroglyph the pretext for a long digression on the pictorial writing of
the Egyptians. He collected information about the hieroglyphs from a
number of sources, notably the then unpublished Greek text of
Horapollo. Like a good humanist, he traced these texts back to their
original source, a lost work by the Stoic Chaeremon.[66] But he said more
about the nature of hieroglyphs than their history. They both caused
pleasure and earned respect, he explained, by their use of the real qualities of natural objects to teach moral and physical lessons. They were a
model of good pedagogy: though sharp and memorable, the hieroglyph
required its readers to work, at least a little, to interpret it:

> the Egyptian soothsayers and priests ... thought it wrong to exhibit the
> mysteries of wisdom to the vulgar in open writing, as we do; but they
> expressed what they thought worthy to be known by various symbols,
> things or animals, so that not everybody could interpret them. But if
> anyone deeply studied the qualities of each object, and the special nature
> and power of each creature, he would at length, by comparing and guess-
> ing what they symbolised, understand the meaning of the riddle.[67]

Festina lente, with its perfect visual embodiment in the natural properties of the dolphin and the anchor, seemed to Erasmus a piece of 'the
mysteries of the most ancient philosophy'.

To explicate a hieroglyph, finally one needed to know the natural
properties of its constituents, the creatures whose images made up the
symbolic vocabulary of the Egyptian sages. Accordingly, Erasmus expa-
tiated at length on the swiftness of the dolphin, quarrying stories from

that beloved omnium gatherum of misinformation, Pliny's *Natural History* (again, he took care to identify Pliny's source, Aristotle):

> Its extraordinary speed can be judged from this, that though its mouth is set far apart from its snout, as it were in the middle of the belly, and this must necessarily greatly delay it in hunting down fish, since it must snatch at them in a twisted and curved-back position, nevertheless there is hardly any fish which can escape its swiftness.[68]

Erasmus thus transformed a single axiom into the strong, if slender, backbone to which he affixed a highly selective reconstruction of ancient culture as whole. He made rhetoric and epic, history and natural philosophy, all teach the same moral. He had Greek and Roman, Egyptian and Christian intellectuals all send the same literary and artistic message. He gave implicit and explicit lessons on how to detect allusions in classical texts. And he used the decoding of the hieroglyph, the discovery of the inner message beneath the apparently difficult surface, as the dominant metaphor for a reading of the classics which always looked for acceptably Christian senses under the surface of pagan writings. One essay – one tiny fragment of a vast and vastly influential book – reveals the shape of the larger enterprise.

Erasmus's work was by no means idiosyncratic. Throughout the sixteenth century, in fact, other northern intellectuals set out to organize and frame basic elements of the classical heritage for students.[69] Some of these works were fairly elementary, like the *Officina* (Workshop) of the Nivernais schoolteacher Ravisius Textor. This provided just what the title promised for the growing lad to adorn his compositions: working materials. Textor assembled short passages from ancient history, and docketed them, not to inform the boy about antiquity, but to provide cases in point of moral and immoral behaviour. The reader encountered not the mountainous Roman history of Livy, hard to scale and sometimes terrifying to contemplate, but a neat and diverting gallery of stories, organized by associative principles easy enough to discern. Men who killed themselves, men who died in latrines, men who were skinned, men who were suffocated, women who died in childbirth, and men who were beheaded follow one another in a Latinate Grand Guignol, unified not by the historical continuity of the past, but the pedagogical and rhetorical needs of the present.[70] The most dramatic and stately works of Latin prose were butchered to make a schoolboy's holiday – or rather to facilitate a schoolboy's work of gaining acquaintance with the range of classical anecdote that a learned person needed to know. This form of contact with a classical world, tamed by its very presentation, proved long-lasting; one of its best-known species took root in the Jesuit colleges of the *ancien régime*, where students read anthologies instead of straight texts, and encountered a castrated – or at least bowdlerized – Martial.

Other efforts to frame the ancient texts for modern use showed far higher intellectual ambitions. As the available texts multiplied and the question of how to read then became more pressing, scholars sought to provide elaborate and systematic arts of reading. Jean Bodin's *Methodus ad facilem historiarum cognitionem*, for example, offered a method for the reading of all historical texts, ancient and modern. Instead or providing an anthology, Bodin instructed the student to make his own, systematically gutting his books for information about which historians he could believe and which constitutions could work for which peoples. His influence was pervasive. Montaigne, in his *Essays*, both responds to the questions Bodin raises and reveals that he had made some sketchy notes on historians of the sort Bodin prescribed. Yet even Bodin sought not to discover the truth about the past as it really was, but to represent it as instructive. He knew, for example, that history was really philosophy taught by concrete examples. And he taught his student to read it in that light, using marginal symbols (*CH* for *consilium honestum*, *CTV* for *consilium turpe utile*) to force each story of a speech or battle into a highly traditional framework.[71]

These textbooks and manuals had a pervasive impact, one less dramatic but far more widely diffused than the teaching of any single master. They continued, and spread across Europe, what in the fifteenth century had been the work of individual masters like Guarino. The young men of the Renaissance, in the main, read their classics at first in a single way: not to search for ancient wisdom as it really was, naked and challenging, but to admire antique *sapientia* as set out in a sort of printed museum – divided into rooms, framed and labelled in ways that predetermined the meaning of the relics displayed.

The general enterprise of modernization that Erasmus and others undertook was hardly new. James Hankins has recently argued that the similar tactics of Decembrio had made it possible for fifteenth-century Milanese intellectuals to read and revere Plato – precisely because they could not see how alien his ideas and values were.[72] Ancient Neoplatonists had done the same for Homer long before, making him palatable to modern readers with a grounding in philosophy.[73] But the mechanically reproduced, universally visible frames of the Erasmian *Adages* and similar works, with their tight union of interpretation and interpreted material, fixed the nature and extent of the sixteenth-century schoolboy's contact with antiquity as a whole. And it domesticated – for most young readers, most of the time – what might otherwise have been the challenge of a non-Christian history and morality. Far more young men in sixteenth-century Europe knew the story of 'Pandora's box' from Erasmus's moralizing account of it than had read the original, less domesticated, account of Pandora's jar in Hesiod.[74]

The humanist's packaging of ancient authorities, ultimately, shaped readers' expectations about important texts in two other vital ways. In the first place, by early in the sixteenth century the humanists had managed to remove many of the medieval commentaries they disliked from distribution. But they did so not by doing away with commentaries altogether, as some modern sources suggest, but by replacing outdated commentaries with modern ones. The glosses of humanist teachers, usually offered first as lessons in classrooms, then rewritten for print, twined themselves like the illuminators' vines around the texts of popular poets like Ovid, Virgil and Juvenal, of major prose texts like Boethius's *Consolatio* and Cicero's *De inventione*, and even around the Bible itself. These commentaries appeared in humanistic, not Gothic, script. They attacked trivial and technical problems, problems of all sorts, often so profusely that they threatened to drown the original texts. And despite the efforts of individual critics, like Poliziano, to stamp out their weed-like growth, they flourished throughout the sixteenth century, and were still being harvested in the variorum editions of the century to come.

The humanist reader in the age of print, accordingly, did not expect his classical text to arrive on his desk neat. The more important its author and subject, the deeper it should be plunged in banks of commentary. Eventually, humanist editors and readers decided that non-classical Latin literary texts also needed glosses; there was no other way to assert their literary claims. Badius Ascensius commented on Book XIII of Virgil's *Aeneid*, which was written by the humanist Maffeo Vegio; Gerardus Listrius commented at length on Erasmus's *Praise of Folly*, which looks in its glossed form exactly like a classical text, and was often printed or bound with genuinely ancient works. Paradoxically, then, the humanist text had returned to the position of the medieval *auctoritas*. Its authoritative glosses were less opaque than the medieval ones; not a Gothic wall, but a classicizing tracery of vines. But the new commentary imprisoned and shaped the text as powerfully as the old ones had. Wreathed in humanist exegesis, the text seemed important not only for its own sake, but also because it was tied once again to a system of instruction and interpretation.

The humanists, finally, made one other vital innovation. Traditional teachers had always stressed the unique virtues and excellences of their authors. Medieval and early Renaissance lecture courses on an ancient writer normally began with a substantial, if stereotypical, account of his life. This set his works into a dramatic historical context – often a fanciful one, to be sure – stressing his high birth, good deeds and close relations with great men. The humanist, by contrast, tended to drama- tize his own life and the circles he himself had moved in. Erasmus, in the *Adages*, lavishly and mendaciously celebrated all the services that Aldo and his merry men had offered him as he worked in their printing shop. He and his associates, like Vives, made their annotated editions of individual texts the occasions for all sorts of dramatic tale-telling about their discoveries of manuscripts, their collaboration with great men of an earlier day, their virtue and their energy.[75]

The humanist text celebrated its editor and his benefactors as elo- quently as its author. And it led the reader to look – much as the modern reader does in a critical study of a major writer – for two sorts of narrative in a single book. An annotated text naturally had as its core a classical tale told by an ancient, which might be poetic or historical or philosophical. Alongside that, however, it wove a double modern narrat- ive by the editor, which might be dutifully rhetorical and philological in its manifest content, but was often alluringly autobiographical in its subtext. Annotated copies of such books reveal the eagerness with which readers – especially those in remote places – scrutinized them for evidence not only about the ancient world, but also about the modern literary circles that had graced the Florence of the Medici or the Louvain of Erasmus. Nothing fascinated the young Lucas Fruterius more in Muret's edition of Catullus, for example, than the material it offered about the grand literary quarrels of Poliziano and Marullus and the more recent polemics of Muret and Pier Vettori.[76] The humanist commentary became the warrant that a text belonged to the high culture of its day; it also linked that text, as firmly as the glosses of Accursius had, to a specific literary and pedagogical regime.

In the Study

Reading, of course, did not end with schooling, as Machiavelli's case shows. Mature individuals could make the technical skills they had mastered in school serve entirely unpredictable purposes. The young Johannes Secundus would prove capable of reading Catullus, and a middle-aged Machiavelli of reading Cicero, in ways that would have shocked any schoolmaster.[77] Secundus's *Basia* and Machiavelli's *Prince* – like many other high literary works, from More's *Utopia* to Mon- taigne's *Essays* – self-evidently could not have been written had their authors not smashed the humanist frame and made off with the ancients, whom they interpreted with freedom and brilliance. These elaborate, but implicit, interpretations of classic texts are too complex, too varied and sometimes too removed from the experience of reading to be described in detail here. But any full history of reading in Renaissance Europe will have to confront them and integrate them with other forms of evidence.

A second qualifying point is also vital. Renaissance readers bought and appreciated a very wide range of texts, some of them in no sense classical or humanistic. Cosimo de' Medici amused himself in two ways in his spare time: by cultivating his olive trees and reading that medieval classic, Gregory the Great's *Moralia in Job*.[78] Federigo da Montefeltro loved the highly scholastic Aristotelian commentaries of Donato Acciaiuoli. He made his library an encyclopaedic collection, which included substantial holdings in theology and other non-humanistic fields. And he made his son memorize not only a new text in a new form, Ptolemy's *Geography*, but also that most medieval of *auctoritates*, a historiated Bible.[79] Giannozzo Manetti read the Hebrew Bible as a humanist, using the best tools of philology to restore the original sense. But he could also read it in the utterly traditional way of the mendicant preacher, as when he found reason in it to predict a terrible fate for a dishonest businessman: 'Io ho voltate molte carte della Scrittura Santa a' mia dì,' he warned; 'tieni questo per certo, che tu hai a essere punito, tu e tua famiglia, d'una punizione che sarà di natura, che sarà esemplo a tutta questa città.'[80] Savonarola – whose public use of the Bible to attack his enemies fascinated Machiavelli – would not have quoted the text differently.[81]

These matters can only be touched on here. In a volume of this kind, moreover, we obviously cannot consider another vital set of data in the records: the many surviving catalogues of personal and public libraries. Like the many varieties of implicit reading embedded in works of literature, the manifold resources that weighed down the humanists' bookshelves require a different and more extensive kind of study.[82] But we can set out and consider evidence relevant to some more circumscribed questions: the circumstances in which mature humanists read, the preparations they made for doing so, and the ways in which the intellectual and the aesthetic came together in their responses to the text.

The humanist sometimes read casually, as we do now. But often, as Machiavelli's letter to Vettori shows, reading in the Renaissance resembled dancing in the same period: an activity governed by a highly complex code of rules and demanding continual attentiveness. In the first place, the humanist read with pen in hand, writing as he moved through his text. Sometimes he had no choice; for often the only way to obtain a book was to copy it. Since the beginnings of Renaissance scholarship in the eighteenth century, scholars have known that Poggio and Niccoli copied the texts they procured from monastic libraries. They had no other way to possess the new texts or give their associates access to them. But it has only recently been discovered that through the second half of the fifteenth century at least, humanists and *cartolai* copied their texts as often as they bought them. Often, to the astonishment of modern editors, they turn out to have copied not manuscript but printed texts of the works they wanted. Of sixteen surviving manuscripts of the *Consolatio ad Liviam*, 'ten certainly and two probably derive from printed editions'; of thirty-one manuscripts of Calpurnius's *Eclogues*, six are copied from the 1471 edition by Sweynheym and Pannartz.[83] And throughout the sixteenth century, humanists often copied out whole Greek and Latin texts.

Modern scholars have often assumed that such activities were pursued for scholarly ends, with publication in view. The humanist copied, in other words, what he intended to edit. Frequently, this interpretation is perfectly sound; but sometimes it derives not from the evidence but from anachronistic assumptions. Writing, after all, was in itself a form of reading, a letter-by-letter homage to the power of the original. The beauty of the script – of which, as we have seen, all humanists were acutely conscious – made it appropriate to the task of appreciating a beautiful text. Trithemius urged that one could not master a text profoundly except by copying it, and many intellectuals far more modern than he shared this view.[84] Joseph Scaliger copied out a uniquely valuable codex of Petronius that belonged to his teacher of Roman law, the great collector Cujas. Modern students of the text of Petronius often berate Scaliger for the ineptitude with which he copied and the carelessness with which he adulterated his unique source with readings drawn from other sources – including printed books. In fact, however, he probably never meant to edit anything more than a few poems attributed to Petronius in the original manuscript. The full transcript, legibly written out in his splendid, informal book hand, was a personal possession, a unique text that he meant to enjoy himself. 'Je l'ayme mieux qu'un imprimé,' he remarked, indicating at once the value he set on his transcript and his lack of interest in reproducing it or producing a text based on it.[85] Just as the schoolboy might know his text word for word because he had memorized and recited it, the mature scholar often knew his because he had copied it out line by line – and enjoyed consulting it not in a form that he shared with others, but in that imposed by his own script as well as his own choice of readings.

The scholar also sharpened his nib for other, more analytical purposes. From Petrarch to Scaliger, scholars wrote in the margins of texts that they had not copied. They compiled technical information; often, they systematically recorded the variant readings they found in other versions of the text. Angelo Poliziano, as is well known, hated the inaccuracy of the editions of the classics that came out in his time. But he also used them meticulously as working materials, filling their margins with textual and exegetical evidence compiled with passion and precision from a vast range of sources. At the ends of volumes he often emulated the Roman scholars of the fourth century AD, entering summary *subscriptiones* which specified the places where and dates when he had worked, the texts he had used, and the names of the young men who had helped him.[86] Casaubon compiled in his copy of the *Corpus Hermeticum* the damning list of coincidences between it and the Bible and other pagan texts that enabled him to prove it inauthentic.[87]

Humanists also responded in writing to the literary and philosophical qualities of their texts. Petrarch's copies of Virgil, Augustine and many other authors mutated as he read and wrote in them into elaborate scripts, discussions between text and margin that sometimes involved several voices.[88] Throughout the fifteenth and sixteenth centuries, humanists inscribed their reactions and interpretations in the margins and blank leaves of their texts; and they often did so with a degree of literary and artistic care that now seems remarkable.

Montaigne thought his summary evaluations of Plutarch and Guicciardini worthy to be included in his *Essays*. Scaliger used most of his books as tools, entering only information. But even he crossed out the whole text of one book that angered him, writing 'cacas' over and over in the margins, and took the time to dispute in correct and bookish Latin with another humanist commentator who provoked him, Melchior Guilandinus, inscribing carefully crafted marginal replies. Gabriel Harvey, whose vast, now-scattered library has been studied with care by G. C. Moore Smith, Virginia Stern and Walter Colman, filled the margins of his books with comments written out in a painstakingly elegant italic hand that became famous – especially among his enemies, who made fun of it. These recorded Harvey's reactions to the texts he read, explained his assessments of collateral sources, and often provided dramatic accounts of the occasions on which he had discussed the texts or heard them discussed or performed in public.[89]

The presence of so many systematic annotations is deeply suggestive. Often, of course, it did mean that the articulate readers was preparing to publish something on the text in question. Scaliger's elaborate notes on Guilandinus were the first draft for an elaborate attack on him; Huet's notes in his copy of Scaliger's *Manilius* were the main source for his full-scale attack on Scaliger.[90] But annotation did not always serve these reassuringly familiar ends. Humanists often insisted on the bindings and title pages of their books that they meant them to serve not only their needs but those of friends as well. 'Angeli Politiani et amicorum', 'A book that belongs to Angelo Poliziano and his friends' – some variant of this declaration of ownership occurs in dozen of cases in the fifteenth and sixteenth centuries, notably Harvey's.

If we examine the care that went into such men's annotation of their books, we may be led to take these formulas strictly and seriously. The humanist created in his book a unique record of his own intellectual development and of the literary circles he had moved in. He often did this, moreover, in a script so elaborately neat and decorative as to suggest that he considered his notes of permanent value. Perhaps whole libraries of such annotations were systematically assembled by men like Harvey, not with publication in view, but as a common reference for members of their circle. Certainly we know that collectors, by the late sixteenth century, prized and competed for printed books that bore the annotations of earlier scholars. The University of Leiden Library, for example, carefully decorated books and manuscripts that came from the library of Scaliger with a printed slip that identified their provenance – often incorrectly, since librarians and others tended to take any set of neat annotations as Scaliger's. Collectors like Huet loved and exhibited their *libri annotati*.

It was not easy to adorn dozens of books with autobiographical narratives, elaborate cross-referencing and thorough discussion of textual details. The humanist had to keep his books in order and to consult many of them at once; he needed to be able to retrieve data from a vast range of sources. By the late sixteenth century, a number of new devices had appeared to make this sort of literary work easier. In particular, the humanist could now use a book wheel – a large vertical wheel, carefully geared to turn slowly and stop whenever necessary. It carried books around on small rotating shelves like passengers in the cars of a ferris wheel. The humanist who owned one could sit quietly, as Ramelli says in his description of such a device, while working through a library of texts. These splendid machines, a number of which survive, were flanked and complemented by other devices in the most advanced libraries. Cujas, for example, had not only a wheel with which he could turn his vast collection of books, but a barber's chair in which he himself could turn rapidly from task to task in his study. Curiously, though, he worked without using any of these devices: 'Il étudioit le ventre contre terre, couché sur un tapis, ses livres autour de lui.'[91] Evidently, then, reading in the Renaissance had something of the expensively dramatic quality that writing now possesses. The sophisticated reader needed a set of elaborate, expensive machines, and once in possession of them, he enjoyed the same advantage – or feeling of advantage – over lesser readers that the possessor of the most up-to-date computer and printer now possesses. Like the computer owner, too, he sometimes used his clever devices not as practical tools that facilitated his work, but as expensive fetishes that imparted glamour to his occupation.

Reading, finally, whether private or public, was often directed to very concrete ends – political as well as intellectual ones. We began with Machiavelli reading history in private, in order to understand his fate. Later, of course, he would read history in public, in a standard Renaissance sense of the term: that is, he would give lectures on Livy to a group of Florentine patricians in the Rucellai gardens.[92] In each case, the conversation with the ancient text had the same end in view: action, practical results, in the present. At the end of the sixteenth century, Gabriel Harvey was only one of many English intellectuals who were evidently paid to read historical texts with men of political influence. Harvey worked through Livy's description of Hannibal with Thomas Smith Jr before Smith went off to die in Ireland while establishing English control and protecting his family's investment. He worked through Livy's account of the origins of Rome with Sir Philip Sidney before Sidney went off on his embassy to the Holy Roman Emperor, Rudolf II. And he probably designed his own, heavily annotated copy of Livy, in which he recorded these readings, as both a memorial to his personal efforts to make knowledge serve power and a source that he could draw from as his own career moved onwards. Harvey's case was hardly isolated; contemporaries singled out the lectures of Henry Cuffe, who read classical texts with Essex, as the inspiration of his doomed rebellion.[93] Hobbes himself would blame the Civil War on classically educated young men who had taken the republican political views of the Greek and Roman historians too zealously to heart. Evidently, reading the ancients could still be a move in the most up-to-date early modern politics. And that sort of reading, pragmatic rather than aesthetic, deserves a prominent and distinctive historical place in any account of the uses of the book in the Renaissance.

Huet: The End of a Tradition

By the middle of the seventeenth century, philosophers had begun to argue that reading alone could not yield certain knowledge about natural or human history. Descartes began his *Discourse on Method* by telling the story of his own disaffection with the humanist education he had received from the Jesuits. Reading about the past, he had learned, could impart only a modest level of sophistication, which one could gain just as well from travel. The zealous reader, like the zealous tourist, learned that different peoples lived by different moral codes and regarded one another, with equal lack of right, as barbarians. Only rigorous reasoning modelled on mathematics could arrive at deeper truths. The humanists proved all too ready to accept these criticisms, or at least to admit that most of the learned young accepted them. Skilled readers and editors of classical texts like J. F. Gronovius and N. Heinsius practised their craft gloomily, aware that the age of philology had passed and a new age of mathematics had replaced it.[94]

No one witnessed these changes more attentively or regretted them more deeply than Huet. By the end of his life, he felt like a revenant, a ghostly witness to the lost world of his youth, in which scholarship had enjoyed a high reputation and attracted men of great ability.[95] Yet he went on editing his classics for the dauphin. He went on collecting and annotating scholarly books in careful Latin, using a small, neat script. And he went on considering books a primary source for knowledge about both the natural and the human sciences. It seems appropriate to close with a vignette from his life.

No vernacular text of Huet's own day appealed to him more deeply than the *Guirlande de Julie*, the manuscript collection of miniatures of flowers and madrigals prepared by the duc de Montausier as a New Year's gift for Julie d'Agennes. Huet lovingly described the presentation manuscript, 'magnificently bound and placed inside a small bag of fragrant Spanish leather', which Julie awoke to find on 1 January 1633/4. And he recalled with delight how one day the duchesse d'Usèz had let him read the work. She brought him to her library, which he described as neither large nor plentiful, but full of well-chosen books 'elegantly bound and decorated, the sort of thing women can appreciate'.[96] And there she locked him in for four of the happiest hours of his life, from dinner to sunset. He felt, as he later recalled, that in reading he actually 'conversed with the men of that time who were most outstanding for their urbanity and wit'.[97] Huet's delight in the physical form of books, his passion for a unique manuscript, his desire to recapture, from the text, the flavour of the social circle which had produced it – all these emotions clearly derive from the tastes and practices of the humanists. So did the physical form and organization of the duchess's library. Even if Latin erudition was on the wane, fine printing, fine binding and humanistic ways of reading could be transferred to the new vernacular classics of the day. Naturally they were systematically retained in the Latin schools of the Holy Roman Empire, the Low Countries and Scandinavia. The humanist approach to reading forms part of the afterlife of the classical heritage, and is rightly associated with the Renaissance. But it had an afterlife of its own as well, in both the high Protestant scholarship of the Refuge and the high vernacular culture of the *ancien régime*. A definitive history of how the humanists read will have to include in its coda Huet and Hardouin, Mme Dacier and Mr Bentley, Montausier and Julie d'Angennes.

8

Protestant Reformations and Reading

Jean-François Gilmont

Was the Reformation the daughter of Gutenberg? The conviction that printing played a fundamental role in the diffusion of Luther's ideas was already widespread in the sixteenth century. In 1526 François Lambert of Avignon went so far as to assert that the appearance of printing in the fifteenth century had been willed by God so that the Reformation could occur: 'Concerning the *ars chalcographica*', he states, 'I wish to add here that it is principally for that reason that God inspired, some years ago, the discovery of that invention so that it might serve to disseminate the truth in our century.'[1] Other Reformers praised the invention enthusiastically. It is traditional to quote Luther's *Tischreden*, where he states: 'Printing is the ultimate gift of God and the greatest one. Indeed, by means of it God wants to spread word of the cause of the true religion to all the Earth, to the extremities of the world.'[2] John Foxe, author of the *Book of Martyrs*, speaks of the 'divine and miraculous inventing of printing'.[3] There was nothing original, what is more, about calling printing 'divine'. The adjective was often used from the moment typography was born: it appears as early as the colophon of the *Catholicon* published in Mainz in 1460.

Historians have quite naturally repeated that the success of the Reformation owed much to printing, a statement that is often a commonplace more than the result of scholarly analysis.

Before discussing Protestant publications, it may be useful to recall that the outbreak of the Reformation coincided with an important revolution in means of communication.[4] Gutenberg's discovery modified the conditions for the circulation of ideas when it accelerated the circulation of texts and reduced the per copy cost. Still, we should guard against exaggerating the immediate impact of that invention on a society that was still largely illiterate. Moreover, the new art only became conscious of its own originality during the course of a gestation period of nearly eighty years.

At its inception, the *ars artificialiter scribendi* was closely modelled on the manuscript; but as printers became more familiar with the new technique, the printed book gradually acquired a personality of its own. That process was completed some time between 1520 and 1540, soon after Luther's revolt against the preaching of indulgences. By that time the printed book had become totally detached from the manuscript model. Printers gradually perceived that reproducing one text in series involved new commercial constraints. The external aspect of the book was revitalized by a title page; print characters became standardized; and many ligatures were abandoned. Above all, there were profound changes in the choices of the texts published, with many more modern authors represented. The major printers also perfected distribution networks, in order to reach readers beyond the narrow circle of their city.

Print shops multiplied rapidly. From Germany they spread first to Italy, then to France and the rest of Europe. Around 1540, only such peripheral regions as England, the Iberian Peninsula, central Europe and Scandinavia were not well equipped with print shops, while Germany, Italy, France and the Seventeen Provinces of the Netherlands all had a dense network of printers.

During the decade from 1530 to 1540, changes took place in libraries as well. This was certainly the case in France, but it is probable that the same was true of the other countries of Europe. The effects of lower book prices began to be felt: the average size of libraries grew notably, and manuscript books began to give way to printed books. As Carla Bozzolo and Ezio Ornato have noted, the book became a more banal object: inventories after death become less precise in their descriptions of books. This is an indication that books were less highly valued. Henceforth owning printed works was current practice.[5]

The spread of print came at the same time as an increased use of the national language in most areas of social life. It is evident that print encouraged that evolution, given that, on the economic plane, the new technique functioned by finding new markets, hence by broadening the reading public.

The diffusion of vernacular languages and the success of printing should probably be connected with more general changes in society. The end of the Middle Ages was marked by the rise of the bourgeoisie. Now that it controlled new economic and commercial sectors, the middle class intended to participate in political decisions that concerned it as well, and it signalled its social success by paying more attention to culture, which it adapted to its own interests. Moreover, the laity had no desire to remain on the edges of the life of the Church.

Printing in the People's Language

The notion of the importance of the printed book in the spread of Protestantism probably goes back to the 'War of the Pamphlets'.[6] Between 1520 and 1523, soon after Luther had raised his voice against the preaching of indulgences, a vast 'press campaign' developed in Germany. Thousands of pamphlets, brief quarto-format publications of only a few pages, at times with illustrations, circulated throughout the Empire. All the Reformation's challenges to the Church were propagated in hastily written, poorly organized, diffuse and redundant publications of this sort. The same texts, presented in the form of sermons, dialogues or letters, were often reproduced from one city to another in what was in fact the first instance of the use of print to arouse public opinion. That flood of ephemeral publications (the German term *Flugschriften* is expressive) soon made Luther's name and ideas known not only in German lands but throughout Europe.

In the countries in which the power structure had remained loyal to the Church of Rome (France, Italy, the Seventeen Provinces) the new religious concepts were also spread by print, but more discreetly. Little books of piety presented Lutheran themes, but avoided being too aggressive in tone, concealing their ideas within a traditional exterior. They did not state, 'In Thee *alone* we put our trust', but 'In Thee we put our trust'. At first such publications came from local presses (in Paris, Venice and Antwerp), but after 1540 printing them became too dangerous, and a pedlars' network was established from a base of operation in neighbouring lands (working from Geneva, Strasbourg and Emden in particular).

One of the Reformers' first concerns was to make the Bible available in the vernacular. Luther was not the only one who did so. In 1530, before Luther had finished his translation, the pastors of Zurich had already brought out a German Bible. A Dutch Bible was printed in Antwerp in 1526. Antonio Brucioli's Italian Bible dates from 1532. Urged on by Guillaume Farel, Pierre-Robert Olivétan made his French translation in 1535, and Miles Coverdale completed his English Bible in the same year. These were only a few of the editions manifestly inspired by Protestantism. The publishing phenomenon that ensued is even more impressive: reprintings followed one another at a steady pace. Before his death in 1546, Luther's German Bible had gone through over 400 total or partial reprintings.

What is more, Luther changed the economy of Wittenberg. In 1517 it was a small university town with only one (thoroughly provincial) print shop. In only a few years, more and more printing houses sprang up to print the flood of Lutheran texts, to the point that Wittenberg rose to the rank of sixth or seventh among centres for printing in Germany.

Much the same occurred in Geneva when the Reformation was proclaimed there and Calvin took up residence in the city. From 1537 to 1550, printing remained a modest affair; but after 1550, when the city's population was around 12,000, there were more and more printers in the city, and they inundated France and neighbouring lands with Protestant publications. The printers' ideological motivations were reinforced by more material interests, and the Geneva archives contain echoes of a number of conflicts arising from ferocious competition. From 1550 to 1562, printing Protestant books in Geneva produced excellent profits.

The organization of the Reformation throughout Europe increased the demand for works for everyday use: Bibles, catechisms, psalters and liturgical works of all sorts. The Protestant printers were also busy, however, printing more erudite works for the use of pastors. Some of these were of a didactic nature: biblical commentaries and theological syntheses such as Melanchthon's *Loci communes* or Calvin's *Institutio christianae religionis* (Institutes of the Christian Religion). Other works arose out of learned controversies, given that doctrinal debate was just as common within the Reformation in the sixteenth century as it was between Catholics and Protestants. With a passion we can hardly imagine, the learned theologians tore one another to bits in the course of never-ending polemics. Printers, of course, turned that rage for dispute to their advantage.

The special case of England suggests another aspect of this flood of printed matter. At the beginning of the century, printing in England was still in its infancy, and the better part of the books sold in English came from the Continent. A group of Reformers in contact with Wittenberg, unsatisfied with Henry VIII's middle-of-the-road position (which may have separated the Anglican Church from Rome, but retained the traditional theology), bombarded England with highly aggressive pamphlets printed in Antwerp. Henry discovered what all the rulers of his century found out: that if it was relatively easy to control the local presses, it was difficult to stop the importation of forbidden books. Mary Tudor had to learn the same lesson, as did the kings of France. Spain was the only exception to this rule: the heavy machinery put into place by the Inquisition succeeded (but at what a price!) in prohibiting heretical books from penetrating the Iberian peninsula.

Henry VIII eventually saw the error of his ways, and encouraged printing in England. In only a few decades, English books were no longer printed in Paris, Rouen or Antwerp, but in London. This facilitated the task of the police, at least as long as printing remained concentrated in the capital city. The exodus of many Protestants when Mary Tudor came to the throne prompted a wave of English publications on the Continent from 1555 to 1558 and an invasion of forbidden books into the British Isles.

In the sixteenth century, all religious groups felt they owed it to themselves to have access to printing, as the policies of dissident religious sects in central Europe demonstrate. Anti-Trinitarians in Poland and Hungary, Bohemian Utraquists and the United Brethren in Moravia all thought it indispensable to have printing presses at their disposition, in order to assert their religious identities. Presses satisfied the sects' internal needs for liturgical, catechetical and spiritual works, but they also supplied weapons of propaganda or counter-propaganda against the other Christian confessions.

The Catholics' fear of the Protestant book testifies to its impact. From the very early years of the Reformation, heretical books were seized everywhere and burned (as they were in Louvain in 1520). At first the police were poorly equipped to act effectively, but a stricter surveillance was slowly put into place. After 1540, book selling through pedlars and the sale of heretical books in Catholic lands became a much more difficult enterprise. A number of itinerant booksellers were imprisoned and sent to the stake, but even that did not stop the flow of books. Catholic authorities began to publish *Indices librorum prohibitorum* for the guidance of both booksellers and the faithful.

An ordinance in Laon in 1565 furnishes a savoury example of the Catholics' fear of heretical books: the decree required all basement windows facing the street to be blocked up, on the pretext that people who had been sent from Geneva threw pamphlets into basements by night. One chronicler noted that this practice had a catastrophic effect: 'Not long after, a good many inhabitants in search of novelty abandoned the Roman Catholic religion to take up the new one, which was then called Lutheran, and all because of those little booklets.'[7] In short, whether we view the book from one side of the confessional divide or the other, it gives every appearance of having been an effective agent for the Protestant Reformation.

The Reformers introduced another novelty that had far-reaching consequences: the use of vernacular languages in liturgy, theological discourse and, above all, the Bible.

The abandonment of Latin did not take place without scholarly debate on the dignity of ancient and modern languages. The first question that scholars posed was whether vernacular languages were capable of serving the domain of the sacred. Contrary to those who intended to continue to surround religion with an aura of mystery, the Reformers preached using the languages that would permit broader communication within the Church and enlarge access to the riches of the scriptural message.[8]

Luther states, significantly: 'I will not be ashamed in the slightest to preach to the uneducated layman and write for him in German.' Stating that he was not ashamed put Luther in a position opposed to a widespread opinion. He insists, however, that with the use of the vernacular, 'Christendom would have reaped no small advantage and would have been more benefited by this than by those heavy, weighty tomes and those *questiones* which are only handled in the schools among learned schoolmen.'[9] Luther shaped the German of his translation of the Bible with true genius, and he touched the people by speaking their language. He states: 'We have to interrogate the mother in her house, the children in the streets, the common man in the market, and consider their mouths to know how they speak in order to translate accordingly. Then they will understand and will note that we are speaking German with them.'[10] Communication with the people was primary with Luther. Curiously, he seems to have been less intent on putting the liturgy into German. He is probably sarcastic when he says of the 'papists': 'They have hidden from us the words of the sacrament, and they have taught us that we should not make them comprehensible to the laity.'[11] It took pressure from disciples more radical than he – Andreas Karlstadt and Thomas Müntzer – to bring Luther to use German in the liturgy, and he never totally rejected the liturgical use of Latin.[12]

Calvin, who was more attracted by humanism than Luther, detached himself from Latin only slowly. One telling detail is that his correspondence with his best francophone friends is entirely written in Latin, both in theological discussions and for news of daily events. His earliest works were written in Latin until the publication (in 1541) of *Le Petit Traicté de la Cène* (Short Treatise on the Holy Supper of Our Lord Jesus Christ). As he himself explained in 1546, he adopted in that work 'a style of instruction, simple and popular, and adapted to the unlearned'. He went on to state: 'I usually write more carefully for those acquainted with Latin. I laboured, however, not only faithfully to express my views, and reduce them within a brief compass, but also to unfold them lucidly and without technicalities.' Calvin adds that in his *Institutes*, which were written in Latin, 'I expose and I confirm more solidly the same doctrine by expressing myself in another and, if I am not mistaken, clearer fashion'.[13]

Théodore de Bèze reiterated Calvin's reservations concerning French.

Writing in 1572 about the translation of one of his theological treatises, he complains of 'the poverty of our language', adding, 'it may well be that the French translation is in some places less easily understood, especially to the commonality, than my original Latin'.[14]

Vernacular languages were evolving fast. Using them to express concepts that had long been polished by ancient languages was not an easy task. As Olivétan proclaims in the introduction to his translation of the Bible, 'to make the French language speak with the eloquence of Hebrew and Greek' was tantamount to 'teaching the sweet nightingale to sing the raucous song of the crow'. We can hear here an echo of Luther, who confided: 'I bleed blood and water to give the Prophets in the vulgar tongue. Good God, what work! How difficult it is to force the Hebrew writers to speak German! Not wishing to abandon their Hebrew nature, they refuse to flow into Germanic barbarity. It's as if the nightingale, losing its sweet song, was forced to imitate the cuckoo and its monotonous note.'[15]

It is clear that there was a trend towards broader popular communication, but the way was not always smooth. Latin remained the technical language of theological debate, and it had an incomparable advantage in international communication. The earliest texts of the German Reformation passed into other linguistic areas in Latin.[16] Similarly, certain of Calvin's treatises were immediately translated into Latin, above all to make them available to the German Reformers. His *Petit traicté de la Cène* is a clear example of this.[17]

The Dangers of Reading

Very soon the panegyrics of 'divine' printing gave way to criticism. Luther even considered printing with outright suspicion, and complained about the superabundance of useless and even harmful books. In 1520 he wrote in *The Christian Nobility of the German Nation Concerning Reform of the Christian Estate*: 'The number of books on theology must be reduced and only the best ones published. It is not many books that make a man learned, nor even reading. But it is a good book frequently read, no matter how small it is. That makes a man learned in the Scriptures and godly.'[18] Throughout his career, Luther expressed more warnings of this sort than praises of printing.

Admittedly, Protestants advocated *scriptura sola*, but that phrase should not be translated as 'the written word and only the written word'. The principle of *scriptura sola* demanded that theological positions be founded on the Bible; its aim was to reject purely human traditions not attested in Scripture. It bore no resemblance to the idea of free examination of Scripture introduced by liberal Protestantism only in the eighteenth century.[19]

Richard Gawthrop and Gerald Strauss have firmly established that Luther did not promote popular reading of the Bible.[20] In the heat of the early combats Luther undeniably expressed a desire 'that every Christian study for himself the Scripture and the pure Word of God'.[21] In *To the Christian Nobility of the German Nation* he insists that children should receive daily lessons in the New Testament, so that they can become familiar with all of its books by the age of nine or ten.[22] After the Peasants' War, however, and under pressure from the proliferation of heterodox interpretations of Scripture, Luther's discourse changed, and he insisted on church control over access to the Bible. The Word enclosed in the Bible would remain a dead letter if it were not transmitted by preaching: 'The Kingdom of Christ', Luther declared in a sermon in 1534, 'is founded on the Word that cannot be seized or comprehended without the two organs of the ears and the tongue.'[23] In 1529, after he had written his two catechisms, Luther insisted that they be put into everyone's hands: 'The catechism is the layman's Bible; it contains the whole of what every Christian must know of Christian doctrine.'[24]

Luther's conception of teaching parallels his thoughts about the catechism. For him, the objective of the school was not to provide access to culture for everyone. The school's function was to form an élite capable of directing civil and religious society. In 1524 he exhorted legislators to found good libraries, assigning to those libraries the dual function of preserving books and offering spiritual and temporal leaders an opportunity to study. There was no hint of popular reading.[25]

Melanchthon's thought evolved in similar ways, moving from an invitation to everyone to read the Bible to promoting the catechism. In the preface to his *Loci communes theologici* (1521) he presents his book as a modest introduction to reading the Bible, and he expresses an ardent hope that 'all Christians be occupied in greatest freedom with the divine Scriptures alone'. In his introduction to the same work in 1543, however, he insists on the need for 'ministers of the Gospel, whose preparation in the schools was God's will. It is they whom he designated as guardians of the Books of the Prophets and the Apostles and of the authentic dogmas of the Church.'[26] When the Reformers found that some of their disciples had outstripped them, they became more prudent, continuing to promote reading, but stressing simple books and keeping control of doctrinal interpretation in their own hands.

Zwingli's exegetic principles evolved between 1522 and 1524 in much the same fashion as Luther's and Melanchthon's.[27] At first Zwingli attempted to attack the stability of the traditional Church through a broad appeal to public opinion, founding his arguments on the doctrine of universal priesthood: all Christians who approach the Bible with humility are capable of interpreting it. He proclaimed this doctrine in public disputations and in several pamphlets in 1522. The situation soon changed, however. The Catholic clergy in Switzerland had been overturned, and the first Anabaptists posed a threat when they invoked the same principles to challenge the legitimacy of the new power. Zwingli made a 180-degree turn. Beginning in 1525, he reserved interpretation of the Bible to competent persons, a group drawn from the political élite and the clerical intelligentsia.

King Henry VIII's attitude also throws light on the social implications of reading the Bible. For a long time Henry forbade all dissemination of the Bible in English. In 1543 he finally gave in to pressure from his entourage, but he accompanied authorization to print the English Bible with significant restrictions, in which he distinguished three categories of persons and of reading matter. 'Everye noble man and gentleman' could not only read the Bible in English, but could also have it read aloud to them and to anyone under their roof. It took only one member of the nobility to authorize free access to Scripture. At the other end of the social scale, reading the Bible in English was totally forbidden to 'woomen or artificers, prentises journeymen serving men of the degrees of yeomen or undre, husbandmen [and] laborers'. People who fell in between those two categories (in practice, the middle class) and noble women 'maie reade to themselves alone and not to others any [Textes] of the Byble or New Testament'. That middle category was thus considered to have enough reading competence not to stray from the narrow path, but it had insufficient authority to dictate to its entourage.[28] Could there be a clearer expression of the political and social stakes involved in reading the Bible?

Nor did the Calvinist tradition leave interpretation to individual tastes; rather, it exercised strict control over exegesis and theological elaboration. For Calvin, not everyone was to have direct access to the Bible. As he explained in a sermon, the Bible is a loaf of bread with a very thick crust. To nourish his people, God wishes 'that the bread be sliced for us, that the pieces be put in our mouths, and that they be chewed for us'. St Paul had shown that 'it is not enough that we read [Scripture] privately, but we must have our ears beaten by the doctrine extracted from it and must be preached to so that we can be instructed'.[29]

Théodore de Bèze provides further evidence of the Calvinists' lack of enthusiasm for moving theology into the market-place. In the dedication to his *Questions et responses chrestiennes* of 1572, Calvin's successor explains that it was only against his better judgement that he had accepted having his Latin treatise translated into French. He states that he felt forced to do so by the curiosity of a public whose mania for throwing itself into the 'labyrinths' of delicate questions he abhorred. Bèze is clear on the subject: theology was a special preserve that required a knowledge of 'all the paths and passages by which one must pass and return'.[30]

One anecdote dating from 1562 seems to me to express the Genevan determination to orient theological reading. The printer Jean Rivery was planning to publish a 'harmony of Scripture', with annotations drawn from a broad range of theologians. The pastors consulted by the city council did not doubt the orthodoxy of the book, but they refused permission for its publication for a subtle reason: the glossator should not have cited Calvin and Bèze, because doing so meant that readers might desert their complete writings for extracts![31] A similar question was raised when the Geneva Bible of 1588 was being prepared, but at that time the question was decided differently. Although the presence of marginal annotations was criticized by some pastors, who denounced readers who read only summaries instead of reading the theologians' commentaries, in the long run the contrary viewpoint prevailed: 'Not everyone has the means to read entire commentaries, nor a judgement firm enough to absorb and carefully choose among their substance.'[32] This was pushing the promotion of good reading habits rather far, and it shows to what extent the great churches of the Protestant Reformation imitated the Catholics in their desire to retain control over theology.

There were only a few marginal dissenting voices. In Zurich the Anabaptists remained faithful to Zwingli's initial position, and espoused a radical interpretation of Scripture: 'After we ourselves have also taken the Scripture in our own hands, and we have interrogated it on all possible points, we have been better instructed, and we have discovered the enormous and shameful errors of the pastors.'[33]

The spiritualists adopted similar positions (though with different emphasis), refusing all intervention from the authorities in their contact with Holy Scripture. For them, the Spirit had priority over the text. In the *Prague Manifest* of 1521, Thomas Müntzer criticized clerics who proposed a Scripture 'stolen on the sly from the Bible with the cleverness of brigands and the cruelty of murderers'. Only the elect would benefit from the Living Word: 'That [will happen] when the seed falls on fertile ground – that is, in hearts filled with the fear of God. That is where the paper and the parchment [are found] on which God inscribes, not with ink, but with his living finger, the true holy Scripture of which the external Bible is the true witness.' Müntzer knew, however, that he lived in a society poorly prepared for individual reading. That is why he wrote, in the introduction to his 'Sermon to the princes' of 1524: 'May

God's servants, zealous and indefatigable, spread the Bible every day by song, reading and preaching.' In accordance with the same logic, he wished for a liturgy that would be offered in a language that the people understood, and he wanted the Bible to be read aloud before the people so that they could truly appropriate it. It is true, however, that Müntzer soon deviated from this ideal, substituting his own preaching for biblical discourse.[34]

Valentin Ickelsamer, a Karlstadt schoolmaster who was a disciple of Müntzer's, was more respectful of the sacred text. In a pamphlet of 1527 he ardently defended reading the Bible: in an exciting epoch of renewal, when the ability to read was more precious than ever before, all Christians could at last read the Word of God for themselves. Better, any Christian could 'be a judge of it, all by himself'. Ickelsamer had asserted in another pamphlet in 1525 that 'the Gospel gives us the freedom to believe and the power to judge'.[35]

Kaspar Schwenkfeld challenged the literal text of the Bible as well as clerical commentaries on it. He explained in a letter in 1527: 'Faith being a spiritual and internal reality . . . it cannot have its source in concrete realities, in speech and external hearing. . . . The communication of the Word of the living God is free. It is not bound to visible things, nor to one minister or one ministry, to one time or one place.'[36] Schwenkfeld was moving in the direction of an individualistic Christianity with looser ties to Scripture.

Positions for and against reading the Bible return us to a fundamental debate. Christianity is defined, in an appeal to two seemingly contradictory means of communication, as a religion of the Word – *logos* – and a religion of the book – *biblos*. (In primitive Christianity, of course, writing down the divine message in no way reflected a desire to set up two parallel types of communication.) The Christian religion was intended to be the living, spontaneous presence of the Word; the Book was there only to make sure of the permanence of the message by offering the Word the guarantee of reliable memory.

From the moment that the practice of reading became widespread, the individual's relation to the text changed. Writing became a means of direct communication. It set up two contradictory positions: on the one hand, there was the conviction that Christ's teaching was simple and had been addressed to all; on the other, fear of heresy led to a desire for control of interpretation through preaching. This created a fundamental debate between the Bible of the ear and the Bible of the eye,[37] between the church of orality and the church of print.[38] By the eve of the Reformation, the debate was already well launched. Luther and Zwingli gave it a new thrust, although they soon softened their emphasis on the promotion of individual reading.

Plural Readings

As the Protestant Reformation spread, written expression never excluded speech. All the Reformers were at once preachers, writers, professors and letter-writers. Speech retained its primacy. The Protestant book had a plural destiny. The Reformers used print deliberately and systematically. Luther soon regretted the overly extended circulation of his books, stating: 'For me, it would be far preferable to increase the number of living books, that is, the number of preachers.'[39]

In the sixteenth century what was new about the book was its proliferation in a world where relationships were still essentially oral. Information circulated by oral and auditory channels: rumour, which fed debate, both public and private; the proclamations of public criers and the calls and come-ons of pedlars; sermons; drama, comic or polemical; letters; street songs and public reading. There were images, spectacles and processions to catch the eye. We need to distance ourselves from the twentieth century and remember that orality was omnipresent.

Society was illiterate. To what extent? The question is nearly insoluble. For Roger Chartier, the lack of documentation makes it impossible to measure literacy rates in Europe before the very end of the sixteenth century.[40] Other scholars have been more optimistic. Rolf Engelsing estimates that around 1500, from 3 to 4 per cent of the population in German lands could read; in the towns that percentage rose to 10 or even 30 per cent.[41] David Cressy puts the literacy rate in England at 10 per cent for men and 1 per cent for women.[42] In a city as cultured as Venice in 1587, 14 per cent of the young (26 per cent of boys, 1 per cent of girls) attended the schools, which gives some idea of the literacy rate in that city.[43] Even if these figures were certain, one would need to keep in mind that there were degrees of literacy. Autograph signatures are often used as proof of a capacity to read, but the relationship between reading and writing is ambiguous, and the connection between being able to sign one's name and mastery of writing cannot be taken as dependable. There is a vast distance between a good reader who can skim pages rapidly and someone who can only painstakingly decipher letters one by one. Basic literacy does not automatically produce silent reading.[44]

The role of printing in the implantation of the Protestant Reformation has been acknowledged ever since the sixteenth century; but just how it played that role has been studied only in recent years. The history of the book has seen a shift of focus from the text to the reader. It is no longer enough to reconstitute the corpus of publications that appeared in a given period, or to identify the networks of printers and pedlars who distributed them. We must also determine how they were read. In what ways were those texts active in their own times?

The most plausible hypothesis is that reading practices continued to overlap. Silent reading, in which contact between a text and its reader takes place in privacy, was certainly practised, but other means of access to writing accompanied it: murmured individual reading, shared reading aloud in a small group, and collective reading of a liturgical nature, where at certain times the minister reads for everyone and at other times each worshipper follows the text in his prayer book as the community sings.

Can we get beyond these generalizations and discern any overall tendencies in this diversity? Obviously, we need to proceed with caution, proposing hypotheses more than certitudes. Certain categories of works seem to have been connected with a specific sort of reading, either exclusive reading aloud or silent reading. In contrast, there are also books that lend themselves alternately to collective and private reading.

Leaving external evidence aside, it may be useful to turn to the book itself and consider its creators' intentions. The material presentation of a book – format, page layout, illustrations, etc. – furnishes valuable indications of the mode of reading that the publisher had in mind. Armando Petrucci spoke to this notion when he drew a distinction among 'bench books, saddlebag books [and] little handbooks'.[45] A book's format guided the reader automatically towards one type of reading or another: a folio volume required the use of a reading stand, but a smaller format, say, a sextodecimo, allowed the reader 'to have it at hand at home; not to be burdened down outside, even better, to stroll unencumbered in the countryside'.[46] This is misleading, however: we have to draw a distinction between the audience for a book (that is, the people who actually read it) and its public (those for whom authors and publishers destine it). Even though the two are closely related, the publisher's projections and the reader's reactions should not be confused.[47]

One interesting example of the uses of print is popular polemics, as with the flood of *Flugschriften* that submerged Germany from 1520 to 1525. 'Press campaigns' of the sort occurred elsewhere in Europe as well: in England around 1540, after the fall of Cromwell;[48] in France after 1561 and throughout the Wars of Religion; and in the Netherlands after 1565, during the conflict that ended with the independence of the United Provinces.[49]

Recent studies, in particular those of Robert W. Scribner, point to a number of convergent indices that suggest that such publications were intended to be read aloud.[50] Stylistic analysis shows the predominance of discourse, sermons and dialogues: rather than written texts, these were spoken exposés. Moreover, the impact of this sort of printed matter on a largely illiterate society cannot be understood without the mediation of speech. This fact is confirmed by the frequent use of pictures (even caricatures) in these works, indicating that oral communication was reinforced by vision. Zwingli reacted to Konrad Grebel's propaganda attacks with a statement that proves them to have been more oral than written: 'They argue in all the corners, streets, shops, wherever they can manage to do it.'[51] The proliferation of pamphlets during the sixteenth century thus represents an indirect written communication rather than a direct one. As Scribner notes: 'The multiplication effect usually attributed to the printed word was just as much a product of the spoken word.'[52]

Catechism developed considerably with the Protestant Reformation and the Catholic Counter-Reformation. When Luther strongly encouraged catechizing from childhood as a way to provide simple Christian teaching, he was establishing a connection with a movement whose roots reached back to the Middle Ages. Like Jean Gerson in the fifteenth century, Luther realized that religious revival was hindered as much by the ignorance of the masses as it was by the inability of many pastors to provide catechetics, and he said as much in the preface to his Large Catechism of 1529.[53] Luther went further in his Small Catechism by creating a model for catechesis within the family. After the basic texts (the Ten Commandments, the Lord's Prayer and the Credo) had been memorized, the father was to comment on them. Quite soon, as we have seen, Luther preferred putting this sort of text into the hands of the faithful, rather than the Bible.

The Calvinist Reformation also assigned catechism an important place, as bibliography confirms. If the Calvinists were responsible for an impressive number of editions of the Bible and the New Testament, these were nothing in comparison to the number of catechisms and psalm books they put out. Our estimates undoubtedly fall short of the real numbers, given that works designed for daily use seldom survive.

Catechizing is an activity in which orality predominates. Memorization precedes explication.[54] The book was perhaps still indispensable: the listening child's eyes followed the written text in silence as the father or the catechist read aloud. In this use of writing the book is a support for memory; it is by no means a place for discovering a new message. Still, this somewhat rigid apprenticeship is not to be scorned; nor should we ignore its effectiveness as an initiation into reading.

Liturgy was another of the Reformers' constant preoccupations. In spite of some resistance, as we have seen, the shift to vernacular languages was taking place everywhere, and congregational singing occupied a prominent place in liturgy. Calvin and Martin Bucer liked their music monodic and simple. In the 1543 edition of the *Institutes* Calvin warned that those singing the psalms should be more attentive to the words than to the melody.[55] Luther was concerned that music fit the text, but he was susceptible to the charms of polyphony.[56]

Liturgical reform required new song collections. In Martin Bucer's Strasbourg and in Calvinist liturgy the psalter was essentially the only form for religious songs. German hymnals, in contrast, were open to other kinds of text. It took several decades to elaborate this musical corpus in Germany, Geneva, England,[57] the Netherlands and elsewhere. The Hussite movement had already shown the way in the fifteenth century.

The first German hymnals were printed in 1524. Around 1550 the Calvinist Reformation began to circulate a three-part collective work that contained a verse psalter (at the time not all the psalms had been translated), the catechism and a missal. When the verse translation of the psalms was completed in 1562, in Geneva alone a vast printing operation produced some 30,000 copies of it in less than two years.[58]

But to what use were these collections put, in particular the ones with musical notation? The discussion in 1551 in Geneva over one such publication attests to a discrepancy between the printed music and the tunes that were actually sung. The vast majority of the faithful could not read music. Some could, however, because we know that at times printing errors produced loud sour notes.[59] This too is proof that the book was primarily used to reinforce memory.

One Czech Catholic remarked in 1588 on what he considered to be the pernicious effects of such song-books. Václav Šturm said of a song-book put out by the United Brethren in 1576: 'Everyone, nobles and peasants, poor and rich, have one at home. Because they sing all [these hymns] in meetings and at home, those who can read only a little use the texts from the hymnal to preach to the people and comment on the hymns.'[60] Hence printing served even a semi-literate public.

The Bible was a work that lent itself to a variety of types of reading. The Reformers' hesitations about permitting uncontrolled access to Holy Scripture led them to connect Bible reading and attendance at sermons. In 1552, when Pierre Navihères was attempting to justify free access to Scripture to his Catholic judges in Lyons, he established a strict relationship between reading and preaching, quoting the Fathers of the Church to argue that 'before coming to the sermon', the faithful should 'read what was to be preached so as to understand it better'.[61]

Lutheran and Calvinist practices probably differed somewhat in this domain. In sixteenth-century Germany and in the Scandinavian countries, editions of the Bible were printed principally for parishes and pastors.[62] In the Netherlands, however, where literacy had made greater strides and print production was proportionally greater, a large number of Bibles penetrated the home.[63] Calvinism, which was more firmly established in a bourgeois, urban setting, was more encouraging to individual reading of the Bible.

Comparison of the formats used by the various groups reveals differences. Lutheran printers preferred the folio format, which suggested a collective, liturgical or familial reading; the Calvinist Reformation published roughly as many Bibles in three formats: folio, quarto and octavo. This was a deliberate policy, given that the 1588 revision of the Bible, carried out under the direction of the Geneva pastors, was put out in the three formats from the outset. This suggests not only collective reading, but also more frequent private consultation.

The use of these Bibles poses another question. The sacred text was accompanied by aids that could themselves be read in multiple ways, thus offering several parallel approaches to the text. Some of these aids were placed at the beginning or end of the text in the form of an introduction, a table of contents or a summary. There were also philological, theological or liturgical marginal notes, which might or might not correspond to a mark in the text itself. One can also find cross-references to parallel passages. How did readers find their way among these various glosses? Was the Bible becoming an object for scholarly consultation? It is interesting to recall that the Catholic authorities feared this 'paratext' of marginal comments to the Bible more than they did the Protestant translations.

Where open combat with the Roman Catholic Church was too dangerous (in Italy, the Netherlands or France), works of piety and spiritual consolation provided a channel through which the Protestant Reformation penetrated, at least during the first half of the sixteenth century. These works, whose presentation was deliberately ambiguous and whose contents were discreetly heterodox, served as a vehicle for religious contestation. Some contained works of the Reformers, at times in faithful translations, at times reworked with various manipulations and interpolations. Lutheran influences dominated Zwinglian tendencies, but not without a certain doctrinal laxity (the Reformed and Reformist attitudes of Luther and Erasmus often overlapped). Some of the more specifically topical evangelical writings – those of Caspar Huberinus and Urbanus Rhegius, for example – were works of consolation in the face of illness or death.[64]

By their very nature, works of piety and consolation were designed for individual reading, as were the manuals of piety of the *Devotio moderna*, but the scant evidence we have of their influence points instead to collective reading, followed by small-group discussions in craftsmen's shops or private houses. Thus several conventicles were discovered in the Netherlands between 1520 and 1540 in which the Bible and spiritual works were read aloud.[65] Italian sources speak of the Protestant infiltration of confraternities devoted to reading edifying texts such as saints' lives, or even controversial works such as those of Savonarola. This occurred even within the cloister: Stefano Boscaia, a Franciscan interrogated by the Inquisition in 1547, admitted to having participated in a collective reading of Francesco Negri's *Tragedia del libero arbitrio*, a text first published in 1546.[66] Analogous situations giving the uneducated access to books can be found throughout Europe.

Beginning around 1545, the ascendancy of Calvin and Geneva lent greater cohesion to religious dissidence in France and the Seventeen Provinces of the Netherlands. Churches were organized (*dressées*, according to the terminology of the day) and provided with at least sketchy notions of worship and discipline. Reading aloud had a place in these. Thus in Tournai in 1561 Jean de Lannoy, a pillar of the Protestant community, 'came three times to the house [of Barbe Aymeries] to read them a chapter of Gospel, the Apocalypse, or others, and afterwards they sang some psalms.... The said upholsterer [de Lannoy] read the Scriptures; he interpreted and explained them as best he could.' The small groups described in such court records at times included as many as twelve participants.[67] The persistence of reading aloud in these Protestant communities was undoubtedly bolstered by individual reading.

Certain sixteenth-century books were used primarily in the silence of a scholar's study. These were works for specialists, people whom Bèze defined as 'already accustomed to and versed in such matters'.[68] Treatises on exegesis and theology, usually written in Latin, were obviously aimed at readers capable of silent reading. In all cases, such books constituted a means of individual communication. This is clear, for example, from a letter written by Valentin Hartung, who was at the time filled with enthusiasm for Calvin's works: 'I read them and reread them, sometimes not without tears, and for the most part with thanksgiving. ... As far as I can, I urge and will always urge all our disciples and our friends to do the same.'[69] The picture Hartung paints is one of solitary reading, both on his part and among his friends.

Such treatises, which appealed to a very restricted audience, were soon translated into the various vernacular languages, probably with less learned preachers in mind. As early as his *Psautier de David* (1524) Lefèvre d'Étaples states in his preface to that work that he hoped to do more than render a service to pious laity: 'And with this, the simple clerics, as they confer and read line by line, will have a better understanding of what they read in Latin.' Were Calvin's exegetic commentaries also translated for less learned ministers? One of the first of them explicitly refers to the 'weak and ignorant': 'It is for them that this translation has been made. . . . May they profit from this exposition as much as those to whom our Lord has given knowledge of languages.'[70] This enlargement of the audience for scholarly books raises a question: were Calvin's *non lettrez* capable of reading? Similar terms – *ignorants*, *illiterati, imperiti ac rudes* – often designated the target audience for publications in the vernacular. In his preface to *The Myrrour, or, Glasse of Christes Passion* (1534), John Fewterer expresses his hope that his translation will prove useful to readers and auditors.[71] Such allusions to texts listened to are too rare for certitude on this point. The question remains open.

Reading aloud might provide a point of departure for oral glosses. When in 1551 the king of Poland, Sigismund Augustus, wanted information about Protestantism, he turned to Francesco Lismanini. Twice a week, on Wednesdays and Fridays, Sigismund invited Lismanini to dine, and asked him to read a few pages from Calvin's *Institutes*.[72] These sessions, which were often limited to a short chapter, usually led to theological discussion.

Texts regarding learned controversies must have been read individually. Fairly soon some essential doctrinal points (in particular, those concerning the Last Supper) created profound divisions among Protestants. Debate, which was often technical, was brought to the public in a large number of pamphlets. The Reformers make it clear in their correspondence how important they considered such publications to be. They did their best to find out, as soon as possible, what their adversaries were up to (if need be, even before their works had come off the presses), so as to prepare the responses they thought indispensable. We can see a good example of this in the correspondence of Joachim Westphal, a Lutheran of strict obedience, with his publisher, Peter Braubach. Feeling himself isolated in Hamburg, Westphal sought a permanent contact in Frankfurt, which was at the time a major publishing centre.[73] The fact that minor works of this sort were seldom reprinted proves that learned theological controversy, as distinct from the more popular pamphlets that circulated during 'press campaigns', was seldom a popular bestseller. By comparison, the success of treatises on exegesis is impressive: such works, which were often voluminous, hence costly, were regularly reprinted.[74]

The Appropriation and Circulation of Texts

On occasion individual reading could have an effect that radiated well beyond the reader, if he became persuaded by the text he had read to the point of propagating the ideas he had found in it. This was a situation that was often repeated during the early years of the Protestant Reformation.

Italy furnishes several examples of this personal dissemination of ideas. In 1541 a group of heretical books, among them the *Unio dissidentium* of Herman Bodius, were seized in the cell of the preacher Giulio da Milano, at the time a member of the Order of St Augustine. One of Giulio's fellow Augustinians noted that many of the people who listened to the sermons that Giulio preached in Bologna in 1538 had followed along with the aid of the *Unio dissidentium* because Giulio's preaching was so closely based on that text. Similarly, in 1558 many forbidden books were found in the possession of the Dominican Giovanni Rubeo. An eyewitness attested that Rubeo had been in the habit of copying passages or even entire pages of Bucer, Bullinger, Zwingli and Calvin, from works he 'kept hidden and locked in a box in his cell', later inserting them into his sermons.[75]

Religious propaganda that spread out in concentric circles in this manner was not unique to Italy, as we have seen in the case of Jean de Lannoy, the upholsterer from Tournai. We are told that after an attentive study of the Bible and Calvin's works Lannoy was capable of discussing 'Scripture without a book because he knew it all by heart'.[76]

Luther considered preaching the normal channel for the diffusion of right doctrine. For him, theological works were not for the common man; their function was to permit 'the theologian and the bishop to be well and abundantly prepared, so that they will be capable of expounding the doctrine of piety'.[77]

Calvin, on the other hand, was happy to see his books circulated widely among his readers. To one correspondent from the duchy of Württemberg who wrote to him in 1554 to express his admiration for Calvin's writings, Calvin replied that he was comforted by the man's statement. 'In this evil century', Calvin wrote, 'there are at least pious and learned men who not only profit from my commentaries in private but seek to spread the benefit they have had from them even further by a loyal effort of hand-to-hand transmission.'[78]

Calvin did not confuse reading aloud with preaching. In 1547, at the beginning of the reign of Edward VI, a collection of homilies had been published in England as an attempt to remedy the lack of culture among the English clergy, who were invited to read them, one Sunday after another, during worship services. In a letter to the duke of Somerset in 1549, Calvin discreetly expressed his disapproval and his preference for real preaching: 'May the people be instructed so as to touch them to the quick,' he wrote, adding, 'I say this ... because it seems to me that there is very little lively preaching in the kingdom, but instead most [preachers] recite as if they were reading.'[79]

How a reader assimilates a text is an eminently personal matter, involving choice and a restructuring of what is written. As Michel de Certeau put it, reading is like 'poaching'.[80] Although writing is necessarily presented as a succession of words, lines and pages designed to be scanned in linear fashion from beginning to end, readers are none the less free to discover that space as they wish. Better, they are not passive when confronted with a text, and they need not necessarily accept its values and ideas.

We find an early reflection of a freer sort of reading in the way sixteenth-century publishers manipulated texts. When certain aspects of a text pleased them, they might reuse that text, sometimes giving it a quite different direction. The *Livre de vraye et parfaite oraison*, a work for Catholic readers that offered highly edited texts by Luther and Farel written between 1528 and 1545 and the Italian version of Calvin's *Catechism* of 1545, which corrected Calvin's doctrine of the Last Supper in a Lutheran direction, are examples of this manipulation that have received scholarly analysis.[81]

Another proof of unorthodox reading styles can be seen in the use that readers made of certain controversial works. Italian readers were delighted to discover Luther's ninety-five theses outlined, for the first time, in the *In praesumptuosas Martini Lutheri conclusiones de potestate papae* of the Dominican Silvestro Mazzolini da Prierio; the author, who was Master of the Sacred Palace, had dutifully reproduced the theses *in toto*, in order to refute them. The authorities in Rome eventually realized that this technique of scholastic polemics had an effect totally opposed to the one they had anticipated, and henceforth they forbade quotations from heretical texts, even when given in order to refute them.[82]

The trials of the Italian Inquisition allow us to move forward a step, and see how readers appropriated the texts they had before their eyes. Silvana Seidel Menchi shows that they tended not to follow the complete argument of a book, but rather to concentrate on one theme and detach it from its context. The Franciscan Stefano Boscaia, whom we have already met, put the complex theological argument of Francesco Negri's *Tragedia del libero arbitrio* in a nutshell when he proclaimed: 'Grace has cut the head off Free Will.' This is an extreme simplification of a highly complex text. Moreover, Italian readers of the time showed a fondness for emphasizing elements in a discourse that referred to daily life. The case of Zuane of Naples, arrested in 1568 for events that reached back to 1562, shows this clearly. Zuane owned a fairly free reworking by Antonio Brucioli of the first three chapters of Calvin's 1536 *Institutes*, an extremely solid text summarizing the fundamental categories of Protestant theology. Zuane claimed, however, that he had retained from it only such peripheral topics as the modes and times for prayer, dietary prescriptions and the cult of images. He added that he had been so deeply affected by these that they had changed his entire life.[83]

The Authority of Writing

Writing was a guarantee of authenticity. What had been true in the early centuries of the Church was equally true in the sixteenth century. Moreover, the authority naturally invested in the Bible was transferred to other forms of religious writings.

The book provided notable support to the operations of the propagators of the Reformation as they approached their listeners, literate and illiterate. In 1543 a Franciscan in Udine, Francesco Garzotto, went about 'always with the Epistles of St Paul in his hand'. The authority that he spontaneously derived from the book put his interlocutors at a disadvantage in any religious discussion. When Pietro Vagnola settled in Grignano Polesine in 1547, to spread Protestant Reformation ideas among the peasants, he was reported to be 'perpetually occupied with the study of the heretical and Lutheran books that he owns and keeps constantly at hand'. When a villager defended the Mass by invoking the authority of tradition, Pietro Vagnola faced him down, displaying the Mass on the printed page. The poor villager confessed to the Inquisitor: 'What do you want; if he proves what he says with books, you have to give up.' In other words, one must submit to the authority of the book.[84]

Circumstances might give a written text more weight in a public situation. In 1543 Charles V convoked a diet at Spires, in an attempt to calm religious discord. This seemed to several Reformers a dangerous enterprise. Bucer suggested to Calvin that they publish a public statement addressed to the emperor: 'A written book [addressed] to the emperor will be read by many others. It will have more weight, and it will be more effective to demand justice by means of a writing, in public as in private. . . . If you hesitate to appeal to the emperor, write to the kings and princes who will gather for the coming diet.' Calvin acquiesced, and he took care that his *Supplex exhortatio ad Carolum Quintum* be printed in thick roman characters and be 'fully readable and of fine appearance'.[85]

Like language for Aesop, the book was the best and the worst of things. In 1556 one citizen of Zug noted, after a confessional conflict that had arisen around the interpretation of a verse of the Bible, 'A lie is as easy to print as the truth.'[86] In the eyes of the Reformers there were too many works that were diffusing errors. In 1554 Calvin complained to Peter Martyr Vermigli 'of that confused forest of books', and he spoke of the urgent need for 'grave commentaries, erudite and solid, coming from pious and right-thinking men gifted with as much authority as judgment'. They alone could 'refute the absurd fantasies of those who confuse everything'.[87]

There was a more serious problem, however, which was the corruption of the Word of God. Luther faced this problem with his German translation of the New Testament. When he first saw unauthorized editions proliferate, he was delighted to see the Word spread far and wide, but he soon changed his mind: those hastily compiled editions were circulating a corrupt text. The last straw, however, was to discover that Hieronymus Emser had borrowed his translation and revised it to put out an edition of the New Testament representing the Catholic point of view.[88] The Calvinists were equally aggressive in their opposition to the French translation of the Bible prepared by Sébastien Castellion. The violence of the reaction was in proportion to the perceived danger, which was that the very foundation of religious discourse might be undermined.

Some perceived the book as a memorial whose audience would outlast its author. Two examples should suffice to show that Calvin and his entourage were aware that print could confer a degree of immortality. The year 1542 had been an extremely difficult one for Calvin, largely because the organization of the church of Geneva was an urgent task that he could not put off. When Farel asked him to write down his lessons on Genesis, Calvin responded that he did not have time to do so: 'If the Lord shall grant me longer life and leisure, perhaps I will set myself about that work. . . . This is my especial end and aim, to serve my generation; and for the rest, if, in my present calling, an occasional opportunity offers itself, I shall endeavour to improve it [the commentary on Genesis], for those who come after us.'[89] Thus in 1542 he stated that immediate service to help his 'generation' was his chief priority, and that a more long-term task for a hypothetical posterity would have to be put off. Two years later, Farel showed that he had learned his lesson. He asked Calvin for a refutation of an Anabaptist work, stating, 'We all know that you are overburdened with work and that you have other topics to treat, not only for the people today but also for posterity, especially in the explication of Scripture.'[90] This dialectic between action through writing in the short and the long term merits more attentive study. For our present purposes it is enough to point out the complexity of the bond between the author and the reader.

The vast increase in the number of texts raises a question that the historians do not seem to have treated as yet: when the Reformers were engaged in controversy, speaking out from the pulpit or in the public squares or blackening pages with small typographical signs, were they aware of the specificity of those media? If we can judge by the texts circulated throughout Germany in the early pamphlets, publications that reproduced spoken discourse much more than they were texts conceived for silent reading, the answer seems to be 'no'.

Francis Higman presents Calvin as a creator of the French language, standing out from his contemporaries by his rejection of a florid style with innumerable incised clauses. The style Calvin proposed is solidly but simply structured – even 'Cartesian', if I may be forgiven an anachronism.[91] Can that analysis be taken any further? Was Calvin conscious of the specificity of the written text as opposed to the spoken word? The way he handled the written text of his sermons is at first sight contradictory: he carefully kept the texts, but refused to circulate them!

Calvin not only agreed to notes being taken while he delivered his sermons, he even encouraged it. In 1549, when Denis Raguenier was installed as director of a secretarial staff charged with taking shorthand notes, it was not the first time Calvin had moved in that direction; for in 1547 he himself had sought a secretary for the same task.[92]

On the other hand, Calvin held back from publishing his sermons. The preface to a first edition (1546) begins: 'Because the author is not accustomed to have his sermons printed ...'. In 1562, toward the end of Calvin's life, another printer, Jacques Roux, confessed that he had obtained Calvin's permission to print his sermons only with 'great difficulty'. Roux added: 'as all who have known him privately will be easily persuaded'. Calvin himself edited only one book of sermons, the *Quatre sermons* of 1552. Conrad Badius, who had published several sets of Calvin's sermons during the latter's lifetime, stated in a preface written in 1557: 'Never did [Calvin] agree to printing or having anyone else print them (with the exception of four, for the relief of the poor faithful who seek the freedom of the Gospel).... The others that have been added to those four since were thanks more to a constrained, forced permission (or rather, by pestering him) than of his free will and consent.'[93]

The publishing history of the *Quatre sermons* provides a first explanation of Calvin's reticence. He did not provide the typesetters with notes taken by his stenographers, but rather with a text that he himself had revised and 'reduced to order'. For stylistic reasons he hesitated to have his sermons reproduced simply as they had been delivered, as confirmed by a letter written in 1546.[94] Farel had not been too pleased with the familiar style of the *Deux sermons* of 1546. He wrote to Calvin: 'I found your two sermons very agreeable, though I might have wished that you had developed your discourses a bit more carefully, as you usually do.'[95]

In his preface to Calvin's *Vingtdeux sermons* of 1554, Jean Girard specifies that Calvin preferred 'to have a few brief comments printed, when the opportunity arose, rather than filling up paper with the long discourses he gives from the pulpit'. Badius said much the same thing in a preface written in 1558: Calvin thought that his homilies had to be put into better order if they were 'to be put in the sight of everyone in that fashion'. His only reason for refusing 'to review them in order to polish them' was lack of time. 'When he wants to put forth [others], he will be quite capable of making completely new, better-fashioned homilies instead of reworking something he has already delivered.' The explanation that Jacques Roux gave in 1562 is less precise, but it too alludes to visual reading. In delivering his sermons, Roux wrote, Calvin 'only wanted to serve the flock that God had committed to his care by teaching it familiarly, not to make Homilies at his leisure to be put before the eyes of everyone'.[96] There is no doubt that Calvin, a master of language, spoken and written, was conscious of different styles. He wanted to give the printer carefully written, concise texts, something that was probably uncommon at the time. But had he intuited the special properties of visual reading? And did he appreciate certain of the demands of texts to be put 'in sight of' or 'before the eyes of everyone'? The summary view of the question that we have just seen would seem to lead to two contradictory interpretations of the history of reading: the Protestant Reformation changed everything; the Protestant Reformation changed nothing!

When the various Protestant churches were established in the late sixteenth century, no revolution in relationships with the written word seems to have taken place. In the religious domain, orality retained its primacy. As Johann Brenz stated, religion depends on preaching. Brenz distinguished three forms of preaching: the most important of them, preaching from the pulpit, was completed by both reading and singing.[97] Startled by the proliferation of heterodox ideas arising out of unsupervised reading, the Reformers took it on themselves to police the theological domain.

Access to the Bible occurred in the worship service and in the family, where readings were punctuated by authorized commentary. Popular reading was encouraged only within the framework of catechetics and liturgical texts. The Reformers were not interested in inviting the faithful to discover new messages, but rather in guaranteeing the stability of an elementary Christian doctrine. For that reason, it was their deliberate policy that the use of silent reading remain limited. Fears of the contentious consequences of free reading were not without foundation. The

Reformation does not seem to have challenged the predominance of orality.

But was that the whole story? Did the first move to place confidence in writing, with the challenge to the medieval ecclesiastical authorities that it brought with it, really leave no trace in Protestant society? When all Christians were invited to read the Bible by themselves, it must surely have weakened the sacralized concept of 'Holy Scripture'.

Moreover, daily contact with the book engendered familiarity with reading. Even though Protestants were solidly controlled on all sides, they were none the less invited to read. Medieval Christianity had hardly ever encouraged appropriation of Holy Writ, either by hearing or by sight. The followers of Luther, Zwingli and Calvin held books in their hands – the Bible, but more often a catechism, a psalter or a liturgical manual. Familiarity with those works was hardly the royal road to silent reading, but it was a modest beginning. The practice of providing the faithful with texts that they already knew by heart, texts either to read or simply to hold in their hands, gradually increased the number of readers.

We still need to ask what was the influence of such practices. Was the later development of reading the result of Protestantism? For a long time there has been little challenge to the accepted idea that the Western world was divided in its relationship to print and reading, and that the roots of that division reached back to the confessional conflicts of the sixteenth century, with the Protestants seen as great consumers of reading matter and the Catholics as more attached to oral traditions. Today's historians of culture are more hesitant about explaining mass literacy by the religious factor alone. Analysis of print production has not yet provided sufficient data to furnish reliable figures on the evolution of that difference in the fifteenth and sixteenth centuries, but it already seems clear that the discrepancy between northern and southern Europe was established before 1517. Important differences between the more largely rural societies in which Lutheranism took hold and the more literate milieus that were won over to Calvinism seem equally clear. Calvinism undeniably found a better welcome in the social strata that already had a certain familiarity with writing. This means that our question shifts. It is no longer sufficient to state that Protestantism promoted reading. We need to investigate how the effects of Protestantism varied according to the milieus that accepted it. As Willem Frijhoff remarks, 'The duty to read proclaimed by the Reformation may thus have led to practices that differed according to the types of society encountered.'[98]

Reading and the Protestant Reformations? Perhaps it would be more accurate to speak of an interplay in reciprocal influences among societies and religions.

9

Reading and the Counter-Reformation

Dominique Julia

The Council of Trent, reacting to reforms establishing Scripture as the one rule of faith (*sola scriptura*), reaffirmed the importance not only of the Bible but also of tradition, the accumulated depository of oral transmission of the faith. The Council decreed on 8 April 1546 that the Roman Catholic Church was to receive, with the same reverence as Scripture (*pari pietatis affectu*), 'the unwritten traditions which, received by the Apostles from the mouth of Christ himself ... have come down even unto us, transmitted as it were from hand to hand'.[1] When the Council insisted on oral transmission of the faith (citing St Paul's Epistle to the Romans, 10:17: 'fides ex auditu, auditus autem per Verbum Christi' (So faith comes from what is heard, and what is heard comes by the preaching of Christ)) at the very moment when print technology was spreading and revolutionizing the relationship to writing in modern societies and the Reformation was promoting a return to the authentic text of Scripture as the only way to combat the corruption of perverted church institutions, it chose an underlying anthropological vision that emphasized instead vital relationships within a community. At the same time, the Council reinforced the distinction between the respective roles of the clergy (henceforth increasingly defined as the priest) and the laity: priests were responsible for preaching to the assembled faithful, for individual spiritual guidance, and for reminding their parishioners, during auricular confession, to heed the demands of the divine Word; the laity's role was to listen, absorb and appropriate the message that an authorized voice had delivered to them. One did not need direct access to the sacred texts to advance on the road to holiness. Thus Catholic reservations concerning solitary reading of print matter had a carefully argued theological and ecclesiological basis. This is something we need to keep in mind in order to comprehend the disciplinary texts decreed at Trent and by authorities in Rome after the Council.[2]

The Conciliar Texts

During that fourth session of the Council in 1546, the bishops who had gathered in Trent established a list of the books of the Bible henceforth to be considered canonical, and they recognized the Latin Vulgate Bible as the one authentic version of Scripture. They also circumscribed what they saw as the correct way to comprehend texts:

> No one, relying on his own skill, shall – in matters of faith, and of morals ... wresting the sacred Scripture to his own senses, presume to interpret the said sacred Scripture contrary to that sense which holy mother Church – whose it is to judge of the true sense and interpretation of the holy Scriptures – hath held and doth hold; or even contrary to the unanimous consent of the Fathers.[3]

This attitude toward the printed book led to a dual policy. On the one hand, books 'on sacred matters' were to be subjected to rigorous controls, and before a text could be printed, the printer or bookseller had to have it examined and approved by the local ordinary. As the prelates separated and prepared to leave Trent, they were concerned with building a barrier to contain the flood of 'suspect or pernicious' books that were spreading bad doctrine, and they entrusted the Pope with seeing through the programme for censorship that a conciliar commission had prepared. In short, they launched the system of the *Index of Prohibited Books*, the first edition of which was promulgated by Paul IV and published in Rome in 1558. Their second policy aimed at making sure that texts would be produced that would impart uniformity to practices throughout the Catholic Church. The decree of 1546 demanded that 'henceforth, the sacred Scripture, and especially the said old and vulgate edition, be printed in the most correct manner possible'.[4] On 4 December 1563 the prelates at Trent also entrusted the Pope with revision of the Breviary and the Missal and with composing a catechism. The unity of Catholicism was to be refashioned around common biblical, liturgical and catechetical texts, all written in Latin.

We might perhaps note two significant absences in the Tridentine texts: they say nothing about prohibiting laymen from reading the

Bible, and they mention no translation of Scripture. This omission was an acknowledgement that open conflict had reigned among the conciliar fathers, and that the papal legates had preferred to leave the question unresolved, given the impossibility of a decision. For even greater reason, there is no mention of translations of liturgical texts in the conciliar documents. The Mass was to be said in Latin, and certain portions of the canon (the consecration, for example) were to be spoken by the celebrant *submissa voce*, in a murmur. It was here that oral *explicationes* took on their full importance: priests were to make sure 'that the sheep of Christ may not suffer hunger, nor the little ones ask for bread, and there be none to break it unto them'; they were to expound 'some portion of those things which are read at mass' and explain 'some mystery of this most holy sacrifice, especially on the Lord's days and festivals'.[5] The Council's insistence on the pedagogical role of parish priests through preaching the Word of God and teaching the catechism thus quite normally and swiftly led to the production of official texts primarily for their use. The Roman Breviary, composed in large part by the Theatines, appeared in 1568. Although that work fully maintained the medieval structure of the traditional liturgy, which was deliberately fashioned as contemplative prayer, and although it did little more than correct the older version, it none the less granted Holy Scripture a larger place in the liturgy of Matins. It did not go as far in that direction, however, as to give the Breviary the didactic and humanist dimension that the general of the Franciscans, Francisco Quiñones, had attempted to introduce into the *Brevarium Romanum* that he had presented to Pope Paul III in 1535. Nor did the new *Missale Romanum* promulgated by Pope Pius V in 1570 give any new prominence to Holy Writ in the celebration of the Mass. For the most part, it repeated the medieval structure of the biblical lessons and pericopes that had been set in place in the late eighth century. In reality, once the Council had decreed that Latin be kept for the celebration of the Eucharist, the main task of the Roman commission of revision consisted less in any thoroughgoing transformation of ritual than in imposing a theologically consistent uniformity on formulas and gestures. The *Catechismus ex Decreto Concilii Tridentini ad parochos*, published in 1566, was explicitly addressed to parish priests, rather than directly to the faithful. It was the priests' task to provide oral explication to their parishioners, so that 'the faithful will be enabled to approach worthily and with salutary effect these inestimable and most holy institutions [the sacraments]'. When the members of the Roman commission, placed under the tutelage of the cardinal-nephew Carlo Borromeo, drew up this practical condensation of theology, they brought together the four traditional parts of catechetical teaching: the Credo, the sacraments, the Decalogue, and the Lord's

Prayer. These 'general heads of Sacred Scripture' would provide 'almost everything that a Christian should learn'. Given its target audience, the Tridentine catechism was the only text whose translation into the vernacular the Council expressly mandated, and it invited the bishops to check its accuracy with particular care.[6]

Bringing the Vulgate up to date, a task mandated as early as the 1546 decree, took longer. When the commission that Sixtus V designated on his accession to the papacy in 1585 had finished its work, the new version (which the Pope himself, persuaded that he should play a critical role, had looked over carefully) was first published, in May 1590. In the preface the Sovereign Pontiff decreed that the present edition, 'reviewed with all possible care', was to be 'regarded as the one that the Council of Trent had proclaimed to be authentic'. When Sixtus V died only four months later (on 27 August 1590), a quite justified fear of Protestant criticism led to withdrawing all extant copies from sale and buying back or exchanging others on a massive scale. A new commission (which included most of the members of the preceding commission, and in which the Jesuit Cardinal Robert Bellarmine played an essential role) took up where the old one had left off, using its dossiers. The new commission's definitive text was promulgated in November 1592 by Clement VIII, and the new official version of the Vulgate was called 'Sistine', maintaining the fiction that Sixtus V himself had felt that the 1590 version was imperfect, and justifying the nearly 5,000 changes that had been made in it.[7] This completed the Council of Trent's programme of texts to be published.

At the same time, the papacy saw to it that these now official texts would be distributed rapidly and surely, in order to compete with the powerful networks of Protestant booksellers. The conciliar texts were immediately adopted in territories under the Spanish crown; in France, where official acceptance was more problematic, the provincial councils called by the metropolitan archbishops soon decreed adoption of the Roman Missal and Breviary (in Bordeaux in 1583, Aix in 1585, and Toulouse in 1590). 'Today', a group of booksellers wrote in 1631, protesting the monopoly over commonly used liturgical books, 'there are not ten [dioceses] among the one hundred and fifteen in France that do not totally follow' the Council.[8] In 1561 Pope Pius IV attempted to respond to the enormous demand for conciliar texts by establishing the Vatican Press, the 'Stamperia del Popolo Romano', and charging it with printing official Church texts, calling Paolo Manuzio from Venice to act as its director. In 1562 a general privilege in the form of a *motu proprio* was accorded the official press, and printers and booksellers who infringed the privilege were threatened with fines and excommunication. The Pope's intentions were made clearer as works inspired by the

Council were published – in particular, with the bull *Quod a nobis* (1568) promulgating the revised Breviary. For one thing, the use of older editions was henceforth forbidden, and the new edition, which was not to be changed in the slightest detail, was to be used universally. For another, in order to guarantee absolute unity in rites, the printing of new texts was to be strictly controlled through selective approval. The Roman printer held a monopoly that he could, with the Pope's approval, delegate to competent and trustworthy printers in the form of local privileges. Thus in Venice Domenico Basa, in collaboration with Luca Antonio Giunti, obtained a privilege in 1567, valid for twenty years, to publish the new Breviary, and in like fashion the Torresino brothers, who directed the Aldine presses, obtained the pontifical privilege to publish the Litany of Our Lady, and received permission from the archbishops of Milan and Naples to sell in their dioceses the liturgical works printed in Venice. The most significant case, as well as the best-known one, is that of Christophe Plantin in Antwerp, who in 1568 obtained the pontifical privilege for the new Breviary for all of the Spanish Netherlands and, in 1570, for the Roman Missal in the Netherlands, Hungary and part of the Empire. Soon, thanks to agreements drawn up between Philip II and the papacy, Plantin devoted a large proportion of his activity to producing liturgical books specifically designed for Spanish territories, given that the cities of the Iberian Peninsula were not among the major typographical centres of the sixteenth century.[9] After the 1590s, the production of liturgical and biblical texts represented more than a quarter of all copies printed by Plantin's presses, and in the 1640s such books accounted for three-quarters of the Plantin firm's production in Antwerp. To cite only one example, the *Missile Romanum* went through seventy different folio editions printed by the Plantin firm between 1590 and 1640, or a total of 31,400 copies.[10]

Even in France, where archives unfortunately do not permit precise measurement of publishing activity or booksellers' sales, the increase in the number of Counter-Reformation editions, in response to strong demand from the dioceses and religious Orders, both old and new, resulted in important economic changes. On the one hand, certain Paris booksellers paid Plantin directly, and furnished him with paper so that he would print Roman liturgical works for them in an edition published with the colophon of the Antwerp house but sold by them, with the profits accruing to them. On the other hand, booksellers' companies were created, and the king, reasserting his sole right to dispense authorizations to print, conceded to them the privilege of publishing the official texts of the Counter-Reformation. Not only did this authorization in theory protect the great Parisian companies (which were founded by notarized contract) from extra-legal competition from provincial booksellers; it also enabled the Paris book dealers to gather together the capital required for large publishing projects. The company members were the wealthiest Paris booksellers, men who were also the principal representatives of the Paris publishing world everywhere abroad, from Frankfurt to the Netherlands and from England to Spain, which meant that they could promise widespread outlets for book production throughout Europe.[11] These changing conditions suggest the enormous size of the market for religious books opened up by the conciliar reforms. The religious book required technical competence on the part of experienced typographers, a sizeable amount of capital and consistently good relations between the booksellers and the political powers (in France the royal privilege substituted for the pontifical one) and the religious authorities.

Reading the Bible

As the church authorities in Rome moved to establish strict control over the official publications of the Counter-Reformation, they also gradually came around to specifying the conditions of access to the sacred texts and, even more, of their translation – something that the conciliar fathers had neglected to do. The *Index of Prohibited Books*, which the Council had entrusted to Pope Pius IV, was finally published in March 1564. The list was preceded by specific rules for permissible use of translations of the Bible. The fourth of these rules contained two essential notions: first, only persons who had obtained the written permission of their bishop or the Inquisitor, 'with the counsel of the parish priest or the confessor', were authorized to read the Bible in translation; second, such permission would be given only to 'learned and pious' men, persons known to the clerics who were dispensing the authorization and who were capable of 'drawing from that reading not harm but some increase of faith and of piety'. Separating the wheat from the chaff thus required clerical judgement of the 'capacities' of the lay potential reader. The injunctions sent out from Rome grew increasingly restrictive: in 1593 Clement VIII published important 'observations' on the rules decreed by Pius IV. Concerning the fourth rule, he withdrew all power from the ordinary bishops to 'give permissions to read or to possess vernacular Bibles or other portions of Holy Writ such as the New Testament or the Old Testament, in whatever language they may have been published'. All later versions of the *Index* until the mid-eighteenth century were to repeat this condemnation of translations of the Bible that in fact prohibited reading them. It remained to be seen how the decrees elaborated by the Roman congregations would be applied in the various Catholic countries. Reactions were of three major kinds. I shall attempt to sketch them, following Bernard Chédozeau.[12]

The first and most restrictive interpretation concerned the states of the Iberian peninsula and the Italian peninsula. In Spain the versions of the *Index* established by the Inquisitors contained in their preambles the rules decreed by Pius IV in 1564 and the observations that Clement VIII had published in the constitution *Sacrosanctum Catholicae Fidei* in 1593. In 1612 the *Index* published by the Inquisitor Bernardo de Sandoval forbade reading 'the Bible and all of its parts, printed or manuscript, in any vernacular language'; it also prohibited reading 'summaries and compendia, even those of a historical nature, of that same Bible or of the books of Holy Scripture written in any vernacular idiom or language'. The *Index* did permit reading 'the Epistles or Gospels that are sung at Mass during the year, provided they not be alone, without an accompanying sermon or declaration composed or to be composed on each one of them for the edification of the faithful'.[13] In 1640 the Inquisitor Antonio de Sotomayor stated in a new edition of the *Index* that he would no longer tolerate such latitude. He included in the prohibition reading

> in the vernacular language the book vulgarly and commonly given as the Epistles and Gospels even if it contains some brief declarations on some parts, and the Gospels, being, as indeed they are, the major part and as if the totality of the holy text in the vernacular language; because of the danger of seeing the ignorant people deceived by a bad interpretation, and for other inconveniences that have been warned about and that have occurred.

As if that prohibition were not clear enough, Sotomayor defined what he meant by 'vulgar' and 'non-vulgar' languages: 'The Hebrew language, Greek, Latin, Chaldean, Syriac, Ethiopic, Persian and Arabic are not vulgar languages. These are to be understood as the original languages, which are not commonly used today in familiar speech, so that the reader may understand that all other languages than these are vulgar.'[14]

This statement could hardly be more categorical. In fact, the very few Spanish Catholic versions of the Bible published after the Council of Trent (all of which are partial) remained in manuscript or were published abroad.[15] The enormous exegetical labours of Spanish Jesuit theologians were published in Latin and, by that token, were restricted to clerical readers. It was only at the very end of the eighteenth century that the inquisitorial vise was loosened, belatedly following the papal brief promulgated by Benedict XIV in 1757, which authorized the use of versions of the Bible in vernacular languages, and made no more mention either of the readers' capacities or of any sort of written permission.[16] The first complete Spanish translation of the Latin Vulgate, which was made by the bishop of Segovia, Felip Scio de San Miguel, a Piarist, appeared in Valencia in ten folio volumes published from 1791 to 1793. The situation seems to have been similar in Portugal: not only was Portugal joined to the Spanish crown politically from 1580 to 1640, but the Portuguese Inquisition exercised the same vigilance as its Spanish counterpart concerning forbidden books.[17] It is hardly surprising, then, that the first (and partial) translations of biblical books all appear after Benedict XIV's brief. The first complete translation of the Latin Vulgate, made by a former member of the Oratory in Portugal, Father Antonio Pereira de Figueiredo, and published in twenty-three volumes from 1778 to 1790, owed much to French publishers, commentators and translators of the seventeenth century, in particular, to the Port-Royal group.[18] On the Italian peninsula, to end the list, all the Roman editions of the *Index* until 1762 repeated Clement VIII's prohibition against reading *Biblia Vulgari quocumque Idiomate conscripta*. The proximity of the papal See easily explains why the most restrictive interpretation triumphed in Italy: in spite of a growing anti-curial sentiment, the various Italian states did not care to hazard a frontal attack on Rome on that point. The first complete translation of the Latin Vulgate into Italian, made by Antonio Martini, appeared in 1769 (the New Testament) and 1776 (the Old Testament), and was approved by Pius VI in 1778. All in all, in the states of the Iberian and Italian peninsulas, for over two centuries direct reading of the Bible was reserved to the clergy, given that the only available text was in Latin.[19]

Even in France the Church tended to restrict translations. Aside from certain religious Orders (the Recollects, for example), from the late sixteenth century through the first half of the seventeenth century the doctors of the Faculty of Theology of Paris displayed a lively and consistent hostility toward translations of Scripture, paradoxically calling on the Spanish or Roman Jesuit theologians to defend their stance. When René Benoist, the parish priest of Saint-Pierre des Arcis, later of Saint-Eustache in Paris, published a French translation of the Bible in 1566, he tried in vain to place his work explicitly in the direct line of the decrees of the Council of Trent by stating that he had accompanied his translation, as those decrees stipulated, with 'annotations necessary for knowledge of the most difficult places and expositions containing brief and familiar resolutions of the passages that have been vitiated and corrupted by the heretics of our own time'. Benoist's translation was immediately placed under interdict by the Faculty of Theology of Paris, which accused him (quite rightly) of having borrowed from the

Geneva Bibles. It was condemned again in Rome in 1575. The initiative caught the eye of Christophe Plantin in Antwerp, who fully understood the importance of the francophone market. In 1572 Plantin obtained a privilege to print the work in Brussels and the approval of four doctors in Louvain. The work finally came out in 1578, without annotations, and from then on the 'Bible of the Louvain Theologians' met with enormous success, in spite of the opposition of the Paris doctors, going through thirteen editions in the decade from 1578 to 1587 alone, several of them in Lyons and Rouen.[20]

During the first half of the seventeenth century, a 'French' Roman Catholic position slowly came to be defined in accordance with the fourth rule of the *Index* of 1564, and (the Paris doctors to the contrary) it was favourable to a controlled reading of the Bible among 'capable' readers. The need for a Catholic translation of Scripture was justified, first, by the religious situation in France, which, after the Edict of Nantes in 1598, was the only Catholic state that was multi-confessional. How were French Catholics to combat the Protestants, who only read French, if they did not have equal weapons? Reading the sacred texts was still not to be permitted to everyone, however. The French Catholic position, which can be found in a number of prefaces, is perfectly summarized in a work by Nicolas Le Maire, *Le Sanctuaire fermé aux profanes ou la Bible défendue au vulgaire* (1651). Stating that 'one of the most important practices of the Church ... consists in concealing the mysteries from the unworthy and distancing the profane from the sanctuary', Le Maire defended the idea that Scripture must not 'be made either common or vulgar'. This is not the same thing as forbidding Bible reading to all the laity. Le Maire defines the requisite capacity negatively: *le vulgaire* was for him not only 'the dregs of the people, who crawl under the feet of the others'; it also included 'the proud, the impure, the ignorant, the weak, the curious, the indiscreet, the unspeakable' – in short, all people who had shown themselves to be incapable of dealing with holy things. Reading the Bible was thus not 'for craftsmen or for women'; nor was it 'for persons of all sorts and conditions'. Returning to patristic requirements for Bible reading, Le Maire stressed the need for humility, which meant rejecting reading 'with no master or interpreter', and consisted in a desire to find 'only instruction and salvation' in reading, in being accustomed 'to envisage spiritual and invisible things', and willing to spend long hours in study and profound meditation. All these qualities, Le Maire insisted, contrasted, trait for trait, with those of 'the vulgar', because 'the people are the grand master of error', and are entombed 'in the shadows of a crass ignorance'. For all these reasons, the Church was right not to give the sacred trust of the Bible into unworthy hands. Here was where the pastoral task of explication came in, a task reasserted by the Council of Trent and delegated to parish priests, the 'doctors' charged with teaching. The example of the early Christian communities, who, lacking the Gospel, took as their sole rule of conduct and faith 'the voice of their pastors and the tradition of their fathers', proved that reading was 'neither necessary nor even useful to everyone'. This was not an authorization of 'the criminal negligence that makes the book of Scripture so little known by everyone and that banishes its reading from most secular families under the pretext of a Christian reverence'.[21]

The position defined by Le Maire was quite probably that of a large proportion of the French episcopate of his day. In 1653 the Assemblée du Clergé charged Father Denys Amelote, an Oratorian, with translating the entire New Testament, a task he completed in 1666. As Amelote wrote in his preface, the aim of his translation was to 'nourish the faithful in dependence from their pastors, and it is destined solely for those who will receive it from the hand of the Church and who will make use of it by [the Church's] light and counsel'.[22]

While that position was spreading in response to a broader demand on the part of urban readers educated in the secondary schools (*collèges*), it was both challenged and weakened by the immense efforts that the 'Messieurs de Port-Royal' and their circle made to put out biblical and liturgical translations. Between 1650 and 1693 the Jansenists offered Catholic laity a complete array of liturgical and biblical texts in French translation. The *Office de l'Église en latin et en français contenant l'office des dimanches et fêtes*, better known as the *Heures de Port-Royal*, was published in 1650. Although this work did not yet provide the Ordinary of the Mass in translation, it did offer translations (from the Hebrew) of fifty-eight psalms and of the hymns of the Church for the entire year, thus making available to the laity many of the prayers sung by the clergy. In 1660 came the *Missel romain, selon le règlement du Concile de Trente: Traduit en français: Avec l'explication de toutes les messes et leurs cérémonies pour tous les jours de l'année*. The author, Joseph de Voisin, a man close to the Port-Royal group, states that he had acted in response to an explicit command of the Princesse de Conti, who wanted to replace the heretics' translation and their explications of the Missal with a complete translation that would give 'the explication of every Mass according to the true meaning of the Church'. Voisin's translation was condemned by the Faculty of Theology of Paris and by Rome, but it was immediately defended by Antoine Arnauld in a book significantly titled *La Traduction et explication du Missel en langue vulgaire autorisée par l'Écriture Sainte, par les Saints Pères et Docteurs de l'Église, par les décrets des Conciles et des Papes, et par l'usage de l'Église gallicane*. In spite of the conflicts that the translation of the Roman Missal had inspired, the years following saw a profusion of *Offices* in translation. One liturgist close to Port-Royal, Nicolas Le Tourneux, published a number of translations, among them *L'Office de la Semaine Sainte* (1674), a work dedicated to Chancellor Le Tellier's wife, and a *Bréviaire romain* that appeared in 1688, two years after Le Tourneux's death. The Port-Royal group was equally productive where translations of the Bible were concerned. Two translations of the Psalms were published in 1665, one of them based on the Hebrew, the other on the Vulgate. In 1667 Louis-Isaac Le Maistre de Sacy put out a *Nouveau Testament*, called 'de Mons', which he translated from the Vulgate and published 'with the differences from the Greek'. Sacy then moved on to translating the Old Testament, which was published, with 'explications', between 1672 and 1693. He followed the same principle from 1696 to 1708 for the books of the New Testament. In all, the collection consisted of thirty-two octavo volumes, each with a preface, the Latin text and a French translation, each verse accompanied by an 'explication' of its literal and 'spiritual' meaning, according to St Augustine's instructions on how to read the Bible. This immense liturgical and biblical effort[23] sprang from a strong conviction, common throughout the Port-Royal movement and well expressed by Sacy in his preface to the Mons New Testament. Reading Scripture, the New Testament in particular, was a moral obligation for all Catholics, even those 'who do not know how to read', who 'are not to be excused for that reason for not knowing what one can learn' through such reading. Following St Augustine's parallel between the Gospels and the Eucharist, Sacy states that reading Scripture is the reception of the Word of God, just as the Eucharist is the reception of his body: hence reading Scripture is preparation for the Eucharist, because the Holy Spirit effects a 'good' reading in the soul of the worshipper so 'disposed' by grace. This view, which makes reading Scripture not a right but a fundamental civic duty for all lay Christians, led to a greater emphasis on the lay state, now endowed with much greater responsibility. Unlike the decrees of the Council of Trent, a view of that sort tended to reduce the gap between the laity and the clergy, imposing on the laity duties once specific to the clergy. The Jansenist attitude shows an acute perception of the transformations that the spread of printed texts had brought to the relationship with writing. Not surprisingly, such a radical approach elicited violent resistance, and produced fractures. One of the principal reasons for the papal bull *Unigenitus* (1713) condemning the *Nouveau Testament en français, avec des réflexions morales sur chaque verset* of Pasquier Quesnel was precisely the author's statement that every Christian – without reservation, women included – had an obligation to read Scripture.[24]

The radical nature of the Jansenist position failed to persuade the French bishops to abandon their defence of a regulated, supervised access to reading Scripture for the laity. In fact, the years between 1670 and 1720 marked the period of greatest intensity in the Catholic Reformation in France. In the same span of years, Latin gradually ceased being a living language in the *collèges*, and its share of publishing production slipped noticeably. Booksellers were more interested in responding to a demand from urban pious milieus who wanted the sacred texts in French. Beginning as early as 1666–70 a number of works were published that had been drawn from Denys Amelote's and Sacy's translations of the New Testament: *Paroles de la Parole incarnée de Jésus-Christ tirées du Nouveau Testament* by the Oratorian Pasquier Quesnel (1668); *Paroles de Notre Seigneur Jésus-Christ tirées du Nouveau Testament* (1668); *La Vie de Jésus-Christ composée de toutes les paroles des Évangélistes* (1669) and *Épîtres et évangiles des dimanches et fêtes* by Father Amelote, and similar works by Sacy and a number of others. Such works attest not only to competition between the two groups that were producing translations, but also to the size of a growing publishing market. Moreover, the Gallican policy of the monarchy (in particular its attitude to Protestants following the revocation of the Edict of Nantes in 1685) definitively closed the way to strict ultramontane positions. The pastoral policy pursued under the leadership of Archbishop Harlay de Champvallon was in reality pastoral instruction through writing, because immense distributions of books, financed by the Caisse des Conversions, were made to the 'new converts'. From October 1685 to January 1687 more than 300,000 copies of scriptural works (among them, Denys Amelote's translation of the New Testament and translations of the Psalms specially made for the occasion), more than 150,000 copies of works relating to the ritual of the Mass and giving the Ordinary in translation, the texts of the decrees of the Council of Trent and the translation of the Council's Catechism (30,000 copies of each) were distributed in French provinces with a sizeable Protestant minority to replace the books that had been taken away from the 'new converts'. The 'gentler way' gave yesterday's heretic the right to a French text of the New Testament with no Latin text, preface or explanatory notes and to translations of the Ordinary of the Mass and the conciliar catechism, a work originally intended for training the clergy. Contrary to the prescriptions of Rule IV of the *Index* of 1565, never at any moment was there any question of the 'capacities' required for reading. How could the old Catholics be refused what had been granted the former Calvinists? The distributions of books that followed the revocation of the Edict of Nantes thus opened a breach that was never closed. Many manuals for Christians appeared that contained the French (at times, the Latin) text of the New Testament, the Psalms, the *Imitation of Christ* and the Ordinary of the Mass. Many missals for lay use were produced as well. It is true that one work, the Old Testament, was conspicuously absent from the list: Sacy's translation had not yet been completed at that date, so it was not included in the distributions. Still, a lay Catholic culture grew up that included reading the New Testament and that escaped the control of parish priests.[25] When the bishop of Arras interrogated him regarding his 'practice ... on the subject of reading the Holy Scripture, and particularly the New Testament',[26] Fénelon, the archbishop of Cambrai, returned to arguments that Nicolas Le Maire had used fifty years earlier, drawn from the same patristic sources, to thunder at the audacity of criticisms that 'dry up hearts, raise minds above their capabilities', and 'teach scorn of simple inner piety'. Fénelon states:

> Christians must be instructed on Scripture before they are given it to read. They must be prepared for it little by little, so that when they read it they will already be accustomed to hearing it and will be filled with its spirit before having seen it written. Reading [Scripture] should be permitted only to simple, docile, humble souls who will seek in it not to satisfy their curiosity or to dispute or criticize but to take nourishment from it in silence. Finally, Scripture must only be given to those who, receiving it from the hands of the Church, will seek in it only the Church's meaning.

Fénelon was forced to admit, however, that times had changed since the first centuries of the Church, and that men

> who bear the name of Christians no longer have the same simplicity, the same docility, the same preparation of mind and heart. . . . The bishops must not flatter themselves concerning their authority. It is so weakened that only traces of it are left in the people's minds. . . . It is not to us that they come to ask counsel, consolation and direction of conscience. Thus that paternal authority, which is so needed in order to moderate minds to a humble docility by the reading of saints' lives, is entirely lacking. In our day everyone is his own casuist, everyone his own doctor, everyone decides, everyone backs the innovators under fine pretexts, against the authority of the Church. People quibble over words, without which meanings are no more than vain phantoms.[27]

In short, enlarging the scope of reading had in fact rendered attempts to control it invalid. The violent conflicts that followed the promulgation of the papal bull *Unigenitus*, which even touched the lower levels of society, soon produced proof.

Reading and the Clergy

When the Council of Trent insisted on the need for better instruction of the clergy in the decree *Cum adolescentium aetas*, it offered an invitation to all bishops to institute a seminary in each diocese that would gather together and train candidates for holy orders. Although the seminary, as formulated by the Council, was soon rivalled and bypassed by the model of the *collège*, and although from that moment on the term 'seminary' included a great variety of forms, ranging from simple boarding schools to teaching centres,[28] during the centuries that followed the Council of Trent, the level of instruction of the parish clergy was undeniably one of the major concerns of the episcopate. A systematic, comparative study of diocesan synodal statutes and of the questionnaires connected with pastoral visits would undoubtedly throw light on variations in the level of implantation of the Catholic Reformation. To keep for the moment to the French example, when French synodal statutes of the first half of the sixteenth century mention books that were considered indispensable for the exercise of the priestly ministry, they of course list Scripture and the synodal statutes themselves, but they also mention two older works, the *Manipulus Curatorum* (a manual of pastoral care by Guy de Montrocher, a Spanish priest of the fourteenth century, that had gone through over 100 editions between the invention of printing and the end of the sixteenth century) and the *Opusculum tripartitum* (a confession manual written by Jean Gerson for 'less well-instructed parish priests').[29] During the latter half of the sixteenth century the parish priest's 'ideal library' grew, at least in newly reformed dioceses. Besides the Roman catechism and the catechism of Peter Canisius, there were recent confession manuals such as the *Directorium* of the Jesuit Juan-Alphonso de Polanco (first published in Louvain in 1554) and the *Enchiridion* of Martin de Azpilcueta, known as Doctor Navarrus (first Spanish edition Coimbra, 1553; first Latin edition Antwerp, 1573). There were also the commentaries or homilies on the Scriptures by the Church Fathers, commentaries on the *Summa* of St Thomas Aquinas (one by François Silvestri, General Master of the Dominicans in the early sixteenth century) and works of anti-Protestant controversy that offered an arsenal of commonplaces. At the height of the Catholic Reformation (that is, between 1650 and 1730) the 'good' parish priest was required to own even more books. As a rule he would have the Bible, and the catechism of the Council of Trent was systematically recommended, but French catechisms were often added, in particular Armand du Plessis de Richelieu's *Instruction du chrétien*. The ecclesiastical authorities also considered the decrees of the Council of

Trent an indispensable vade-mecum. Beyond these basics, French prelates of the latter half of the seventeenth century invited their priests to procure French-language versions of three sorts of works: commentaries or homilies on Holy Writ by the Church Fathers (with a particular insistence on St Gregory's *Moralia* and his *Regula pastoralis* (The Pastoral Care)), books of moral theology that might be considered 'professional' reading (St Charles Borromeo's instructions to confessors, the *Avvertimenti ... per li confessori*; the *Summa casuum conscientia* (Summa of Cases of Conscience) of the Spanish Jesuit Francisco Toledo), and spiritual reading matter (chiefly Thomas à Kempis's *Imitation of Christ*, the *Guia de pecadores* (Sinner's Guide) of Luis de Granada, and François de Sales's *Introduction à la Vie dévote* (Introduction to the Devout Life)).[30] The immense pedagogical efforts of the Counter-Reformation were thus aimed at turning parish clergy into men of study and of the book.

What the bishops were really doing was trying to persuade the priests under their authority to keep up the good habits they had acquired in the seminaries under the guidance of the new priestly congregations (Eudists, Oratorians, Sulpicians and Lazarists). This was the thrust of the daily schedules they proposed. To pick one example, Félix Vialart de Herse, bishop of Châlons-sur-Marne, specified in a *Mandement du bon emploi que les ecclésiastiques et principalement les curés, tant des villes que de la campagne doivent faire de leur temps* that the priest should spend three hours in the morning and two in the evening in studies. Every morning from eight to eleven he should prepare himself to teach catechism or to give the Sunday sermon, study cases of conscience concerning 'the most useful things and [those] that occur the most in practice', study the rubrics of the Missal, the Breviary and the Ritual, prepare himself for the next ecclesiastical conference and write a summary of his studies. In the afternoon from four to six he was expected to continue his morning studies, then take up 'reading some book of piety' (a short list of appropriate works was provided), 'reading a little at a time in order to grasp the meaning and encourage himself to devotion'. These times reserved for study and reading did not excuse the priest from other times given over to meditation, for instance, self-examination after morning prayer (from 5.30 to 6), when he was invited to apply his mind to 'considering some point of piety', perhaps with the aid of a 'book that may serve that purpose, such as the Meditations of Beuvelet, Hayneuve, Grenade, du Pont, or their like'. In the evening before retiring, and again when he awoke the next morning, he was advised to reread 'the point of piety to be considered'.[31] This rise in the number of books in clerical libraries was inconceivable without a regulated use of reading and conformity in practices.[32] This was the precise aim of ecclesiastical conferences.

The ecclesiastical conferences, which developed after the second half of the seventeenth century in particular, were instituted to support the parish clergy's intellectual interests, produce a common discourse, and to establish practices specific to parish clergy as a group. They were periodic gatherings that generally took place once a month during the months that the roads were passable, attended by the parish priests and curates from ten to twenty parishes, with the dean of the parochial district as group leader. Matters of dogma and Holy Writ were discussed, but the participants also raised questions related to the exercise of their ministry (liturgy, administration of the sacraments, cases of conscience) or questions specific to the sacerdotal state ('ecclesiastical virtues'). The bishop set the yearly agenda of topics for discussion, and distributed a printed text to be discussed, along with a list of books recommended for each topic. Every priest was invited to do serious preparation for each conference. After each session its 'results' were sent to the episcopal chancellery in the form of *devoirs* (compositions) that were read and 'corrected' by the vicars general.[33] Although the conferences met with unequal success, they set up a mode of work specific to priests that was guided by recourse to the same manuals and a common store of reports on studies, and they created a group language.[34]

As the network of seminaries grew, pastoral care came to be supported by an entire religious literature of manuals of theology, confessors' manuals, sermon collections and spiritual texts that were destined for all priests, rather than uniquely for learned clerics or graduates in theology. Enormous quantities of this literature, written by secular priests or by members of the new priestly congregations (Jesuits, Oratorians, Lazarists, Sulpicians), were published in Paris, to be distributed in the provinces through specialized catalogues published at regular intervals by booksellers who were themselves often closely connected with an Order or a Congregation, a seminary or a spiritual current.[35] In the provinces the bishop usually held a general privilege for printing books for the use of his diocese. Pontchartrain wrote to Monsignor de Grignan, bishop of Carcassonne:

> Monsieur: I approve infinitely of all that you tell me you are doing [to further] the instruction of the parish priests of your diocese and to establish among them a perfect uniformity of doctrine and discipline. All your sentiments on the topic are worthy of the title that adorns you, and I know not how to praise too highly intentions as pure and as upright as your own. I count myself happy to be able to second them by according you the privilege that you ask of me for the printing of the books about which you speak.[36]

In the seat of every important diocese a bishop's printer was granted the privilege of 'printing, selling and distributing all the *Jubilees*,

Prayer-books, Catechisms, Indulgences, Psalters, Processionals, Pastoral Letters, [and] *Ordonnances* and all works printed in the said diocese, recognition of which is the right of my said Lord [bishop] and his officers'.[37] The bishop's printer might also serve as the distributor of books he had not printed that were destined for the use of the clergy. In 1693, for instance, Jacques Seneuze printed at the end of his edition of the decrees of the diocese of Châlons-sur-Marne an 'Abrégé de bibliothèque pour les ecclésiastiques' (short list for a clerical library) of some ninety titles. It is hardly surprising to see in that ideal library the entire arsenal of texts that the bishops of the Catholic Reformation thought every 'good' priest should own. The list included the Bible and its great commentators from the late sixteenth and early seventeenth centuries (Maldonat, Estius, Jansenius, Menocchio); theological *summae* (St Thomas's, but also more modest manuals for seminary use such as the so-called Grenoble *Théologie*); works on ecclesiastical history (Baronius, Godeau, Fleury); and such Tridentine texts as the decrees and the catechism of the Council in both Latin and French. It also offered an entire pastoral literature of sermon collections, confessors' manuals and catechisms (given that 'most of the bishops' had 'each made a catechism, more than twelve sorts will be offered'); texts from ecclesiastical conferences (those of Luçon, La Rochelle, Périgueux, Besançon and Langres); and spiritual texts (Saint-Jure, Rodriguez, Luis de Granada, Beuvelet's *Meditations*). The Bible and the New Testament in Latin, St Thomas's *Summa*, the *Lives of the Saints* and the *Imitation of Christ* (in both Latin and French) were listed 'in various editions, formats, and prices'. Moreover, if Mabillon's two-volume folio edition of St Bernard (in twenty-four books) was beyond the reach of some priests' purses, 'there are other different editions at a good price'. Seneuze advertised that he sold 'all the books proposed for those who aspire to the ecclesiastical state or who are in the greater or lesser seminary' and 'all books proper for divine service, both of the Roman use and of the diocese of Châlons'. He announced that over and above the catalogue listings his shop contained

all books, principally those printed in France, such as Sermonaries, Homilies, Sermons, Ecclesiastical Conferences, Catechisms, Casuistry, Meditations and other Books of spirituality and devotion. Also Commentaries on Holy Writ, Fathers of the Church, Greek and Latin, old and new; Historians both ecclesiastical and secular; Theologians, Councils, Canonists, Controversists, Philosophers and Works of Jurisprudence ancient and new.[38]

The picture shifts when we move from libraries proposed for parish priests to the books they actually owned. Certain clerical devotional societies concentrated on reading. For example, the Grande Congréga-tion Académique of Molsheim, whose members were former students of the Jesuit school, and some two-thirds of whom were ecclesiastics, met in common devotion to the Virgin. Beginning in 1670 the Congrégation put out a yearly publication as a New Year gift for the edification of each of the members,[39] in the process offering the whole tradition of Jesuit spirituality for priestly meditation.[40] The Marian Congregation of Molsheim is not an isolated example,[41] but we cannot take its encour-agement of reading to have been the general rule. According to the vicar general of the diocese of Strasbourg, writing in 1697, 'The clergy of Alsace does not apply itself to anything and would not open a book in an entire year.'[42] Similarly, the anonymous author of a 'Mémoire pour servir à l'établissement des conférences dans le diocèse d'Auxerre' wrote in 1696: 'Study is something so extraordinary in the countryside and even in the towns that except for a few sermonaries the parish priests read and study nothing.'[43] These writers probably exaggerated, and in order to grasp the presence of the book in priests' lives and gauge the impact of the Catholic Reformation on the body of priests, we need to turn to such documents as notarial inventories and mentions of books in the records of pastoral visits.

Present space limitations permit only a few observations. During the last quarter of the seventeenth century, priestly libraries were still modest, but we can begin to see a discernible difference between the 'libraries' of priests who had been trained in the seminaries (a group whose composition corresponds fairly well to the prelates' demands as these were reflected in the synodal statutes and ordinances) and the very few books owned by the priests of the older generation. Records of the pastoral visits of Henry de Laval from 1674 to 1679 tell us that in the diocese of La Rochelle the older parish priests owned at best a Bible or a New Testament and a few old manuals of theology. The younger priests, on the other hand, always had a Bible, often accompanied by a commentary, works of the Fathers or the Doctors of the Church (St Gregory, St Bernard, St Augustine), and almost always the *Summa* of St Thomas Aquinas. Catechisms, spiritual works and manuals of theology rounded out a collection that, although it seldom included more than ten or fifteen volumes, none the less represented the beginnings of a theological culture.[44] Analysis of the records of diaconal visits in the diocese of Reims in the same period show a similar improvement in the quality of priestly libraries and a similar difference between generations. In 1698 in the diaconate of La Montagne, near Reims, Bibles, the decrees of the Council of Trent and Roman cat-echisms are the rule in parish libraries. Two-thirds of the parish priests owned a more or less complete edition of the *Summa* of St Thomas

Aquinas, one-third owned an edition of St Bernard and modern commentaries on Holy Scripture; the rest of their 'libraries' were made up of works of moral theology, usually recent works directly applicable to their ministry. Although the average number of books that priests owned undeniably fell short of the prelates' desires, their owners' conformity to the demands formulated in the diocesan ordinances is striking.[45]

Jean Quéniart's analysis of notarial inventories of clerical libraries in the cities and towns of western France fully corroborates these findings. At the end of the seventeenth century, 30 per cent of parish priests owned fewer than ten works at their death. Some had none, and others owned only a *Life of the Saints* and a few books of personal piety, a Missal or a Breviary, a collection of sermons or two, and, on occasion, the decrees of the Council of Trent. Only 5 per cent of these libraries contained more than a 100 volumes. A decisive turning point came in this region during the first quarter of the eighteenth century, when within a generation the proportion of those who owned more than a 100 books rose to 45 per cent of inventories, and three-quarters of the priests owned at least twenty books. Around 1755–60, 60 per cent of priests owned more than 100 books, a figure that rises to 75 per cent on the eve of the French Revolution, when nine out of ten priests owned more than fifty volumes. More than a century after the Council of Trent, the seminaries had finally succeeded in turning the priest into a man of studies. The contents of these libraries continued to emphasize practical works, however. Books of moral theology replaced the great scriptural commentaries of the seventeenth century (a change that parallels the development of the ecclesiastical conferences). These men of God chose texts oriented toward the exercise of their ministry, such as catechisms, sermons and confession manuals, as well as texts of spiritual meditation to provide food for thought and help them guide their flocks.[46] Luciano Allegra comes to similar conclusions in his analysis of parish libraries in the archdiocese of Turin in the eighteenth century, but he also stresses the strong influence of Jansenist thought among Piedmontese priests from works that they read in translation from the French.[47]

We would of course need a broader sample to reach any definitive conclusions. The degree to which the Catholic Reformation took root among the clergy varied enormously according to country and region, as it encountered resistance from the benefice structure and from family strategies. For example, on the Italian peninsula reform of the secular clergy was not really launched until the eighteenth century.[48] This still does not tell us what parish priests and curates made of their reading. It is fair to say, quoting Michel de Certeau, that most of them 'produced' a church by concentrating on the 'conservation of Christian fidelity' and the elimination of popular superstitions. In his role as an educator, the parish priest gradually became 'an agent by which the Church is differentiated from other groups'.[49]

Two contrasting examples testify to this role. At one end of the scale was Jean Meslier, priest of a parish in Champagne in the seventeenth century, whose anti-Christian 'thoughts and sentiments' (which owed their posthumous fame to Voltaire and d'Holbach) arose out of a study of Scripture and patristic literature encouraged by ecclesiastical conferences in the diocese of Reims. None the less, in the opinion of Meslier, a priest who professed a materialist faith, parish priests were not 'totally useless, because all well-regulated republics need masters who teach the virtues and instruct men in good conduct'.[50] At the other end of the scale there was Gilles Guillaume, priest of the parish of Semoine in the diocese of Troyes and a contemporary of Meslier's. We can only guess what it meant to him when he copied into the parish registers for the year 1718 a letter that the Jesuit Jean-Joseph Surin had written in 1630 to his colleagues in La Flèche describing an encounter with an illiterate young man in a stage-coach that was taking Surin back to Paris from Rouen. Did Guillaume share Surin's certitude that spiritual treasures are revealed to the humblest human creatures and that the simplest people, who have no formal knowledge of Scripture, often know the way to salvation better than doctors of theology? At the very least, Guillaume displayed some anxiety concerning his own mission as a parish priest when he chose to copy this singular text.[51]

Reading among the Faithful

Circumscribing what the faithful read is a much more complex and delicate task. We need to distinguish among periods, countries and regions, town and countryside, and social milieus. Between the sixteenth and the eighteenth centuries a considerable enlargement of the world of readers, the result of advances in schooling, both in the urban setting (through the development of charity schools) and rural areas (from the efforts of reforming bishops), had led to a broader range of products offered for the edification of students. Any given text – including Scripture, the *Imitation of Christ*, or missals – was circulated in a number of formats, from an edition in finely chiselled letters to one in rough characters, from a simple Latin version to annotated editions with 'explications' or translations, from a volume bound in morocco leather with the owner's crest to the book with a simple paper cover, and from the copper-plate engravings of the Royaumont Bible, to which Louis-Isaac Le Maistre de

Sacy added a summary of the biblical text, to the simple woodcuts of the *Figures de la Sainte Bible* that appeared in the *Bibliothèque bleue* of Troyes (in the seventeenth century, three-quarters of all illustrated books were religious).[52] Multiple forms led to plural appropriations, and in ways that should be elucidated. We are better informed about the spiritual reading of monks, however, than we are about the reading habits of the laity. A vast distance separated members of the élite – nobility of the blood or of the robe – who received individual counsel from their spiritual advisers on the books required for their spiritual development and on the best ways to read them[53] from the common people of the cities or villages, who received massive amounts of images, broadsides and pamphlets during missions. We should take special care to investigate how and by what stages pastoral guidance through the written word accompanied (when it did not replace) a more immediately striking form of instruction by sight and hearing. One decisive moment came (in France at any rate) during the latter half of the seventeenth century, when the ecclesiastical hierarchy opted resolutely to broaden schooling without necessarily assessing what the long-term consequences of that move would be. Fénelon, who was sent as a missioner to the Protestants of Aunis and Saintonge in the years immediately following the revocation of the Edict of Nantes, gives witness to this change. Fénelon accorded 'capital' importance to the senses, arguing that the king ought to authorize the 'new converts' to sing psalms 'on Sundays in the church before Mass and after Vespers'. This was roughly what 'missionaries do in country areas for certain canticles on the mysteries that they have the peasants sing after the liturgy. . . . [The peasants] need something that strikes the senses, that consoles them and that seems to bring us closer to them.'[54] Fénelon soon realized, however, that this pastoral policy of seducing Protestants by luring them back to the fold 'imperceptibly' by edification had its limits. A mission was temporary; it might 'astonish' the people, shake them up momentarily, even induce a 'violent state',[55] but it was incapable of implanting religion in their hearts: 'Everything that goes by jolts shakes the tree without uprooting it.'[56] What was needed was continuous preaching, and that required 'edifying parish priests who know how to instruct', because 'peoples nourished by heresy are won over only by the spoken word'.[57] The function of that instruction, which the parish priest was to impart 'affectionately' by explaining the Gospel, was to guide reading and provide it with a framework. For Fénelon, conversions could be made durable by two means: the first was schools ('If one does not establish good schools for both sexes as soon as possible, we will have to begin over from the beginning'); the second was profuse distributions of the New Testament. He stipulates, however, that 'large print is necessary; they will be unable to read small letters. It is too much to hope that they will buy Catholic books; it's already much to expect them to read ones that cost them nothing. Most of them are unable to buy them.'[58] In a similar vein, Fénélon recommended Claude Fleury's *Catéchismes historiques*, a work that 'would be very useful'.[59] Because, as Fénélon insisted, 'it is no small affair to change the sentiments of an entire people', and because it was difficult 'to persuade the ignorant, through clear and formal passages to be read every day, to [return to] the religion of their ancestors',[60] the Church – and the king – deliberately opted for a pastoral policy that was based on the book but on the book adapted to the reading level ('large print') of the common people.

The volume of print religious book production need not detain us long. Henri-Jean Martin has established figures for Paris: between 1600 and 1650, during a period of prosperity marked by a spectacular rise in the number of print editions (600 for the year 1644 alone, as opposed to around 150 for the decade 1600–9), books on religious subjects accounted for an ever larger proportion of total production, rising from 30 per cent to 50 per cent. (The latter figure was probably even higher on the Iberian and Italian peninsulas.) Marked changes also took place within print religious book production. Although Scripture and patrology seem to have occupied only a modest place, the proportion of catechisms and sermon collections increased; as works of anti-Protestant controversy declined, their place was taken by polemics between Jesuits and Jansenists on grace and frequent communion. Above all, an entire literature of spirituality emerged, in a pious 'invasion' analysed by Henri Bremond in his monumental *Histoire littéraire du sentiment religieux en France*.[61] Not only were there ecclesiastical texts like the many translations of the *Imitation of Christ*, the Life and Works of St Teresa of Avila, the works of Luis de Granada and the treatises of the Spaniards La Puente and Rodriguez; there were also the works of the great French spiritual writers: Capuchins such as Father Joseph and Yves de Paris (*Introduction à la vie spirituelle*) and Jesuits such as Binet, Suffren, Caussin, Poiré, Hayneuve, Le Moye and Surin.[62]

Booksellers' inventories after death confirm this picture. During the seventeenth century the religious book (theology, controversy, piety) quite often represented over half the stock in their warehouses.[63] Figures for the press runs of the most intensely used books – Books of Hours, the *Imitation of Christ*, catechisms or little devotional books such as *L'Ange conducteur* by the Jesuit Jacques Coret – could reach as high as 5,000 to 10,000 copies.[64] On the eve of the French Revolution, the liberalization of the privilege and the introduction of simple permissions (decree of 30 August 1777) brought a number of older works into the public domain, thus permitting historians to evaluate the enormous numbers of religious books reprinted in the French provinces. Such works represented 63 per cent of the 1,363,700 copies reprinted between 1778 and 1789. Nearly one-half of these (45 per cent, or 569,000 copies) were liturgical texts in translation (*Journée du Chrétien, Offices de la Sainte Vierge, Offices de l'Église*, psalm-books, the *Petit paroissien* and more) or collections of songs and prayers (*Formulaire de prières chrétiennes à l'usage des Ursulines, Cantiques spirituels sur les principaux mystères de notre religion*, etc.). Devotional books such as manuals for the perfect Christian accounted for nearly one-third of religious book production. These were works of edification, often written by Jesuits to guide the faithful on the ways of salvation. One of these was *L'Âme pénitente ou le Nouveau Pensez y bien* of Father Barthélemy Baudrand (12,150 copies reprinted); another was Coret's bestseller, *L'Ange conducteur dans la dévotion chrétienne en faveur des âmes dévotes*, a work first published in Liège in 1683 and reprinted in sixteen cities, for the most part in Lorraine, for a total of 99,700 copies. Finally, 20.8 per cent of the reprinted works were Books of Hours of all sorts (283,500 copies), among them the *Heures royales, Heures dédiées à Monseigneur le Dauphin* and *Heures nouvelles dédiées à Madame la Dauphine.*[65] As this massive quantity of books attests, at the end of the eighteenth century, Christian acculturation was accomplished largely through writing, especially because many of these texts were explicitly aimed at instruction in reading for the schools, as shown by such titles as *Cantiques syllabaires français, Office de la Sainte Vierge suivi d'une méthode facile pour apprendre les lectures et prononciations françaises, Heures nouvelles d'école, Demi-psautier à l'usage des écoles*, etc.

Collective use of such texts is a topic that deserves a few brief remarks. The seventeenth-century 'companies' made up of pious members of the élite practised collective reading. From their earliest sessions the members of the Compagnie du Saint-Sacrement (most of whom were royal office-holders) read together passages of the *Imitation of Christ* and the *Spiritual Combat (Combattimento spirituale)* of the Theatine Lorenzo Scupoli; the 'spiritual lectures' attended by the members of the Compagnie de Limoges were devoted to explication of the New Testament or a work of piety. Books and booklets circulated within the network of devotional societies, and biographies of deceased members, such as the *Vie de Monsieur de Renty* (1651) by the Jesuit Jean-Baptiste Saint-Jure, offered a model to encourage unity among them and help them focus their endeavours. Outside the limited circle of members, broadsides circulated information to parish confraternities and other charitable organizations regarding activities that the societies supported (foreign missions, for instance) and solicited funds.[66] In the

Marian Congregations founded by the Jesuits an entire series of Hours, Offices and Spiritual Exercises (published first in Latin, later in French) encouraged piety among the members, and with the rise of public libraries the propagation of religion by the book soon spread, especially in northern Europe, for example, among married and unmarried crafts-men in Antwerp and Cologne.[67] More modest urban confraternities of penitents, of the Holy Sacrament or of the Holy Virgin had their own breviaries, each of which was reprinted as needed. Among these were an *Office de la Glorieuse Vierge Marie* published for the 'companies of secular penitents', an *Heures de pénitens*, a *Bréviaire à l'usage des peni-tents blancs de Grenoble* and an *Office du Très Saint Sacrement*. Famil-ies carefully preserved such volumes, passing them on as a legacy from a father or a male relative, and on occasion a poorer member might purchase one from a deceased brother's widow. A detailed survey of editions of confraternal liturgical texts has yet to be made.[68]

Catechisms

The methods and the customs governing catechetics varied considerably, as did the manuals written for the priests and schoolmasters who were charged with such instruction. Although catechetics underwent phases of expansion and retraction before becoming a widespread custom in the nineteenth century, use of the catechism in schools is clearly attested as early as the sixteenth century. In northern Italy, confraternities of Christian doctrine inspired by the Compagnia dei Servi dei Puttini in Carità founded by Castellino da Castello in 1539 backed a massive effort to promote catechism through Sunday schools, particularly during the final years of the sixteenth century. Teaching methods varied enor-mously. In the diocese of Milan, although Christian doctrine was still primarily learned 'by heart', methods of inculcation encouraged reading as well. These included using personal copies of a catechism booklet that began with an alphabet in the same type-face as the catechism itself, having students sit side by side to learn to read the catechism a few words at a time and supporting the teacher by providing a 'chancellor' who taught children to read and write gratis. But if in Milan or Pavia Sunday schools helped to encourage an embryonic ability to read (thanks in part to an environment in which the master–pupil relationship was extremely conducive to learning), elsewhere doctrinal instruction was purely oral. There was no question of alphabets for the children to look at or books they might own; they learned by recitation and memoriza-tion. This was the case in Bologna and Cremona, where lessons were based exclusively on listening to the schoolmaster.[69]

As for the Society of Jesus, in 1554 Ignatius of Loyola drew up for Peter Canisius, who was at the time dean of the Faculty of Theology of Vienna, a programme of studies on three levels, aimed at implanting the doctrine of Catholic truth among heretics. On the most elementary level, children and 'the common people who are . . . not too capable of subtleties' were to be provided with a catechism or a book of Christian doctrine summarizing the basic truths of Christianity. Parish priests with less intellectual preparation were to be given 'short and well written' pamphlets to help them counsel their flocks and lead them to accept the right doctrine and reject the wrong. Better-prepared and more cultivated minds would be offered 'the sound theology which is taught in the universities'.[70]

Peter Canisius responded to Ignatius's injunction by publishing three catechisms, each on a different level. The first was a *Summa doctrinae christianae*, a volume of some 200 pages written in Latin, destined (in theory) for the use of Christian children (*pueritia*), which appeared in 1555. This text, which was divided into five parts, was dense to begin with, thanks to the length of its responses to the various questions, and in 1566 it was augmented (in a so-called post-Tridentine version) by a long development on justification. In 1577 this catechism was reworked by the Louvain theologian Pierre Busée, who furnished a full apparatus of scriptural and patristic authorities in support of the responses. At this point this *Summa* had become a treatise of theology of four quarto volumes more nearly corresponding to the high-level summary of theology that Ignatius of Loyola had called for. Be that as it may, a *Catechismus minimus* was published in Ingolstadt in 1556. This work, destined for small children who were learning to read and were beginning their study of Latin, was divided into fifty-two questions, and was accompanied by the basic prayers and a Latin grammar. The series was completed by the publication in Cologne of a *Parvus catechismus catholicus* for the use of schoolchildren, soon called *minor* to distinguish it from the other two publications. It included 124 questions, reflecting the arrangement of the *Summa*.[71] The success of Canisius's catechisms, which went through a large number of editions in both Latin and the vernacular, in German-language countries[72] and French-speaking lands alike,[73] was aided by the expansion of the Jesuit schools, as witnessed by the places of publication, which corresponded to the sites of *collèges* in which the books were immediately put to use. The *Catechismus parvus* was in fact used (and taught by rote) in the elementary schools in the first to third grades. It was usually presented in the vernacular, while the longer catechism was taught to the more advanced classes in Latin.[74] Even in France, Canisius's catechisms rapidly replaced the ones prepared by Edmond Auger (also offered in three versions), works that followed Calvin's catechism step by step and provided direct refutations in French. This parallel method was judged harmful, because it failed to emphasize the importance of certain doctrinal tenets, and 'openly' introduced youth to heresy. Canisius's catechism, on the other hand, treated 'Christian justice' (emphasizing the sins), works of charity, and the fruits and gifts of the Holy Spirit.[75] Thanks to its theological conformity to the decrees of the Council of Trent and its pedagogical clarity, Canisius's catechism became the standard reference manual for generations of Catholic schoolchildren who attended the secondary schools.

In France the Church was quick to try to make Catholic doctrine (which was memorized more than it was always comprehended) accessible to children, and in the seventeenth century the division of the catechism into several levels of difficulty was frequently reflected in diocesan manuals. In 1646 Jean-François de Gondi, archbishop of Paris, had three catechisms written, one 'for the little children', the second 'for those more advanced in age and capacity', and a third 'for learning how to make one's first communion'.[76] The 1676 catechism 'of the three Henrys' (Henry de Laval, bishop of La Rochelle; Henry de Barillon, bishop of Luçon; and Henry Arnauld, bishop of Angers) was a triple volume containing a 'little catechism' of twenty-seven pages for the youngest children, a second catechism of ninety-three pages for 'young people' of seven or eight years old and more who were preparing for first communion, and a 'great' catechism of 382 pages addressed largely to parish priests to help them prepare the instruction they were expected to impart to their flocks in sermons and catechism classes.[77] The Paris parish of Saint-Nicolas du Chardonnet was a veritable pedagogical laboratory that inspired a number of reformist experiments. Not only were its children separated into three levels (youngest, middle and older), it also developed an entire series of specific pedagogical materials to supplement its catechism classes. The teacher's explanations were backed up by copper-plate engravings representing the Christian mysteries (which were changed according to the liturgical calendar), and the children received leaflets bearing short summaries of the current lesson. Brief lessons about feast-days matched the children's level of understanding: the 'littlest of those who read in French' gave the responses to the first questions; the second and third parts, which gave the reasons for the Church's celebration of those solemnities, were assigned to the middle classes; the older students, 'more capable than the others', gave the responses concerning the rewards awaiting those who properly fulfilled 'the moral practices of these solemnities'. In this instance instructional materials were thought through and written according to a specific pedagogy differentiating schoolchildren according to their abilities. Jean-Baptiste de La Salle was to borrow many of the ideas worked out at Saint-Nicolas du Chardonnet and use them in his own Christian schools.[78]

Although adapting catechetical instruction to the capacities of different learner groups was broadly shared as an objective,[79] we cannot generalize from the method worked out in one pilot project in one Paris parish. During the centuries that we call the early modern period, the Church long continued to practice a purely oral catechism, in which only the priest or the schoolmaster had a manual in his hands. What mattered to the Church was that the faithful be instructed in the tenets of their religion. Certain bishops even had catechisms published in patois. After his first pastoral visit, François-Placide de Baudry de Piencourt, bishop of Mende, had a catechism prepared in *langue d'oc*, 'in order to make more intelligible to the peoples of the mountains the first verities of religion, knowledge of which is necessary to salvation, and of which many of them are unaware because of the difficulty of comprehending them in the French language'. For the bishop, this was like giving 'milk to those who, one might say, are still in the infancy of Christianity'.[80] Soon after his arrival in the diocese of Auch in 1746, Bishop Jean-François de Montillet had a catechism prepared in French to be taught in the *langue vulgaire* almost everywhere in his diocese. In the second edition of this manual he speaks in glowing terms of the progress that had already been made:

> What a spectacle, both for the faithful and for ourselves, to see more than half of the young persons, even of the country parishes where almost no one knew how to read, none the less reciting the entire catechism! Those who were the least able to learn by heart, [have been] carefully taught a summary of all that it is necessary to know about our mysteries, about the commandments of the Church [and] about the sacraments and the dispositions required for receiving them worthily!

In the second edition of this catechism, however, he found it necessary to shorten a certain number of questions and responses 'relative to the limited facility of country people', to shorten the prayers to adapt them 'to the memory and the capacity of the majority of the children', and 'to give the French a turn of phrase and expressions that can be rendered, word for word, in the idiom customary in this diocese, so that the translation will be everywhere the same, because the smallest difference in this sort of thing disconcerts children'.[81] Here catechetics is simple recitation, in which the children's memories are filled with the questions and responses. In the eighteenth century there was a notable difference in this regard between catechisms published in the south of France, which were for the most part of this type, and those of the north and north-east of France, where a catechism was a school-book designed to be read before being committed to memory.[82] Charles de Caylus, bishop of Auxerre, stressed that the catechism taught by the parish priest in the church profited greatly from the catechism lessons of the schoolmaster in the elementary school:

> It is evident that the children who are taught to read have a much more open mind for understanding and retaining the principles of the faith taught to them. We see all too often how difficult it usually is to get into the heads of the children, and even of older people who cannot read, the essential verities of religion, and how easily they forget what has been taught them in the catechism classes once they no longer attend. To the contrary, those who know how to read are always able to call back to mind, by reading, what would otherwise be effaced from memory.[83]

The catechists increasingly raised the question of the relationship between memorization and genuine access to meaning. This was what led Claude Fleury to the historical method, and his *Catéchisme historique contenant en abrégé l'histoire et la doctrine chrétienne* was a veritable Copernican revolution in catechetics. What Fleury objected to most was the style of the diocesan catechisms of his time: 'One cannot deny that the style of the catechisms is extremely dry and that children have a good deal of difficulty retaining them and even more in understanding them. First impressions are the strongest, however, and throughout their lives many will retain a secret aversion for the instruction that so wearied them in their childhood.' The catechisms' basic defect, Fleury declared, was that they had been composed by 'theologians nourished in the schools who did nothing but extract out of various theological treatises the definitions and divisions they judged most necessary, and translate them into the vernacular tongue without changing their style'. The method and style of scholastic theology, Fleury continued, was only appropriate for those who had studied 'logic and the other parts of philosophy, as theologians usually do'. Fleury opted instead for an understanding of the meaning of Christian truths:

> Knowing certain words by heart without comprehending their meaning is not the same as believing. One does not believe with the mouth but with the heart. . . . One cannot say, I believe in 'the mystery of the Trinity' with no idea of what it is [or] if the memory is burdened only with the sound of words as unknown as those of a foreign language. That is just what scholastic language is for all who have not studied it.

Fleury constantly looked back to the experience of all the past centuries. For him, religion must be taught through 'narration and simple deduction of the facts on which the dogmas and precepts of morality were founded'. Narration was important, because 'everyone can understand and retain a story. . . . Above all, it is children who are most avid for them.' Thanks to Fleury, narration (that is, stories) became the core of catechism. This was not the old *histoires* or saints' lives that had stressed the supernatural, but rather *Histoire Sainte*, the history of the Christian religion.[84] This was an important discovery, and it is easy to see why Fleury's *Catéchisme historique* soon became a bestseller, and why it continued to sell well into the mid-nineteenth century. Moreover, other catechisms (that of Bossuet, bishop of Meaux, for one) immediately borrowed from Fleury's innovation by incorporating the history of salvation into their exposés of dogma.[85]

What the Illiterate Read

Claude Fleury consciously chose to accompany his historical catechism with illustrations, 'so that it may serve as both a catechism and an illustration of sacred history'. Pictures, he acknowledged, were 'very appropriate for striking the imagination of children and fixing [things in] their memory; it is the writing of ignorant people'. He admitted to drawing inspiration from the 'excellent invention' of abridged tales from the Old and New Testaments 'accompanied by illustrations'. Many children had in fact been introduced to reading by *Figures de la Bible*, a genre that combined images representing the various episodes of Holy Scripture and a commentary. As Fleury remarked, however, 'books filled with illustrations are too expensive to be commonly used by the poor, who are most in need of such instruction'.[86] The copper-plate engravings of the Royaumont Bible were out of the reach of modest fortunes, but collective use was one solution: the Royaumont Bible was read out loud in the 'grand séminaire' of Autun run by the Sulpicians,[87] in the Jesuits' 'petit séminaire' of the Hospice of Bicêtre (to which the young Nicolas Rétif was sent),[88] and in the charity schools of the Faubourg Saint-Antoine.[89] Aside from this costly volume, which would have been the property of the school or seminary, there was a full range of more modest publications that included the *Figures de la Bible* of the *Bibliothèque bleue* of Troyes. An edition of that sort may well have helped one youngster from Troyes named Grosley to learn to read under the vigilant supervision of Marie, an elderly and illiterate servant who memorized the text accompanying the pictures.

> A half hour every evening was devoted to reading the *Figures de la Bible*. I had to begin every sentence over and over until she understood it and

could grasp its meaning, thus getting me to understand it as well. When I read without pausing for the periods and commas, she would hit the book with the end of her distaff and tell me to stop.[90]

It is harder to evaluate the possible impact of the enormous numbers of pamphlets and booklets distributed during missions. Missions very probably relied primarily on the spoken word and on spectacle as ways to arouse, convert and reconcile an entire parish community. Still, as the missioners travelled on their circuits, they were accompanied by booksellers and notions-sellers who distributed a pious bric-à-brac of prayer beads, medals and images, but also brochures and books written in the interest of prolonging the effects of the mission. In Brittany between 1640 and 1660 a notions-seller named Guillaume Yvonnic accompanied missions led by the Jesuit Julien Maunoir for some fifteen years, distributing booklets that contained spiritual songs in Breton.[91] We can find the same sort of spiritual literature in the catalogues of booksellers in Vannes, Morlaix and Quimper in the late seventeenth and eighteenth centuries.[92] In his *Manuel de la Mission à l'usage des Capucins de la province de Paris* (1702), Father Albert de Paris advised missioners not to distribute books themselves, 'but just tell some printer of the locality where we will hold the mission, and he will not fail to prepare himself for it'. At times booksellers put out a 'catalogue of books it is advisable to stock for a mission'. One of these was a printer from Sées who followed the missions in Normandy of the Jesuit Pierre Sandret. In 1719 the printer advertised a dozen or so titles that would be available where the mission was to take place and that included prayer books, hymnals and titles such as *Guide du Salut, Règlement des familles* and *Leçons du Calvaire pour apprendre à se préparer à une bonne mort*.[93] In Franche-Comté the missioners of Beaupré conducted 260 missions during the first half of the eighteenth century, and at least two booksellers from the Jura, Denis Raillard from Salins and Jean-Baptiste Tonnet from Dôle, regularly followed their tours. Estate inventories show that the book remained a rare object in eighteenth-century Jura society: 23 per cent of merchants, 19 per cent of craftsmen, but only 6 per cent of peasants of various categories owned books. These books were overwhelmingly religious (from 70 to 90 per cent of the books listed by title), and missions very probably played a major role in their distribution.[94] The Jesuit missions in Alsace and Germany were accompanied by similar distributions of pious literature. Here the booklets resembled catechisms, insisting on the strong points of Catholic doctrine, on devotional practices traditional in the Rhineland and other German lands (the Five Wounds of Christ, for example), and on the importance of such Jesuit saints as St Francis Xavier and St Ignatius.[95]

To judge from the number of copies that have been preserved, these
booklets must have been distributed in enormous quantities. The
account books of one minor bookseller in Rodez, Pierre Leroux, enable
us to trace his dealings with a 'package man' from Murat (in the
Auvergne), Michel Chappat, who was 'following the most reverend
fathers of the mission'. Between 1670 and 1678 Leroux sent Chappat
3,425 mission booklets, 1,500 hymnals, 500 prayer sheets, 150 Angelus
booklets and a number of copper-plate engravings. This precise
accounting pertaining to one locality allows us to imagine the masses of
booklets that must have been distributed.[96]

What use did people make of this literature? The pamphlets prepared
for Jesuit missions in Germany are so insistent on St Ignatius's powers
against the evil influence of devils that they suggest that mission booklets might at times have served to accompany rites to repel the forces of
evil. The missioners worked to introduce 'good' books as a way of substituting orthodox practices (prayers and regular attendance at Mass)
for superstitious or magical practices. In his *Bouquet de la Mission*
(1700) Jean Leuduger, a scholastic attached to the cathedral of Saint-
Brieuc who led many missions in Brittany, clearly states that his work
offered 'a summary of all that is said in the sermons, dialogues, lectures
and other exercises of the mission ... so that you can remember what
you have learned in the missions and can, from time to time, renew the
good sentiments and holy resolutions that you made at that time'.[97]
Leuduger devotes an entire chapter of his *Bouquet* to spiritual reading.
He gives the traditional advice handed down through the ages since the
Fathers of the Church on how to 'taste' and 'savour' texts. He also furnishes a list of 'good' books, ranging from the Jesuit Paul de Barry's
Pensez-y bien and the *Imitation of Christ* to the equally time-honoured
collections of spiritual writings by such authors as François de Sales,
Luis de Granada, Alfonso Rodriguez and Lorenzo Scupoli. He even
invites the illiterate to own good books:

> Even if you do not know how to read, do not fail to have good books so
> that you can have them read to you by others. The good Armelle Nicolas,
> who died at Vannes in the odour of sanctity, did just that. She always
> carried *The Imitation of Christ* with her, and when she found someone
> who knew how to read, she would beg him to read her a few lines from
> her book, after which she would pause to reflect on them.[98]

How common was the exemplary spirituality that we see in this
illiterate but pious woman? The men and women who may have shared
her experience have not passed on word of it to us.

10

Reading Matter and 'Popular' Reading: From the Renaissance to the Seventeenth Century

Roger Chartier

How texts found 'popular' readers in the Renaissance, the period between the mid-fifteenth and the mid-seventeenth centuries, has long been related in ways that follow in the wake of Lucien Febvre's and Henri-Jean Martin's pioneering work in the history of the book, *L'Apparition du livre*.[1] The first task of that history was to define the various populations of readers, male and female, by reconstructing the presence of the book within different social groups in a given city or region. The answer to the question, 'Who read?' depended on sociological analysis of book ownership. The answer to the question, 'Who read what?' depended on a definition of global bibliographical categories of titles and genres and their distribution within each social group.

There were several corollaries to this. First, such an approach gave preference to massive sources that lent themselves to a serial, quantitative treatment of homogeneous, repetitious and comparable data, which explains the importance of estate inventories and printed catalogues of library sales. Second, beyond a basic division of people into literate and illiterate, it encouraged the construction of indices of a number of cultural disparities according to the presence or absence of books, the number of works owned, and the nature of the titles that were mentioned in inventories and catalogues.

Such investigations (there have been many more of them concerning the eighteenth century than previous centuries) produced notable results. Monographic studies, in general focused on one city, showed books to have been more common in crafts and merchant circles than might be expected. In Valencia between 1474 and 1550, where one-third of estate inventories mention books, books are listed in 14 per cent of the inventories of textile workers and 10 per cent of those of other manual workers.[2] In Amiens from 1503 to 1576 one out of five of all inventories notes the presence of books; one out of ten (more precisely, 11 per cent of inventories) in the case of merchants and crafts-men.[3] In Canterbury between 1620 and 1640 one-half of the inventories made after death of personal goods show printed matter: 45 per cent of the inventories of people in the clothing trades do so, 36 per cent for the building trades, and 31 per cent of rural yeomen.[4] Throughout Europe in the cities of the Renaissance, books were not foreign objects in popular circles. Admittedly, only a minority owned books, but that minority was never negligible, and at times it included a sizeable proportion of the population studied.

Should we be satisfied with this first sampling? Perhaps not. The distribution of book ownership as registered in inventories after death or sale catalogues can be misleading. For one thing, it takes into account only works sufficiently valuable to be thought worth mentioning in an inventory of personal possessions or a listing of items to be sold at public auction. For another, it gives no indication of books that readers did not own but might have borrowed, read in someone else's house, or heard someone else read. Finally, it sets up rigid divisions and cultural distinctions, whereas even in the Renaissance the same texts and the same books often circulated in all social milieus. This means that we need to replace the notion that the titles and genres found among the possessions of craftsmen and merchants must be considered 'popular' reading matter with an approach that attempts to discern the ways in which different readers used and read the same texts.

Shared Reading

Two propositions underlie such a project. First, it is clear that 'popular' readers owned books that were not specifically aimed at them. Menoc-chio, the Friuli miller, read the Bible in the vernacular, *Il fioretto della Bibbia*, a translation of the *Golden Legend*, *Il cavallier Zuanne de Mandavilla* (an Italian translation of John Mandeville's *Voyages*) and Boccaccio's *Decameron*. What makes Menocchio a 'popular' reader is thus not the corpus of works that he read, but rather his way of reading them, understanding them and appropriating their texts to serve his own personal cosmos.[5]

In similar fashion, the workers, craftsmen and merchants in the diocese of Cuenca who were interrogated by the Inquisition between 1560 and 1610 read the same works as their wealthier compatriots: books of devotion, saints' lives and chivalric romances (*caballerías*).[6] Thus we will have to re-evaluate the judgement that the public for chivalric romances was basically aristocratic.[7] That notion, which has been widely accepted in literary history, was arrived at in three stages. The first was to demonstrate an aristocratic *afición* for the genre on the basis of individual pieces of evidence (letters, memoirs and autobiographical accounts such as the Life of Teresa of Avila[8]) and to demonstrate its success among nobles at court and in the army. The second stage was to note that nobles developed a taste for a sublimated, nostalgic image of a free, independent and errant chivalric life just as the aristocracy was becoming a fixed feature of the court and had settled in the city. The third stage was to declare that the few attestations of popular reading of the *caballerías* were fictional. Chief among these instances is the scene in part 1, chapter 23, of *Don Quixote*, where harvesters gathered in Juan Palomeque's inn listen to a reading of three books that neither they nor the innkeeper had bought, but that they had found in a trunk that a traveller had left behind: Bernardo de Vargas's *Los cuatro libros del valeroso caballero don Cirongilio de Tracia*, *La primera parte de la grande historia del muy animoso y esforzado principe Felixmarte de Hircania* by Melchor de Ortega, and the *Crónica del Gran Capitán Gonzalo Hernández de Córdoba y Agilar: Con la vida del caballero Diego García de Paredes*. One critic stated categorically: 'The romances were read by the upper or noble class, and perhaps by a few particularly well-to-do members of the bourgeoisie. Certainly they were not read by, nor to, the peasants.'[9]

The declarations of people brought before the courts of the Inquisition oblige us to revise that judgement. In the diocese of Cuenca between 1560 and 1610 seven workers, six merchants and one craftsman – fourteen of the seventeen people under accusation who mention that sort of reading matter – declare that they have read *caballerías*. These readers are young (two-thirds of them are under thirty) and for the most part (twelve out of seventeen) unmarried. Age and marital status thus define a public for chivalric romances, as opposed to a more bourgeois and even younger reading public for classical and humanistic literature (given the presence of students in the Latin schools), or the public for works of devotion (manuals of religious instruction, saints' lives, books of prayers) that was on the whole much more numerous (ninety-one readers, male and female), older and made up largely of widows and widowers and married people of all levels of society.

Sara T. Nalle's exemplary analysis teaches us two things. First, cultural divisions are neither necessarily nor perhaps even in the majority of cases determined by socio-professional status. Age, marital status and schooling (elsewhere, a shared religious affiliation, membership in a group, residence in the same locality) can define the specific identity of a reading public more accurately than social condition, strictly speaking. Second, Nalle shows that no reading matter was exclusive to any one group. Just as devotional literature was not the special province of popular readers, so chivalric romances (in spite of their large format and high price) were not exclusive to the élites of nobility and wealth. Even if humbler folk did not themselves own such works, they might – like Cervantes's harvesters – have heard them read.

The Popular Market for Print

We must look at practices more than distribution, at ways of reading more than at book ownership, to find a second reason for popular reading. It has to do with the strategies of the book business. Throughout Europe (earlier in some countries than in others) audacious bookseller-publishers invented a popular market for print matter. Several things were needed to reach a 'popular' clientele ('popular' both numerically and in the sense that it included the humblest sorts of readers, craftsmen, shopkeepers, retail merchants and village élites).[10] These included publishing techniques that lowered manufacturing costs, hence lowered per copy sale price; distribution of print works by pedlars in both urban and rural areas; and a choice of texts or genres that would appeal to the greatest possible number of readers, among them the least affluent readers. Publishing strategies of this sort led to the diffusion, among 'popular' readers, of texts that had already had a more limited circulation in another print form among readers of higher social levels and with more literate backgrounds and of texts put out simultaneously in different forms for different publics.

This was the case, for example, with the *romances* offered for reading (and singing) in the dual form of *pliegos sueltos* (the oldest of which contains a *romance* dating from 1510) and anthologies. The *Cancionero general* of Hernando del Castillo (1511) contains forty-eight such works; it was followed by the *Cancionero de romances* published by Martín Nucio in Antwerp (1547 or 1548), the *Romances nuevamente sacados de historias antiguas de la crónica de España* (Seville, c.1549), the *Silva de romances* (Saragossa, 1551) and the *Silva de varios romances* (Barcelona, 1561).[11] The twofold circulation (of individual texts printed on one sheet in quarto format and of collections of several tens or even hundreds of poems in one work) introduced several elements into these works: borrowings between the oral tradition and a fixed, printed form, among the various print versions that were copied from one another, among various generations of texts from the *romancero viejo* to the *romances nuevos* that were composed in the late sixteenth century by more literary poets (Lope de Vega and Góngora among them) or the *romances de ciego* or the *romances de cordel* written between the seventeenth and the nineteenth centuries by authors who wrote specifically with the urban lower classes in mind.[12] In these multiple trajectories, where very soon 'the *romance* is the base of the literary culture of nearly all social levels, because everyone had heard, read, sung and memorized *romances*',[13] the invention of one particular publishing formula, the *pliego suelto*, played a decisive role. Originally offered as a booklet of eight pages or four pages (that is, one sheet or half a sheet in quarto format),[14] it was the primary vehicle for the broad circulation of the *romance* in all its forms. The format obliged the print object to adjust to the poetic form, but it also set constraints on new works[15]. Such works swelled the packs of wares sold by ambulant merchants and blind pedlars,[16] and it put within the reach of all readers, even the least affluent, a repertory of texts that lent themselves to multiple uses, as an accompaniment to work or celebration, as an aid for learning to read, or simply as a way to pass time agreeably.

The broadside ballads of sixteenth-century England were similar to the Spanish *pliegos sueltos poéticos* in many ways. Such ballads, with religious or lay texts printed on one side of a printer's sheet and sold by pedlars (like Autolycus in Shakespeare's *The Winter's Tale*), made up a poetic and publishing genre with an extremely broad distribution.[17] Their popularity is clear from the large number of such publications (estimated at 3,000 in the sixteenth century), from the near-monopoly of the market established in the early seventeenth century by five booksellers of the Stationers' Company (known as the 'ballad partners') who cornered broadside production, and from the ballad makers' spontaneous borrowings from print forms. The texts of many handwritten ballads are preserved in the archives of the Star Chamber, which was charged with responsibility (between 1603 and 1625) for pursuing authors of 'diffamous libels' and 'lascivious, infamous or scandalous ballads' aimed at magistrates, officials or vicars. The ballads display two major traits: on the one hand, they attest to the originality of compositions that sprang from a tavern culture, where someone who could write (a schoolmaster, a barrister, a lettered traveller) captured a collective creation that did not always bother with formal rules and was aimed at very specific targets. On the other hand, manuscript ballads written to be distributed, sung and posted up imitated the form of the printed ballads, at times adapting their text to circumstances, imitating their two-column layout and using the same melodies.[18] As with the Spanish *romances*, the print publication of these poems had a marked effect on both tradition and oral creation, thanks to the forms and the texts it offered.

In the 1620s ballad publishers, profiting from their many advantages (control over the pedlars' networks, ownership of copyright – more precisely, of 'rights in copies' – of widely circulated texts, and a knowledge of the most profitable clientele), invented and exploited a new commercial outlet, the penny chapbook trade. This new formula was fairly rigidly defined. It covered three classes of print objects: 'small books' of twenty-four pages in octavo or duodecimo format (that is, one and a half sheets or one sheet), 'double books' of twenty-four pages in quarto format (three sheets), and 'histories', which had between thirty-two and seventy-two pages (from four to nine sheets). In the seventeenth century, 'small books' sold for 2*d*. or 2½*d*., the 'double books' for 3*d*. or 4*d*., and the histories for 5*d*. or 6*d*.[19] The penny chapbooks included in their repertory older texts taken from other genres and traditions, both religious and secular ('penny godlinesses' and 'penny merriments'), adapted and at times abridged.[20] The publishing strategy of the London ballad partners was thus quite close to that of their contemporaries, the bookseller-publishers of Troyes in the late sixteenth century who invented a similar formula with the *Bibliothèque bleue*.[21]

Contrasting Appropriations

'Popular' readers did not have a 'literature' that was exclusively theirs during the Renaissance. Everywhere in Europe texts and books circulated throughout the social world, shared by readers of very different social conditions and cultures. This means that we need to look at the different uses of the same genres, the same works and often – although in editorial forms aimed at quite different publics – the same texts. The essential question shifts from popular reading to popular print practices.

This question is part of a broader perspective that historians might formulate as: How can we grasp chronological and social variations in the process of constructing meaning as it operates where the 'world of the text' meets the 'world of the reader'? (to use Paul Ricoeur's terms[22]).

Ricoeur's hermeneutical and phenomenological approach offers valuable assistance in defining a history of reading practices. In the first place it helps to counter the most peremptory structuralist and semiotic formulations that locate signification exclusively within the automatic and impersonal functioning of language, and it obliges us to consider reading as the act by means of which a text takes on meaning and acquires efficacy. Without a reader, the text is merely virtual; it has no true existence: one might 'believe that reading is added onto the text as a complement it can do without. . . . Our earlier analyses should suffice to dispel this illusion. Without the reader who accompanies it, there is no configuring act at work in the text; and without a reader to appropriate it, there is no world unfolded before the text.'[23]

When reading is restored to its full power of effectuation, it is seen in two dimensions and through two references. In its individual dimension, reading requires a phenomenological description that views it as a dynamic interaction, a response to the solicitations of the text and a 'labour' of interpretation. This sets up a gap between the text and reading, which, because of its capacity for invention and creativity, is never totally subjected to the injunctions of the work.[24] In its collective dimension, reading has to be characterized as a dialogue, a relationship between the 'textual signals' that each specific work emits and a collectively shared 'horizon of expectations' that governs its reception. The signification of the text – rather, its significations – thus depends on criteria of classification, on the corpus referred to, and on the interpretive categories of its various successive or simultaneous audiences.[25]

Finally, taking Paul Ricoeur as our guide allows us to comprehend reading as an 'appropriation'. This is true in two senses: first, appropriation designates the 'effectuation' or 'actualization' of the semantic possibilities of the text; second, it sees interpretation of the text as a mediation that enables the reader to reach self-comprehension and construct 'reality'.

This perspective is essential, but it cannot satisfy a historian completely. Its first limitation, which is also the limitation of its basic references (a phenomenology of the act of reading, on the one hand; an aesthetic of reception, on the other), is that it considers texts as if they existed in themselves, irrespective of any material form. To counter that abstraction of the text, we need to recall that the form in which a text is presented for reading also plays a part in the construction of meaning. Versions of the 'same' literal text are not the 'same' when the physical support that transmits it to readers, listeners or spectators varies. Hence there has been renewed interest in disciplines such as bibliography that focus on the expressive function of the non-verbal resources of the book (or any other written object) and on 'the relation of form to meaning', as D. F. McKenzie puts it.[26] By implication, moreover, the phenomenological and hermeneutic approach supposes a universality of reading.

Everywhere and in all times, reading is thought of as an act of pure intellection and interpretation, an act whose concrete modalities have no importance. To counter that projection of universality into reading, we need to stress that reading is a practice with multiple differentiations varying with time and milieu, and that the signification of a text also depends on the way it is read: aloud or silently, in solitude or in company, in private or in public, etc.

A history of reading and readers, popular or otherwise, is thus an account of the historicity of the process of the appropriation of texts. It considers the 'world of the text' as a world of objects or forms whose structures, devices and conventions bear meaning and constrain the production of meaning. Similarly, it considers the 'world of the reader' to be constituted by the 'community of interpretation' (the expression is Stanley Fish's[27]) to which that reader belongs and which defines a shared group of competencies, habits, codes and interests. Hence we must consider both the material aspects of written objects and the behaviour of reading subjects.

Reading Aloud, Silent Reading

Our search for the 'popular' readers of the Renaissance necessarily leads us to investigate the strategies that are available to reconstruct their reading practices. The first of these strategies looks to representations of the modalities and the effects of reading as constructed by the texts. Between the fifteenth and the seventeenth centuries such representations were organized on the basis of a competition (which was also a trajectory) between reading aloud and silent reading. In the literature of Golden-Age Spain, for example, reading aloud is an ordinary, expected and projected means for appropriating works – works of all genres. As Margit Frenk has shown, the implication that a reader is reading aloud, oralizing a text for a public of listeners, is not exclusive to such poetic genres as *romances*, *villancicos*, *lírica cancioneril*, epic poems or poetry in the Italian style. It was presumably also the reading style for humanist comedy (as in the prologue to *Celestina*), chivalric romances ('Que trata de lo que vera el que lo leyere o lo oira el que lo escuchare leer' (Which deals with what any reader of these pages will see for himself, and anyone who has this read to him will hear), Cervantes writes in the title of part 2, chapter 66, of *Don Quixote*), pastoral romances, *novelas cortas* and history texts (Bernal Diaz del Castillo says as much in the prologue to his *Historia verdadera de la conquista de la Nueva España*: 'Mi historia, si se imprime, cuando la vean e oyan, la daran fe verdadera' (If my history is printed, people will really believe it when they see or hear it)).[28] The practice of oralized reading that the texts describe or were designed for created (at least in the cities) a broad public of popular 'readers' that included semi-literates and illiterates who, thanks to the mediation of a reading voice, became familiar with the works and the genres of a learned literature shared well beyond lettered milieus:

> Given the continued importance of the voice in the transmission of texts, the public for written literature was not limited to its 'readers', in the modern sense of the term, but also included a large number of auditors. Every print piece or manuscript was like a hub from which innumerable receptions might emanate, either when [the text] was read orally or when it served as a basis for memorization or free repetition. The high illiteracy rate was not in itself an obstacle to the existence of a very large audience. If in a given family or community one person knew how to read, that was sufficient for virtually any text to be widely enjoyed.[29]

This first image, which identifies the 'popular' with a text circulation covering an entire society, contrasts with another image that recognizes the advance of silent (hence potentially solitary) reading, not only in lettered milieus but also among humble folk. Much was at stake. Because silent reading swept away the distinction – which was always clear in reading aloud – between the world of the text and the world of the reader, and because it gave unheard-of persuasive force to the fabulations of fictional texts, silent reading wove a dangerous spell.[30] The vocabulary used to speak of it used verbs of wonderment such as 'to enchant', 'to marvel at', 'to charm' (*encantar, maravillar, embelesar*). Authors represented silent reading as more apt to make people believe the incredible than the living voice when it recited or read. Cervantes agreed. In *El casamiento engañoso* Campuzano does not relate or read the 'colloquy' he has written on 'the things that those dogs, or whatever they were, said'. He has Peralta read it for himself: ' "I will sit down in this chair", said the Captain, "while you read, if you care to, these dreams or follies." ' It is as if the reader's imagination could be captured more easily by a silent reading; as if the *Coloquio de los perros* could be made more believable by eliminating all mediation between the text that relates it and the reader.

The many decrees that the authorities in Castile put out prohibiting fictional literature should probably be understood as a reflection of their fear of a reading practice that blurred the borderline between the real and the imaginary in readers' minds. In 1531 a royal decree forbade the exportation 'to the Indes' of *romances* and of 'vain or profane stories as are *Amadis* and others of that sort'. In 1543 another royal decree repeated the prohibition, and forbade the printing, sale and possession in the colonies of 'romances that treat of profane and fabulous matters and fictional stories'. In 1555 the Cortés of Valladolid demanded the extension to Spain of the prohibition of 'all books that have been invented in the same vein as [*Amadis de Gaula*], as well as writings and farces about love and other vanities'.[31] As B. W. Ife has shown, suspicion of fiction was rooted in a Neoplatonic hostility to the seductions of illusion and to the appeal of bad examples. It was also based, however, on fear of the growth of silent reading, a form of reading that made readers vulnerable, and that weakened their resistance. That same perception probably explains the Junta de Reformación's refusal in 1625 to grant further permissions to print novels or theatrical works.[32]

Publishing Formulas and Text Types

A second way to define 'popular' reading is based on a hypothesis of labour. As D. F. McKenzie puts it: 'New readers make new texts, and their meanings are a function of their new forms.'[33] When texts were presented in a new way and in a new physical guise that transformed their format, their page layout, the ways in which the text was sectioned and the illustrations, they reached new, broader and less learned audiences, and they took on new significations far removed from the ones their authors had intended or their original readers had constructed. The books of the *Bibliothèque bleue* in France and chapbooks in England offered texts that had already been published in other forms and for other readers, but by giving them a new form, they put such texts within the economic and intellectual reach of new readers, who did not read in the same ways as learned readers. The new public's reading style called for brief, self-contained sequences clearly separated from one another; it demanded the use of images, at times borrowed from another work, that clarified the meaning of the text and served as an aid to memorization. It required repetition more than invention: each new text was a variation on already known themes and motifs. This led the bookseller-publishers of the *Bibliothèque bleue* and the chapbooks to an explicit classification of their titles according to type or format. In England, for instance, 'small godly books' were clearly distinguished from 'small merry books', 'double books' and 'histories'.[34] Reading style also dictated an implicit arrangement of pedlars' books into genres. The *Bibliothèque bleue* offered chivalric romances, fairytales, the literature of *gueuserie* (roguery), civility books and how-to-do-it books. We might add to the list (although in the seventeenth century the generic designation of *Bibliothèque bleue* excluded such works) religious works such as saints' lives, *noëls*, devotional manuals and almanacs.[35]

In Castile the *pliegos sueltos* (and the Catalonian *plecs*[36]) combined a particular publishing formula, a repertory of texts and certain predetermined notions about the reading public. The *pliego* was perfectly adapted to the scope and resources of print-shops whose production capacity long remained limited. In one day a print-shop that possessed only one press could print perhaps 1,250 or 1,500 copies of one print sheet, and the original definition of the *pliego* was, precisely, 'one sheet of paper of its normal size, folded twice so as to obtain eight pages'.[37] Even when the *pliego* was extended to four or five print sheets, economic and technological constraints on printing in Spain dictated the choice of texts to be published in that format. Texts had to be brief, to promise a broad circulation, and (as in France and England at a later date) to belong to an immediately identifiable genre. In sixteenth- and seventeenth-century Spain, that meant *romances* (*antiguos* or *nuevos*), *relaciones de sucesos*, whose annual production greatly increased beginning in the last decade of the sixteenth century,[38] and, from the mid-seventeenth century on, *comedias sueltas*. Because they circulated both traditional works and new works on all levels of society (including popular readers or listeners), the *pliegos* reinforced the notion of a public divided into the *vulgo* and the *discreto*. Admittedly, as a category, the *vulgo* does not immediately or necessarily refer to a 'popular' public, in the strictly social sense of the term. In a literary rhetoric explicitly formulated in the dual prefaces ('Al vulgo' and 'Al discreto lector') of *Guzmán de Alfarache* (1599), *vulgo* was a term that disparaged readers (or spectators) who lacked aesthetic judgement or literary competence.[39] In Golden-Age Castile, however, such 'ignorant' persons made up a sizeable market. This was a market for comedy. First, Lope de Vega wrote in his *Arte nuevo de hacer comedias en este tiempo* (1609): 'Since the common people (*el vulgo*) pay, it is just to speak to them as stupid in the aim of pleasing them.' Second, it was a market for inexpensive print pieces sold by blind pedlars and purveying the genres most likely to attract a broad public. Such texts included the poems of the *cancioneros*, accounts of extraordinary happenings or current news items, and showy pieces like the *comedias*. The existence of this public among the *vulgo* (which is not only postulated but verified) dictated strategies for writing learned works; it also governed the choice of texts and the editorial decisions of booksellers who published works for a broader market.

We find the same combination of a publishing formula, a specific category of texts, and the perception of a multiple public that was 'popular' in both its size and its composition in the production of French *occasionnels*.[40] Three characteristics gave unity to these sixteenth- and seventeenth-century booklets, whose production peaked between 1570 and 1630: their material form, their means of circulation and their titles. These were generally short works in octavo format, printed on one sheet or possibly even a half sheet (giving sixteen or eight pages for the booklet). This meant that one press could print 1,250 or 2,500 copies in a day. Such works were distributed in urban areas (at first, in Paris) by pedlars and itinerant merchants. The majority of these texts were presented as *histoires* or *discours*, two terms that seem to have been interchangeable at the time. Their titles give an indication of their typical register: when they relate extraordinary happenings, they make heavy use of adjectives such as 'prodigious', 'marvellous', and 'awesome' (*prodigieux, merveilleux, admirable*); when they promise thrills and chills, they use such terms as 'dreadful', 'fearsome', 'cruel', 'bloodthirsty', 'terrible', 'barbarous' and 'inhuman' (*épouvantable, effroyable, cruel, sanguinaire, terrible, barbare, inhumain*); and they elicit pity with 'lamentable' and 'pitiful' (*lamentable, pitoyable*). They insist on the authenticity of the events they relate by proclaiming them *vrais* or *véritables*.

Texts composed for publication as *occasionnels* all obey the same structural constraints. They begin with a theological or moral maxim; next comes a story to illustrate the generalization; the text ends with an explicit statement of the religious 'lesson' that the reader should have drawn from the tale. The introductory passage and the final sentence illustrate the definition of the *discours* as a secular, printed form of Christian preaching. Whether they warn against dancing or duels, clandestine marriages and concealed pregnancies, pacts with the devil and heretical conversions, the 'stories' of the *occasionnels* operate like *exempla*, relying on the threat of terrible punishments and eternal damnation. They were weapons in the hands of a pastoral tradition inherited from the Middle Ages and brandished by means of a broad-scale use of print pieces.

The *occasionnels* were instruments used to denounce Protestantism, to Christianize mores and to win over (or back) souls. Some *occasionnels* express that aim through statements of repentance and professions of faith made by criminals, male and female, as they go to meet their fate. This explains why the quantity of these booklets (many of them in support of the radical Catholicism of the League) rose during the Wars of Religion and during the first third of the seventeenth century, when the Roman Catholic Church was intent on imprinting the decrees of the Council of Trent on people's minds and bodies. Hence the *occasionnels* of the years from 1570 to 1630 use narratives presented as 'true' and 'new' in the service of a political and religious cause (the Catholic Counter-Reformation), even though, more often than not, they were reworkings of older plots and motifs taken from traditional *exempla* and saints' lives or even from traditional tales.

The persuasiveness of such texts depended on the credibility that their readers granted them. The singular or extraordinary events they related had to be thought to be true. Several techniques were used to enhance credibility: citation of decrees and sentences extracted from the registers of the courts of justice, declarations of witnesses (gentlemen, clergy, secular and regular, notables) whose rank or station lent weight to their words, an accumulation of details such as names and localities in order to lend an air of reality. Less often, the author claims to have actually seen what he describes. If this claim is rare, it is probably because the extraordinary events that the *occasionnels* related belonged to forms of logic other than simple statement of fact. Extraordinary events were usually held to be warnings, announcements or punishments. Disorders of nature such as comets, floods and the appearance of monsters foretold events or chastisements willed by God (or thought to reflect the malevolence of the devil, acting as agent of divine ire). In a few cases, natural phenomena, although still presented as extraordinary, were given no sign value, and were described as simple curiosities to be noted, classified by natural philosophy and compared with other, similar phenomena. As Lorraine Daston suggests, this aspect of the *occasionnels* (and of artisans' books of secrets[41]) becomes a somewhat paradoxical and unexpected source of the modern notion of scientific fact.[42]

Reading Styles

Despite their differences, *pliegos*, *occasionnels*, volumes in the *Bibliothèque bleue* and chapbooks all illustrate the validity of an approach that begins from print objects themselves and attempts to reconstitute, on the one hand, the types of texts that lent themselves to publication in those forms and, on the other, the readers (and reading styles) that their publishers had in mind. Can we take one further step and document more directly the ways humble folk appropriated the texts that they bought, borrowed or listened to? This is a difficult task because, unlike the reading styles of the learned and the lettered, 'popular' reading has left no traces on the print objects themselves. Careful scrutiny of the marginal notes that Gabriel Harvey, a professional reader in the service of various aristocratic patrons, made in his copy of Livy has made it possible to reconstruct how he read,[43] and similar annotations in Jean Bodin's *Universae Naturae Theatrum* made by university professors give a notion of the uses and interpretations of that work,[44] but this recourse seem totally unavailable to historians of the poorest members of society. Similarly, historians lack anything like the first-person accounts of reading left by some popular readers of the eighteenth century who wrote the stories of their lives.[45]

In the countries that experienced the courts of the Inquisition (to the misfortune of their populations and the good fortune of later historians), the declarations that the accused made to their judges have seemed to offer a good substitute for autobiographies. It has been thought possible to use the records of the Inquisition to reconstitute popular ways of reading, either on the scale of the individual (with Menocchio), of a geographical community (the diocese of Cuenca), or even on the level of the reception of a single author's works (in Italian readers' interpretations of Erasmus's works[46]). Historians have been strongly tempted to use such materials to describe the reading style of all humble readers as if they were all like Menocchio and as if the specificity of 'popular' reading lay in a dislocation of texts, a decontextualization of fragments and an adherence to literal meaning. The fragmented, sequential organization of print pieces published for the broad popular market seemed to support that analysis.

That view is surely pertinent. It calls for prudence, however, to the extent that the practices it takes as specifically popular were also those (though in other modalities) of learned reading. The two objects emblematic of learned reading in the Renaissance – the reading wheel, which enabled one person to read several books simultaneously, and the commonplace book, in which the reader could enter under its various headings the quotations, notes and observations that he had collected – were vehicles for a style of reading that proceeded by extracts, displacements and comparisons and that invested the text read (or listened to) with the weight of absolute authority. If all lettered readers did not participate in the culture of the commonplace books (Montaigne, for one, did not),[47] that culture none the less dictated the way the majority of lettered readers organized their readings. Are we to take Menocchio as a plebeian, awkward, clumsy practitioner of that intellectual technique? Should we think that even though he belonged within 'popular' culture (in the broader sense of the village community), his reading habits were far from popular? In any event, questions such as these should put us on guard against overly hasty, overly global social categorizations of the morphological traits of reading practices.

These questions also invite us to pursue an investigation that is only in its earliest stages and, as Lisa Jardine and Anthony Grafton suggest to historians of the book, whom they consider overly timid,[48] to connect the study of texts, reading, the book and the interpretation of texts. A programme of the sort, which governs a new approach to humanist reading,[49] can serve as a guide for grasping, as far as possible, the unrecorded reading styles of anonymous readers. This is not an easy task, and a number of dangers lurk in it. One, for example, is to take representations for actual practices; another is to restrict the category of 'popular' to an overly narrow social sense; a third is to reinscribe the construction of meaning within the text alone (and the object that bears the text), even after postulating its autonomy. All these are reefs that are not easy to avoid when sources are few and we take insufficient precautions. Still, we must navigate among them if we want to construct a better, more intelligible picture of communities of readers, publishing genres and modalities of interpretation.

11

Was there a Reading Revolution at the End of the Eighteenth Century?

Reinhard Wittmann

For as long as the world has existed, there have been no phenomena so remarkable as the reading of novels in Germany and the Revolution in France. They have evolved more or less simultaneously, and it is not beyond the bounds of probability that novels have been just as much the cause of unhappiness to people in secret as the terrible French Revolution has been publicly.[1]

In his comparison between the political upheavals in western Europe and a reading revolution in central Europe, the conservative Swiss bookseller Johann Georg Heinzmann expressed a conviction shared by many of his contemporaries in 1795: it was not the Jacobins who dealt the fatal blow to the *ancien régime* in Germany, it was readers.

This momentous transformation in the function of reading, previously a widespread cultural practice, was greeted with enthusiasm by revolutionary zealots, but it met with the disapproval of moderate Enlightenment thinkers wearing troubled expressions. It was bitterly opposed by reactionary, conservative and clerical strata of society and by groups representing the interests of the state, but it was refuted by no one. In this respect, too, Britain and France in particular were ahead of central Europe. From as early as the eighteenth century, German travellers had been reporting a conspicuous change in reading habits. In Britain, roof-tilers had newspapers passed up to them during their meal breaks, and in the French capital one observer remarked that everyone in Paris is reading ... Everyone, but women in particular, is carrying a book around in their pocket. People read while riding in carriages or talking walks; they read at the theatre during the interval, in cafés, even when bathing. Women, children, journeymen and apprentices read in shops. On Sundays people read while seated at the front of their houses; lackeys read on their back seats, coachmen up on their boxes, and soldiers keeping guard.[2]

A few years later, however, Germany (in the context of this chapter 'Germany' denotes a linguistic and cultural area rather than a political area or territory) was also completely gripped by this cultural revolution. Indeed, it seemed that this degree of social transformation was not achieved anywhere more than in central Europe, where a previously unknown illness now broke out and spread very rapidly. It was initially a single infection, a 'reading bug' that quickly escalated into a collective 'reading epidemic'. In 1796, the Erfurt clergyman Johann Rudolf Gottlieb Beyer made a record of its main symptoms, observing

readers of books who rise and retire to bed with a book in their hand, sit down at table with one, have one lying close by when working, carry one around with them when walking, and who, once they have begun reading, are unable to stop until they have finished. But they have scarcely finished the last page of a book before they begin looking round greedily for somewhere to acquire another one; and when they are at their toilet or at their desk or some other place, if they happen to come across something that fits with their own subject or seems to them to be readable, they take it away and devour it with a kind of ravenous hunger. No lover of tobacco or coffee, no wine drinker or lover of games, can be as addicted to their pipe, bottle, games or coffee-table as those many hungry readers are to their reading habit.[3]

The infection that contemporary observers were correctly diagnosing, but were unable to treat, has been termed a 'reading revolution' by modern researchers. The term implies an interpretive model that conceives the secular change as a revolutionary transition from 'intensive' to 'extensive' reading. Drawing on sources taken from the Protestant north and middle regions of Germany, Rolf Engelsing has described a process by which the intensive reading of a small collective canon of texts, mostly of a religious kind and primarily the Bible, that were familiar, normative and repeatedly recited, was replaced with an extensive form of reading. In a modern, secularized and individual way, extensive reading was characterized by an eagerness to consume new and varied reading materials for information, and for private entertainment in particular.

Clearly, there was not a rapid and comprehensive substitution of the traditional approach to reading for a more modern one. Even if we prefer not to use the term 'reading revolution', nevertheless it remains doubtful whether, at the end of the *ancien régime*, the reading habits of a constantly expanding public could be quantitatively or qualitatively differentiated according to social stratum or region throughout Europe. From then on, more extensive reading habits came increasingly to be the obligatory and dominant cultural norm; traditional intensive reading was increasingly regarded as obsolete and socially inferior. However, it is not so easy to identify the causes of this transformation: 'intensive', repetitive reading could be a ritual devoid of meaning, while 'extensive' reading could be performed with passionate intensity.

In order to understand this process, one so momentous for the cultural history of Europe, to grasp its causes and its development, its influence and its consequences, and to some extent to get closer to the reality of the eighteenth-century reader, we need to carry out a comprehensive initial examination of a large number of sources, together with a careful interpretation of them. Researchers in Europe have endeavoured to do this, especially in the last two decades, albeit by very different means. On the whole, though, we are just as at the beginning, and we have for a long time lacked a sophisticated picture of the processes involved.[4] Even this chapter can provide no more than a rough outline.

The World of Readers

We can only give a suggestion of the varied and closely interwoven conditions and premises of reading in the eighteenth century, together with the political, economic, sociological and cultural changes it underwent. The population of the German linguistic area must have almost doubled between 1700 and 1800, to about 25 million (excluding the Habsburg Empire), reaching a high point in the last third of the century. At the same time, a clear, if initially only gradual, trend toward urbanization began, even though around 80 per cent of the population continued to live on the land. In all the territories belonging to the politically very fragmented Holy Roman Empire of the German nation, the social status and structure of the nobility and peasantry remained largely unchanged until the end of the century, but within the bourgeoisie situated in between there were important processes of transformation, emancipation and differentiation that ultimately led to the breakup of feudal society.

The 'bourgeoisie' was not a unified order in the sense of a *tiers état*. On the contrary, it continued to comprise the traditional urban, middle and upper strata of society occupied by merchants, guild-masters and the highest-ranking craftsman; in addition to these, there was a similarly urban, innovative and entrepreneurial economic bourgeoisie. However, the 'educated bourgeoisie', consisting of scholars or 'intellectuals', as well as officials with an academic training, played an especially significant role. The restricted political area occupied by the Empire, had a large number of small courts and imperial cities acting as administrative centres, so there were more of these élites than in the other countries of Europe. Their opportunities for social advancement worsened considerably at the beginning of the eighteenth century, because the comparatively lively social mobility of the Baroque period came to a standstill, the feudal system became decrepit, and the new bourgeois agents of culture increased in number, but no longer found adequate employment. Excluded once more from leadership positions, these 'free-floating intellectuals' constituted a potential for unrest through their more and more explicit questioning of the traditional system.

This development was embedded in the familiar pan-European embourgeoisement of society, culture and literature. It represented the historical achievement of the Enlightenment movement, with its new value system, its ideal of equality based on natural law, its spirit of utilitarian efficiency, and an intensive striving for education that served to demarcate the nobility, but primarily for social advancement under the dominant themes of reason, humanity, tolerance and virtue. Jürgen Habermas has outlined this change in consciousness, using his theory of the 'structural transformation of the public sphere'. According to this theory, bourgeois identity emerged with a new public sphere that was independent of the courts, a 'sphere of private people assembled into a public' that questioned the monopoly of information and interpretation enjoyed by the authorities of Church and State, and developed new, anti-feudal structures of intercourse and communication, initially through literature but then politically too. Individual identity replaced status bestowed by birth. It was first and foremost within the intellectual sphere that this identity sought to win and maintain the autonomy to which it aspired. The characteristic feature of this bourgeois individuality was the way it discovered and liberated subjectivity, and strove toward constant communication, in order to expand its restricted sphere of experience.

No medium could perform this function better than the printed word. Written culture and literature became the training ground for self-understanding and reasoning, while books and reading acquired a new status in the public consciousness. For the first time the bourgeoisie now had at its disposal enough time and purchasing power for reading.

Reading acquired an emancipatory function, and became a productive social force: it expanded one's moral and intellectual horizon. It made of the reader a useful member of society, allowed him to command his range of duties better, and was even an aid to his social career. The printed word became the vehicle of bourgeois culture.

In previous centuries, the book had been principally regarded as an authoritarian medium with an impersonal claim to power. It was seen as an indispensable factor of social discipline imposed by the State and the Church. It was not until the general change in attitudes in the eighteenth century that people recognized the capacity of printed matter to 'completely penetrate the reader's subjective life'.[5] Precisely because the mechanically duplicated text could be read in its complete uniformity, far more automatically than any manuscript, it drew new readers hook, line and sinker into the imagined world of the book. To do so, of course, there was a fundamental prerequisite: namely, literacy.

Without even approximate figures for the whole of Europe, the extent of reading and writing at the end of the eighteenth century can only be guessed at. What are the criteria for selection? What use are rough approximations of an 'elementary reading ability', deduced from a limited school education, if during a whole lifetime this ability is never converted into reading *practice*? Do we count among 'readers' people who are able to scribble their signature at the bottom of a bill of sale? Or those who pore over their catechism in an effort to decipher it? Or could 'readers' include any illiterate person who listens eagerly and attentively to another person who is reading aloud? We must take gender differences between readers into account (female literacy centred more on reading than writing), differences in religion, but in particular differences between readers in the town and those in the country. The only country for which we have accurate figures is Sweden, where the entire adult population of around 1.3 million had a semblance of reading and writing ability. But Sweden is a unique case; for the remaining countries of Europe the rough figures and contemporary accounts that are available to a large extent give the same picture. For Britain, the 'nation of readers' (Samuel Johnson), E. Burke estimated that the reading public in the 1790s amounted to 80,000. Out of a total population of 6 million, this constitutes less than 1.5 per cent. Even by 1788 a quarter of all British parishes were still without a school. The figures for France are just as vague: in the 1780s around 9.6 million people were able to write their name, but even there the proportion of illiterate people around 1789 was still thought to be a good 60 per cent.

In central Europe in the eighteenth century there was undoubtedly a dramatic *relative* increase in the number of readers. We can assume that they doubled, if not trebled, but only at a very low level. Contemporary accounts differ enormously in their assumptions, and there is a similar variation in the sources of information.[6] In 1773 Friedrich Nicolai reckoned that the 'learned' public in Germany amounted to 20,000 people (that is, around 0.01 per cent of the population). Jean Paul numbered the readers of *belles-lettres* at 300,000 towards the year 1800, or about 1.5 per cent of the entire population. However, these two sets of figures – from before and after the 'reading revolution'? – differ by a factor of more than 100. Researchers today, on the other hand, give far higher figures, estimating that, around 1770, 'potential' readers accounted for 15 per cent of the population over six years old, and 25 per cent in 1800.[7] Here is a far more realistic supposition (in spite of the fact that the average print run is fixed too high): with an estimated 25 million inhabitants in Germany and an average first print run of 2,500 copies, a book was bought by 0.01 per cent of the population, and read by about 0.1 per cent.[8] Complaints levelled by contemporaries at the 'reading mania' raging through all classes of society were without doubt an 'ideological falsification'.[9] A truly numerical or quantitative democratization of reading did not come about for approximately another 100 years. We have at our disposal more accurate statistics for the number of actual readers in the duchy of Württemburg, which can serve as a case study (albeit not as a representative one). In his study of *Das gelehrte Wirtemberg* in 1790, Bathasar Haug conducted a careful census of the class of dignitaries within the duchy who for the most part must also have been the agents of literary culture in their society: 834 clerics, 388 curates and scholarship-holders in Tübingen, 452 lawyers (who probably included higher-ranking officials), 218 doctors and apothecaries, 300 officers (two-thirds of them from the nobility), around 200 graduate students, 75 merchants in Stuttgart and around 450 in the country, and finally, 1,324 *Schreiber* ('clerks') – that is, middle-ranking officials without a university education.[10] If we add to these 4,000 members of the property-owning and educated bourgeoisie a further 2,000 women and young people and a few hundred nobles, we arrive at a figure of around 7,000 'extensive' readers in Würtemburg in the last years of the eighteenth century – a little over 1 per cent of the population as a whole. Those who practised the traditional mode of reading continued to revert to the edifying 'old solaces', the Bible, the catechism and the calendar.

However, it would be a mistake for us to assign only a marginal role, culturally or within society as a whole, to the regularly reading public in Germany, which numbered approximately 300,000 people, or 1.5 per cent of the adult population. For this (initially very small) ferment of new readers started some momentous cultural and political chain reactions.

Old and New Forms of Reading in the Eighteenth Century

How did reading evolve in the eighteenth century? To answer this question, we would need to have a more sophisticated model of the history of readers to work with, one that took account of both the diachronic sequence of events, together with its intermediate stages, *and* instances of synchronic overlap. Reading evolved into an individual process independent of social class. The class to which people belonged scarcely determined their access to reading any more: 'The literary public of the pre-revolutionary era was still largely élitist, homogeneous and closed. Between 1789 and 1815 it was independent of social class, heterogeneous and open.'[11]

The most widespread form of interaction with the printed word continued to be 'unruly' reading, a mode of reading that was naïve, non-reflexive and undisciplined, and for the most part performed aloud. It constituted the sole form of reading among the rural population and a large section of the urban lower classes too. Given that they worked week in, week out, from sunrise to sunset, six days a week, there was neither the time nor the motivation for these people to read. For the static world of the rural populace, from the stable-boy to the large farm-holder, reading was a social practice or technique of domination that was superfluous to their daily lives. If they had a rudimentary reading ability, they applied it to reading blood-letting tables, rules for the weather and sowing, and devotional works sold at market and by pedlars, as well as chapbooks both spiritual and secular in character. Many provincial publishers, particularly those in Germany, published dozens of these little chapbooks. However, like the *Bibliothèque bleue* in France, even the chapbook 'was not necessarily bought to be read, or at least not to be read carefully, precisely, and within an attention to the letter of the text', but 'a person of weak reading skills, who could assimilate only brief, elementary bits at one time, could find satisfaction in a minimally cohesive text without attaching too much importance to its incoherent aspects'.[12] In fact, with time the contents of these booklets underwent textual modifications that anticipated the change in reading habits.

This 'unruly' form of reading could, however, be linked to a collective 'alfabetismo di gruppo' (Italo Sordi) – in other words, a well-developed capacity to listen, implying an indirect 'literalization' without any literacy education. It was promoted by a hierarchical form of communication, the lecture: in most family circles, religious texts were recited by the father of the house or the children, while in public places such as inns or markets, those who could read, including teachers and priests, distributed political and other new publications. In the last years of the eighteenth century, Enlightenment thinkers largely failed in their intensive efforts to transform 'unruly' reading into a socially integrative 'useful' form of reading among the rural population using an authoritarian method of teaching people to read.

This situation underwent a permanent change following the trauma of the French Revolution. An elementary interest in the sensational news about freedom, equality and fraternity began to spread beyond the towns. Backstreet lawyers, schoolmasters who had abandoned their duties, rebellious students, ecclesiastical reformers, innkeepers and coach-house owners read newspapers aloud in schools or taverns, and encouraged noisy debate. All this helped considerably to motivate people to learn to read for themselves (measures taken by the counter-revolutionary authorities to control opinion had much the same effect), to the discomfort of the leading political and social classes, who were increasingly determined to oppose this intellectual emancipation.

A quicker and earlier change in reading habits occurred among the urban classes than in the rural lower and middle classes, in particular among domestic workers, lackeys and barbers, chambermaids, employees in trade and craft industries, and among the middle ranks and some lower ranks in the army. This group possibly constituted up to a quarter of the urban population. It also enjoyed the necessary preconditions for reading: namely, that precious resource, light, together with brief times for reading throughout the day, and often when there were free meals and lodging, a small budget for a lending library too. By emulating the ruling class, the workers also acquired its fashionable reading habits, in particular its extensive consumption of *belles-lettres*. In the city the printed word was a natural component part of daily urban life: posters on houses, public notices on walls, town criers and market criers with their declarations, the ubiquitous newspapers in the smoke rooms and taverns. In the progressive England of 1740, Richardson's *Pamela* was already regarded as the 'culture-heroine of a very powerful sisterhood of literate and leisured waiting-maids'.[13] After an interval of several decades, this literary emancipation came about in Germany as well. In 1781 a Viennese author noted a true passion for *belles-lettres* among chambermaids: 'Not satisfied with this alone, they also play the part of sentimental souls, demand the rights to *belles-lettres*, read comedies, novels and poems conscientiously, and learn entire scenes, passages or verses off by heart, and even argue about the sorrows of young Werther.' These reading tastes could no longer be disciplined by a moralizing work like the *Little Book of Morals for the People* (Lavater, 1773). Long hours of idleness on guard duty encouraged reading in the urban army, as one observer lamented in 1780:

'Even the musketeers in the large towns have library books brought to them at the main guardroom.' Apart from novels, the preferred reading materials in the garrisons were racy stories and pamphlets.

Socially, 'unruly' reading was in decline, but in percentage terms it was still prevalent. Its opposite had always been 'scholarly' reading. Among the intellectual élites a 'modern', cursory reading to gain information was not the only current form. An extensive, poly-historical and encyclopaedic mode of reading had also become estab-lished by the seventeenth century. However, from the middle of the eighteenth century onwards, the scholarly bookworm who remained oblivious to the world as he pored over his folios was looked upon as a figure of ridicule. His knowledge of books, which stubbornly resisted any form of pragmatism, was contrary to the enlightened bourgeois world-view. The ponderous, pedantic thinker reading within the con-fines of his room was replaced by the learned and versatile 'petit maître' who was more superficial in his pursuit of the sciences.

Enlightenment ideology, on the other hand, propagated 'useful' reading for both traditional and new agents of culture. Between 1720 and 1750 the main vehicles of this reading propaganda were the *Moralische Wochenschriften* ('moral weeklies') that appeared princip-ally in the commercial towns of the Protestant north. In addition to Leipzig, Hamburg played the decisive role as the gateway for British Enlightenment thought. Following the model of the 'moral weeklies' such as the *Spectator*, *Tatler* and *Guardian*, these publications dissemi-nated a specifically bourgeois 'message of virtue' and the cultural ideal of the Enlightenment, opposed to the *galant* life-style of the court. Using such programmatic titles as *Der Patriot, Der Weltbürger, Der Vernünft-ler, Der Biedermann, Der Menschenfreund, Der Freygeist, Der Gesel-lige* and *Die vernünftigen Tadlerinnen* and the reader-oriented strategies of the earlier edifying books, they now conveyed secular information from this world, in an effort to pass the time in an entertaining way. For both the well-to-do tradesman and the ambitious student, the well-mannered woman and the honest official, reading material that was both socially useful and at the same time promoted individual morality was no idle pleasure but actually a moral duty.

This strategy was particularly effective among the female reading public. With their increasing economic prosperity, the wives and daugh-ters of the bourgeoisie had more free time available for reading. Up to the beginning of the eighteenth century, their reading canon had been almost exclusively confined to edifying religious writings (even if such restrictions were not always effective), but it was now allowed to expand. The 'moral weeklies' recommended several 'women's libraries', which were not intending to educate any 'femme savante', but merely presupposed a 'relative education, narrowly confined to a range of domestic duties'. However, they undoubtedly quenched the female thirst for knowledge with travel stories and fables, even with British family novels. The teaching of literacy skills to youngsters was pursued with a similar level of commitment. As childhood was now recognized as a properly defined stage in life, greater attention was given to what children and young adults actually read. From 1760 onwards, an intensive method of teaching the young generation of the bourgeoisie to read was implemented. This had scarcely any impact among young students, who did not have very much time and who had always had a more extensive and secularized mode of reading.

This 'useful' form of reading not only considered the text as a moralizing allegory, as a guide to achieving the perfection of the individual, it later developed within the rising bourgeois public, thanks in particular to the institution of the reading society (see below), into a form of reading oriented toward communication and reflection, with the aim of shaping the social identity of the bourgeoisie through reading. Even Jean Jacques Rousseau, in his home town of Geneva, contrasted this stage of 'rational' reading, which was practised in a useful and pragmatic way, with the diversionary reading matter popular in the city of Paris:

> The Frenchman reads a lot, but only new books; or to be precise, he leafs through them, not in order to read them, but in order to be able to say that he has read them. The Genevan does not read good books; he reads them and thinks at the same time; he does not appreciate them but he understands them.[14]

Following the example of the Encyclopaedists, this kind of reading was regarded even by some German Enlightenment thinkers as an act of liberation from a feudal obscurantism. On the part of the bourgeoisie it promoted a new, collective self-understanding that was based on a secular argumentation and was freeing itself from the religious and legal doctrinaire discourse of the feudal structures of the *ancien régime*. The bourgeois individual was thus able to keep his sense of direction, and gain a new corporative, social and cultural identity. Obviously, this 'rational' way of reading was a male preserve. With their growing economic prosperity, men had more and more time for reading. They were interested not only in information related to their trade or profession, but also in new political publications and works of diversion.

The role played by the German nobility in all this was relatively minor. We have clearly to distinguish their reading habits, which we have only little knowledge of, even today. In France, right up to the end of the century, the landed gentry still possessed very few books. Similarly, in Germany the 'Krautjunker' (country nobleman), whose homes contained perhaps several dozen books, faced a small circle of educated patrons of literature, who, like the educated bourgeoisie, modernized their roles as readers. Among the courtly nobles and especially the landed gentry, the number of book lovers who had amassed valuable collections was extremely small. None of them played more than a minimal role in the 'reading revolution'.

As previously mentioned, the process of modernizing reading habits sprang not so much from the residences and courts as from the Protestant commercial towns of northern and central Germany. The Catholic regions of the Empire did not begin to participate in the process until later. Unlike the Protestants, they lacked the tradition of individual Bible reading, a quasi-religious act providing a fundamental stimulus to reading.

> In Catholic areas the clerics are the necessary intermediaries between the Word of God and the faithful, and no other book has a similar existential importance to that of the Bible for the Reformed, the Bible whose presence in each family is verified, and the text of which could be recited to oneself after learning it by heart from multiple recitals and readings.[15]

Of course, even among the Catholic population, popular mass-market publications such as calendars and leaflets were in circulation, and it was not strictly forbidden for laymen to pore over the Bible. However, in contrast to the early Protestant argument, which held that writing prevailed over tradition (*sola scriptura*), here oral mediation via the authority of teaching had absolute precedence. Nevertheless, for the role of the popular book, this only applied to the wider strata of religious believers. The clergy and the monasteries, by contrast, had always constituted a literary public *sui generis*. Libertine reading matter was especially popular in religious cities, as it was in France. But a far more significant role was played by the monastic libraries, which, right up to the period of secularization at the beginning of the nineteenth century, were the locus of a late and prestigious burgeoning of scholarly life.

It was also at this point that reading began to be modernized. From 1780, serious complaints about the reading of novels by seminarists were increasingly heard in Catholic regions; but, by contrast, the ridicule directed at members of the clergy who could not read grew conspicuously rare. A new generation of readers among the clergy had their first modern reading experiences in the monastery or the seminary. The progressive journal, the *Zuschauer in Bayern* (Spectator in Bavaria) reported the change that took place between the old and new generations of Bavarian clergymen: 'the old generation takes snuff, smokes tobacco, drinks and reads nothing. The young generation is modernizing, reading, beginning to acquire taste, and to think.'

Remarkably quickly, albeit between two and three decades behind the Protestants, educated Catholics adapted to the new ways of reading, along with the wider public, and did so in a radically secularizing manner:

> Nothing is more keenly coveted, printed, sold, read and recommended, than precisely those writings in which religion is discredited. They pass through everyone's hands. They are reprinted. Some of them go out of stock in the first three months. The Normalschulen and press freedom enable even the common man to read everything that is hatched and published by these writing fanatics. There are public schools where the teachers recommend them to their pupils and read out extracts to them. Young girls take them into church with them. Young boys learning grammar are familiar with them. Clergymen – and God willing only the lowest, only those upon whom one does not bestow trust – put them up in their bookcases.[16]

While Bible reading among Protestants became increasingly rare, first in the towns, the processes of acculturation and de-regionalization and the 'reading mania' spread among Catholics, including those in the metropolises. A perfect example of this was Josephinian Vienna, with its deluge of anticlerical pamphlets. Clergymen who were hostile to reading resorted in their sermons and pamphlets to the old Baroque model for criticizing this reading mania. They feared, not without justification, that reading would lead to a general process of secularization and de-Christianization.

The 'Reading Mania'

Around 1770 even this model of reading, one which fitted with Enlightenment doctrine, and in which the social aspect of education played a central role, changed and became more sophisticated. Though a rapid process of modernization which also began to break free of the constraints of rationalism, the criteria for its reception, which were both authoritarian and academic, became more emotional and individual. This marked the beginning of a particularly decisive phase in the history of reading, one that remained especially virulent for several decades: that of a 'sentimental' or 'empathetic' form of reading. This form of reading was mid-way between, on the one hand, an individual passion that isolated the reader from society and his environment and, on the other, a hunger for communication through reading. This 'overwhelming desire to make new contact with the lives behind the printed page'[17] led to a completely new and incredibly intensive familiarity, even an imaginary friendship between author and reader, the producer of literature and its recipient. The isolation and anonymity felt by the reader who was emotionally aroused yet isolated was compensated by his awareness that reading made him part of a community of like-minded people. Undeniably, this form of reading was – in the sense of a 'revolution' in reverse – far more 'intensive' than before, and not in the least 'extensive'.

In Britain, France and Germany respectively, this culturally very significant process is specifically associated with the names Richardson, Rousseau, Klopstock and Goethe. At the root of the new relationship that existed between author, text and reader was Samuel Richardson (1689–1761). His novels *Pamela, or Virtue Rewarded* (1740) and *Clarissa* (1747–8) were received with greater enthusiasm than any representative of this literary genre before him. It was primarily a female readership who responded enthusiastically to *Pamela*. In this novel Richardson portrayed specifically the world of women's experience with a precision previously unheard of, whether by virtue of its domestic details or the intimacy of a love affair, using the form of letters, the subjective medium of articulation *par excellence*. All this helped to make *Pamela* into a work that 'could be praised from the pulpit and yet attacked as pornography, a work that gratified the reading public with the combined attractions of a sermon and a striptease'.[18]

In France, too, this reading matter created a considerable stir, as Diderot's *Éloge de Richardson* (1761) showed. But it was not until the work of Jean Jacques Rousseau (1712–78) appeared that the passion kindled by Diderot's book turned into a conflagration. Rousseau demanded to be read

> as if he were a prophet of divine truth ... What set the reading of Rousseau apart from his religious forebears – be it Calvinist, Jansenist or pietist reading – was the invitation to read the most suspect kind of literature, the novel, as if it were the Bible ... Rousseau ... wanted to penetrate life through literature, his own life and that of his readers.[19]

Conversely, his readers hungered for this kind of reading matter, 'not in order to enjoy literature, but better to master life, in particular family life, and precisely according to Rousseau's ideas'.[20]

La Nouvelle Héloïse (1761), probably the top bestseller of the *ancien régime* and reprinted at least seventy times by 1800, unleashed an overwhelming response, including floods of tears and extreme despondency. Robert Darnton emphasizes that the readers of pre-revolutionary France threw themselves into texts with a passion that we can barely imagine, that is 'as alien to us as the lust for plunder among the Norsemen or the fear of demons among the Balinese'[21] – or simply like the ecstasy of teenagers at pop concerts?

In Germany this revolution took place in a significant intermediate stage. Here, the female readership in particular needed a link between purely religious and purely worldly reading material. This was Friedrich Gottlieb Klopstock's (1724–1803) biblical epic *The Messiah*, published after 1749. It dealt with an edifying and, even for women, perfectly permitted subject, that of the life of Christ, but it did so from a sentimental perspective and in a boldly subjective way. Readers seized upon it at the moment they were preparing to emancipate themselves from traditional scholarly and religious reading materials, and it was abandoned immediately this emancipation was achieved, at which point they dealt with poetry and *belles-lettres* so naturally and casually that they no longer comprehended how 'Klopstock's *Messiah* could have once meant so much to them.'[22] The success enjoyed by C. F. Gellert's works is similarly explained. In the first bourgeois novel in Germany, his *Life of the Swedish Countess of G* (1746), the author's moral and religious intention was above all suspicion, which allowed the reader to devour the story's events all the more greedily.

A crucial breakthrough ultimately came in 1774, with Goethe's bestseller *The Sorrows of Young Werther*, the young Napoleon's favourite book. In contrast to Rousseau, however, its author placed not the slightest value on any kind of intimacy with the reader. Nevertheless, a proportion of his largely youthful reading public interpreted this tragic love story, in which bourgeois morality on earth was no longer propagated but exposed, as something other than a work of art. In line with the traditional concept of the 'useful' and edifying text, they constructed it as an invitation to emulate. A wave of suicides among *Werther* readers was the disastrous consequence of this misinterpretation. However, the great majority of readers were content to identify with the hero on a merely superficial level, turning Werther's clothing (a blue tailcoat and yellow breeches) into a symbol of rebellious youth, and bought cult objects such as the famous Werther cup. Finally, a small minority succeeded in objectifying the story aesthetically, distinguishing between the world of reading and everyday reality.

The example of *Werther* illustrated the sophistication of the new reading public who were trying out various forms of interaction with literary texts, new modes and rituals of reading. Both social and solitary forms of reading assumed new functions. The main reading public for *belles-lettres*, namely women, preferred a mode of collective reading that for them was a means of direct communication. However, the authoritative, 'frontal' method of reading aloud used by the *paterfamil-ias*, priest or teacher was now replaced by a gregariousness legitimized and formalized by reading, whose significance lay in the 'experience of empathetic role-playing',[23] or in other words a controlled and disciplined common mastering of literary texts. An exemplary case was a day described by Luise Mejer in 1784, in a letter to her friend, Heinrich Christian Boie. She worked as a lady's companion at Tremsbüttel in Holstein, at the residence of the Countess of Stolberg, whose husband and brother-in-law were successful writers:

> Breakfast is at ten o'clock. Then Stolberg reads out a chapter from the Bible, and a song from Klopstock's *Lieder*. Everyone retires to his or her bedroom. Then I dip into the *Spectator* or *Physiognomy*, and a few books the Countess has given me. She comes downstairs while Lotte translates, and I spend an hour reading her Lavater's *Pontius Pilate*. While she has her Latin lesson, I copy for her or read myself until dinner is served. After dinner and coffee, Fritz reads from the *Lebensläufen*, then Lotte comes downstairs and I read Milton with her for an hour. Then we go back upstairs and I read to the Count and Countess from *Plutarch* until teatime at around nine o'clock. After tea Stolberg reads a chapter from the Bible and one of Klopstock's *Lieder*, then it's 'goodnight'.[24]

Luise Mejer assessed this excessive kind of reading, which was both intensive and extensive in character, as follows: 'Here people are stuffed with reading matter in the same way that geese are stuffed with noodles.'

As a counterpart to the gregarious and communicative form of reading, solitary reading too assumed new qualities, characterized by quiet, peaceful appreciation. The body as a medium of textual experience was relegated to second place, and 'unruly' reading was disciplined. Quiet and relaxation while reading were now regarded as bourgeois virtues and as the prerequisite for aesthetic appreciation. By no longer putting himself at the mercy of the text, the reader remained master of himself and consequently free to interact with the text in a controlled way.[25] The immobility required from then on when reading at one's desk posed difficulties for more than just a few men, who continued to prefer the most casual positions. Literacy teaching at the end of the eighteenth century regarded the physically accentuated practice of reading aloud solely from a dietetic viewpoint, describing 'the acting of walking, in which the effort required causes the blood to circulate, prevents the bodily fluids from coagulating, and wards off illnesses and feelings of weariness. During rainy or unhealthy weather, or when we are ill, we have to take refuge in reading aloud as a substitute for the pleasures and benefits of a walk in the open air.'[26] Furthermore, as it internalized all emotions, quiet reading itself encouraged the reader to withdraw into the realm of the imagination.

The intensity conferred by closeted reading was further heightened by the 'sentimental' practice of reading in natural surroundings, in the open countryside, which for a time became a popular setting for the academically educated bourgeoisie, as an ostentatious retreat from society. It reflected the bourgeoisie's precarious position between, on the one hand, its revolt against the norms of late feudal society and, on the other, its humiliating consciousness of the fragility of its social prestige. This pointed escape from society, from the unreasonable demands of the court, from the town and from daily duties, into a sentimental retreat with a literary vade-mecum, conferred a particular intensity to the experience of reading by creating an interplay between the idyll of the surrounding landscape and imagined destinies. Readers liked to enjoy 'beautiful places' to the full by reading beautiful passages.

However, the principal location for reading continued to be the private domestic sphere, the bourgeois living space. The new cultural practice was integrated into daily life. Hitherto, the only people who had spent the hours of darkness unhealthily bent over folios had been scholars. Now, however, the evenings and nights also became available as free time for the literary public to enjoy reading. A change came about in the bourgeois attitude to time: once the day and time were structured and 'departmentalized', people gradually learned to alternate effortlessly between the imaginative world of reading and daily life, and the risk of confusing separated spheres of life with each other was reduced.[27]

The manufacturers of luxury items made 'reading furniture' available for the first time: *chaises longues* with an inbuilt reading desk, convertible furniture for the lady of rank, furniture that could serve simultaneously as a dressing table, a dining table, a desk for reading and writing, comfortable 'English chairs for reading or sleeping', and many others.[28] Women could procure clothing to match: the *liseuse*, a warm yet light house-frock or two-piece for imaginative journeys. For *galant* rococo ladies the boudoir had been a private space to which they could retire, but for the new bourgeois woman it was a 'closet' for reading, a refuge of female independence. It coupled the act of withdrawing from society with that of giving free rein to feelings. It 'was not used to conceal lovers, but to keep them out'.[29] It no longer contained courtly decorations, just reading materials and a writing desk, complete with letter-writing equipment. Just as popular among the female reading public was the habit of reading in bed, as can be inferred from contemporary accounts (often containing highly erotic allusions).

By the end of the eighteenth century, only a small proportion of the reading public had succeeded in achieving the highest, 'adult' stage in the literary culture of reading, namely 'by effecting the transition to the fictional world solely through the imagination',[30] and in integrating reading into everyday reality. They read hermeneutically, as an autonomous artistic practice, no longer in order to confirm already familiar truths within the range of their own expectations, but to discover new and unknown ones. These competent readers of classical national literature were few in number, and have remained so right up to the present day. This was why Friedrich Schiller rejected the search for a 'Volksdichter' (national poet): 'There is now a very large gap between the *élite* of a nation and its *masses*.' Jean Paul referred to a similar division, describing German readers around 1800 as follows:

> In Germany there are three types of reading public: 1. the broad, almost completely uncultured and uneducated one of libraries, 2. the learned scholarly public consisting of professors, students and critics, and 3. the cultured public consisting of men of the world and educated women, artists and members of the upper classes, among whom at least frequent contact and journeys form the rudiments of an education. (Of course, these three categories of public often communicate with one another.)[31]

The great majority of readers practised a quasi-pubescent variant of sentimental reading, a 'narcotic' (as the philosopher J. G. Fichte put it) and often escapist 'reading mania'. This practice was at the heart of contemporary discussions.

Around 1780 this new epidemic began to spread rapidly, again emanating from central and northern Germany outwards, and particularly among the younger, female audience. The debate in the newspapers and journals, sermons and pamphlets, at the end of the century even detected it 'among classes who otherwise did little or no reading, and who even now do not read in order to teach and educate themselves, but do so simply for the purpose of personal entertainment' (in the words of the Bavarian Enlightenment thinker L. Westenrieder).

The authorities of Church and State were not alone in taking offence at the new reading mania. Even progressive Enlightenment thinkers regarded it as a principal obstacle to the emancipation they were striving to bring out in a disciplined and rational way. This socially harmful practice would, they believed, lead to vices that conflicted with the bourgeois, Protestant work ethic, and belonged within the world of the nobility and the court: idleness, luxury, boredom. Initially, however, the case against reading was brought mainly on dietetic and sociomedical grounds. While Tissot's *On the Health of Scholars* (1786) merely warned of the health risks to scholars who spent all their time in their rooms, in the pedagogues' tracts of the late eighteenth century the 'masturbation' debate was linked to the debate about reading. Both were counted among the harmful 'secret sins of youth':

> the obligatory position, the lack of all physical movement when reading, combined with the violent alternation of imaginings and feelings [create] limpness, bloatedness and constipation of the intestines, in a word hypochondria, which has a recognized effect on the genitals of both sexes, particularly of the female sex [and creates] coagulations and defects in the blood, excitation and exhaustion of the nervous system, as well as conditions of langour and weakness in the whole body.[32]

Instructions on reading in the late Enlightenment condemned reading as a socially useless diversion: 'To read a book merely in order to kill time is an act of high treason toward humanity because one is belittling a medium that was designed for loftier purposes.'[33] Instead of being 'a method of educating toward independence', in the sense intended by Immanuel Kant in his definition of Enlightenment, it served 'merely to shorten time and maintain a condition of eternal dependency'.[34]

Reading Tastes and the Book Trade

The fundamental changes in the cultural practice of reading naturally had direct effects on the book trade that modernized both its forms of communication and its products. From the second half of the eighteenth century onwards, the book was consistently regarded as a cultural commodity, and with the transition from the barter economy that until then had been dominant to a monetary economy, the market was realigned according to capitalist principles. Starting with Leipzig and the booksellers of Saxony and northern Germany, the trend toward strictly sales-oriented book production led to a new market of demand, and even to new forms of advertising. The number of booksellers in the provincial towns also increased conspicuously, and a new generation of publishers pursued Enlightenment as a business. For this they were denounced by conservative publicists as the principal cause of the reading revolution.

At the same time the role of the author became professional, and in Germany the 'freier Schriftsteller' (freelance writer) emerged, on the one hand insisting on the autonomy of his creativity, and on the other having to subordinate himself to the laws of the emergent anonymous traffic in goods. This necessity for self-prostitution on the market before an anonymous public induced the author to have intensive contact with the recipient of his work, and vice versa, leading to a spiritual community created by the book.

The book market now tended to deal with a reading public that was unlimited, heterogeneous and anonymous, whose reading tastes and needs were becoming increasingly sophisticated, and who were interested in both specialist books for advancing their professional careers *and* political information, in bloody horror stories *and* spiritual comfort. Nevertheless, these special, overlapping interests were matched by the homogenization of reading tastes transcending former class boundaries. The same moving family story was read both by the noblewoman and by her maids-in-waiting; the same horror story was read by the high-ranking official in the judiciary and the tailor's apprentice alike. However, they were all able to rise to the level of the canonized national literature. While the anonymous reader was at the mercy of market supply, he also made collective demands of this market that could not be ignored without risk of commercial failure.

The fluctuations in the market and reading tastes are (despite inadequate statistics) reflected in the Leipzig book fair catalogue that represented the transregional book trade throughout the entire century. The sheer expansion in the volume of production after 1760 shows the remarkable growth in a public hungry for reading matter. In 1765 the book fair catalogue recorded 1,384 titles; in 1775, 1,892 titles; in 1785, 2,713; in 1790, 3,222; in 1795, 3,257; and in 1800, 3,906 titles. Total annual production may have comprised almost double that number around 1800. The growth in the number of new publications was matched by the rapid decline in Latin, which for centuries had been the dominant language among scholars. At the book fairs the proportion of titles written in Latin fell from 27.7 per cent in 1740 to 3.97 per cent in 1800. Similarly there was a change in the hierarchy of subject areas: the overwhelming superiority of theology and religion rapidly diminished, indicating both the secularization of learning and the disaffection of the Protestant reading public with the edifying literature of the time. At the same time, there was an increase in the percentage of modern subjects like geography, natural history, politics, education and above all *belles-lettres*. The latter, which in 1740 had constituted only 6 per cent of the book supply at the fairs, had increased to 16.5 per cent by 1770, and to 21.45 per cent by 1800, reaching the highest position of all subjects. This increase was mostly attributable to the novel, whose market share more than quadrupled from 2.6 per cent of the book supply in 1740 to 11.7 per cent in 1800.

It was not only the number of titles that increased, but also the number of copies. Of course, average print runs did not increase to the same extent, owing to the reprinting of titles and the growth of lending libraries. Far larger print runs were achieved by newspapers than by books at the very end of the century, following the trauma of the

French Revolution: the renowned *Hamburgischer Correspondent* reached 25,000 copies in 1798, rising to as many as 51,000 copies in 1801. At an average of ten readers per copy, this would have amounted to half a million readers. The print runs for more sophisticated literary journals, on the other hand, were lower by far (for instance, Wieland's *Teutscher Merkur*, with its 1,500 copies).

In the last third of the eighteenth century, book prices proved to be an obstacle to the rapid expansion of the reading public, especially the prices of the much sought-after *belles-lettres*. During this period, prices increased around eight- or ninefold, which was attributable to book-seller's practices, net retailing and low break-even quantities, but also to ever-increasing demand. For the price of one novel, a family in Germany (like Britain) could afford to feed itself for two weeks. For this reason most people among the newly emerging reading public, includ-ing the ranks of the bourgeois middle classes, switched to the lending libraries and reading societies in order to satisfy their reading require-ments, or at least bought the reprinted editions that were produced in the south of the Empire and were far cheaper than the original editions printed in northern and central Germany. In this way the reprint has played a central role in the expansion of the reading public, and in the spread of new reading tastes even in Catholic upper Germany – in fact, especially there.

Of course, the book as an object also changed. In an effort to promote an extensive and quick form of reading, progressive publishers tried in vain to introduce the elegant roman type in place of Gothic print, those 'ghastly runes' and that 'angular, scroll-filled monks' script' (as J. J. Bertuch described it). Such attempts to modernize largely failed, making the readers of *belles-lettres* all the more eager for the texts to have an elegant and pleasing appearance. They had to be provided with a number of copper plates and vignettes, decorations and tailpieces. An integral part of the gripping novel was the illustration, best of all those by Daniel Chodowiecki, the incomparably talented portrayer of bour-geois life. The aversion to thick tomes grew: 'books create scholars, pamphlets create human beings' went the new motto.

The beginning of the bourgeois culture of reading in the age of Enlightenment also saw the introduction of the octavo format. Throughout the following decades, books became slimmer and slimmer, and the octavo, duodecimo and even the dainty sextodecimo grew to be the preferred formats for readers of *belles-lettres*. The content matched the dainty exterior most perfectly in the case of almanacs. The poetry chapbook was the medium of a literary culture that, in line with the French model, gave rise to over 2,000 of these often pleasantly, even luxuriously, produced little volumes: literary chapbooks, scientific ones for the popular and specialist markets, and political and satirical ones. Jean Paul, a favourite writer of the late eighteenth century, commented on this change:

> Heavens! If I think of the old folios weighing many pounds, covered in boards, leather or brass bindings and clips, the fireside armchairs, uphol- stered in leather and fitted with nails of brass, in which the scholar spent his sedentary life; and if I now compare these to the little pocket books: one really cannot complain. Pigskin has been replaced by moroccan leather; the edges are now of gold, not brass; the clips and clasps have made way for silk-cloth cases; and instead of the chain tied to the old tomes in libraries, there is now a little silk instruction book for stamping.[35]

It was not the educative and informative literature of 'real facts', the travelogues and works of natural history, that occupied the highest position in the public taste and simultaneously constituted the main objects of the critics of the reading mania; it was rather the principal new genres of 'extensive' reading, the periodicals and novels. The latter in particular encouraged a 'rapid, inattentive, almost unconscious kind of reading habit'.[36] However, it may seem paradoxical that 'the most powerful vicarious identification of readers with the feelings of fictional characters that literature had seen should be produced by exploiting the qualities of print, the most impersonal, objective, and public of the media of communication'.[37]

As is well known, the polemic against the reading of novels has a long tradition stretching back to the *Amadis de Gaule*, though it is always described as a perversion confined to a privileged minority. However, with the multiplication of the production and reception of the novel in the late eighteenth century, the mania for reading novels assumed a sociopolitical dimension for the first time. In Germany the Easter trade fair of 1803 alone launched no fewer than 276 new novels, a figure that neither France nor Britain could come near. The deluge of novels covered all nuances of taste. In 1805 the *Allgemeine Literatur- Zeitung* took stock of the main trends in the production of novels in Germany since 1775, the year Johann Martin Miller's *Siegwart* was published: the sentimental, the comical, the psychological, the era of the passion novel, the chivalric or visionary romance, the ghost story, the magic novel, the novel of secret orders and courtly cabals, the domestic era, the era of the brigand, the thief and the rogue. A substantial pro- portion (around 40 per cent) of these new publications consisted of translations, primarily from English. An entire generation seemed to have caught the 'reading bug', that very generation that was meant to be continuing the struggle for bourgeois emancipation, yet was spend- ing its time indulging in the narcotic habit of reading. Moral criticism thus acquired an eminently political dimension. Some progressive authors deplored the fact that, in the case of young students and men, such reading material destroyed the autonomy of reason and the desire for emancipation – 'and without the slightest indignation they watch the murdering of freedom of thought and the press'. By exciting and unleashing the power of the imagination, reading released the reader from concrete sensory perception and the world of experience, at the risk of total disillusionment, even nihilism. Women with a passion for novels were reproached for escaping into passive and sentimental pleasures at the very moment when the bourgeois family was assigning a new and important range of duties to them. Complaints were also heard from conservative quarters in innumerable variations that such novels stimulated the reader's imagination, corrupted his sense of morality, and distracted him from his work. Immanuel Kant stated it succinctly: 'Besides causing many other upsets to a person's nature, reading novels also makes a habit of diversion.'

Besides novels, the reading matter preferred by the new reading public was periodicals. There had already been complaints about the 'untimely new newspaper craze' since the end of the seventeenth century, but even this now assumed a new dimension. The desire for daily news, for journalistic information about topical political and ecclesiastical, literary and economic events, spread far beyond the bourgeois classes. This was also true of pamphlets, in so far as the barriers of censorship gave way. When the reforming emperor Joseph II introduced press freedom in Austria, the consequence was a unique 'thaw', due to more than 1,200 brochures, pamphlets and loose sheets that were published in the years 1781 and 1782 alone. By the end of the century, the absolute dominance of politics united all strata of readers according to the conditions specific to each group. The lower classes had the sensational new publications read to them in the markets and the inns, while the upper classes devoured them at the commercial notice stalls, or else discussed them in a well-mannered way at reading societies. Evidently, however, the 'reading mania' had not taken hold of an entire generation, but seemed to have reached a new stage, as the masonic clergyman K. A. Ragotzky reported in 1792:

> But now it really is the case that a new, universal and far more powerful reading fashion than any before it has spread not just throughout Germany but over the whole of Europe too, attracting all classes and strata of society, and suppressing almost every other kind of reading matter. This is the reading of newspapers and political pamphlets. It is at present certainly the most widespread reading fashion there has ever been ... From the regent and the minister down to the woodcutter on the street and the peasant in the village tavern, from the lady at her toilet to the

cleaning maid in the kitchen, everyone is now reading newspapers. They
calculate the hour when the mail will arrive, and besiege the post office in
order to be the first there when the mailbag is opened ... A lady of taste
must have read at least the latest pages in the *Moniteur* the *Journal de
Paris* or the *Gazette de Leide* before she goes to her tea circle, and with the
company of gentlemen whom this common spirit assembles more assiduously around the tea table and who exchange news in the *Chronique du
mois*, the *London Chronicle*, the *Morning Post*, or the two Hamburg
newspapers, and those of Frankfurt or Bayreuth; while the smith sits on
his anvil and the cobbler on his stool, temporarily laying down his
hammer or his awl to read the *Strassburger Kriegsbothen*, the *Brünner
Bauern-Zeitung* or the *Staats-Courrier*, or has his wife read them to him.[38]

   In Germany the revolution in reading literature did not prevent the
formation of a political consciousness. On the contrary, it promoted
anti-feudal, anti-Church and altogether anti-authoritarian tendencies
that manifested themselves in fashionable *belles-lettres* just as frequently
as they did in the political commentaries. Unfortunately the role played
by clandestine reading in Germany has not yet been fully explored. As
Robert Darnton has shown, using the rich sources of the *Société
typographique* in Neuchâtel, obscene and irreligious books were
particularly sought after in France, even among the middle class of
officials and administrators.

Lending Libraries and Reading Societies

The new mode of reading also assumed new forms of organization.
Facing the highly organized market was not only the mass of anonymous book buyers, but also the institutionalized reader. This form of
organization was characteristic of the bourgeoisie on the road to emancipation in the eighteenth century, and took two parallel directions: on
the one hand, the commercial *lending library* and, on the other, the
non-commercial *reading societies*. In Germany as well as Britain and
France both forms of organization were vehicles for the reading revolution.[39] Nevertheless, the public libraries, the libraries of monastery,
town, court and most universities (with the exception of Göttingen)
played next to no part in satisfying this new desire for reading. On the
contrary, in so far as it was possible, they even checked its progression.
The Ducal Library Decree in the Thuringian town of Gotha held that
'Anyone wanting to take a closer look at a book must request it from
the librarian who will then show it to him and, should the need arise,
authorize him to read it'.
   If we leave aside one or two precursors, the heyday of the lending

library everywhere in Europe began in 1750. In Britain, their number increased to 'not less than one thousand' by 1801, according to *Monthly Magazine*. In 1761 the bookseller Quillan founded the first French lending library in the Parisian rue Christine. The *loueurs de livres* multiplied very rapidly during the 1770s and 1780s. Following several precursors in Berlin, there is evidence in the German-speaking area that the first lending libraries were established in Frankfurt-am-Main and Karlsruhe in the 1750s. In the majority of towns and markets, even the smaller ones, there was at least one lending library in operation by the 1780s and 1790s. Around 1800 Leipzig had nine such establishments, Bremen ten and Frankfurt-am-Main as many as eighteen. But even in a small town like Prussian Oranienburg the postmaster lent more than 12,000 volumes, and allowed readers to consult around 100 newspapers for a charge. The lending libraries were the ideal partners for the extensive consumption of reading material that was spreading among the middle classes. Anyone who, for social, financial or local reasons had no opportunity to join a reading society was here able to satisfy his need for literature of all kinds, even with only a limited purchasing power and motivation. This applied especially to those large sections of the public to whom the reading societies essentially remained closed, although it was precisely they who were the worst affected by the 'reading mania': students and craftsmen's apprentices, young girls and women, socially marginal groups who had in part benefited from a university education, such as private tutors, common soldiers and clerks.

The same contemporary voices that were raised against the fatal reading epidemic began to attack the lending libraries that they considered to be the main breeding grounds of this vice. They were regarded as 'brothels and houses of moral perdition' that infected everyone – the young and the old, the upper classes and the lower – with their 'spiritual poison'. Lending libraries with a stock of predominantly *belles-lettres*, including chivalric romances, stories of brigands or ghosts, along with sentimental love stories and family novels, were often disparagingly called *Winkeletablissements* ('backstreet establishments'). Often their stocks were outdated, and ranged from a few dozen titles to over a thousand volumes. This early type of purely entertaining consumer library was frequently run by antiquarian booksellers, bookbinders or complete newcomers to the trade; but many serious booksellers in the smaller towns felt the need to bring their supplies into line with the prevailing taste. In Württemburg in 1809, nine-tenths of all lending libraries in the small market towns were this kind of humble establishment, with stocks of between 100 and 600 volumes. But even in the larger towns, reading tastes were by no means superior.

However, in the early history of the institution, this widely decried type of library can be contrasted with another type, modelled on the reading societies, which competed with them and occasionally even evolved from one of them. The stocks kept by these *Lesekabinette* or 'museums' betray encyclopaedic aspirations. The entire range of the contemporary book market was represented here, including specialist science publications, editions of the works of major writers, even foreign-language publications. In addition, a frequently affiliated journal-reading circle would supply periodicals from home and abroad. These firms displayed a self-understanding that was characteristic of the late Enlightenment, despite their otherwise commercial motives, and could more than stand up against the few inadequate public and university libraries. In the main cities of trade and education – Vienna, Frankfurt or Dresden, for instance – these institutions added reading rooms, where reference books could be consulted, exhibition rooms for displaying news publications, and in some cases for *objets d'art* and crafts, and music rooms and salons where refreshments were offered.

In spite of these 'lofty' institutions, the calls to have these 'dens of political and moral perdition' supervised grew even louder, particularly in the wake of the French Revolution. Around 1800, in all the German states, either a total ban was enforced on all lending libraries (as happened in Austria between 1799 and 1811), or at least a set of strict controls (the Wöllner Edict of 1788 in Prussia, and of 1803 in Bavaria).

From the beginning of the nineteenth century onwards, the lending libraries overtook the reading societies everywhere. This development testifies to the individualization and simultaneous anonymity of literary reception. Literary discussions conducted within a familiar circles of friends were succeeded by an individual form of reading practised in isolation, partly escapist and partly devoted to social climbing, that required commercial mediation.

In contrast to the lending libraries, the reading societies were self-managed organizations set up for the purpose of making reading material available to their members at a low cost and without commercial interests. A particular section of the bourgeoisie of the late Enlightenment who, in its criticism of the reading mania, deplored the anti-social practice of reading in solitude as an idle and socially harmful habit, saw in these clubs a centre for the achievement of emancipation, but also doubtless for mutual discipline and control. Here, a supervised form of reading based on common standards was practised, a collective assimilation and appropriation of reading matter. Evidently the reading societies were at the intersection of two decisive achievements along the way to bourgeois emancipation: on the one hand, extensive reading (in general the financial wherewithal of an individual did not extend to satisfying his desire for reading) and, on the other, the aspiration to create a social organization of this new reading public of private individuals in a comparably autonomous form.

Reading societies first began to evolve in the seventeenth century, with joint subscriptions to newspapers and later on to journals as well. These reading circles served to satisfy the craving for political information, and often continued until well into the nineteenth century, in the absence of any other institutions. With this mode of circulation, each member remained in his own private world, without regulated communication of what they read. From the 1770s onwards, more tightly run forms of organization became prominent: *Lesebibliotheken* ('reading libraries') emerged, in which the procured reading materials were collected in a single room and made available for use – periodicals and also an increasing number of books. For the purposes of acquiring and issuing books on loan, for finances and administration, guidelines needed to be drawn up, and a managerial committee had to be appointed; it was in this way that the first associative structures began to emerge. The place where the books were kept soon became a place where they were collected, and readers came together there to discuss what they had read and to form their opinions. A clearly widespread need for such places of communication about and through reading matter led to a boom in new institutions, particularly in the commercial towns of Protestant Germany. By 1770 thirteen reading societies were established, but by 1780 around fifty new ones had emerged, as many as 170 between 1780 and 1790, reaching 200 new societies in the last decade of the century. By 1810 another 130 were added, but by 1820 only a further 34. Unfortunately, these impressive statistics are not matched by corresponding data on the life-span of these societies.

Undoubtedly, their special appeal at the end of the eighteenth century was associated with the expansion in their stock of entertaining literature. A growing number of *Lesebibliotheken* and *cabinets littéraires* had other rooms added to their reading rooms, so that people could chat and smoke, and servants could serve refreshments, and it was not uncommon for other club rooms to be added for honourable diversions such as billiards and other games. Although there was mostly no reference in the statutes of these reading societies to class restrictions, nevertheless social homogeneity was guaranteed by the fact that a majority decision was needed before a new member could be accepted. On this evidence at least, the often proclaimed 'equality of all classes' was a mere fiction.

These readings societies, often called 'Harmonie', 'Societät', 'Museum',

'Ressource' or 'Kasino', helped the property-owning and educated bourgeoisie, as well as aristocratic officials, to broaden their social contacts. Reading soon became a secondary consideration in these carefully selected meeting places. Membership figures could range from two dozen in the case of the smaller societies, through 100 (in Bonn or Worms), 180 (in Frankfurt-am-Main), to 400 in Hamburg, or as many as 452 in the case of the particularly active people of Mainz.

Similarly, there was considerable variation in the size and composition of their stocks of reading materials. To begin with, edifying, moralistic and didactic texts predominated, as well as periodicals and works of popular science. In the specialist reading societies – those of doctors and lawyers, preachers, teachers and economists – there were mainly publications specific to their professions. Towards the end of the century, entertaining reading matter, and novels in particular, became increasingly popular within the more gregarious reading societies. Many societies entertained the ambition of owning a particularly wide stock of topical publications, ranging from almanacs, the major review organs, and the latest travelogues, to the political dailies, including those published in French and English.

If we take as our average a membership of 100, the reading societies altogether gained an audience of around 50,000 people between 1770 and 1820, and had great significance for both the political education and the reading culture of this élite. This seems to be an almost ideal exemplification of Habermas's model – in its discussions about reading matter, a public consisting of educated private individuals had managed to reach a consensus about its cultural and political interests. This élite may have constituted 7 per cent of all readers, but only a thousandth of the total population. Nevertheless, this did not prevent the authorities from regarding these autonomous circles with a certain suspicion. The war against the 'reading mania' also turned its attention to the reading societies as places where extensive reading was learned through practice. They were licensed, and their stocks of books were placed under supervision. The Catholic territories had a particularly suspicious attitude towards organized reading. The dioceses of Mainz, Trier and Würzburg issued prohibitions, especially from 1789 onwards; in Bavaria, reading societies had already been accused of harbouring *illuminati*, and were dissolved in 1786; in Austria, after a long period of surveillance, the authorities eventually came to the same decision in 1789. The justification used in Hanover in 1799 to put all reading societies under police supervision was significant. Once again, they constituted a moral and political danger, specifically the danger that disorder, slovenliness, and probably diseases of the cornea and other ill-nesses arise in some families if the first-form schoolboy can study his *Portier des chartreux*, inexpensively and in complete tranquillity, if the girl of marriageable age can do the same with her *Sopha* and *Ecumoire*, and the young housewife with her *Liaisons dangereuses*. As one has been able to procure these and similar writings in our native language since the time of the 'Great Enlightenment' in Germany, so they can be easily made available to all classes and at all levels through the libraries and the reading societies, if these 'factories of the Enlightenment' remain outside public supervision.

It is still unclear whether the reading societies really did play such an essential role in forming bourgeois public opinion, as the opponents of the Enlightenment maintained at the time, and as researchers believe today. The fact that their appearance changed around 1800 was due not only to acts of repression by the authorities, but to the new status of reading which did not in the least develop that comprehensive and explosive social force that many feared. Instead, reading became a cul-tural activity like others – in accordance with the situation, oriented toward education, diversion, information or as the last bastion against the demands of the outside world. The reading societies had been the site of social discourse; they had now become centres of sociability. In this new form some of them survived for the whole of the nineteenth century, and some of them have even persisted until the present day.

Was there a reading revolution at the end of the eighteenth century? In this rough outline I have attempted to show that, in spite of all limitations, the answer to this question is yes. The development of indi-vidual and communal reading during this time testifies to the ambiva-lent role played by the book and by print in social discipline and rationalization in the early modern period. On the one hand, knowledge of the cultural practice of reading was able massively to support this process of social formation, but on the other hand, it also offered the most seductive means individually to escape the unreasonable demands of society. Bourgeois rationalists were convinced that the way to imma-nent and transcendent well-being could be followed by reading. Their tireless propaganda on behalf of a useful form of reading acquainted the rising bourgeoisie with this cultural practice, which they regarded as an original form of communication. Its opponents, married to tradition, attacked reading with the same vehemence, because in their view it was synonymous with original sin: he who read ate from the forbidden tree of knowledge.

However, within a few decades, both of them were completely over-taken by events. Around 1800, the public was largely anonymous, unhomogeneous and fragmented – in short, modern – and an education

Reinhard Wittmann

in reading had long ceased to have a hold on the public. Readers did not read whatever was recommended to them by the authorities and the ideologues, but whatever satisfied their intellectual, social and private needs. The genie had irretrievably escaped from the bottle.

12

New Readers in the Nineteenth Century: Women, Children, Workers

Martyn Lyons

In the nineteenth century, the reading public of the Western world achieved mass literacy. The advances made towards general literacy in the age of Enlightenment were continued, to create a rapidly expanding number of new readers, especially for newspapers and cheap fiction. In revolutionary France, about half the male population could read, and about 30 per cent of women.[1] In Britain, where literacy rates were higher, male literacy was about 70 per cent in 1850, and 55 per cent of females could read.[2] The German Reich was 88 per cent literate in 1871.[3]

These figures hide considerable variations between town and country, and between the highly literate capital cities and the rest of the country. In Paris, for example, on the eve of the French Revolution, 90 per cent of men and 80 per cent of women were able to sign their wills; and in 1792, two out of three inhabitants of the popular *faubourg* St Marcel could read and write.[4] Such high levels of literacy, however, were found only in the largest western European cities before the mid-nineteenth century. Nevertheless by the 1890s, 90 per cent literacy had been almost uniformly reached, and the old discrepancy between men and women had disappeared. This was the 'golden age' of the book in the West: the first generation which acceded to mass literacy was also the last to see the book unchallenged as a communications medium, by either the radio or the electronic media of the twentieth century.

This expansion of the reading public was accompanied by the spread of primary education. Progress in education, however, tended to follow, rather than precede, the growth of the reading public. Primary education only became effectively free, general and compulsory in England and France after the 1880s, when those countries were already almost completely literate.

Meanwhile, the shorter working day provided more leisure time for reading. In 1910, for instance, the *Verein für Socialpolitik* found that most German workers associated leisure only with Sundays.[5] But the working day had been getting gradually shorter in Germany since 1870, and by the end of the century, a ten-hour day was normal. In England, a nine-hour day was the rule by 1880. Even the working classes could begin to join the ranks of the new reading public.

The new public devoured cheap novels. In the eighteenth century, the novel was not regarded as a respectable art-form, but in the first quarter of the nineteenth century, its status was assured. It became the classic literary expression of triumphant bourgeois society. In the early years of the nineteenth century, novels were rarely produced in print runs of more than 1,000 or 1,500 copies. By the 1840s, editions of 5,000 copies were more common, while in the 1870s, the cheapest editions of Jules Verne appeared in editions of 30,000.[6] In the 1820s and 1830s, Walter Scott had done much to enhance the reputation of the novel, and had become an international success in the process. By the 1870s, Jules Verne was beginning to reach the global readership that made him a colossus of the growing popular fiction market. The mass production of cheap popular fiction integrated new readers into national reading publics, and helped to make those reading publics more homogeneous and unified.

The publishers, who had now 'arrived' for the first time as a body of professional specialists, fully exploited the new opportunities for capitalist investment. Cheap monthly instalments could reach a wider public than the traditional, well-bound, three-decker novel. The serialization of fiction in the press opened up a new market, and made the fortune of authors like Eugène Sue, Thackeray and Trollope. A new relationship was created between the writer and his or her public. American readers, it was reported, crowded the docksides to greet the ship bringing the next instalment of Dickens's *The Old Curiosity Shop*, so eager were they to learn the fate of the heroine, Little Nell. The French public first read Marx's *Das Kapital* in weekly instalments, published in 1872. In a famous essay of 1839, Sainte-Beuve warned that this 'industrialization of literature' could never produce great art.[7] The lure of profit, however, would not be denied.

The new readers of the nineteenth century were a source of profit, but they were also a source of anxiety and unease for social élites. The 1848 revolutions were partly blamed on the spread of subversive and socialist literature, which reached the urban worker and a new audience in the countryside. In 1858 the British novelist Wilkie Collins coined the phrase 'The Unknown Public' to describe 'the lost literary tribes' of 3 million lower-class readers, 'right out of the pale of literary civilisation'.[8] He referred to the readers of illustrated penny magazines, which offered a weekly fare of sensational stories and serials, anecdotes, readers' letters, problem pages and recipes. The readers of the penny novels included many domestic servants and shop-girls, 'the young lady classes'. According to Collins, 'the future of English fiction may rest with this Unknown Public, which is now waiting to be taught the difference between a good book and a bad'. England's new readers, who never bought a book or subscribed to a library, provided middle-class observers with a sense of discovery, tinged with fear.

The Female Reader: Occupying a Space of her Own

Women formed a large and increasing part of the new novel-reading public. The traditional discrepancy between male and female literacy rates was narrowed, and finally eliminated by the end of the nineteenth century. The gap had always been the widest at the lowest end of the social scale. In Lyons at the end of the eighteenth century, day-labourers and silk-workers were twice as literate as their wives; but in artisan trades like baking, where the wife might be responsible for the accounting, and frequent contact with the public was required, women were the equals of their literate male partners.[9]

Perhaps more women than we realize could already read. The signature test, commonly used by historians to measure literacy, hides from view all those who could read, but were still unable to sign their own name. This group was essentially female. The Catholic Church had tried as far as possible to encourage people to read, but not to write. It was useful for parishioners to be able to read the Bible and their catechism, but the ability to write as well might have given peasants an undesirable degree of independence in the eyes of the clergy. Perhaps for this reason, many women could read but not sign or write. In some families, there was a rigid sexual division of literary labour, according to which the women would read to the family, while the men would do the writing and account-keeping.

Girls' education continued to lag behind that of boys everywhere in Europe. At the end of the eighteenth century, only 9 per cent of pupils in Russian state schools were girls, and in Spanish Navarre in 1807, boys' schools outnumbered girls' schools by two to one. In France, the first *écoles normales d'institutrices* were not established until 1842, but by 1880, over two million French girls attended school.

The provision of more formal schooling for girls therefore seemed to follow, rather than precede, the growing feminization of the reading public. Expanding opportunities for female employment (for example, as teachers, shop assistants or postal clerks) and gradually changing expectations of women did more to raise the level of female literacy. The nineteenth century witnessed the growth of a thriving female magazine industry and the emergence of a comparatively new phenomenon: the blue-stocking. Women writers, pilloried mercilessly by satirical journals like *Le Charivari* as a threat to domestic stability, made their mark. The notoriety of a few individuals like George Sand should not disguise the more general literary contributions made by women everywhere in the nineteenth century. The *femme des lettres* had arrived.

The role of the female reader was traditionally that of a guardian of custom, tradition and family ritual. In Protestant families in Australia, for instance, the family Bible was usually handed down from generation to generation through the female line. In it were recorded births, marriages and deaths, so that it remained a symbol of Christian tradition and family continuity.[10]

Similarly, Pierre-Jakez Hélias, recalling his own childhood near Plozevet, in Finistère, towards the beginning of the twentieth century, told us that the *Vie des Saints* had been part of his mother's trousseau:

> In the house, aside from my mother's prayer books and a few collections of hymns, there were only two large volumes. One of them, which was kept permanently on the window sill, was Monsieur Larousse's French dictionary . . . the other was closed into the cupboard that my mother had received as a wedding gift. It was *The Lives of the Saints*, written in Breton.[11]

This account links a series of cultural dichotomies. The Lives of Saints was a specifically female preserve, and the maternal wedding chest was a hoard of religious knowledge, in opposition to the Larousse, a treasury of lay wisdom. The *Vie des Saints* (or *Buhez ar zent*) represented Catholic France, while Larousse was an emblem of secular republicanism. Hélias's mother's chest was, at the same time, Breton-speaking territory, while the window sill supporting Larousse was a kind of altar devoted to the French language. The traditional image of the woman reader tended to be of a religious, family-oriented reader, far removed from the central concerns of public life.

The new women readers of the nineteenth century, however, had other, more secular tastes, and new forms of literature were designed for their consumption. Among the genres destined for this new market of readers were cookery books, magazines and, above all, the cheap popular novel.

Among cookery manuals, *La Cuisinière bourgeoise* takes pride of place in early nineteenth-century France. Thirty-two editions of this title, or of *La Nouvelle Cuisinière bourgeoise*, were produced between 1815 and 1840, the years of its greatest popularity. The total print run produced in this period was probably about 100,000 copies, which made it a bestseller of the Restoration.[12]

La Cuisinière bourgeoise typified the cooking of the Enlightenment, embodying a more scientific approach to dietetics and a rejection both of aristocratic luxury and of the coarse taste of the lower classes. *La Cuisinière bourgeoise* was published with a set of instructions, which defined specifically bourgeois gestures and table manners. Advice was given on correct seating arrangements, on the roles of husband and wife at table, on the proper subjects of mealtime conversation, and on various rituals of collective consumption. Bread, for example, was to be broken not cut in peasant fashion; wine, the book firmly insisted, could be taken neat immediately after the soup course, but decorum thereafter dictated that it be watered. In these ways, the nineteenth-century bourgeoisie was encouraged to invent its own distinctive style of social behaviour, or its own gestural code, which would allow it to recognize its own, and to identify interlopers.

Unlike its rivals, *Le Cuisinier royal* and *Le Cuisinier impérial*, *La Cuisinière bourgeoise* was female, and the book was usually edited by women. This did not mean that publishers expected bourgeois women to read and use *La Cuisinière bourgeoise*. The book included not only recipes and advice on entertaining, but also all the household duties of domestic servants, for whom the manual was especially written. According to the preface to the 1846 edition, the mistress of the house 'can have it read to her domestic servants from time to time ... which will save her the trouble of repeating the same instructions over and over again. In this respect, this book is indispensable for bachelors, who always risk encountering inept domestics.'[13] The book's real readership was thus even more democratic than its title implied; it was destined not just for the personal use of the *bourgeoise*, but also for those who sought to serve her better.

Recipes and advice on etiquette were incorporated into women's magazines, alongside fashion news. The *Journal des Dames et des Modes* lasted from 1797 until 1837, carrying engravings and descriptions of both male and female outfits. It was followed in the 1840s by journals like the *Journal des demoiselles* and *La Toilette de Psyché*. Gradually, fashion magazines began to reach a more popular readership

– a trend indicated perhaps in France when *femme* replaced *dame* in magazine titles. By 1866, *La Mode illustrée* had a print run of 58,000, with its combination of fiction, household hints and sumptuously illustrated fashion pages.[14]

From time to time, attempts were made to launch journals which were not just aimed at female readers, but which actively promoted feminist causes. *La Voix des femmes* was an ambitious daily which appeared for three months in 1848. In the Third Republic, *La Droit des femmes* urged the re-establishment of divorce and educational facilities for girls. *La Fronde* was entirely produced by women, between 1897 and 1903.

Weekly illustrated magazines flourished during the Second Empire in France, many of them based on English antecedents like the *Penny Magazine* or the *Illustrated London News*. *Le Journal illustré*, for example, was an illustrated weekly, established in 1864, with eight pages in folio format. One or two pages were taken up with an illustration, and other features included views of Paris, puzzles, some European news, society chat and a *causerie théâtrale*. In 1864, an entire issue written by Alexandre Dumas and Gustave Doré boasted a circulation of 250,000.[15] Such weeklies, costing ten centimes and sold at street kiosks, were becoming an integral part of mass urban culture.

Les Veillées des chaumières catered more specifically for female readers, and promised something more moral and uplifting than its competitors. Costing only 5 centimes per issue, it offered novels as bonuses for subscribers, and at times included three different *feuilletons*. It did not, however, ignore the potential drawing power of large melodramatic illustrations. The serialized *Fédora la nihiliste* opened in 1879 with a full-page illustration, in which a fur-coated Tsar presided, godlike, above the clouds, with sword and sceptre, accompanied by a half-naked winged figure holding a shining crucifix. Below, a masked figure holding a smoking revolver lay transfixed by a sword. Fédora could not destroy a monarch who enjoyed divine protection. *Les Veillées des chaumières* had two columns of text, with very few breaks except chapter headings. Only in the twentieth century did women's magazines discover the value of breaking up the text, and of interspersing it with illustrated advertisements. In so doing, it was offering a kind of fragmented reading, more perfectly attuned to the interrupted working rhythm of a modern housewife.

For contemporary publishers, the woman reader was above all a consumer of novels. They offered series like the *Collection des meilleurs romans français dédiés aux dames* (Werdet in Paris), or fiction for *le donne gentili* (Stella in Milan). Such titles were making a claim to respectability, attempting to reassure both male and female purchasers that the contents were suitable for delicate eyes. They tried to corner a particular sector of the market, but at the same time, they encouraged the growth of a female reader's subculture. This development ultimately restricted, rather than expanded, sales, and the practice was rarely continued beyond the Restoration period. Nevertheless, to create a series defined by its public, rather than its material contents, was a new development in publishing.

In Stendhal's correspondence, the author emphasized the importance of the female reader for the novelist. Novel-reading, he claimed, was the favourite activity of French provincial women: 'There's hardly a woman in the provinces who doesn't read her five or six volumes a month. Many read fifteen or twenty. And you won't find a small town without two or three reading rooms (*cabinets de lecture*).'[16] While the *femmes de chambre* read authors like Paul de Kock in small duodecimo format, Stendhal continued, the *femmes de salon* preferred the more respectable novel in octavo, which aspired to some kind of literary merit.

Although women were not the only readers of novels, they were regarded as a prime target for popular and romantic fiction. The feminization of the novel-reader seemed to confirm dominant preconceptions about the female's role and about her intelligence. Novels were held suitable for women, because they were seen as creatures of the imagination, of limited intellectual capacity, both frivolous and emotional.[17] The novel was the antithesis of practical and instructive literature. It demanded little, and its sole purpose was to amuse readers with time on their hands. Above all, the novel belonged to the domain of the imagination. Newspapers, reporting on public events, were usually a male preserve; novels, dealing with the inner life, were part of the private sphere to which nineteenth-century bourgeois women were relegated.

This carried a certain danger for the nineteenth-century bourgeois husband and *paterfamilias*: the novel could excite the passions, and stimulate the female imagination. It could encourage romantic expectations that appeared unreasonable; it could make erotic suggestions which threatened chastity and good order. The nineteenth-century novel was thus associated with the (supposedly) female qualities of irrationally and emotional vulnerability. It was no coincidence that female adultery became the archetypal novelistic form of social transgression in the period, from Emma Bovary to Anna Karenina and Effi Briest.

The threat which fiction posed to sensitive girls was emotionally described by a reader herself, subsequently 'redeemed' from her errors. Charlotte Elizabeth Browne, daughter of a Norwich clergyman, was only seven when she innocently encountered *The Merchant of Venice*. 'I drank a cup of intoxication under which my brain reeled for many a year,' she wrote in 1841.

I revelled in the terrible excitement that it gave rise to; page after page
was stereotyped upon a most retentive memory, without an effort, and
during a sleepless night I feasted on the pernicious sweets thus hoarded in
my brain. . . . Reality became insipid, almost hateful to me; conversation,
except that of literary men . . . a burden; I imbibed a thorough contempt
for women, children, and household affairs, entrenching myself behind
invisible barriers. . . . Oh how many wasted hours, how much of unprofitable labour, what wrong to my fellow-creatures, must I refer to this
ensnaring book! My mind became unnerved, my judgement perverted, my
estimate of people and things wholly falsified. . . . Parents know not what
they do, when from vanity, thoughtlessness, or overindulgence, they
foster in a young girl what is called a poetical taste.[18]

As a result of this harrowing experience, Charlotte issued strict warnings
to parents about protecting the young from dangerous reading.

The seductive potential of the sentimental novel was ironically treated
by Brisset in the opening scenes of his *Le Cabinet de lecture*, published
in 1843. The bearded and hunchbacked Madame Bien-Aimé, who keeps
the reading room, advises a writer: 'You have, to entice your female
readers, some sentimental insights to seduce them, some deliciously
entangled phrases, the most chaste and shameless thoughts, followed by
whirlwinds of passion to enrapture them, frenzied ravings and fiery out-
bursts!'[19] In Brisset's story, a young *grisette* asks for a gothic novel with
castles and dungeons, with a happy romantic ending, to read after
work. Then a fashionable, married *Parisienne*, tired of chaste, sentimental heroines, promises to send her maid to collect something stronger.
The novelist immediately resolves to seduce both the *couturière* and the
rich *Parisienne*. The novel itself, by implication, is a means of seduction.

Reading had an important role in female sociability. In pubs and
cabarets, men discussed public affairs over a newspaper; fiction and
practical manuals, in contrast, changed hands through exclusively
female networks. One Bordeaux writer commented in 1850: 'These
days society is split into two great camps; on one side the men, who
smoke and gamble, on the other the women and young girls, whose life
is divided between reading novels and music.'[20] When the two genders
came together as readers, the woman was often in a position of tutelage
to the male. In some Catholic families, women were forbidden to read
the newspaper. More frequently, a male would read it aloud. This was a
task which sometimes implied a moral superiority and a duty to select
or censor material.

While the man was expected to read the political and sporting news,
women appropriated the sections of the newspaper devoted to *faits
divers* and serialized fiction. The territory of the newspaper was thus
thematically divided according to gender-based expectations. The

roman-feuilleton, or serialized novel, was a subject of everyday conversation among women readers, and many would cut out the episodes as they were published, and paste or bind them together. The improvised novels so created could be passed on through many female hands. As a shoemaker's daughter from the Vaucluse, born in 1900, explained:

> I used to cut out the serials from the journal and rebind them. We women passed them round between us. On Saturday evening, the men went to the café, and the women used to come and play cards at our house. The main thing was, that's when we swapped our serials, things like *Rocambole* or *La Porteuse de pain.*[21]

In this way, women who might never have bought a book improvised their own library of cut-out, re-sewn and often-shared texts.

Oral historians who have interviewed women about their reading practices in the period before 1914 have become familiar with a few common attitudes. The commonest female response, looking back on a lifetime's reading, is to protest that there had never been any time for reading. For women, and for their mothers, 'I was too busy getting on with my duties', or 'Mother never sat down idle'. Peeling potatoes, embroidery, making bread and soap left no time for recreation, in the memory of many working-class women. As children, they recalled that they feared punishment if they were caught reading. Household obligations came first, and to admit to reading was tantamount to confessing neglect of the woman's family responsibilities. The idealized image of the good housekeeper seemed incompatible with reading.

Working-class women, however, *did* read, as oral historians have also discovered – magazines, fiction, recipes, sewing patterns – but they persisted in discrediting their own literary culture. Those interviewed frequently described their own fiction-reading as 'trash' or 'nonsense-reading'. Reading was condemned as a waste of time, which offended against a rather demanding work ethic. Such women, interviewed by Anne-Marie Thiesse in France, and by myself and Taksa in Sydney, denied their own cultural competence.[22] They accepted conventional expectations of the woman as housekeeper, intellectually inferior and a limited reader. Those who violated these stereotypical patterns read in secret. For them, books provided furtive enjoyment (*les plaisirs dérobés*).

One young girl who struggled for her independence as a reader and a woman was Margaret Penn, autobiographical author of *Manchester Fourteen Miles.* First published in 1947, the book described the author's life near the northern city of Manchester in about 1909.

Margaret, or Hilda as she called herself, had illiterate and devoutly

Methodist parents. She read all the family's correspondence aloud, and
she read the Bible to her parents. Using the local co-operative library,
she began, as a young teenager, to borrow novelettes. Her parents,
however, objected to her reading anything except the Bible and books
from Sunday school. They further wanted to confine her reading to
Sunday.

Hilda, however, persuaded the local Anglican vicar to give his
approval to her borrowing from the co-operative library. She read
Robinson Crusoe and *Tess of the D'Urbervilles*, which would have
shocked her parents, as would her choice of the best-selling Victorian
melodrama *East Lynne*. Her parents, however, were forced to accept
the advice of the vicar, but her illiterate mother remained suspicious of
any book that Hilda would not read aloud. Hilda refused to go meekly
into domestic service as her parents demanded. Instead, aged thirteen,
she left for Manchester to begin work as an apprentice dressmaker. She
had encountered constant attempts to prevent her from indulging in
'idle reading'. Her difficulties were severe, since her parents would at
first tolerate nothing but religious reading. Her crime was aggravated by
the fact that she was a girl, who had no business thinking about educating or improving herself. Hilda's father blamed reading for her
refusal to accept her destiny. He was probably correct to see a connection between reading and Hilda's independence, but reading was a
symptom, not a cause, of Hilda's desire for liberation.

Women of the middle or lower-middle classes rarely faced such obs-
tacles as readers. Even if they could not afford to buy books regularly,
they became regular customers at public lending libraries. This was especially true in large cities. In the popular libraries sponsored by the *Société
Franklin*, from the end of the Second Empire onwards, women formed a
small minority of provincial borrowers. In Cette in 1872, 94 per cent of
library readers were men, in Pau 80 per cent and in Rouen in 1865, 88
per cent. In the lending libraries of the Paris *arrondissements*, however,
in the 1880s and 1890s, there was a substantial proportion of women
readers – about half of the total in the first and eighth *arrondissements*
(the Louvre and the *faubourg* St Honoré), and about one-third in Batign-
olles.[23] Unemployed women, described by librarians as *propriétaires* or
rentières, reinforced the demand for novels and recreational reading in
the late nineteenth-century lending libraries.

As never before, the female reader compelled recognition, from novel-
ists and publishers, from librarians, and from parents keen to discour-
age time-wasting or to protect their daughters from imaginative fancy
or erotic stimulation. She appeared more and more frequently in literary
and pictorial representations of reading.

The female reader was a recurrent subject for nineteenth-century painters like Manet, Daumier, Whistler and Fantin-Latour. Fantin-Latour's female readers read alone and in peace, completely absorbed in their books. In Whistler's versions of readers, again usually female, books are never quite as absorbing as the pink-covered review is for the reader in Fantin-Latour's *Portrait de Victoria Dubourg* (1873). But Whistler did paint his half-sister reading at night, with lamp and cup of coffee beside her. This was a modern portrayal of reading, and one in a bourgeois setting (*Reading by Lamplight*, 1858). In general, though, Whistler's readers recline in languid poses, like his wife, lying in bed with a book on her lap in *The Siesta*.

Manet tended to distinguish very clearly between male and female reading practices. In his *Liseur* of 1861, the artist Joseph Gall is painted in the style of a Tintoretto self-portrait, deep in meditation over a large and heavy tome. He is a bearded, paternal figure, engaged in serious and erudite reading.

Manet's *La Lecture de l'illustré* of 1879, however, presented a different, and modern view of the female reader. A young girl, elegantly dressed, is sitting outside a café, casually flipping through the pages of an illustrated magazine. She reads alone, without concentration, and purely for entertainment, her eyes and attention wandering towards the street scene in front of her. At the same time, she is close to a common stereotype of the female reader, destined to be an eternal consumer of light, trivial and romantic reading matter.

The realist Bonvin painted peasant women, nuns and servant girls bending silently over large quarto illustrated volumes. His subjects have often interrupted their work to read, since they are often still dressed in apron and white cap, or have purposefully rolled up their sleeves (*Femme lisant*, 1861, and *La Lecture*, 1852). The inspiration of the Dutch masters is evident in Bonvin's thick-textured garments and in his use of light and shade. His art, however, has a quality of *reportage*. He often painted his working-class readers from behind, as though he was peeping over their shoulder, without disturbing their evident concentration. He painted as an observer capturing a slice of popular life. His women are very private readers – the maid reading her employer's letters could not be otherwise (*La Servante indiscrète*, 1871). They read as a respite from their labour. They read alone, and they are almost always female.

Although Fantin-Latour often represented the act of reading as an element of female companionship in bourgeois households, the painted image of the woman reader was increasingly that of a solitary individual. Reading aloud, in contrast, was a practice more common to the male society of the pub or the workshop. The female readers of the nineteenth century can be associated with the development of silent, individual reading, which relegated oral reading to a world that was disappearing. Perhaps the female reader was more than this: a pioneer of modern notions of privacy and intimacy.

The Child as a Reader: From Classroom Learning to Reading for Pleasure

The expansion of primary education in nineteenth-century Europe encouraged the growth of another important sector of the reading public: the children. For much of the century, though, educational provision remained rudimentary. In France, the Guizot Law of 1833 indicated a trend, but did not bring about an immediate transformation in primary education. Not until the Ferry reforms of the 1880s in France, and the 1870 Education Act in England and Wales, was primary education in any sense universal. These developments had important repercussions for reading and publishing. Children's magazines and other literature blossomed, and appealed to the pedagogical concerns of educated families. The demand for school texts began to assume a larger share of the book market, helping to make the fortune of publishers like Hachette.

In France, free, universal primary education was not available until the 1880s. The educational reforms of Bonaparte had been directed principally at secondary education, and thus had little impact outside the ranks of the bourgeoisie. The Guizot Law of 1833 laid down a blueprint for a primary school in every municipality in France, but it was some time before this goal was achieved. The number of primary schools in existence certainly rose after 1833, but it had already begun to increase in response to demand in the 1820s.

Setting up a school was only the first step; the largest problem was to persuade the local inhabitants to attend. In 1836, only 8 per cent of children in the Dordogne attended school; in 1863, the attendance rate in the Vienne was only 6 per cent.[24] Even in rural communes where a primary school existed, it would be completely deserted at harvest time. A survey carried out in 1863 revealed that almost a quarter of French children in the nine to thirteen age-group never attended school, and that a third of the rest attended only for six months in the year.[25] It need hardly be said that figures like this apply only to boys' schooling.

School equipment was rudimentary. Often schools had no tables and no books. Frequently, there was not even a classroom either. Guizot's inspectors found that the school in Lons-le-Saunier, for instance, was also used as an armoury and as a public dance-hall.[26] Elsewhere, lessons were held in the teacher's house, where he might have the catechism recited while he prepared his dinner. Many schools were damp, badly lit and poorly ventilated. In the Meuse, one inspector was shocked to find that the teacher's wife had just given birth in the classroom.

The teachers relied on collecting fees from parents. This was not an easy task. Some teachers were paid in food, or were forced to take sup- plementary jobs as grave-diggers or choirmasters. The lack of qualified personnel put an intolerable burden on urban schools. In Montpellier, in 1833, there were between 100 and 220 students per class.[27] In this overcrowded situation, the system of mutual education was popular. The eldest and, it was assumed, the best student was appointed monitor, and entrusted with the instruction of his peers.

In Britain, as in France, educational opportunities for working-class children were sparse and unreliable for most of the nineteenth century. Only with the Education Acts of 1870, 1876 and 1880 did it become compulsory to attend school, at least up to the age of ten. Even until 1880, the decision to fine reluctant parents was left to the discretion of local authorities. The normal age of apprenticeship was fourteen, but this required an initial payment which not everyone could afford. Many had abandoned schooling long before this age. They had started work as errand-boys or farm-hands as soon as practical, which usually meant at any time after their eighth birthday. The education of the working-class child was always secondary to the needs of the family economy.

Tom Mann, future labour leader and trade unionist, continued a family tradition typical of coal-mining communities. In 1865, at the age of nine, he started work in a colliery farm, after only three years of formal schooling. His mother was dead, and his father a colliery clerk. Family survival depended on the sacrifice of his school years.

In the countryside, a range of seasonal activities made schooling an intermittent affair. As late as 1898, Her Majesty's Inspector De Sausmarez commented that

> In addition to the regular harvest, children are employed in potato-digging, pea-picking, hopping, blackberrying and nutting, and fruit and daffodil gathering, and where ... a boy can earn ten shillings in one week in picking blackberries, it is not surprising if his parents consider him more profitably employed than in struggling with the analyses of sentences.[28]

In the north of England, where agricultural wages were higher, this was less of a problem.

The British example shows that those taught in the mutual or monit- orial system learned to read according to a rigorous discipline, and under strict religious supervision. The Lancaster schools, supported by the Dissenters, and promoted by the British and Foreign School Society, were outstripped by the Anglican schools, which followed the similar Bell system. In both, teachers were trained only superficially, but they were entrusted with the instruction of their leading pupils, or monitors, who led their classes. The monitors, often aged no more than thirteen, might each be responsible for between ten and twenty children, giving them tasks and maintaining discipline. In Lancaster schools, each pupil had a number, and they were marched to their desks in military fashion. In 1846 a government-sponsored system of teacher training was inaugurated, which began to supplant the monitors.

Beginners started to read and write in a sand-tray, before progressing to slates. To avoid the expense of books, children learned to read from cards. In large groups, they were made to chant syllables, words and sentences 'as if they were poetry', as one student recalled.[29] Children spent hours copying letters and words, to perfect their handwriting. Teachers were especially well trained in syntax and etymology, and the children were never required to compose anything original. As they learned to recognize individual words from cards, they learned to read without ever having touched a book. Reading lessons insisted on the mechanical memorization of a few texts – those which inspectors would later use to test the child's reading competence. Reading thus demanded grim patience and endlessly repetitive exercises. Most children must have regarded it as a miserable experience. So, too, did reformers like Matthew Arnold, who later campaigned for a more 'humanizing' form of instruction.

'Reading is a key to the treasures of Holy Writ,' pronounced an Oxfordshire vicar in 1812, before insisting that the teaching of writing and arithmetic might dangerously encourage the career expectations of the rural poor.[30] In mutual schools, even arithmetic was taught in a religious context. In 1838 the Central Society for Education recommended mathematical examples on the following model: 'There were twelve apostles, twelve patriarchs and four evangelists; multiply the patriarchs and the apostles together and divide by the evangelists.'[31]

Teaching the young to read had to be compatible with religious orthodoxy and the continued inculcation of social subordination. For T. B. Macaulay in 1847,

> The statesman may see, and shudder as he sees, the rural population growing up with as little civilization, as little enlightenment as the inhabitants of New Guinea, so that there is at every period a risk of a jacquerie.[32]

In English village schools, seven-year-old girls were caned for not curtseying to the squire's wife or the vicar's wife.[33] The monitorial schools thus aimed at mass literacy, combined with the kind of obedience and regular work discipline needed for nineteenth-century capitalist society.

They were not necessarily successful. In working-class areas of East London, Sunday schools were more popular than monitorial schools, because they were cheap, familiar and well integrated into the neighbourhood. So too, were dame-schools, where the rudiments of reading and writing were taught informally, in the homes of local women often accused by the authorities of being no more than child-minders. In dame-schools, religious instruction was almost completely absent. In spite of the effort made by London's monitorial schools, the attendance at the monitorial school in Bethnal Green in the early 1820s was only 21 per cent of its capacity. Furthermore, in 1812, 20 per cent of the poor of Spitalfields confessed to having no religious beliefs at all, and nearly half of them possessed no Bible.[34]

Learning to read and write from the Bible was common practice in Protestant countries in the nineteenth century. There was an increasing demand, however, for a more secular pedagogical literature, which publishers rushed to satisfy. In France, seventeenth- and eighteenth-century authors still provided the standard texts recommended to children. The educational market, for example, helps to account for the position of La Fontaine's *Fables* at the top of the bestseller lists in at least the first half of the nineteenth century. Between 1816 and 1850, the *Bibliographie de France* recorded 240 editions of La Fontaine, and probably close to 750,000 copies were produced in this period.[35]

Robinson Crusoe enjoyed a global popularity, and was produced in various versions adapted to the needs of children of different ages. The same was true of Buffon's *Histoire naturelle*, which appeared as *Le Petit Buffon* and *Buffon des enfants*. The best-selling *Voyage du jeune Anacharsis en Grèce*, by the *abbé* Barthélemy, first published in 1788, was the young student's guide to ancient Greek civilization. The author, a historian of antiquity and a connoisseur of ancient languages, had known the art critic Winckelmann, and was an expert numismatist. The fictional journey taken by Anacharsis served as a vehicle for a discussion of Greek art, religion and science in the period of Philip of Macedon. In the course of his trip through the islands, the hero has conversations with philosophers, and observes a wide range of Greek institutions. This book was often abridged; it was especially popular in the 1820s.

The emergence of a flourishing industry in children's literature was part of the process Philippe Ariès has called the 'invention of childhood' – the definition of childhood and adolescence as discrete phases of life with unique problems and needs. In the first part of the nineteenth century, however, the specific needs of the child-reader were recognized only for the purpose of imposing a strictly conventional moral code. Much of early nineteenth-century children's literature was therefore rigorously didactic.

Bérenger's *La Morale en action*, for example, had eighty editions listed by the *Bibliographie de France* for 1816–60, and it was regularly reprinted throughout the century. Caron's Amiens edition had 137 reprints between 1810 and 1899. The work, adopted by secondary schools, had as its subtitle 'Faits mémorables et anecdotes instructives'. It was a compilation of short moral tales, usually about little children.

The stories had exotic settings to capture the young imagination, and they all had a happy, moral ending. They advanced a chiefly secular morality, emphasizing kindness to animals, courage, honesty and fidelity. They warned against avarice and gambling, and like most children's literature of the period, stressed family solidarity. Many stories in *La Morale en action* featured wealthy merchants, and praised the utility of commerce, while condemning ostentatious wealth and reckless social climbing. *La Morale en action* carried a traditional message, transposed into a bourgeois setting, in which Catholicism played an unobtrusive role.

Forms of children's literature also began to prosper and develop by stimulating young appetites for fantasy and magic, and among these were the increasingly popular fairy-tales. Fairy-tales underwent a constant process of transformation by authors and publishers, as they were rewritten, edited, cut or reinvented to suit readers of different ages and different moral standards. Fairy-tales are texts without texts, because they have always been part of a complex interchange between high literature and an ancient oral tradition. They are not only texts without texts, but almost texts without authors: the stories are familiar to all, but every version may be different. The peasant folk-tales of the past were universally re-baptized 'fairy-tales' by the romantic nineteenth century: a change which signified their importance as literature destined exclusively for the young. Like many other aspects of traditional folk culture, fairy-tales were 'infantilized'. In their reading tastes, children were becoming the peasants of the twentieth century.

Perrault's tales had drawn both on erudite texts and on oral tradition, but had been recast to point a contemporary moral, and conform to standards of *bienséance*. The tales had been sanitized, cured of impropriety, coarseness or overt sexuality, to meet the demands of polite seventeenth-century society. This process of textual transformation continued.

Publishers sweetened the folk-tales they inherited for nineteenth-century children. The second part of *La Belle au bois dormant*, dealing with the ogress, was often suppressed by the end of the century, so that the marriage of the prince and La Belle becomes the ending.

Little Red Riding Hood, to take another example, had always posed a problem for moralists. It could be interpreted as a cautionary tale, and modern Freudians have read it as a warning to young girls against erotic temptations posed by wolf-like sexual predators. It was, however, the only one of Perrault's tales which did not have a happy ending. In the seventeenth century, popular publishers had already amended Perrault's ending, in order to punish the wolf. Many variations appeared for the endings of fairy-tales like this one, including the appearance of the friendly, paternal woodcutter beloved of the Grimm brothers. Perrault's tales thus survived, but not always in the version that he had given them. Independent oral versions coexisted with nineteenth-century texts of fairy-tales. In the oral versions of *Le Petit Chaperon rouge* collected by nineteenth- and twentieth-century folklorists, only seven out of thirty-five French versions had a happy ending.[36] Perrault's versions appeared much more frequently in oral tales after Perrault was selected as a primary school text in France in 1888. Once again, therefore, the 'literary' fairy-tale, having drawn on popular oral tradition, was influencing and contaminating what remained of that folk culture.

The brothers Grimm, whose first collection was published in 1812, also claimed to tap an oral, peasant-based tradition. They responded to the romantic period's desire to give Germany a unique folk culture and a national literature. In practice, however, their sources were neither peasant in origin nor exclusively German: they consisted of their close circle of friends and relatives in Hesse, many of whom were of French Huguenot descent, and familiar with the tales of Perrault.

The impact of the Grimms on this corpus of children's literature was to soften the theme of conflict between child and parent. They could not tolerate the expulsion of Hansel and Gretel from their home by both parents. A sympathetic father was introduced; and in the fourth edition of their stories in 1840, the children's mother became a stepmother. This assured that *no* natural parents appeared malevolent in the story.

Stories which suggested that crime paid, like *Puss-in-Boots*, were omitted from their anthology. They introduced more fairy-tale clichés – friendly hunters, beautiful princesses and the fairies themselves, who populated this sugary and predictable world. At the same time, brutality was intensified against the villains of the tales. Rumpelstiltskin thus met a violent death, instead of flying away on a spoon. The Grimms thereby reinforced the moral message and family values. In addition, they interpolated several religious references. Hansel and Gretel did not, in the Grimms' version, rely entirely on their own ingenuity to escape the dangers that trapped them: instead, they appealed to God. In the fifth edition of the stories, in 1843, the wicked witch was described as 'godless' for good measure.[37]

The Grimms were hailed as the inventors of a national literary monument. They had successfully adapted for children the traditions they

inherited and discovered. At the same time, the Grimms adapted themselves, reworking their stories from one edition to another. The literature of fairy-tales, like the popular culture in which they had once been
embedded, was never fixed or static. It was a dynamic body of texts,
always open to assimilation and contamination, by new publishers, new
fashions and the perceived needs of new audiences.

Advances in lithography permitted new scope and inventiveness for
publishers of the elementary ABCs studied by Ségolène Le Men.[38] These
reading primers were destined chiefly for domestic consumption; their
leading illustration might depict an idealized scene in which young children gather around their mother's knee to study the ABC. (In spite of
such propaganda by publishers, learning to read took place more and
more in the classroom rather than at home.)

The pedagogical technique of illustrated ABCs was usually a linear one.
In other words, the infant began at the letter A, and worked alphabetically through a series of examples to Z. He or she would, as at school,
learn first the shape of individual letters, then syllables and would finally
recognize entire words. The lavish illustrations could be used to recapitu-
late each lesson, and test the student on what had been learned. The illustration, in other words, had an important role in the memorizing process.
Sometimes the image accompanied a text, but remained separated from it.
At other times, more inventive visual techniques were adopted: text was
superimposed on illustration, for example, or perhaps the text itself was
transformed into an image. To delight the infant further, individual letters
were given human form, dancing, bending, or falling into their place in an
animated anthropomorphic alphabet.

For older students, a children's press emerged. In 1857, Hachette
launched *La Semaine des enfants*, costing only ten centimes for an issue
of eight pages, including the novels of the comtesse de Ségur as *feuilletons*. In 1864, Hetzel created the *Magasin d'éducation et de
récréation*, which ran to thirty-two pages for fifteen centimes, and was
to include many Jules Verne novels.

Le Magasin d'éducation et de récréation was to appear twice per
month from 1864 to 1915. Its authors tried to remain neutral in politics
and religion, but family solidarity and an underlying French patriotism
were constant themes. The periodical catered to a bourgeois audience,
which proved very susceptible to the formulas of authors like Jules
Verne – his faith in science and his heroes who were models (mostly
Anglo-Saxon models) of self-control and self-discipline. The tone was
secular and republican, but it remained socially conservative.

For Hetzel, the *Magasin d'éducation et de récréation* had a dual
responsibility to amuse and to instruct. The cover itself announced
this ambiguity of intention. The plump infant illustrated there, with

spectacles and a paper knife, already has the reading manner of an adult. This was to be serious literature, but at the same time, literature for children. Hetzel himself advertised Jules Verne's stories as works with a serious scientific purpose, and claimed that they demonstrated the power of science and human energy to overcome all adversity. His publicity was idealistically aimed at the family as a whole, envisaging 'la lecture en commun faite au coin du feu'.[39] Even so, his discourse on Verne emphasized his pedagogic value, and invited a scientific and positivist reading of *Les Voyages extraordinaires*.

Neither Verne himself nor his illustrators fully echoed these sentiments. Verne treated topical scientific themes, in geology, astronomy and exploration, but at the same time he invented a new kind of adventure novel for adolescents. A dichotomy of aims potentially existed in Verne's novels, in which the spirit of fantasy and adventure struggled to transcend their scientific and pedagogical purpose. For Isabelle Jan, this created the profound misunderstanding which lay at the heart of the relationship between Verne and his publisher Hetzel.[40]

This contrast is much more plausible if the illustrators of *Le Magasin d'éducation et de récréation* are considered, as well as the publisher and authors. The engravings provided by Bennett and Riou for Verne's stories were an integral part of the magazine and of the subsequent novels. They stress the action of the plot and all that is fantastic in Verne's detailed descriptions of natural phenomena. The composition often centres on a bright nucleus of light in the foreground, but they are engravings with great depth, which lead the reader further into a world of mystery. They stress movement and adventure, and their purpose is imaginative rather than educational. Riou exploited the shipwrecks, tempests and maelstroms of Verne's imagination, without making them part of a geography lesson. Riou's illustrations tended to suggest not human mastery of the elements, but rather man's fragility in the face of powerful natural forces. Perhaps this served to enhance all the more the sang-froid of the Vernian hero. At any rate, his illustrations offered adolescents an alternative reading to that proposed by Hetzel's advertising. While Riou invited a youthful reader to imagine Verne's fiction as pure adventure, Hetzel invited a different, more utilitarian view from the adults who were, after all, the ones who paid the subscriptions.

The Working Classes: Prescribed Reading, Improvised Reading

The new readers of the nineteenth century also included the lower-middle classes, aspiring artisans and the white-collar workers who swelled the clientele of lending libraries everywhere. Public lending libraries were especially well-advanced in Britain. Legislation of 1850 gave local councils the right to levy one penny in local taxation to finance library facilities. This gave Great Britain its distinctively decentralized public library system, and by 1980, there were 553 municipal libraries in the country. In 1902, Leeds, with a population of 400,000, boasted a central library, and fourteen branches open all day, with lending and newspaper rooms. This fast development of public libraries in Britain was a product of dense urbanization and a degree of administrative decentralization unmatched on the European continent.[41]

Public lending libraries had a philanthropic and a political purpose. Like factory schools, they were instruments of social control, designed to incorporate a sober working-class élite into the value system of the ruling classes. Charles Dickens, opening the Manchester Library in 1852, saw libraries as a guarantee of social harmony. Dickens expected to hear from the working man

> the solid and nervous language to which I have often heard such men give utterance to the feelings of their breasts, how he knows that the books stored here for his behoof will cheer him through many of the struggles and toils of his life, will raise him in his self-respect, will teach him that capital and labour are not opposed, but are mutually dependent and supporting (hear, hear and applause), will enable him to tread down blinding prejudice, corrupt misrepresentation, and everything but the truth, into the dust (applause).[42]

As Dickens himself was well aware, there was considerable reader resistance to the libraries' attempts to provide moral and edifying literature. Instead of attracting working-class readers, lending libraries in Britain and France catered rather for women, students and white-collar workers. These new workers overwhelmingly demanded recreational literature, in preference to practical manuals and works of instruction.

There was nevertheless a great demand for continuing adult education, although workers in France often felt this was thwarted by clerical interference and short library opening hours. In 1862 a group of bronze workers, returning from the London Exhibition, complained that the arts relied too heavily on mythological and allegorical subject matter, and the love intrigues of gods and heroes, 'ne relevant presque toujours que de la ruse, de la force, quand ils ne sont pas épiquement incestueux'.[43] French national history, they claimed, was a better field for subjects which would encourage the intellectual development of ordinary Frenchmen. A section of the working class therefore rejected a culture which fed them only religious history and antique mythology.

Middle-class library reformers continued to recommend the classics to working-class readers. When Agricol Perdiguier compiled a list of basic books for a workers' library in 1857, many of his selections reflected this choice.[44] His list included Homer and Virgil, the Bible, Fénélon, Corneille, Molière, Racine and La Fontaine. This would have pleased the liberal library reformers of the Société Franklin. He went further, however, in insisting on some history of the French Revolution, Eugène Sue's *Mystères de Paris*, Hugo's *Notre-Dame de Paris*, and Sand's *Le Compagnon de la tour de France*.

The popular reader, often patronizingly known as 'le grand enfant', had a mind of his own. A lithographer, Girard, set up a *bibliothèque populaire* in the third *arrondissement* of Paris, and tried to evade municipal surveillance for as long as possible. At Le Creusot in 1869, one twenty-eight-year-old worker, Dumay, formed a *bibliothèque démocratique* which organized support for a republican candidate in 1869, and for a 'no' vote in the 1870 plebiscite.[45] Two popular libraries had been set up in the industrial city of St Étienne in 1866, which the city notables and clerical élite attempted to bring under control.[46] The workers' choice of literature was offensive, because it included Voltaire and Rousseau, as well as George Sand and Eugène Sue, who were accused of attacking marriage and justifying suicide and adultery. Rabelais was considered a dangerous author, as were Michelet for *La Sorcière*, Renan for *La Vie de Jésus* and Lamennais for *Les Paroles d'un croyant*. Enfantin, Louis Blanc, Fourier and Proudhon also had their place in these workers' libraries, and suggest that working-class readers struggled to form their own literary culture, free of bourgeois, bureaucratic or Catholic control.

A gradual reduction in the working day allowed greater opportunities for reading among the working classes. In England, a fourteen-hour day was commonplace in the early nineteenth century, but by 1847, the textile industry had won a ten-hour day. By the 1870s, London artisans normally worked a fifty-four-hour week. In Germany, on the other hand, a reduction of daily working hours to twelve was achieved very slowly after 1870. In 1891, the maximum working day for German women was limited by law to eleven hours. Shortly before the First World War, the Reich Statistical Office determined that of 1.25 million workers whose conditions were regulated, 96 per cent worked fewer than ten hours, although only 38 per cent worked fewer than nine hours.[47] In iron and steel works a double-shift system still operated, which necessitated a twelve-hour day.

These conditions explain why leisure was seen principally in terms of physical recuperation, and why, when asked what they did in their leisure time, German workers almost invariably thought of Sundays.

Although they enjoyed reading, their favourite occupation, according to the *Verein für Sozialpolitik*, was going for walks in the fresh air.

The daily burden of work dictated reading habits and library borrowings. In the winter, borrowings from German libraries with a high proportion of workers rose regularly, while in the summer months it declined. In many occupations, the winter working day was shorter. In times of slump and unemployment, workers also tended to borrow more library books.[48]

The German Social Democratic Party gave a high priority to workers' education, in the spirit of Karl Liebknecht's slogan, coined in 1872, 'Knowledge is Power! – Power is Knowledge!'. The party's education committee recommended titles of books for lending libraries, and published ten-pfennig booklets, written in popular style, to help with the interpretation of plays and operas. These, however, enjoyed little success.

Employers, too, made their own attempts to control the leisure pursuits of a new, lower-class reading public. The industrialists of eastern France, for example, played a major role in the movement to create popular lending libraries at the end of the Second Empire. In Germany there are some striking examples of successful factory libraries. In the book hall of the Rhine Steel Works in Duisburg-Meiderich, the proportion of workers who asked for readers' cards rose from 17 per cent of all workers in 1908 to 47 per cent in 1911. The Krupp Company library in Essen was an exceptional example of a factory library. Established in 1899, the Krupp library had over 61,000 volumes by 1909. By that year, 50 per cent of the Krupp work-force borrowed books, mainly from the very richly provided *belles-lettres* section.[49] This was regarded as one of the finest lending libraries in Germany.

Employers and library reformers hoped that by providing suitable literature, and by encouraging the reading habit, they could soften social tensions. Working-class readers, it was hoped, could be weaned away from drink and from dangerous literature with tendencies towards socialism, excessive superstition or obscenity. A range of useful literature, to promote 'rational recreation', would incorporate the more intelligent members of the working class into a consensus of bourgeois values. Liberal philanthropy of this kind seemed to be working in Britain and the United States. Continental observers were impressed by the apparent quiescence of Lancashire operatives during the cotton famine; liberal philanthropists believed there was a lesson to be learned here. Perhaps popular libraries could contribute towards social stability.

Readers, however, resisted the diet of useful and moral literature which they were offered. A model library catalogue produced by the Société Franklin in 1864 recommended that two-thirds of library stock should consist of works of instruction.[50] The German Social Democrats, at the turn of the century, promoted proletarian education by means of libraries oriented towards the social sciences. Readers might begin to use popular libraries for entertaining fiction, but they would be expected to 'advance' to the classics of socialism, Kautsky and eventually *Das Kapital*. The Dresden librarian Griesbach declared that the main task of the workers' librarian was to 'lead the reader from reading entertainment to reading non-fiction material'.[51] In Britain, in the 1830s, both Utilitarians and Evangelicals urged the provision of 'improving' literature for working-class readers. With these severely educational aims in mind, the Society for the Diffusion of Useful Knowledge launched its *Library of Useful Knowledge*, concentrating on biography and natural science.

This educational optimism, however, was doomed to disappointment, as working-class readers overwhelmingly chose the recreational literature offered by lending libraries, whether they were employers' or trade union institutions. By the 1840s, the Society for the Diffusion of Useful Knowledge was bankrupt. In German workers' libraries, there was an enormous discrepancy between the actual tastes of readers and the expectations of the Social Democratic Party. Of almost 1.1 million borrowings from German workers' libraries recorded between 1908 and 1914, 63 per cent were in the *belles-lettres* category. Another 10 per cent were from the youth section, which included fairy-tales, children's tales and humorous fiction. The same pattern is found in Vienna, where fewer than 2 per cent of readers asked for social science literature at the Arbeiterzentralbibliotek de Wien-Favoriten in 1909–10.[52]

In France, too, popular practices failed to conform to the norms of librarians. In the 1880s and 1890s, more than half the borrowings from Parisian municipal libraries were of novels (see tables 1 and 2).[53] The librarians sponsored by the Société Franklin complained regularly that their customers rejected serious works in favour of Alexandre Dumas or Hugo's *Notre-Dame de Paris*.

One stratum of the working class, however, did embark on the hard struggle to emancipate itself from ignorance and dependence. Webb estimates over two-thirds of the British working class could read before 1870.[54] Their thirst for knowledge was only partly satisfied by the Mechanics' Institutes, which spread useful knowledge and moral improvement to an artisan élite.

Workers' autobiographies describe their determination to overcome poverty and material hardship, in order to understand their world. Thomas Wood, a Yorkshire mechanic, rented a newspaper for a penny a week when he was sixteen, after the paper was a week old, and he read it by firelight because he could not afford a candle. It was

Table 1   Categories of books borrowed from the municipal libraries in Paris, 1882[a]

Category	Per cent
History and biography	8
Geography and travel	10
Science, arts, education	11
Poetry, drama, literary history	13.5
Novels	55
Music	2.5

[a] Total number of recorded borrowings: 363,322.
Source: Martyn Lyons, *Le Triomphe du livre: Une histoire sociologique de la lecture dans la France du XIXe siècle* (Paris: Promodis, 1987), p. 190.

Table 2   Users of the public libraries in Paris, by profession, 1885–1894[a]

Profession	Per cent
'Rentiers', landlords, women 'of no profession'	24
Shopkeepers, manufacturers, merchants	4.5
Liberal professions, teachers, students	12
Clerks, office-workers, shop assistants	31
Caretakers	5
Workers/labourers	13.25
Soldiers	8
Artists	2.25

[a] 3,847 recorded borrowers.
Source: Lyons, *Le Triomphe du livre*, p. 187.

significant that the paper he read was the radical Chartist *Northern Star*. Winifred Foley, general maid, was beaten by her nonagenarian mistress for reading *Uncle Tom's Cabin*.[55] Maxim Gorky, who had no formal education, carried on reading, although he was working fourteen hours a day, in a bakery in Kazan in 1887 – one of the places he ironically called *My Universities*.

Thomas Cooper, shoemaker, Chartist and public lecturer, wrote of his own attempts at self-education:

> I thought it possible that by the time I reached the age of 24 I might be able to master the elements of Latin, Greek, Hebrew and French; might get well through Euclid, and through a course of algebra; might commit the entire *Paradise Lost*, and 7 of the best plays of Shakespeare to

memory; and might read a large and solid course of history, and of religious evidences; and be well acquainted also with the current literature of the day. I failed considerably, but I sped on joyfully.[56]

Cooper was an honourable failure, reading every morning from 3 or 4 to 7 a.m., and also during meals, with a book propped up in front of him, and then from 7 p.m. until too exhausted to go on, always reciting some text while working at his cobbler's stall. In 1828, aged twenty-one, Cooper had a complete physical breakdown, and was confined to bed for several months.

The profusion of working-class autobiographies like Cooper's in the nineteenth century is one clear indication of the growing self-awareness and mastery of the printed word among individual workers who had experienced little formal tuition. Proletarian autobiographers were an articulate élite. In spite of their exaggerated modesty and humble origins, most of them wrote of personal struggles which had led to success. Some had become trade unionists, others journalists; most described the hard road towards individual and collective emancipation. To some extent, therefore, their writing can be situated within the ambiguous ideology of 'self-improvement' – ambiguous because it was expounded by middle-class writers, promising upward social mobility which would blur or cross class boundaries.

Middle-class radicals believed that the pursuit of knowledge was open to all who were ready to apply a little self-discipline. Thomas Cooper had accepted this aim, but it led him to imprisonment in Stafford Gaol in the Chartist crisis of 1842. Nevertheless, a self-educated working-class intelligentsia emerged, which recognized the importance of the written word. To this group fell the enormous burden of elaborating and disseminating a working-class political ideology. They followed a long tradition of serious reading in the British labouring community, which fed on Milton and Bunyan in the seventeenth century and Paine and Volney among radical texts of the eighteenth century.

Reading was central to the ethos of self-improvement. Working-class autobiographers rarely failed to give a description of their reading, and many of them outlined the detailed reading programmes which had guided and improved them. When the Lancashire hand-loom weaver Samuel Bamford discovered what he called 'the blessed habit of reading', he set out on a course which led him to parliamentary reform agitation, journalism and later to a career as a public poetry reader. 'What a wasted life is his', wrote the cabinet-maker James Hopkinson, 'who has no favourite book, no store of thought or happy recollection (*sic*), of what he has done, experienced or read'.[57] The eager search for book knowledge was vital to the intellectual emancipation on which political action was based; it also provided the knowledge and discipline required for moral, rational self-improvement. Willie Thom read Walter Scott, 'the Wizard of Waverley', in his moments of relaxation as a young factory weaver in Aberdeen in 1814. Books, he wrote, provided 'glimpses, – the only glimpses afforded us of true, and natural, and rational existence'.[58]

These proletarian readers had quite distinctive methods of literary appropriation. Although many of them attended formal school, their attendance was usually brief and irregular. The need to earn a living as soon as possible, or to travel in search for work, precluded sustained periods of schooling. The autobiographers were on the whole auto-didacts, men who had taught themselves most of what they knew. 'My education was very meagre,' wrote the Chartist John James Bezer; 'I learnt more in Newgate than at my Sunday school'.[59] Samuel Bamford and many others wrote works whose titles included the proud phrase 'Written by Himself', to stress their independence and the remarkable nature of their self-taught achievement.

Educational deprivation led autodidacts to treat schooling sometimes with abuse, sometimes with exaggerated respect. The rich ambivalence of the autodidact's response to formal education is exposed in Maxim Gorky's classic account, *My Universities*. Gorky's title is ironic: his real teachers, he claimed, were his companions and his various work-places up and down the Volga, the drunken labourers, fruit-growers, bakers and itinerants he encountered on his journeys through Russia. He learned, too, from clandestine political meetings addressed by students and travelling lecturers, improvised in backrooms and private lodgings, where Gorky could satisfy his thirst for knowledge and discussion. His attention wavered between these lectures and the attractions of the Volga.

> I did not find J. S. Mill very fascinating, and soon realized that I was very well acquainted with the basic principles of economics – I had learned them from direct experience of life and they were engraved on my skin . . .
> It was boring at those readings and I wanted to go off instead to the Tartar quarter, where good-hearted, friendly people lived their own pure and clean lives.[60]

He accused intellectuals of romanticizing the brutal, ignorant life of the people of Russia, but he himself talked of 'the heroic poetry of everyday life' among the Volga navvies.

Gorky well knew, however, that he had more to learn than the navvies could teach him. He had travelled to Kazan in 1884, when he was still under twenty years old, specifically intending to obtain a place at university. He never succeeded, but his attitude to formal learning remained ambiguous, for he wrote: 'I would have endured even torture in return for the happy opportunity of studying in a university.'[61] Although he found the Kazan students patronizing, he respected their learning, and freely acknowledged the sincerity of their desire for change.

The autodidacts pursued their desire for study and self-improvement with a determination that was sometimes obsessive. Indeed, it had to be, if they were to overcome the immense material handicaps that stood in their way. Poverty, lack of time and lack of privacy made study impossible for all except the most dedicated.

Cramped housing conditions forced many working-class readers to take to the woods and fields. The English labourer-poet John Clare worked outdoors, composing his work secretly in the fields. He would hide behind hedges and dykes, to scribble down his thoughts on the crown of his hat.[62]

Lack of light was another problem in working-class homes, Windows were rare in early nineteenth-century England, and candles were expensive. For W. E. Adams, candles and rushlights 'did scarcely more than make the darkness visible'. 'It was almost as well', he continued, 'that the general body of the people could not read for persistent efforts to turn the advantage to account after sunset would almost certainly have ruined half the eyes of the country.'[63] There was very little gas lighting in British working-class houses before 1850. The family of Jean-Baptiste Dumay, at Le Creusot, shared this difficulty. They could only afford to light their oil-lamp at the evening meal. Dumay used to read by the glow of the coal-stove.

Industrialization was to produce a very clear distinction between leisure and work. The discipline of industrial labour and the regular rhythm of work it imposed made reading more difficult. It is no coincidence that the majority of autodidact autobiographers were craftsmen and artisans. Their work rhythm was irregular; it oscillated between slack intervals and very active periods; and it permitted impromptu holidays which became impossible for factory hands in the early phrases of industrialization. According to William Aitken, 'the hours of labour in cotton mills, when I was a piecer, were so protracted that improvement of the mind was almost an impossibility'.[64] But the anonymous Stonemason, when employed as a roundsman, had taught the horse the route, and could read as he travelled.[65]

The literary culture of the autodidacts was of a specific kind. Although their early reading was frequently eclectic and indiscriminate, they tended to impose a stern discipline on their own reading. They confessed to a ravenous appetite for literature of all sorts, which they admitted in retrospect was poorly directed. Thomas Cooper was also slightly ashamed to recall that he had 'often diverged into miscellaneous reading', by which he meant authors like Disraeli and Boswell, travel literature and the *London Magazine*. In Gorky's case, this literary bulimia was extremely dangerous. In Tsarist Russia, ravenous and indiscriminate consumers of novels were bound to arouse police suspicion.

The autodidact's aim, as William Lovett's autobiography eloquently proclaimed, was threefold: bread, knowledge and freedom. Self-improvement – material, moral and intellectual – was a very demanding objective. It required serious application and self-abnegation. Time had to be set aside for the acquisition of knowledge; money had to be saved for the purchase of books; sleep was sacrificed; health deteriorated, friendships were put at risk by the fervent determination to read and to know. The goal of self-improvement was often inspired by a Noncon-formist Protestant faith; and it often went hand in hand with the taking of the 'pledge' to abstain from alcohol. This, too, was a sign of self-discipline and a desire to distinguish oneself from fellow-workers.

Reading, however, was a necessary instrument for self-education and self-mastery. The autodidacts' reading was concentrated and purpose-ful. It was, in many ways, an 'intensive' mode of reading, relying heavily on repetition, recitation and oralization as aids to memory. Autodidacts had a specifically ardent and determined relationship with their texts. They read repetitively, closely rereading the few texts at their disposal and, in their own well-worn phrase, 'committing them to memory'. They taught themselves through memorization, which often depended on reading and reciting aloud. Their relationship with the printed word occasionally resembled the 'intensive' mode of literary appropriation, encountered by historians in eighteenth-century Germany and Puritan New England.[66]

One distinguishing feature of the world of the 'intensive' reader was the frequency of reading aloud. Oralization was a very common way of absorbing the message of the Bible, and this was often how children were taught to read. John Buckmaster recalled that the Scriptures were read out morning and night by his grandmother.[67] Alexander Murray, a young Scottish shepherd and future professor of oriental languages at Edinburgh, also learned to recite the Bible at an early age.[68]

Oral reading, however, occurred in secular, as well as religious, con-texts. For Charles Shaw the potter, oralization added an essential dimension to the act of reading. As he remembered,

> no tea-meeting would have been complete without recitations ... I began
> to enjoy the literary charms of certain recitations, not only when reciting

them in public, but they sent their music through my daily drudgery. In the midst of this, when opportunity served, I recited a few verses or lines aloud, and found they were always more inspiring when I heard them than when I simply said them to myself.[69]

Reading aloud was an essential part of the culture of the work-place. In 1815 Thomas Carter worked for a tailor near Grosvenor Square, in London. He recalled:

I became their news-purveyor; that is, I every morning gave them an account of what I had just been reading in the yesterday's newspaper. I read this at a coffee-shop, where I took an early breakfast on my way to work.[70]

He read Cobbett's *Register*, the *Black Dwarf* and the *Examiner*, leading radical titles of the turbulent period after the Napoleonic wars. Martin Nadaud had an almost identical experience in Paris in 1834: 'Tous les matins', he wrote, 'on me demandait dans la salle du marchand de vin de lire à haute voix le *Populaire* de Cabet.'[71] He read Socialist brochures aloud to his comrades, and oral reading was thus an important part of working-class politicization and self-education.

George Seaton, an apprentice-saddler in Newcastle-upon-Tyne, read the *Black Dwarf* aloud to fellow-workers who gathered at the village cross of Bellingham for the purpose, as James Burn recalled of 1817.[72] W. E. Adams remembered Sunday morning readings of O'Connor's *Northern Star* in a local shoemaker's kitchen.[73] Perdiguier recalled oral reading of Racine and Voltaire among French carpenters in the early 1820s.[74]

The intense concentration required by the autodidact could sometimes only be achieved by a certain posture, and in the right surroundings. Thomas Carter needed a great deal of sensual stimulation. He usually read sitting on the floor in the 'Oriental', or tailor's posture, in a vegetable store-room full of the aroma of herbs and onions, which he needed to stimulate his concentration.[75]

Whatever gestures or odours were needed to stimulate the brain, an effort of memory was required, and autodidact readers frequently began by memorizing parts of the Bible at home. Alexander Murray had to do this secretly, because as a child, he was not permitted to open or touch the family Bible. Nevertheless, he

soon astonished all our honest neighbours with the large passages of Scripture I repeated before them. I have forgot too much of my biblical knowledge, but I can still rehearse all the names of the Patriarchs from Adam to Christ, and various other narratives seldom committed to memory.[76]

By the age of eleven, he boasted, his memory earned him the local reputation of 'a living miracle'.

Thomas Cooper, however, whose assiduous reading programme has already been outlined, is a more striking example of the intense effort at memorization by recitation made by the autodidacts. Cooper employed every available moment to acquire learning. He worked from the early hours of the morning until too exhausted to go on, reading, reciting and memorizing poetry, or mathematical theorems for much of the day. He memorized Shakespeare, Milton, Coleridge and the Romantic poets by constant daily oral repetition.

Cooper was perhaps an extreme case: but many others appropriated their literary culture in a similar manner. Samuel Bamford, for example, read Homer 'with an absorbed attention which soon enabled me to commit nearly every line to memory'.[77] William Cobbett learned grammar by copying his textbook, learning it by heart, and repeating it to himself daily on sentry duty.[78] Ebenezer Elliott, the 'Corn-Law Rhymer', knew the Bible by heart by the time he was twelve years old, and when he was sixteen, could recite Books 1, 2 and 6 of *Paradise Lost*.[79]

The private memo-book or notebook was another intimate method of appropriating a literary culture and conducting a personal dialogue with the text. Samuel Bamford copied works of Milton, 'and this I did', he tells us, 'not only on account of the pleasure which I felt in their repetition, and in the appropriation – so to speak – of the ideas, but also as a means for the improvement of my handwriting'.[80] Cooper made notes on Gibbon and religious works as he read them, and recorded all his reading in a journal. Maxim Gorky used his notebook for writing down anything he could not understand, and Robert Owen, aged twelve, transcribed Seneca's moral precepts, to ponder on solitary walks.[81] The memo-book was thus not merely an aid to memory; it also served to conduct a personal debate with the text, to absorb it and refute it. It was an essential part of the process of self-education and self-improvement.

The working-class autodidacts thus adopted a style of intensive reading which was peculiar to their time and to their needs. It answered their serious purpose and determination to succeed with meagre resources.

The Persistence of Oral Reading

The peasantry was only partly integrated into the nineteenth-century European reading public. A recent oral history survey conducted in

France suggested that, during the Belle Époque, all white-collar workers and 80 per cent of shopkeepers bought a daily newspaper. Two-thirds of urban workers interviewed bought a daily newspaper, but only one out of five peasants did so.[82]

In the cities, the book had become an object of everyday consumption, but sections of the peasantry still belonged to a traditional mode of reading. For them, books were still respected and rare possessions, encountered most often in a religious context. They were the 'generations of listeners', who had not yet become 'generations of readers', for whom reading was often a collective experience, integrated into an oral culture.

Oral reading still persisted, in spite of the trend towards individual, silent reading. It was often encountered by Mayhew, the assiduous observer of London street life.[83] Costermongers would persuade someone to read to them from an illustrated periodical or Sunday newspaper, being careful to save it afterwards to use as a wrapper for their merchandise. In London taverns Mayhew found young boys hired to recite the most popular scenes from Shakespeare. When the editor of the very bourgeois *Sydney Gazette* attacked his more plebeian rival, *The Australian*, in 1825, he ridiculed the way it was read aloud in a cramped settler's hut, with the entire family and servants gathered together for the occasion, at the end of a long day's labour.

On the streets of London, song-sellers sold song-sheets by the yard, *chaunters* sang their ballads for sale, and others hawked parodies, satires and 'gallows literature', offering the 'last confessions' of condemned criminals. Much of this street literature was designed to be read or sung aloud.

Oral reading still survived, too, in middle-class circles. Kilvert, the diarist and Shropshire parson (with an erotic interest in the young girls of his parish), often visited his parishioners to read aloud to them. He participated in public recitals, or 'penny readings', at which 'There were sixty people standing outside the school. They were clinging and clustering around the windows, like bees, standing on chairs, looking through the windows, and listening, their faces tier upon tier.'[84]

This love of the recital of familiar pieces, of the orality and music of poetry, was part of a traditional, or 'intensive', relationship between the reader/listener and the printed word. This relationship was disappearing in the nineteenth century. Its passing was lamented by conservatives who regretted the way that individual, silent reading was dissolving traditional forms of sociability. The mellow atmosphere of Hans Thoma's painting, *Evening: The Artist's Mother and Sister in the*

Garden (1868), expresses this nostalgia. The mother reads, presumably from a Bible, to daughter and son, in a deliberately idealized image of two generations of German piety. This longing to put reading practices back, once again, into a religious and family context is a symptom of the nineteenth-century transition from 'intensive' to 'extensive' reading practices.

13

Reading to Read: A Future for Reading[*]

Armando Petrucci

Reading, understood as an activity of acculturation or delight for the literate person, has a secure future, to the degree that we can be certain that in the near future the other, fundamental and correlative communicative activity proper to literate society – writing – will be practised. As long as people produce written texts (in one form or another) the complementary activity of reading will continue to be practised by at least some portion, large or small, of the Earth's population.

It seems certain that in the near and not-so-near future the cultured segments of human society will continue to produce writing. Our world today produces a broader variety and a much greater amount of written matter than in 1900 or 1950, and more than in all past centuries. These texts were produced for the most part, if not in all cases, for a broad range of purposes, for immediate or delayed reading and within a socially limited or a far-reaching audience. It is hard to see how or why such an activity, which is essential to the operation of bureaucracies, to agencies of information and to manufacturing, should or could cease to exist. In short, people (or some people) will continue to read as long as there are men and women (the same ones or different ones) who will continue to write and be read. Moreover, everything indicates that this situation will last, at least for some time.

[*]*Lire pour lire: La lecture littéraire* is the title (taken from a work by Georges Perec) of a special issue of *Textuel*, 7 (1990), a periodical put out by the University of Paris VII, edited by Bernard Sarrazin and Robert Strick. This issue contains a series of essays pertaining to personal reading, literary reading and reading in the schools.

According to Robert Pattison, 'Literacy from the age of the pharaohs forward has never collapsed but only changed.'[1] We can suppose that it will continue to change without disappearing.

Hence this is not the question that a historian-prophet or an analyst of the sociocultural behaviour of the masses would find most interesting. They might prefer other, more subtle questions: In the near future, what type of reading activity will people engage in? How broadly will reading be practised across the social spectrum? What will it relate to? What importance will it have in society, and what functions will it serve? Will the demand for reading matter grow or decline? How will the various sociocultural areas of the planet react to reading? Finally, is it true, as recently stated, that 'the *activity* of reading loses ground proportionally as the *operation* of reading is increasingly universalized'?[2]

How Much do People Read, and Where do they Read?

Historians have never been very good prophets. As we know, they have had enough difficulty scrutinizing and interpreting the past, and they would have even more if they tried to predict the future. No one should expect them suddenly to become seers. None the less, although it is permissible to hazard some predictions on the mechanisms of human behaviour in a domain as complex as acculturation, we can only do so through an analysis of data on literacy, on the production of texts and the demand for them, and on world-wide circulation of printed matter during the last decade.

One point requires clarification. A question like the one raised in the opening paragraph (and that motivates the present study) must be treated in the perspective of the entire world, not only of the developed countries of Europe and America. This is in part because the future of reading will be played out not where it is a habitual, consolidated practice, but where it is not, and in part because new demands, new products and new reading practices can only come from 'frontier' zones where reading, among the masses or among the élites, is now only in the formative stage, just beginning to spread; in sociocultural situations that are absolutely new with respect to the past and in lands of long-standing illiteracy. Basically (or above all) this is also true because, as one historian of literature recently wrote, displaying both courage and sincerity, 'From now on the more rigorous (or even simply the more honest) intellectuals cannot be satisfied with giving an account of Western privilege; they will have to measure themselves against the *other*, against someone who is *different* and who cannot always be exorcised by invoking the madness or barbarity of backwardness.'[3]

Data from UNESCO investigations present a picture of rapid change and of great variations from one region of the globe to another. These are some of their findings:

1. Literacy rates are gradually rising, but in absolute terms the number of illiterates is continually growing and has now reached over a billion. In 1980 world illiteracy stood at 28.6 per cent, or 824 million persons; in 1985 that rate had declined slightly (to 28 per cent), but the number of illiterates had risen to 889 million. The areas in which illiteracy is most widespread are above all in Africa (in some countries of Arab culture and in others with a predominantly rural economy), in Latin America (Guatemala, Ecuador, Peru, Haiti, Bolivia) and in Asia, in particular in Muslim countries (Pakistan, Afghanistan, Saudi Arabia). These are extreme cases, but illiteracy is also widespread in nearly all the African countries, in many Latin American countries and in a number of Asian countries. Moreover, even in many of the so-called developed countries there are high percentages of resurgent illiteracy and of primary illiteracy among immigrants, concentrated for the most part in the big cities. The United States is a case apart. There illiteracy rates reflect a social distribution and are high among blacks, Latino-Americans and the urban under-classes. Investigations and literacy campaigns in the last two decades have produced little or no result.

2. Persistent illiteracy in large areas of the world cannot be attributed to low incomes alone, but has political and ideological origins as well. Certain regimes (Haiti, for instance, or Peru) have chosen not to promote mass education; others, in Muslim countries for instance, oppose the education of women. One of the consequences of female illiteracy in countries with a strong religious ideology is in fact an uncontrolled demographic rise, which in turn contributes to keeping the overall illiteracy rate high. The only mass literacy campaigns that have succeeded are in countries (Cuba, Vietnam, Sandinista Nicaragua) that, following the Soviet example, have engaged women in the educational process and launched campaigns to encourage birth control.

3. Book production is strongly on the rise throughout the world: in the two giants (the United States and, until 1989, the Soviet Union), in Europe and even (but only in the last decade) in other parts of the world. In 1975 total book production stood at 572,000 titles; in 1980 the figure had risen to 715,000; in 1983 it was 772,000. In the early 1980s Europe, with 18 per cent of the world's population, was still producing 45.6 per cent of the world's books; the Soviet Union, with 8.1 per cent of world population, produced 14.2 per cent of books; the

United States, with 7.5 per cent of world population, produced 15.4 per cent of books. That distribution will undoubtedly change in the near future, but it will not change either radically or very fast.

4. In 1982, 8,220 daily newspapers were produced in the world, 4,560 of them in the so-called developed countries (the United States accounted for 1,815 of them). Per capita circulation figures were much higher in countries with long-standing traditions of reading and information: Great Britain had a newspaper circulation of 690 copies per 1,000 population; Japan, 571; Sweden and East Germany, 496; the Soviet Union, 400; France, 205.

5. Book circulation figures in public libraries furnish analogous data. According to a survey made in 1980, the United States led the list with 986 million volumes lent in that year, followed by the Soviet Union with 665 million and Great Britain with 637 million (making it first in worldwide library circulation when books borrowed are calculated in relation to population). Next in total numerical library circulation came France, with 89 million books borrowed annually, Denmark with 79 million and Sweden with 77 million (for the last two countries the figures for per capita book borrowing are high, as with Great Britain).

If we leave aside recent phenomena that are above all connected with positive political changes in areas or countries in Latin America, Africa and Asia, it is thus clear that the highest figures for book production, book distribution and daily periodical circulation occur in the countries with the highest literacy rates and the greatest economic strength, in particular, in certain European countries with a long-standing cultural tradition. The areas where the circulation of written texts is smaller or nearly non-existent are the ones that are not only more economically depressed, but the ones where demographic pressures are strongest and women are kept out of the educational process.[4]

Control and Limits

During the last century, nearly all mass campaigns to encourage literacy in the more developed or ex-colonial countries, whether on the national or supranational level (for example, under UNESCO sponsorship), have emphasized reading over writing.[5] That choice was quite obviously deliberate, the result of the pedagogical vocation of institutions everywhere that have elaborated the ideologies and methodologies of learning. These include the school systems of the bourgeois states and the Roman Catholic Church, which, even though they are in competition, agree on this point; libraries, particularly in the Anglo-Saxon countries, which have fostered the democratic ideology of public reading; and the publishing industry, which is more interested in creating an ever-larger reading public than it is in encouraging writers. Something else lay behind a universal choice common to all authorities and powers: an awareness that, before the advent of television, reading was the best means for diffusing values and ideologies and the one easiest to regulate, once controls had been established for the processes of the production and, above all, the distribution of texts. Writing is instead an individual skill and is totally free; it can be done in any fashion, anywhere and to produce anything the writer wants; it is beyond the reach of any control or, at the limit, of any censorship.

It is true, however, that at the highest levels of official culture, written production can be controlled, either brutally or subtly. Michel Foucault made this point trenchantly in a lecture of miraculous clarity over twenty years ago.[6] In comparison, control over reading seems much more direct, simpler and certainly less painful. All that it needs in order to function is to control the reading matter of the public that is learning to read and that is being educated (hence being indoctrinated), authoritatively turning it towards a specific corpus – a fixed canon – of works rather than to others. That canon can be broad or narrow, more liberal or more restrictive, but it has to be imposed (precisely) as a canon: that is, as an indisputable value that must be accepted as such.

According to current definitions of the term 'canon', it is a 'list of works or authors proposed as a norm, as a model'.[7] Every written culture has had one or more canons, which were considered valid either absolutely or as specific to a certain milieu (religious, literary, etc.). Even our Western European literary tradition has elaborated a canon sufficiently broad to satisfy the needs of the publishing industry, but also rigid enough to reproduce the ideological, cultural and political values on which the West's vision of the world has been based for some two centuries, and which includes authors and works from Homer to the *maîtres à penser* of the Collège de France.

How was this canon elaborated? We need to return to Michel Foucault and to the list of factors – in his words, 'procedures' – that determine the 'order of discourse' of our own culture. Foucault starts from the hypothesis that 'in every society the production of discourse is at once controlled, selected, organized, and redistributed according to a certain number of procedures, whose role is to avert its powers and its dangers, to cope with chance events, to evade its ponderous, awesome materiality'.[8]

These procedures are prohibition, division and rejection, the will to truth, commentary, disciplines, sociocultural rituals, recognized doctrine and educational systems. Foucault was analysing the production of texts, but if you turn his analysis around, all that he wrote can also be applied to the use of the text – that is, to reading, which in an organized written culture is subjected to analogous if not identical procedures of exclusion and control as text production. Foucault himself observed:

> We tend to see, in an author's fertility, in the multiplicity of commentaries and in the development of a discipline so many infinite resources available for the creation of discourse. Perhaps so, but they are none the less principles of constraint, and it is probably impossible to appreciate their positive, multiplicatory role without first taking into consideration their restrictive, constraining role.[9]

In a United States guided by the spirit of Franklin D. Roosevelt's 'New Deal' during the 1930s and 1940s, the typically Anglo-Saxon ideology of the public library as a fundamental instrument of democracy was reinforced and widely implemented. Library science textbooks and sociological studies concerning basic education or reading stated that the preferred repertory of positive reading matter, useful to both individuals and the community, was one based on standard works that had met with the approval of generations of authoritative intellectuals and that reflected a higher system of values. Today we read this sort of statement with some embarrassment, but at the time such thoughts were widely current and highly influential on many levels. The impression we get now is that in a progressive, democratic, American ideology, reading is consciously understood as an instrument of social formation and control, precisely because it is limited to a recognized and homogeneous canon of authors and works backed by the authority of tradition.

Canon and Classification

A cultural and ideological attitude of that sort gave rise (and still gives rise) to lists of works recommended for public reading libraries and for individual readers. These lists form a veritable canon, proposed in catalogues and specialized reviews and furthered by an entire normative and pedagogical apparatus that the book industry (authors, publishers and editors, 'intellectocrats', journalists and librarians) pours out daily in Rome, Paris, New York, London, Tokyo or New Delhi for the enlightenment of the real or potential reader. The result is a reader who is always guided and 'in-formed', moulded to the use of a written culture whose first priority is sales, and is thus substantially homogeneous.

Since their rise in the sixteenth century, the bibliographical sciences have displayed a profound ideological bias, masked by a penchant for abstract, objective technology. For centuries they have helped to elaborate criteria for the selection or exclusion of texts, and have offered them for the organization of written culture in the West. By the same token, they have developed hierarchies of value and dependence that, once mechanically introduced into the structures for the preservation and use of books and subsequently repeated automatically, have themselves become authoritative, hence not open to question by the common reader, by public opinion, or by the so-called public, which, in the end, reads and buys books.

Even today, in the United States and in the world, the most widespread system for the classification and collocation of books is the one elaborated in 1876 by Melvil Dewey, at the time a young librarian. The Dewey Decimal System presents (and in a certain sense, ingenuously imposes) a vision of human knowledge that is both archaic and modernized. It divides knowledge into ten overall categories: 000, Generalities (reference works and encyclopaedias); 100, Philosophy and Psychology; 200, Religion; 300, Social Sciences; 400, Language; 500, Natural Sciences and Mathematics; 600, Technology (Applied Sciences); 700, The Arts; 800, Literature and Rhetoric; 900, Geography and History. These categories are in turn divided into subcategories numbered 0 to 9, thus setting up 100 'divisions' than can in turn be broken down into subsections, themselves divisible by ten and so on practically ad infinitum. Precisely because of its mathematical simplicity, the Dewey Decimal System enables any library, public or private, to classify and shelve all books with relative ease. What I want to emphasize, however, is that in this system the hierarchy of subject matters (philosophy and religion first, religion after philosophy, history and geography grouped together, literature as a separate category and so forth) shows, on the one hand, a perpetuation of earlier schemes of knowledge and, on the other, a deliberate application of the secular, scientifically oriented values of American culture of the time and of Western positivistic culture in general. The persistence of the Dewey Decimal System for the classification of books can thus be considered a significant symptom of the continued existence of mechanisms of constraint regulating the distribution, circulation and even the use of books in our culture.

It might perhaps be instructive to consider briefly two Italian examples of the application of the Dewey Decimal System, one historical and well known, the other more recent and extremely widespread. In 1969 the publisher Giulio Einaudi put out a 'systematic catalogue' of books arranged by subject matter in the interest of offering 'an essential choice of volumes for anyone intending to form a library', public or private. The *Guida alla formazione di una biblioteca* was a resounding success,[10] in part because it came out when political tensions had reached historical proportions in Italy during a time of growing progressive and leftist movements, when cultural (and in particular political) essays responded to the curiosities of a vast gamut of readers, young readers in particular. Einaudi's guide listed some 5,000 works, arranged in an order inspired by Dewey's, but modified and updated, in particular by fusing together some of Dewey's categories, focusing others more precisely, shifting still others, and in general offering a more contemporary vision of knowledge than Dewey's by-then outdated model.[11] An essay by Delio Cantimori, a leading Italian intellectual, printed in an appendix to the *Guida* seemed to contradict these forward-looking changes, however. Rather than fulfilling the usual pedagogical role of explaining the aims of the volume, Cantimori referred instead to a rigidly and organically authoritarian vision of knowledge, of the book and of reading, according to which the library's function was to 'teach reading' to those unable to read and to 'give solid and healthy nourishment' to those who hungered for it.[12]

An overall scheme that was at once informative and formative also underlay the great universal *Bibliografia*, which came out in 1984 as the twelfth and final volume of the *Enciclopedia europea* published by Livio Garzanti.[13] The basic system used in this bibliography is much more fully articulated than Dewey's classification (with twenty-one major sections rather than ten), but it is founded on similar organizing principles, and it presents a traditional, hierarchical vision of knowledge, listing reference works first, continuing with philosophy and religion, giving the humanistic and literary disciplines before the scientific and technical ones, and so forth. Even in this case, in other words, we see a scheme that analyses and presents the canon of Western culture with serene certainty, displaying no doubts or hesitations.

A Crisis in Reading, a Crisis in Production

The production and circulation of texts in book form within the framework of written culture in the Western tradition seems thus far to paint a picture of a harmoniously homogeneous continent, where a universally accepted canon reigns and universally respected rules of order pertain. This appearance is contradicted, however, by recurrent symptoms of destabilization and continual cries of alarm that point to crises in both publishing and reading. Both these sectors display obvious contradictions, show a growing uncertainty regarding programmes, and are urgently requesting state intervention. Is there in fact a crisis of reading and of the book? And if so, exactly what is it?

Here again we need to analyse and establish some distinctions. Oddly enough, the loudest cries of alarm come from areas where the production and distribution of printed texts is the liveliest and where printing reaches the broadest variety of social groups – the United States and Europe – rather than from Africa or Latin America. Japan is a case apart.

In the United States, the country that heads the list for world-wide production of books and printed matter and one that has an extremely powerful and well-organized publishing industry (which is nevertheless obsessed by the idea that crisis lurks at every turn), the problems that are considered the most urgent are an increase in illiteracy in urban areas and a gradual decline in the level of preparation of students in public secondary schools and universities, problems that are in reality two aspects of the same phenomenon.

According to Robert Pattison, there is a growing tendency in the American school system to separate an élite instruction, located in and imparted by the costliest, best-equipped colleges and universities and based in official culture and an absolute respect for traditional linguistic customs, from popular education, which is more technically oriented and objectively inferior. 'We have', Pattison affirms, 'one literacy of power and business and another still-forming literacy of popular vigor.'[14] If such a separation were to pit one class and one form of literacy against the other, Pattison states, 'it would be the end of the American experiment'.[15] The United States is the country that displays the most striking difference between a youth culture attuned to the mass media and focused on rock music, the cinema, television and electronic games (and only secondarily on reading, which is limited, moreover, to contemporary fiction – in particular, science fiction and the comic strips), and a more traditional youth culture founded on reading books, on seeing plays and high-quality films, on listening to classical music, and on a more strictly complementary use of the new media technologies.

In the United States the struggle against massive urban illiteracy has always been based on programmes to reinforce book reading and extend its social range. As early as 1966 Robert McNamara founded an association aimed especially at young children called 'Reading is Fundamental', which today has some 100,000 participants scattered throughout the United States. In more recent years Barbara Bush promoted a 'Foundation for Family Literacy', which enjoyed generous support from the federal government. The year 1989 was proclaimed the 'Year of the Young Reader', and 1991 the 'Year of the Lifetime Reader'. To end the list, on 6 February 1990, the United States Senate approved a 'National Literacy Act' that allocated substantial federal funds to creating a federally sponsored structure to combat illiteracy throughout the United States and to co-ordinate existing private and local initiatives.

Other sources state, however, that the United States is undergoing a crisis not only of mass illiteracy, but also of quality reading that involves the reading matter of the so-called strong readers who read avidly and by conviction and who determine public opinion. In the quite subjective opinion of one expert regarding the publishing business in the United States, out of a population of some 236 million people, there are only some 15,000–16,000 'quality' readers of the sort, not including the 500–600 people who read poetry. This expert's statement is obviously ironical, and cannot be taken as true, but its gist is shared by other authoritative witnesses whom I have had occasion to question on the subject. Be that as it may, the very fact that this opinion could be expressed and published (not to mention shared) shows how urgent the so-called crisis of the book market is felt to be in the United States, over and above the real problems of the book industry.[16]

Europe presents a different aspect of the problem. European publishing firms, great and small, live in a state of convulsive crisis, moving frantically from one merger to another, from one team of owners to another, and from one search for additional capital to another, all the while waiting for the mythical advent of European unification and keeping a wary eye on what is happening in the promising but chaotic market of the countries of Eastern Europe and the former Soviet Union.

In Europe the book is not yet treated uniquely as merchandise, and there are leading cultural figures and smaller publishing firms that are doing their best to keep this from happening. One typical reaction was the discussion prompted in France by the deregulation (in French, *libéralisation*) of book prices in 1979, which delivered the price of books to the laws of the market-place. (The Lang Law of 1 January 1982 subsequently annulled this provision, and standardized book prices throughout France.)

The old myths die hard on the Continent, but it is also true that European publishing, following publishing in the United States, is faced with a widespread deculturation that has had an effect on book production on all levels, and that has conditioned the choice of texts, their editing and translation, and their graphic presentation. The result has been a chase after the author or the book that guarantees success, a frantic creation of 'instant books', a passive reliance on authors of the past (as in the so-called rediscovery of the classics, at times with original text and translation on facing pages) and so forth. This radical change in orientation and procedures, which was launched above all by major publishing houses that are undergoing continual transformation and are devastated by ceaseless changes in personnel and programmes, has failed to conquer new market niches or a new public, in part because of a ferocious, relentless competition, both national and continental. In a situation of this sort, the nations with a weaker publishing industry (Italy, for one) face greater difficulties than countries with a stronger, better-equipped publishing industry (Great Britain, Germany, Spain).

In spite of these difficulties, publishers in Europe (Italy included) have in recent years put out an ever-increasing number of publications, diversified their products and published many translations. The publishing industry, all things considered, seems to be more lively and more dynamic than it was, say, thirty years ago. Still, it has not managed to create a reliable, expanding market share, and (like publishing in the United States) it lives in fear of a gradual (worse, a sudden) decline in an already limited reading public.

Japan is a special case, because the Japanese people make up the greatest concentration of 'strong' readers known today, and those readers are served by a publishing industry that is correspondingly modern, highly organized and sophisticated, in which some 5,000 publishing firms produce nearly 40,000 titles per year, for an overall production of about 1.5 billion copies annually.

The Japanese reader reads a lot because he or she is highly acculturated and considers it a duty to be informed and formed by written culture, but also because schools and universities in Japan enjoy an undisputed prestige. The publishing sectors with the highest sales figures are textbooks, escapist and informational literature, and comic strips; prices are extremely low. Taken as a whole, the Japanese phenomenon is an example of widespread mass reading with characteristics of induced consumption. It is probably unique, deriving from the authoritarian and hierarchical nature of Japanese society, hence it is not easily exportable elsewhere.

Contestation of the Canon

What we have seen so far are the superficial and most evident aspects of the crisis of transformation that reading as a traditional sociocultural practice is facing in developed countries. In the last decade or more, there have been other challenges to the basic principles and the moral justifications of what might be defined as the Western ideology of reading (or its 'order of reading'). For the first time, the persistence of that ideology – even its chances for survival into the new century – has been questioned. Such challenges consist either in a weakness in supply – that is, in production – or in unexpected new rises in demand. Combined or chaotically superimposed, these end up challenging the authority of a universal canon of written texts that has never before been so sweepingly denied.

On the supply side, publishing, dominated by the terror of a market crisis continually perceived as imminent, has 'gone mad', in the sense that it has lost, on all levels, but especially on the highest levels, the context within which it could move with relative certainty. It has fallen back on offering the public products of a *Triviallitteratur* and classics with parallel translations, journalistic 'instant books' of the worst sort, books for hobbyists, philosophical or linguistic essays, collections of jokes, volumes of poetry, mysteries, science fiction, books on politics, histories of customs or of sex, and lightweight romances. All these have been published indistinguishably. Neither the publisher's imprint nor the way the work is marketed nor the price discriminates among them, or brings any sort of order to the mass of texts that are produced every day. These procedures contrast markedly with the ways in which all other products are marketed, from foodstuffs to house furnishings, clothing, automobiles, etc., where design, presentation, the distribution chain and, above all, price serve to orient the purchaser and establish predictable differences. In any supermarket the average buyer is capable of distinguishing (by price if by no other means) a fine wine from a table wine. The supermarket would be trying to cheat the customer if this were not so. For some time now, what the major publishers have been doing as they operate within the book market is a form of obfuscation based on obliterating every criterion of selection. It might be considered a genuine fraud perpetrated on the reader-consumer.

The reader-consumer reacts in an equally irrational manner. Because the institutions (the schools in particular) that have always maintained and diffused both the traditional canon for reading and traditional values have lost their forward motion and their capacity to influence people, the reader behaves in a highly disorganized and unpredictable way within the market. He or she buys or does not buy, chooses or refuses to choose, prefers one type of book today and another tomorrow, is seduced on one occasion by a reduced price, on another by the graphic presentation of a book, on still another by a passing interest or by a publicity blitz. In short, the reader too begins to lose all criteria of selection, which makes it hard to programme production rationally on the basis of predictable public tastes. Tastes remain solidly consistent only within the declining numbers of the so-called strong readers, who read a good many books per year and who, in every society, make up the most conservative (hence the most stable) portion of the universe of readers. Because their numbers are limited, however, they do not much interest the major publishers, either in the United States or in Europe.

To complicate the picture, broader and increasingly self-aware sectors of the public, seemingly less conditioned by market concerns than by their own particular ideological orientations, are beginning to express an explicit rejection of the traditional canon. Something of the sort is occurring in what was formerly East Germany, once a book-market paradise with a very high number of habitual readers who had been trained to subscribe to a traditional canon pruned by censorship, and who had benefited from a widespread education in the consumption of reading matter (as was true in all the countries of Eastern Europe before 1989) in fulfilment of a policy of mass culture that had strong state support. Today those same readers categorically refuse the classics, the novels and the authors of the Marxist sub-canon that the local publishing industry produces, and devour avidly and chaotically whatever the West German book market offers in the way of *Triviallitteratur*, hobby books, mysteries, science fiction, travel books, etc. Publishing houses are in crisis in East Germany: famous firms are closing, the writers' association has dissolved, and in the environs of Leipzig the world's first book dump has been created, a noteworthy novelty in the contemporary urban landscape, and perhaps an omen of a more widespread but as yet underground rejection.[17]

From Leipzig we shift to Stanford, the prestigious California university that was the site (in 1988) of an explicit contestation of the canon of obligatory readings required of students in nearly all American universities, a canon representing the classical paradigm of European culture from Homer to Goethe. What were the Stanford students demanding? And what are the students – above all the black, Asiatic and Hispanic students – who are following their example all over the United States demanding? They call for changes in that canon; they want it made less Eurocentric and more 'American'; they want African and South American authors included in it; they want literature courses to be less closed and traditional in their repertories and more open to current events and contemporary concerns; they want cultures other than the traditional Western, 'white' culture to have equal access to university-level study. In short, they want to see other canons added to the one canon that has until now been imposed as the only one. The academic establishment in the United States reacted to this movement and to its demands in ways that were often critical and in some instances strongly negative. The defence of the traditional canon of Eurocentric culture, which begins with the ancient Greeks and ends with Sartre and Foucault (and which, moreover, is the canon that provides the foundation for what I am writing and you are reading), has been, and continues to be, implacable. When I observed to one respected professor who teaches in California that a European canon in a new, multi-racial situation like North America's was absurd, he answered with utter candour that in his opinion American culture is essentially European, and cannot be otherwise.

The fact remains, however, that in many universities the movement against the canon has met with success, and in others it is gaining strength. It has posed a serious problem, not only for the administrators and professors of literature in some big American universities, but also for all written culture in the United States, for its publishing industry (which has not as yet picked up the challenge implicit in the movement), and for its values and its tradition.[18] If the twilight of the canon of Western written culture has indeed arrived, its decline began in Leipzig and at Stanford. In what may turn out to be the near future, we may be forced to recall those dates and those places.

Other Readings

Stanford was certainly not the first place, and this was not the first time, that a canon of written texts sanctioned by tradition has ever been contested, in whole or in part. It has happened at least twice in Western European history: first, between the third and the fifth centuries, when Christian culture rebelled against the pagan tradition and substituted its own canon for the Greek and Latin pagan authors, then between the fourteenth and fifteenth centuries, when the Italian humanists rejected the canon of university and scholastic culture and replaced it with another repertory of authors, for the most part in the Latin and Greek classical traditions. In both these cases, rejection was not total: Christians did not renounce Virgil; nor did the humanists give up the Fathers of the Church; and as time passed a portion of the previous canon was reabsorbed into the new one that had replaced it. Undeniably, however, in both these cases changes in the canon were accompanied by the rise of new ways of producing written testimony, new models for the book and new reading practices. Perhaps we can perceive some sign of a change in models of production and in practices in what is taking place before our eyes.

There have always been some individuals or small groups on the fringes of the system of written culture who reject the current canon. This has occurred when intellectuals playing the role of critic attempted to find and impose new texts, and set up new authorities in opposition to the old ones; it has also occurred when subordinate readers attempted to make their cultural marginalization into a coherent system of values and texts that was totally different from the official system. To keep to Italian examples, that is what the now legendary Menocchio, the late-sixteenth-century miller from Friuli, attempted to do,[19] and many others, known and unknown.

Similar situations occur in the contemporary world, especially among the young and the elderly, two categories of consumers of the book who lack social power, but often read a good deal because they have large amounts of free time. They almost never succeed in subjecting their reading to a programme or making it fit in an orderly way into a predetermined canon, partly because their economic and social weakness does not permit them access to a private library or the means to create one. Thus they read freely and chaotically whatever they find at hand, mixing genres and authors, disciplines and levels, and unaware of the official canon and its hierarchy of values, which they contest (albeit unconsciously) and which does not determine their choices.

Are such readers ignoring the canon in order to contest it, or contesting it in order to ignore it? The rejection of the canon observable in day-by-day ordinary reading (which operates outside the more prominent organized protests such as the one at Stanford) is caught between the horns of that dilemma. These are practices that quite simply demand a freedom to read unencumbered by all canons, existent or possible. Thus they refuse all canons, unlike the Stanford students, who wanted to institutionalize other canons, and unlike the 'strong' readers of East Germany, who simply prefer other canons.

As long ago as 1961, Eugenio Montale, who was clearly a man of the past, but also an acrimonious observer of his own day, noted a difference in attitudes toward reading between study practices and consumeristic practices; between reading in order to learn, remember and form one's mind, and reading just to read, to pass the time, for simple amusement. He stated:

> In particular, fewer and fewer books are read, while the number of readers of periodicals, newspapers, reviews, manifests posted on walls and other printed material is fairly high. But the readers of the fleeting daily publications do not read: they see, they look. They look with comic-strip attention even when they really know how to read: they look and they throw away.[20]

In America today, certain openly consumeristic reading practices reject all systems of values and all pedagogical attitudes in the name of absolute freedom. According to a survey conducted by the American sociologist Elizabeth Long of seventy local book clubs unaffiliated with any sponsoring organization in Houston, Texas (the most future-oriented city in the United States today), some groups insisted on choosing from a repertory that might be defined as 'trash' and that included mysteries, science fiction, westerns and so on. The members of these book clubs included university professors (not of humanistic disciplines, however), professional people and business people, all of whom demanded the right not to be 'snobs', and defended their refusal to be conditioned by any external source of suggestions in their choice of reading matter. Their aim was simply entertainment.[21]

Thanks to pressure from what I might define as the new mass readers, even in public libraries in the United States, once temples of traditional and official culture and the instruments of its diffusion, systems of classification that have always been based on the foundations of Western knowledge have begun to be modified. The Dewey Decimal System is being abandoned in favour of other types of organization that take into consideration the needs and tastes of the reader as consumer. In one Detroit library, for example, the subject areas of the new classification are Classics; The Arts, Today's World; People and Lands; Humour; Sports; Hobbies; Personal Life (which includes religion and psychology); The Family, The House, Group Activities; Work; Technology; and Information.[22] Compared to what we are accustomed to finding in a typical public library, this listing lacks the grand, traditional sectors into which the written culture of our own early training was divided: the sciences, literature, history, philosophy and politics. Nor can we take it for granted that the new modes of organization have the same contents organized differently. We get the impression that not only is demand changing (see the free-wheeling readers of the Houston reading clubs), but supply as well, and that certain types of text are no longer proposed for reading, because they will soon not even be printed, at least not in large enough quantities to respond to mass demand.

Reading Disorders

It seems evident that precisely in the most culturally advanced parts of the world (the United States and Europe) a mode of mass reading that some have hastily dubbed 'postmodern' is gaining ground. This is an 'anarchical, egotistical, egocentric' mode of reading based on the one imperative, 'I read what I want'.[23]

As we have seen, this movement arose above all out of a crisis in the institutional and ideological structures that up to now have sustained a pre-existent 'order of reading'. Those structures include the schools, where that order was a pedagogy of reading set within a determined repertory of authoritarian texts; the Catholic Church, as a propagandist for reading with devotional and moral aims; and a progressive and democratically oriented culture, which saw reading as an absolute value for the formation of the ideal citizen. This movement, however, was also the direct result of a higher mass literacy rate, of greater access to the book on the part of a much larger number of readers as compared with fifty or even thirty years ago, and of a supply-side crisis in the publishing industry linked with a new demand chaotic in terms of both tastes and sheer numbers. The resulting situation much resembles the crisis in reading as a social habit and the crisis of the book as an instrument of that habit that occurred during the course of the eighteenth century in Europe, when new mass readers raised new questions, and the publishing industry could muster only timid and antiquated responses to their growing needs, and when the traditional divisions between so-called popular books and cultural books evaporated in the face of the practices of many middle-class readers and even of some of the newly literate city-dwellers.

Reading today, unlike in the past, is no longer the principal available instrument for acculturation. In mass culture it has been undermined by television, which has spread rapidly to become almost universal in the past thirty years. In 1955, 78 per cent of families in the United States owned a television set; in 1970 the figure had grown to 95 per cent, and in 1985 it had reached 98 per cent. In the same period, the number of daily newspapers declined in American society: more than 2,500 daily papers were published in 1910, by 1945 these had declined to 1,750, and in 1985 to 1,676.[24] Some differences notwithstanding, the same is true in Europe and Japan. Overall, it is fair to say that throughout the world today, the role of mass information and education that for centuries was fulfilled by printing, hence by reading, has been transferred to the audio-visual media, which means (as the name indicates) to listening and viewing.

For the first time, then, the book and other print products confront a public, real and potential, that gathers information in other ways and has learned other processes of acculturation (precisely, from the audio-visual media). Moreover, it is a public accustomed to reading messages in movement, that in many cases writes and reads messages produced electronically (by computer, televideo, fax), and that gets its acculturation from instruments and processes that are not only costly, but also highly sophisticated, which it has mastered or which it uses in ways completely different from those of the normal reading process. The new reading practices of the new readers necessarily coexist with this genuine revolution in mass cultural behaviour and cannot help but be influenced by it.

The use of remote-control devices has given television spectators the power to change channels instantly, jumping from a film to a debate, from a game show to a news programme, from a commercial announcement to a soap opera and so on, in a bewildering succession of images and episodes. In the unprogrammed disorder generated by this practice, new programmes and individualized spectacles are created out of non-homogeneous juxtaposed fragments. The only author of these creations is the individual television viewer. No such spectacle fits within the framework of an organic and coherent television culture; each one is in effect both an act of dependence and an act of rejection, and in either case they spring from situations that in part reflect total deculturation and in part are original cultural creations. 'Zapping' is an absolutely new and individual technique of audio-visual consumption and creation. The consumer of media culture who practises it has grown accustomed to receiving a message made of disjointed bits and pieces. Above all, judged from a rational and traditional viewpoint, that message has no 'meaning'. It is none the less a message that demands a minimum of attention if one is to follow and to enjoy it, and a maximum of tension and sportive participation to create it.

This increasingly widespread media practice is the exact contrary of reading understood in the traditional sense, which is linear and progressive. It is fairly close, though, to the transverse, desultory, interrupted sort of reading style – now slow, now fast – of deculturated readers. It is also true that the same creative television spectator is usually capable of following the thread of the immense, fluvial plots of the daily 'soap operas', the new epic compilations of our time, encyclopaedic syntheses of consumeristic living, each of which is the equivalent of a novel of over a thousand pages or one of the great epic poems of the past in twelve books or more.

The practice of zapping and the interminable plots of the soap operas have created potential readers who not only know no 'canon' or 'order of reading', but have not acquired the respect, traditional in book readers, for the order of the text, which has a beginning and an end, and is thus intended to be read in a precise sequence established by someone other than the reader. Such new readers, however, are also capable of following an extremely long serial sequence of events, provided those events reflect the mythical hyperrealism typical of narrative fiction of a so-called popular sort.

Modes of Reading

The traditional order of reading consisted (and still consists) not only of a unified, hierarchical repertory of texts both readable and 'to be read', but also of specific rituals for the readers' behaviour and for the use of books that require environments with special furnishings and particular equipment and instruments. In the millennial history of reading, rigid, professional, ordered practices of reading have always been opposed by free, relaxed, unregulated practices. In thirteenth- and fourteenth-century Europe, for example, the professionals of written culture read seated at a bench, surrounded by books, reading stands and a variety of instruments, in contrast to the freer reading habits in court society and the unconstrained modes of reading unfettered by rules of the bourgeois 'people' who read in the vernacular.

Throughout its reign, the dominant order of reading dictated certain rules about how to read in a civilized manner and how readers should comport themselves. Those rules derived directly from the didactic practices of pedagogy of the early modern age, and they were immediately applied in the bourgeois school when it was institutionalized between the nineteenth and twentieth centuries. They proclaimed that the reader must be seated in an erect position with his arms resting on a table and the book in front of him. Reading must be done with maximum attention, without moving, making noise, annoying others or taking up too much space. One should read in an orderly fashion, following the text section by section, turning pages carefully without rumpling them or folding them down and without mistreating or damaging the book. The reading rooms of Anglo-Saxon public libraries, places sacred to reading 'for all', were planned on the basis of those principles. Consequently, they are practically identical to the traditional reading rooms of libraries designed for study, work and research.

In short, according to such principles and models, reading is a serious and demanding activity requiring effort and attention. It often takes place in a group, always in silence and following rigid rules of behaviour. Other modes of reading (alone, anywhere in the house, in total liberty) are of course known and even acknowledged, but as secondary; they are grudgingly tolerated, but felt to be potentially subversive, because they involve attitudes of scarce respect for the venerable texts of the canon.

According to a survey of a totally unscientific sampling of Italian readers, nearly all of middling to high culture, conducted by Pietro Innocenti, the reading habits of Italians, at least in the age, class and socio-literate levels that he sampled, have remained on the whole traditional. Few of the eighty persons he interviewed showed any desire to read outdoors; twelve reported that they preferred to read at a table or a desk; four mentioned the library. Their preferred place for reading, however, was at home in a room of their own (when they had one). Some preferred reading in bed, some in an armchair, and several mentioned trains as an excellent place to read, almost on a par with the domestic armchair. In short, these responses referred to a code of reading behaviour of the nineteenth and twentieth centuries connected with practices (the train excepted) that had been established centuries before in early modern Europe. They reflect no substantive innovation.[25]

The conventionality and traditional nature of the reading habits of the people whom Pietro Innocenti interviewed can perhaps be explained by their high educational level, their social class and average age, or the fact that they were cultured Europeans. It is certainly not by chance that the only young woman under twenty in the sampling (her formal schooling had ended with elementary school) reported preferences and habits in clear contrast to those of the others: her favourite position for reading was lying flat on a rug.[26]

Young people under twenty potentially, and by nature, represent a public that rejects the canon – any canon – and prefers anarchical choices. In reality, that age-group also rejects the rules of behaviour that are the obvious corollary of every canon. As one commentator recently wrote, 'The young claim to read everything, always and wherever they find it. Comic strips have this characteristic; they adapt to any environment.'[27]

The impression one gets by frequenting places of higher learning in the United States – in particular, certain university libraries (if I can generalize from personal and relatively casual experience) – is that there, as elsewhere, young readers are changing the rules of reading behaviour that until now have somewhat rigidly conditioned reading practice. A European observer finds it all the more telling when such changes are found in libraries, because it means that the traditional model no longer holds up even where it once found triumphal consecration.

How can we describe the new *modus legendi* of young readers? First of all, the body takes totally free positions determined by individual preferences: a reader can stretch out on the floor, lean against a wall, sit under (yes, under) a reading room table, sit with his or her feet up on a table (the oldest and most widespread stereotype) and so on. Second, the 'new readers' either almost totally reject the normal supports for the operation of reading – the table, the reading stand, the desk – or else they use them in inappropriate (that is, unintended) ways. Rather than as places to put an open book, such supports tend to be used as places to rest the reader's body, legs or arms in an infinite series of variations on physical positions for reading. Finally, the new *modus legendi* also includes a physical relationship with the book that is much more intense and direct than in traditional modes of reading. The book is constantly manipulated, crumpled, bent, forced in various directions and carried on the body. One might say that readers make it their own by an intensive, prolonged and violent use more typical of a relationship of consumption than of reading and learning.

The new mode of reading influences the social role of the book and its presence in contemporary society, helping to change these with respect even to the recent past. The ways in which books are preserved illustrate this. According to the traditional rules of behaviour the book was supposed to be kept in a special place (the library), or, if in a private setting, in special pieces of furniture (free-standing or built-in bookshelves, shelved cabinets, etc.). Today books in a private house (and increasingly in libraries as well, where non-book materials are fast accumulating) cohabit with a large number of other objects of information and formation, many of them electronic, and with the many technological or purely symbolic gadgets that fill the living space of the young and characterize their life-style. The book is the least costly of these objects; it is also the most easily manipulated (its pages can be written on, drawn on or highlighted) and the most fragile. Its means of preservation bear a strict relationship to those of its use: the more their uses are casual, inventive and free, the more books have no permanent place or predictable arrangement. The book is preserved – in so far as it is – among and with other objects in a mobile and infinitely varied and variable arrangement. It shares the fate of those other objects, which are in great part inexorably ephemeral.

All this ends up influencing reading habits. The short lifetime of the book and the absence of a precise collocation for it (hence the uncertainty of ever being able to put one's hands on it) make difficult, if not impossible, an operation that was common in the past: rereading. Rereading was strictly related to a concept of the book as a text to be meditated on, learned, respected and remembered, not of the book as an object uniquely for instant use, to be consumed, mislaid or even tossed out once it has been read.

Some years ago Hans Magnus Enzensberger, after first announcing that 'reading is an anarchic act', attacked the authoritarianism of the critical-interpretive tradition, and called for absolute liberty for the reader: 'The reader is always right, and no one can take away the freedom to make whatever use of a text which suits him.' Enzensberger continues:

> This freedom also includes the right to leaf back and foreward, to skip whole passages, to read sentences against the grain, to misunderstand them, to reshape them, to spin sentences out and embroider them with every possible association, to draw conclusions from the text, of which the text knows nothing, to be annoyed at it, to be happy because of it, to forget it, to plagiarize it and to throw the book in which it is printed into the corner at any time he likes.[28]

The Absence of Canons and New Canons

Today the 'order of reading' characteristic of Western written culture, on the levels of both the repertory of texts and the practices for their use and preservation, shows serious symptoms of dissolution. A production system that is behaving irrationally, concentrating on grasping maximum profit in the least time, with no thought to the future, contributes strongly to this trend. At the same time, the fact that books (and other print products) coexist within the same media system as audio-visual devices marginalizes books, which have already been weakened by what is in essence their inability to adapt to new times, new practices, and new learning methods that depend less and less on traditional written matter. Another factor that contributes to the decline of the book is the rise of the new reading practices just described of the 'anarchical reader', a figure that for the moment is more common among the young, but that is destined to proliferate and, in all probability, to become the prevailing model in the near future.

There is another anomalous and potentially 'anarchical' figure who corresponds to the new readers and their innovative reading practices. It is the consumeristic writer who produces texts of para-literature, rewrites other people's texts, churns out lightweight romantic fiction and mysteries, or patches together articles for second-tier periodicals, often anonymously or as a member of an editorial team. This is not a new phenomenon in the long history of Western written culture. Writers of the sort have surfaced in all times of crisis in book production, of a suddenly expanded reading public, or of widely divergent levels in the product. One example is late eighteenth-century France, on the eve of the French Revolution.[29] In the various phases of the history of this ambiguous figure, he or she has often played an active role in contesting the current cultural (and political) system, just as his counterpart, the 'anarchical' reader, may do in the future, and in part has already done.

All that has been said so far pertains especially, if not exclusively, to the developed Western world, which includes not only Europe but the United States, the Soviet Union (at least until 1989), Japan and a few other scattered cultural areas. It is not valid for other strong cultural traditions that until now have continued to identify proudly with their own specific textual canons and that possess their own rituals for reading. Chief among these is the Islamic world, which possesses a cultural wealth and an extensive patrimony of written culture that it does not seem disposed to renounce, even when its traditions seem to conflict with a consumeristic Westernization. Nor is it valid for China, which, although it can boast a wealth of written products on various levels, is still a closed cultural universe respectful of a firmly dogmatic tradition.

The fact that the world is divided into cultural areas that differ notably from one another, even in the area of the production and use of written culture, is certainly nothing new. It has always been the case. Differences in written products and reading practices among various areas were a good deal more pronounced in the distant past (even the recent past) than they are now. For precisely that reason, however, the problem of a future for reading – unified or multiple – becomes urgent now, when tendencies operating within a media-driven culture work increasingly to form monopolies and annul diversities in both markets and products.

In summary, in so far as we can foretell the future, it seems that, on the one hand, the general weakening of the Western canon and its admixture, in multi-racial situations and moments of conflict, with other repertories and, on the other hand, the affirmation on the individual plane, if not on the level of small groups, of 'anarchical' practices is turning reading into a fragmented and diversified activity totally without rules. This is the precise opposite of what is happening in the electronic mass media, television in particular, where a 'canon' of programmes is rapidly becoming uniform throughout the world, and where the viewing public (of all cultural traditions) is just as rapidly being levelled, even though the guerilla warfare of 'zapping' has begun to introduce anarchical, individual disorder within an ironclad 'order of video'.

In reality, it seems mistaken (although perhaps inevitable) to wonder at this point whether or not there are signs that the future of reading matter and reading as they are delineated here – that is, as a complex of individual practices, personal choices and rejections of rules and hierarchies; of productive chaos and undisciplined consumption; of *métissages* between different repertories and highly diverse but parallel levels of production – will be positive. Reading is a broad and complex phenomenon. In the next decade or two, as we move from the second to the third millennium, its direction will undoubtedly become clear. Only in fifty or a hundred years will we know where reading has led us, and, if we still care to, be able to give our judgement.

Not now; it is too soon.

Notes

Introduction

1 Michel de Certeau, 'Lire: un braconnage', in *L'Invention du quotidien*, vol. 1 of *Arts de faire* (1980), new edn, ed. Luce Giard (Paris: Gallimard, 1990), pp. 279–96, at p. 251; quoted here from 'Reading as poaching', in *The Practice of Everyday Life*, trans. Steven F. Rendall (Berkeley: University of California Press, 1984), pp. 165–76, at p. 174.

2 Certeau, *L'Invention du quotidien*, p. 274; *Practice of Everyday Life*, pp. 170–1.

3 Paul Ricoeur, *Temps et récit*, (3 vols, Paris: Seuil, 1985), vol. 3, *Le Temps raconté*, pp. 228–63; trans. into English by Kathleen Blamey and David Pellauer as *Time and Narrative*, (Chicago: University of Chicago Press, 1984–8), 3:157–79.

4 Stanley Fish, *Is There a Text in this Class? The Authority of Interpretive Communities* (Cambridge, Mass.: Harvard University Press, 1980).

5 D. F. McKenzie, *Bibliography and the Sociology of Texts*, The Panizzi Lectures, 1985 (London: British Library, 1986), p. 20.

6 Roger Stoddard, 'Morphology and the book from an American perspective', *Printing History*, 17, 9 (1987): 2–14.

7 Plato, *Phaedrus* 275E, quoted here from Plato, trans. Harold North Fowler, Loeb Classical Library (Cambridge, Mass.: Harvard University Press and London: William Heinemann, 1982), pp. 565–7.

8 Ibid., p. 567.

9 To cite only one work, see the classic study of E. G. Turner, *Athenian Books in the Fifth and Fourth Centuries B.C.* (London: University College Publications, 1952), revised as 'I libri nell'Atene del V e IV secolo A.C.', trans. Manfredo and Lucia Manfredi, in *Libri, editori e pubblico nel mondo antico: Guida storica e critica*, ed. Guglielmo Cavallo, 2nd edn (Rome and Bari: Laterza, 1992), pp. 5–24.

10 B. M. W. Knox, 'Silent reading in antiquity', *Greek, Roman and Byzantine Studies*, 9 (1968): 421–35.

11 Aristophanes, *Frogs* 52–3, quoted here from *Aristophanes*, trans. Benjamin Bickley Rogers, Loeb Classical Library (Cambridge, Mass.: Harvard University Press and London: William Heinemann, 1961), 2:52–3.

12 It should be noted that Plato was a good deal more open to writing, even favourable to it, when it did not relate to philosophical discourse or discussion of 'truth'. This point is made and fully discussed in Giovanni Cerri, *Platone sociologo della comunicazione* (Milan: Il Saggiatore, 1991).

13 Xenophon, *Memorabilia* 4.2.10, quoted here from *Memorabilia and Oeconomicus*, trans. E. C. Marchant, Loeb Classical Library (Cambridge, Mass.: Harvard University Press and London: William Heinemann, 1959), p. 275.

14 On the verbs connected with various manners of reading, see Pierre Chantraine, 'Les verbes grecs signifiant "lire" ', in *Mélanges Henri Grégoire*, Annuaire de l'Institut de Philologie et d'Histoire Orientales et Slaves, 10 (4 vols, Brussels: Secretariat des Éditions de l'Institut, 1950), 2:115–26, and the works of Jesper Svenbro. See also Gian Franco Nieddu, 'Decifrare la scrittura, "percorrere" il testo: Momenti e livelli diversi dell'approccio alla lettura nel lessico dei Greci', *Giornale italiano di filologia*, 40 (1988): 17–37; D. J. Allan, 'Anagignosko and some cognate words', *Classical Quarterly*, n.s. 30 (1980): 244–51.

15 On the various stages in the transfer from an oral culture to a completely written culture, see Luigi Enrico Rossi, 'L'ideologia dell'oralità fino a Platone', in *Lo spazio letterario della Grecia antica*, ed. Giuseppe Cambiano, Luciano Canfora and Diego Lanza (3 vols in 6 pts, Rome: Salerno, 1992–6), vol. 1: *La production e la circolazione del testo*, part 1, *La polis* (1992), pp. 77–106.

16 See Luciano Canfora, *La biblioteca scomparsa*, 8th edn, La memoria, 140 (Palermo: Sellerino di Giorganni, 1986); trans. into English by Martin Ryle as *The Vanished Library*, Hellenistic Culture and Society, 7 (Berkeley: University of California Press, 1989).

17 Robert Nicolai, 'Le biblioteche dei ginnasi', *Nuovi annali della Scuola speciale per archivisti e bibliotecari*, 1 (1987): 17–48.

18 Mario Citroni, 'Le raccomandazioni del poeta: Apostrofe al libro e contatto col destinatario', *Maia*, n.s. 38 (1986): 11–46.

19 Polybius, *Histories* 11.1a.2, quoted here from *The Histories*, trans. W. R. Paton, Loeb Classical Library (6 vols, London: William Heinemann and New York: G. P. Putnam's Sons, 1925), 4:227.

20 Gioia M. Rispoli, 'Declamazione e lettura nella teoria retorica e grammaticale greca', *Koinonia*, 15/2 (1991): 93–133.

21 On problems involving the transmission of Latin texts in earlier ages, see Oronzo Pecere, 'I meccanismi della tradizione testuale', in *Lo spazio letterario di Roma antica*, ed. Guglielmo Cavallo, Paolo Fedeli and Andrea Giardina (5 vols, Rome: Salerno, 1989–91), vol. 3: *La recezione del testo* (1990), pp. 297–386.

22 Johannes Diethart and Christian Gastgeber, 'Sechs eindringliche Hinweise für den byzantinischen Leser aus der Kommentarliteratur zu Dionysios Thrax', *Byzantinische Zeitschrift*, 86–7 (1993–4): 386–401.

23 Evelyne Patlagean, 'Discours écrit, discours parlé à Byzance aux VIIIᵉ–XIᵉ siècles', *Annales ESC*, 34 (1979): 264–78. This article also contains a number of acute observations on written culture in Byzantium.

24 A basic text regarding reading practices in this period is Franco Alessio, 'Conservazione e modelli di sapere nel medioevo', in *La memoria del sapere: Forme di conservazione e scritture organizzative dall'antichità a oggi*, ed. Pietro Rossi (Rome and Bari: Laterza, 1988).

25 Francesco Petrarca, 'De librorum copia', in *De remediis utriusque fortunae* 1.43, ed. Gianfranco Contini, in *Mostra di codici petrarcheschi laurenziani, Firenze, Maggio–Ottobre 1974* (Florence: Olschki, 1974), pp. 75–81, at p. 79, quoted here from 'Many Books', in *Petrarch's Remedies for Fortune Fair and Foul*, trans. Conrad H. Rawski (5 vols, Bloomington and Indianapolis: Indiana University Press, 1991), 1:138–42, at p. 142.

26 On this question and others concerning relationships among the book, reading and the public in the final centuries of the Middle Ages, see Armando Petrucci, 'Il libro manoscritto', in *Letteratura italiana*, gen. ed. Alberto Asor Rosa (8 vols, Turin: Einaudi, 1982–91), vol. 2: *Produzione e consumo* (1983), pp. 499–524.

27 Ann Moss, *Printed Common-Place Books and the Structuring of Renaissance Thought* (Oxford and New York: Clarendon Press, 1996).

28 Lisa Jardine and Anthony Grafton, ' "Studied for action": how Gabriel Harvey read his Livy', *Past and Present*, 129 (November 1990): 30–78, esp. p. 34.

29 Ann Blair, *The Theater of Nature: Jean Bodin and Renaissance Science* (Princeton, NJ: Princeton University Press, 1997).

30 Ruth B. Bottigheimer, 'Bible reading, "Bibles", and the Bible for children in early modern Germany', *Past and Present*, 139 (1993): 66–89.

Chapter 1 Archaic and Classical Greece: The Invention of Silent Reading

This chapter is a distillation of two works, to which the reader is referred for more a complete treatment of the question: Jesper Svenbro, *Phrasikleia: Anthropologie de la lecture en Grèce ancienne* (Paris: La Découverte, 1988); trans. in English by Janet Lloyd as *Phrasikleia: An Anthropology of Reading in Ancient Greece* (Ithaca, NY: Cornell University Press, 1993); Svenbro, 'La lecture à haute voix: Le témoignage des verbes grecs signifiant "lire" ', in *Phoinikeia grammata: Lire et écrire en Méditerranée*, ed. Claude Baurain, Corinne Bonnet and Véronique Krings (Namur: Société des études classiques, 1991), pp. 539–48.

1 Pierre Chantraine, 'Les verbes grecs signifiant "lire" ', in *Mélanges Henri Grégoire*, Annuaire de l'Institut de Philologie et d'Histoire Orientales et Slaves, 10 (4 vols, Brussels: Secretariat des Éditions de l'Institut, 1950), 2:115–26.

2 Sophocles, fr. 144 Nauck².

3 Theocritus, *Idyllia* 18.47–8.

4 Epicharmus, fr. 224 Kaibel.

5 See Carlo Gallavotti, 'Letture epigrafiche', *Quaderni Urbinati di cultura classica*, 20 (1975): 172–7; Bernhard Forssman, 'ANNEMOTA in einer dorischen Gefässinschrift', *Münchener Studien zur Sprachwissenschaft*, 34 (1976): 39–44.

6 Hesychius, s.v. *annemein* (= *ananemein*); *Scholia to Pindar* 3.222.16–17 Drachmann.

7 Werner Peek, *Grieschische Vers-Inschriften*, vol. 1 (Berlin: Akademie-Verlag, 1955), no. 1210, 1–3.

8 See Émile Benveniste, 'Actif et moyen dans le verbe', in *Problèmes de linguistique général* (2 vols, Paris: Gallimard, 1966), 1:168–75.

9 Chantraine, 'Les verbes grecs signifiant "lire" ', p. 115.

10 'Of reading and writing, they learned only enough to serve their turn': Plutarch, *Life of Lycurgus* 16.6, quoted here from *Plutarch's Lives*, trans. Bernadotte Perrin, Loeb Classical Library (Cambridge, Mass.: Harvard University Press and London: William Heinemann, 1959), 1:257.

11 Alcman, fr. 40 Page.

12 Hermippus, fr. 88 Wehrli.

13 For the magistrate called a *nomoidos*, see Strabo 12.2.9.

14 Simonides, fr. 37.11–12 Page; Herodotus 1.173.

15 Hesiod, *Works and Days* 224, 213.

16 Plutarch, *Life of Lycurgus* 13.1–4.

17 André Magdelain, *La Loi à Rome: Histoire d'un concept*, Collection d'études latines, série scientifique, 34 (Paris: Belles Lettres, 1978), p. 17.

18 Plato, *Theaetetus* 143c.

19 See Demosthenes, XXI, *Against Meidias* 8, 10, etc.

20 Peter Herrmann, 'Teos und Abdera im 5. Jahrundert v. Chr.: Ein neues Fragment der Teiorum Divae', *Chiron*, 11 (1981): 1–30, esp. pp. 8, 11.

21 Chantraine, 'Les verbes grecs signifiant "lire" ', p. 126.

22 Hesychius, s.v. *epineimato*.

23 Pindar, *Olympian Odes* 10.1.

24 Chantraine, 'Les verbes grecs signifiant "lire" ', p. 115.

25 For this phrase, see Hippocrates, *On Regimen* 1.23.

26 *Anecdota Graeca*, 2.793–5 Bekker. See also Liddell–Scott–Jones, s.v. *stoikheion*, 2.1.

27 Xenophon, *Memorabilia* 1.6.14.

28 Aesop, *Fables*, 276 Chambry.

29 For these two verbs, see Chantraine, 'Les verbes grecs signifiant "lire" ', pp. 122–6 and 118, respectively. For the sense, 'to have relations with', see Plutarch, *Life of Solon* 20.4, and Xenophon, *Anabasis* 1.2.12, etc.

30 Gorgias, fr. 11.8 Diels-Kranz.

31 Pindar, fr. 152 Bowra, etc.

32 Michel Charles, *Rhétorique de la lecture* (Paris: Seuil, 1977), p. 9.

33 See Aeschines, *Prosecution of Timarkhos*, and the analysis of that work in K. J. Dover, *Greek Homosexuality* (Cambridge, Mass.: Harvard University Press, 1978), pp. 42–6.

34 Michel Foucault, *L'Usage des plaisirs*, vol. 2 of *Histoire de la sexualité* (3 vols, Paris: Gallimard, 1976–82), pp. 205–69; trans. into English by Robert Hurley, as *The Use of Pleasure*, vol. 2 of *The History of Sexuality* (3 vols, New York: Viking Books, 1980–6), pp. 187–227.

35 See n. 5 above.

36 Plato, *Phaedrus* 242c.

37 Plato, *Republic* 2.9.366e.

38 Gerhard Pfohl, *Greek Poems on Stones*, Textus minores, 36 (Leiden: Brill, 1967), vol. 1: *Epitaphs: From the Seventh to the Fifth Centuries B.C.*, no. 15.

39 Margherita Guarducci, *Epigrafia greca* (3 vols, Rome: Istituto Poligrafico dello Stato, 1967–74), vol. 3: *Epigrafi di carattere privato* (1974), p. 482.

40 Mario Burzachechi, 'Oggetti parlanti nelle epigrafi greche', *Epigraphica*, 24 (1962): 3–54.

41 Maria Letizia Lazzarini, *Le formule delle dediche nella Grecia arcaica*, Atti della Accademia nazionale dei Lincei, Memorie, Classe di scienze morali, storiche e filologiche, 8th ser., vol. 19, fasc. 2 (Rome: Accademia nazionale dei Lincei, 1976), no. 658.

42 See, for example, the classic article of Josef Balogh, ' "Voces paginarum": Beiträge zur Geschichte des lauten Lesens und Schreibens', *Philologus*, 82 (1927): 84–109, 202–40, and the critique of that article in B. M. W. Knox, 'Silent reading in antiquity', *Greek, Roman and Byzantine Studies*, 9 (1968): 421–35.

43 Plato, *Crito* 54d; quoted here (edited) from Plato, trans. Harold Worth Fowler, Loeb Classical Library (Cambridge, Mass.: Harvard University Press and London: William Heinemann, 1982), vol. 1: *Euthyphro, Apology, Crito, Phaedo, Phaedrus*, p. 191.

44 Plato, *Sophist* 263e–264a; *Theaetetus* 189e–190a.

45 Plato, *Apology* 31d; quoted from Fowler trans., 1:115. See also Plato, *Theages* 128d; *Phaedrus* 242b–c.

46 Daimonion is the diminutive of *daimon*, literally, 'distributor' (from *daiesthai*, 'to distribute').

47 Eric Alfred Havelock, 'Dikaiosune: an essay in Greek intellectual history', *Phoenix*, 23 (1969): 49–70.

48 Knox, 'Silent reading in antiquity', pp. 432–5.

49 Euripides, *Hippolytus* 874–8; quoted here from *Hippolytus*, in *Children of Heracles, Hippolytus, Andromach, Hecuba*, ed. and trans. David Kovacs, Loeb Classical Library (Cambridge, Mass., and London: Harvard University Press, 1995), p. 209.

50 Aristophanes, *Knights* 118–27; quoted here from *Aristophanes*, trans. Benjamin Bickley Rogers, Loeb Classical Library (Cambridge, Mass.: Harvard University Press and London: William Heinemann, 1982), vol. 1: *The Acharnians, The Knights, The Clouds, The Wasps*, p. 135.

51 Paul Saenger, 'Silent reading: its impact on late medieval script and society', *Viator*, 13 (1982): 367–414, esp. p. 378.

52 Ibid., pp. 378–80, 383–4, 405.

53 Plutarch, *Life of Solon* 29.

54 See Charles Segal, *Interpreting Greek Tragedy: Myth, Poetry, Text* (Ithaca, NY: Cornell University Press, 1986); consulted in French as *La Musique du Sphinx: Poésie et structure dans la tragédie grecque*, trans. Catherine Malamoud (Paris: La Découverte, 1987), pp. 263–98.

55 George Thomson, *Aeschylus and Athens: A Study in the Social Origins of Drama*, 2nd edn (New York: Haskell House, 1967), pp. 181–3.

56 Homer, *Odyssey* 15.167–70; quoted here from Thomson, *Aeschylus and Athens*, p. 181.

57 Plato, *Timaeus* 72a–b, quoted here from Thomson, *Aeschylus and Athens*, p. 182.

58 Thomson, *Aeschylus and Athens*, p. 183.

59 Sir Arthur Wallace Pickard-Cambridge, *Dithyramb, Tragedy and Comedy*, 2nd edn, rev. T. B. L. Webster (Oxford: Clarendon Press, 1962), p. 88.

60 Aristotle, *De sensu et sensibilibus* 437b, quoted here from 'On sense and sensible objects', from *Parva Naturalia*, in *On the Soul, Parva Naturalia, On Breath*, trans. W. S. Hett, Loeb Classical Library (Cambridge, Mass.: Harvard University Press and London: William Heinemann, 1957), p. 223.

61 Aristotle, *De sensu et sensibilibus* 437b, quoted here from 'On sense and sensible objects', p. 223. See also Empedocles, fr. B89 Diels-Kranz.

62 Alexander of Aphrodisias, *Commentaria De sensu Aristotelis* 56.12.
63 See Samuel Sambursky, *The Physical World of the Greeks*, trans. Merton Dagut (London: Routledge and Kegan Paul, 1956), pp. 126–8.
64 Leucippus, fr. A9 Diels-Kranz.
65 The quotations that follow are taken from Aeschylus, *Seven Against Thebes* 432–4, 103, 465–9, 646–8; quoted here from *The Suppliant Maidens, The Persians, Prometheus Bound, The Seven Against Thebes*, trans. Herbert Weir Smyth, Loeb Classical Library (Cambridge, Mass.: Harvard University Press and London: William Heinemann, 1988), pp. 357–9, 331, 361, 375.
66 Herodotus, 1.124, 187; 2.102, 106, 133, 136, 141; 3.88; 4.91; 5.60, 61, 90, 92; 6.77; 7.228; 8.22, 136.
67 Plato, *Phaedrus* 275d; Fowler trans., p. 565.
68 Euripides, *Hippolytus* 865, 877, 878–80; quoted here from the Kovacs trans., p. 209.
69 Plato, *Phaedrus* 275c–276a. See also Plato, *Philebus* 38e–39a.
70 Pindar, *Olympian Odes* 10.1–3; quoted here from *The Odes of Pindar*, trans. Sir John Sandys, Loeb Classical Library (Cambridge, Mass.: Harvard University Press and London: William Heinemann, 1961), p. 111.
71 Aristotle, *Poetics* 4.1149a16.
72 Aeschylus, *Prometheus Bound* 788–9. The quotations that follow come from *The Suppliants* 178–9, 991–2; *Eumenides* 273–5; *Coephori* 450. These passages are quoted here from the Smith translation: *Prometheus Bound*, p. 287; *Suppliant Maidens*, p. 99; *Eumenides*, p. 299; *Libation-Bearers*, p. 203.
73 Plato, *Phaedrus* 276d.
74 Athenaeus of Naucratis 8.276a; 10.448b, 453c–454a (= Callias, fr. 31 Edmonds); quoted here from *The Grammatical Play*, in *The Fragments of Attic Comedy*, ed. and trans. John Maxwell Edmonds (3 vols, Leiden: Brill, 1957), 1:179. See also Egert Pöhlmann, 'Die ABC-Komödie des Kallias', *Rheinisches Museum*, 114 (1971): 230–40.
75 Euripides, fr. 382 Nauck².
76 Callias, *The Grammatical Play*, in *Fragments of Attic Comedy*, 1:181.
77 Sophocles, fr. 117 Nauck².

Chapter 2   Between *Volumen* and Codex: Reading in the Roman World

1 Alan E. Astin, *Cato the Censor* (Oxford: Clarendon Press and New York: Oxford University Press, 1978), pp. 135–7.
2 Plutarch, *Cato the Elder* 20.7; quoted here from 'Cato Major', in *Plutarch's Lives*, trans. Bernadotte Perrin, Loeb Classical Library (Cambridge, Mass.: Harvard University Press and London: William Heinemann, 1959), 2:363.
3 See Naphtali Lewis, *Papyrus in Classical Antiquity* (Oxford: Clarendon Press, 1974), pp. 85–7.
4 Livy 40.29.6.
5 Lewis, *Papyrus*, p. 88; Tiziano Dorandi, 'Lucilio, fr. 798 Krenkel', *Studi italiani di filologia classica*, n.s. 63 (1982): 216–18; *idem*, 'Glutinatores', *Zeitschrift für Papyrologie und Epigraphik*, 50 (1983): 25–8.

6 John Van Sickle, 'The book-roll and some conventions of the poetic book', *Arethusa*, 13 (1980): 5–42, esp. p. 12.

7 Scevola Mariotti, *Lezioni su Ennio*, 2nd edn enlarged (Urbino: Quattro-Venti, 1991), pp. 17–23.

8 Plutarch, *Cato the Elder* 68.2–70.2; *Plutarch's Lives*, trans. Perrin, 8:401–9.

9 Cicero, *De finibus bonorum et malorum* 3.7.

10 On conquered libraries and, more generally, on private libraries in Rome between the late Republic and the first centuries of the Empire, see, for example, Horst Blanck, *Das Buch in der Antike* (Munich: Beck, 1992), pp. 152–60.

11 On books and libraries in the age of Cicero, see Oronzo Pecere, 'I meccanismi della tradizione testuale', in *Lo spazio letterario di Roma antica*, ed. Guglielmo Cavallo, Paolo Fedeli and Andrea Giardina (5 vols, Rome: Salerno, 1988–91), vol. 3: *La ricezione del testo* (1990), pp. 314–19.

12 Cicero, *Epistolae ad Quintum fratrem* 3.5.6, quoted here from *The Letters to his Brother Quintus*, trans. W. Glynn Williams, Loeb Classical Library (Cambridge, Mass.: Harvard University Press and London: William Heinemann, 1979), p. 595.

13 Cicero, *Brutus* 65, 122, 129, 133.

14 Cicero, *Epistolarum ad Atticum* 2.20.6.

15 Ibid., 1.20.7; 2.1.12.

16 Ibid., 4.10.1, 14.1; Cicero, *De finibus bonorum et malorum* 3.7.

17 Paul Zanker, *Augustus und die Macht der Bilder* (Munich: Beck, 1987), pp. 35–8; trans. into English by Alan Shapiro as *The Power of Images in the Age of Augustus* (Ann Arbor: University of Michigan Press, 1988).

18 Catullus 14.17–18; Cicero, *Orationes Philippicae* 2.21. See also T. P. Wiseman, 'Looking for Camerius: the topography of Catullus 55', *Papers of the British School at Rome*, 48 (1980): 6–16.

19 Cicero, *Tusculanae disputationes* 4.6.

20 Ibid., 1.6.

21 Cicero, *De finibus bonorum et malorum* 5.52.

22 Elizabeth Rawson, *Intellectual Life in the Late Roman Republic* (Baltimore and London: Johns Hopkins University Press, 1985), p. 49. For the Republican age, however, Rawson postulates too broad an extension of reading practices.

23 E. A. Lowe, *Codices Latini Antiquiores: A Paleographical Guide to Latin Manuscripts prior to the Ninth Century* (11 vols, Oxford: Clarendon Press, 1934–66), vol. 3, no. 385.

24 Catullus 22. See also Leopoldo Gamberale, 'Libri e letterature nel carme 22 di Catullo', *Materiali e discussioni per l'analisi dei testi classici*, 8 (1982): 143–69.

25 R. D. Anderson, P. J. Parsons and R. G. M. Nisbet, 'Elegiacs by Gallus from Qasr Imbîm', *Journal of Roman Studies*, 49 (1979): 125–55.

26 Lowe, *Codices Latini Antiquiores*, 2nd edn (1972), vol. 2, no. 223, and *Supplement* (1971), no. 1721.

27 Erich Auerbach, *Literatursprache und Publikum in der lateinischen Spätantike und im Mittelalter* (Berne: Francke, 1958), p. 178; quoted here from *Literary Language and its Public in Late Latin Antiquity and in the Middle Ages*, trans. Ralph Mannheim (Princeton, NJ: Princeton University Press, 1993), p. 239.

28 Paul Veyne, 'The Roman Empire', in *A History of Private Life*, ed. Philippe Ariès and Georges Duby (5 vols, Cambridge, Mass., and London: The Belknap Press of Harvard University Press, 1987–91), vol. 1: *From Pagan Rome to Byzantium*, trans. Arthur Goldhammer (1987), pp. 5–234, at p. 18.

29 On public libraries in Rome, see Blanck, *Das Buch in der Antike*, pp. 160–78.

30 Volker Michael Strocka, 'Römische Bibliotheken', *Gymnasium*, 88 (1981): 298–329, esp. p. 315.

31 Blanck, *Das Buch in der Antike*, pp. 120–9.

32 Gellius, *Noctes Atticae* 18.4.11.

33 Henri-Jean Martin, *Histoire et pouvoirs de l'écrit* (Paris: Perrin, 1988), p. 81; trans. into English by Lydia G. Cochrane as *The History and Power of Writing* (Chicago: University of Chicago Press, 1994), pp. 71–2.

34 For examples, see Henri Irénée Marrou, *Mousikos aner: Études sur les scènes de la vie intellectuelle figurant sur les monuments funéraires romains* (Grenoble: Didier et Richard, 1938), pp. 24–197.

35 See Salvatore Settis, 'La colonna', in Salvatore Settis, Adriano La Regina, Giovanni Agosti and Vincenzo Farinella, *La colonna traiana* (Turin: Einaudi, 1988), pp. 45–255, esp. pp. 107–14.

36 Petronius, *Satyricon* 58.7; quoted here from *Satyricon*, trans. Michael Heseltine, rev. E. H. Warmington (Cambridge, Mass.: Harvard University Press and London: William Heinemann, 1987), p. 125.

37 R. P. Duncan-Jones, 'Age-rounding, illiteracy and social differentiation in the Roman Empire', *Chiron*, 7 (1977): 335–53.

38 Quintilian, *De institutione oratoria* 1.1.25–34.

39 Petronius, *Satyricon* 75.4; Heseltine trans., p. 175.

40 Although in some ways it has been superseded and in other ways it invites criticism, an article that continues to provide a useful collection of materials on this topic is Josef Balogh, ' "Voces paginarum" ', *Philologus*, 82 (1927): 84–109 and 202–40.

41 In general, see Kenneth Quinn, 'The poet and his audience in the Augustan age', in *Aufstieg und Niedergang der römischen Welt*, ed. Hildegard Temporini and Wolfgang Haase (Berlin and New York: Walter de Gruyter, 1972–96), vol. 2: *Principat*, 30.1, *Sprache und Literatur*, ed. Wolfgang Haase (1982), pp. 75–180, esp. pp. 155–8.

42 Quintilian, *De institutione oratoria* 1.8.1; Butler trans., 1:147.

43 Gellius, *Noctes Atticae* 18.4.2; quoted here from *The Attic Nights of Aulus Gellius*, trans. John C. Rolfe, Loeb Classical Library (3 vols, Cambridge, Mass.: Harvard University Press and London: William Heinemann, 1984), 3:307.

44 For such testimony, see Francesco di Capua, 'Osservazioni sulla lettura e sulla preghiera ad alta voce presso gli antichi', *Rendiconti dell'Accademia di Archeologia, Lettere e Belle Arti di Napoli*, n.s. 28 (1953): 59–62.

45 Jules Marouzeau, 'Le style oral latin', *Revue des études latines*, 10 (1932): 147–86.

46 Quintilian, *De institutione oratoria* 9.4.138; 11.2.33; Butler trans., 4:231.

47 On interpunction, see Rudolf Wolfgang Müller, 'Rhetorische und syntaktische Interpunktion: Untersuchungen zur Pausenbezeichnung im antiken Latein', inaugural dissertation, Tübingen, 1964. See also Malcolm B. Parkes, *Pause and Effect: An Introduction to the History of Punctuation in the West* (Berkeley: University of California Press, 1993), pp. 9–19.

48 Henri-Jean Martin, 'Pour une histoire de la lecture', *Revue française d'histoire du livre*, n.s. 16 (1977): 583–610, at p. 585.
49 See Quinn, 'The poet and his audience', pp. 158–65.
50 U. E. Paoli, *'Legere e recitare'*, *Atene e Roma*, n.s. 3 (1922): 205–7, at p. 206.
51 Paolo Fedeli, 'I sistemi di produzione e diffusione', in *Lo spazio letterario di Roma antica*, vol. 2: *La circolazione del testo*, pp. 349–67.
52 B. M. W. Knox, 'Silent reading in antiquity', *Greek, Roman and Byzantine Studies*, 9 (1968): 421–35; Santiago Mollfulleda, 'La lectura, ¿eslabon entre la lengua escrita y la hablada?', *Revista española de linguistica*, 18 (1988): 38ff.
53 Horace, *Satires* 1.6.122; 2.5.68; St Augustine, *Confessions* 6.3.3 (describing St Ambrose reading).
54 Roger Chartier, 'Du livre au lire', in *Pratiques de la lecture*, ed. Roger Chartier (Paris and Marseilles: Rivages, 1985), pp. 61–82.
55 Apuleius, *Metamorphoses* 1.1.1: quoted from *Metamorphoses (The Golden Ass)*, trans. J. Arthur Hanson, Loeb Classical Library (2 vols, Cambridge, Mass., and London: Harvard University Press, 1989), 1:3.
56 Lucian, *Adversus Indoctum et libros multos ementem* 2–4, 7, 18–19, 24; quoted here from 'The Ignorant Book-Collector', in *Lucian*, trans. A. M. Harmon, Loeb Classical Library (Cambridge, Mass.: Harvard University Press and London: William Heinemann, 1960), pp. 173–212, at pp. 177, 179, 197, 185.
57 Pliny, *Epistolae* 9.23.2.
58 Juvenal, *Satires* 6.451; quoted here from *Juvenal and Persius*, trans. G. G. Ramsay, Loeb Classical Library (Cambridge, Mass.: Harvard University Press and London: William Heinemann, 1941), p. 121.
59 Ovid, *Metamorphoses* 9.522–5.
60 Ibid., 6.576–83.
61 Ovid, *Epistulae heroidum* 3.1–4.
62 Ovid, *Ars amatoria* 2.745–6; 3.45–8.
63 The passages that follow are discussed in Mario Citroni, 'Le raccomandazioni del poeta: Apostrofe al libro e contatto col destinatario', *Maia*, n.s. 38 (1986): 111–46.
64 E. G. Turner, *Greek Manuscripts of the Ancient World*, 2nd edn rev. and enlarged, ed. P. J. Parsons, Bulletin Supplement, Institute of Classical Studies, 46 (London: University of London, 1987), p. 96.
65 Ovid, *Tristia* 2.471–92.
66 Mario Citroni, 'Marziale e la letteratura per i Saturnali (Poetica dell'intrattenimento e cronologia della pubblicazione dei libri)', *Illinois Classical Studies*, 14 (1989): 201–26, at p. 205.
67 Mario Citroni, *Poesia e lettori in Roma antica* (Rome and Bari: Laterza, 1995), pp. 442–3.
68 On this literature, see Citroni, 'Marziale', pp. 206–26, at p. 226.
69 For a discussion of a broad sample of this sort of material, see Francesco De Martino, 'Per una storia del "genere" pornografico', in *La letteratura di consumo nel mondo greco-latino,* Atti del Convegno internazionale, Cassino, 14–17 settembre 1994, ed. Oronzo Pecere and Antonio Stramaglia (Cassino: Università degli studi di Cassino, 1996), pp. 293–341.
70 Longus, *Daphnis and Chloe*, Proem. 3, quoted here from *Daphnis and Chloe, Parthenius, etc.*, trans. George Thornley, rev. J. M. Edmonds, Loeb

Classical Library (London: William Heinemann and New York: G. P. Putnam's Sons, 1924), p. 9.

71 On the reading public for these texts, see, among other works, Tomas Hägg, *Den Antika romanen* (Uppsala: Bokförlager Carmina, 1980), trans. into English as *The Novel in Antiquity* (Berkeley: University of California Press, 1983), pp. 90–101; Kurt Treu, 'Der Antike Roman und sein Publikum', in *Der Antike Roman: Untersuchungen zur literarischen Kommunikation und Gattungsgeschichte*, ed. Heinrich Kuch (Berlin: Akademie-Verlag, 1989), pp. 178–97; E. L. Bowie, 'Les lecteurs du roman grec', in *Le monde du roman grec*, Actes du Colloque international tenu à l'École Normale Supérieure, Paris, 17–19 décembre 1987, ed. Marie-Françoise Baslez, Philippe Hoffmann and Monique Trédé (Paris: Presses de l'École Normale Supérieure, 1992), pp. 55–61.

72 Photius, *Bibliotheca* cod. 166.111a–b.

73 Brigitte Egger, 'Zu den Frauenrollen im griechischen Roman: Die Frau als Heldin und Leserin', in *Groningen Colloquia on the Novel*, vol. 1 (Groningen: Egbert Forsten, 1988), pp. 33–66.

74 Lucian, *Imagines* 9.

75 Paolo Fedeli, in *Petronio Arbitro: I racconti del 'Satyricon'*, ed. Paolo Fedeli and Rosalba Dimundo, Omikron, 31 (Rome: Salerno, 1988), pp. 7–15.

76 Apuleius, *Metamorphoses* 9. 30.1; Hanson trans., 2:181.

77 Ibid., 1.1.1.

78 Albert Henrichs, ed., *Die Phoinikikà des Lollianos: Fragmente eines neuen griechischen Romans* (Bonn: R. Habelt, 1972).

79 According to the Byzantine lexicographer Suidas: see *Suidae Lexicon*, ed. Ada Adler (5 vols, Lipsiae: in aedibus B. G. Tevbneri, 1928–38), 4:724.

80 Parkes, *Pause and Effect*, p. 12.

81 *The Oxyrynchus Papyri* (London: Egypt Exploration Society), vol. 62 (1974), no. 3010.

82 Gellius, *Noctes Atticae* 9. 4.1–5, Rolfe trans., 2:163.

83 E. G. Turner, *Greek Papyri: An Introduction*, 2nd edn (Oxford: Clarendon Press, 1980), p. 204.

84 Nicholas Horsfall, 'The origins of the illustrated book', *Aegyptus*, 63 (1983): 199–216.

85 *Papiri dell'Istituto Papirologico 'G. Vitelli'*, Quaderni dell'Accademia delle Arti del Disegno, 1 (Florence: Accademia delle Arti del Disegno, 1988), pp. 32–3.

86 Albert Hartmann, 'Eine Federzeichnung auf einem Münchener Papyrus', in *Festschrift für Georg Leidinger zum 60. Geburtstag am 30. Dezember 1930* (Munich: Hugo Schmidt, 1930), pp. 103–8.

87 *Oxyrynchus Papyri*, vol. 62, no. 3001.

88 Ibid., vol. 22 (1954), no. 2331.

89 On this point, especially in relation to increased numbers of readers, see Citroni, *Poesia e lettori*, pp. 442–59.

90 Martial 1.117.10–17; 4.72.2; 13.3.4.

91 Martial 1.2.1–4; 14.184, 186, 188, 190, 192.

92 Lowe, *Codices Latini Antiquiores*, vol. 2, no. 207.

93 The classic work on this topic is Colin H. Roberts and T. C. Skeat, *The Birth of the Codex* (London: Published for the British Academy by Oxford University Press, 1983). On the ongoing debate, see Michael McCormick,

'The birth of the codex and the apostolic life-style', *Scriptorium*, 39 (1985): 150–8; Joseph van Haelst, 'Les origines du codex', in *Les débuts du codex*, Actes de la journée d'études organisée à Paris les 3 et 4 juillet 1985 par l'Institut de Papyrologie de la Sorbonne et l'Institut de recherche et d'histoire des textes, ed. Alain Blanchard (Turnhout: Brepols, 1989), pp. 13–35; William V. Harris, 'Why did the codex supplant the book-roll?', in *Renaissance Society and Culture: Essays in Honor of Eugene F. Rice, Jr.*, ed. John Monfasani and Ronald G. Musto (New York: Italica Press, 1991), pp. 71–85; T. C. Skeat, 'Irenaeus and the four gospel canon', *Novum Testamentum*, 34 (1992): 194–99; *idem*, 'The origin of the Christian codex', *Zeitschrift für Papyrologie und Epigraphik*, 102 (1994): 263–8.

94 See Hägg, *Novel in Antiquity*, pp. 154–65, at p. 162; *La narrativa cristiana antica: codici narrativi, strutture formali, schemi retorici*, XXIII Incontro di studiosi della antichità cristiana, [Rome] 5–7 maggio 1994, Studia ephemeridis 'Augustinianum', 50 (Rome: Institutum Patristicum 'Augustinianum', 1995).

95 Cyril of Jerusalem, *Procatechesis* 14 (PG 33. 356A–B).

96 St Augustine, *Soliloquia* 1.10.7, ed. W. Hörmann, (CSEL 89) (Vienna: Hoelder-Pichler-Tempsky, 1986), p. 26.

97 See *Vie de Sainte Mélanie*, ed. and trans. Denys Gorce, Sources Chrétiennes, 90 (Paris: Cerf, 1962), pp. 174, 178, 180, 188. On St Melania's relationship to written culture, see Andrea Giardina, 'Melania, la santa', in *Roma al femminile*, ed. Augusto Fraschetti (Rome and Bari: Laterza, 1994), pp. 277–83.

98 Armando Petrucci, 'Dal libro unitario al libro miscellaneo', in *Società romana e impero tardoantico*, ed. Andrea Giardina (4 vols, Rome and Bari: Laterza, 1986), vol. 4: *Tradizione dei classici, transformazioni della cultura*, pp. 173–87, at p. 179.

99 Ibid., p. 186.

100 Cassiodorus, *Institutiones* 1.3.1.

101 Skeat, 'Origin of the Christian Codex', pp. 265–6.

102 St Jerome, *Praefationes in Ezechael* (PL 38. 996A).

103 Cassiodorus, *Institutiones* 1.15.12.

104 On this process, see Hélène Toubert, 'Formes et fonctions de l'enluminure', in *Histoire de l'édition française*, ed. Henry-Jean Martin and Roger Chartier (4 vols, Paris: Promodis, 1989), vol. 1: *Le Livre conquérant: Du moyen âge au milieu du XVIIᵉ siècle*, pp. 110–14.

105 Cassiodorus, *Institutiones* 1.31.2.

Chapter 3   Reading, Copying and Interpreting a Text in the Early Middle Ages

I am grateful to Professor D. Ganz, Dr A. Grotans, Dr P. Saenger, G. Tunbridge and Dr R. Zim for helpful comments and valuable suggestions, and to members of the Colloquium of the Center for Medieval Studies at the University of Minnesota for stimulating discussion. I remain solely responsible for the views expressed.

1 This definition of the *officia grammaticae* appears in various forms in the writings of grammarians from late antiquity, and in additions to manuscripts of this later period containing grammatical texts. An expanded version of the text (from the preface to the treatise known as the 'Anonymus ad Cuimnanum' in St Paul in Lavanttal, Stiftsbibliothek, MS 26.2.16, fol. 23) together with a brief account of the tradition is printed by M. Irvine, 'Bede the grammarian, and the scope of grammatical studies in eighth-century Northumbria', *Anglo-Saxon England*, 15 (1986): 15–44. See also H.-I. Marrou, *Histoire de l'éducation dans l'antiquité*, 6th edn (Paris: Seuil, 1965), pp. 406–10.

2 For the most part a reading was preferred eclectically on the subjective basis of its intrinsic interest without regard to other witnesses or to textual tradition. Occasionally a reader collated the text with other copies: for example, in Vatican, Biblioteca apostolica, MS Vatican lat. 3363, fol. iii, where St Dunstan records a reading of Boethius's *De consolatione philosophiae* which 'quidam codices habent'; see M. B. Parkes, *Scribes, Scripts and Readers: Studies in the Communication, Presentation and Dissemination of Medieval Texts* (London and Rio Grande, OH.: Hambledon Press, 1991), pp. 259–62.

3 See St Augustine, *De doctrina christiana* II. iv. The author of the seventh-century grammar of the Irish language justified his work on the grounds that it had been made necessary by the consequences of the Tower of Babel; see *Auraicept na n-Éces*, ed. A. Ahlqvist, *The Early Irish Linguist*, (Helsinki: Societas Scientiarum Fennica, 1982), p. 47.

4 The standard collection of texts is *Grammatici latini*, ed. H. Keil (Leipzig, 1857–70). See especially L. Holtz, *Donat et la tradition de l'enseignement grammaticale: étude sur l'Ars Donati et sa diffusion (IVe–IXe siècle)* (Paris: CNRS, 1981) and references; C. Lambot, 'La Grammaire latine selon les grammairiens latins du IVe et du Ve siècle', *Revue Bourgignonne publiée par l'Université de Dijon*, 28 (1908). Supplements to this tradition available to assist the process of *discretio* in the ninth century are also discussed by V. Law, *The Insular Latin Grammarians* (Woodbridge, Suffolk: Boydell & Brewer, 1932).

5 See esp. H.-I. Marrou, *Saint Augustin et la fin de la culture antique* (Paris: Boccard, 1958).

6 See the remarks by Marrou, *Histoire de l'éducation dans l'antiquité*, pp. 446–7.

7 'Omnis qui nomen vult monachi vindicare, litteras ei ignorare non liceat': Ferreolus, *Regula*, ii (*Patrologia series latina*, ed. J. P. Migne (hereafter referred to as *PL*), lxvi, 959). Examples of exhortations include that of St Paul in 1 Tim. 4:13; 'viva lectio est vita bonorum': Gregory the Great, *Moralia in Job*, xxiv, 8, 16 (*PL*, lxxvi, 295). Cf. D. Illmer, *Formen der Erziehung und Wissenvermittlung im frühen Mittelalter* (Munich: Arbeo, 1971).

8 Dhuoda, *Manuel pour mon fils*, ed. P. Riché (Paris: Cerf, 1975).

9 P. Riché, 'Le Psautier, livre de lecture élémentaire', in *Études merovingiennes*, Actes des journées de Poitiers 1952 (Paris, 1953), pp. 253–6; A. Petrucci, 'Scrittura e libro nell'Italia altomedievale', *Studi medievali*, 10 (1969): 157–207, esp. pp. 164ff.

10 Gregory the Great, *Dialogi*, i, prol. 9; cf. *Moralia in Job*, xxx, 37; *Homeliae in Evangelia*, xxxviii, 15; xxxix, 10; *Homeliae in Ezekiel* II.vii.3.

11 ... grammaticorum autem doctrina potest etiam proficere ad vitam dum
    fuerit in meliores usus assumpta': Isidore, *Libri sententiarum*, III.xiii.3
    (*PL*, lxxxiii, 698); see J. Fontaine, *Isidore de Seville et la culture classique
    dans l'Espagne wisigothique* (Paris: Études Augustiniennes, 1959), 2:787;
    J. Leclercq, 'Pédagogie et formation spirituelle du VIᵉ au IXᵉ siècle', in
    La Scuola nell'occidente latino dell'alto medioevo, Settimane di studio
    di Centro Italiano di Studi sull'alto medioevo, 19 (Spoleto, 1972),
    pp. 255–90.
12 On the ideal of the *vir eloquentissimus* see O. Seeck, *Geschichte des Unter-
    gangs der antiken Welt*, vol. 4 (Berlin, 1911), pp. 168–204; Marrou, *Saint
    Augustin et la fin de la culture antique*, pp. 3–9, 85–9.
13 Cf. Aulus Gellius, *Noctes Atticae* xiii, 31.5.
14 'Qui autem ad hujusmodi provehitur gradum, iste erit doctrina et libris
    imbutus, sensuumque ac verborum scientia perornatus, ita ut in distinction-
    ibus sententiarum intelligat ubi finiatur junctura, ubi adhuc pendet oratio,
    ubi sententia extrema claudatur. Sicque expeditus vim pronuntiationis
    tenebit, ut ad intellectum omnium mentes sensusque promoveat, discer-
    nendo genera pronuntiationum, atque exprimendo sententiarum proprios
    affectus, modo indicantis voce, modo dolentis, modo increpantis, modo
    exhortantis, sive his similia secundum genera propriae pronuntiationis':
    Isidore, *De ecclesiasticis officiis* II.xi.2 (*PL*, lxxxiii, 791). See M. Banniard,
    'Le Lecteur en Espagne wisigothique d'après Isidore de Seville: de ses fonc-
    tions à l'état de la langue', *Revue des études Augustiniennes*, 21 (1975):
    112–44. Hildemar, a monk of Corbie in the ninth century, discussed this
    passage from Isidore in his commentary on the Rule: see *Expositio Regulae
    ab Hildemaro tradita*, [ed. R. Mittermüller] (Regensburg and New York,
    1880), pp. 427ff. Copies of texts to be read aloud in the liturgy, before
    chapter, or in the refectory, usually exhibit more careful attention to punc-
    tuation than most, and frequently have accents placed over syllables to be
    stressed. See the examples cited by M. B. Parkes *Anglo-Saxon England*, 26,
    'Raeden, areccan, smeagan: how the Anglo-Saxons read', (1997), 1–22,
    esp. 7–8.
15 Fifteen copies of Terence survive from the ninth to the eleventh centuries:
    see *Texts and Transmission: A Survey of the Latin Classics*, ed. L. D.
    Reynolds (Oxford: Clarendon Press, 1983), p. 418. On the suitability of
    reading Terence to improve a student's eloquence, see Quintilian, *Institutio
    oratoria*, I.xi.12.
16 Hrotsvit's purpose was to redress the balance of Terence's representation of
    women and to emphasize the chastity of Christian virgins; see *Hroswitha of
    Gandersheim*, ed. A. L. Haight (New York, 1965).
17 On monastic *lectio* and *meditatio*, see Cassian, *Collatio* xiv.10; J. Leclercq,
    The Love of Learning and the Desire for God (New York: Fordham Univer-
    sity Press, 1961), pp. 18–22; P. Riché, *Éducation et culture dans l'occident
    barbare*, 6ᵉ–8ᵉ siècle (Paris: Seuil, 1962), pp. 161–2.
18 *La Règle de Saint Benoît*, ed. A. De Vogüé and J. Neufville (Paris: Cerf,
    1971–2), ch. 48. This injunction is repeated in later customaries: for
    example, the Constitutions of Lanfranc, ed. M. D. Knowles, *Corpus consue-
    tudinum monasticum*, vol. 3 (Siegburg: Schmidt, 1967), p. 5.
19 See J. Fontaine, 'Fins et moyens de l'enseignement ecclésiastique dans l'Es-
    pagne wisigothique', in *La Scuola nell'occidente latino dell'alto medioevo*,
    Settimane di studio del centro italiano di studi sull'alto medioevo, vol. 19
    (Spoleto, 1972), pp. 145–202, esp. pp. 180–1, 187–90.

20 Isidore, *Libri sententiarum* III.xiv.9 and 8 (*PL*, lxxxiii, 689).

21 This development is outlined in M. B. Parkes, *Pause and Effect: An Intro-
    duction to the History of Punctuation in the West* (Aldershot: Scolar Press,
    1992; Berkeley: University of California Press, 1993).

22 Although the existence of documents in antiquity and the development of
    forms of abbreviation such as the *notae iuris* and the Tironian notes indicate
    that writing was regarded as a medium of record (especially for administra-
    tive purposes), in general it was perceived primarily as a record of the
    spoken word, not as an autonomous manifestation of language: cf. H. C.
    Teitler, *Notarii and Exceptores* (Amsterdam, 1985); D. Ganz, 'On the
    history of Tironian notes', in *Tironische Noten*, ed. Ganz, Wolfenbütteler
    Mittelalter-Studien, 1 (Wiesbaden, 1990), pp. 35–51.

23 Isidore, *Etymologiae*, I.iii.1; contrast St Augustine, *De Trinitate* x.19. See
    Parkes, *Pause and Effect*.

24 Riché, 'Le Psautier, livre de lecture élémentaire'; A. Lorcin, 'La Vie scolaire
    dans les monastères d'Irland au Vᵉ–VIIᵉ siècle', *Revue du moyen âge latin*,
    1 (1945): 221–36.

25 See, for example, R. I. Page, 'The study of Latin texts in late Anglo-Saxon
    England: 2 The evidence of English glosses', in *Latin and the Vernacular
    Languages in Early Medieval Britain*, ed. N. P. Brooks (Leicester: Leicester
    University Press, 1982), pp. 141–65.

26 *Thesaurus palaeohibernicus*, ed. W. Stokes and J. Strachan (repr. Dublin:
    Institute for Advanced Studies, 1975), 1:399, no. 118a15; 2:117, no. 64a18;
    H. D. Meritt, *Old English Glosses (a Collection)* (New York: MLA, 1945),
    p. 35, nos 28, 334.

27 *Thesaurus*, 1:22, no. 17d6; Meritt, *Old English Glosses*, p. 33, no. 256.

28 *Thesaurus*, 1:248, nos 73a9–10; 1:416, no. 123b2.

29 *Die althochdeutschen Glossen*, ed. E. Steinmeyer and E. Sievers, vol. 2
    (Berlin, 1882), p. 38, no. 11; p. 76, nos 66, 54; p. 164, no. 31; p. 71,
    no. 53; p. 77, no. 3. On the syntactical glosses of Anglo-Saxon scribes, see
    G. R. Wieland, *The Latin Glosses on Arator and Prudentius in Cambridge
    University Library MS Gg. 5.35* (Toronto: Toronto University Press, 1983).

30 Meritt, *Old English Glosses*, p. 4, nos 30, 49, 52.

31 Notably Würzburg, Universitätsbibliothek, M.P.th.f.12; Milan, Biblioteca
    Ambrosiana, MS C 301 inf.; Oxford, Bodleian Library, MS Auct.F.4.32.

32 The most recent account is by M. Korhammer, 'Mittelalterliche Konstruk-
    tionshilfen und ae Wortstellung', *Scriptorium*, 37 (1980): 18–58. See
    further, n. 37 below.

33 R. Wright, 'On editing texts written by romance speakers', in *Linguistic
    Studies in Medieval Spanish*, ed. R. Harris-Northall and T. O. Cravens
    (Madison, 1991), pp. 191–208.

34 Cf. B. Bischoff, 'A propos des gloses de Reichenau, entre latin et français,
    in his *Mittelalterliche Studien*, vol. 3 (Stuttgart: Hiersemann, 1981),
    pp. 234–43.

35 M. C. Diaz y Diaz, *Las primeras glosas hispanicas* (Barcelona: 1978);
    J. Fortacin Piedrafita, 'Glosas morfosintácticas en el codice emilianense 60',
    Revista de investigacion (1980): 67–89.

36 *De arte metrica et de schematibus et tropis*, ed. C. B. Kendall in *Beda,
    Opera didascalica*, vol. 1, Corpus Christianorum series latina, 123A (Turn-
    hout: Brepols, 1975), p. 142; Alcuin's list of figures (*PL*, ci, 857) puts even
    more emphasis on those which affect word order.

37 The theory of the *circumstantiae rerum*, or *periochas*, has been traced back

to Hermagoras (*Fragmenta*, ed. D. Matthes (Leipzig: Teubner, 1962), pp. 13ff.); and in Fortunatianus, *Ars rhetoricae* ii. 1; Victorinus, *In rhetorica Ciceronis*; the late eighth-century collection known as the *Anecdotum Parisinum* in Paris, Bibliothèque nationale, MS lat. 7530; and in the eighth- or ninth-century Pseudo-Augustine, *De rhetorica*, vii; all printed in *Rhetores latini minores*, ed. C. Halm (Leipzig, 1863), pp. 103, 226, 586 and 141. A ninth-century writer reports that the questions (see below) were apparently used by John the Scot in his teaching (*Vitae Vergilianae*, ed. J. Brummer (Leipzig: Teubner, 1912), p. 62). On the use of the *circumstantiae* in the *accessus* literature, see the summary account by A. J. Minnis, *Medieval Theory of Authorship* (London: Scolar, 1984), pp. 15–19 with references. On the use of the *circumstantiae* with syntax markers, see Parkes, in *Anglo-Saxon England*, 26, 4–5, with further references.

38 From a text 'Quomodo vii circumstantiae rerum in legendo ordinande sint' printed in *Die Schriften Notkers und seine Schule*, ed. P. Piper (Freiburg-im-Briesgau, 1882), vol. 1, pp. xv–xvi (a tenth-century copy is in Zurich, Zentralbibliothek, MS C 98, fol. 38ᵛ); a comparable example is quoted by H. Hagen, *Anecdota Helvetica* (Leipzig, 1870), p. xliii, from a ninth-century copy of an anonymous commentary on Donatus in Berne, Burgerbibliothek, MS 432.

39 For example, by Ekkehart IV of St Gall in glosses to the text of Orosius and elsewhere; see E. Dümmler, 'Ekkehart IV von St Gallen', *Zeitschrift für deutsches Altertum und deutsche Literatur*, 14 (1869): 23; *Der Liber benedictionum Ekkeharts IV*, ed. J. Egli (St Gall: Fehr'sche, 1909), p. xlviii, n. 2.

40 See Parkes, *Scribes, Scripts and Readers*, pp. 1–18, 104–12.

41 See Donatus, *Ars maior* II. 2; Holtz edn, p. 603): 'Littera est pars minima uocis articulata' (cf. Priscian, *Institutiones grammaticae* I.3; I.7–8). An anonymous insular treatise in St Paul in Lavanttal, Stiftsbibliothek, MS 25.2.16, in a gloss on this passage from Donatus emphasizes the perception of letters as a *written* phenomenon: 'Vocis duae sunt partes: articulata et confusa. Articulata est que scribi potest, quae sub est articulis, id est digitis qui scribent, vel quod artem habeat et exprimat. Confusa est quae scribi non potest' (fol. 54ᵛ). The beginner copied letters to enable him or her to register their *figurae*, and pronounced them to register their *potestates*.

42. The term *litterae absolutae* was used by Boniface, Epistola 63, *S. Bonifatii et Lullii Epistolae*, ed. M. Tangl, MGH, Epistolae selectae, vol. 1 (Berlin: Weidmann, 1916; 2nd edn 1955), p. 131.

43 For details in what follows, see Parkes, *Scribes, Scripts and Readers*, pp. 1–18. Conscious linguistic analysis of a different kind appears in an eighth-century Irish copy of a commentary on verse (Paris, Bibliothèque nationale, MS lat. 11411, fol. 123), where quotations to illustrate *metaplasmus* are presented according to metrical feet rather than parts of speech: for example, *dumpela . gode . saeuit . hiempseta . quosuso . rion* (=Aeneid, iv. 52, 'dum pelago desaeuit hiemps et aquosus orion').

44 See, for example, Parkes, *Pause and Effect*, plate 11.

45 Paris, Bibliothèque Nationale, MS lat. 12132 was copied at Reims in the second half of the ninth century from Paris, MS lat. 2630, itself copied in Italy in the sixth century. On the relationship between the two, see J. Vezin, 'Hincmar de Reims et Saint-Denis à propos de deux manuscrits du *De Trinitate* de Saint Hilaire', *Revue d'histoire des textes*, 9 (1979): 289–98; Parkes, *Pause and Effect*, plates 49 and 50 with transcriptions, translations and commentary.

46 *Grammatici latini*, ed. Keil, 7:54. 1–13. For a recent account of the general situation, see R. Wright, *Late Latin and Early Romance in Spain and Carolingian France* (Liverpool: Cairns, 1982), pp. 104–44, with references.

47 A scribe's personal language system was not merely his 'native language', but would have incorporated all the various elements of his own linguistic experience, both spoken and written; this would have included both Latin and, perhaps, more than one vernacular or variety of a single vernacular language. By the second half of the ninth century, his experience of Latin may well have been influenced by a conscious revival of Latin by Paul the Deacon or by Alcuin, such as those postulated by Wright, and by D. Norberg, 'À quelle époque a-t-on cessé de parler latin en Gaule', *Annales*, 21/2 (1966): 346–56.

48 Leiden, Bibliotheek der Rijksuniversiteit, MS Lipsius 7 (facs. of fol. 291ᵛ in E. Châtelain, *Paléographie des classiques latins* (Paris, 1884–1900), plate cxlii) was copied from Leiden, MS Vossianus lat. 2°, 61 (facs. of fol. 80ᵛ in ibid., plate cxli of the same portion of text).

49 Compare the accounts of *praepositiones loquelares* in Pompeius, *Commentum in artis Donati* (*Grammatici latini*, ed. Keil, 5: 271, 21) and in Pseudo-Sergius, *Explanationes* (ed. Keil, 4: 517, 6). See also Parkes, *Scribes, Scripts and Readers*, p. 26 and notes.

50 Gregory the Great, *In Iob*, iv, *praejatio*.

51 'Hoc totum corpus litterae et tamquam corpus homini' (*PL*, xcvi, 958A–B); 'Ecce hominem integrem corpore anima et spiritu. Ecce et librum integrem historia tropologia et mystice intellegentur' (ibid., 962C).

52 Augustine, *De doctrina christiana* II.vi.7; III.ix.13 and xxvii.38.

53 *De schematibus et tropis* II. ii (xii), ed. Kendall, pp. 161–9; Boniface, *Epistola* 34, Tangl edn, p. 59.

54 See R. H. and M. A. Rouse, 'Bibliography before print: the medieval *De viris illustribus*', in *The Role of the Book in Medieval Culture*, ed. P. Ganz, Bibliologia, 3 (Turnhout: Brepols, 1986), 1:133–53.

55 'Spiritus sanctus infinitos in ea constituit intellectus ideoque nullius expositoris sensus sensum alterius aufert': John the Scot, *De divisione naturae* (*PL*, cxxii, 690, 696); cf. Smaragdus de Saint Mihiel, *Diadema monachorum*, iii (*PL*, cii, 598A). For a survey of the exegesis of this period, see C. Spicq, *Esquisse d'une histoire de l'exégèse latine au moyen âge* (Paris, 1944), pp. 10–60.

56 *De clericorum institutione*, praef. (*PL*, cvii, 296).

57 Ibid., III, vii and xiii (*PL*, cvii, 384C, 389C): cf. Augustine, *De doctrina christiana* III.x.14 and xxix.49; and also 2. Tim. 3:16.

58 *De clericorum institutione*, III. xi (*PL*, cvii, 387B): cf. Augustine, *De doctrina christiana* III.ii.2 and xxviii.39.

59 See, for example, the discussion of glosses to Boethius, *De consolatione philosophiae*, III, metre xii, by Parkes, in *Anglo-Saxon England*, 26 15–17; see also D. K. Bolton, 'The study of the "Consolation of Philosophy" in Anglo-Saxon England', *Archives d'histoire doctrinale et littéraire du moyen âge*, 44 (1977): 33–78; F. Troncarelli, *Tradizioni perdutè: la 'Consolatio philosophiae' nell'alto medioevo* (Padua, 1981).

60 On the interest in Martianus Capella, see G. Glauche, 'Die Rolle der Schulautoren im Unterricht von 800 bis 1100', in *La Scuola nell'occidente latino dell'alto medioevo*, pp. 617–36, esp. pp. 621–4; C. Leonardi, 'I codici di Marziano Capella', *Aevum*, 33 (1959): 433–89; 34 (1960): 1–99, 411–524; M. L. W. Laistner, 'Martianus Capella and his ninth-century

commentators', *Bulletin of the John Rylands Library*, 9 (1925): 130–8. The *Mythologiarum ad Catum presbyterum libri tres* is in Fulgentius Planciades, *Opera*, ed. R. Helm (Leipzig, 1898); on his influence see M. L. W. Laistner, *The Intellectual Heritage of the Early Middle Ages* (Ithaca, NY: Cornell University Press, 1957), pp. 202–15. The work of 'Mythographus II' is in *Scriptores rerum mythicarum Latini libri tres*, ed. G. H. Bode (Celle, 1834); see M. Manitius, *Geschichte der lateinische Literatur des Mittelalters*, vol. 2 (Munich: Beck, 1923), pp. 656–60.

61 From Oxford, Bodleian Library, MS Laud Misc. 135, fol. 134ᵛ, from Würzburg: for details see Parkes, *Pause and Effect*, plate 65.

62 The different interpretations of this passage indicated by the punctuation of other copies and their relationship to the development of punctuation as a feature of the pragmatics of the written manifestation of language are discussed in Parkes, *Pause and Effect*, ch. 7.

63 For facsimiles of early vernacular texts, see E. Monaci, *Facsimili di documenti per la storia delle lingue e delle letterature romanze* (Rome, 1910); *Schrifttafeln zum althochdeutschen Lesebuch*, ed. H. Fischer (Tübingen: Niemeyer, 1966); the series Early English Manuscripts in Facsimile (Copenhagen: Rosenkilde & Bagge, 1951–); the oldest Irish glosses in *Epistolae Beati Pauli glosatae glosa interlineali*, ed. L. C. Stern (Halle, 1910); 'Cambrai Homily' in New Palaeographical Society, *Facsimiles of Ancient MSS &c.*, ed. E. M. Thompson, G. F. Warner et al., ser. II (London: New Palaeographic Society, 1913–30), plate 10(b). On the influence of glossaries see Palaeographical Commentary in *The Épinal, Erfurt, Werden and Corpus Glossaries*, Early English Manuscripts in Facsimile, 22, ed. B. Bischoff et al. (Copenhagen: Rosenkilde & Bagger, 1988). On the layout of verse, see Parkes, *Pause and Effect*, ch. 8; *Mise en page et mise en texte du livre manuscrit*, ed. H.-J. Martin and J. Vezin (Paris: Cercle de la Librairie-Promodis, 1990), pp. 147–53, 165–8.

64 Parkes, *Scribes, Scripts and Readers*, pp. 1–18.

Chapter 4   The Scholastic Model of Reading

1 A good point of departure for a study of the evolution of the technique of reading during the Middle Ages might be a thought that Henri-Jean Martin expressed in 'Pour une histoire de la lecture', *Revue française d'histoire du livre*, 16 (1977): 583–610, at p. 583: 'Our ancestors had a completely different idea of the reading of texts from ours, which means that they conceived of the organization of the page and the book in totally different ways. Even more, they had another vision of the relationship between written discourse and spoken discourse. There would certainly be an entire history to be elaborated therein.' For a general approach to the problem, see Guglielmo Cavallo, ed., *Libri e lettori nel medioevo: Guida storica e critica*, Biblioteca Universale Laterza, 296 (Rome and Bari: Laterza, 1977).

2 The Greek term *didascalicon* refers to the act of teaching or instructing. See Hugues de Saint-Victor, *L'Art de lire: Didascalicon*, ed. and trans. Michel Lemoine (Paris: Cerf, 1991).

3 *PL*, 213.713–18.

4 Marcel Jousse, *La Manducation de la Parole* (Paris: Gallimard, 1976).

5 See Paul Saenger, 'Silent reading: its impact on late medieval script and society', *Viator*, 13 (1982): 367–414; *idem*, 'Manières de lire médiévales', in *Histoire de l'édition française*, ed. Henri-Jean Martin and Roger Chartier (4 vols, Paris: Promodis, 1982), vol. 1: *Le Livre conquérant: Du moyen âge au milieu du XVIIe siècle*, pp. 131–41.

6 Armando Petrucci, 'Lire au moyen âge', *Mélanges de l'École française de Rome: Moyen âge–temps modernes*, 96 (1984): 603–16, at p. 604.

7 Ibid.

8 Marie-Dominique Chenu, *Introduction à l'étude de saint Thomas d'Aquin*, 2nd edn, Université de Montréal, Publications de l'Institut d'Études Médiévales, 11 (Montreal: Institut d'Études Médiévales, 1954), p. 67; quoted from *Toward Understanding Saint Thomas*, ed. and trans. A. M. Landry and D. Hughes (Chicago: Regnery, 1964), p. 80.

9 *Ionnis Saresberiensis Episcopi Carnotensis Metalogicon libri IIII* Recognovit ... Clemens C. C. I. Webb (Oxford: Clarendon Press, 1919), pp. 53–4, quoted here from *The Metalogicon of John of Salisbury: A Twelfth-Century Defense of the Verbal and Logical Arts of the Trivium*, ed. and trans. Daniel D. McGarry (Berkeley and Los Angeles: University of California Press, 1955), pp. 65–6.

10 See Charles Vulliez, 'Le vocabulaire des écoles urbaines des XIIe et XIIIe siècles à travers les "summae dictaminis" ', in *Vocabulaire des écoles et des méthodes d'enseignement au moyen âge*, Actes du colloque Rome, 21–22 octobre 1989, ed. Olga Weijers, CIVICIMA: Études sur le vocabulaire intellectuel du moyen âge, 5 (Turnhout: Brepols, 1992), pp. 86–101, esp. p. 94.

11 See Vincenzo Colli, 'Termini del diritto civile', in *Méthodes et instruments du travail intellectuel au moyen âge: Études sur le vocabulaire*, ed. Olga Weijers, CIVICIMA: Études sur le vocabulaire intellectuel du moyen âge, 3 (Turnhout: Brepols, 1990), pp. 231–42: Colli states: 'The historians of law usually classify these as *lecturae*, in contrast to marginal *glossae*. In the twelfth century exegetic texts of this sort were similarly called *glossae*. At the time the term *lectura* did not designate a written account of what the student had learned in class. *Lectura* referred to the method of teaching, to the way of reading a text, hence of interpreting it.' In the same age we can also find *lectura* used in the sense of reading a text unconnected with teaching. Robert of Melun writes in the prologue to his *Sententiae*: 'What does one seek in reading (*lectura*), if it is not deep comprehension of a text?' See *Oeuvres de Robert de Melun*, ed. Raymond M. Martin, Spicilegium Sacrum Lovaniense, 21 (4 vols, Louvain: Spicilegium Sacrum Lovaniense, 1932–52), vol. 3, pt 1: *Sententiae*, p. 11.

12 See Olga Weijers, *Terminologie des universités au XIIIe siècle*, Lessico Intellettuale Europeo, 39 (Rome: Ateneo, 1987), p. 300: 'The term *lectura* also refers to the method of teaching mentioned: the commented reading of texts. But, unlike *lectio*, *lectura* never signifies one lesson. It is a series of lessons on a specific subject, that is, teaching in the form of formal lectures. As *lectio* did at the beginning, *lectura* means "reading"; "the act of reading", hence the teaching of masters or bachelors based on certain texts. The term may be followed by a genitive indicating the matter taught, as in *lectura* "Ut nullus admittatur ad lecturam extraordinariam in jure civili odicis", or by in and the ablative, for example.'

13 Gabriella Severino Polica, 'Libro, lettura, "lezione" negli studia degli ordini mendicanti (sec. XIII)', in *Le scuole degli ordini mendicanti* (Todi: Accademia Tudertina, 1978), pp. 375–413.

14 See Joy Taylor, *Reading and Writing in the First School* (London: Allen and Unwin, 1973); Michael T. Clanchy, *From Memory to Written Record: England, 1066–1307* (Cambridge, Mass.: Harvard University Press, 1979), pp. 34–45; Walter J. Ong, *Orality and Literacy: The Technologizing of the Word*, 4th edn (London and New York: Methuen, 1987); Giulio d'Onofrio, 'Theological ideas and the idea of theology in the early Middle Ages (9th–11th centuries)', *Freiburger Zeitschrift für Philosophie und Theologie*, 38/3 (1991): 273–97.

15 See B. Munk-Olsen, 'Les classiques latins dans les florilèges médiévaux antérieurs au XIII⁰ siècle', *Revue d'histoire des textes*, 9 (1979): 47–122, esp. p. 56.

16 See D'Onofrio, 'Theological ideas and the idea of theology', pp. 278–9: 'Thus the monastic libraries of the ninth to eleventh centuries were, over the years, more and more filled with new, but unoriginal exegetical treatises, compounded of extracts from patristic texts, held together by short connecting sentences. From Alcuin to the time of Anselm, there is a true flourishing of exegetical compilations from patristic sources, often even copies of each other, of little interest for a modern reader. At first sight, in fact, no trace of a reflection on the methodology of theological investigation is to be found in these texts.'

17 Robert de Melun, *Sententiae* 7.5–6.

18 On memory, see Mary Carruthers, *The Book of Memory: A Study of Memory in Medieval Culture*, Cambridge Studies in Medieval Literature, 10 (Cambridge and New York: Cambridge University Press, 1990); Janet Coleman, *Ancient and Medieval Memories: Studies in the Reconstruction of the Past* (Cambridge and New York: Cambridge University Press, 1992).

19 [William of Ockham], *Dialogus inter militem et clericum* (A Dialogue between a Knight and a Clerk), cited in Jürgen Miethke, 'Die Mittelalterlichen Universitäten und das gesprochene Wort', *Historische Zeitschrift*, 251/1 (1990): 1–44, esp. p. 35.

20 *Magistri Petri Lombardi Sententiae in IV libris distinctae*, 3rd edn (2 vols, Grottaferrata [Rome]: Editiones Collegii S. Bonaventurae ad Claras Aquas, 1971–), vol. 1, pt 1, p. 4.

21 Richard H. Rouse, 'Cistercian aids to study in the thirteenth century', *Studies in Medieval Cistercian History*, 2 (1976): 123–34; *idem*, 'La diffusion en Occident au XIII⁰ siècle des outils de travail facilitant l'accès aux textes autoritatifs', International colloquia of La Napoule (France), Islam and the West in the Middle Ages, 1 (25–8 October 1976), in 'Medieval education in Islam and the West', *Revue des études islamiques*, 44 (1976): 115–47; *idem*, 'Le développement des instruments de travail au XIII⁰ siècle', in *Culture et travail intellectuel dans l'Occident médiéval* (Paris: CNRS, 1981), pp. 115–44; *idem* and Mary A. Rouse, '*Statim invenire*: schools, preachers and new attitudes to the page', in *Renaissance and Renewal in the Twelfth Century*, ed. Robert L. Benson and Giles Constable with Carol Lanham (Cambridge, Mass.: Harvard University Press, 1982), pp. 201–335; *idem*, 'La naissance des index', in *Histoire de l'édition française*, ed. Martin and Chartier, vol. 1: *Le Livre conquérant*, pp. 77–85; Malcolm B. Parkes, 'The influence of the concepts of *ordinatio* and *compilatio* on the development of the book', in *Medieval Learning and Literature: Essays Presented to Richard William Hunt*, ed. J. J. G. Alexander and M. T. Gibson (Oxford: Clarendon Press, 1976), pp. 115–41.

22 See Ivan Illich, *Du lisible au visible: La naissance du texte: un commentaire*

du *'Didascalicon' de Hugues de Saint-Victor*, trans. Jacques Mignon, trans. rev. by Maud Sissung (Paris: Cerf, 1991), p. 13; available in English as *In the Vineyard of the Text: A Commentary to Hugh's Didascalicon* (Chicago: University of Chicago Press, 1993). Writing around 1128, Hugh states, in Jerome Taylor's translation of the work's opening sentence, *Omnium expetendorum prima est sapientia*: 'Of all things to be sought, the first is wisdom' (quoted in Illich, *In the Vineyard*, p. 13).

23 See Charles B. Schmitt, 'Auctoritates, repertorium, dicta, sententiae, flores, thesaurus and axiomata: Latin Aristotelian florilegia in the Renaissance', in *Aristoteles: Werk und Wirkung: Paul Moraux gewidmet* (2 vols, Berlin and New York: W. de Gruyter, 1985–7), vol. 2: *Kommentierung, Überlieferung, Nachleben*, pp. 515–37.

24 D. A. Callus, *Introduction of Aristotelian Learning to Oxford, Proceedings of the British Academy*, 29 (1943). Callus states: 'As in the higher Faculties of Theology, Law, and Medicine, so in the Faculty of Arts, the *Abbreviationes*, *Extracta*, or *Summae*, as they were generally called, gained no little favour among students. The aim of the treatises, commentaries, and *quaestiones*, which represented in varying degrees the method and technique of medieval university teaching, was an attempt to grasp the author's thought and to discover the profound meaning of his doctrine with all its implications. The *abbreviationes* were meant to offer to beginners a summary of the contents of their text-books. In the Faculty of Arts the *abbreviationes* may possibly have been used as the text-books through which the *cursor* introduced novices to the Aristotelian *corpus*; or perhaps they were simply intended as a practical aid in private study. In either case they were in constant use in the schools as the starting-point in philosophical training. They presented in a concise form the fundamental philosophical notions which were supposed to be required by all who attempted the study of the text itself' (p. 275).

25 See Jacqueline Hamesse, 'Le vocabulaire de la transmission orale des textes', in *Vocabulaire du livre et de l'écriture au moyen âge*, Actes de la table ronde, Paris 24–26 septembre 1987, ed. Olga Weijers, CIVICIMA: Études sur le vocabulaire intellectuel du moyen âge, 2 (Turnhout: Brepols, 1989), pp. 168–94.

26 Claude Lafleur, *Quatre introductions à la philosophie au XIIIe siècle: Textes critiques et étude historique*, Université de Montréal, Publications de l'Institut d'Études Médiévales, 23 (Montreal: Institut d'Études Médiévales and Paris: J. Vrin, 1988).

27 See Palémon Glorieux, 'L'enseignement au moyen âge: Techniques et méthodes en usage à la Faculté de Théologie de Paris, au XIIIe siècle', *Archives d'histoire doctrinale et littéraire du moyen âge*, 35 (1963): 65–186.

28 Jacqueline Hamesse, 'Les autographes à époque scolastique', in *Gli Autografi medievali: Problemi paleografici e filologici*, Atti del Convegno, Erice, 25 settembre–2 ottobre 1990, ed. Paolo Chiesa and L. Pinelli, Quaderni di cultura mediolatina, 5 (Spoleto: Centro Studi Alto Medioevo, 1994).

29 *Monumenta Ordinis Fratrum Praedicatorum Historica* (Rome: In Domo Generalitia, 1896–), vol. 4: *Acta capitulorum generalium* (1899), recensuit Benedikt Maria Reichert, p. 80.

30 See Saenger, 'Manières de lire médiévales'.

31 See Hamesse, 'Le vocabulaire de la transmission orale des textes'.

32 *Chartularium Universitatis Parisiensis*, ed. Henri Denifle and Émile Châtelain (4 vols, Paris: Delalain, 1889–97), vol. 3 (1894), p. ix.

33 We know that this was not the case at Oxford, however, where courses of

studies were much longer than elsewhere, which perhaps explains why exercises were more numerous there, and why students had more time to memorize the prescribed materials. See Malcolm B. Parkes, 'The provision of books', in *The History of the University of Oxford* (8 vols, Oxford: Clarendon Press, 1984–92), vol. 2: *Late Medieval Oxford*, ed. J. I. Catto and Ralph Evans (1992), pp. 407–83: 'Undergraduates reading for the first degrees in the faculty of arts did not need books, since they were required to hear lectures in which a master or a bachelor read out a prescribed text sentence by sentence, and explained and commented on each one as he went along' (p. 407).

34 Jordan of Saxony, *Die Konstitutionen des Predigerordens unter Jordan von Sachsen*, ed. Heribert Christian Scheeben, Quellen und Forschungen zur Geschichte des Dominikanerordens in Deutschland, 38 (Cologne: Albertus-Magnus-Verlag and Leipzig: O. Harrassowitz, 1939), p. 76.

35 Humbert de Romans, *Opera de vita regulari*, ed. Joachim Joseph Berthier (2 vols, Turin: Marietti, 1956), vol. 1: *Expositio regulae beati Augustini*, ch. 144, 'De studio philosophiae'; available in English as *The Explanation of the Rule of St. Augustine, according to Blessed Humbert* (Akron: D. H. McBride [1900]).

36 See Franz Ehrle, *Historia bibliothecae Romanorum Pontificum tum Bonifatianae tum Avenionensis*, Biblioteca dell'Accademia storico-giuridica, 7 (Rome: typis Vaticanis, 1890), p. 180. The source of this statement is a famous passage in Petrarch's *Rerum memorandarum libri*, 2.91, where he describes John's taste for tables and summaries: see Francesco Petrarca, *Rerum memorandarum libri*, critical ed. Giuseppe Billanovich, Edizione Nazionale delle opere di Francesco Petrarca, V, Ia (Florence: G. C. Sansoni, 1943), p. 102.

37 Pope John XXII, Sermon IV (2 Feb. 1332), p. 2. See also 'Sermon de la Chandeleur', in *Les Sermons de Jean XXII sur la vision béatifique*, ed. Marc Dykmans, Pontificia Universitas Gregoriana: Miscellanea Historiae Pontificiae, 34 (Rome: Presses de l'Université Grégorienne, 1973), pp. 149.11–150.3.

38 For example, Pope John XXII asked the Dominican Giovanni Dominici of Montpellier to prepare a summary of St Thomas's *Summa Theologica* for him (Vat. Borgh. 116–19) and used a *tabula* of the same work (Vat. lat. 814) on which he made annotations. See Anneliese Maier, 'Annotazioni autografe di Giovanni XXII in codici vaticani', in *Ausgehendes Mittelalter: Gesammelte Aufsätze zur Geistesgeschichte des 14. Jahrhunderts*, Storia e letteratura, 97, 105, 138 (3 vols, Rome: Edizioni di Storia e Letteratura, 1964–77), 2:87–8.

39 This manuscript is preserved in the Vatican Library under the code Urbin. lat. 207. See *Codices Urbinates latini*, recensuit Cosimus Stornajolo, Bibliothecae Apostolicae Vaticanae codices manu scripti recensiti iussu Leonis XIII Pont. Maximi (3 vols, Rome: typis Vaticanis, 1902), 1:199–200.

40 Vatican Library, Urbin. lat. 207, fol. 218ʳ.

41 See Jacqueline Hamesse, 'Parafrasi, florilegi e compendi', in *Lo spazio letterario del medioevo: 1. Il medioevo latino*, ed. Guglielmo Cavallo, Claudio Leonardi, Enrico Menestò (5 vols, Rome: Salerno, 1992–), vol. 3: *La ricezione del testo* (1995), pp. 197–220.

42 *Dictionary of the Middle Ages*, gen. ed. Joseph R. Strayer (13 vols, New York: Scribner, 1982–9), s.v. 'anthologies' by A. G. Rigg, 1:317.

43 See Paul Oskar Kristeller, *Medieval Aspects of Renaissance Learning: Three*

Essays, ed. and trans. Edward P. Mahoney, Duke Monographs on Medieval and Renaissance Studies, 1 (Durham, NC: Duke University Press, 1974), pp. 106–7.

44 See Charles B. Schmitt, *Aristotle and the Renaissance,* Martin Classical Lectures, 27 (Cambridge, Mass.: published for Oberlin College by Harvard University Press, 1983): 'Many students today rely on outlines, summaries, and textbook accounts of required readings; so too it was in the Renaissance. The set philosophical texts of the Renaissance university were various writings of Aristotle, usually read in Latin translation. Then, as today, a vast – even vaster – collection of supplementary literature grew up around the prescribed writings. Many of the forms were carryovers from the Middle Ages; on the other hand, the age of printing both allowed and encouraged the development of new types of interpretive literature. I estimate that the number of miscellaneous works of Aristotelian inspiration published from the beginning of printing to 1650 surpasses the number of editions of the text and the various translations taken together. These include commentaries, collections of *sententiae,* compendia, textbooks, orations, introductions, *quaestiones,* paraphrases, *tabulae,* independent treatises, theses, and several other types of works' (pp. 44–5).

45 See Charles B. Schmitt, 'Philosophy and science in sixteenth-century Italian universities', in *The Renaissance: Essays in Interpretation* (London and New York: Methuen, 1982; repr. London: Variorum, 1984), p. 315: 'The fundamental Aristotelian textbooks for Catholic Europe during the first third of the seventeenth century were the commentaries prepared by the Jesuits of the University of Coimbra.' See also Schmitt, 'Auctoritates, repertorium, dicta, sententiae, flores, thesaurus, and axiomata'.

46 An exaggerated use of university-based reading techniques, which reduced the literary production of authors by inciting them to cultivate the art of discussion, later inspired Descartes to return to the sources. Reading the canonical authors inspired Descartes to write 'meditations', a genre that contrasted strongly with the question method that had flourished during the Middle Ages, which had privileged argumentation over in-depth explication of a text based on personal reflection. Descartes explains his method in *Réponses aux secondes objections,* 9.122: 'That is why I wrote "Meditations" rather than "Disputations", as the philosophers have done, or "Theorems and Problems", as the geometers would have done. In so doing I wanted to make it clear that I would have nothing to do with anyone who was not willing to join me in meditating and giving the subject attentive consideration' (quoted here from 'Second Set of Replies', in *The Philosophical Writings of Descartes,* trans. John Cottingham, Robert Stoothoff and Dugald Murdoch (2 vols (Cambridge and New York: Cambridge University Press, 1984), 2:112).

47 See Joseph de Ghellinck, 'Un évêque bibliophile au XIVe siècle: Richard Aungerville de Bury (1345): Contribution à l'histoire de la littérature et des bibliothèques médiévales', *Revue d'histoire ecclésiastique,* 18 (1922): 271–312, 482–508. When he was bishop of Durham, Richard made the works in his library available to lettered fellow citizens: 'It is permissible to conclude that a good number of the works cited or used by the men of letters of Durham were accessible to them thanks to acquisitions made by the bibliophile bishop, and that one might, by conjecture (because the catalogue to that library seems to have been lost), reconstitute the contents of the shelves on the sciences, profane literature and philosophy' (p. 495).

48 Quoted in ibid., p. 505.
49 Martin, 'Pour une histoire de la lecture', p. 602. It is certainly not by chance that the followers of the *Devotio moderna* in northern Europe (Brothers of the Common Life and the canons of Windesheim) spearheaded a return to the monastic reading style. As heirs of a spiritual movement that had slowly taken root within the cloister and had reached out to the cultivated laity (whose numbers were increasing within the commercial middle class), the Brothers undertook to substitute individual meditation and direct contact with God for collective liturgical prayer. In that aim, many of their early works were inspired by certain patristic works. The style of reading they advocated was necessarily slow, given that the reader was expected to stop every few lines for self-interrogation and dialogue with God. The Latin of these texts continued the medieval tradition as well. Groups of this sort faced a problem when they tried to extend their teaching to other circles: one need only read the *Imitation of Christ*, for example, to see that access to such works was not easy, but rather required a constant manipulation of abstract notions. This explains why the Brothers of the Common Life (who, incidentally, often made their living as copyists) founded many secondary schools, and strove to provide a solid classical culture in them.

Chapter 5   Reading in the Later Middle Ages

1 P. Saenger, 'The separation of words and the order of words: the genesis of medieval reading', *Scrittura e Civiltà*, 14 (1990): 49–74.
2 See Monique-Cécile Garand, 'La scriptorium de Guibert de Nogent', *Scriptorium*, 31 (1977): 3–29, esp. p. 15 and plates 1–3; *idem*, 'Analyse d'écritures et macrophotographie: les manuscrits originaux de Guibert de Nogent', *Codices manuscripti*, 1 (1975): 112–23, esp. plates 1–3.
3 Rudolf Goy, *Die Überlieferung der Werke Hugos von St. Viktor*, Monographien zur Geschichte des Mittelalters, 14 (Stuttgart: 1976), p. 135, no. 8, and plate 2.
4 See Ernst S. Rothkopf, 'Incidental memory for information in text', *Journal of Verbal Learning and Verbal Behavior*, 10 (1971): 608–13.
5 Prologue to Hugh of Saint Victor's *De tribus maximis circumstantiis gestorum*, ed. William M. Green, in 'Hugo of Saint Victor: *De tribus maximis circumstantiis gestorum*', *Speculum*, 18 (1943): 490.
6 Charles Henry Buttimer, ed., *Hugh de Saint Victor: Didascalicon, de studio legendi*, Studies in Medieval and Renaissance Latin, 10 (Washington, DC: Catholic University Press, 1939), pp. 57–8.
7 Ibid., p. 58; cf. *Ars Victorini grammatici*, in Keil, *Grammatici latini*, 6:188.
8 Roger Baron, ed., *Hugonis de Sancto Victore opera propraedentica* (Notre Dame, Ind.: University of Notre Dame Press, 1966), p. 127.
9 Carlo de Clercq, 'Le *Liber de rota verae religionis* d'Hugues de Fouilloi', *Bulletin du Cange*, 29 (1959): 219–28, with two plates; *idem*, 'Hugues de Fouilloy imagier de ses propres oeuvres?', *Revue du nord*, 45 (1963) with four plates.
10 John of Salisbury, *Metalogicon*, i.24, ed. Clement C. J. Webb (Oxford: Clarendon Press, 1929), pp. 53–4.
11 Ibid., i.20.
12 Ibid., i.21; Webb edn, pp. 50–1.

13 See Monique-Cecilé Garand, 'Manuscrits monastiques et scriptoria aux XIe et XIIe siècles', in A. Gruys and J. P. Gumbert, eds, *Codicologica*, 3 (1980), pp. 16–18.

14 Microfilm, at the Institut de Recherche et d'Histoire des Textes; *France: Manuscrits datés*, vol. 5 (1965), 56 and plates 236 and 242. I am indebted to the staff of the IRHT for enabling me to consult the two volumes of this manuscript in Paris.

15 J.-M. Déchanet, 'Un recueil singulier d'opuscules de Guillaume de Saint-Thierry: Charleville 114', *Scriptorium*, 6 (1952): 196–212 and plates 24–5; idem, 'Les Divers etats du texte de la *Lettre aux Frères du Mont-Dieu* et le problème de la préface dans Charleville 114', *Scriptorium*, 11 (1957): 63–86 and plate 12; *France: Manuscrits datés*, 5 (1965), 43, 51 and plates 10–11.

16 See François Dolbeau, 'Anciens possesseurs des manuscrits hagiographiques latins conservés à la Bibliothèque Nationale de Paris', *Revue d'histoire des textes*, 9 (1979), plate 3. The examples cited by Dolbeau have been supplemented by a list kindly provided to me by Patricia Stirnemann.

17 A. H. Bredero, 'Un Brouillon du XIIe s.: l'autographe de Geoffroy d'Auxerre', *Scriptorium*, 13 (1958): 27–60 and plates 8–10.

18 Jean Leclercq, 'Iconographie de Saint Bernard', *Analecta S. Ord. Cisterciens Cisterciens.*, plate 2; idem, *Recueil des études sur Saint Bernard* (Rome: Edizioni di Storia e Letteratura, 1962–6), 1:9n3, 77, 215, 247, 263.

19 For reference to the appropriate plates, see Déchanet, 'Les divers états du texte', p. 85, n. 39.

20 These marks are present in Charleville, BM 196c. I am indebted to Mme Anne-Véronique Raynal for indicating them to me.

21 Richalm, *Liber revelationum de insidiis et versutiis daemonum adversus homines*; cf. Bernard Pez, *Thesaurus anectdorum novissimus* (Augsberg: M. and J. Veith, 1721–29), vol. 1, pt 2, col. 390.

22 See Usmer Berlière, *L'Ascèse bénédictine des origines à la fin du XIIIe siècle* (Paris: Desclée De Brouwer, 1927).

23 Jean Mabillon, *Sancti Bernardi abbatis primi clare-vallicensis Opera omnia* (Paris, 1690), 2:219–20.

24 *De interiore domo*, 24; in *PL*, 184, cols 520B–C, cited by Jean Leclercq, 'Aspect spirituel de la symbolique du livre au XIIe siècle', in *L'Homme devant Dieu: mélanges offerts au Père Henri de Lubac*, Études publiées sous la direction de la Faculté de théologie S. J. de Lyon-Fourvière, 56–8 (Paris: Aubier, 1963–4), 2:64. Absalon de Springkirsbach, *Sermo 25*; in *PL*, 211, col. 1518C, cited in ibid.

25 Richard Rouse, 'La diffusion en occident au XIIIe siècle des outils de travail facilitant l'accès aux textes autoritatifs', *Revue des études islamiques*, 44 (1976): 118 and 120–3.

26 Monique-Cécile Garand, 'Auteurs latins et autographes des XIe et XIIe siècles', *Scrittura e civiltà*, 5 (1981): 98 and plate 1.

27 Petrus Cellensis, *Tractatus de disciplina claustrali*, ch. 19 (*de lectione*); in *PL*, 202, cols 1125–6; Gérard de Martel, *Pierre de Celle: l'école de Cloître*, Sources chrétiennes, 240 (Paris: Cerf, 1977), pp. 233–6.

28 De Martel, *Pierre de Celle*, pp. 74–8 with two plates.

29 Gérard de Martel, 'Recherches sur les manuscrits des sermons de Pierre de Celle', *Scriptorium*, 33 (1979): 3–17 and plate 1.

30 Léopold Delisle, *Matériaux pour l'édition de Guillaume de Jumièges préparée par Jules Lair* (s.l., 1910), pp. 485–7.

31 Quintilian, *Institutiones oratoriae* 10.3.19–20.

392   Notes to Pages 126–8

32 Edmond René Labande, *Guibert de Nogent: autobiographie* (Paris: Belles lettres, 1981), pp. 136–9.
33 Ibid., pp. 144–5.
34 *PL*, 156.340.
35 See Garand, 'Auteurs latins et autographes', pp. 88–97.
36 Labande, *Guibert de Nogent*, pp. 136–7.
37 André Boutemy, 'Odon d'Orléans et les origines de la bibliothèque de l'abbaye de Saint-Martin de Tournai', in *Mélanges dédiés à la mémoire de Félix Grat* (2 vols, Paris, 1946–9), 2:179–222. For an example of the scriptorium of Saint-Martin's, see Paris, BN NAL 2195; *France: Manuscrits datés*, 4/1 (1981), 231 and plate 17. *Prosodiae* include *traits d'union* and acute accents to denote the double *ii*. Paris, BN NAL 2195, a Psalter copied at Saint-Martin's in 1107, was canonically separated with *prosodiae* including *traits d'union* and the acute accent on the double *ii*.
38 Josephus-Maria Canivez, ed., *Statuta capitulorum generalium ordinis cisterciensis* (8 vols, Louvain: Bureaux de la Revue, 1933–41), i:26.
39 Jean Leclercq, 'Saint Bernard et ses secrétaires', *Revue bénédictine*, 61 (1951): 208–28; cf. Bernard, *Epistula*, 89; in *PL*, 182, cols 220–1.
40 R. W. Southern, ed., *The Life of Saint Anselm Archbishop of Canterbury by Eadmer* (London: T. Nelson, 1962), pp. viii–xxiv; *idem, Saint Anselm and his Biographer: A Study of Monastic Life and Thought 1059–1130* (Cambridge: Cambridge University Press, 1963), pp. 367–74; the frontispiece is a plate of the first leaf of the text.
41 For an overview, see P. Bloch, 'Autorenbild', in Engelbert Kirschbaum, ed., *Lexikon der christlichen Ikonographie*, vol. 1 (Rome: Herder, 1968), pp. 232–4.
42 Wolfram von den Steinen, *Notker der Dichter und seine geistige Welt* (Bern: A. Francke, 1948), vol. 2, plates 1–3.
43 Jean Leclercq, 'Aspects littéraires de l'oeuvre de Saint Bernard', *Cahiers de civilisation médiévale*, 1 (1958): 440 and plates 3 and 4.
44 S. J. P. Van Dijk, *The Myth of the Aumbry: Notes on Medieval Reservation Practice and Eucharistic Devotion with Special Reference to the Findings of Dom Gregory Dix* (London: Burns and Oates), p. 80, plate 10.
45 John J. O'Meara, 'Giraldus Cambrensis: In topographia Hiberniae', *Proceedings of the Royal Irish Academy*, 52C4 (1949): 151–2.
46 Examples include the Gospels of Henry III, Bremen, Universitätsbibliothek b. 21, originating from Echternach; facsimile (Wiesbaden, *c.*1980); Paris, BN lat. 8551, fol. 1, a Gospel Book from Trèves written in 1002–14; *France: Manuscrits datés*, 3 (1974), 87; reproduction, Paris, BN Collection Porcher; Reims, BM 9, fol. 23, reproduction, Paris, BN Collection Porcher.
47 Luba Eleen, *The Illustrations of the Pauline Epistles in French and English Bibles of the Twelfth and Thirteenth Centuries* (Oxford: Clarendon Press, 1982), plates 54, 55, 59, 61, 100.
48 *Beschreibendes Verzeichnis der Illuminierten Handschriften in Österreich*, 4/2 (1911), plates 58 and 60.
49 Pierre Petitmengin and Bernard Flusin, 'Le livre antique et la dictée: nouvelles recherches', in *Mémorial André-Jean Festugière: antiquité païenne et chrétienne*, ed. Enzo Lucchesi and H. D. Saffrey, Cahiers d'orientalisme, 10 (Geneva: Droz, 1984), pp. 247–62, plates 61, 71 and 103; A. I. Doyle, 'Further observations on Durham Cathedral MS A.IV.34', in *Litterae Tex-*

tuales: Essays Presented to G. I. Lieftinck, ed. J. P. Gumbert and M. J. M. De Haan (Amsterdam: Van Gendt, 1972–6),1:35–47.

50 Neil R. Ker, 'Copying an exemplar: two manuscripts of Jerome on Habakkuk', in *Miscellanea codicologica F. Massai dicata*, ed. Pierre Cockshaw, Monique-Cécile Garand and Pierre Jodogne, Les publications de Scriptorium, 8 (Ghent: E. Story Scientia, 1979), 1:203–10 and plates 30–3.

51 Waitz, ed., *Hermani liber de restauratione s. Martini Tornacensis*, in *MGH: Scriptores*, vol. 14 (1983), pp. 312–13.

52 *Lexikon der Christlichen Ikonographie* (Rome: Herder, 1968–76), 6:442, 446.

53 See Paul Saenger, 'Word separation and its implications for manuscript production', in the proceedings of the Wolfenbüttel seminar of 12–14 Nov. 1990, in *Die Rationalisierung der Buchherstellung im Mittelalter und in der frühen Neuzeit*, ed. Peter Rück, (Marburg an der Lahn: Institut für Historische Hilfswissenschaften, 1994).

54 See, for example, Dorothee Klein, 'Autorenbild', in *Reallexikon zur deutschen Kunstgeschichte*, vol. 1 (Stuttgart, 1937), p. 1312; Paris, BN lat. 415, fol. 1.

55 For a plate of a well-spaced stationer's exemplar, see Louis J. Bataillon, Bertrand G. Guyot and Richard H. Rouse, *La Production du livre universitaire au moyen âge: exemplar et pecia* (Paris: CNRS, 1988). Vernacular exemplars were similarly well separated; see, for example, Paris, BN fr. 794 (s. xiii in.), described by Mario Roques, 'Le manuscrit français 794 de la Bibliothèque Nationale et le scribe Guiot', *Romania*, 73 (1952): 177–99. I am indebted to Geneviève Hasenohr for this reference.

56 Petrarch, *Epistolae familiares*, xxiii, 19, ed. G. Martelotti, in *Petrarca: Prose* (Milan: A. Ricciardi, 1955), p. 1016; *Epistolae variae*, xv, ed. Joseph Fracassetti, in *Francisci Petrarcae: Epistolae de rebus familiaribus et variae* (3 vols, Florence: Le Monnier, 1859–63), 3:332–3; Conrad H. Rawski, *Petrarch: Four Dialogues for Scholars* (Cleveland, OH.: Press of Western Reserve University, 1967), pp. 78 and 138.

57 For examples, see Paris, BN lat. 1160, fol. 3 and London, BL Add. 20694, fol. 189 (St Mark); Janet Backhouse, *Book of Hours* (London: British Library, 1986), p. 20, plate 13.

58 Harry Levin and Ann Buckler Addis, *The Eye–Voice Span* (Cambridge, Mass.: MIT Press, 1979), pp. 71–6 and 79.

59 In the use of imposition, texts were copied in out-of-sense sequence; see G. I. Lieftinck, 'Mediaeval manuscripts with imposed sheets', *Het Boek*, ser. 3, 34 (1960–1): 210–20; Pieter Obbema, 'Writing on uncut sheets', *Quaerendo*, 7 (1978): 337–54. For related earlier examples of mechanical copying, see W. M. Lindsay, *Palaeographia latina*, 2:26–8 and 4:84–5; Doyle, 'Further observations on Durham Cathedral MS AIV. 34'.

60 Robert J. Scholes, 'On the orthographic basis of linguistic constructs: morphology', in *Literacy and Language Analysis*, ed. R. J. Scholes (Hillsdale, NJ: Erlbaum, 1993).

61 G. L. Bursil-Hall, *Speculative Grammars of the Middle Ages* (The Hague, Mouton, 1971), pp. 258 and 276; *idem, Thomas of Erfurt: Grammatica speculativa: An Edition with Translation and Commentary* (London: Longman, 1972), pp. 56, 57, 91–3.

62 Johannes de Balbis, *Catholicon* (Mainz, n.d.), ff. 12, 18, 24.

63 See Charles Thurot, 'Notices et extraits de divers manuscrits latins pour

servier à l'histoire des doctrines grammaticales au moyen âge', *Notices et extraits des manuscrits de la Bibliothèque nationale et autres bibliothèques*, 22/2 (1868): 341–50.

64 Remigio Sabbadini, 'Sulla Constructio', *Revista di filogia e d'instruzione classica*, 25 (1897): 102. See also Paris, BN lat. 11386, fol. 30 (s. 14); Thurot, 'Notices et extraits', p. 344.

65 For an example, see C. H. Talbot, 'The archetypes of Saint Bernard's *Sermons super Cantica*', *Scriptorium*, 8 (1954): 231.

66 In commentaries on Aristotle's discussion in the *De sophisticis elenchis* of the fallacies of composition and division, modist grammarians set forth the rule, lifted out of context from Priscian, that adjectives naturally preceded nouns, and adverbs naturally preceded verbs, reducing the ambiguity of written prose much as *prosodiae* reduced the ambiguity of the individual word; Alain de Libera, 'De la logique à la grammaire: Remarques sur la théorie de la détermination chez Roger Bacon et Lambert d'Auxerre' in *De Ortu Grammaticae: Studies in Medieval Grammar and Linguistic Theory in Memory of Jan Pinborg*, ed. G. L. Bursill-Hall, Sten Ebbesen and Konrad Koerner, Studies in the History of Language (Amsterdam: J. Benjamins, 1990), pp. 209–26.

67 Jacques Monfrin, 'Les traducteurs et leur public en France au moyen âge', in *L'Humanisme médiéval dans les littératures romanes du XIIe au XIVe siècle: Colloque organisé par le Centre de Philologie et de la Littérature romane de l'Université de Strasbourg du 29 janvier au 2 février 1962*, ed. Anthime Fourrier, Actes et Colloques, 3 (Paris: Klincksieck, 1964), p. 261.

68 This process has been studied by modern psychologists and psycholinguists; see Samuel Fillenbaum, 'Memory for gist: some relevant variables', *Language and Speech*, 9 (1966): 217–27; Jacqueline Struck Sachs, 'Recognition memory for syntactic and semantic aspects of connected discourse', *Perception and Psychophysics*, 2 (1967): 437–42; John R. Anderson, 'Verbatim and prepositional representation of sentences in immediate and long-term memory', *Journal of Verbal Learning and Verbal Behavior*, 13 (1974): 149–62; Eric Wanner, *On Remembering, Forgetting, and Understanding Sentences: A Study of the Deep Structure Hypothesis*, Janua linguarum, series minor, 170 (The Hague: Mouton, 1974).

69 For examples of this proto-cursive writing, see the writing of Albertus Magnus, in S. Harrison Thomson, *Latin Bookhands of the Later Middle Ages* (Cambridge: Cambridge University Press, 1969), no. 38; cf. that of Thomas Aquinas, in Antoine Dondaine, *Secrétaires de Saint Thomas* (Rome: S. Tommases, 1956), plates 36–8.

70 Albert d'Haenens, 'Écrire en couteau dans la main gauche: un aspect de la physiologie de l'écriture occidentale au XIe et XIIe siècles', in Rita Lejeune and Joseph Deckers, eds, *Clio et son regard: Mélanges d'histoire de l'art et d'archéologie offerts à Jacques Stiennon à l'occasion de ses vingt-cinq ans d'enseignement à l'université de Liège* (Liège: 1982), pp. 129–41; Obbema, 'Writing on uncut sheets', p. 353. The frontispiece of the Pierpont Morgan Library manuscripts of the *Bible moralisée* shows a scribe holding the page with his knife as he writes to dictation.

71 Jean Porcher, *Medieval French Miniatures*, trans. Julian Brown (New York: Abrams, 1960), p. 93.

72 Nicolas of Lyra, prologue to his *Postillae* on the book of Genesis, *Postilla super totam Bibliam* (Strassburg, 1492); repr. Frankfurt, 1971), fol. Ci^v.

73 '[N]ihilominus testimonium perhibeo vobis quale positum est in epistola mea Ad fratres de Monte Dei quod Scripturas Sacras nullus unquam plene intelliget qui non affectus scribentium induerit': Jean Gerson, *Oeuvres complètes*, ed. P. Glorieux (10 vols, Paris: Desclée, 1960), 5:334.

74 Humbert of Romans, *Expositio Regulae B. Augustini*, in Joachim Joseph Berthier, *Humbertus de Romanis: Opera de vita regulari* (2 vols, Rome: A. Befanier, 1888–9), 1:186.

75 *Chartularium Universitatis Parisiensis*, ed. H. Denifle and E. Châtelain (4 vols, Paris, 1889–97), 1:386; César Egasse du Boulary, *Historia Universitatis Parisiensis* (Paris, 1665–1773), 4:159; Hastings Rashdall, *The Universities of Europe in the Middle Ages*, ed. F. M. Powicke and A. B. Emden (Oxford: Clarendon Press, 1936), p. 423, nn. 1–2.

76 Pierre Dubois, *De recuperatione Terre Sancte*, ed. Angelo Diotti (Florence, L. S. Olschki, 1977), p. 163.

77 In 1271, Jean d'Orléans, chancellor of Notre-Dame, mentions 'libros tradendos et recuperandos pauperibus scolaribus in theologica studentibus'; Alfred Franklin, *Les Anciennes Bibliothèques de Paris* (Paris, 1867–73), 1:8, n. 5; cf. 1:9, n. 1; Rashdall, *Universities of Europe*, p. 423. At the Sorbonne in the fifteenth century, thirty manuscripts of the *Sentences* of Peter of Lombard were available for borrowing; see Jeanne Vielliard, 'Le registre de prêt de la bibliothèque du Collège de Sorbonne au XVᵉ siècle', *Mediaevalia Lovaniensia*, 6 (1978): 291.

78 A. Tuilier, 'La bibliothèque de la Sorbonne et les livres enchâinés', *Mélanges de la Bibliothèque de la Sorbonne*, 2 (1981): 22–3 and 26.

79 Cf. James J. Murphy, 'The double revolution of the first rhetorical textbook published in England: the *Margarita eloquentiae* of Gulielmus Traversagnus (1479)', *Texte: Revue de critique et de théorie littéraire* (1989), pp. 367–76.

80 The *Regiensis Livy*, Vat. reg. lat. 792, for example, had not been divided into chapters.

81 L. D. Reynolds, *Texts and Transmissions: A Survey of the Latin Classics* (Oxford: Clarendon Press, 1983), p. 209.

82 Malcolm B. Parkes, 'The influence of the concepts of *ordinatio* and *compilatio* on the development of the book', *Medieval Learning and Literature: Essays Presented to Richard William Hunt*, ed. J. J. G. Alexander and M. T. Gibson (Oxford: Clarendon Press, 1976), pp. 124–5; Daniel A. Callus, 'The Tabula super originalia patrum' of Robert Kilwardby O.P.', in *Studia medievalia in honorem R. J. Martin* (Bruges: De Tempe, 1948), pp. 243–70; Richard W. Hunt, 'Chapter headings of Augustine *De trinitate* ascribed to Adam Marsh', *Bodleian Library Record*, 5 (1954): 63.

83 Parkes, 'Concepts of *ordinatio* and *compilatio*', pp. 118–22; Richard H. Rouse and Mary A. Rouse, *Preachers, Florilegia and Sermons: Studies on the Manipulus florum of Thomas of Ireland* (Toronto: Pontifical Institute of Medieval Studies, 1979), pp. 7–36.

84 Robert Marichal, 'L'Écriture latine et la civilisation occidentale', L'Écriture et la psychologie des peuples (Paris: A Colin, 1963), pp. 237–40; Parkes, 'Concepts of *ordinatio* and *compilatio*', p. 121; *idem, Pause and Effect: An Introduction to the History of Punctuation in the West* (Aldershot: Scolar Press, 1992; Berkeley: University of California Press, 1993), p. 44.

85 Paris, BN lat. 4436 and lat. 4523.

86 For example, the *Tragedies* of Seneca copied in 11397, Paris, BN

lat. 8824. This system was used to attach Nicolas of Lyra's *Postillae* to the text of the Bible in the Strasbourg edition of 1492 (see above, n. 72).

87 D. F. McKenzie, 'Speech–Manuscript–Print', in *New Directions in Textual Studies*, ed. D. Oliphant and R. Bradford (Austin, Tex.: Harry Ransom Humanities Research Center, University of Texas at Austin, 1990), p. 104.

88 Paul Saenger and Michael Heinlen, 'Incunable description and its implications for the analysis of fifteenth-century reading habits', in *Printing the Written Word: The Social History of Books, c.1450–1520*, ed. Sandra Hindman (Ithaca, NY: Cornell University Press, 1992), p. 249.

89 Paul of Burgos, *Additiones ad postillam Nicolai de Lyra*, could be used only in this manner. For manuscripts of this text, see Friedrich Stegmüller, *Repertorium Biblicum medii aevi* (11 vols, Madrid, 1940–61), 4:197.

90 Georges Dogaear and Marguerite Debae, *La Librairie de Philippe le Bon: Exposition organisée à l'occasion du 500ᵉ anniversaire de la mort du duc* (Brussels: Bibliothèque Albert Ier, 1967), plate 33.

91 Malcolm B. Parkes, 'Tachygraphy in the Middle Ages: writing techniques employed for *Reportationes* of lectures and sermons', *Medioev e Rinascimento*, 3 (1989): 159–69.

92 For an Italian example of the fourteenth century, see Astrik L. Gabriel, *Garlandia: Studies in the History of the Mediaeval University* (Frankfurt: Knecht, 1969), plate 25; for a French example of the thirteenth and fourteenth centuries, Paris, Bibliothèque de la Sorbonne 31, fol. 278, reproduced on the cover of the exhibition catalogue *La Vie Universitaire parisienne au XIIIᵉ siècle* (Paris: Bibliothèque de la Sorbonne, 1974); Astrik L. Gabriel, *Student Life in Ave Maria College, Mediaeval Paris: History and Chartulary of the College*, Publications in Mediaeval Studies, 14 (Notre Dame, Ind.: University of Notre Dame Press, 1955), plates 25 and 26. Duns Scotus was painted in the fourteenth century instructing students with books; Jacques Guy Bougerol, *Saint Bonaventure et la sagesse chrétienne* (Paris: Seuil, 1963), p. 150. In the second half of the fifteenth century, the same iconography of the classroom is common in early printed books; see, for example, Guilhelmus of Gouda as a teacher: Leonide Mees, *Bio-bibliographia Franciscana neerlandica ante saeculum XVI* (3 vols, Nieuwkoop: B. De Graaf, 1974), 3:77, ill. 92.

93 A. Van Hove, 'La bibliothèque de la faculté des arts de l'Université de Louvain', in *Mélanges d'histoire offerts à Charles Moeller à l'occasion de son jubilé de 50 années de professorat à l'Université de Louvain 1863–1913* (2 vols, Louvain: Bureau du Recueil, 1914), 1:616. See also Gerhardt Powitz, 'Modus scolipetarum et reportistarum: pronuntiatio and fifteenth-century university hands', *Scrittura e civiltà*, 12 (1988): 201–11.

94 The university wanted the professor to lecture in the manner of a preacher delivering a sermon: *Chartularium Universitatis Parisiensis*, 3:39, 642 and 646. In the fourteenth and fifteenth centuries, the iconography of the preacher differed from that of the professor in that the preacher was usually shown speaking extemporaneously without a written text before him; see, for examples, Paris, BN lat. 646B, fol. 1; lat. 17294, fols 65ᵛ and 66ᵛ; lat. 17716., fol. 43; fr. 147, fol. 1; fr. 177, fol. 315; fr. 244, fol. 1; and fr. 824, fol. 1. The effort to enliven the style of lecturing seems not to have taken hold, and in 1454, Cardinal Estouteville rescinded the prohibition of *legere ad pennam* – that is, reading lectures word for word: *Chartularium Universitatis Parisiensis*, 4:727.

95 Jean Destrez, *La Pecia dans les manuscrits universitaires du XIIIe et du XIVe siècle* (Paris: J. Vautrain, 1935); Bataillon, Guyot and Rouse, *La Production du livre universitaire au moyen âge.*

96 At the University of Bologna in the fourteenth century, doctors disputing questions were obliged to deposit their manuscripts for inspection and transcription: H. Denifle, *Archiv für Literature- und Kirchengeschichte des Mittelalters* (Graz, 1955–6), 4:321–2. At Angers the lectures of the professor were made available for transcription by the library of the university: Célestin Port, 'La bibliothèque de l'Université d'Angers', in *Notes et notices angevines* (Angers: 1879), p. 34. The documents first published by Port have been re-edited by Marcel Fournier: *Les Statuts et privilèges des universités françaises*, vol. 1 (Paris: Laresse et Force, 1890), pp. 387–9. The hypothesis of transcriptions being made prior to oral presentation has been dismissed out of hand by Kantorowicz (see n. above), but it would account for medieval miniatures which appear to show students silently reading from the very texts from which the professor is lecturing: for example, Paris, BN lat. 14023, fols 2 and 123. In about 1300, an English theologian requested his pupils to submit their arguments in writing before redacting his lecture, an indication of the degree to which graphic communication may have paralleled and even anticipated oral presentation: P. Glorieux, *La Littérature quodlibétique* (Kain Revue des Philosophiques et Theologiques 1925–35), 1:52. On the relationship between oral arguments and their published versions, see also Jean Acher, 'Six disputations et un fragment d'une répétition orléanaises', in *Mélanges Fitting* (Montpellier, 1907), 2:300–1. In French law courts, written arguments also regularly amplified oral presentations. In the mid-fifteenth century, Thomas Basin suggested that the oral arguments were therefore superfluous and could be discontinued; see P. Guilhiermoz, 'De la persistance du caractère oral dans la procédure civile française', *Nouvelle revue historique de droit français et étranger*, 13 (1889): 21–65. The written pleas were especially needed in cases too complex to be understood orally. The court used the terms *dit de bouche* and *dit en escriptures* to distinguish between the two modes of presenting arguments, the logical structure of which closely paralleled the scholastic *quaestiones* of the law schools. The task of recording the oral pleas was assigned to a scribe and not to the reporter, who was one of the judges.

97 See, for example, Gozzoli's portrait of Saint Bonaventure: Bougerol, *Saint Bonaventure*, p. 163, and the representation of *scientia*, Paris, BN fr. 541, fol. 108. In the sixteenth century, Geoffrey Whitney chose as an emblem of silence the scholar dressed in an academic gown poring over an open book: Raymond B. Waddington, 'The iconography of silence and Chapman's *Hercules*', *Journal of the Warburg and Courtauld Institutes*, 33 (1970): 97.

98 Martin Grabmann, 'Abkürzende Bearbeitungen der Aristotelischen Schriften: *Abbreviationes, Summulae, Compendia, Epitomata*', in *Sitzungsberichte der Bayerischen Akademie der Wissenschaften: Philosophisch-historische Abteilung*, pt 5 (1939), pp. 54–104. Nicolas of Lyra stated specifically that the differences between the Hebrew Old Testament and the Vulgate, noted in the *Postillae*, could be more easily read (*expeditius videri*) in his *Tractatus de differentia*: Herman Hailperin, *Rashi and the Christian Scholars* (Pittsburgh: University of Pittsburgh Press, 1963), p. 285, n. 22.

99 Dubois, *De recuperatione Terre Sancte*, p. 163.

100 Hailperin, *Rashi and the Christian Scholars*, p. 139.

101 The customary of the Augustinian convent of Springiersbach-Rolduc, written *c.*1229, described as sub-audible singing and reading what we would call mumbling or murmuring that did not violate the silence: Stephanus   Weinfürter,   *Consuetudines   canonicorum   regularium Springirsbacenses Rodenses*, CCCM 48 (Turnhout: Brepols, 1978), pp. 18, 67, 78, 82, 101. The *Liber Ordinis Sancti Victoris Parisiensis* set down rules for small groups of monks to practice liturgical recitation and the singing of psalms in a relatively quiet manner which was held not to violate the general silence: Luc Jocqué and Ludo Milis, *Liber ordinis Victoris Parisiensis*, CCCM 61 (Turnhout: Brepols, 1984), pp. 145, 147 and 149.

102 John W Clark, *The Care of Books* (Cambridge: Cambridge University Press, 1961), pp. 145–64. For a fifteenth-century miniature depicting such a library, see François Dolbeau, 'Les usagers des bibliothèques', in *Histoire des bibliothèques françaises*, vol. 1, ed. André Vernet (Paris: Promodis, 1989), p. 394.

103 H. W. Garrod, 'The library regulations of a medieval college', *Library*, ser. 4, 8 (1927): 315. For the growth of reference collections, see the bibliography provided by Richard H. Rouse, 'The early library of the Sorbonne', *Scriptorium*, 21 (1967): 60.

104 Rouse, 'Early Library of the Sorbonne', p. 59.

105 Van Hove, 'La bibliothèque de la faculté des arts de l'Université de Louvain', pp. 602–25.

106 Léopold Delisle, *Le Cabinet des manuscrits de la Bibliothèque nationale* (3 vols, Paris: Imprimerie Nationale, 1868–91), 2:181, no. 6.

107 See the statutes of the library of the University of Angers: Port, 'La bibliothèque de l'université d'Angers', p. 28, and of Oxford: Henry Anstey, *Munimenta academica* (London: Longmans, 1868) 1:263–6.

108 F. J. McGuigan and W. I. Rodier, 'Effects of auditory stimulation on covert oral behavior during silent reading', *Journal of Experimental Psychology*, 76 (1965): 649–55; Robert W. Weisberg, *Memory, Thought, and Behavior* (New York: Oxford University Press, 1980), pp. 235–6, cf. pp. 159–60. In ancient libraries, oral reading was an accepted practice; see Optatus, bishop of Mileve, *Contra Parmenianum Donatistam*, 7.1; ed. Karl Ziusa, CSEL, 26 (Vienna, 1893), p. 165.

109 Berthier, *Humbertus de Romanis*, 1:421; K. W. Humphreys, *The Book Provisions of the Medieval Friars* (Amsterdam: Erasmus Booksellers, 1964), p. 136.

110 Anstey, *Munimenta academica*, 1:263–4.

111 Port, 'La bibliothèque de l'université d'Angers', p. 31.

112 Delisle, *Le Cabinet des manuscrits*, 2:201, correctly asserted that the text as given in Claude Héméré's manuscript *Sorbonae origines* dated from the establishment of a new building for the library *c.*1483. However, the inference drawn by Delisle that these rules were intended solely for printed books is not supported by fifteenth-century documentary evidence. Precedents for each of the Sorbonne regulations can be found in rules established for the fifteenth century. Moreover, in 1493, the Sorbonne library was still acquiring manuscript books; see Franklin, *Les Anciennes Bibliothèques de Paris*, 1:256, n. 8. Manuscript and printed books were regularly

intermixed in medieval libraries: see Dominique Coq, 'L'incunable, un bâtard du manuscrit', *Gazette du livre médiéval*, 1 (1981): 10–11.

113 Eugène Müntz, *La Bibliothèque du Vatican au XVe siècle d'après des documents inédits* (Paris, 1887), p. 140.

114 Rouse and Rouse, *Preachers, Florilegia and Sermons*; Pieter F. J. Obbema, 'The Rooklooster register evaluated', *Quaerendo*, 7 (1977): 325–53.

115 Saenger and Heinlen, 'Incunable description', pp. 239–50.

116 At Oxford, Angers and Paris: Anstey, *Munimenta academica*, 1:139–40; Port, 'La bibliothèque de l'université d'Angers', p. 32; Delisle, *Le Cabinet des manuscrits*, 2:201.

117 P. Saenger, 'Coupure et séparation des mots sur le Continent', in *La Mise en page et mise en texte du livre manuscrit*, ed. Henri-Jean Martin and Jean Vezin (Paris: Cercle de la Libraire–Promodis, 1990), pp. 450–5.

118 After 1320, the quodlibet was no longer an important vehicle for discussing controversial issues. All of Ockham's writings were circulated as private tracts, and were not intended for oral delivery to students in the classroom. On the demise of the quodlibet, see Gordon Leff, *Paris and Oxford Universities in the Thirteenth and Fourteenth Centuries: An Institutional and Intellectual History* (New York: Wiley, 1968), p. 249.

119 It was perhaps for this reason that in 1259 the Dominicans forbade bringing to class any book other than the one being read by the professor in his lecture: *Chartularium Universitatis Parisiensis*, 1:386.

120 Anne Hudson, 'A Lollard quaternion', *Review of English Studies*, n.s. 22 (1971): 442.

121 *Chartularium Universitatis Parisiensis*, 1:486 and 543.

122 Ibid., 2:271.

123 Ibid., 2:576.

124 See n. 106 above.

125 Robert Gaguin reported the chaining of the books in a letter sent to Guillaume Fichet: Charles Samaran et al., *Auctarium chartularii Universitatis Parisiensis*, vol. 3 (Paris: Delalain, 1935), pp. 259–60. Gaguin's report is confirmed by a letter of 1479 of Jean d'Estouteville to the rector of the University of Paris: 'Le Roy m'a chargé faire decloüer et defermer tous les livres de Nominaux qui ja pieça furent sceelez et cloüez par M. d'Avranches ès colleges de la dite Université à Paris et que je vous fisse sçavoir que chascun y estudiast qui voudrait': du Boulay, *Historia Universitatis Parisiensis*, 5:739.

126 Geoffroy of Beaulieu, *Sancti Ludovici vita*, in *Recueil des historiens des Gaules et de la France*, vol. 20 (Paris, 1840), pp. 14–15; idem, *Vie de Saint Louis par le confesseur de la reine Marguerite*, ibid., pp. 79–80.

127 Bernard Guenée, 'La culture historique des nobles: le succès des *Faits des Romains*, XIIIe–XVe siècles', in *La Noblesse au moyen âge XIe–XVe siècles: essais à la mémoire de Robert Boutruche*, ed. Philippe Contamine (Paris: Presses Universitaires de France, 1976), p. 268.

128 Gaston Paris and A. Jeanroy have written of the *Chronique* of Villehardouin that it has 'l'air d'avoir été parlé, comme il était destiné à être écouté': Paris and Jeanroy, *Extraits des chroniqueurs français* (Paris, 1912), p. 6.

129 Joinville speaks of having 'fait escrire' his book *Histoire de Saint Louis*, ch. 1. He expected his book to be read aloud to listeners who would 'orrez': ch. 7 and *passim*. The author of the *Roman de Lancelot* is shown

in a miniature dictating: Paris, BN fr. 342, fol. 150, copied in 1274. In 1298, Marco Polo dictated *La Description du monde*, ed. Louis Hambis (Paris: Klincksieck, 1955), p. 2.

130 Only this process explains the textual variants, such as transposition of lines and stanzas, found in Provençal poetry. Guillaume de Machaut described this process of oral composition and dictation when he declared in the *Livre du voir-dit*, 'Quant j'eus fiat le dit et le chant, ... Je le fis escrire et noter': ed. Paulin Paris (Paris, 1875), p. 80. A thirteenth-century Spanish miniature depicts the *Cantigas* in praise of Holy Mary being dictated to a scribe: Robert I. Burns, 'Christian-Islamic Confrontation in the West,' *American Historical Review*, 76 (1971): 1416 (bottom left). Portraits also exist of scribes who appear to be taking down troubadour lyrics: Hendrik Van der Werf, *The Chansons of the Troubadours and Trouvères* (Utrecht: A. Oosthoek, 1972), plates 3 and 4.

131 See the recent discussion of twelfth-century Provençal texts by Laura Kendrick, *The Game of Love: Troubadour Wordplay* (Berkeley: University of California Press, 1988), p. 35. An analogous phenomenon is the difficulty in separating words when writing which early twentieth-century French peasants evinced; see Marcel Jousse, *L'Anthropologie du geste* (Paris, Gallimard, 1974–8), 1:340.

132 Dag Norberg, *Manuel pratique de Latin médiéval* (Paris: Picard, 1968), p. 90.

133 See Kendrick, *Game of Love*, pp. 31–2 and 195–6.

134 *Fillastre* and *maistre* are good examples; the 's' was no longer pronounced at the end of the Middle Ages.

135 In French, *devoir* became *debvoir*; *fevre* became *febvre*. In English, the 'b' was introduced into debt. See Albert C. Baugh, *A History of the English Language* (New York: Appleton, 1957), p. 250, and J. Vachek, 'English orthography: a functionalist approach', in W. Haas, ed., *Standard Languages, Spoken and Written* (Manchester: Manchester University Press, 1982), pp. 37–56. Under the influence of humanism, departures from phonetic orthography in French reached their zenith in the first half of the sixteenth century, but began to disappear after 1550, when Jacques Peletier, Louis Meigret and Jean Antoine Baif led a campaign for the restoration of spelling that accurately expressed the sounds of words.

136 For an example, see Paris, BN fr. 794, described by Roques, 'Le manuscrit français 794 de la Bibliothèque nationale et le scribe Guiot', Romania, 73 (1952).

137 Paul Saenger, 'Colard Mansion and the evolution of the printed Book', *Library Quarterly*, 45 (1975): 405–18.

138 D. J. A. Ross, *Alexander Historiatus: A Guide to Medieval Illustrated Alexander Literature* (London: Warburg Institute, 1963), pp. 69–71.

139 Monfrin, 'Les traducteurs et leur public en France au moyen âge', p. 255.

140 Georges Tessier, *Diplomatique royale française* (Paris: Picard, 1962), p. 305.

141 Louis XI empowered his secretaries to imitate his hand in order to speed the flow of letters: Joseph Vaesen and Étienne Charavay, *Lettres de Louis XI roi de France* (Paris: Société de l'histoire de France, 1909), p. vi; Robert Henri Bautier, 'Les notaires et secrétaires du roi des origines au milieu du XVIe siècle', in André Lapeyre and Rémy Scheurer, eds, *Les Notaires et secrétaires du rois sous les règnes de Louis XI, Charles VIII et Louis XII:*

notices personnelles et généalogies (Paris: Bibliothèque Nationale, 1978), p. xxvii.

142 Tessier, *Diplomatique royale française*, frontispiece.

143 Pierre Bersuire's translation of Livy's *History of Rome* and Jean of Sy's translation of the Bible with Latin commentary are the principal literary monuments of King John's reign; see Delisle, *Le Cabinet des manuscrits*, 1:16.

144 Monfrin, 'Les traducteurs et leur public en France au moyen âge', pp. 260–2.

145 Delisle, *Le Cabinet des manuscrits*, 1:201; Claire Richter Sherman, *The Portraits of Charles V of France (1338–80)* (New York: New York University Press, 1969), p. 13.

146 Sherman, *Portraits of Charles V*, fig. 11. Cf. a miniature depicting King Solomon as a teacher: Rosy Schilling, 'The master of Egerton 1070: hours of René d'Anjou', *Scriptorium*, 8 (1954): plate 26.

147 Paul Saenger, 'Books of hours and the reading habits of the later Middle Ages', *Scrittura e Civiltà*, 14 (1990): 153.

148 On the vocabulary for monastic reading, see S. J. P. van Dijk, 'Medieval terminology and methods of psalm singing', *Musica Disciplina*, 6 (1952): 9–10; Carolo A. Lewis, *The Silent Recitation of the Canon of the Mass*, Excerpta ex dissertatione ad Lauream in Facultate Theologica Universitatis Gregorianae (Bay Saint Louis, Miss., 1962); Saenger, 'Books of hours', pp. 143–5.

149 Saenger, 'Books of hours', p. 146; Jouvenal des Ursins stated that he had been instructed by Charles VII to go 'en vos chambres des comptes, du Trésor de vos chartres et ailleurs pour veoir les lettres et chartres necessaires' for writing the *Traictie compendieux contre les Anglois*: cited by P. S. Lewis, 'War propaganda and historiography in fifteenth-century France and England', *Transactions of the Royal Historical Society* (1965), p. 16.

150 For Christine de Pisan as a writer, see Paris, BN fr. 603, fol. 1; fr. 835, fol. 1; and fr. 1176, fol. 1. For Froissart, see BN fr. 86, fol. 11.

151 Dogaear and Debae, *La Libraire de Philippe le Bon*, plate 39.

152 Jean Barthelemay used *écrire* in this sense: Paris, BN fr. 9611, fol. 1. Jean du Chesne, in the prologue to his translation of the *Commentaries* of Julius Caesar, referred to the 'Commentaries que César mesmes escript de sa main', and qualified Caesar as an 'escripvain': BL, Royal 16 G. viii. Lefèvre, *L'Histoire de Jason* (Frankfurt-am-Main: Athenäum, 1971), p. 125, referred to Philip the Good of Burgundy as the 'père des escripvains'. In the mid-fourteenth century, however, Pierre Bersuire had found no ready French translation for the Latin *scriptor*, meaning author; see Jean Rychner, 'La traduction de Tite-Live par Pierre Bersuire', in *L'Humanisme médiéval dans les littéraires romaines du XIIe au XIVe siècle*, ed. Fourrier, pp. 170–1.

153 Antoine Thomas, *Jean de Gerson et l'éducation des dauphins de France: étude critique suivie du texte de deux de ses opuscules et de documents inédits sur Jean Majoris précepteur de Louis XI* (Paris, E. Droz, 1930), pp. 50–1.

154 See, for example, Jean Mansel's *Fleurs des histoires*, in which the saints' lives are arranged 'en ordre selon le A. B. C. pour plus legerement trouver ceulx donc len vouldra lire': Paris, BN fr. 57, fol. 9. On the early introduction of such tables into vernacular texts, see F. Avril, 'Trois manuscrits des

402   Notes to Pages 142–4

collections de Charles V et de Jean de Berry', *Bibliothèques de l'Ecole des Chartes*, 127 (1969): 293.

155 Sherman, *Portraits of Charles V*, pp. 42ff.

156 For an example of vernacular *banderolles*, see Michel François, 'Les rois de France et les traditions de l'abbaye de Saint-Denis à la fin du XVᵉ siècle', in *Mélanges dédiés à Félix Grat*, plates 7 and 8; Pierre Champion, *Louis XI* (Paris, H. Champion, 1928), 2, plate 20. In the sixteenth century, Martin Luther considered the *banderolle* as part of the iconography of the Resurrection; see Catherine Delano Smith, 'Maps as art and science: maps in sixteenth-century Bibles', *Imago Mundi*, 42 (1990): 67.

157 An early example of *cursiva formata* used for an essentially literary text is Paris, Archives nationales, Registre JJ 28, dating from the reign of Philip the Fair. For literary texts, the script was first used regularly in the reign of Charles V; see, for example, Paris, BN fr. 16993. Cf. Léopold Delisle, *Recherches sur la librairie de Charles V* (Paris: Champion, 1905), p. 230.

158 Paul Saenger, 'Geoffroy Tory et le nomenclature des écritures livresques françaises du XVᵉ siècle', *Le Moyen-âge*, ser. 4, 32 (1977): 493–520.

159 Geoffroy Tory, *Champ fleury*, ed. Gustave Cohen (Paris: Charles Bosse, 1931), fol. 72.

160 However, a recently acquired Chicago, Newberry Library MS 116, contains Netherlandish texts written in the scripts usually reserved for French vernacular books.

161 G. I. Lieftinck, 'Pour une nomenclature de l'écriture livresque de la periode dite gothique', in *Nomenclature des écritures livresque du IXᵉ au XVIᵉ siècle* (Paris: CNRS, 1954), pp. 23–4, suggests that *lettre bâtarde* was invented between 1420 and 1430, but his earliest dated example is 1436. Vernacular examples date from as early as 1441; Gerhard Eis, *Altdeutsche Handschriften* (Munich, 1949), pp. 82–3.

162 The term *lettre bourguignonne* has been suggested by G. I. Lieftinck, *Manuscrits datés conservés dans les Pays-Bas*, vol. 1 (Amsterdam, North Holland, 1964), p. xv. For examples of Aubert's script, see Dogaear and Debae, *La Librairie de Philippe le Bon*, nos 64, 162 and *passim*.

163 For example, Gothic *textualis* was used in the Bible of Louis XI, Paris, BN lat. 25. In an extensive survey of hundreds of fifteenth-century vernacular literary manuscripts from the circle of the royal court and the great nobility, I have found only a single example of a literary text written in *textualis*, Paris, BN fr. 19919.

164 See, for example, the use of capitalization and punctuation in Guillaume Fillastre's *Toison d'Or*, Paris, BN fr. 139.

165 Erich Auerbach, *Literary Language and its Public in Late Latin Antiquity and in the Middle Ages*, trans. R. Manheim (Princeton: Princeton University Press, 1965), pp. 299–302.

166 Franz Steffens, *Lateinische Paläographie* (Leipzig: Teubner, 1411), no. 103.

167 See, for example, Lieftinck, 'Pour une nomenclature', p. 33.

168 Silvia Rizzo, *Il lessico filologico degli umanisti* (Rome: Storia & Letteratura, 1973), pp. 104–5.

169 Erasmus, *De recta latini graecique sermonis pronuntiatione*, ed. M. Cytowska in *Opera omnia Desiderii Erasmi Roterodami*, ser. 1, vol. 4 (Toronto: University of Toronto Press, 1973), p. 38.

170 Terence O. Tunberg, 'The Latinity of Lorenzo Valla's *Gesta Ferdinandi Regis Aragonum*', *Humanistica Lovaniensia*, 37 (1988): 71–8.

171 For a French example written in Italian humanistic script, see Baltimore, Walters Art Gallery W. 452. I am indebted to Lilian Randall for this reference.

172 Henri Bornecque, *La Prose métrique dans la correspondance de Cicéron* (Paris, 1898), p. 205.

173 See, for example, Chicago, Newberry Library, f. 101.1.

174 Tory, *Champ fleury*, fos 65ᵛ–66, cited Byzantine grammarians for this use of punctuation. Cf. Aurelio Roncaglia, 'Note sulla punteggiatura medievale e il segno di parentesi', *Lingua nostra*, 3 (1941): 6–9.

175 The term and symbol of the parenthesis are known in the fourteenth century, but it was used in the classical sense only in humanistic manuscripts of the fifteenth century.

176 The parenthesis was used in manuscripts in semi-humanistic script in France in the reign of Louis XI. Tardif included it among the signs of punctuation in his treatise on grammar. In about 1500 the Parisian printer Jean Petit used the parenthesis in his editions of scholastic texts. At the end of the fifteenth century, the parenthesis was also used in vernacular texts, e.g. Paris, BN fr. 15456–7. The humanistic ideal of written eloquence is reflected by Guillaume Leseur, who wrote of royal historiographer Jean Chartier as a 'très suffisant et elégant orateur' who 'a bien sçeu escripte': Guillaume Leseur, *Histoire de Gaston IV, comte de Foix*, ed. Henri Courteault (Paris, 1893–6), 1: p. xxiv.

177 Paris, BN lat. 10922, fol. 58ᵛ; Thurot, 'Notices et extraits de divers manuscrits latins', p. 416.

178 Marichal, 'L'écriture latine', p. 231.

179 Jean Froissart, *Chroniques*, prologue to book 1.

180 G. W. Coopland, ed., *Philippe de Mezières, Chancellor of Cyprus: Le songe du vieil pèlerin* (Cambridge: Cambridge University Press, 1969), 1:102.

181 Paul Saenger, 'The education of Burgundian princes 1435–1490', (Ph.D. diss., University of Chicago, 1972), pp. 179–267.

182 Paul Saenger, 'John of Paris: principal author of the *Quaestio de potestate papae*', *Speculum*, 56 (1981): 41–55.

183 Pierre des Gros, *Jardin des nobles*: Paris, BN fr. 193.

184 See Saenger, 'Books of hours', pp. 148, 153–4.

185 For example, Guillaume Fillastre, *L'Histoire de la Toison d'Or*, Paris, BN fr. 140, fol. 78, left it to his readers to judge whether an individual prince's highest loyalty should be to his family or to the *chose publique*.

186 Paulin Paris, *Les Manuscrits françois de la Bibliothèque du roi* (Paris, 1836–48), 4:131–5.

187 Paris, BN lat. 6607.

188 Paul Saenger, 'The earliest French resistance theory: the role of the Burgundian court', *Journal of Modern History*, suppl. 51 (1979): 1225–49.

189 See, for example, a dog's tail suggesting anal penetration, Paris, BN lat. 12054 (s. 12), fol. 330ᵛ.

190 A typical example illustrates a fifteenth-century copy of the French translation of Valerius Maximus, *Facta et dicta memorabilia*; Robert Melville, *Erotic Art of the West* (London, Weidenfeld and Nicholson, 1973), fig. 116. The miniature is misdated to the sixteenth century in the caption and the text. For other examples, see Edward Lucie Smith, *Eroticism in Western Art* (London: Praeger, 1972). These manuscripts are the direct antecedents of late fifteenth- and sixteenth-century erotic art, notably that of Hieronymus Bosch; see Anthony Bosman, *Jérôme Bosch* (Paris,

Marabout, 1962), p. 16; Otto Brusendorf and Poul Henningsen, *Love's Picture Book: The History of Pleasure and Moral Indignation from the Days of Classical Greece until the French Revolution* (Copenhagen, Veta, 1960); Eduard Fuchs, *Geschichte der Erotischen Kunst* (Munich, A. Langer, 1912), p. 175. The bordello was usually represented as a public bath.

191 *Les Cent Nouvelles Nouvelles*, ed. Franklin P. Sweetser (Geneva: Droz, 1966), p. 22.

192 For a description of the surviving manuscript, see Pierre Champion, *Les Cent Nouvelles Nouvelles* (Paris: Droz, 1928), pp. xcvi–cxvii, and J. Gerber Young and P. Henderson Aitken, *A Catalogue of the Manuscripts in the Library of the Hunterian Museum in the University of Glasgow* (Glasgow: J. Maclehose and Sons, 1908), pp. 201–3.

193 J. Harthan, *The Book of Hours* (New York, Crowell, 1977), pp. 24, 26. Sotheby's November 1990 sale, lot no. 140, purchased by Pierre Berès. I am grateful to Chirsopher de Hamel for this reference.

194 A. Grunzweig, 'Quatre lettres autographes de Philippe le Bon', *Revue belge de philologie et d'histoire*, 4 (1925): 431–7.

195 *Thomas à Kempis et la dévotion moderne*, Bibliothèque Royale exhibition catalogue (Brussels: Bibliothèque Royale Albert Ier, 1971), p. 34.

196 Paris, Arsenal 5205, fol. 'F'.

197 Paris, Arsenal 5206, fol. 174.

198 Paris, BN fr. 982, fol. 51^v. A similar emphasis on private piety existed in England: Pantin, 'Instructions for a devout and literate layman', in Medieval Learning and Literature: Essays Presented to Richard William Hunt, eds. J. J. G. Alexander and N. T. Gibson (Oxford, Clarendon Press, 1976), pp. 406–7.

199 Paris, BN fr. 982, fol. 56.

200 Paris, BN fr. 407, fol. 5.

201 Paris, BN fr. 407, fol. 7.

202 Jacques Toussaert, *Le Sentiment religieux en Flandre à la fin du moyen âge* (Paris: Plon, 1963), pp. 351–2.

203 See, for example, Poitiers, BM 95, fos 104 and 139^v.

Chapter 6 Reading in the Jewish Communities of Western Europe in the Middle Ages

1 For an overview of the exercise of self-government among Jews before the modern age, see Salo Wittmayer Baron, *The Jewish Community: Its History and Structure to the American Revolution* (3 vols, Philadelphia: Jewish Publication Society of America, 1942); Louis Finkelstein, *Jewish Self-Government in the Middle Ages*, 2nd edn (New York: Jewish Theological Seminary of America, 1964); Simon Schwarzfuchs, *Kahal: La communauté juive de l'Europe médiévale*, Présence et mémoire juive, 2 (Paris: Maisonneuve et Larose, 1986).

2 On this point, see Anne-Marie Chartier and Jean Hébrard, *Discours sur la lecture 1880–1980* (Paris: Bibliothèque publique d'information, Centre Georges Pompidou, 1989), pp. 15–74.

3 See Armando Petrucci, 'La concezione cristiana del libro fra VI e VII secolo', *Studi medievali*, 3rd ser., 14 (1973): 961–84, repr. in *Libri e lettori nel medioevo: Guida storica e critica*, ed. Guglielmo Cavallo, Biblioteca Universale Laterza, 296 (Rome and Bari: Laterza, 1977), pp. 3–26.

For analogous phenomena as observed by anthropologists in primitive (or pre-literate) societies, see, for example, *Literacy in Traditional Societies*, ed. Jack Goody (Cambridge: Cambridge University Press, 1968), pp. 16–18.

4 There is now a vast literature on the *Chronicle of Ahima'az*. An English translation is to be found in *The Chronicle of Ahima'az*, trans. with an introduction and notes by Marcus Salzman (New York, 1924; repr. 1966). For a brief survey, see the bibliography listed in Robert Bonfil, 'Tra due mondi: Prospettive di recerca sulla storia culturale degli Ebrei dell'Italia meridionale nell'alto medioevo', in *Italia Judaica*, Atti del I° Convegno Internazionale, Bari, 18–22 maggio 1981 (Rome: Ministero per i beni culturali e ambientali, 1983), pp. 135–58.

5 *Meghillath Ahimá 'az*, ed. Benjamin Klar, 2nd edn rev. (Jerusalem: Sifrey Tarshish, 1974), p. 30. On the Christian idea of the female pollution of cult objects, see, for example, Gratian, *Decretum*, dist. 23, ch. 25 (prohibiting women from touching sacred utensils) and Rufinus's commentary on denying women entry into church, a prohibition established by Gregory the Great and reiterated by Gratian: 'Because woman is the only animal to menstruate, in contact with her blood fruit fails to mature, wine sours, the grass wilts, the trees drop their fruit, iron rusts, the air darkens, and if dogs lick that blood they are stricken with rabies.' For this quotation and remarks on related passages, see Alain Boureau, *La Papesse Jeanne* (Paris: Flammarion, 1988, 1993), pp. 44–5.

6 For example, see the story of the trick played by Rabbi Silano on a Palestinian preacher discussed and analysed in Bonfil, 'Tra due mondi'.

7 The notion of 'secular' requires quotation marks because nothing in the Middle Ages was totally secular.

8 On the exercise of ecumenical authority from centres situated in the Muslim East, see S. D. Goitein, *A Mediterranean Society: The Jewish Communities of the Arab World as Portrayed in the Documents of the Cairo Geniza* (6 vols, Berkeley: University of California Press, 1967–93), vol. 2: *The Community*, pp. 5–10. On the transfer of the Jews in the West from the area of Palestinian hegemony to that of Babylonian hegemony, see Bonfil, 'Tra due mondi'.

9 See Thomas Docherty, *On Modern Authority: The Theory and Condition of Writing, 1500 to the Present Day* (Hassocks, Sussex: Harvester Press and New York: St Martin's Press, 1987), pp. 2–43; David Weiss Halivni, *Midrash, Mishnah and Gemara: The Jewish Predilection for Justified Law* (Cambridge, Mass.: Harvard University Press, 1986).

10 See R. W. Southern, *The Making of the Middle Ages* (New Haven, Conn., and London: Yale University Press, 1953), pp. 170–84.

11 The most recent and most complete study of the *Book of Yossippon* is David Flusser's introduction to his critical edition of the work, *The Yossippon [Josephus Gorionides]* (2 vols, Jerusalem: Mosad Byalik, 1978–80). The text of the work is in vol. 1.

12 On Donnolo and his work, see Andrew Sharf, *The Universe of Shabbetai Donnolo* (New York: Ktav Publishing House, 1976); Giuseppe Sermoneta, 'Il neo-platonismo nel pensiero dei nuclei ebraici stanziati nell'Occidente latino (riflessioni sul "Commento al Libro della Creazione" di Rabbi Sabetai Donnolo', in *Gli ebrei nell'Alto Medioevo*, Spoleto, 30 marzo–5 aprile 1978, Settimane di studio del Centro Italiano di studi sull'alto

medioevo, 26 (2 vols, Spoleto: Centro Italiano di studi sull'alto medioevo, 1980), 2:867–925.

13 On the process of urbanization of the Jews, see Salo Wittmayer Baron, *A Social and Religious History of the Jews*, 2nd edn (18 vols, New York: Columbia University Press, 1952), 4:150–227, 312–52; Irving Abraham Agus, *Urban Civilization in Pre-Crusade Europe: A Study of Organized Town-Life in Northwestern Europe during the Tenth and Eleventh Centuries Based on the Responsa Literature* (2 vols, Leiden: Brill, 1965); *idem*, The Heroic Age of Franco-German Jewry (New York: Yeshiva University Press, distribution Bloch, 1969); H. H. Ben-Sasson, 'The "northern" European Jewish community and its ideals', *Journal of World History*, 11 (1968): 208–19.

14 The considerations that follow cannot all be found, line by line, in the studies mentioned in the previous note. They should be understood instead as preliminary results from a new reading of the sources that should appear shortly.

15 *Sefer Ḥasidim*, ed. Jehuda Wistinetzki (Frankfurt am Main: M. A. Wahrmann, 1924), p. 6. For a full bibliography and further information on the *Sefer Ḥasidim* and its sociocultural context within the Jewish community in the Rhine region, see Ivan G. Marcus, *Piety and Society: The Jewish Pietists of Medieval Germany*, Études sur le judaïsme médiéval, 10 (Leiden: Brill, 1981); *idem*, 'Hierarchies, religious boundaries and Jewish spirituality in medieval Germany', *Jewish History*, 1/2 (1986): 7–26; Peter Schäfer, 'The ideal of piety of the Ashkenazi Hasidim and its roots in Jewish tradition', *Jewish History*, 4/2 (1990): 9–23.

16 *Sefer Ra'avià*, 1.179, emphasis added.

17 'Meir Bar-Ilan, Rishumah shel I-Yediath ha-Keriah al Keriath Meghilla Ve-Hallel' (The influence of the inability to read on ritual readings of the Megillah and of the Hallel), *Proceedings of the American Academy for Jewish Research*, 53 (1987), Hebrew section, pp. 11–12.

18 See Daniel Jeremy Silver, *Maimonidean Criticism and the Maimonidean Controversy, 1180–1240* (Leiden: Brill, 1965); H. H. Ben-Sasson, 'The Maimonidean controversy', in *Trial and Achievement: Currents in Jewish History* (Jerusalem: Keter Publishing House, 1974), pp. 230–42.

19 See A. S. Halkin, 'Yedaiah Bedershi's Apology', in *Jewish Medieval and Renaissance Studies*, ed. Alexander Altmann (Cambridge, Mass.: Harvard University Press, 1967), pp. 165–84.

20 For a rapid overview of these arguments, see Patrick Girard, 'Le peuple du livre brûlé', in *Censures: De la Bible aux larmes d'Éros* (Paris: Centre Georges Pompidou, Bibliothèque publique d'information, 1987), pp. 24–31.

21 One notable example of this phenomenon is in the case of Salomon ben Adret, on whom, see Halkin, 'Yediah Bedershi's Apology'.

22 It should be superfluous to rehearse the chronology of the connection between the Christian cultural establishment and the persecution of books, which began with the foundation of the University of Paris and the publication of the papal bull *Parens Scientiarum* in 1231. On this topic, see, for example, 'La censure du livre: quelques dates', in *Censures: De la Bible aux larmes d'Éros*, pp. 214–16.

23 See Silver, *Maimonidean Criticism*, pp. 15–17.

24 For a reconstruction of these events, see Robert Bonfil, introduction (in

Hebrew) to the photostatic reprint of the *editio princeps* (1475) of the *Sefer Nofet Tsufim* of Messer Leon (Judah ben Yehiel) (Jerusalem: National and University Library, 1981), pp. 15–18.

25 See Robert Bonfil, *Rabbis and Jewish Communities in Renaissance Italy*, trans. Jonathan Chapman (Oxford and New York: Oxford University Press, 1990), pp. 67–75 and *passim*; *idem*, 'Le savoir et le pouvoir: Pour une histoire du rabbinat à l'époque prémoderne', trans. Patrick Michel, in *La Société juive à travers l'histoire*, ed. Shmuel Trigano (4 vols, Paris: Fayard, 1992–3), 1:115–95.

26 The logic inherent in that sort of policy is what motivates Jorge of Burgos in Umberto Eco's *The Name of the Rose*. Since Jorge is blind, he is not subject to the thousands of distractions that come from visual representations of reality. The result is that he 'sees' better than anyone else the 'danger' of an ambivalent attitude that permits access to the contents of certain books to some people and forbids it to others, and he chooses to destroy the ambivalence, which means destroying those contents. See Umberto Eco, *The Name of the Rose*, trans. William Weaver (San Diego, New York and London: Harcourt Brace Jovanovich, 1983).

27 In the metaphor suggested in *The Name of the Rose*, burning the books is thus transformed, by the inexorable working out of historical destiny, into the destruction of the abbey itself.

28 In this connection, see Antonio Rotondò, 'La censura ecclesiastica e la cultura', in *Storia d'Italia*, ed. Ruggiero Romano and Corrado Vivanti (6 vols, Turin: Einaudi, 1972–6), vol. 5: *I documenti* (1973), pp. 1397–1492. On the censorship of Hebrew books, see William Popper, *The Censorship of Hebrew Books* (1899), repr. edn, introduction by Moshe Carmilly-Weinberger (New York: Ktav Publishing House, 1969); Paul F. Grendler, 'The destruction of Hebrew books in Venice, 1568', *Proceedings of the American Academy of Jewish Research*, 45 (1978): 103–30; Benjamin Ravid, 'The prohibition against Jewish printing and publishing in Venice and the Difficulties of Leone Modena', in *Studies in Medieval Jewish History and Literature*, ed. Isadore Twersky, Harvard Judaic Monographs, 2– (2 vols, Cambridge, Mass.: Harvard University Press, 1979–84), 1:135–53.

29 For the text of this ordinance and an English translation (quoted here), see Finkelstein, *Jewish Self-Government*, pp. 301, 304.

30 See, for example, Antonio Rotondò, 'Cultura umanistica e difficoltà di censori: censura ecclesiastica e discussioni cinquecentesche sul platonismo', in *Le Pouvoir et la plume: incitation, contrôle et répression dans l'Italie du XVIe siècle*, Actes du colloque international organisé par le Center Interuniversitaire de Recherche sur la Renaissance italienne et l'Institut Culturel Italien de Marseille, Aix-en-Provence, Marseille, 14–16 mai 1981 (Paris: Université de la Sorbonne nouvelle, 1982), pp. 15–50; Nicola Longo, 'Fenomeni di censura nella letteratura italiana del Cinquecento', in ibid., pp. 275–84.

31 Robert Bonfil, 'Some reflections on the place of Azariah de Rossi's *Meor Enayim* in the cultural milieu of Italian Renaissance Jewry', in *Jewish Thought in the Sixteenth Century*, ed. B. D. Cooperman (Cambridge, Mass.: Harvard University Center for Jewish Studies, distribution Harvard University Press, 1983), pp. 23–48.

32 See Rotondò, 'Cultura umanistica e difficoltà di censori'; Longo, 'Fenomeni di censura'.

33 See Chartier and Hébrard, *Discours sur la lecture*.

34 See Docherty, *On Modern Authority*.

35 See, for example, Walter J. Ong, *Orality and Literacy: The Technologizing of the Word*, 4th edn (London and New York: Methuen, 1987), p. 122; Armando Petrucci, 'Pouvoir de l'écriture, pouvoir sur l'écriture dans l'Italie de la Renaissance', *Annales ESC*, 43 (1988): 823–47.

36 See Elizabeth Armstrong, *Before Copyright: The French Book-Privilege System, 1498–1526* (Cambridge and New York: Cambridge University Press, 1990).

37 Meir Benayahu, *Haskamah u-reshuth bi-defussey Venezia* (Copyright, Authorization and Imprimatur for Hebrew Books Printed in Venice) (Jerusalem: Makhon Ben Zvi and Mossad Ha-Rav Kook, 1971).

38 See Kenneth R. Stow, 'The burning of the Talmud in 1553, in the light of sixteenth century Catholic attitudes toward the Talmud', *Bibliothèque d'humanisme et Renaissance*, 34 (1972): 435–59.

39 See the discussion between Antonio Rotondò and Marino Berengo in *Le Pouvoir et la plume*, pp. 303–4, 305–6.

40 See Annabel M. Patterson, *Censorship and Interpretation: The Conditions of Writing and Reading in Early Modern England* (Madison: University of Wisconsin Press, 1984). Patterson states: 'It is to censorship that we in part owe our very concept of "literature" ' (p. 4).

41 For an investigation of this phenomenon in Italy, see Robert Bonfil, 'Le biblioteche degli ebrei d'Italia nell'epoca del Rinascimento', in *Manoscritti, frammenti e libri ebraici nell'Italia dei secoli XV–XVI*, Atti dell'VII° Congresso Internazionale dell'Associazione Italiana per lo Studio del Giudaismo, San Miniato (Pisa), November 1988 (Rome: Carucci, 1991), pp. 137–50.

42 See Robert Bonfil, 'Can medieval storytelling help understand Midrash? The story of Paltiel: a preliminary study on history and Midrash', in *The Midrashic Imagination: Jewish Exegesis, Thought, and History*, ed. Michael Fishbane (Albany: State University of New York Press, 1993), pp. 228–54.

43 For a modern edition, see *The Iggeres of Rav Sherirà Gaon*, trans. and ed. Natan David Rabinowich (Jerusalem: H. Vagshal, 1988, 1991).

44 The *Epistle of Rav Sherirà* explicitly lists the texts that gradually become 'open'.

45 Bonfil, 'Tra due mondi'.

46 See, for example, Guglielmo Cavallo, 'Aspetti della produzione libraria nell'Italia meridionale longobarda', in *Libri e lettori nel medioevo*, pp. 99–129.

47 Moses Avigdor Shulvass, a pioneer in this as in many other fields, remarks on this difference in the preface to one of the very few studies that scholars of Judaic history have devoted to the topic of reading: See Shulvass, 'Le-Toledoth ha-Sefer bi-Tehum Tarbuth ha-Yahaduth ha-Ashkenazith be-yemey ha-Beinayim' (For the history of the book in the cultural sphere of Ashkenazi Judaism), in *Samuel K. Mirsky Jubilee Volume*, ed. Simon Gerson Bernstein and Gershon A. Churgin (New York: Jewish Theological Seminary of America, 1958), pp. 337–49; repr. in Shulvass, *Bi-Tsvat ha-Doroth* (In the Grip of Centuries) (Tel-Aviv and Jerusalem: M. Newman and New York: Ogen Publishing Company, 1960), pp. 9–22.

48 Goitein, *Mediterranean Society*.

49 See Baron, *Social and Religious History*; Agus, *Urban Civilization in Pre-*

Crusade Europe; *idem*, *The Heroic Age of Franco-German Jewry*; Sasson, 'The "northern" European Jewish community'.

50 Bonfil, 'Le Savoir et le pouvoir'.

51 Midrash *Genesis Rabbah*, ed. Theodor-Albeck (Jerusalem: Wahrmann Books, 1965), p. 1.

52 On this question, which is part of a more general antithesis between the Law and Christ at the heart of Pauline thought, see Marcel Simon, *Verus Israel: Étude sur les relations entre Juifs et Chrétiens dans l'Empire Romain (135–425)* (Paris: E. de Boccard, 1948; 2nd edn 1964), pp. 96–7; trans. into English by H. McKeating as *Verus Israel: A Study of the Relations between Christians and Jews in the Roman Empire, 135–425* (Oxford and New York: published for the Littman Library by Oxford University Press, 1986), pp. 72–5.

53 Robert Bonfil, 'La Sinagoga in Italia come luogo di riunione e di preghiera', in *Il Centenario del Templo Isrealitico di Firenze: Atti del Convegno, 24 ottobre 1982* (Florence: Giuntina, 1985), pp. 36–44.

54 On community organization in general, see Baron, *Jewish Community*; Schwarzfuchs, *Kahal*.

55 See Roger Chartier, 'Urban reading practices, 1660–1780', in his *The Cultural Uses of Print in Early Modern France*, trans. Lydia G. Cochrane (Princeton, NJ: Princeton University Press, 1987), pp. 183–239; Chartier and Hébrard, *Discours sur la lecture*, pp. 81–167.

56 On the sociological model, see, for example, Karl Polanyi, *The Livelihood of Man*, ed. Harry W. Pearson, Studies in Social Discontinuity (New York: Academic Press, 1977), p. 55.

57 *The Responsa of Rabbenu Gershom Meor Hagolah*, ed. with introduction and notes by Shlomo Eidelberg (New York: Yeshiva University, 1955), no. 66, pp. 153–4. It is true, as Eidelberg rightly notes, that several decades later not everyone accepted that statement as axiomatic, *sic et simpliciter*. See the quotation from the *Responsa* of Rabbi Meir of Rothenburg (thirteenth century), ibid., Prague edn, no. 179, which assumes as axiomatic that 'a man is accustomed to lend his own books to scholars'.

58 *Sefer Ḥasidim*, no. 309, p. 99; no. 1215, p. 303, etc.

59 On the custom of bequeathing books to the synagogue, see, for example, the case of Bonaiuto da Bagnacavallo, who left a four-volume Bible to the synagogue situated in the house of Musetto da Padova 'ut omnes volentes legere possint et discere'. The document is published in Roberto Cessi, 'La condizione degli ebrei banchieri in Padova nel secolo XIV', *Bollettino del Museo Civico di Padova*, 6 (1907); repr. in Cessi, *Padova medievale: Studi e documenti*, ed. D. Gailo (Padua, 1985), document 1, p. 329.

60 Vat. Urb. 22/1.

61 Isaiah Sonne, 'Book lists through three centuries', *Studies in Bibliography and Booklore*, 2 (1955–6): 3–19, esp. pp. 7–9.

62 Shulvass, *Bi-Tsvat ha-Doroth*, pp. 21–2.

63 Ibid.

64 See, for example, Sonne, 'Book lists through three centuries'.

65 For bibliographic references, see Bonfil, *Rabbis and Jewish Communities*, pp. 272–80; Zipora Baruchson, 'ha-Sifriyot ha-Peratiyot shel Yehoudey Duksut Mantua' (The Private Libraries of North Italian Jews at the Close of the Renaissance: Chapters in the History of the Book and Reading Interests as Reflected in the History of the Book Lists of Mantuan Jews at the

end of the Sixteenth Century), Ph.D. diss., Bar Ilan University, 1985 (in Hebrew with summary in English). Baruchson has subsequently published several specialized articles, the most recent of which is 'Tefutsat Sefarim Kitvey Kodesh ve-Sifrut Classit be-Sifriyot Yehudey Italia' (The circulation of texts of a religious nature and of classical literature in the libraries of Jews of the Italian Renaissance), *Italia*, 8 (1989): 87–99 of the Hebrew section, where the reader will also find Baruchson's earlier articles listed. See also Jean-Pierre Rothschild, 'Quelques listes de livres hébreux dans des manuscrits de la Bibliothèque Nationale de Paris', *Revue d'histoire des textes*, 17 (1987): 291–346, which mentions Rothschild's previous studies among many others.

66 Philippe Ariès, 'L'histoire des mentalités', in *La Nouvelle Histoire*, ed. Jacques Le Goff, Roger Chartier and Jacques Revel (Paris: Retz, 1978), pp. 402–22.

67 One typical example is Mosè ben Joab Rieti, who lived in Florence during the sixteenth century. In his collection of poetry manuscripts, studied some years ago by Umberto Cassuto, Rieti interlards sacred verse with poems that we, with our modern sensitivities, would call simply pornographic. See Umberto Cassuto, *Gli Ebrei a Firenze nell'età del Rinascimento* (1918; repr. Florence: Olschki, 1965), pp. 340–6.

68 Robert Bonfil, 'Changing mentalities of Italian Jews between the period of the Renaissance and the Baroque', *Italia*, 11 (1994): 61–79.

69 Examples include such important medieval works of Hebraic theology as the *Book of Beliefs and Convictions* of Sa'adià Gaon (tenth century), the *Kuzarì* of Judah ha-Levi, and Maimonides' *The Guide of the Perplexed*.

70 Whatever stand one takes in the lively discussion in recent years over the importance of Latin in defining degrees of literacy, that controversy does not seem to me to affect this conclusion. See, for example, Franz H. Bäuml, 'Varieties and consequences of medieval literacy and illiteracy', *Speculum*, 55 (1980): 237–65. For a recent summary of the question, see Dennis Howard Green, 'Orality and reading: the state of research in medieval studies', *Speculum*, 65 (1990): 267–80. I might recall that for the Roman Catholic Church, Latin was decidedly a sacred language: see Irven Michael Resnick, 'Lingua Dei, lingua hominis: sacred language and medieval texts', *Viator*, 21 (1990): 51–74.

71 See Robert Muchembled, *Popular Culture and Elite Culture in France, 1400–1750*, trans. Lydia G. Cochrane (Baton Rouge and London: Louisiana State University Press, 1985), p. 166.

72 Typical examples of books for female consumption are prayer formularies, the *Haggadah* for Passover (accompanied by a vernacular translation), and little manuals of precepts aimed specifically at women.

73 See Yosef Hayim Yerushalmi, *From Spanish Court to Italian Ghetto: Isaac Cardoso, A Study in Seventeenth-Century Marranism and Jewish Apologetics* (New York and London: Columbia University Press, 1971; repr. Seattle: University of Washington Press, 1981).

74 See, for example, B. D. Weinryb, *The Jews of Poland: A Social and Economic History of the Jewish Community in Poland from 1100 to 1800* (Philadelphia: Jewish Publication Society of America, 1973), pp. 107–18.

75 Abraham Stahl, 'Ritualistic reading among Oriental Jews', *Anthropological Quarterly*, 52/2 (1979): 115–20; Harvey E. Goldberg, 'The Zohar in

southern Morocco: a study in the ethnography of texts', *History of Religions*, 29 (1990): 233–58.

76 Aaron of Lunel, for example, mentions reading the Maxims of the Fathers (Pirke Avoth) in the synagogue: see Aaron ben Nathan of Lunel, *Sefer ha-Manhiq* (Rulings and Customs), ed. Yitzhak Raphael (2 vols, Jerusalem: Mosad Harav Kook, 1978), par. 65, pp. 189–90.

77 Meghillah, 32a. In this connection, see Eric Werner and L. Kravitz, 'The silence of Maimonides', *Proceedings of the American Academy for Jewish Research*, 53 (1986): 179–201.

78 It seems that printed *Meghilloth* were circulated by Italian printers, but unfortunately none has come down to us. The fact is mentioned by Rabbi Mosè Provenzali in one of his manuscript *responsa*.

79 See Roger Chartier, 'From ritual to the hearth: marriage charters in seventeenth-century Lyons', in *The Culture of Print: Power and the Uses of Print in Early Modern Europe*, ed. Roger Chartier, trans. Lydia G. Cochrane (Cambridge: Polity Press and Princeton, NJ: Princeton University Press, 1989), pp. 174–90.

80 Martyn Lyons, *Le Triomphe du livre: Une histoire sociologique de la lecture dans la France du XIXe siècle* (Paris: Promodis-Cercle de la Librairie, 1987), p. 222.

81 Colette Sirat with Michèle Dukan, *Écriture et civilisations*, Études de paléographie hébraïque (Paris: Institut de recherche et d'histoire des textes, 1976), esp. pp. 2–20; Malachi Beit-Ariè, *Hebrew Codicology: Tentative Typology of Technical Practices Employed in Hebrew Dated Medieval Manuscripts*, Études de paléographie hébraïque (Paris: Institut de recherche et d'histoire des textes, 1977).

82 Use of the small format for books of devotion is not really an exception to this generalization. On the one hand, small-format books of piety existed in both the Christian and the Jewish camps; on the other, the Jewish manuscript tradition shows a strong continuity in this connection from the Middle Ages on.

83 One image of a seated reader (Parma, Biblioteca Palatina, ebr. 3596, fol. 3^v) is reproduced in Thérèse and Mendel Metzger, *La Vie juive au moyen âge, illustrée par les manuscrits hébraïques enluminés du XIIIe au XVIe siècle* (Fribourg: Office du Livre, 1982), no. 146. For other examples, see the images (London, BL, Add. 14762, fol. 7^v), reproduced in ibid., no. 175; (Jerusalem, Israel Museum, MS Rothschild, fol. 44^v), reproduced in ibid., no. 266, p. 190.

84 See Lyons, *Le Triomphe du livre*, pp. 223, 240–8; Chartier and Hébrard, *Discours sur la lecture*, pp. 397–453.

85 Chartier and Hébrard, *Discours sur la lecture*, rightly stressed this difficulty.

86 The most important of these are Leon Modena's autobiography, for which see *The Autobiography of a Seventeenth-Century Venetian Rabbi: Leon Modena's Life of Judah*, ed. and trans. Mark R. Cohen (Princeton, NJ: Princeton University Press, 1988), and the memoirs of Glückel Hameln, discussed below. On Glückel and other Jewish women, see Natalie Zemon Davis, 'Fame and secrecy: Leon Modena's Life as an early modern autobiography', in ibid., pp. 50–70.

87 *Passover Haggadah*, London, BL, or. 2884, fol. 17^v. This manuscript has been reproduced in a number of studies – for example, in Rezalel Narkiss,

Hebrew Illuminated Manuscripts (Jerusalem: Keter, 1969), pp. 58–9; Metzger and Metzger, *La Vie juive au moyen âge*, no. 103, p. 72.

88 See, for example, Carlo Ginzburg, 'High and low: the theme of forbidden knowledge in the sixteenth and seventeenth centuries', *Past and Present*, 73 (1976): 29–41.

89 *Passover Haggadah*, London, BL, Add. 14761, fol. 28^v; reproduced in Metzger and Metzger, *La Vie juive au moyen âge*, no. 378.

90 *Passover Haggadah*, London, BL, Add. 14762, fol. 6; reproduced in Narkiss, *Hebrew Illuminated Manuscripts*, p. 125.

91 Jerusalem, Jewish National and University Library, 8° 4450; reproduced in Metzger and Metzger, *La Vie juive au moyen âge*, no. 96.

92 It is hard to tell whether the beardless figures in this miniature represent children or women; if they were women, one would expect to see some sort of curtain dividing male and female space. That distinction is clearly shown, however.

93 Darmstadt, Hessische Landes- und Hochschulbibliothek, Cod. or. 8, fol. 37^v; reproduced in Narkiss, *Hebrew Illuminated Manuscripts*, p. 127 and in Metzger and Metzger, *La Vie juive au moyen âge*, nos. 169 and 170.

94 For in-depth studies of Mantuan libraries, see Baruchson, 'ha-Sifriyot ha-Peratiyot' and 'Tefutsat Sefarim Kitvey Kodesh'.

95 See Bonfil, 'Le biblioteche degli ebrei d'Italia'.

96 See Lyons, *Le Triomphe du livre*, and the bibliography therein.

97 That is to say, this development needs to be seen in relation to Western Europe's higher degree of modernity as compared to the East.

98 A systematic study (beyond the scope of the present volume) of the origin and dissemination of this stereotype would undoubtedly give extremely interesting results.

99 Chartier, 'Urban reading practices', pp. 219–39; Martine Poulain, 'Scènes de la lecture dans la peinture, la photographie, l'affiche de 1881 à 1889', in Chartier and Hébrard, *Discours sur la lecture*, pp. 427–53.

100 To develop this theme would lead us far from the topic of the present study. On a superficial level, the phenomenon is familiar. The specific weight of medieval texts in the definition of Jewish thought, even in the universities, is, for example, far greater than the corresponding literature on the definition of non-Jewish identity. The works of Maimonides and Judah ha-Levi, not to mention the meteoric success of the medieval *kabbalah*, are still very much a part of Jewish philosophic discourse.

101 Chava Turniansky, 'Le-toledoth ha-'Teitch-Humesh', 'Humesh mit hibber' (For the history of translations of the Pentateuch into Yiddish)', in *Iyyunim be-Sifruth: Devarim … likhvod Dov Sadan …* (Essays in Honor of Dov Sadan) (Jerusalem: Zalman Shazar Center, 1988), pp. 21–58.

102 For this development among Jewish scholars, see E. Toitou, 'Shitato ha-parshanit shel Rashbam al reka ha-metsiut ha-historit shel zemano' (The exegetic method of Rashbam in its historical context), in *Iyyunim be-sifrut hazal, be-mikra uve-toledot Israel* (Studies in Rabbinic Literature, Bible and Jewish History in Honour of Ezra Zion Melamed) (Ramat-Gan: Bar llan University Press, 1982), p. 62.

103 *Die Memoiren der Glückel von Hameln, 1645–1719*, ed. David Kaufmann (Frankfurt am Main, 1896). This work has been translated, in part or in whole, into German, English, Dutch, Hebrew, French and Italian. See *Mémoires de Glückel Hameln*, trans. L. Poliakov (Paris, 1971); *Memorie*

di Glückel Hameln, trans. V. Luccattini Vogelmann (Florence: Giuntina, 1984). For the English translations, see Davis, 'Fame and secrecy', p. 55, n. 13.

104 Chava Turniansky, 'The literary sources of Glückel Hameln's Memoirs', in *Keminhag Ashhkenazz u-Polin: Festschrift for Chone Smeruk,* ed. Chava Turniansky et al. (Jerusalem: Zalman Shazar Center, 1992), pp. 153–79.

105 I might add, in this connection, that the typology of this segment of Jewish society should be added to the ones customarily considered by students of 'oral literature': see Albert Bates Lord, *The Singer of Tales,* Harvard Studies in Comparative Literature, 24 (Cambridge, Mass.: Harvard University Press, 1960; repr. New York: Atheneum, 1970); Ruth Finnegan, 'What is oral literature anyway? Comments in the light of some African and other comparative material', in *Oral Literature and the Formula,* ed. Benjamin A. Stoltz and Richard S. Shannon (Ann Arbor: Center for the Coordination of Ancient and Modern Studies, University of Michigan, 1976), pp. 127–66; Green, 'Orality and reading'.

106 Lyons, *Le Triomphe du livre,* pp. 231–6.

107 See Chartier, 'Urban reading practices', p. 222.

108 Michel Picard, *La Lecture comme jeu: Essai sur la litérature* (Paris: Minuit, 1986), p. 46.

109 Chartier, 'Urban reading practices', p. 224.

110 See Lyons, *Le Triomphe du livre,* p. 233.

111 In virtue of their presumed congenital 'lightness', women were in fact tacitly authorized by 'orthodox' law to read texts considered prohibited to men. This means that no men could have imported into the 'sacred' internal space things that would normally have been excluded from it. In a further inversion of the medieval structure, the only persons allowed to take on that role were the men of the governing élites. One notable example that merits study in this connection is the Italian baroque poetess Sara Coppia Sulam. *Mutatis mutandis,* Glückel played a similar role in her cultural context. Finally, careful observation of the behaviour of modern embodiments of 'orthodox' Jewish society shows that the sociological model continues to our own day.

112 The first text of this sort to have been published seems to have been printed in Egypt in 1740, the second in Venice in 1777. From that date on, innumerable editions were printed, and they are still being published today.

113 On this point, see Giuseppe Sermoneta, 'Aspetti del pensiero moderno nell'Ebraismo italiano tra Rinascimento e età barocca', in *Italia Judaica: 'Gli Ebrei in Italia tra Rinascimento ed età barocca',* Atti del II Convegno internazionale, Genova 10–15 giugno 1984 (Rome: Ufficio centrale per i beni archivistici, divisione studi e pubblicazioni, distribuzione e vendita, Istituto poligrafico e Zecca dello Stato, 1986), pp. 17–35.

Chapter 7   The Humanist as Reader

1 N. Machiavelli, *Opere,* vol. 3: *Lettere,* ed. F. Gaeta (Turin: UTET, 1984), pp. 425–6; English translation taken from *The Portable Machiavelli,* ed. P. Bondanella and M. Musa (Harmondsworth: Penguin, 1979), pp. 68–9.

2 See the fine account in M. Lowry, *The World of Aldus Manutius* (Ithaca, NY: Cornell University Press, 1979).

3 E. Panofsky, *Renaissance and Renascences in Western Art* (Stockholm: Almqvist & Wiksell, 1960); E. Garin, *L'umanesimo italiano* (Florence: Olschki, 1952); and *idem, Medioevo e Rinascimento* (Bari and Rome: Laterza, 1980). For some reflections on this body of literature, see A. Grafton, *Defenders of the Text* (Cambridge, Mass., and London: Harvard University Press, 1991), ch. 1.

4 Budé characteristically described this practice as due to the 'ignorantia Accursii vel saeculi potius Accursiani, quae hac aetate ridicula est'; see E. H. Kantorowicz, *The King's Two Bodies* (Princeton, NJ: Princeton University Press, 1957), p. 126.

5 Petrarch, 'Posteritati', in *Opere*, ed. G. Ponti (Milan, 1968), pp. 886–900.

6 Erasmus, *Methodus*, ed. and trans. G. B. Winkler, *Ausgewählte Werke*, ed. W. Welzig, vol. 3 (Darmstadt: Wissenschaftliche Buchgesellschaft, 1967), p. 50.

7 E. P. Goldschmidt, *Hieronymus Münzer und seine Bibliothek* (London: Warburg Institute, 1938), pp. 35–7.

8 See in general *La Production du livre universitaire au moyen âge: Exemplar et pecia*, ed. L. J. Bataillon et al. (Paris: CNRS, 1988), esp. the articles by H. V. Schooner ('La production du livre par la pecia', pp. 17–37) and R. H. Rouse and M. A. Rouse ('The book trade at the University of Paris, ca. 1250–ca.1350', pp. 41–114).

9 *Seniles*, 6.5, quoted by A. Petrucci, 'Libro e scrittura in Francesco Petrarca', in *Libri, scrittura e pubblico nel Rinascimento*, ed. A. Petrucci (Bari and Rome: Laterza, 1979), p. 5.

10 B. L. Ullman, *The Origin and Development of Humanistic Script* (Rome: Storia & Letteratura, 1960); J. Wardrop, *The Script of Humanism* (Oxford: Oxford University Press, 1963); M. Meiss, 'Toward a more comprehensive Renaissance paleography', in *The Painter's Choice* (New York: Harper & Row, 1976), pp. 151–75; *Libri scrittura e pubblico nel Rinascimento*, ed. Petrucci. For Poggio see E. Walser, *Poggius Florentinus* (Leipzig: Teubner, 1914), pp. 104–10.

11 For a classic case study see B. L. Ullman, *The Humanism of Coluccio Salutati* (Padua: Antenore, 1963). For more general information see C. Bec, *Les Livres des florentins (1413–1608)* (Florence: Olschki, 1984).

12 For the Vatican see J. Bignami Odier and J. Ruysschaert, *La Bibliothèque Vaticane de Sixte IV à Pie XI* (Vatican City: Vatican Library, 1973); for San Marco see J. Onians, *Bearers of Meaning* (Princeton, NJ: Princeton University Press, 1988), ch. 20.

13 M. Baxandall, *Giotto and the Orators* (Oxford: Oxford University Press, 1971).

14 For a reproduction see Federigo da Montefeltro, *Lettere di stato e d'arte (1470–1480)* (Rome: Storia & Letteratura, 1949), frontispiece.

15 Ibid., pp. 115–16.

16 E. P. Goldschmidt, *The Printed Book of the Renaissance* (Amsterdam, 1974).

17 A. Petrucci, 'Alle origini del libro moderno: libri di banco, libri da bisaccio, libretti da mano', in *Libri, scrittura e pubblico nel Rinascimento*, ed. Petrucci, pp. 139–56.

18 F. Anzelewsky, *Dürer-Studien* (Berlin: Deutscher Verlag für Kunstwissenschaft, 1983), pp. 182–5.

19 P. de Nolhac, *Les Correspondants d'Alde Manuce* (Rome, 1888), p. 26.

20 A. Petrucci, ' "L'antiche e le moderne carte": *Imitatio* e *renovatio* nella

riforma grafica umanistica', in *Renaissance- und Humanistenhandschriften*, ed. J. Autenrieth et al. (Munich: Oldenbourg, 1988), pp. 4–5.

21 C. Mitchell, *A Fifteenth-Century Italian Plutarch* (London: Phaidon, 1961).

22 Petrucci, ' "L'antiche e le moderne carte" ', p. 11.

23 *The Medici Aesop*, ed. E. Fahy (New York: Abrams, 1989).

24 For the case of Pliny, see L. Armstrong, 'The illustrations of Pliny's *Historia naturalis* in Venetian manuscripts and early printed books', in *Manuscripts in the First Fifty Years after the Invention of Printing*, ed. J. B. Trapp (London: Warburg Institute, 1983), pp. 97–106.

25 For Maximilian, see J.-D. Müller, *Gedechtnus* (Munich, 1982). For other case studies, see M. B. Winn, 'Antoine Vérard's presentation manuscripts and printed books', in *Manuscripts in the First Fifty Years after the Invention of Printing*, ed. Trapp, pp. 66–74; P. Spunar, 'Der humanistische Kodex in Böhmen als Symbol der antiken (fremden) Kultur', in *Renaissance- und Humanistenhandschriften*, ed. Autenrieth et al., pp. 99–104.

26 E. H. Gombrich, 'From the revival of letters to the reform of the arts', in *Essays in the History of Art Presented to Rudolf Wittkower* (London: Phaidon, 1967), pp. 71–82.

27 For two perspectives on the importance of the middleman, see R. C. Darnton, *The Kiss of Lamourette* (New York: Norton, 1990), pp. 107–87; L. Hellinga, 'Manuscripts in the hands of printers', in *Manuscripts in the First Fifty Years after the Invention of Printing*, ed. Trapp, pp. 3–11.

28 W. Benjamin, 'Unpacking my library', in *Illuminations*, trans. H. Zohn (London, 1970), pp. 59–67.

29 See, most influentially, E. Eisenstein, *The Printing Press as an Agent of Change* (Cambridge: Cambridge University Press, 1979).

30 M. A. Rouse and R. H. Rouse, *Cartolai, Illuminators and Printers in Fifteenth-Century Italy*, UCLA University Research Library, Department of Special Collections, Occasional Papers, 1 (1988).

31 For advertising in the age of manuscripts, see *Der Deutsche Buchhandel in Urkunden und Quellen*, ed. H. Widmann et al. (Hamburg: Hauswedell, 1965), 1: 15–16, and H. Widmann, *Geschichte des Buchhandels vom Altertum bis zur Gegenwart* (Wiesbaden: Harrassowitz, 1975), 1: 37.

32 Rouse and Rouse, *Cartolai, Illuminators and Printers*, p. 58.

33 For further evidence of the pervasiveness of these practices, see Armstrong, 'Illustrations of Pliny's *Historia naturalis*'.

34 Vespasiano da Bisticci, *Vite de uomini illustri del secolo xv* (Florence, 1938), p. 108–9. On Vespasiano see G. M. Cagni, *Vespasiano da Bisticci e il suo epistolario* (Rome: Storia & Letteratura, 1969), and A. C. de la Mare, 'Vespasiano da Bisticci, Historian and Bookseller', PhD. diss., London University, 1965.

35 Vespasiano, *Vite*, p. 528.

36 Ibid., p. 539.

37 Ibid., p. 112.

38 See *Claudii Ptolemaei Geographiae Codex Urbinas Graecus 82*, ed. J. Fischer, SJ, *Tomus prodromus* (Leiden, Leipzig and Turin, 1932).

39 Vespasiano, *Vite*, pp. 108–9, 524.

40 C. Koeman, *Joan Blaeu and his Grand Atlas* (Amsterdam: 1970).

41 *Opus epistolarum Des. Erasmi Roterodami*, ed. P. S. Allen et al. (Oxford: Oxford University Press, 1908–56), 1: 439.

42 *Correspondance de Jacques Dupuy et de Nicholas Heinsius (1646–1656)*,

ed. H. Bots (The Hague, 1971), p. 78; F. F. Blok, *Nicolaas Heinsius in dienst van Christina van Zweden* (Delft: Ursulapers, 1949), pp. 92–9.

43 See *The Auction Catalogue of the Library of J. J. Scaliger*, ed. H. J. de Jonge (Utrecht: HES, 1977).

44 See E. Diehl, *Bookbinding: Its Background and Technique* (New York: Dover, 1980); A. Hobson, *Humanists and Bookbinders* (Cambridge: Cambridge University Press, 1990); and J. B. Trapp's review in *TLS*, 17 May 1991.

45 Vat. lat. 1626, fol. 2^r, in *Miniature del Rinascimento* (Vatican City: Vatican Library, 1950), plate 1.

46 Vat. lat. 2094, fol. 8^r, in ibid., plate 3. Two other splendid examples from the Vatican are a copy of Cicero's *Orationes* (Vat. lat. 1742) and of Virgil (Urb. lat. 350).

47 Vat. lat. 3870; see G. Morello, *Raffaello e la Roma dei Papi: Catalogo della Mostra* (Vatican City: Vatican Library, 1986), p. 75.

48 Lowry, *World of Aldus Manutius*.

49 Reproduced in S. Hindman, *Pen to Print* (College Park, Md., 1977), plate 79; see ibid., pp. 190–2.

50 On the case of Maximilian I see ibid., pp. 181–9; L. Silver, 'Prints for a prince', in *New Perspectives on the Art of Renaissance Nuremberg*, ed. J. Chipps Smith (Austin: Archer M. Hontington Art Gallery, University of Texas, 1985): Müller, *Gedechtnus*.

51 Cf. Vespasiano's comment on Bessarion: 'In tutto il tempo ch'egli era istato nella corte di Roma, sempre faceva iscrivere libri in ogni facultà, così in greco come in latino. E non solo iscriveva, ma comperava tutti i libri ch'egli non aveva; e grande parte di quello che gli avanzava delle sue rendite, ispendeva in libri a uno fine laudabile': *Vite*, pp. 159–60. In this case, of course, the praise was entirely justified, considering the remarkable learning, taste and enterprise which Bessarion showed as a collector. See also Benjamin, 'Unpacking my library'.

52 P. de Nolhac, *Pétrarque et l'humanisme* (Paris: Champion, 1899); B. L. Ullman, *Studies in the Italian Renaissance* (Rome: Storia & Letteratura, 1955).

53 E. P. Goldschmidt, *Hieronymus Münzer und seine Bibliothek* (London, 1938).

54 See Benjamin, 'Unpacking my library', for a fine discussion of the ways that books become a collection.

55 A. Traversari, *Epistolae*, 7.1.

56 Guarino, *Epistolario*, ed. R. Sabbadini (Venice: a spesa della Società, 1915–19), 2: 270.

57 Fahy, introduction, in *The Medici Aesop*.

58 A. Grafton and L. Jardine, *From Humanism to the Humanities* (London and Cambridge, Mass.: Harvard University Press, 1986), pp. 53–7.

59 P. D. Huet, *Commentarius de rebus ad eum pertinentibus* (Amsterdam, 1718), curiously describes the provision of a running paraphrase as a novelty called for by Montausier (pp. 286–93).

60 See in general Grafton and Jardine, *From Humanism to the Humanities*. For the classical world see above all R. Kaster, *Guardians of Language* (Chicago and London: University of Chicago Press, 1987). Several of the articles by P. O. Kristeller collected in his *Renaissance Thought and its Sources*, ed. M. Mooney (New York: Columbia University Press, 1979), emphasize the massive continuity of the arts curriculum through the centuries. Rich

primary evidence is assembled and surveyed in the six volumes so far published of the *Catalogus translationum et commentariorum*, founded by Kristeller and F. Cranz and now edited by V. Brown (Washington, DC: Catholic University of America Press, 1960–).

61 M. Baxandall, *Painting and Experience in Fifteenth-Century Italy* (Oxford: 1972); *idem*, *The Limewood Sculptors of Renaissance Germany* (New Haven, Conn., and London: Yale University Press, 1980).

62 G. Güldner, *Das Toleranz-Problem in den Niederlanden im Ausgang des 16. Jahrhunderts* (Lübeck and Hamburg: Matthiesen, 1968), pp. 97–8, 103, 110–111. Of his opponent Coornhert, who had misread him, Lipsius significantly wrote: 'Mittatur senex in scholas.' See more generally Grafton and Jardine, *From Humanism to the Humanities*, esp. pp. 11–12 and n. 30.

63 Grafton and Jardine, *From Humanism to the Humanities*, ch. 1.

64 See in general J. Chomarat, *Grammaire et rhétorique chez Erasme* (Paris: Belles Lettres, 1981).

65 Erasmus, *Adagiorum chiliades* (Basle: Froben, 1536), II.i.1, p. 355; I have also used the helpful translation and notes of M. M. Phillips, *Erasmus on his Times* (Cambridge: Cambridge University Press, 1965).

66 Erasmus, *Adagiorum chiliades*, p. 356: 'Scripsit his de rebus Plutarchus in commentario de Osiride et Chaeremon apud Graecos, testimonio Suidae, cuius ex libris excerpta suspicor ea, quae nos nuper conspeximus huius generis monimenta.' Cf. P. W. van der Horst, *Chaeremon* (Leiden: Brill, 1984).

67 Erasmus, *Adagiorum chiliades*, pp. 355–6.

68 Ibid., p. 357.

69 For Erasmus's many other, similar works, see Chomarat, *Grammaire et rhétorique chez Erasme*.

70 See W. J. Ong, 'Commonplace rhapsody: Ravisius Textor, Zwinger, and Shakespeare', in *Classical Influences on European Literature, A.D. 1500–1700*, ed. R. R. Bolgar (Cambridge: Cambridge University Press, 1976), pp. 91–126.

71 See J. H. Franklin, *Jean Bodin and the Sixteenth-Century Revolution in the Methodology of Law and History* (New York and London: Columbia University Press, 1963).

72 J. Hankins, *Plato in Fifteenth-Century Italy* (Leiden: E. J. Brill, 1990), vol. 1, pt 2. See also his fascinating typology of fifteenth-century ways of reading, 1: 18–26. See more generally L. A. Jardine, *Erasmus, Man of Letters: The Construction of Charisma in Print* (Princeton, 1993). My thanks to Professor Jardine for allowing me to see the manuscript before it appeared, and for helpful conversations.

73 R. C. Lamberton, *Homer the Theologian* (Berkeley: University of California Press, 1986).

74 D. Panofsky and E. Panofsky, *Pandora's Box*, 2nd edn (New York: Pantheon, 1962).

75 Erasmus, *Adagiorum chiliades*, II.i.1, pp. 357–61 (a digression added to the original text). See more generally L. Jardine's forthcoming book on Erasmus and his generation; I owe much both to the manuscript and to conversations with Jardine.

76 A. Grafton, *Joseph Scaliger*, vol. 1 (Oxford University Press, 1983), pp. 97–8.

77 P. Godman, 'Literary classicism and Latin erotic poetry of the twelfth century and the Renaissance', in *Latin Poetry and the Classical Tradition*, ed. P. Godman and O. Murray (Oxford: Oxford University Press, 1990), pp. 149–82; J. H. Hexter, *The Vision of Politics on the Eve of the Reformation* (New York: Basic Books, 1973).

78 Vespasiano, *Vite*, p. 281.

79 Ibid., pp. 83–122.

80 Ibid., p. 469.

81 See also Hankins, *Plato in Fifteenth-Century Italy*.

82 For some samples, see Bec, *Les Livres des florentins*; Ullman, *Humanism of Coluccio Salutati*; P. Kibre, *The Library of Pico della Mirandola* (New York: Columbia University Press, 1936).

83 M. D. Reeve, 'Manuscripts copied from printed books', in *Manuscripts in the First Fifty Years after the Invention of Printing*, ed. Trapp, pp. 12–13; cf. C. F. Bühler, *The Fifteenth-Century Book* (Philadelphia: University of Pennsylvania Press, 1960).

84 J. Trithemius, *In Praise of Scribes*, ed. K. Arnold, trans. R. Behrendt (Lawrence, Kans.: University of Kansas Press, 1974), p. 60: 'Fortius enim, que scribimus, menti imprimimus, quia scribentes et legentes ea cum morula tractamus.'

85 Scaliger's MS is now Leiden University, MS Scal. 61; see K. Müller's editions of Petronius's *Satyricon* (Munich: Heimeran, 1961, 1965, 1978), M. D. Reeve, 'Petronius', in *Texts and Transmission*, ed. L. D. Reynolds (Oxford: Oxford University Press, 1983), pp. 295–300.

86 I. Maïer, *Les Manuscrits d'Ange Politien* (Geneva: Droz, 1965); R. Ribuoli, *La collazione polizianea del Codice bembino di Terenzio* (Rome: Storia & Letteratura, 1981); J. N. Grant, *Studies in the Textual Tradition of Terence* (Toronto: University of Toronto Press, 1986).

87 Grafton, *Defenders of the Text*, ch. 6.

88 De Nolhac, *Pétrarque et l'humanisme*; G. Billanovich, 'Petrarch and the textual tradition of Livy', *Journal of the Warburg and Courtauld Institutes*, 14 (1951); C. Quillen, *Rereading the Renaissance: Petrarch, Augustine and the Language of Humanism* (Ann Arbor, 1998). For an insightful case study of a richly personalized book, see J. C. Margolin, 'Laski, lecteur et annotateur du "Nouveau Testament" d' Érasme', in *Scrinium Erasmianum*, ed. J. Coppens, vol. 1 (Leiden: Brill, 1969), pp. 93–128.

89 See G. C. Moore Smith, *Gabriel Harvey's Marginalia* (Stratford-upon-Avon: Shakespeare Head Press, 1913); V. Stern, *Gabriel Harvey* (Oxford: Oxford University Press, 1979); W. Colman is preparing a comprehensive edition of Harvey's marginalia.

90 A. Grafton, 'Rhetoric, philology and Egyptomania in the 1570s: J. J. Scaliger's invective against M. Guilandinus's *Papyrus*', *Journal of the Warburg and Courtauld Institutes*, 42 (1979): 167–94; Huet, *Commentarius*, pp. 291–2.

91 See L. Jardine and A. Grafton, ' "Reading for action": how Gabriel Harvey read his Livy', *Past and Present*, 129 (1990): 30–78; the description of Cujas at work comes from *Scaligerana*, ed. P. Des Maizeaux (Amsterdam, 1740), 1: 75.

92 F. Gilbert, *Machiavelli and Guicciardini* (Princeton, NJ: Princeton University Press, 1965).

93 On all these points, see Jardine and Grafton, ' "Reading for action" '.

94 Grafton, *Defenders of the Text*, pp. 1–3.

95 *Huetiana* (Amsterdam, 1723), p. 3: 'Je puis donc dire que j'ai vû fleurir et mourir les Lettres, et que je leur ai survécu.'

96 Huet, *Commentarius*, p. 295.

97 Ibid.; cf. *Huetiana*, pp. 104–5, for another account.

Chapter 8   Protestant Reformations and Reading

1 François Lambert, *Commentarii de prophetia, eruditione et linguis* (Strasbourg, 1526).

2 Martin Luther, *Werke, Kritische Gesammtausgabe, Tischreden* (6 vols, Weimar: Böhlau, 1912–21), vol. 1 (1912), p. 523, no. 1038.

3 John Foxe, *The Acts and Monuments of John Foxe (Book of Martyrs)*, ed. Stephen Reed Cattley, preliminary dissertation by George Townsend (8 vols, London, 1837–41), 3:720.

4 On this entire question, see Jean-François Gilmont, introductory chapter in *La Réforme et le livre: L'Europe de l'imprimé (1517–v.1570)*, ed. Jean-François Gilmont (Paris: Cerf, 1990), pp. 19–28.

5 Carla Bozzolo and Ezio Ornato, 'Les bibliothèques entre le manuscrit et l'imprimé', in *Histoire des bibliothèques françaises* (4 vols, Paris: Promodis-Cercle de la Librairie, 1989–92), vol. 1, ed. André Varnet, pp. 333–47, esp. p. 346.

6 For all aspects of the development of the Protestant book and its influence on the Reformation, see *La Réforme et le livre*, ed. Gilmont, a collective work in which some fifteen authors present a detailed picture of the Protestant book throughout sixteenth-century Europe.

7 Antoine Richart, *Mémoires sur la Ligue dans le Laonnais* (Laon, 1869), p. 492, quoted in Francis M. Higman, 'Le domaine français, 1520–1562', in *La Réforme et le livre*, ed. Gilmont, pp. 105–54, at p. 146.

8 See Herman A. P. Schmidt, *Liturgie et langue vulgaire: Le problème de la langue liturgique chez les premiers réformateurs et au concile de Trente*, trans. from the Dutch by Suitbert Caron, Analecta gregoriana, 53 (Rome: Universitas Gregoriana, 1951); Vittorio Coletti, *Parole dal pulpito: Chiesa e movimenti religiosi tra latino e volgare nell'Italia del Medioevo e del Rinascimento*, Collana di saggistica, 6 (Casale Monferrato: Barietti, 1983).

9 Martin Luther, *Werke*, vol. 6 (1888), p. 203, quoted here from 'Treatise on good works, 1520', trans. W. A. Lambert, rev. James Atkinson, in *Luther's Works* (55 vols, St Louis: Concordia and Philadelphia: Fortress Press, 1958–67), vol. 44: *The Christian Society*, ed. James Atkinson (1966), pt 1, pp. 15–144, at p. 22.

10 Ibid., vol. 30, pt 2 (1909), p. 637.

11 Ibid., vol. 6 (1888), p. 362.

12 Marc Lienhard, *Martin Luther, un temps, une vie, un message* (Paris: Le Centurion and Geneva: Labor et Fides, 1983), pp. 188–95. See also John L. Flood, 'Le livre dans le monde germanique à l'époque de la Réforme', in *La Réforme et le livre*, ed. Gilmont, pp. 29–104, esp. pp. 80–3.

13 John Calvin, *Opera quae supersunt omnia*, vol. 12 (1874), col. 316; quoted here from a letter to Theodore Vitus, 17 March 1546, in *Selected Works of John Calvin: Tracts and Letters*, ed. Henry Beveridge and Jules Bonnet (7 vols, Grand Rapids, Mich.: Baker Books), vol. 5: *Letters, part 2: 1545–1553*, ed. Jules Bonnet, trans. David Constable, p. 40.

14 Théodore de Bèze, *Correspondance*, ed. Hippolyte Aubert (Geneva: Droz, 1960–), vol. 13, ed. Alain Dufour and Béatrice Nicollier, Travaux d'humanisme et Renaissance, 229 (1988), p. 19.

15 Luther, *Werke: Briefwechsel* (18 vols, Weimar: Böhlau, 1930–85), vol. 4 (1933), p. 484.

16 Higman, 'Le domaine français', pp. 132–3.

17 Calvin, *Opera*, vol. 11 (1873), col. 804.
18 Luther, *Werke*, vol. 6 (1888), p. 461, quoted here from 'To the Christian nobility of the German nation concerning the reform of the Christian estate', trans. Charles M. Jacobs, rev. James Atkinson, in *Luther's Works*, vol. 44, pt 2, pp. 115–219, at p. 205.
19 Joseph Lecler, 'Protestantisme et "libre examen": Les étapes et le vocabulaire d'une controverse', *Recherches de science religieuse*, 57 (1969): 321–74.
20 Richard L. Gawthrop and Gerald Strauss, 'Protestantism and literacy in early modern Germany', *Past and Present*, 104 (1984): 31–55, esp. pp. 32–43. See also Rolf Engelsing, *Der Bürger als Leser: Lesergeschichte in Deutschland, 1500–1800* (Stuttgart: Metzler, 1974), p. 37.
21 Luther, *Werke*, vol. 10, pt 1/1 (1910), p. 728.
22 Ibid., vol. 6 (1888), p. 461; 'To the Christian nobility', p. 206.
23 Ibid., vol. 37 (1910), p. 512. See Lienhard, *Martin Luther*, p. 326.
24 Luther, *Tischreden*, vol. 5 (1919), no. 6288.
25 Luther, *Werke*, vol. 15 (1899), p. 49.
26 Philipp Melanchthon, *Werke in Auswahl*, ed. Robert Stupperich (Gütersloh: Bertelsmann, 1951–), vol. 2, pt 1 (1978), pp. 17, 189. See also ibid., pp. 193–4.
27 Arnold Snyder, 'Word and power in Reformation Zurich', *Archiv für Reformationsgeschichte*, 81 (1990): 263–85.
28 *The Statutes of the Realm, Printed by Command of His Majesty King George the Third*, vol. 3 (London, 1817), p. 896; reprint edition (Buffalo, NY: William S. Hein, 1993).
29 Calvin, *Opera*, vol. 55, cols 151, 160. See also Philippe Denis, 'La Bible et l'action pastorale', in *Le Temps des Réformes et la Bible*, ed. Guy Bedouelle and Bernard Roussel, Bible de tous les temps, 5 (Paris: Beauchesne, 1989), pp. 514–44, esp. pp. 517–18.
30 Théodore de Bèze, *Questions et responses chrestiennes* (Geneva, 1572), repr. in Bèze, *Correspondance*, 13:19–21.
31 Geneva, Archives d'État, Reg. Cons. LVII, fols 154^r, 159^r.
32 *Registres de la Compagnie des pasteurs de Genève au temps de Calvin*, ed. R. M. Kingdon and J. F. Bergier, Travaux d'humanisme et Renaissance, 55– (12 vols, Geneva: Droz, 1962–), vol. 5: *1583–1588* (1976), p. 347.
33 See Denis, 'La Bible et l'action pastorale', p. 531. See also *The Mennonite Encyclopedia* (5 vols, Hillsboro, Kan.: Mennonite Brethren Publishing House, 1955–90), s.v. 'Bibelstunde' by Harold S. Bender, 1:322–4.
34 See Marianne Schaub, *Müntzer contre Luther: Le droit divin contre l'absolutisme princier* (Thomery: A l'enseigne de l'arbre verdoyant, distribution Paris: A. Colin, 1984), pp. 78–80; Bernard Roussel, 'Des protestants', in *Le Temps des Réformes*, ed. Bedouelle and Roussel, pp. 309–26, esp. pp. 314–18.
35 Quoted in Gawthrop and Strauss, 'Protestantism and literacy', p. 42.
36 See Roussel, 'Des protestants', pp. 318–30.
37 Guy Bedouelle, 'Le débat catholique sur la traduction de la Bible en langue vulgaire', in *Théorie et pratique de l'exégèse*, Colloque international d'histoire de l'exégèse biblique au XVIe siècle, ed. Irena Backus and Francis Higman (Geneva: Droz, 1990), pp. 39–59. See also Guy Bedouelle and Bernard Roussel, 'L'écriture et ses traductions: Éloge et réticences', in *Le Temps des Réformes*, pp. 463–88, esp. pp. 471–6.

38 Bernard Chédozeau, *La Bible et la liturgie en français: L'Église tridentine et les traductions bibliques et liturgiques, 1600–1789* (Paris: Cerf, 1990).

39 Luther, *Werke: Briefwechsel*, vol. 2 (1931), p. 191.

40 Roger Chartier, 'The practical impact of writing', in *A History of Private Life*, ed. Philippe Ariès and Georges Duby (5 vols, Cambridge, Mass., and London: The Belknap Press of Harvard University Press, 1987–91), vol. 3: *Passions of the Renaissance* (1989), ed. Roger Chartier, trans. Arthur Gold-hammer, pp. 111–59, esp. pp. 111–12.

41 Rolf Engelsing, *Analphabetentum und Lektüre: Zur Sozialgeschichte des Lesens in Deutschland zwischen feudaler und industrieller Gesellschaft* (Stuttgart: Metzler, 1973), p. 20. See also Robert W. Scribner, 'How many could read? Comments on Bernd Moeller's "Stadt und Buch" ', in *Stadtbürgertum und Adel in der Reformation* (The Urban Classes, the Nobility, and the Reformation: Studies on the Social History of the Reformation in England and Germany), ed. Wolfgang J. Mommsen (Stuttgart: Klett-Cotta, 1979), pp. 44–5.

42 David Cressy, *Literacy and the Social Order: Reading and Writing in Tudor and Stuart England* (Cambridge and New York: Cambridge University Press, 1980), p. 176.

43 Paul F. Grendler, 'The organization of primary and secondary education in the Italian Renaissance', *Catholic Historical Review*, 71/2 (1985): 185–205, esp. p. 204.

44 Roger S. Schofield, 'The measurement of literacy in pre-industrial England', in *Literacy in Traditional Societies*, ed. Jack Goody (Cambridge: Cambridge University Press, 1968), pp. 311–25.

45 Armando Petrucci, 'Alle origini del libro moderno: Libri da banco, libri da bisaccia, libretti da mano', *Italia medioevale e umanistica*, 12 (1969): 295–313.

46 Jean Crespin, in a sextodecimo edition of *The Iliad* (Geneva, 1559).

47 See Natalie Zemon Davis, 'Printing and the people', in *Society and Culture in Early Modern France* (Stanford, Calif.: Stanford University Press, 1975), pp. 192–3.

48 Little print evidence of this campaign has survived: see David M. Loades, 'Le livre et la Réforme anglaise avant 1558', in *La Réforme et le livre*, ed. Gilmont, pp. 269–300, esp. pp. 280–1.

49 Craig E. Harline, *Pamphlets, Printing and Political Culture in the Early Dutch Republic*, International Archives of the History of Ideas, 116 (Dordrecht and Boston: Nijhoff, 1987). On reading aloud, see pp. 65–6.

50 Robert W. Scribner, *For the Sake of Simple Folk: Popular Propaganda for the German Reformation*, Cambridge Studies in Oral and Literate Culture, 2 (Cambridge and New York: Cambridge University Press, 1981); *Flugschriften als Massenmedium der Reformationszeit*, Beiträge zum Tübinger Symposium 1980, ed. Hans-Joachim Köhler, Spätmittelalter und frühe Neuzeit, 13 (Stuttgart: Klett-Cotta, 1981).

51 Quoted in Snyder, 'Word and power', p. 274.

52 Robert W. Scribner, *Popular Culture and Popular Movements in Reformation Germany* (London and Ronceverte, W. Va.: Hambledon Press, 1987), pp. 65, 54–60, at p. 65.

53 M. Browet-Duquène and Omer Henrivaux, 'L'oeuvre catéchétique de Luther', in *Luther aujourd'hui*, ed. H. R. Boudin and A. Houssiau, Cahiers de la Revue théologique de Louvain, 11 (Louvain-le-neuve: Peeters, 1983),

pp. 89–110. See also *Aux origines du catéchisme en France*, Actes du colloque historique, Paris 11–12 mars 1988, ed. Pierre Colin et al., Relais-études, 6 (Paris: Desclée, 1989), a conference that concerned Catholic catechetics alone, however.

54 Gawthrop and Strauss, 'Protestantism and literacy', pp. 36–8.

55 W. Stanford Reid, 'The battle hymns of the Lord: Calvinist psalmody of the sixteenth century', *Sixteenth-Century Essays and Studies*, 2 (1971): 36–54. On Bucer, see René Bornert, *La Réforme protestante du culte à Strasbourg au XVIᵉ siècle, 1523–1598: Approche sociologique et interprétation théologique*, Studies in Medieval and Reformation Thought, 28 (Leiden: Brill, 1981), pp. 469–84.

56 Patrice Veit, 'Martin Luther, chantre de la Réforme: sa conception de la musique et du chant d'église', *Positions luthériennes*, 30 (1982): 47–66. On communication by means of singing, see Scribner, *Popular Culture*, pp. 60–2.

57 Rivkah Zim, *English Metrical Psalms: Poetry as Praise and Prayer 1535–1601* (Cambridge and New York: Cambridge University Press, 1987).

58 For a lively description of this process, see G. Morisse, 'Le Psautier de 1562', *Psaume: Bulletin de la recherche sur le psautier huguenot*, 5 (1991): 105–27. See also the classic article of Eugénie Droz, 'Antoine Vincent: La propagande protestante par le psautier', in *Aspects de la propagande religieuse* (Geneva: Droz, 1957), pp. 276–93.

59 Pierre Pidoux, 'Les origines de l'impression de musique à Genève', in *Cinq siècles d'imprimerie genevoise*, Actes du colloque international sur l'histoire de l'imprimerie et du livre à Genève, 27–30 avril 1978, ed. Jean-Daniel Candaux and Bernard Lescaze (2 vols Geneva: Société d'histoire de l'archéologie, 1980–1), 1:97–108.

60 Quoted in Mirjam Bohatcová, 'Le livre et la Réforme en Bohême et en Moravie', in *La Réforme et le livre*, ed. Gilmont, pp. 393–416, at p. 409.

61 Jean Crespin, *Histoire des martyrs persécutez et mis a mort pour la vérité de l'Évangile* (3 vols, Toulouse, 1885–9), 1:687. This work was first published in 1564.

62 Gawthrop and Strauss, 'Protestantism and literacy', p. 40; Anne Riising, 'Le livre et la Réforme au Danemark et en Norvège 1523–1540', in *La Réforme et le livre*, ed. Gilmont, pp. 441–58, esp. p. 444; Remi Kick, 'Le livre et la Réforme dans le royaume de Suède', in ibid., pp. 459–78, esp. p. 472.

63 Andrew G. Johnston, 'L'imprimerie et la Réforme aux Pays-Bas, 1520–c.1555', in *La Réforme et le livre*, ed. Gilmont, pp. 155–86, esp. p. 170.

64 Gunther Franz, *Huberinus-Rhegius-Holbein: Bibliographische und druckgeschichtliche Untersuchung der verbeitesten Trost- und Erbauungsschriften des 16. Jahrhunderts*, Bibliotheca humanistica et reformatoria, 7 (Nieuwkoop: De Graaf, 1973).

65 Johnston, 'L'imprimerie et la Réforme aux Pays-Bas', pp. 179–80.

66 Silvana Seidel Menchi, in Seidel Menchi and Ugo Rozzo, 'Livre et Réforme en Italie', in *La Réforme et le livre*, ed. Gilmont, pp. 327–74, esp. pp. 369–72.

67 Gérard Moreau, *Histoire du protestantisme à Tournai jusqu'à la veille de la Révolution des Pays-Bas*, Bibliothèque de la Faculté de philosophie et lettres de l'Université de Liège (Paris: Belles Lettres, 1962), p. 151.

68 Bèze, *Correspondance*, 13:19.

69 Calvin, *Opera*, vol. 13 (1875), cols 591–3.

70 John Calvin, *Commentaire sur la première épistre aux Corinthiens* (Geneva, 1547), p. 4.
71 See Alfred W. Pollard and G. R. Redgrave, *A Short-Title Catalogue of Books Printed in England, Scotland, and Ireland and of English Books Printed Abroad 1475–1640*, 2nd rev. edn begun by W. A. Jackson and F. S. Ferguson, completed by Katharine F. Pantzer (3 vols, London: Bibliographical Society, 1976–91), vol. 2 (1986), p. 25, no. 14553.
72 Lorenz Hein, *Italienische Protestanten und ihr Einfluss auf die Reformation in Polen während der beiden Jahrzehnte vor dem Sandomir Konsens 1570* (Leiden: Brill, 1974), p. 35.
73 Herwarth von Schade, *Joachim Westphal und Peter Braubach: Briefwechsel*, Arbeiten zur Kirchengeschichte Hamburgs, 15 (Hamburg: Wittig, 1981).
74 See Jean-François Gilmont, *Jean Crespin: Un éditeur réformé du XVIᵉ siècle*, Travaux d'humanisme et Renaissance, 186 (Geneva: Droz, 1981), p. 205.
75 Seidel Menchi, 'Livre et Réforme en Italie', p. 348.
76 Moreau, *Histoire du protestantisme*, p. 137.
77 Luther, *Werke*, vol. 54 (1915), p. 179.
78 Calvin, *Opera*, vol. 15 (1876), col. 214.
79 Ibid., vol. 13 (1875), cols 70–1. On this collection of homilies, see Philip Hughes, *The Reformation in England* (3 vols, London: Hollis and Carter, 1950–4), vol. 2 (1953), p. 95.
80 Michel de Certeau, 'Lire: braconnage et poétique de consommateurs', *Projet*, 124 (1978): 447–57, repr. with the title 'Lire: un braconnage' in de Certeau, *L'Invention du quotidien*, vol. 1 of *Arts de faire* (Paris: Gallimard, 1980), pp. 279–96; trans. in English by Steven F. Rendall as 'Reading as poaching', in *The Practice of Everyday Life* (Berkeley: University of California Press, 1984), pp. 165–76.
81 Francis M. Higman, 'Luther et la piété de l'église gallicane: *Le Livre de vraye et parfaicte oraison*', *Revue d'histoire et de philosophie religieuse*, 63 (1983): 91–111. See also Higman, 'Les traductions françaises de Luther, 1524–1550', in *Palaestra typographica*, ed. Jean-François Gilmont (Verviers: Aubel, 1984), pp. 11–56. On Calvin's *Catechism* in Italian, see Silvano Cavazza, 'Libri in volgare e propaganda eterodossa: Venezia 1543–1547', in *Libri, idee e sentimenti religiosi nel Cinquecento italiano*, ed. Alessandro Biondi and Adriano Prosperi (Modena: Panini, 1987), pp. 9–28, esp. pp. 18–19.
82 See Ugo Rozzo, 'La fabrication et la circulation du livre', the first section of Seidel Menchi and Rozzo, 'Livre et Réforme en Italie', pp. 327–45.
83 See Seidel Menchi, in Seidel Menchi and Rozzo, 'Livre et Réforme en Italie', pp. 369–72.
84 Ibid., pp. 368–9.
85 Calvin, *Opera*, vol. 11 (1873), cols 634–5.
86 Quoted in Jane O. Newman, 'The Word made print: Luther's 1522 *New Testament* in an age of mechanical reproduction', *Representations*, 11 (1985): 95–133, at p. 97.
87 Calvin, *Opera*, vol. 15 (1876), col. 220.
88 On the effect of printing on the accuracy of religious texts, see Newman, 'The Word made print'.
89 Calvin, *Opera*, vol. 11 (1873), col. 418, quoted here from *Tracts and Letters*, vol. 4, pt 1: *1528–1545*, p. 339.
90 Calvin, *Opera*, vol. 11, cols 681–2.
91 Francis M. Higman, *The Style of John Calvin in his French Polemical Treat-*

ises (London: Oxford University Press, 1967). See also Higman, 'Theology in French: religious pamphlets from the Counter-Reformation', *Renaissance and Modern Studies*, 23 (1979): 128–46, esp. p. 128.

92 Calvin, *Opera*, vol. 21 (1879), col. 70; vol. 12 (1874), col. 540. See also Hanns Rükert, 'Einleitung', in *Supplementa calviniana* (8 vols, Neukirchen: Neukirchener Verlag, 1936–61), vol. 1: *Predigten über des 2. Buch Samuelis* (1961), pp. ix–xx; Rodolphe Peter, Introduction to *Supplementa calviniana*, vol. 6: *Sermons inédits*, ed. Rodolphe Peter (1971), p. xxxiv.

93 Calvin, *Opera*, vol. 32 (1887), cols 449–50; vol. 35 (1887), cols 521–54; vol. 25 (1882), col. 598. See also ibid., vol. 35 (1887), col. 589.

94 Ibid., vol. 8 (1870), cols 373–4; vol. 12 (1874), col. 401.

95 Ibid., vol. 12 (1874), col. 302.

96 Ibid., vol. 25 (1887), cols 589, 521–4. The preface to Calvin, *Vingtdeux sermons* (Geneva: Girard, 1554) is not given in Calvin's *Opera*.

97 Patrice Veit, 'Le chant, la Réforme et la Bible', in *Le Temps des Réformes*, ed. Bedouelle and Roussel, pp. 659–82, esp. p. 661.

98 Willem Frijhoff, 'Naissance d'un public réformé', in *Le Grand Atlas des littératures* (Paris: Encyclopaedia universalis, 1990), p. 293.

Chapter 9   Reading and the Counter-Reformation

1 'Decree Concerning the Canonical Scriptures', quoted from *The Canons and Decrees of the Sacred and Oecumenical Council of Trent*, trans. J. Waterworth (London: Dolman, 1848), p. 18.

2 On these questions, see Bernard Chédozeau, *La Bible et la liturgie en français: L'Église tridentine et les traductions bibliques et liturgiques, 1600–1789* (Paris: Cerf, 1990). For an analysis of certain aspects of the attitudes of the post-Tridentine Catholic Church toward tradition and writing, see Philippe Boutry, 'Tradition et écriture: de la théologie aux sciences sociales', *Enquête, anthropologie, histoire, sociologie*, no. 2, 2nd semester (1995), pp. 39–57.

3 'Decree Concerning the Edition, and the Use, of the Sacred Books', in *Canons and Decrees*, pp. 19–20. See also Victor Baroni, *La Contre-Réforme devant la Bible: La question biblique* (Lausanne: La Concorde, 1943), esp. pp. 81–132.

4 'Decree Concerning the Edition, and the Use, of the Sacred Books', p. 20.

5 Decree of the twenty-second session of the Council of Trent, *De sacrificio missae* (Doctrine on the Sacrifice of the Mass), 17 September 1562; ch. 8: 'On not celebrating the Mass every where in the vulgar tongue; The mysteries of the Mass to be explained to the people', quoted here from *Canons and Decrees*, p. 158. During the twenty-fourth session, 11 November 1563, canon VII of the decree, 'On the Sacrament of Order' (which, incidentally, repeats ch. 2 of the fifth session, 17 June 1546, 'On Preachers of the Word of God, and on Questions of Alms'), enjoined the parish priests 'during the solemnization of mass, or the celebration of the divine offices' to explain 'in the said vulgar tongue, on all festivals, or solemnities, the sacred oracles, and the maxims of salvation; and that, setting aside all unprofitable questions, they endeavour to impress them on the hearts of all, and to instruct them in the law of the Lord'. See *Les Conciles oecuméniques*, vol. 2, pt 2,

ed. Paul Christophe and Francis Frost (Paris: Desclée, 1994), pp. 1494, 1552; quoted here from *Canons and Decrees*, p. 214.

6 *Catechism of the Council of Trent for Parish Priests Issued by Order of Pope Pius V*, ed. and trans. John A. McHugh and Charles J. Callan (Rockford, Ill.: Tan Books, 1982), pp. 141, 9. On the production of official texts by the Council of Trent, see Guy Bedouelle, 'La Réforme catholique', in *Le Temps des Réformes et la Bible*, ed. Guy Bedouelle and Bernard Roussel, Bible de tous les temps, 5 (Paris: Beauchesne, 1989), pp. 327–68.

7 Bedouelle, 'La Réforme catholique', pp. 350–5.

8 On the question of the pontifical privilege, see Denis Pallier, 'Les impressions de la Contre-Réforme en France et l'apparition des grandes compagnies de libraires parisiens', *Revue française d'histoire du livre*, 31 (April–June 1981): 215–73, at p. 268.

9 On the geography of the major centres for printing in the sixteenth century, see Jean-François Gilmont, 'Les centres de la production imprimée aux XVᵉ et XVIᵉ siècles', in *Produzione e commercio della carta e del libro secc. XIII–XVIII*, Atti della 'Ventitreesima Settimana di Studi', 15–20 aprile 1991, ed. Simonetta Cavaciocchi (Florence: Le Monnier, 1992), pp. 343–64.

10 Jan Materné, 'The *Officina Plantiniana* and the dynamics of the Counter-Reformation, 1590–1650', in *Produzione e commercio*, ed. Cavaciocchi, pp. 481–90. See also Robert M. Kingdon, 'The Plantin breviaries: a case study in the sixteenth-century business operations of a publishing house', *Bibliothèque d'humanisme et Renaissance: travaux et documents*, 22 (1960): 133–50.

11 I am following here the argument in Pallier, 'Les impressions de la Contre-Réforme en France'.

12 See Chédozeau, *La Bible et la liturgie en français*; Bernard Chédozeau, 'La Bible française chez les Catholiques', in *Les Bibles en français: Histoire illustrée du moyen âge à nos jours*, ed. Pierre Maurice Bogaert (Turnhout: Brepols, 1991), pp. 134–68.

13 Rule IV, *Index librorum prohibitorum* of Sandoval, quoted in Chédozeau, *La Bible et la liturgie en français*, p. 84.

14 Rule V of the *Index* of Sotomayor, quoted in Chédozeau, *La Bible et la liturgie en français*, p. 85. Both Sandoval and Sotomayor forbade the translation into the vernacular of the 'prayers at various hours' that were part of divine liturgy. The *Index* of 1667 explicitly condemns the *Heures de Notre-Dame latin français*, a liturgical text for the use of the faithful.

15 See *Dictionnaire de la Bible* (5 vols, Paris: Letouzey et Ané, 1926–), s.v. 'Versions de la Bible; Espagnoles', vol. 2, cols 1956–65.

16 By that date the use of vernacular versions of the Bible was authorized 'provided that they be approved by the Holy See or published with annotations drawn from the Fathers of the Church or from learned Catholic writers'. The Spanish Inquisition promulgated an analogous decree on 20 December 1782, or some twenty-five years after the Roman brief.

17 On this point, see Francisco Béthencourt, 'Les visites inquisitoriales de contrôle des livres', in *Culture et société dans l'Europe moderne et contemporaine: Yearbook of the Department of History and Civilization*, ed. Dominique Julia (Florence: Istituto Universitario Europeo, 1992), pp. 17–34. See also Béthencourt, *L'Inquisition à l'époque moderne: Espagne, Italie, Portugal, XVᵉ–XIXᵉ siècle* (Paris: Fayard, 1995).

18 See José Adriano de Freitas Carvalho, 'La Bible au Portugal', in *Le Siècle des Lumières et la Bible*, ed. Yvon Belaval and Dominique Bourel, La Bible de tous les temps, 7 (Paris: Beauchesne, 1986), pp. 253–65. I have chosen not to mention the Portuguese version of the Bible published in Batavia between 1681 and 1759 under the auspices of the Danish Royal Mission by João Ferreira d'Almeida, a Portuguese Calvinist missionary.

19 On Italian versions of the Bible, see Pietro Stella, 'Produzione libraria religiosa e versioni della Bibbia in Italia tra età dei lumi e crisi modernista', in *Cattolicesimo e Lumi nel Settecento italiano*, ed. Mario Rosa (Rome: Herder, 1981), pp. 99–125.

20 On the Bible 'of the Louvain Theologians', see Chédozeau, *La Bible et la liturgie en français*, pp. 110–13; Jean-François Gilmont, 'La Bible française chez les Catholiques au seizième siècle', in *Les Bibles en français*, ed. Bogaert, pp. 91–101.

21 Nicolas Le Maire, *Le Sanctuaire fermé aux profanes ou la Bible défendue au vulgaire* (1651), quoted from Chédozeau, *La Bible et la liturgie en français*, pp. 200–6, which also provides an excellent analysis of this work.

22 *Le Nouveau Testament*, trans. Denys Amelote (1666); quoted from Chédozeau, *La Bible et la liturgie en français*, p. 207.

23 See the works of Bernard Chédozeau already cited, and *idem*, 'La publication de l'écriture par Port-Royal, première partie: 1653–1669' and 'Deuxième partie: L'Ancien Testament de la "Bible de Sacy": 1672–1693', *Chroniques de Port-Royal*, 33 (1984): 35–42; 35 (1986): 195–203, respectively.

24 Bull *Unigenitus*, propositions 79–85; given in Chédozeau, *La Bible et la liturgie en français*, pp. 219–21.

25 On this point, see Jean Orcibal, *Louis XIV et les protestants* (Paris: Vrin, 1951); Bernard Chédozeau, 'Les distributions de livres aux nouveaux convertis et leurs incidences sur le statut du laïc catholique', *XVIIe siècle*, 154 (January–March 1987): 39–51.

26 Letter of Guy de Sève de Rochechouart, bishop of Arras, to Fénelon, 1 February 1707, in *Correspondance de Fénelon*, ed. Jean Orcibal, with the collaboration of Jacques Le Brun and Irénée Noye (15 vols to date, Paris: Klincksieck and Geneva: Droz, 1972–), vol. 12 (1990), p. 270.

27 Letter of Fénelon to Guy de Sève de Rochechouart, 1 February 1707, ibid., pp. 270–84, at pp. 283–4.

28 On the various forms of seminary, see Dominique Julia, 'L'éducation des ecclésiastiques en France aux XVIIe et XVIIIe siècles', in *Problèmes d'histoire et de l'éducation*, Actes des Séminaires de l'École Française de Rome et de l'Université de Rome-La Sapienza (Rome: École Française de Rome, 1988), pp. 141–205.

29 Jean Gerson's *Opusculum tripartitum* combined three unconnected brief didactic treatises on the Ten Commandments, the art of confession and the art of dying well that had been annexed to the synodal statutes of the diocese of Poitiers in 1544, then translated into French in the synodal statutes of the diocese of Cahors in 1558, and translated into the *langue d'oc* in similar statutes of the diocese of Rodez in 1556. According to Nicole Lemare, *Le Rouergue flamboyant: La clergé et les fidèles du diocèse de Rodez, 1417–1563* (Paris: Cerf, 1988), pp. 434–6, during the first half of the sixteenth century Gerson's book was a 'convenient' solution to the problem of training the clergy, and its didactic clarity had made it the basis for Catholic preaching.

30 On the evolution of prescribed reading for parish priests, see Dominique Julia and Denis McKee, 'Les confrères de Jean Meslier: Culture et spiritualité du clergé champenois au XVIIe siècle', *Revue d'histoire de l'Église de France*, 49 (1983): 61–86.

31 *Mandement* of 25 September 1657, published in *Statuts, Ordonnances, Mandemens, Règlemens, et Lettres Pastorales imprimez par order de Monseigneur L'Illustrissime et Révérendissime Messire Louis-Ant^{ne} de Nouailles, Évêque Comte de Chaalons Pair de France* (Châlons-sur-Marne: Jacques Seneuze, 1963), pp. 107–10. Matthieu Beuvelet, *Méditations sur les principales vérités chrétiennes et ecclésiastiques … composées pour l'usage du séminaire établi par Mgr l'archevêque de Paris à l'église paroissiale de Saint-Nicolas du Chardonnet* (Paris, 1654) was a bestseller of priestly literature in the seventeenth century. 'Grenade' is Luis de Granada; 'Du Pont' is the Jesuit Luis de La Puente.

32 In a letter condemning a book titled *Apologie pour les casuistes*, Félix Vialart de Herse, bishop of Châlons-sur-Marne, first invited his parish priests to draw from the science 'of the legitimate administration of the sacraments, and from the faithful conduct of souls' by a 'familiar and devout reading' of a series of books. He recommended that 'in order to acquire practice in this', they 'assiduously attend the conferences' of their diaconate, and prepare themselves for them 'with care'. See 'Quatrième lettre au clergé du diocèse contenant la condamnation du livre intitulé *Apologie pour les Casuistes*', 25 September 1655, in *Statuts, Ordonnances, Mandemens*, p. 261.

33 On the organization of ecclesiastical conferences, see Louis Pérouas, *Le Diocèse de La Rochelle de 1648 à 1724: Sociologie et pastorale* (Paris: SEVPEN, 1964), pp. 254–6; Charles Berthelot du Chesnay, *Les Prêtres séculiers en Haute-Bretagne au XVIIIe siècle* (Rennes: Presses Universitaires de Bretagne, 1984), pp. 427–32; Jean-Marie Gouesse, 'Assemblées et associations cléricales: Synodes et conférences ecclésiastiques dans le diocèse de Coutances aux XVIIe et XVIIIe siècles', *Annales de Normandie*, 24 (1974): 37–71; Julia and McKee, 'Les confrères de Jean Meslier'.

34 See Michel de Certeau, *L'Écriture de l'histoire* (Paris: Gallimard, 1975), pp. 208–9, trans. into English by Tom Conley as *The Writing of History* (New York: Columbia University Press, 1988).

35 On this point, see Henri-Jean Martin, *Livre, pouvoirs et société à Paris au XVIIe siècle (1598–1701)*, Histoire et civilisation du livre, 3 (Geneva: Droz, 1969).

36 Letter of Chancellor Pontchartrain to the bishop of Carcassonne, 4 March 1711: Paris, BN, fr., MS no. 21133, fols 208^v–209. The books printed by the bishops had to be in conformity with 'good doctrine and public order'. See also the letter of Chancellor Pontchartrain to François Bochart de Saron de Champigny, bishop of Clermont, 27 July 1708: Paris, BN, fr., MS no. 21128, fol. 791^v. At the time of the conflict over the bull *Unigenitus*, public order was indeed disturbed by the bishops' pastoral letters.

37 Privilege for thirty years granted on 27 November 1681 to the bookseller Jacques Seneuze, 'printer to the Count Bishop of Châlons'.

38 'Abrégé de bibliothèque pour les ecclésiastiques qui se trouve chez Jacques Seneuze, Imprimeur de Monseigneur, avec les prix au plus juste', in *Statuts, Ordonnances, Mandemens*.

39 See Louis Châtellier, *Tradition chrétienne et renouveau catholique dans le*

cadre de l'ancien diocèse de Strasbourg, 1650–1770 (Paris: Ophrys, 1981), pp. 164–5, 390–2. Between 1701 and 1790, eighty-six such New Year's gifts were printed. Nearly half of these (forty, or 46.5 per cent) were spiritual guides or works of morality, fourteen were explications of Holy Scripture, eleven were books of religious history. Beginning in the mid-eighteenth century they emphasized the Fathers of the Church, spiritual writers and French seventeenth-century Doctors of the Church. On the social composition of this group, see Châtellier, 'La Congrégation académique de Molsheim et la société alsacienne à la fin du dix-huitième siècle', *Société d'histoire et d'archéologie de Molsheim et environs, Annuaires* (1980): 89–97.

40 Of fifty-five identifiable authors of these books, thirty belonged to the Society of Jesus. The library of the Grand Séminaire of Strasbourg contains a complete collection of 'Étrennes de la Congrégation de Molsheim'.

41 Such Congregations were particularly common in Germany and Central Europe. See Émile Villaret, *Les Congrégations mariales*, vol. 1: *Des origines à la suppression de la Compagnie de Jésus (1540–1773)* (Paris: Beauchesne, 1947), pp. 485–92.

42 Quoted in Châtellier, *Tradition chrétienne*, p. 165.

43 Archives of the Département de l'Yonne, G 1622.

44 See Pérouas, *Le Diocèse de La Rochelle*, pp. 263–4.

45 For a detailed analysis of the content of such libraries, see Julia and McKee, 'Les confrères de Jean Meslier', pp. 73–8.

46 See Jean Quéniart, *Les Hommes, l'Église et Dieu dans la France du XVIIIᵉ siècle* (Paris: Hachette, 1978), pp. 69–77.

47 Luciano Allegra, *Ricerche sulla cultura del clero in Piemonte: Le biblioteche parrocchiali nell'Arcidiocesi di Torino sec. XVII–XVIII* (Turin: Deputazione subalpina di Storia Patria, 1978).

48 See Gaetano Greco, 'Fra disciplina e sacerdozio: Il clero secolare nella società italiana del Cinquecento al Settecento', in *Clero e società nell'Italia moderna*, ed. Mario Rosa (Bari: Laterza, 1992), pp. 45–113.

49 Certeau, *L'Écriture de l'histoire*, pp. 203–12; quoted here from *The Writing of History*, p. 185.

50 Jean Meslier, *Oeuvres complètes*, ed. Jean Deprun, Roland Desné and Albert Soboul (3 vols, Paris: Anthropos, 1970–2), 2:32.

51 Michel de Certeau, 'L'illettré éclairé', in his *La Fable mystique XVIᵉ–XVIIᵉ siècles* (Paris: Gallimard, 1982, 1987); trans. into English by Michael B. Smith as 'The enlightened illiterate', in *The Mystic Fable* (Chicago: University of Chicago Press, 1992), pp. 206–40.

52 On the literary genre of the *Figures de la Bible*, see Max Engammare, 'Les figures de la Bible: Le destin oublié d'un genre littéraire en image (XVIᵉ–XVIIᵉ siècle)', *Mélanges de l'École Française de Rome: Italie et Méditerranée*, 106 (1994): 549–91.

53 On spiritual direction and spiritual reading, seventeenth-century correspondence (that of Fénelon in particular) is enlightening. See Fénelon, *Correspondance de Fénelon*.

54 Fénelon, letter to the duchesse de Beauvilliers, 16 January 1686, in *Correspondance de Fénelon*, vol. 2 (1972), pp. 20–1.

55 Ibid., p. 21.

56 Fénelon, letter to the minister, Seignelay, La Rochelle, 29 June 1687, in ibid., p. 58.

57 Fénélon, letter to the minister, Seignelay, La Tremblade, 8 March 1686, in ibid., p. 32.
58 Ibid., p. 33.
59 Fénélon, letter to the minister, Seignely, June 1687, in ibid., p. 57.
60 Fénélon, letter to Bossuet, La Tremblade, 8 March 1686, in ibid., p. 34.
61 Henri Bremond, *Histoire littéraire du sentiment religieux en France depuis la fin des Guerres de Religion jusqu'à nos jours* (11 vols, Paris: Bloud et Gay, 1924–33). Two volumes are available in English translation: *A Literary History of Religious Thought in France from the Wars of Religion down to our Own Times*, vol. 1: *Devout Humanism*; vol. 2: *The Coming of Mysticism (1590–1620)*, trans. K. L. Montgomery (New York: Macmillan, 1928–30).
62 See Henri-Jean Martin, 'Classement et conjonctures', in *Histoire de l'édition française*, ed. Henri-Jean Martin and Roger Chartier (4 vols, Paris: Promodis, 1982), vol. 1: *Le Livre conquérant: Du moyen âge au milieu du XVIe siècle*, pp. 429–57, esp. p. 449.
63 See, for example, Louis Desgraves, 'L'inventaire du fonds de livres chez J. Mongiron-Millanges en 1672', *Revue française d'histoire du livre* (1973): 125–71; Gregory Hanlon, *L'Univers des gens de bien: Culture et comportement des élites urbaines en Agenais-Condomois au XVIIe siècle* (Bordeaux: Presses Universitaires de Bordeaux, 1989), which analyses (pp. 312–17) the inventory of the Agen bookseller Jean Jacques Bru in 1689. I do not discuss Henri-Jean Martin's study of Nicolas, a Calvinist bookseller in Grenoble, because although Nicolas sold a number of Catholic works on theology and spirituality, he is perhaps atypical in the context of places where religious books were sold. See Henri-Jean Martin and Anne-Marie Lecocq, *Livres et lecteurs à Grenoble: Les registres du libraire Nicolas 1645–1668*, Histoire et civilisation du livre, 10 (2 vols, Geneva: Droz, 1977).
64 To offer only two examples: Jean-François Behourt, a Rouen printer who died in 1759, left 200,000 copies of books of piety, 33,000 of them books of hours, 15,000 song-books and 12,000 catechisms. See Jean Quéniart, *L'Imprimerie et la librairie à Rouen au XVIIIe siècle* (Paris: Klincksieck, 1969), p. 137. The estate inventory of Étienne Garnier, a bookseller-printer in Troyes who died in 1789, shows that 42.7 per cent of his stock (or 189,672 copies) were religious books. Psalters, saints' lives and pilgrimage books, collections of songs and *noëls*, and catechisms were prominent among them. See Henri-Jean Martin, 'Culture écrite et culture orale: culture savante et culture populaire', in *Le Livre français sous l'ancien régime* (Paris: Promodis-Cercle de la Librairie, 1987), pp. 149–86, esp. pp. 160–5.
65 Julien Brancolini and Marie-Thérèse Bouyssy, 'La vie provinciale du livre à la fin de l'ancien régime', in *Livre et société dans la France du XVIIIe siècle* (2 vols, Paris and The Hague: Mouton, 1965–70), 2:3–37. The information in the two manuscripts on which this study is founded (Paris, BN, fr., nos 22018, 22019) is published in Robert L. Dawson, *The French Booktrade and the 'Permission simple' of 1777: Copyright and Public Domain with an Edition of the Permit Registers*, Studies on Voltaire and the Eighteenth Century, 301 (Oxford: Voltaire Foundation, 1992). On the fortunes of *L'Ange conducteur*, see Michel Vernus, 'Un best-seller de la littérature religieuse: L'Ange conducteur du XVIIe au XIXe siècle', in *Actes du 109e Congrès national des Sociétés Savantes*, Dijon, 1984, Section d'histoire

moderne et contemporaine (Paris: CTHS, 1984), vol. 1: *Transmettre la foi: XVIᵉ–XIXᵉ siècles*, pt 1: *Pastorale et prédication en France*, pp. 231–44.

66　See Alain Tallon, *La Compagnie du Saint-Sacrement, 1629–1667* (Paris: Cerf, 1990), pp. 37–47. Spiritual reading together is also attested in Milanese devotional confraternities of the late sixteenth and early seventeenth centuries: see Riccardo Bottoni, 'Libri e lettura nelle confraternite milanesi del secondo Cinquecento', in *Stampa, libri e letture a Milano nell'-età di Carlo Borromeo*, ed. Nicola Raponi and Angelo Turchini (Milan: Vita e Pensiero, 1992), pp. 247–77.

67　See Louis Châtellier, *L'Europe des dévots* (Paris: Flammarion, 1987), p. 137.

68　See Bernard Dompnier and F. Hernandez, 'Les livres de piété des pénitents du XVIIIᵉ au XIXᵉ siècle: La négation de la Révolution?', *Provence historique*, 39 (1989): 257–71; Marie-Hélène Froeschlé-Chopard, 'La dévotion du Rosaire à travers quelques livres de piété', *Histoire, Economie, Société*, 10 (1991): 299–316.

69　See Xenio Toscani, 'Le "Scuole della dottrina cristiana" come fattore di alfabetizzazione', *Società e Storia*, 26 (1984): 757–81; Paul F. Grendler, 'Borromeo and the Schools of Christian Doctrine', in *San Carlo Borromeo: Catholic Reform and Ecclesiastical Politics in the Second Half of the Sixteenth Century*, ed. John M. Headley and John B. Tomaro (London: Associated University Press and Washington, D.C.: Folger Shakespeare Library, 1988), pp. 158–71.

70　Ignatius of Loyola, letters to Peter Canisius, 13 August 1554, in French translation in Ignatius of Loyola, *Écrits* (Paris: Desclée, 1991), p. 893, quoted here from *Letters of St Ignatius of Loyola*, selected and translated by William J. Young (Chicago: Loyola University Press, 1959), pp. 344–7.

71　On the Canisius catechisms, see Otto Braunsberger, *Enstehung und erste Entwicklung der Katechismen des Seligen Petrus Canisius aus der Gesellschaft Jesu* (Freiburg-im-Breisgau and St Louis, Mo.: Herder, 1893).

72　On editions of Canisius's catechisms in Latin and German, see *S. Petri Canisii Catechismi Latini et Germanici*, critical edition, Fridericus Streicher, Societatis Jesu Selecti Scriptores, 2 (Rome: Pontificia Universitas Gregoriana, Monachii Bavariae: Off. Salesiana, 1933), 1:1, 2.

73　On the circulation of Canisius's works in French-speaking lands, see Guy Bedouelle, 'L'influence des catéchismes de Canisius en France', in *Aux origines du catéchisme en France*, Actes du colloque historique, Paris, 11–12 mars 1988, Institut supérieur de pastoral catéchétique, département de l'Institut Catholique de Paris, ed. Pierre Colin et al., Relais-Études, 6 (Paris: Desclée, 1989), pp. 67–86.

74　See, for example, 'Ordo et Ratio Studiorum Quinque Classium' by Father Jacob Ledesma, prefect of studies at the Collegio Romano in 1564, in Ladislaus Lukács, *Monumenta paedagogica Societatis Iesu*, Monumenta historica Societatis Iesu, 92 (7 vols, Rome: Monumenta historica Societatis Iesu, 1965–92), vol. 2 (1974), pp. 757–62. At the Roman college, the catechism was taught on Fridays in two half-hour sessions. The younger children recited their memorized catechism to their teachers every day; the older children, once or several times a week. See ibid., vol. 3 (1974), p. 371.

75　See the Acts of the Congregation of the province of Aquitaine for 1576, cited in Lukács, *Monumenta paedagogica*, vol. 4 (1981), pp. 287–8. In 1571 Canisius's 'little catechism' was taught in French in the colleges of Chambéry, Lyons, Tournon and Avignon.

76 See Elisabeth Germain, 'Du prône au catéchisme dans le diocèse de Paris', in *Aux origines du catéchisme,* ed. Colin et al., pp. 106–19.

77 See Pérouas, *Le Diocèse de La Rochelle,* pp. 276–7.

78 On catechetics in the parish of Saint-Nicolas du Chardonnet, see Dominique Julia, 'La leçon de catéchisme dans l'*Escole Paroissiale* (1654)', in *Aux origines du catéchisme,* ed. Colin et al., pp. 160–87.

79 See, for example, *Catéchismes, ou Abrégez de la doctrine chrétienne, cy-devant intitulez Catéchisme de Bourges,* written by Joachim Trotti de La Chétardie, the *curé* of Saint-Sulpice in Paris in the late seventeenth century. The Paris edition of 1707 states: 'Monseigneur our prelate has desired that the questions and the responses be clear and short, as one will find them here, and that they be held to exactly, almost never varying [since he is] persuaded that nothing imprints itself better in the mind of children than the same things repeated and inculcated frequently and in the same terms.... He hopes that this summary will bear all the more fruit for his having seen, in long and well-meditated experience, that children are capable of this but are capable of no more, for their ideas and their expressions have been studied [as well as] what is easy or difficult for them to grasp, retain and repeat. This work has kept to that.'

80 See *Catéchisme abrégé de la doctrine chrétienne imprimé par l'ordre de Monseigneur l'évêque de Mende pour l'usage de son diocèse* (2 vols, Mende, 1684), introductory 'Mandement' of the bishop to his parish priests.

81 'Avertissement de Monseigneur l'Archevêque d'Auch sur la nouvelle édition du Catéchisme à l'usage de son Diocèse', 4 August 1764, in *Catéchisme à l'usage du diocèse d'Auch,* 1764 edn.

82 To give three examples, the rules for schools in the diocese of Toul, decreed on 10 March 1695 by Henri de Thyard de Bissy, direct teachers to have the catechism recited twice a week, and to make sure 'that every child has his catechism'. A pastoral instruction of Pierre Sabatier, bishop of Amiens, dated 25 July 1707, requires that teachers be capable of teaching 'the entire catechism with facility and without needing to hold the book in their hand, something that seems indecent on the part of those who should be perfectly instructed in what they are teaching to others'. Sabatier adds that the catechism book should be 'the first French book after the ABC'. In 1744 the synod of the diocese of Boulogne decided that the 'catechism will be the first reading book for children who have learned the alphabet'.

83 Charles de Caylus, *Avis et instructions sur les ordonnances publiées dans le synode tenu au Palais épiscopal les 18 et 19 juin 1738* (Paris, 1742), p. 168.

84 All these quotations are from Claude Fleury, 'Du dessein et de l'usage du catéchisme', in the preface to his *Catéchisme historique contenant en abrégé l'histoire et la doctrine chrétienne* (Paris, 1683).

85 On this topic, see François Brossier, S. Duguet, Elisabeth Germain and Jean Joncheray, *Catéchismes, mémoires d'un temps, 1687: Les manuels diocésains de Paris et de Meaux (Bossuet),* Cahiers de l'Institut Supérieur de pastorale catéchétique, 1 (Paris: Desclée, 1988).

86 Fleury, 'Du dessein et de l'usage du catéchisme'.

87 The Royaumont Bible was read in the Autun seminary during the years 1680–92; see the letter of Monsieur Tronson to Mr Le Vayer de Bressac, director of the seminary of Autun, 14 December 1692, in Louis Tronson, *Correspondance de M. Louis Tronson,* ed. L. Bertrand (3 vols, Paris: Victor Lecoffre, 1904), 1:161–2.

88 Nicolas Restif de la Bretonne, *Monsieur Nicolas, ou Le coeur humain*

dévoilé (6 vols, Paris: Pauvert, 1959), 1:187; ed. and trans. into English by Robert Baldick as *Monsieur Nicolas, or, The Human Heart Laid Bare* (London: Barrie and Rockliff, 1966).

89 Citoyen Renaud, *Mémoire historique sur la ci-devant communauté des écoles chrétiennes du faubourg Saint-Antoine* (Paris, 1804), p. 20.

90 *Vie de M. Grosley, écrite en partie par lui-même, continuée et publiée par l'abbé Maydieu, chanoine de l'Église de Troyes en Champagne, dédiée à un inconnu* (Paris, 1787), p. 14. The *collèges* of Troyes used the *Figures de la Bible*, very probably in the *Bibliothèque bleue* format, as a textbook.

91 Xavier-Auguste Séjourné, *Histoire du vénérable serviteur de Dieu Julien Maunoir* (2 vols, Paris: H. Houdin, 1885), 2:214.

92 Gwennole Le Menn, 'Les catalogues des libraires bretons (1695–1746)', *Mémoires de la Société d'Histoire et d'Archéologie de Bretagne*, 42 (1985): 301–11.

93 See Madeleine Foisil, 'Un jésuite normand missionnaire en Basse-Normandie: Pierre Sandret, 1658–1738', *Annales de Bretagne et des Pays de l'Ouest*, 81 (1974): 537–52.

94 See Jean-Baptiste Bergier, *Histoire de la communauté de prêtres mission-naires de Beaupré et des missions faites en Franche-Comté depuis 1676 jusqu'en 1850* (Besançon: Cyprien Monnat, 1853); Michel Vernus, 'La diffusion du petit livre de piété et de la bimbeloterie religieuse dans le Jura (au XVIIIe siècle)', in *Actes du 105e Congrès national des Sociétés Savantes, Caen 1980*, Section d'histoire moderne et contemporaine (Paris: CTHS, 1983), 1:127–41.

95 See Louis Châtellier, 'Livres et missions rurales au XVIIIe siècle: L'exemple des missions jésuites dans les pays germaniques', in *Le Livre religieux et ses pratiques: Études sur l'histoire du livre religieux en Allemagne et en France à l'époque moderne*, ed. Hans Erich Bödeker, Gérald Chaix and Patrice Veit, Veröffentlichungen des Max-Planck-Instituts für Geschichte, 101 (Göttingen: Vandenhoeck and Ruprecht, 1991), pp. 183–93.

96 Private archives of M. Carrère, Rodez, 'Livre de comptes du libraire Leroux'. Michel Chappat was also called a *quinquiller* (hardware vendor).

97 Jean Leuduger, *Le Bouquet de la mission, ou, L'Abrégé des vérités et maximes que l'on enseigne dans les missions*, revised, corrected, and enlarged by the author (Rennes, 1700). The quotation is taken from the 'Préface aux peuples de la campagne'. Louis-Marie Grignion de Montfort trained for mission work with Jean Leuduger: see J. B. Blain, *Abrégé de la vie de Louis-Marie Grignion de Montfort*, ed. Louis Pérouas (Rome: Centre International Montfortain, 1973), pp. 146–8.

98 Leuduger, *Le Bouquet de la mission*, p. 308.

Chapter 10   Reading Matter and 'Popular' Reading: From the Renaissance to the Seventeenth Century

1 Lucien Febvre and Henri-Jean Martin, *L'Apparition du livre*, L'évolution de l'humanité (Paris: Albin Michel, 1958); trans. into English by David Gerard as *The Coming of the Book: The Impact of Printing 1450–1800*, ed. Geoffrey Nowell-Smith and David Wootton, new edn (London and New York: Verso, 1990).

2 Philippe Berger, 'La lecture à Valence de 1474 à 1560: Évolution des com-

portements en fonction des milieux sociaux', in *Livres et lecture en Espagne et en France sous l'ancien régime*, Colloque de la Casa de Velazquez (Paris: ADPF, 1981), pp. 97–101; *idem, Libro y lectura en la Valencia del Renacimiento*, trans. Amparo Balanzá Pérez (Valencia: Alfons el Magnánim, Institució Valenciana d'Estudis i Investigació, 1987).

3 André Labarre, *Le Livre dans la vie amiénoise du XVIᵉ siècle: L'enseignement des inventaires après décès, 1503–1576* (Paris and Louvain: Nauwelaerts, 1971).

4 Peter Clark, 'The ownership of books in England, 1560–1640: the example of some Kentish townsfolk', in *Schooling and Society: Studies in the History of Education*, ed. Lawrence Stone (Baltimore: Johns Hopkins University Press, 1976), pp. 95–111, table 4.4, p. 101.

5 Carlo Ginzburg, *Il formaggio e i vermi: Il cosmo di un mugnaio del '500* (Turin: Einaudi, 1976); trans. into English by John and Anne Tedeschi as *The Cheese and the Worms: The Cosmos of a Sixteenth-Century Miller* (Baltimore: Johns Hopkins University Press, 1980).

6 Sara T. Nalle, 'Literacy and culture in early modern Castile', *Past and Present*, 125 (November 1989): 65–96.

7 Maxime Chevalier, 'El público de las novelas de caballerías', in *Lectura y lectores en la España de los siglos XVI y XVII* (Madrid: Turner, 1976), pp. 65–103.

8 Marcel Bataillon, 'Santa Teresa, lectora de libros de caballerías', in *Varia lección de clásicos españoles* (Madrid: Gredos, 1964), pp. 21–3.

9 Daniel Eisenberg, 'Who read the romances of chivalry?', *Kentucky Romance Quarterly*, 20 (1973): 209–33, repr. in Eisenberg, *Romances of Chivalry in the Spanish Golden Age*, Juan de la Cuesta Hispanic Monographs, 3 (Newark, Del.: Juan de la Cuesta, 1982), pp. 89–118, at p. 105.

10 On the various definitions of 'popular', see Lawrence Levine, 'The folklore of industrial society: popular culture and its audience', *American Historical Review*, 97/5 (1992): 1369–99, esp. p. 1373; Roger Chartier, 'Popular appropriations: the readers and their books', in Roger Chartier, *Forms and Meanings: Texts, Performances, and Audiences from Codex to Computer* (Philadelphia: University of Pennsylvania Press, 1995), pp. 83–97.

11 For a summary, see Paloma Díaz-Mas, 'Prólogo', in *Romancero*, ed. Paloma Díaz-Mas, with a preliminary study by Samuel G. Armistead, Biblioteca clásica (Barcelona: Crítica, 1994), pp. 1–50.

12 See Antonio Rodriguez Moñino, *Nuevo Diccionario bibliográfico de pliegos sueltos poéticos (siglo XVI)*, edition corrected and updated by Arthur L. F. Askins and Víctor Infantes (Madrid: Castalia, 1997); *idem, Manual bibliográfico de cancioneros y romanceros* (4 vols), vols 1 and 2: *Impresos durante el siglo XVI*, ed. Arthur L. F. Askins (Madrid: Castalia, 1973); Giuliana Piacentini, *Ensayo de una bibliografía analítica del romancero antiguo: Los Textos (siglos XV y XVI)* (2 vols, Pisa: Giardini, 1981–6), vol. 2: *Cancioneros y romanceros* (1986). On *romances nuevos* and the *pliegos sueltos* in the seventeenth century, see Maria Cruz García de Enterría, *Sociedad y poesía de cordel en el Barroco* (Madrid: Taurus, 1973).

13 Díaz-Mas, 'Prólogo', p. 32.

14 The definition of the *pliego* can be extended beyond its original form. The outside limit of the *pliego suelto* was thirty-two pages, 'and even more' (that is, four print sheets or more) according to Antonio Rodriguez Moñino (*Nuevo Diccionario bibliográfico*, p. 15); thirty-two pages (four sheets) according to Maria Cruz García de Enterría (*Sociedad y poesía de*

cordel, p. 61); thirty-two pages 'and even more' according to Joaquín Marco, *Literatura popular en España en los siglos XVIII y XIX (Una aproximación a los pliegos de cordel)*, Persiles, 102 (Madrid: Taurus, 1977), p. 33.

15 Víctor Infantes, 'Los pliegos sueltos poéticos: Constitución tipográfica y contenido literario (1482–1600)', in *En el Siglo de Oro: Estudios y textos de literatura áurea* (Potomac: Scripta Humanistica, 1922), pp. 47–58.

16 Jean-François Botrel, 'Les aveugles colporteurs d'imprimés en Espagne', pt 1: 'La confrérie des aveugles de Madrid et la vente des imprimés du monopole à la liberté du commerce (1581–1836)', and pt 2: 'Les aveugles considérés comme mass-média', *Mélanges de la Casa de Velazquez*, 9 (1973): 417–82 and 10 (1974): 233–71.

17 Tessa Watt, *Cheap Print and Popular Piety, 1550–1640* (Cambridge and New York: Cambridge University Press, 1991).

18 Adam Fox, 'Ballads, libels and popular ridicule in Jacobean England', *Past and Present*, 145 (November 1994): 47–83.

19 Margaret Spufford, *Small Books and Pleasant Histories: Popular Fiction and its Readership in Seventeenth-Century England* (London: Methuen, 1981; Athens, Ga.: University of Georgia Press, 1982).

20 Tessa Watt, 'The development of the chapbook trade', in *Cheap Print and Popular Piety*, pp. 257–95.

21 On the *Bibliothèque bleue*, see Roger Chartier, *Lectures et lecteurs dans la France d'ancien régime* (Paris: Seuil, 1987), pp. 110–21, 247–70, and 271–351; trans. into English by Lydia G. Cochrane as *The Cultural Uses of Print in Early Modern Europe* (Princeton, NJ: Princeton University Press, 1987), pp. 170–9, 240–64, 265–342.

22 Paul Ricoeur, *Temps et récit* (3 vols, Paris: Seuil, 1983–5), vol. 3: *Le Temps raconté* (1985), pp. 228–63; trans. into English by Kathleen Blamey and David Pellauer as *Time and Narrative* (Chicago: University of Chicago Press, 1984–8), 3:157–79.

23 Ricoeur, *Le Temps raconté*, p. 239; *Time and Narrative*, 3:164.

24 Wolfgang Iser, *Der Akt des Lesens: Theorie ästhetischer Wirkung* (Munich: Wilhelm Fink, 1976); trans. into English as *The Act of Reading: A Theory of Aesthetic Response* (Baltimore: Johns Hopkins University Press, 1978).

25 Hans Robert Jauss, *Literaturgeschichte als Provokation der Literaturwissenschaft* (Frankfurt am Main: Suhrkamp, 1970); trans. into English by Timothy Bahti as *Toward an Aesthetic of Reception* (Minneapolis: University of Minnesota Press, 1982).

26 D. F. McKenzie, *Bibliography and the Sociology of Texts*, The Panizzi Lectures, 1985 (London: British Library, 1986). See also Roger Chartier, 'Textes, formes, interprétations', in preface to the French translation of this same work, *La Bibliographie et la sociologie des textes* (Paris: Cercle de la Librairie, 1991), pp. 5–18; 'Texts, forms, and interpretations', in Roger Chartier, trans. into English by Lydia G. Cochrane as *On the Edge of the Cliff: History, Language, Practices* (Baltimore and London: Johns Hopkins University Press), pp. 81–9.

27 Stanley Fish, *Is There a Text in this Class? The Authority of Interpretive Communities* (Cambridge, Mass., and London: Harvard University Press, 1980), pp. 1–17.

28 Margit Frenk, ' "Lectores y oidores": La difusión oral de la literature en el Siglo de Oro', in *Actas del Septimo Congreso de la Asociación Internacional de Hispanistas, publicadas por Giuseppe Bellini* (Rome: Bulzoni, 1982),

1:101–23. See also idem, *Entre la voz y el silencio (La lectura en tiempos de Cervantes)* (Alcalá de Henares: Centro de Estudios Cervantinos, 1997).

29 Frenk, ' "Lectores y oidores" ', pp. 115–16.

30 B. W. Ife, *Reading and Fiction in Golden-Age Spain: A Platonist Critique and some Picaresque Replies* (Cambridge and New York: Cambridge University Press, 1985).

31 Ibid., pp. 16–17.

32 Jaime Moll, 'Diez años sin licencias para imprimir comedias y novelas en los reinos de Castilla: 1625–1634', *Boletín de la Real Academia de España*, 54 (1974): 97–103; D. W. Cruickshank, ' "Literature" and the book-trade in Golden-Age literature', *Modern Language Review*, 73/4 (1978): 799–824.

33 McKenzie, *Bibliography and the Sociology of Texts*, p. 20.

34 Spufford, *Small Books and Pleasant Histories*, pp. 91–101. For an example of a catalogue, see ibid., pp. 262–7.

35 Henri-Jean Martin, 'Culture écrite et culture orale, culture savante et culture populaire dans la France d'ancien régime', *Journal des savants* (July–December 1975): 225–82.

36 Joana Escobedo, *Plecs poètics catalans del segle XVII de la Biblioteca de Catalunya* (Barcelona: Biblioteca de Catalunya, 1988).

37 Antonio Rodriguez Moñino, *Poesía y cancioneros (siglo XVI)* (Madrid: Real Academia Española, 1968), pp. 31–2. For Pedro M. Cátedra and Victor Infantes, 'the authentic, original *pliego*' was one print sheet folded twice, giving eight quarto-format pages. They add, however: 'We must admit that every [additional] page distanced the original product from its initial condition.' See Pedro M. Cátedra and Victor Infantes, 'Estudio', in *Los pliegos sueltos de Thomas Croft (siglo XVI)* (Valencia: Primus Calamus, Albatros, 1983), pp. 11–48, at pp. 25–6.

38 Mercedes Agulló y Cobo, *Relaciones de sucesos*, vol. 1: *Años 1477–1619*, Cuadernos Bibliográficos, 20 (Madrid: CSIC, 1966).

39 Edward Calverley Riley, 'Author and reader', in *Cervantes's Theory of the Novel* (Oxford: Clarendon Press, 1962), pp. 81–115; Maria Cruz Garcia de Enterría, 'Lectura y rasgos de un público', *Edad de Oro*, 12 (1993): 119–30.

40 Jean-Pierre Seguin, *L'Information en France avant la périodique: 517 canards imprimés entre 1529 et 1631* (Paris: Maisonneuve et Larose, 1964). For an example of such print pieces, see Roger Chartier, 'La pendue miraculeusement sauvée: Étude d'un occasionnel', in *Les Usages de l'imprimé (XVᵉ–XIXᵉ siècle)*, ed. Roger Chartier (Paris: Fayard, 1987), pp. 83–127; trans. into English by Lydia G. Cochrane as 'The hanged woman miraculously saved: an *occasionnel*', in *The Culture of Print* (Cambridge: Polity Press, 1989), pp. 59–91.

41 William Eamon, 'Arcana disclosed: the advent of printing, the books of secrets tradition, and the development of experimental science in the sixteenth century', *History of Science*, 22/2, no. 56 (1984): 111–50.

42 Lorraine Daston, 'Marvelous facts and miraculous evidences in early modern Europe', *Critical Inquiry*, 18/1 (1991): 93–124.

43 Lisa Jardine and Anthony Grafton, ' "Studied for action": how Gabriel Harvey read his Livy', *Past and Present*, 129 (November 1990): 30–78.

44 Ann Blair, 'Humanist methods in natural philosophy: the commonplace book', *Journal of the History of Ideas*, 53/4 (1992): 541–51.

45 For examples of such memoirs and autobiographies in France, see Valentin Jamerey-Duval, *Mémoires: Enfance et éducation d'un paysan au XVIIIᵉ siècle*, introduction by Jean-Marie Goulemot (Paris: Le Sycomore, 1981);

Jacques-Louis Ménétra, *Journal de ma vie: Jacques-Louis Ménétra, compagnon vitrier au XVIIIᵉ siècle*, presented by Daniel Roche (Paris: Montalba, 1982); trans. into English by Arthur Goldhammer, with a foreword by Robert Darnton and an introduction and commentary by Daniel Roche, as *Journal of My Life* (New York: Columbia University Press, 1986); Anne Fillon, 'Louis Simon, étaminier (1741–1820) dans son village du Haut Maine au siècle des Lumières', thèse de troisième cycle, Université du Maine, 1982.

46 Silvana Seidel Menchi, *Erasmo in Italia 1520–1580* (Turin: Bollati Boringhieri, 1987), pp. 286–321.

47 See Francis Goyet, *Le Sublime du 'lieu commun': L'invention rhétorique dans l'Antiquité et à la Renaissance* (Paris: Champion, 1996).

48 Jardine and Grafton, ' "Studied for action" ', p. 73, n. 148.

49 See Lisa Jardine, *Erasmus, Man of Letters, The Construction of Charisma in Print* (Princeton, NJ: Princeton University Press, 1993).

Chapter 11   Was there a Reading Revolution at the End of the Eighteenth Century?

1 J. G. Heinzmann, *Appel an meine Nation: Über die Pest der deutschen Literatur* (Bern, 1795; repr. Hildesheim: Olm, 1977), p. 139.

2 Quoted from W. Krauss, 'Über den Anteil der Buchgeschichte an der Entfaltung der Aufklärung', in *Zur Dichtungsgeschichte der romanischen Völker* (Leipzig, 1965), pp. 194–312.

3 J. G. Beyer, 'Über das Lesen, insofern es zum Luxus unserer Zeiten gehört', in *Acta Academiae Electoralis Moguntinae Scientiarum Utilium*, vol. 12 (Erfurt, 1794), p. 7.

4 In France there is a predominance of quantitative analyses of posthumous inventories and library catalogues which permit only relatively global conclusions to be drawn. They often record what was collected, but not what was read. Well-thumbed and suspicious material was often not singled out, and frequently catalogues represent an obsolete stock accumulated by generations, awarding space to the traditional agents of culture and cultural context in preference to innovative materials. In Germany, however, even these limited findings are not widely available, and the mostly theoretical models lack empirical substantiation.

5 I. Watt, *The Rise of the Novel* (Harmondsworth: Penguin, 1957), p. 174.

6 Cf. R. Engelsing, *Analphabetentum und Lektüre* (Stuttgart: Metzler, 1973), pp. 62ff.

7 R. Schenda, *Volk ohne Buch: Studien zur Sozialgeschichte der popularen Lesestoffe 1770–1910* (Frankfurt am Main: Klostermann, 1970), p. 445.

8 H. Kiesel and P. Münch, *Gesellschaft und Literatur im 18. Jahrhundert* (Munich: Beck, 1977), p. 160.

9 Schenda, *Volk ohne Buch*, p. 88.

10 B. Haug, *Das gelehrte Wirtemberg* (Stuttgart, 1790), pp. 26–32.

11 A. Martino, *Die deutsche Leihbibliothek: Geschichte einer literarischen Institution (1756–1914)* (Wiesbaden: Harrassowitz, 1990), p. 52.

12 R. Chartier, 'The Bibliothèque bleue and popular reading', in Chartier, *The Cultural Uses of Print in Early Modern France* (Cambridge: Polity Press, 1987), pp. 251f.

13 Watt, *Rise of the Novel*, p. 52.

14 J. J. Rousseau, *La Nouvelle Héloïse*, p. 695.

15 R. Chartier, 'Du livre au lire', in *Pratiques de la lecture*, ed. Chartier (Paris: Payot et Rivages, 1993), p. 91.

16 J. A. Wiessenbach, *Vorstellungen über den Krieg, den man itzt gefährlichen Schriften anzukündigen hat; an alle so wohl geistliche, als weltliche Oberkeiten* (Augsburg: Joh. Nep. Styx, 1793), pp. 7f.

17 R. Darnton, 'Readers respond to Rousseau: the fabrication of romantic sensitivity', in Darnton, *The Great Cat Massacre and Other Episodes in French Cultural History* (New York: Basic Books, 1984), p. 226.

18 Watt, *Rise of the Novel*, p. 196.

19 Darnton, 'Readers respond to Rousseau', p. 226.

20 Ibid., p. 234.

21 Ibid., p. 244.

22 R. Engelsing, 'Die Perioden der Lesergeschichte in der Neuzeit', *Archiv für Geschichte des Buchwesens*, 10 (1970): 143.

23 E. Schön, *Der Verlust der Sinnlichkeit oder die Verwandlungen des Lesers: Mentalitätswandel um 1800* (Stuttgart: Klett-Cotta, 1987), p. 327.

24 L. Mejer, letter to H. C. Boie of 1 January 1784; quoted in Ilse Schreiber (ed.), *Ich war wohl klug, daß ich dich fand. H. C. Boies Briefwechsel mit Luise Mejer 1777–1785* (Munich, 1961), p. 275.

25 Cf. Schön, *Der Verlust der Sinnlichkeit*, p. 326.

26 J. A. Bergk, *Die Kunst, Bücher zu lesen: Nebst Bemerkungen über Schiften und Schriftsteller* (Jena: Hempel, 1799), p. 69.

27 Cf. Schön, *Der Verlust der Sinnlichkeit*, p. 328.

28 Cf. Eva Maria Hanebutt-Benz, ed., *Die Kunst des lesens: Lesemöbel und Leseverhalten vom Mittelalter bis zur Gegenwart*, exhibition catalogue (Frankfurt am Main, 1985), pp. 109ff.

29 Watt, *Rise of the Novel*, p. 213.

30 Schön, *Der Verlust der Sinnlichkeit*, p. 167.

31 Jean Paul, *Briefe und bevorstehender Lebenslauf: Konjektural-Biographie, sechste poetische Epistel*; quoted from Jean Paul, *Werke*, ed. Norbert Miller, vol. 4 (Munich: Hanser, 1962), p. 1070.

32 Karl G. Bauer, *Über die Mittel, dem Geschlechtstrieb eine unschädliche Richtung zu geben* (Leipzig, 1791), p. 190.

33 Bergk, *Die Kunst, Bücher zu lesen*, p. 59.

34 Ibid., p. 407.

35 Jean Paul, *Kleine Nachschule zu ästhetischen Vorschule*, vol. 1: *Miserkordias-Vorlesung*; quoted from Jean Paul, *Werke*, ed. Norbert Miller, vol. 5 (Munich: Hanser, 1963), p. 495.

36 Watt, *Rise of the Novel*, p. 54.

37 Ibid., p. 234.

38 'Über Mode-Epoken in der Teutschen Lektüre', *Journal des Luxus und der Moden* (November 1972): 549–58.

39 Cf. Martino, *Die deutsche Leihbibliothek*, p. 57.

Chapter 12   New Readers in the Nineteenth Century: Women, Children, Workers

1 François Furet and Jacques Ozouf, *Lire et écrire: L'alphabétisation des français de Calvin à Jules Ferry* (2 vols, Paris, 1977). Trans. into English as *Reading and Writing: Literacy in France from Calvin to Jules Ferry* (Cambridge: Cambridge University Press, 1982).

2 Roger Schofield, 'Dimensions of illiteracy in England, 1750–1850', in Harvey J. Graff, ed., *Literacy and Social Development in the West: A Reader* (Cambridge: Cambridge University Press, 1981), pp. 201–13.

3 Dieter Langewiesche and Klaus Schonhoven, 'Arbeiterbibliotheken und Arbeiterlektüre in Wilhelminischen Deutschland', *Archiv für Sozialgeschichte*, 16 (1976): 140.

4 Daniel Roche, *Le Peuple de Paris: Essai sur la culture populaire au 18ᵉ siècle* (Paris: Aubier-Montaigne, 1981), pp. 206–9.

5 Langewiesche and Schonhoven, 'Arbeiterbibliotheken und Arbeiterlektüre', p. 136.

6 Martyn Lyons, *Le Triomphe du livre: Une histoire sociologique de la lecture dans la France du XIXᵉ siècle* (Paris: Promodis, 1987).

7 C.-A. Ste-Beuve, 'De la littérature industrielle', in *Portraits contemporains* (5 vols, Paris, 1869–76), vol. 2 (1869), pp. 444–71.

8 Wilkie Collins, 'The unknown public', in *Victorian Fiction: A Collection of Essays*, ed. I. B. Nadel (New York: Garland, 1986).

9 R. Chartier, D. Julia and M.-M. Compère, *L'Éducation en France du XVIᵉ au XVIIIᵉ siècle* (Paris: Société d'édition d'enseignement supérieur, 1976), pp. 102–5.

10 Martyn Lyons and Lucy Taksa, *Australian Readers Remember: An Oral History of Reading, 1890–1930* (Melbourne and New York: Oxford University Press, 1992), ch. 3.

11 Pierre-Jakez Hélias, *The Horse of Pride: Life in a Breton Village*, trans. J. Guicharnaud (New Haven, Conn.: Yale University Press, 1978), p. 96.

12 Lyons, *Le Triomphe du livre*, p. 101.

13 Anon. [Audin-Rouvière], *La Cuisinière bourgeoise* (Paris, 1846), 'advice'.

14 Evelyne Sullerot, *La Presse feminine* (Paris, 1963).

15 *Le Journal illustré*, no. 8 (3–10 April 1864).

16 Stendhal, *Correspondance*, ed. Paupe-Chéramy (3 vols, Paris, 1908), 3:89–92.

17 Lise Quéffelec, 'La lecteur du roman comme lectrice: Stratégies romanesques et stratégies critiques sous la Monarchie de Juillet', *Romantisme*, 16/53 (1986): 9–21.

18 Cited in Richard D. Altick, *The English Common Reader: A Social History of the Mass Reading Public, 1800–1900* (Chicago: University of Chicago Press, 1957), pp. 112–13.

19 M.-J. Brisset, *Le Cabinet de lecture* (2 vols, Paris, 1843), 1:10.

20 Georges Duby, ed., *Histoire de la France urbaine*, vol. 4: *La Ville de l'âge industriel: Le cycle haussmannien* (Paris: Seuil, 1983), p. 366.

21 Anne-Marie Thiesse, *Le Roman du quotidien: Lecteurs et lectures populaires à la belle époque* (Paris: Le Chemin Vert, 1984), p. 22.

22 Ibid. and Martyn Lyons and Lucy Taksa, ' "If Mother caught us reading!": impressions of the Australian woman reader, 1890–1933', *Australian Cultural History*, 11 (1992): 39–50.

23 Lyons, *Le Triomphe du livre*, p. 186.
24 Furet and Ozouf, *Lire et écrire*, 2:32–3 and 263.
25 Maurice Gontard, *Les Écoles primaires de la France bourgeoise, 1833–1875* (Toulouse, n.d.), pp. 162–9.
26 P. Lorain, *Tableau de l'instruction primaire en France* (Paris, 1837), pp. 2–5.
27 Antoine Prost, *Histoire de l'enseignement en France, 1800–67* (Paris: A. Colin, 1968), p. 113.
28 Pamela Horn, *Education in Rural England, 1800–1914* (Dublin: Gill and Macmillan, 1978), p. 138.
29 Ibid., p. 146.
30 Ibid., p. 116.
31 Ibid., p. 118.
32 Ibid., p. 53.
33 Ibid., p. 120.
34 Phillip McCann, *Popular Education and Socialization in the 19th century* (London: Methuen, 1977), pp. 28–30.
35 Lyons, *Le Triomphe du livre*, p. 95.
36 Catherine Velay-Vallantin, 'Le miroir des contes: Perrault dans les bibliothèques bleues', in *Les Usages de l'imprimé*, ed. R. Chartier (Paris: Fayard, 1987), p. 168.
37 John M. Ellis, *One Fairy Story Too Many: The Brothers Grimm and their Tales* (Chicago: University of Chicago Press, 1985), p. 193.
38 S. Le Men, *Les Abécédaires français illustrés du 19ᵉ siècle* (Paris: Promodis, 1984).
39 *Magasin d'éducation et de récréation*, 4 (1865–6): 371.
40 Isabelle Jan, 'Childrens' literature and bourgeois society since 1860', *Yale French Studies*, 43 (1969): 57–72.
41 Jean Hassenforder, *Développement comparé des bibliothèques publiques en France, en Grande-Bretagne et aux États-Unis dans la seconde moitié du XIXᵉ siècle (1850–1914)* (Paris: Cercle de la Libraire, 1967).
42 Charles Dickens, *Speeches*, ed. K. J. Fielding (Oxford: Clarendon Press, 1960), pp. 152–4.
43 Georges Duveau, *La Pensée ouvrière sur l'éducation pendant la Seconde République et le Second Empire* (Paris, 1948), p. 185.
44 Agricol Perdiguier, *Livre du compagnonnage* (Paris, 1857), 1:231ff.
45 Jean-Baptiste Dumay, *Mémoires d'un militant ouvrier du Creusot (1841–1905)*, ed. Pierre Ponsot (Grenoble: Maspéro, 1976), pp. 116–18.
46 Roger Bellet, 'Une bataille culturelle, provinciale et nationale, à propos des bons auteurs pour bibliothèques populaires', *Revue des sciences humaines*, 34 (1969): 453–73.
47 Langewiesche and Schonhoven, 'Arbeiterbibliotheken und Arbeiterlektüre', p. 136.
48 Ibid., p. 138.
49 Ibid., pp. 150–1.
50 Lyons, *Le Triomphe du livre*, p. 182.
51 Langewiesche and Schonhoven, 'Arbeiterbibliotheken und Arbeiterlektüre', p. 163.
52 Ibid., p. 167.
53 Lyons, *Le Triomphe du livre*, p. 190.
54 R. K. Webb, *The British Working-Class Reader, 1790–1848: Literacy and Social Tension* (London: Allen & Unwin, 1955), p. 22.

55 John Burnett, ed., *Useful Toil: Autobiographies of Working People from the 1820s to the 1920s* (Harmondsworth: Penguin, 1977), pp. 231, 308.

56 Thomas Cooper, *The Life of Thomas Cooper, Written by Himself* (London: Hodder & Stoughton, 1872, 1897), p. 57.

57 Jocelyne Baty Goodman, ed., *Victorian Cabinet-Maker: The Memoirs of James Hopkinson, 1819–1894* (London: Routledge & Kegan Paul, 1968), p. 83.

58 William Thom, *Rhymes and Recollections of a Handloom Weaver*, 2nd edn (London: Smith and Elder, 1845), p. 13.

59 John James Bezer, 'Autobiography of one of the Chartist rebels of 1848', in *Testaments of Radicalism: Memoirs of Working-Class Politicians, 1790–1885*, ed. David Vincent (London: Europa, 1977), p. 157.

60 Maxim Gorky, *My Universities* (Harmondsworth: Penguin, 1983), pp. 31–2.

61 Ibid., p. 95.

62 J. W. and Anne Tibble, eds, *The Prose of John Clare, Including the Autobiography, 1793–1824* (London: Routledge & Kegan Paul, 1951), p. 32.

63 William Edwin Adams, *Memoirs of a Social Atom* (2 vols, London: Hutchinson, 1903), 1:44–5.

64 William Aitken, 'Remembrances and the struggles of a working man for bread and liberty', *Ashton-under-Lyne News*, 25 September 1869, p. 3b.

65 David Vincent, *Bread, Knowledge and Freedom: A Study of 19th Century Working-Class Autobiography* (London: Europa, 1981), p. 124.

66 David D. Hall, 'The uses of literacy in New England, 1600–1850', in William L. Joyce et al., *Printing and Society in Early America* (Worcester, Mass.: American Antiquarian Society, 1983); Rolf Engelsing, *Der Burger als Leser: Lesergeschichte in Deutschland, 1500–1800* (Stuttgart: Metzler, 1974).

67 John Buckley (pseud.), *A Village Politician: The Life Story of John Buckley*, ed. J. C. Buckmaster (London: Fisher Unwin, 1897), p. 2.

68 George L. Craik, *The Pursuit of Knowledge under Difficulties* (London: Bell, 1876), pp. 248–9.

69 Charles Shaw, *When I was a Child* (Firle, Sussex: Caliban Books, 1977), pp. 220–1 (facsimile reprint of anon. 1903 edn).

70 Thomas Carter, *Memoirs of a Working Man* (London: Charles Knight, 1845), pp. 186 and 191.

71 Martin Nadaud, *Les Mémoires de Léonard, ancien garçon maçon* (Paris, n.d.), p. 96.

72 James Dawson Burn, *The Autobiography of a Beggar-Boy*, ed. D. Vincent (London: Europa, 1978; 1st edn, 1855), pp. 93–4.

73 Adams, *Memoirs*, 1:164.

74 Agricol Perdiguier, *Mémoires d'un compagnon* (Moulins, 1914), p. 137.

75 Carter, *Memoirs of a Working Man*, p. 135.

76 Quoted in Craik, *Pursuit of Knowledge*, pp. 248–9.

77 Samuel Bamford, *Early Days*, ed. W. H. Chaloner (London: Cass, 1967; 1st edn, 1848–9), pp. 192–4.

78 William Cobbett, *The Autobiography of William Cobbett*, ed. William Reitzel (London: Faber and Faber, 1967), p. 27.

79 Ebenezer Elliott, 'Autobiography', *Athenaeum*, 1/1159 (12 January 1850): 46–9.

80 Bamford, *Early Days*, p. 210.

81 Robert Owen, *The Life of Robert Owen, Written by Himself, with Selections from his Writings and Correspondence*, vol. 1 (London, 1857), p. 14.

82 Thiesse, *Le Roman du quotidien*, p. 19.

83 Henry Mayhew, *London Labour and the London Poor*, ed. J. D. Rosenberg (4 vols, New York: Dover, 1968), 1:25.

84 Francis Kilvert, *Kilvert's Diary: Selections*, ed. William Plomer (3 vols, London: Cape, 1977), 1:301–2.

Chapter 13   Reading to Read: A Future for Reading

1 Robert Pattison, *On Literacy: The Politics of the Word from Homer to the Age of Rock* (New York: Oxford University Press, 1984), p. 202.

2 Roland Barthes and Antoine Compagnon, 'Lettura', in *Enciclopedia Einaudi* (16 vols, Turin: Einaudi), vol. 8 (1979), pp. 176–99, at p. 198.

3 Romano Luperini, 'Tendenze attuali della critica in Italia', *Belfagor*, 46 (1991): 365–76, at p. 376.

4 The data discussed here are taken from Armando Petrucci, *Scrivere e no: Politiche della scrittura e analfabetismo nel mondo d'oggi* (Rome: Editori Riuniti, 1989), pp. 45–81.

5 See Barthes and Compagnon, 'Lettura', p. 178.

6 Michel Foucault, *L'Ordre du discours: Leçon inaugurale au Collège de France prononcée le 2 décembre 1970* (Paris: Gallimard, 1971); trans. into English by A. M. Sheridan Smith as 'The discourse on language', in *The Archaeology of Knowledge and the Discourse on Language* (New York: Pantheon Books, 1972), pp. 215–37.

7 *Lessico universale italiano* (26 vols, Rome: Istituto Enciclopedia Italiano), s.v. 'Canone'.

8 Foucault, *L'Ordre du discours*, pp. 10–11; quoted here from 'Discourse on language', p. 216.

9 Foucault, *L'Ordre du discours*, p. 38; quoted from 'Discourse on language', p. 224.

10 *Guida alla formazione di una biblioteca pubblica e privata: Catalogo sistematico e discografia. Con un commento di Delio Cantimori, una lettera di Salvatore Accardo e una documentazione sull'esperienza di Dogliani* (Turin: Einaudi, 1969). (A second edition, edited by Paolo Terni, Ida Terni and Piero Innocenti, was published in 1981 in the series Piccola biblioteca Einaudi, no. 123.)

11 Ibid., p. 2.

12 Ibid., p. 551.

13 *Enciclopedia europea* (12 vols, Milan: Garzanti, 1984), vol. 12: *Bibliografia. Repertorio. Statistiche*. The bibliography occupies pp. 7–928.

14 Pattison, *On Literacy*, p. 201.

15 Ibid., p. 207.

16 See Furio Colombo, *Il destino del libro e altri destini*, Temi, 16 (Turin: Bollati Boringhieri, 1990), pp. 11–34. For the American's opinion, see p. 94. My data on the situation of publishing in the United States was gathered from a survey of *Publishers Weekly: The International News Magazine of Book Publishing* (New York) for 1990 and 1991, January to April.

17 See G. Ambrosino, *Il manifesto*, 30 April 1991, p. 10.

18 See Remo Ceserani, *Il manifesto*, 26 April 1991, p. 10.

19 See Carlo Ginzburg, *Il formaggio e i vermi: Il cosmo di un mugnaio del'500* (Turin: Einaudi, 1976). Trans. into English by John and Anne Tedeschi as

The Cheese and the Worms: The Cosmos of a Sixteenth-Century Miller (Baltimore and London: Johns Hopkins University Press, 1980).

20 Eugenio Montale, 'I libri nello scaffale', in *Auto-da-fé: Cronache in due tempi* (Milan: Il Saggiatore, 1966), pp. 96–100; this quotation, dated 24 October 1961, is on p. 96.

21 Elizabeth Long, 'Reading groups and the postmodern crisis of cultural authority', *Cultural Studies*, 1 (1987): 306–27. On new, individualistic and free sorts of reading, see also Anne-Marie Chartier and Jean Hébrard, *Discours sur la lecture (1880–1980)* (Paris: Bibliothèque publique d'information, Centre Georges Pompidou, 1989), pp. 507–10. For the situation in Russia in recent years, see Chiara Basoli, 'Nuova editoria a Mosca', *Belfagor*, 46/6 (1991): 667–80.

22 Anna Rita Zanobi, 'Dewey sugli scaffali', *Biblioteche oggi*, 5/1 (1987): 84–8.

23 See Piero Innocenti, *La pratica del leggere*, Quaderni di *Biblioteca oggi*, 4 (Milan: Biblioteca oggi, 1989), p. 12.

24 Melvin L. DeFleur, 'How massive are mass-media?', *Syracuse Scholar*, 10/1 (1990): 14–34. As early as 1963, however, Ronald Morris, an English scholar, stated that reading had lost ground with respect to television and the other non-written means of communication, and that the process had accelerated in the preceding ten years. See Ronald Morris, *Success and Failure in Learning How to Read*, 3rd edn, ed. David McKay (Harmondsworth: Penguin, 1973), p. 25.

25 Innocenti, *La pratica del leggere*, pp. 219–315.

26 Ibid., p. 271, n. 61.

27 Fatima Marini-Marinucci, *Il testo, il lettore: Analisi teorico-pratica della comprensione* (Rome: A. Armando, 1979); quoted in Innocenti, *La pratica del leggere*, p. 152.

28 Hans Magnus Enzensberger, 'Una modesta proposta per difendere la gioventù dalle opere di poesia', in his *Sulla piccola borghesia: Un capriccio 'sociologico' seguito da altri saggi* (Milan, 1983), pp. 15–16, at p. 20, quoted here from 'A modest proposal for the protection of young people from the products of poetry', in *Mediocrity and Delusion: Collected Diversions*, trans. Martin Chalmers (London and New York: Verso, 1992), pp. 3–18, at p. 11.

29 On this question, see Roger Chartier, *Les Origines culturelles de la Révolution française* (Paris: Seuil, 1990), pp. 73–80, 98–102; trans. into English by Lydia G. Cochrane as *The Cultural Origins of the French Revolution*, Bicentennial Reflections on the French Revolution (Durham, NC, and London: Duke University Press, 1991), pp. 56–61, 70–3.

Select Bibliography

1. General Studies

Alfabetismo e cultura scritta: Con alcune contributi su psicologia e storia. Edited by A. Bartoli Langeli and A. Petrucci. Bologna: Il Mulino, 1978.

Die Almanach- und Taschenbuchkultur des 18. und 19. Jahrhunderts. Edited by Paul Gerhard Klussmann and York Gothart Mix. Wiesbaden: Harrassowitz, 1996.

'Autodidaxies XVI*e*–XIX*e* siècle'. Edited by Willem Frijhoff. *Histoire de l'éducation*, 70 (May 1996).

Barbier, Frédéric and Catherine Bertho Lavenir. *Histoire des médias: de Diderot à l'Internet.* Paris: Armand Colin, 1996.

Bialostocki, Jan. *Bücher der Weisheit und Bücher der Vergänglichkeit: Zur Symbolik des Buches in der Kunst.* Heidelberger Akademie der Wissenschaften. Heidelberg, Schwetzingen: K. F. Schimper, 1984. Translated into French by Christiane F. Kopylov as *Livres de sagesse et livres de vanités: Pour une symbolique du livre dans l'art.* Paris: Centres et Institut d'Études du Livre, 1993.

Biblioteca: Metafore e progetti. Edited by Giusi Baldissone. Milan: Franco Angeli, 1994.

La Bibliothèque: Miroir de l'âme, mémoire du monde. Edited by Richard Figuier. Paris: Autrement, 1991.

Bladeren in andermans hoofd: Over lezers en leescultuur. Edited by Theo Bijvoet, Paul Koopman, Lisa Kuitert and Garrelt Verhoeven. Nijmegen: Sun, 1996.

Blumenberg, Hans. *Die Lesbarkeit der Welt.* Frankfurt: Suhrkamp, 1981.

The Book Encompassed: Studies in Twentieth-Century Bibliography. Edited by Peter Davison. Cambridge: Cambridge University Press, 1992.

Bottigheimer, Ruth B. *The Bible for Children: From the Age of Gutenberg to the Present.* New Haven, Conn., and London: Yale University Press, 1996.

Canfora, Luciano. *Libro e libertà.* Rome and Bari: Laterza, 1994.

Chartier, Roger. *L'Ordre des livres: Lecteurs, auteurs, bibliothèques en Europe entre XIV*e* et XVIII*e* siècle.* Aix-en-Provence: Alinéa, 1992. Translated into

English by Lydia G. Cochrane as *The Order of Books: Readers, Authors, and Libraries in Europe between the Fourteenth and Eighteenth Centuries*. Cambridge: Polity Press, 1994.

Chartier, Roger. 'Le message écrit et ses réceptions: Du *codex* à l'écran'. *Revue des sciences morales et politiques*, 2 (1993): 295–313.

Chartier, Roger. *Forms and Meanings: Texts, Performances, and Audiences from Codex to Computer*. Philadelphia: University of Pennsylvania Press, 1995.

Chartier, Roger. *Culture écrite et société: L'ordre des livres (XIVᵉ–XVIIIᵉ siècles)*. Paris: Albin Michel, 1996.

Chartier, Roger. *Le Livre en révolutions*. Paris: Textuel, 1997.

Colportage et lecture populaire: Imprimés de large circulation en Europe, XVIᵉ–XIXᵉ siècles. Edited by Roger Chartier and Hans-Jürgen Lüsebrink. Paris: IMEC/La Maison des Sciences de l'Homme, 1996.

Darnton, Robert. 'First steps toward a history of reading'. In *The Kiss of Lamourette: Reflections in Cultural History* (New York and London: Norton, 1990), pp. 154–87.

Darnton, Robert. *Censorship in Comparative Perspective, France, 1789–East Germany, 1989*. The Adams Helms Lecture, 1994. Stockholm: Svenska Bokförläggareföreningen et Ordfront, 1995.

Eisenstein, Elizabeth. *The Printing Press as an Agent of Change: Communications and Cultural Transformations in Early Modern Europe*. Cambridge: Cambridge University Press, 1979. In an abridged version as *The Printing Revolution in Early Modern Europe*. Cambridge: Cambridge University Press, 1983.

Entre la palabra y el texto: Problemas en la interpretación de fuentes orales y escritas. Edited by Luis Díaz G. Viana and Matilde Fernández Montes. Oiartzun: Sendoa, 1997.

Escolar, Hipólito. *Historia del libro*. Madrid: Fundación Sánchez Ruipérez, 1996.

Escribir y leer en Occidente. Edited by Armando Petrucci and Francisco M. Gimeno Blay. Valencia: Universitat de Valencia, 1995.

Espaces de la lecture. Edited by Anne-Marie Christin. Paris: Retz, 1988.

The Ethnography of Reading. Edited by Jonathan Boyarin. Berkeley: University of California Press, 1993.

L'Europe et le livre: Réseaux et pratiques du négoce de librairie XVIᵉ–XIXᵉ siècles. Edited by Frédéric Barbier, Sabine Juratic and Dominique Varry. Paris: Klincksieck, 1996.

Gender and Reading: Essays on Readers, Texts, and Contexts. Edited by Elizabeth Flynn and Patrocinio P. Schweickert. Baltimore: Johns Hopkins University Press, 1986.

Gilmont, Jean-François. *Le Livre, du manuscrit à l'ère électronique: Notes de bibliologie*. 2nd edn. Liège: CEFAL, 1993.

Gimeno Blay, Francisco M. 'Quemar libros ... qué extraño placer!'. *Eutopías 2a época*, 104 (1995).

Goody, Jack. *The Domestication of the Savage Mind*. Cambridge: Cambridge University Press, 1977.

Goody, Jack. *The Interface between the Written and the Oral*. Cambridge: Cambridge University Press, 1987.

Graff, Harvey J. *The Legacies of Literacy: Continuities and Contradictions in Western Culture and Society*. Bloomington and Indianapolis: Indiana University Press, 1987.

Grafton, Anthony. *The Footnote: A Curious History.* Cambridge, Mass.: Harvard University Press, 1997.

Hall, David D. 'Readers and reading in America: historical and critical perspectives'. *Proceedings of the American Antiquarian Society,* 103/2 (1994): 337–57.

Hanebut-Benz, Eva Maria. *Die Kunst des Lesens: Lesemöbel und Leseverhalten vom Mittelalter bis zur Gegenwart.* Frankfurt: Museum für Kunsthandwerk, 1985.

Histoire de l'édition française. Edited by Roger Chartier and Henri-Jean Martin. 4 vols. Paris: Promodis, 1982–6. New edn, Paris: Fayard-Cercle de la Librairie, 1989–91.

Histoire des bibliothèques françaises. 4 vols. Paris: Cercle de la Librairie, 1988–92.

Histoires de la lecture: un bilan des recherches. Actes du colloque des 29 et 30 janvier 1993, Paris. Edited by Roger Chartier. Paris: IMEC/La Maison des Sciences de l'Homme, 1995.

Histoires du livre: nouvelles orientations. Actes du colloque du 6 et 7 septembre 1990, Göttingen. Edited by Hans-Erich Bödeker. Paris: IMEC /La Maison des Sciences de l'Homme, distribution Distique, 1995.

Un'idea di biblioteca. Edited by Enzo Esposito. Naples: CUEN, 1996.

Iser, Wolfgang. *Der Akt des Lesens: Theorie ästhetischer Wirkung.* Munich: Wilhelm Fink, 1976. In English translation as *The Act of Reading: A Theory of Aesthetic Response.* Baltimore: Johns Hopkins University Press, 1978.

Il linguaggio della biblioteca. Edited by Mauro Guerrini. Milan: Bibliografica, 1996.

Literacy and Social Development in the West: A Reader. Edited by Harvey J. Graff. Cambridge and New York: Cambridge University Press, 1981.

Literacy in Historical Perspective. Edited by Daniel P. Resnick. Washington, D.C.: Library of Congress, 1983.

Literacy in Traditional Societies. Edited by Jack Goody. Cambridge: Cambridge University Press, 1968.

'Literatura popular: Conceptos, argumentos y temas'. Edited by María Cruz García de Enterría. *Anthropos: Revista de Documentación Científica de la Cultura,* 166–7 (May–August 1995).

Le Livre et l'historien: Études offertes en l'honneur du Professeur Henri-Jean Martin. Edited by Frédéric Barbier, Anne Parent-Charon, François Dupuigrenet-Desroussilles, Claude Jolly and Dominique Varry. Geneva: Droz, 1997.

Livre et lecture en Russie. Edited by Alexandre Stroev. Paris: IMEC/La Maison des Sciences de l'Homme, 1996.

'O livro e a leitura'. Edited by João Luís Lisboa. *Cultura: Revista de história e teoria das ideias,* 2nd ser., 9 (1997).

Manguel, Alberto. *A History of Reading.* London: HarperCollins, 1996.

McKenzie, D. F. *Bibliography and the Sociology of Texts.* The Panizzi Lectures, 1985. London: British Library, 1986. In French translation as *La Bibliographie et la sociologie des textes.* Introduction by Roger Chartier. Paris: Cercle de la Librairie, 1991. Translated into English by Lydia G. Cochrane as 'Texts, forms, and interpretations'. In Roger Chartier, *On the Edge of the Cliff: History, Language, Practices* (Baltimore and London: Johns Hopkins University Press, 1997), pp. 81–9.

McKenzie, D. F. 'Speech–manuscript–print'. In *New Directions in Textual*

Studies, edited by Dave Oliphant and Robin Bradford, (Austin, Tex.: Harry Ransom Humanities Research Center, University of Texas at Austin, 1990), pp. 86–109.

Martin, Henri-Jean. *Histoire et pouvoirs de l'écrit*. With the collaboration of Bruno Delmas. Preface by Pierre Chaunu. Paris: Librairie Académique Perrin, 1988. Translated into English by Lydia G. Cochrane as *The History and Power of Writing*. Chicago and London: University of Chicago Press, 1994.

Masson, André. *Le Décor des bibliothèques du moyen âge à la Révolution*. Geneva: Droz, 1972.

La memoria del sapere: Forme di conservazione e strutture organizzative dall'-Antichità a oggi. Edited by Pietro Rossi. Rome and Bari: Laterza, 1988.

Milde, Wolfgang. 'Metamorphosen: Die Wandlung des Codex durch den Leser oder der dritte Aspekt der Handschriftenkunde: Ein Überblick'. *Gutenberg Jahrbuch*, 70 (1995): 27–36.

'*Los muros tienen la palabra*': *Materiales para una historia de los graffiti*. Edited by Francisco M. Gimeno Blay and María Luz Mandingorra Llavata. Valencia: Universitat de Valencia, 1997.

Nies, Fritz. *Bahn und Bett und Blütenduft: Eine Reise durch die Welt der Leserbilder*. Darmstadt: Wissenschaftliche Buchgesellschaft, 1991. Translated into French as *Imagerie de la lecture: Exploration d'un patrimoine millénaire de l'Occident*. Paris: Presses Universitaires de France, 1995.

Ong, Walter J. *Orality and Literacy: The Technologizing of the Word*. London and New York: Methuen, 1982.

Petrucci, Armando. *La scrittura: Ideologia e rappresentazione*. Turin: Einaudi, 1986.

Petrucci, Armando. *Le scritture ultime: Ideologia della morte e strategie dello scrivere nella tradizione occidentale*. Turin: Einaudi, 1995.

A Potencie of Life: Books in Society: The Clark Lectures, 1986–1987. Edited by Nicolas Barker. London: British Library, 1993.

Le Pouvoir des bibliothèques: La mémoire des livres en Occident. Edited by Marc Baratin and Christian Jacob. Paris: Albin Michel, 1996.

The Practice and Representation of Reading in England. Edited by James Raven, Helen Small and Naomi Tadmor. Cambridge and New York: Cambridge University Press, 1996.

'Pratiche di scrittura e pratiche di lettura nell'Europa moderna'. *Annali della Scuola Normale di Pisa*. Classe di Lettere e Filosofia, ser. 3, 23/2 (1993): 375–823.

Pratiques de la lecture. Edited by Roger Chartier. Marseille: Rivages, 1985. New edn, Paris: Payot et Rivages, 1993.

Reading in America: Literature and Social History. Edited by Cathy Davidson. Baltimore: Johns Hopkins University Press, 1989.

Reynolds, Leighton D. and Nigel G. Wilson. *Scribes and Scholars: A Guide to the Transmission of Greek and Latin Literature*. Oxford: Oxford University Press, 1968. 2nd edn rev. Oxford: Clarendon Press, 1974.

Rose, Jonathan. 'Rereading the common reader: a preface to a history of audiences'. *Journal of the History of Ideas*, 53 (1992): 47–70.

Saenger, Paul. 'Physiologie de la lecture et séparation des mots'. *Annales ESC*, 44 (1989): 939–52.

Storia e teoria dell'interpunzione. Atti del Convegno internazionale di Studi (Firenze, 19–20 maggio 1988). Edited by E. Cresti, N. Maraschio and L. Toschi. Rome: Bulzoni, 1992.

Sulle vie della scrittura: Alfabetizzazione, cultura scritta e istituzioni in età moderna. Atti del Convegno di Studi (Salerno, 10–12 marzo 1987). Edited by Maria Rosaria Pelizzari. Naples: Edizioni Scientifiche Italiane, 1989.

Il testo letterario: Istruzioni per l'uso. Edited by Mario Lavagetto. Rome and Bari: Laterza, 1996.

Texts and Transmission: A Survey of the Latin Classics. Edited by Leighton D. Reynolds. Oxford: Clarendon Press, 1983.

Tous les savoirs du monde: Encyclopédies et bibliothèques, de Sumer au XXIe siècle. Edited by Roland Schaer. Paris: Bibliothèque Nationale de France/Flammarion, 1996.

Transcrire les mythologies: tradition, écriture, historicité. Edited by Marcel Detienne. Paris: Albin Michel, 1994.

Wittmann, Reinhard. *Geschichte des deutschen Buchhandels: Ein Überblick*. Munich: Beck, 1991.

2. Greece and Rome

Alexandrie IIIe siècle avant J.-C.: tous les savoirs du monde ou le rêve d'universalité des Ptolémées. Edited by Christian Jacob and François de Polignac. Paris: Autrement, 1992.

Le biblioteche nel mondo antico e medievale. Edited by Guglielmo Cavallo. 2nd edn. Rome and Bari: Laterza, 1989.

Binder, Gerhard. 'Öffentliche Autorenlesungen: Zur Kommunikation zwischen römischen Autoren und ihrem Publikum'. In *Kommunikation durch Zeichen und Wort*, edited by Gerhard Binder and Konrad Ehlich, vol. 4 of *Stätten und Formen der Kommunikation im Altertum* (Trier: Wissenschaftlicher Verlag, 1995), pp. 265–332.

Blanck, Horst. *Das Buch in der Antike*. Munich: Beck, 1992.

Canfora, Luciano. *La biblioteca scomparsa*. Palermo: Sellerio, 1986. Translated into English by Martin Ryle as *The Vanished Library*. Berkeley: University of California Press, 1989.

Canfora, Luciano. 'Lire à Athènes et Rome'. *Annales ESC*, 44 (1989): 925–37.

Cavallo, Guglielmo. 'Libro e cultura scritta'. In *Storia di Roma*, edited by Arnaldo Momigliano and Aldo Schiavone, 4 vols in 7 pts (Turin: Einaudi, 1988–93), vol. 4: *Caratteri e morfologie* (1989), pp. 693–734.

Cavallo, Guglielmo. 'Testo, libro, lettura'. In *Lo spazio letterario di Roma antica*, edited by Guglielmo Cavallo, Paolo Fedeli and Andrea Giardina, 5 vols (Rome: Salerno 1989–91), vol. 2: *La circolazione del testo*, pp. 307–41.

Cavallo, Guglielmo. 'Libri scritti, libri letti, libri dimenticati'. *Settimane di studio del Centro italiano di studi sull'alto medioevo*, 38: 'Il secolo di ferro: Mito e realtà del secolo X' (1991): 759–802.

Cavallo, Guglielmo. 'Gli usi della cultura scritta nel mondo romano'. In *Princeps Urbium: cultura e vita sociale dell'Italia romana* (Milan: Libri Scheiwiller, 1991), pp. 171–251.

Cavallo, Guglielmo. 'Discorsi sul libro'. In *Lo spazio letterario della Grecia antica*, edited by Giuseppe Cambiano, Luciano Canfora and Diego Lanza, (Rome: Salerno, 1994), vol. 1: *La produzione e la circolazione del testo*, pt 3: *I Greci e Roma*, pp. 613–47.

Cavallo, Guglielmo. 'Donne che leggono, donne che scrivono'. In *Vicende e figure femminili in Grecia e a Roma*, Atti del Convegno: Pesaro, 28–30 aprile, edited by Renato Raffaelli (Ancona: Commissione per le pari opportunità tra uomo della Regione Marche, 1995), pp. 517–26.

Cavallo, Guglielmo. 'Iniziali, scritture distintive, fregi: morfologie e funzioni'. In *Libri e documenti d'Italia dai Longobardi alla rinascita delle città*, edited by Cesare Scalon (Udine: Arti Grafiche Friulane, 1996), pp. 15–33.

Cavallo, Guglielmo. 'Veicoli materiali della letteratura di consumo: maniere di scrivere e maniere di leggere'. In *La letteratura di consumo nel mondo greco-latino*, Atti del convegno internazionale, Cassino, 14–17 settembre 1994, edited by Oronzo Pecere and Antonio Stramaglia (Cassino: Università degli Studi di Cassino, 1996), pp. 11–46.

Citroni, Mario. *Poesia e lettori in Roma antica*. Rome and Bari: Laterza, 1995.

Les Débuts du codex. Edited by Alain Blanchard. Turnhout: Brepols, 1989.

Dupont, Florence. *L'Invention de la littérature: De l'ivresse grecque au livre latin*. Paris: La Découverte, 1994.

Fehrle, Rudolf. *Das Bibliothekwesen im alten Rom: Voraussetzungen, Bedingungen, Anfänge*. Wiesbaden: Reichert, 1986.

Frasca, Rosella. *Educazione e formazione a Roma: Storia, testi, immagini*. Bari: Dedalo, 1996.

Gamble, Harry Y. *Books and Readers in the Early Church: A History of Early Christian Texts*. New Haven, Conn., and London: Yale University Press, 1995.

Gil Fernandez, Luis. *La palabra y su imagen: La valoración de la obra escrita en la antigüedad*. Madrid: Universidad Complutense, 1995.

Giovè Marchioli, Nicoletta. *Alle origini delle abbreviature latine: Una prima ricognizione (I secolo a.C.–IV secolo d.C.)*. Messina: Sicania, 1993.

Harris, William V. *Ancient Literacy*. Cambridge, Mass., and London: Harvard University Press, 1989.

Knox, B. M. W. 'Silent reading in antiquity'. *Greek, Roman, and Byzantine Studies*, 9 (1968): 421–35.

Jacob, Christian. 'La bibliothèque et le livre: Formes de l'encyclopédisme alexandrin'. *Diogène*, 178 (1997): 64–85.

Libri, editori e pubblico nel mondo antico: Guida storica e critica. Edited by Guglielmo Cavallo. Rome and Bari: Laterza, 1977.

Literacy and Power in the Ancient World. Edited by Alan K. Bowman and Greg Woolf. Cambridge and New York: Cambridge University Press, 1994.

Literacy in the Roman World. Ann Arbor: Department of Classical Studies, University of Michigan, 1991.

Lledó, Emilio. *El surco del tiempo: Meditaciones sobre el mito platónico de la escritura y la memoria*. Barcelona: Crítica, 1992.

Lledó, Emilio. *La memoria del Logos*. Madrid: Taurus, 1996.

McDonnel, Myles. 'Writing, copying and autograph manuscripts in ancient Rome'. *Classical Quarterly*, n. s., 46 (1996): 469–91.

Robb, Kevin. *Literacy and Paideia in Ancient Greece*. Oxford and New York: Oxford University Press, 1994.

Roberts, Colin H. and T. C. Skeat. *The Birth of the Codex*. London: Published for the British Academy by Oxford University Press, 1987.

Salles, Catherine. *Lire à Rome*. 'Appendice (paléographique, papyrologique et codicologique)' by René Martin. Paris: Belles Lettres, 1992.

Les Savoirs de l'écriture en Grèce ancienne. Edited by Marcel Detienne. Villeneuve-d'Ascq: Presses Universitaires de Lille, 1988.

Scheid, John and Jesper Svenbro. *Le Métier de Zeus: Mythe du tissage et du tissu dans le monde grec et romain*. Paris: La Découverte, 1994. Translated into English by Carol Volk as *The Craft of Zeus: Myths of Weaving and Fabric*. Cambridge, Mass.: Harvard University Press, 1996.

Small, Jocelyn Penny. *Wax Tablets of the Mind: Cognitive Studies of Memory and Literacy in Classical Antiquity.* London and New York: Routledge, 1997.

Svenbro, Jesper. *Phasikleia: Anthropologie de la lecture en Grèce ancienne.* Paris: La Découverte, 1988. Translated into English by Janet Lloyd as *Phrasikleia: An Anthropology of Reading in Ancient Greece.* Ithaca, NY: Cornell University Press, 1993.

Thomas, Rosalind. *Oral Tradition and Written Record in Classical Athens.* Cambridge and New York: Cambridge University Press, 1989.

Thomas, Rosalind. *Literacy and Orality in Ancient Greece.* Cambridge and New York: Cambridge University Press, 1993.

Thompson, Dorothy J. 'Language and literacy in early Hellenistic Egypt'. In *Ethnicity in Hellenistic Egypt*, edited by Per Bilde, Troels Engberg-Pedersen, Lise Hannestad and Jan Zahle (Aarhus: Aarhus University Press, 1992), pp. 39–52.

Valette-Cagnac, Emmanuelle. *La Lecture à Rome: Rites et pratiques.* Paris: Belin, 1997.

Voice into Text: Orality and Literacy in Ancient Greece. Edited by Ian Worthington. Leiden and New York: Brill, 1996.

Zanker, Paul. *Die Maske des Sokrates: Das Bild des Intellektuellen in der antiken Kunst.* Munich: Beck, 1995. Translated into English by Alan Shapiro as *The Mask of Socrates: The Image of the Intellectual in Antiquity.* Berkeley: University of California Press, 1996.

3. The Middle Ages

Alexandre-Bidon, Danièle. 'La lettre volée: Apprendre à lire à l'enfant au moyen âge'. *Annales ESC*, 44 (1989): 953–92.

Banniard, Michel. *Viva voce: Communication écrite et communication orale du IVe au IXe siècle en occident latin.* Paris: Institut des Études Augustiniennes, 1992.

Bartoli Langeli, Attilio. 'I libri dei frati: La cultura scritta dell'Ordine dei Minori'. In *Francesco d'Assisi e il primo secolo di storia francescana* (Turin: Einaudi, 1997), pp. 283–305.

Bäuml, Franz H. 'Varieties and consequences of medieval literacy and illiteracy'. *Speculum*, 55 (1980): 237–65.

Buc, Philippe. *L'Ambiguïté du livre: Prince, pouvoir et peuple dans les commentaires de la Bible au moyen âge.* Paris: Beauchesne, 1993.

Das Buch als magisches und als Repräsentationsobjekt. Edited by Peter Ganz. Wiesbaden: Harrassowitz, 1992.

Das Buch in Mittelalter und Renaissance. Edited by Rudolf Hiestand. Düsseldorf: Droste, 1994.

Camille, Michael. 'Seeing and reading: some visual implications of medieval literacy and illiteracy'. *Art History*, 8 (1985): 26–49.

Cavallo, Guglielmo. 'Dallo scriptorium senza biblioteca alla biblioteca senza scriptorium'. In *Dall'eremo al cenobio*, edited by Giovanni Pugliese Carratelli (Milan: Scheiwiller, 1987), pp. 331–422.

Cavallo, Guglielmo. 'Scrivere leggere memorizzare le Sacre Scritture'. In *Morfologie sociali e culturali in Europa fra tarda antichità e alto medioevo*, Settimane di studio del Centro italiano di studi sull'alto medioevo, 45 (Spoleto: Centro di studi sull'alto medioevo, 1998).

Cerquiglini-Toulet, Jacqueline. *La Couleur de la mélancholie: La fréquentation des livres au XIVe siècle, 1300–1415*. Paris: Hatier, 1993. Translated into English by Lydia G. Cochrane as *The Color of Melancholy: The Uses of Books in the Fourteenth Century*. Baltimore and London: Johns Hopkins University Press, 1997.

Clanchy, Michael T. *From Memory to Written Record: England 1066–1307*. 2nd edn. Oxford: Blackwell and Cambridge, Mass.: Harvard University Press, 1993.

Der Codex im Gebrauch. Edited by Christel Meier, Dagmar Hüpper and Hagen Keller. Munich: Wilhelm Fink, 1996.

Coleman, Janet. *Public Reading and the Reading Public in Late Medieval England and France*. Cambridge and New York: Cambridge University Press, 1966.

Dagenais, John. *The Ethics of Reading in Manuscript Culture: Glossing the Libro de buen amor*. Princeton, NJ: Princeton University Press, 1994.

The Early Medieval Bible: Its Production, Decoration, and Use. Edited by Richard Gameson. Cambridge and New York: Cambridge University Press, 1994.

La Face cachée du livre médiéval: L'histoire du livre vue par Ezio Ornato, ses amis et ses collègues. Rome: Viella, 1997.

Frioli, Donatella. 'La "grammatica della leggibilità" nel manoscritto cisterciense: L'esempio di Aldersbach'. *Studi medievali*, 3rd ser., 36 (1995): 743–76.

Gimeno Blay, Francisco M. 'Analfabetismo y alfabetización femeninos en la Valencia del Quinientos'. *Estudis*, 19 (1993): 59–101.

Goldberg, P. J. P. 'Lay book ownership in late medieval York: the evidence of wills'. *Library*, 6th ser., 16/3 (1994): 181–9.

Green, D. H. *Medieval Listening and Reading: The Primary Reception of German Literature, 800–1300*. Cambridge and New York: Cambridge University Press, 1994.

Grundmann, Herbert. 'Litteratus-Illiteratus: Der Wandel einer Bildungsnorm vom Altertum zum Mittelalter'. *Archiv für Kulturgeschichte*, 40 (1958): 1–65.

Heresy and Literacy, 1000–1530. Edited by Peter Biller and Anne Hudson. Cambridge and New York: Cambridge University Press, 1994.

Hillgarth, J. N. *Readers and Books in Majorca, 1229–1550*. 2 vols. Paris: CNRS, 1991.

Hunger, Herbert. *Schreiben und Lesen in Byzanz: Die byzantinische Buchkultur*. Munich: Beck, 1989.

Huot, Sylvia Jean. *The Romance of the Rose and its Medieval Readers: Interpretation, Reception, Manuscript Transmission*. Cambridge and New York: Cambridge University Press, 1993.

Hyde, J. K. *Literacy and its Uses: Studies on Late Medieval Italy*. Manchester and New York: Manchester University Press, 1994.

Illich, Ivan. *In the Vineyard of the Text: A Commentary to Hugh's Didascalicon*. Chicago: University of Chicago Press, 1993. Translated into French by Jacques Mignon as *Du lisible au visible: la naissance du texte: un commentaire du 'Didascalicon' de Hugues de Saint-Victor*. Translation revised by Maud Sissung. Paris: Cerf, 1991.

Irvine, Martin. *The Making of Textual Culture: 'Grammatica' and Literary Theory, 350–1100*. Cambridge and New York: Cambridge University Press, 1994.

Keller, Hagen. 'Vom "heiligen Buch" zur "Buchfürhrung". Lebensfunktionen der Schrift im Mittelalter'. *Frühmittelalterliche Studien*, 26 (1992): 1–31.

Lerer, Seth. *Chaucer and his Readers: Imagining the Author in Late Medieval England*. Princeton, NJ: Princeton University Press, 1993.

Libri e lettori nel Medioevo: Guida storica e critica. Edited by Guglielmo Cavallo. Rome and Bari: Laterza, 1977, 1989.

Lucas, Peter J. *From Author to Audience: John Capgrave and Medieval Publication*. Dublin: University College Dublin Press, 1997.

McKitterick, Rosamond. *The Carolingians and the Written Word*. Cambridge and New York: Cambridge University Press, 1989.

Manuscripts and Readers in Fifteenth-Century England: The Literary Implications of Manuscript Study. Essays from the 1981 conference at the University of York. Edited by Derek Pearsall. Cambridge: D. S. Brewer and Totowa, NJ: Biblio Distribution Services, 1983.

Mise en page et mise en texte du livre manuscrit. Edited by Henri-Jean Martin and Jean Vezin. Paris: Cercle de la Librairie-Promodis, 1990.

Obbema, Pieter. *De middeleeuwen in handen: Over de boekcultuur in de late middeleeuwen*. Hilversum: Verloren, 1996.

Parkes, Malcolm B. 'The influence of the concepts of *ordinatio* and *compilatio* in the development of the book'. In *Medieval Learning and Literature: Essays Presented to Richard William Hunt*, edited by J. J. G. Alexander and M. T. Gibson (Oxford: Clarendon Press, 1976), pp. 115–41.

Parkes, Malcolm B. *Scribes, Scripts and Readers: Studies in the Communication, Presentation and Dissemination of Medieval Texts*. London and Rio Grande, Oh.: Hambledon Press, 1991.

Parkes, Malcolm B. *Pause and Effect: An Introduction to the History of Punctuation in the West*. Aldershot: Scolar Press, 1992; Berkeley: University of California Press, 1993.

Petrucci, Armando. 'Le bibliotheche antiche'. In *Letteratura italiana*, gen. ed. Alberto Asor Rosa (8 vols, Turin: Einaudi, 1982–91), vol. 2: *Produzione e consumo* (1983), pp. 527–54.

Petrucci, Armando. 'Il libro manoscritto'. In *Letteratura italiana*, vol. 2: *Produzione e consumo*, pp. 499–524.

Petrucci, Armando. 'Lire au moyen âge'. *Mélanges de l'École française de Rome: Moyen âge–temps modernes*, 96 (1984): 603–16.

Petrucci, Armando. 'Storia e geografia delle culture scritte (dal secolo XI al secolo XVIII)'. In *Letteratura italiana*, gen. ed. Alberto Asor Rosa (Turin: Einaudi, 1982–91), vol. 7: *Storia e geografia*, pt 2: *L'età moderna* (1988), pp. 1193–1292.

Petrucci, Armando. *Writers and Readers in Medieval Italy: Studies in the History of Written Culture*. Translated by Charles M. Radding. New Haven, Conn., and London: Yale University Press, 1995.

Pomposia monasterium modo in Italia primum: La biblioteca di Pomposa. Edited by Giuseppe Billanovich. Padua: Antenore, 1994.

La Production du livre universitaire au moyen âge: Exemplar et pecia. Actes du symposium tenu au Collegio San Bonaventura de Grottaferrata en mai 1983. Edited by Louis J. Bataillon, Bertrand G. Guyot and Richard H. Rouse. Paris: CNRS, 1988.

Reynolds, Suzanne. *Medieval Reading: Grammar, Rhetoric and the Classical Text*. Cambridge and New York: Cambridge University Press, 1996.

The Role of the Book in Medieval Culture. Proceedings of the Oxford International Symposium, 26 September–1 October 1982. Edited by Peter Ganz. Turnhout: Brepols, 1986.

Rouse, Richard H. 'Cistercian aids to study in the thirteenth century'. *Studies in Medieval Cistercian History*, 2 (1976): 123–34.

Rouse, Richard H. and Mary A. Rouse. *Preachers, Florilegia and Sermons: Studies on the Manipulus florum of Thomas of Ireland.* Toronto: Pontifical Institute of Medieval Studies, 1979.

Saenger, Paul. 'Silent reading: its impact on late medieval script and society'. *Viator*, 13 (1982): 367–414.

Saenger, Paul. 'Books of hours and the reading habits of the late Middle Ages'. *Scrittura e Civiltà*, 9 (1985): 239–69.

Saenger, Paul. 'The separation of words and the order of words: the genesis of medieval reading'. *Scrittura e Civiltà*, 14 (1990): 49–74.

Saenger, Paul. *Space between Words: The Origins of Silent Reading.* Stanford, Calif.: Stanford University Press, 1997.

Saint-Victor, Hugues de. *L'Art de lire: Didascalicon.* Edited and translated by Michel Lemoine. Paris: Cerf, 1991.

Scalon, Cesare. *Produzione e fruizione del libro nel basso medioevo: il caso Friuli.* Padua: Antenore, 1995.

Schriftkultur und Reichsverwaltung unter den Karolingern. Referate des Kolloquiums der Nordrhein-Westfälischen Akademie der Wissenschaften am 17.–18. Februar 1994 in Bonn. Edited by Rudolf Schieffer. Abhandlungen der Nordrhein-Westfälischen Akademie der Wissenschaften, 97. Opladen: Westdeutscher, 1996.

Sicard, Patrice. *Diagrammes médiévaux et exégèse visuelle: Le Libellus de formatione arche de Hughes de Saint-Victor.* Paris and Turnhout: Brepols, 1993.

Sirat, Colette. *Du scribe au livre: Les manuscrits hébreux au moyen âge.* Paris: CNRS, 1994.

Sirat, Colette, Michèle Dukan, Claude Heymann, Carsten L. Wilke and Monique Zerdoun. *La Conception du livre chez les piétistes ashkénazes au moyen âge.* Geneva: Droz, 1996.

Stock, Brian. *The Implications of Literacy: Written Language and Models of Interpretation in the Eleventh and Twelfth Centuries.* Princeton, NJ: Princeton University Press, 1983.

Supino Martini, Paola. 'Scrittura e leggibilità in Italia nel secolo IX'. In *Libri e documenti d'Italia: Dai Longobardi alla rinascita delle città*, edited by Cesare Scalon (Udine: Arti Grafiche Friulane, 1996), pp. 35–60.

The Uses of Literacy in Early Medieval Europe. Edited by Rosamund McKitterick. Cambridge and New York: Cambridge University Press, 1990.

Viva vox und ratio scripta: Mündliche und schriftliche Kommunikationsformen in Mönchtum des Mittelalters. Edited by Clemens M. Kasper and Klaus Schreiner. Münster: LIT, 1997.

Vocabulaire du livre et de l'écriture au moyen âge. Actes de la table ronde, Paris, 24–6 September 1987. Edited by Olga Weijers. CIVICIMA: Études sur le vocabulaire intellectuel du moyen âge, 2. Turnhout: Brepols, 1989.

Vox intexta: Orality and Textuality in the Middle Ages. Edited by A. N. Doane and Carol Braun Pasternack. Madison: University of Wisconsin Press, 1991.

The Whole Book: Cultural Perspectives on the Medieval Miscellany. Edited by Stephen G. Nichols and Siegfried Wenzel. Ann Arbor: University of Michigan Press, 1996.

Women and the Book: Assessing the Visual Evidence. Edited by Jane H. M.

Taylor and Lesley Smith. London: British Library and Toronto: University of Toronto Press, 1997.

Zumthor, Paul. *La Lettre et la voix de la 'littérature' médiévale*. Paris: Seuil, 1987.

4. The Renaissance and the Reformation

Ambrosoli, Mauro. 'Lettori e chiosatori delle edizioni a stampa di Pier de' Crescenzi tra 1474 e 1561'. *Rivista storica italiana*, year 96, no. 2 (1984): 360–413.

Balsamo, Luigi. *Produzione e circolazione libraria in Emilia (XV–XVIII sec.): Studi e ricerche*. Rome: Casanova, 1983.

Bath, Michael. *Speaking Pictures: English Emblem Books and Renaissance Culture*. London and New York: Longman, 1993.

Bec, Christian. *Les Livres des Florentins (1413–1608)*. Florence: Olschki, 1984.

Benedict, Philip. 'Bibliothèques protestantes et catholiques à Metz au XVIᵉ siècle'. *Annales ESC*, 40 (1985): 343–70.

Bennett, H. S. *English Books and Readers, 1558–1603*. Cambridge: Cambridge University Press, 1965.

Bennett, H. S. *English Books and Readers, 1475 to 1557*. Cambridge: Cambridge University Press, 1970.

Berger, Philippe. *Libro y lectura en la Valencia del Renacimiento*. Translated by Amparo Balanzá Pérez. Valencia: Alfons el Magnánim, Institució Valenciana d'Estudis i Investigació, 1987.

Blair, Ann. 'Humanist methods in natural philosophy: the commonplace book'. *Journal of the History of Ideas*, 53/4 (1992): 541–51.

Blair, Ann. *The Theater of Nature: Jean Bodin and Renaissance Science*. Princeton, NJ: Princeton University Press, 1997.

Bonfil, Robert. *Rabbis and Jewish Communities in Renaissance Italy*. Translated by Jonathan Chapman. Oxford and New York: Oxford University Press, 1990.

Bottigheimer, Ruth B. 'Bible reading, "Bibles" and the Bible for children in early modern Germany'. *Past and Present*, 139 (1993): 66–89.

Bouza-Alvarez, Fernando J. 'La Biblioteca des Escorial y el orden de los saberes en el siglo XVI'. In *El Escorial: Arte, poder y cultura en la corte de Felipe II*, Cursos de Verano El Escorial 1988 (Madrid: Universidad Complutense, 1988), pp. 81–99.

Bouza-Alvarez, Fernando J. *Del escribano a la biblioteca: La civilización escrita europea en la Alta Edad Moderna (Siglos XV–XVII)*. Madrid: Sintesis, 1992.

Bouza-Alvarez, Fernando J. 'Monarchie en lettres d'imprimerie: typographie et propagande au temps de Philippe II'. *Revue d'histoire moderne et contemporaine*, 41/2 (1994): 206–20.

Brown, Cynthia Jane. *Poets, Patrons, and Printers: Crisis of Authority in Late Medieval France*. Ithaca, NY, and London: Cornell University Press, 1995.

Burkardt, Albrecht. 'Reconnaissance et dévotion: Les vies des saints et leurs lectures au début du XVIIᵉ siècle à travers les procès de canonisation'. *Revue d'histoire moderne et contemporaine*, 43/2 (1996): 214–33.

Burke, Peter. *The Fortunes of the Courtier: The European Reception of Castiglione's Cortegiano*. Cambridge: Polity Press, 1995; University Park: Pennsylvania State University Press, 1996.

Castillo Gómez, Antonio. *Escrituras y escribientes: Prácticas de la cultura escrita en una ciudad del Renacimiento*. Las Palmas de Gran Canaria: Fundación de Enseñanza Superior a Distancia, 1997.

Cayuela, Anna. *Le Paratexte au Siècle d'Or: Prose romanesque, livres et lecteurs en Espagne au XVIIᵉ siècle*. Geneva: Droz, 1996.

La censura libraria nell'Europa del secolo XVI. Convegno internazionale di studi Cividale del Friuli, 9–10 novembre 1995. Edited by Ugo Rozzo. Udine: Forum, 1997.

Certeau, Michel de. 'La Lecture absolue. Théorie et pratiques des mystiques chrétiens, XVI–XVIIᵉ siècle'. In *Problèmes actuels de la lecture*, edited by Lucien Dällenbach and Jean Ricardou (Paris: Clancier-Guénaud, 1982), pp. 65–79.

Châtelain, Jean-Marc. *Livres d'emblèmes et de devises: une anthologie (1531–1735)*. Paris: Klincksieck, 1993.

Châtelain, Jean-Marc. 'Livres d'emblème et livre du monde'. *Revue française d'histoire du livre*, 86–7 (1995): 87–104.

Chevalier, Maxime. *Lectura y lectores en la España de los siglos XVI y XVII*. Madrid: Turner, 1976.

Chrisman, Miriam Usher. *Lay Culture, Learned Culture, Books and Social Change in Strasbourg, 1480–1519*. New Haven, Conn., and London: Yale University Press, 1982.

Ciappelli, Giovanni. 'Libri e letture a Firenze nel XV secolo: Le 'ricordanze' e la ricostruzione delle biblioteche private'. *Rinascimento*, 2nd ser., 29 (1996): 267–91.

Les Croates et la civilisation du livre. Edited by Henrik Heger and Janine Matillon. Paris: Presses de l'Université de Paris-Sorbonne, 1986.

Crofts, Richard A. 'Books, reform and the Reformation'. *Archiv für Reformationsgeschichte*, 71 (1980): 21–36.

Crofts, Richard A. 'Printing, reform and the Catholic Reformation in Germany (1521–1545)'. *Sixteenth Century Journal*, 16 (1985): 369–81.

La Cultura del Renaixement: homenatge al Pare Miguel Batllori. Monografies Manuscrits, 1. Bellaterra: Monografies Manuscrits, 1985.

Davis, Natalie Zemon. *Society and Culture in Early Modern France*. Stanford, Calif.: Stanford University Press, 1975.

Davis, Natalie Zemon. 'Beyond the market: books as gifts in sixteenth-century France'. *Transactions of the Royal Historical Society*, 33 (1983): 69–88.

Donna, disciplina, creanza cristiana dal XV al XVII secolo: Studi e testi a stampa. Edited by Gabriella Zarri. Rome: Storia e Letteratura, 1996.

Frenk, Margit. ' "Lectores y oídores": La difusión oral de la literatura en el Siglo de Oro'. In *Actas del Septimo Congreso de la Asociación Internacional de Hispanistas, publicadas por Giuseppe Bellini* (Rome: Bulzoni, 1982), pp. 101–23.

Frenk, Margit. *Entre la voz y el silencio (La lectura en tiempos de Cervantes)*. Alcalá de Henares: Centro de Estudios Cervantinos, 1997.

Gaisser, Julia Haig. *Catullus and his Renaissance Readers*. Oxford: Clarendon Press and New York: Oxford University Press, 1993.

Gawthrop, Richard L. and Gerald Strauss. 'Protestantism and literacy in early modern Germany'. *Past and Present*, 104 (1984): 31–55.

Gilmont, Jean-François. *Jean Calvin et le livre imprimé*. Geneva: Droz, 1997.

Ginzburg, Carlo. *Il formaggio e i vermi: Il cosmo di un mugnaio del '500*. Turin: Einaudi, 1976. Translated into English by John and Anne Tedeschi as *The Cheese and the Worms: The Cosmos of a Sixteenth-Century Miller*. Baltimore: Johns Hopkins University Press, 1980, 1992; New York: Penguin Books, 1982.

Goyet, Francis. 'A propos de "ces pastissages de lieux communs" (le rôle des notes de lecture dans la genèse des *Essais*)'. *Bulletin de la Société des Amis de Montaigne*, 5–6 (1986): 11–26; 7–8 (1987): 9–30.

Goyet, Francis. *Le Sublime du 'lieu commun': L'invention rhétorique dans l'Antiquité et à la Renaissance*. Paris: Champion, 1996.

Grafton, Anthony. *Defenders of the Text: The Traditions of Scholarship in an Age of Science, 1450–1800*. Cambridge, Mass., and London: Harvard University Press, 1991.

Grafton, Anthony. 'Is the history of reading a marginal enterprise? Guillaume Budé and his books'. *Papers of the Bibliographical Society of America*, 91 (June 1997): 139–57.

Higman, Francis M. *La Diffusion de la Réforme en France, 1520–1565*. Geneva: Labor et Fides, 1992.

Hirsch, Rudolf. *Printing, Selling and Reading, 1450–1550*. Wiesbaden: Harrasowitz, 1967.

Ife, B. W. *Reading and Fiction in Golden-Age Spain: A Platonist Critique and some Picaresque Replies*. Cambridge and New York: Cambridge University Press, 1985.

Infantes, Victor. *En el Siglo de Oro: Estudios y textos de literatura áurea*. Potomac: Scripta Humanistica, 1992.

Jardine, Lisa. *Erasmus, Man of Letters: The Construction of Charisma in Print*. Princeton, NJ: Princeton University Press, 1993.

Jardine, Lisa and Anthony Grafton. ' "Studied for action": how Gabriel Harvey read his Livy'. *Past and Present*, 129 (November 1990): 30–78.

Kintgen, Eugene R. *Reading in Tudor England*. Pittsburgh: University of Pittsburgh Press, 1996.

Labarre, André. *Le Livre dans la vie amiénoise du XVIe siècle: l'enseignement des inventaires après décès (1503–1576)*. Paris and Louvain: Nauwelaerts, 1971.

Libri, scrittura e pubblico nel Rinascimento: Guida storica e critica. Edited by Armando Petrucci. Rome and Bari: Laterza, 1979.

El libro antiguo español. Actas del primer Coloquio Internacional (Madrid, 18 al 20 de diciembre de 1986). Edited by María Luisa López-Vidriero and Pedro M. Cátedra. Salamanca: Universidad de Salamanca, Biblioteca Nacional de Madrid, Sociedad Española de Historia del Libro, 1988.

El libro antiguo español. Actas del segundo Coloquio Internacional (Madrid, 18 al 20 de diciembre de 1986). Edited by María Luisa López-Vidriero and Pedro M. Cátedra. Salamanca: Universidad de Salamanca, Biblioteca Nacional de Madrid, Sociedad Española de Historia del Libro, 1992.

El libro antiguo español III: El libro en palacio y otros estudios bibliográficos. Edited by María Luisa López-Vidriero and Pedro M. Cátedra. Salamanca: Universidad de Salamanca, Patrimonio Nacional, Sociedad Española de Historia del Libro, 1996.

Le Livre dans l'Europe de la Renaissance. Actes du XXVIIIe colloque international d'études humanistes de Tours. Edited by Pierre Aquilon and Henri-Jean Martin. Paris: Promodis-Cercle de la Librairie, 1988.

'Les livres des Espagnols à l'époque moderne'. *Bulletin Hispanique*, 99/1 (January–June 1997).

Maiello, Francesco. *Storia del Calendario: La misurazione del tempo, 1450–1800*. Turin: Einaudi, 1994.

Margolin, Jean-Claude, Jean Pendergrass and Marc Van der Poel. *Images et lieux de mémoire d'un étudiant du XVIᵉ siècle: Étude, transcription et commentaire d'un cahier de latin d'un étudiant néerlandais*. Paris: Guy Trédanel, 1991.

Marín Martínez, Tomás. 'Estudio introductorio'. In *Catálogo Concordado de la Biblioteca de Hernando Colón*, edited by Tomás Marín Martínez, José Manuel Ruiz Asencio and Klaus Wagner, Fundación MAPFRE-América and Cabildo de la Catedral de Sevilla (Madrid: MAPFRE), vol. 1 (1993), pp. 19–352.

Moll, Jaime. *Estudios sobre el libro español de los siglos XVI al XVIII*. Madrid: Arco/Libros, 1994.

Moss, Ann. *Printed Common-Place Books and the Structuring of Renaissance Thought*. Oxford and New York: Clarendon Press, 1996.

Nelson, William. 'From "Listen, Lordings" to "Dear Reader" '. *University of Toronto Quarterly: A Canadian Journal of the Humanities*, 46/2 (1976–7): 110–24.

Newman, Jane O. 'The Word made print: Luther's 1522 *New Testament* in an age of mechanical reproduction'. *Representations*, 11 (1985): 95–133.

Pardo Tomás, José. *Ciencia y censura: La Inquisición española y los libros científicos en los siglos XVI y XVII*. Madrid: Consejo Superior de Investigaciones Científicas, 1991.

Patterson, Annabel M. *Censorship and Interpretation: The Conditions of Writing and Reading in Early Modern England*. Madison: University of Wisconsin Press, 1984.

Pedraza Gracia, Manuel José. *La producción y distribución del libro en Zaragoza 1501–1521*. Zaragosa: Institución Fernando el Católico (Consejo Superior de Investigaciones Científicas), 1997.

Peña Diaz, Manuel. *Cataluña en el Renacimiento: Libros y lenguas (Barcelona, 1473–1600)*. Lleida: Milenio, 1996.

Peña Diaz, Manuel. *El laberinto de los libros: Historia cultural de la Barcelona del Quinientos*. Madrid: Fundación Sánchez Ruipérez, 1997.

Print and Culture in the Renaissance: Essays on the Advent of Printing in Europe. Edited by Gerald P. Tyson and Sylvia S. Wagonheim. Newark: University of Delaware Press and London and Toronto: Associated University Press, 1986.

Printing the Written Word: The Social History of Books, circa 1450–1520. Edited by Sandra Hindman. Ithaca, NY, and London: Cornell University Press, 1991.

Quondam, Amedeo. 'La letteratura in tipografia'. In *Letteratura italiana*, gen. ed. Alberto Asor Rosa (8 vols in 13 pts, Turin: Einaudi, 1882–91), vol. 2: *Produzione e consumo* (1983), pp. 555–686.

La Réforme et le livre: L'Europe de l'imprimé (1517–v.1570). Edited by Jean-François Gilmont. Paris: Cerf, 1990.

Richardson, Brian. *Print Culture in Renaissance Italy: The Editor and the Vernacular Text, 1470–1600*. Cambridge and New York: Cambridge University Press, 1994.

Rico, Francisco. 'La *Princeps* del *Lazarillo*: Título, capitulación y epigrafes de un texto apócrifo'. In *Problemas del Lazarillo*. Madrid: (Cátedra, 1988), pp. 113–51.

Rozzo, Ugo. *Linee per una storia dell'editoria religiosa in Italia (1465–1600)*. Udine: Arti Grafiche Friulane, 1993.

Rozzo, Ugo. *Biblioteche italiane del Cinquecento tra Riforma e Controriforma.* Udine: Arti Grafiche Friulane, 1994.

Schmitt, Charles B. *Aristotle and the Renaissance.* Cambridge, Mass.: Published for Oberlin College by Harvard University Press, 1983.

Scribner, R. W. *For the Sake of Simple Folk: Popular Propaganda for the German Reformation.* Cambridge and New York: Cambridge University Press, 1981.

Seidel Menchi, Silvana. *Erasmo in Italia, 1520–1580.* Turin: Bollati Boringhieri, 1987.

Sherman, William H. *John Dee: The Politics of Reading and Writing in the English Renaissance.* Amherst: University of Massachusetts Press, 1995.

Soman, Alfred. 'Press, pulpit and censorship in France before Richelieu'. *Proceedings of the American Philosophical Society,* 120/6 (1976): 439–63.

Stampa, libri e letture a Milano nell'età di Carlo Borromeo. Edited by Nicola Raponi and Angelo Turchini. Milan: Vita e Pensiero, 1992.

Strauss, Gerald. *Luther's House of Learning: Indoctrination of the Young in the German Reformation.* Baltimore: Johns Hopkins University Press, 1978.

Trovato, Paolo. *Con ogni diligenza corretto: La stampa e le revisioni editoriali dei testi letterari italiani (1470–1570).* Bologna: Il Mulino, 1991.

Veit, Patrice. 'Piété, chant et lecture: Les pratiques religieuses dans l'Allemagne protestante à l'époque moderne'. *Revue d'histoire moderne et contemporaine,* 37/4 (1990): 624–41.

Zedelmaier, Helmut. *Bibliotheca Universalis und Bibliotheca Selecta: Das Problem der Ordnung des gelehrten Wissens in der frühen Neuzeit.* Cologne, Weimar and Vienna: Böhlau, 1992.

5. From the Classical Age to the Enlightenment

Abramovici, Jean-Christophe. *Le Livre interdit: De Théophile de Viau à Sade.* Paris: Payot et Rivages, 1996.

Achinstein, Sharon. *Milton and the Revolutionary Reader.* Princeton, NJ: Princeton University Press, 1994.

Alvarez Barrientos, Joaquín, François Lopez and Inmaculada Urzainqui. *La República de las Letras en la España del siglo XVIII.* Madrid: Consejo Superior de Investigaciones Cientificas, 1995.

Ankarcrona, Anita. *Bud på böcker: Bokauktioner i Stockholm, 1782–1801.* Stockholm: Stockholm University, 1989.

Appel, Charlotte. 'Læsning og læsefærdighet i 1600-tallets Danmark: Problemer og perspektiver for et nyt forskningsfelt'. *Nordisk Tidskrift fö Bochoch biblioteksväsen,* 79 (1992).

Barber, Sigmund J. *'Amadis de Gaule' and the German Enlightenment.* Berne and New York: Peter Lang, 1984.

Barbu, Daniel. 'Loisir et pouvoir: Le temps de la lecture dans les pays roumains au XVIIIᵉ siècle'. *Revue des études sud-est européennes: Mentalités-civilisations,* 28/1–4 (1990): 17–27.

Beckmann, Friedhelm. *Französische Privatbibliotheken: Untersuchungen zu Literatursystematik und Buchbesitz im 18. Jahrhundert.* Frankfurt: Buchhändler-Vereinigung GmbH, 1988.

Benedict, Barbara M. *Making the Modern Reader: Cultural Mediation in Early Modern Literary Anthologies.* Princeton, NJ: Princeton University Press, 1996.

Bennett, H. S. *English Books and Readers, 1603 to 1640*. Cambridge: Cambridge University Press, 1970.

Berger, Günter. *Der komisch-satirische Roman und seine Leser: Poetik, Funktion und Rezeption einer niederen Gattung im Frankreich des 17. Jahrhunderts*. Heidelberg: Carl Winter, 1984.

Berger, Günter. 'Littérature et lecteurs à Grenoble aux XVIIe et XVIIIe siècles: le public littéraire dans une capitale provinciale'. *Revue d'histoire moderne et contemporaine*, 23/1 (1986): 114–32.

Berthold, Christian. *Fiktion und Vieldeutigkeit: Zur Erstehung moderner Kulturtechniken des Lesens im 18. Jahrhundert*. Tübingen: Niemeyer, 1993.

Bibliotheken und Aufklärung. Edited by Werner Arnold and Peter Vodosek. Wolfenbütteler Schriften zur Geschichte des Buchwesens, 14. Wiesbaden: In Kommission bei Otto Harrassowitz, 1988.

Les Bibliothèques au XVIIIe siècle. Edited by Louis Trénard. Bordeaux: Société des Bibliophiles de Guyenne, 1989.

Björkman, Margareta. *Läsarnas nöje: Kommersiella Lånbibliotek i Stockholm, 1783–1809*. Uppsala: Uppsala University, 1992.

Bolufer Peruga, Mónica. 'Espectadores y lectoras: Representaciones y influencia del público femenino en la prensa del siglo XVIII'. *Cuadernos de Estudio del Siglo*, 18/5 (1997).

De Bonne Main: La communication manuscrite au XVIIIe siècle. Edited by François Moureau. Paris: Universitas and Oxford: Voltaire Foundation, 1993.

Books and their Readers in Eighteenth-Century England. Edited by Isabel Rivers. Leicester: Leicester University Press and New York: St Martin's Press, 1982.

Bracht, Edgar. *Der Leser im Roman des 18. Jahrhunderts*. Frankfurt and New York: Peter Lang, 1987.

Braida, Lodovica. *Le guide del tempo: Produzione, contenuti e forme degli almanacchi piemontesi nel Settecento*. Turin: Deputazione Subalpina di Storia Patria, 1989.

Braida, Lodovica. *Il commercio delle idee: Editoria e circolazione del libro nella Torino del Settecento*. Florence: Olschki, 1995.

Brewer, John. *The Pleasures of the Imagination: English Culture in the Eighteenth Century*. London: HarperCollins and New York: Farrar Straus Giroux, 1997.

Brouwer, Han. 'Rondom het boek: Historisch onderzoek naar leescultur, in het bijzonder in de achttiende eeuw: Een overzicht van boronnen en benaderingen: Resultaten en problemen'. *Documentatie-Blad Werkgroep Achttiende Eeuw*, 20/1 (1988): 51–120.

Brouwer, Han. 'Lezen in de provincie: Zwolle in de late achttiende en negentiende eeuw'. In *De productie, distributie en consumptie van cultuur*, edited by J. J. Kloek and W. W. Mijnhardt (Amsterdam, 1991), pp. 127–34.

Bücherkataloge als buchgeschichte Quellen in der frühren Neuzeit. Edited by Reinhard Wittmann. Wiesbaden: In Kommission bei Otto Harrassowitz, 1984.

Buch und Buchhandel in Europa im achtzehnten Jarhundert / The Book and the Book Trade in Eighteenth-Century Europe. Fünftes Wolfenbütteler Symposium (1–3 November 1997). Edited by Giles Barber and Bernhard Fabian. Hamburg: Dr. Hauswedell and Co., 1981.

Buch und Leser. Vorträge d. 1. Jahrestreffens d. Wolfenbütteler Arbeitskreises für Geschichte d. Buchwesens, 13. u. Mai 1976. Edited by Herbert G. Göpfert. Hamburg: Hauswedell, 1977.

Buch und Sammler: Private und öffentliche Bibliotheken im 18. Jahrhundert. Colloquium der Arbeisstelle 18. Jahrhundert Gesamthochschule Wuppertal, Universität Münster, Düsseldorf vom 26.–28. September 1977. Heidelberg: Carl Winter Universitätsverlag, 1979.

Capp, Bernard. *English Almanacs 1500–1800: Astrology and the Popular Press.* Ithaca, NY: Cornell University Press, 1979.

Carlsson, Akrne. *Böcker i bohuslänska bouppteckingar, 1752–1808.* Göteborg: Göteborg University, 1972.

Cátala Sanz, Jorge Antonio and Juan José Boigues Palomares. 'Bibliotecas nobiliarias: Una primera aproximación a las lecturas de la nobleza valenciana del siglo XVIII'. *Estudis,* 14 (1989): 103–44.

Cerda Díaz, J. *Libros y lectura en la Lorca del siglo XVII.* Murcia: Caja de Murcia, 1986.

Chartier, Roger. *Lectures et lecteurs dans la France d'ancien régime.* Paris: Seuil, 1987.

Chartier, Roger. 'Loisir et sociabilité: Lire à haute voix dans l'Europe moderne'. *Littérature classique,* 12: *La Voix et le texte,* pp. 127–47. Translated into English by Carol Mossman as 'Leisure and Sociability: Reading Aloud in Early Modern Europe'. In *Urban Life in the Renaissance,* edited by Susan Zimmerman and Ronald F. E. Weissman (Newark: University of Delaware Press and London and Toronto: Associated University Press, 1989), pp. 103–20.

Châtelain, Jean-Marc. 'Lire pour croire: Mises en texte de l'emblème et art de méditer au XVIIe siècle'. *Bibliothèque de l'École des Chartes,* 150 (1992): 321–51.

Clerici, Luca. *Il romanzo italiano del Settecento: Il caso Chiari.* Venice: Marsilio, 1997.

La Communication par l'imprimé au XVIIIe siècle/Communication through the Printed Word in the Eighteenth Century. Edited by Jeroom Vercruysse. Archives et Bibliothèques de Belgique/Archief – en Bibliotheekwezen in België, 54/1–4 (1983).

Couton, Georges. *Écritures codées: essais sur l'allégorie au XVIIe siècle.* Paris: Aux Amateurs de Livres, distribution Klincksieck, 1990.

Curto, Diogo Ramada. *O discurso político em Portugal (1600–1650).* Lisbon: Centro de Estudos de História e Cultura Portuguesa, Projecto Universidade Aberta, 1988.

Dall'erudizione alla politica: Giornali, giornalisti ed editori a Roma tra XVII e XX secolo. Edited by Marina Caffiero and Giuseppe Monsagrati. Milan: Franco Angeli, 1997.

Damien, Robert. *Bibliothèque et État: Naissance d'une raison politique dans la France du XVIIe siècle.* Paris: Presses Universitaires de France, 1995.

Darnton, Robert. *The Business of the Enlightenment: A Publishing History of the 'Encyclopédie', 1775–1800.* Cambridge, Mass., and London: The Belknap Press of Harvard University Press, 1979.

Darnton, Robert. 'Readers respond to Rousseau: the fabrication of romantic sensitivity'. In *The Great Cat Massacre and Other Episodes in French Cultural History* (New York: Basic Books, 1984), pp. 214–56.

Darnton, Robert. *Édition et sédition: L'univers de la littérature clandestine au XVIIIe siècle.* Paris: Gallimard, 1991.

Darnton, Robert. *Gens de lettres, gens du livre.* Paris: Jacob, 1992.

Darnton, Robert. *The Forbidden Best-Sellers of Pre-Revolutionary France*. New York and London: W. W. Norton, 1995.

Davidson, Cathy N. *Revolution and the Word: The Rise of the Novel in America*. Oxford and New York: Oxford University Press, 1986.

DeMaria, Robert, jr. *Samuel Johnson and the Life of Reading*. Baltimore and London: Johns Hopkins University Press, 1997.

Dibon, Paul. *Regards sur la Hollande du Siècle d'Or*. Naples: Vivarium, 1990.

La Diffusion et la lecture des journaux de langue française sous l'ancien régime/Circulation and Reception of Periodicals in the French Language during the Seventeenth and Eighteenth Century. Proceedings of the International Congress, Nijmegen, 3–5 June 1987. Amsterdam and Maarsen: APA-Holland University Press, 1988.

Drévillon, Hervé. *Lire et écrire l'avenir: L'astrologie dans la France du Grand Siècle (1610–1715)*. Seyssel: Champ Vallon, 1996.

Droixhe, Daniel. *Le Marché de la lecture dans la Gazette de Liège à l'époque de Voltaire: Philosophie et culture commune*. Liège: Vaillant-Carmanne, 1995.

Ducreux, Marie-Elisabeth. 'Livres d'hommes et de femmes, livres pour les hommes et pour les femmes: Réflexions sur la littérature de dévotion en Bohême au XVIIIᵉ siècle'. In *Husitství, Reformace, Renasance: Sborník k 60. narozeninám Frantiska Smahela*, edited by Jaroslav Pánek, Miloslav Políkva and Noemi Rejchrtová (3 vols, Prague: Historicky ústav, 1994), 3: 915–45.

Dutu, Alexandru. *Les Livres de sagesse dans la culture roumaine: Introduction à l'histoire des mentalités sud-est européennes*. Bucharest: AIESEE, 1971.

Dutu, Alexandru. *Humanisme, Baroque, Lumières: L'exemple roumain*. Bucharest: Editura Stiintifica si Enciclopedica, 1984.

Dutu, Alexandru. *Dimensiunea umana a istoriei: directii istoria mentalitatitor*. Bucharest: Meridiane, 1986.

L'Editoria del'700 e i Remondini. Edited by Mario Infelise and Paola Marini. Bassano del Grappa: Ghedina e Tassotti, 1992.

'Editoria e commercio librario nelle capitali italiane d'ancien régime'. Edited by Maria Iolanda Palazzolo. *Roma moderna e contemporanea: Rivista interdisciplinare di storia*, 2/2 (1994).

Eisenstein, Elizabeth L. *Grub Street Abroad: Aspects of the French Cosmopolitan Press from the Age of Louis XIV to the French Revolution*. Oxford and New York: Clarendon Press, 1992.

Engelsing, Rolf. 'Die Perioden der Lesergeschichte in der Neuzeit: Das statistische Ausmass und die soziokulturelle Bedeutung der Lektüre'. *Archiv für Geschichte des Buchwesens*, 10 (1970): 944–1002.

Engelsing, Rolf. *Der Bürger als Leser: Lesergeschichte in Deutschland, 1500–1800*. Stuttgart: Metzler, 1974.

L'Épreuve du lecteur: Livres et lectures dans le roman d'ancien régime. Actes du VIIIᵉ Colloque de la Société d'Analyse de la Topique Romanesque (Louvain-Anvers, 19–21 mai 1994). Edited by Jan Herman and Paul Pelckmans. Louvain and Paris: Peeters, 1996.

Feather, John. *The Provincial Book Trade in Eighteenth-Century England*. Cambridge and New York: Cambridge University Press, 1985.

François, Étienne. 'Livre, confession et société en Allemagne au XVIIIᵉ siècle'. *Revue d'histoire moderne et contemporaine*, 29/3 (1982): 353–75.

Frieiro, Eduardo. *O diabo na livraria do Cônego*. Belo Horizonte: Itatiaia Limitida and São Paulo: Editora da Universidade de São Paulo, 1981.

Furet, François and Jacques Ozouf. *Lire et écrire: L'alphabétisation des Français de Calvin à Jules Ferry*. 2 vols. Paris: Minuit, 1977. Vol. 1 translated into English as *Reading and Writing: Literacy in France from Calvin to Jules Ferry*. Cambridge and New York: Cambridge University Press, 1982.

Les Gazettes européennes de langue française (XVIIe–XVIIIe siècle). Table ronde internationale, Saint-Étienne, 21–23 mai 1992. Edited by Henri Duranton, Claude Labrosse and Pierre Rétat. Saint-Étienne: Publications de l'Université de Saint-Étienne, 1992.

Goodman, Dena. *The Republic of Letters: A Cultural History of the French Enlightenment*. Ithaca, NY, and London: Cornell University Press, 1994.

Göpfert, Herbert G. *Vom Autor zum Leser: Beiträge zur Geschichte des Buchwesens*. Munich: Hanser, 1977.

Gough, Hugh. *The Newspaper Press in the French Revolution*. London: Routledge & Kegan Paul and Chicago: Dorsey Press, 1988.

Goulemot, Jean-Marie. *Ces Livres qu'on le lit que d'une main: Lecture et lecteurs de livres pornographiques au XVIIIe siècle*. Aix-en-Provence: Alinéa, 1991; Paris: Minerve, 1994. Translated into English by James Simpson as *Forbidden Texts: Erotic Literature and its Readers in Eighteenth-Century France*. Philadelphia: University of Pennsylvania Press, 1994.

Guedes, Fernando. *O livro e a leitura em Portugal: Subsídios para a sua história: séculos XVIII–XIX*. Lisbon and São Paulo: Verbo, 1987.

Guttormsson, Loftur. 'Island: Læsefærdighed og folkedannelse, 1540–1800'. In *Nordisk kulturhistoria: Läskunnighet och folkbildning före folskoleväsendet* (3 vols, Jyväskylä: Yliopista, 1981).

Hall, David D. 'Introduction: the uses of literacy in New England, 1600–1850'. In *Printing and Society in Early America*, edited by William L. Joyce, David D. Hall, Richard D. Brown and John B. Hench (Worcester, Mass.: American Antiquarian Society, 1983), pp. 1–47.

Hall, David D. *Worlds of Wonder, Days of Judgment, Popular Religious Belief in Early New England*. New York: Knopf, 1989; Cambridge, Mass., and London: Harvard University Press, 1990.

Hall, David D. *Cultures of Print: Essays in the History of the Book*. Amherst: University of Massachusetts Press, 1996.

Hansen, João Adolfo. *A sátira eo engenho: Gregório de Matos e a Bahia do século XVII*. São Paulo: Companhia das Letras, 1989.

Hébrard, Jean. 'La scolarisation des savoirs élémentaires à l'époque moderne'. *Histoire de l'éducation*, 38 (1988): 1–58.

Hesselmann, Peter. *Simplizissimus Redivivus: Eine kommentierte Dokumentation der Rezeptionsgeschichte Grimmelshausens im 17. und 18. Jahrhundert, 1667–1800*. Frankfurt: Klostermann, 1992.

Houston, R. A. *Scottish Literacy and the Scottish Identity: Illiteracy and Society in Scotland and Northern England 1600–1800*. Cambridge and New York: Cambridge University Press, 1985.

Infelise, Mario. *L'Editoria veneziana nel'700*. Milan: Franco Angeli, 1997.

The Invention of Pornography: Obscenity and the Origins of Modernity, 1500–1800. Edited by Lynn Hunt. New York: Zone Books; distribution Cambridge, Mass., by MIT Press, 1993.

Jarrick, Arne. *Mot det moderna förnuftet: Johan Hjerpe och andra småborgare i upplysningstidens Stockholm*. Stockholm: Tiden, 1992.

Jouffroy-Gauja, Françoise and Jean Haechler. 'Une lecture de l'Encyclopédie: Trente-cinq ans d'annotations par un souscripteur anonyme'. *Revue française d'histoire du livre*, 96–7 (1997): 329–76.

Kalender? Ey, wie viel Kalender! Literarische Almanache zwischen Rokoko und Klassizismus. Edited by York-Gotthart Mix. Wolfenbüttel: Herzog August Bibliothek, 1986.

Kloek, J. J. and W. W. Mijnhardt. 'The eighteenth-century revolution in reading: a myth?'. In *Transactions of the Seventh International Congress of the Enlightenment* (Oxford: Voltaire Foundation, 1989), 2:645–51.

Labrosse, Claude. *Lire au XVIIIe siècle: La Nouvelle Héloïse et ses lecteurs.* Lyons: Presses Universitaires de Lyon, 1985.

Leal, Idelfonso. *Libros y bibliotecas en Venezuela colonial (1633–1767).* 2 vols. Caracas: Academia Nacional de la Historia, 1978.

'Lectura, Inquisición y Sociedad en el Antiguo Régimen'. *Historia Social*, 14 (1992): 85–119.

'Lecture et réécriture'. Special issue of *Cahiers de littérature du XVIIe siècle*, 10 (1988). Edited by Alain Viala.

Lectures de Raynal: L'histoire des deux Indes en Europe et en Amérique au XVIIIe siècle. Actes du Colloque de Wolfenbüttel. Edited by Hans-Jürgen Lüsebrink and Manfred Tietz. Oxford: Voltaire Foundation, 1991.

Lefèvre, Martine. 'Bibliothèques et lecteurs à la Bastille au XVIIIe siècle'. *Bulletin du bibliophile*, 2 (1994): 33–368.

Lesegesellschaften und bürgerliche Emanzipation: Ein europäischer Vergleich. Edited by Otto Dann. Munich: Beck, 1981.

'Lesekulturen im 18. Jahrhundert'. Special issue of *Aufklärung*, 6/1 (1992). Edited by Hans Erich Bödeker.

Leselust: Niederländische Malerei von Rembrandt bis Vermeer. Edited by Sabine Schulze. Stuttgart: Verlag Gerd Hatje, 1993.

Lesen und Schreiben im 17. und 18. Jahrhunderts: Studien zu ihrer Bewertung in Deutschland, England, Frankreich. Edited by Paul Goetsch. Tübingen: Gunter Narr Verlag, 1994.

Leser und Lesen im 18. Jahrhundert. Colloquium der Arbeitsstelle Achtzehntes Jahrhundert Gesamthochschule Wuppertal (24–6 Oktober 1975). Heidelberg: Carl Winter Universitätsverlag, 1977.

Lesewut, Raudbruck und Bücherluxus: Das Buch in der Goethe-Zeit. Düsseldorf: Goethes-Museums Düsseldorf, Anthona und Katharrina Kippenberg Stiftung, 1997.

Lext, Gösta. *Bok och samhälle i Göteborg, 1720–1809.* Göteborg: Elanders, 1950.

Libro, editoria, cultura nel Settecento italiano. Rome: Materiali della Società italiana di studi sul secolo XVIII, 1988.

'Libros, libreros y lectores'. *Revista de Historia Moderna: Anales de la Universidad de Alicante*, 4 (1984).

Lisboa, João Luis. *Ciência e Política: Ler nos finais do Antigo Regime.* Lisbon: Instituto Nacional de Investigação Científica, 1991.

Le Livre religieux et ses pratiques: Études sur l'histoire du livre religieux en Allemagne et en France à l'époque moderne/Der Umgang mit dem religiösen Buch: Studien zur Geschichte des religiösen Buches in Deutschland und Frankreich in der frühen Neuzeit. Edited by Hans Erich Bödeker, Gérald Chaix and Patrice Veit. Göttingen: Vandenhoech and Ruprecht, 1991.

Loueiro, Olímpia Maria da Cunha. *O livro e a leitura no Porto no Século XVIII.* Porto: Colecção Centro de Estudos D. Domingos de Pinho Brandão, 1994.

Love, Harold. *Scribal Publication in Seventeenth-Century England.* Oxford: Clarendon Press and New York: Oxford University Press, 1993.

MacCarthy, John A. 'Lektüre und Lesertypologie im 18. Jahrhundert (1730–1770): Ein Beitrag zur Lesergeschichte am Beispiel Wolfenbüttels'. *Internationales Archiv für Sozialgeschichte der deutschen Literatur*, 8 (1983): 35–82.

McKitterick, David. 'Customer, reader, and bookbinder: buying a Bible in 1630'. *Book Collector*, 40/3 (1991): 382–406.

Le Magasin de l'univers: The Dutch Republic as the Centre of the European Book Trade. Papers presented at the International Colloquium held at Wassenaar, 5–7 July 1990. Edited by C. Berkvens-Stevelinck, H. Bots, P. G. Hoftijzer and O. S. Lankhorst. Leiden: Brill, 1992.

Marchesini, Daniele. *Il bisogno di scrivere: Usi della scrittura nell'Italia moderna*. Rome and Bari: Laterza, 1992.

Markussen, Ingrid and Vagn Skovgaard-Petersen. 'Læsefæredighed og læsebehov i Danmark ca. 1550 til 1850'. In *Nordisk kulturhistoria: Läskunnighet och folkbildning före folskoleväsendet* (3 vols, Jyväskyl: Yliopista, 1981).

Martin, Henri-Jean. *Livre, pouvoirs et société à Paris au XVIIe siècle (1598–1701)*. Geneva: Droz, 1969.

Martin, Henri-Jean. *Le Livre français sous l'ancien régime*. Paris: Promodis-Cercle de la Librairie, 1987.

Martin, Henri-Jean and Anne-Marie Lecocq. *Livres et lecteurs à Grenoble: Les registres du libraire Nicolas (1645–1668)*. 2 vols. Geneva and Paris: Droz, 1977.

Maza, Sarah. *Private Lives and Public Affairs: The Causes Célèbres of Prerevolutionary France*. Berkeley: University of California Press, 1993.

Milliot, Vincent. *Les 'Cris de Paris', ou, Le peuple travesti: Les représentations des petits métiers parisiens (XVIe–XVIIIe siècles)*. Paris: Publications de la Sorbonne, 1995.

Milliot, Vincent. *Paris en bleu: Images de la ville dans la littérature de colportage (XVIe–XVIIIe siècles)*. Paris: Parigramme, 1996.

Negroni, Barbara de. *Lectures interdites: Le travail des censeurs au XVIIIe siècle, 1725–1774*. Paris: Albin Michel, 1995.

Neveu, Bruno. *Érudition et religion aux XVIIe et XVIIIe siècles*. Paris: Albin Michel, 1994.

Öffentliche und private Bibliotheken im 17. und 18. Jahrhundert: Raritätenkammern, Forschinginstrumente oder Bildungsstätten? Edited by Paul Raabe. Bremen and Wolfenbüttel: Jacobi, 1977.

Papacostea-Danielopolu, Cornelia and Lidia Demény. *Carte si tipar in Societatea Româneasca si Sud-Est Europeana (Secolele XVII–XIX)*. Bucharest: Eminescu, 1985.

Pasta, Renato. *Editoria e cultura nel Settecento*. Florence: Olschki, 1997.

Pleijel, Hilding. *Våra äldsta folkböker*. Lund: Gleerup, 1967.

Popkin, Jeremy. *Revolutionary News: The Press in France, 1769–1792*. Durham, NC, and London: Duke University Press, 1990.

Produzione e circolazione libraria a Bologna nel Settecento: avvio di un'indagine. Atti del V Colloquio, Bologna, 22–3 Febbraio 1985. Bologna: Istituto per la Storia di Bologna, 1987.

Prüsener, Marlies. 'Lesegesellschaften im achtzehnten Jahrhundert: Ein Beitrag zur Lesergeschichte'. *Archiv für Geschichte des Buchwesens*, 13 (1973): 370–594.

Publishing and Readership in Revolutionary France and America. A Symposium at the Library of Congress sponsored by the Center for the Book and the

European Division. Edited by Carol Armbruster. Westport, Conn.: Greenwood Press, 1993.

Raabe, Mechtild. *Leser und Lektüre im 18. Jahrhundert: Die Ausleihbücher der Herzog August Bibliothek Wolfenbüttel 1714–1799.* 4 vols. Munich, London, New York and Paris: K. G. Saur, 1989.

Raabe, Paul. *Bücherlust und Lesefreuden: Beiträge zur Geschichte des Buchwesens im 18. und frühen 19. Jahrhundert.* Stuttgart: Metzler, 1984.

Raven, James. *Judging New Wealth: Popular Publishing and Responses to Commerce in England, 1750–1800.* Oxford: Clarendon Press and New York: Oxford University Press, 1992.

Revolution in Print: The Press in France, 1775–1800. Edited by Robert Darnton and Daniel Roche. Berkeley: University of California Press, in collaboration with the New York Public Library, 1989.

Roche, Daniel. *Le Peuple de Paris: Essai sur la culture populaire au XVIIIe siècle.* Paris: Aubier-Montaigne, 1981. Translated into English by Marie Evans and Gwynne Lewis as *The People of Paris: An Essay in Popular Culture in the Eighteenth Century.* Berkeley: University of California Press, 1987.

Roche, Daniel. *Les Républicains des lettres: Gens de culture et lumières au XVIIIe siècle.* Paris: Fayard, 1988.

'Round table/Table ronde/Runder Tisch: Manners of reading/Manières de lire/Formen des Lesens'. In *Transactions of the Ninth International Congress on the Enlightenment* (Oxford: Voltaire Foundation, 1996), 2: 731–59.

Saisselin, Rémy G. 'After the battle: imaginary in the eighteenth century'. *Studies on Voltaire and the Eighteenth Century,* 311 (1993): 115–41.

Salman, Jeroen and Garrelt Verhoeven. 'The Comptoir-Almanacs of Gillis Joosten Saeghman'. *Quaerendo,* 23/2 (1993): 93–114.

Sandin, Bengt. *Hemmet, gatan, fabriken eller skolan: Folkundervisning och beruppfostran i svendka städer, 1600–1850.* Lund: Arkiv, 1986.

Sauvy-Wilkinson, Anne. 'Lecteurs du XVIIIe siècle: Les abonnés de la *Bibliothèque universelle des romans*: première approche'. *Australian Journal of French Studies,* 22/1 (1986): 48–60.

Schlup, Michel. 'Sociétés de lecture et cabinets littéraires dans la principauté de Neuchâtel (1750–1800): De nouvelles pratiques de lecture'. *Musée neuchâtelois,* 24 (1987): 81–144.

Schlup, Michel. 'La lecture et ses pratiques dans la principauté de Neuchâtel au XVIIIe siècle à travers quelques écrits personnels'. *Musée neuchâtelois,* 4 (1996): 263–72.

Schön, Erich. *Der Verlust der Sinnlichkeit oder die Verwandlungen des Lesers: Mentalitätswandel um 1800.* Stuttgart: Klett-Cotta, 1987.

Siegert, Reinhart. *Aufklärung und Volkslektüre exemplarisch dargestellt an Rudolph Zacharias Becker und seinem 'Noth- und Hülfsbüchlein'.* Frankfurt: Vereinigung, 1978.

Smout, T. C. 'Born again at Cambusling: new evidence on popular religion and literacy in eighteenth-century Scotland'. *Past and Present,* 97 (1982): 114–27.

Sociétés et cabinets de lecture entre Lumières et Romantisme. Actes du colloque organisé à Genève par la Société de Lecture le 20 novembre 1993. Geneva: Société de Lecture, 1995.

Spufford, Margaret. 'First steps in literacy: the reading and writing experience of the humblest seventeenth-century spiritual autobiographers'. *Social History,* 4 (1979): 407–35.

Spufford, Margaret. *Small Books and Pleasant Histories: Popular Fiction and its Readership in Seventeenth-Century England*. London and Athens, Ga.: Methuen, 1981.

Tóth, István György. *Mivelhogy magad írást nem tudsz.... Az írás térhódítása a müvelödésben a kora újkori Magyarországon*. Budapest: MTA Történettudományi Intézete, 1996.

Trouille, Mary Seidman. *Sexual Politics in the Enlightenment: Women Writers Read Rousseau*. Albany: State University of New York Press, 1997.

Unseld, Siegfried. *Goethe und seine Verlegen*. Frankfurt am Main and Leipzig: Insel, 1991, 1993. Translated into English by Kenneth J. Northcott as *Goethe and his Publishers*. Chicago: University of Chicago Press, 1996.

Les Usages de l'imprimé (XVe–XIXe siècle). Edited by Roger Chartier. Paris: Fayard, 1987. Translated into English by Lydia G. Cochrane as *The Culture of Print: Power and the Uses of Print in Early Modern Europe*. Cambridge: Polity Press, 1989.

'Les usages du manuscrit'. *XVIIe siècle*, 192/3 (1996).

Van Selm, Bert. ' "Almanacken, lietjes, en somwijl wat wonder, wat nieus": Volkslectuur in de Noordelijke Nederlanden (1480–1800): Een onbekende grootheid'. *Leidschrift*, 5/3 (1988–9): 33–68.

Van Selm, Bert. *Inzichten en vergezichten: Zes beschouwingen over het onderzoek naar de geschiedenis van de Nederlandse boekhandel*. Amsterdam: De Buitenkant, 1992.

Velculescu, Catalina. *Carti populare si cultura românesca*. Bucharest: Minerva, 1984.

Velculescu, Catalina. *Intre scriere si oralitate*. Bucharest: Minerva, 1988.

Villalta, Luiz-Carlos. 'Os clérigos e os livros nas Minas Gerais da segunda metade do século XVIII'. *Acervo*, 8/1–2 (1995): 96–106.

'La voix au XVIIe siècle'. Edited by Patrick Dandrey. *Littératures classiques*, 23 (1990).

Ward, Albert. *Book Production, Fiction, and the German Reading Public, 1740–1800*. Oxford: Clarendon Press, 1974.

Warner, Michael. *The Letters of the Republic: Publication and the Public Sphere in Eighteenth-Century America*. Cambridge, Mass., and London: Harvard University Press, 1990.

Watt, Ian. *The Rise of the Novel: Studies in Defoe, Richardson and Fielding* (1957). New edn, Berkeley: University of California Press, 1967.

Watt, Tessa. *Cheap Print and Popular Piety, 1550–1640*. Cambridge and New York: Cambridge University Press, 1991.

Weil, Françoise. *L'Interdiction du roman et de la librairie, 1728–1750*. Paris: Aux Amateurs de Livres, 1986.

Weruaga Prieto, Angel. *Libros y lectura en Salamanca: Del Barroco a la Ilustración (1650–1725)*. Salamanca: Junta de Castilla y León de Cultura y Turismo, 1993.

The Widening Circle: Essays on the Circulation of Literature in the Eighteenth Century. Edited by Paul J. Korshin. Philadelphia: University of Pennsylvania Press, 1976.

Willke, Ingeborg. *ABC-Bücher in Schweden: Ihre Entwicklung bis Ende des 19. Jahrhunderts und ihre Beziehungen zu Deutschland*. Stockholm: Svenska Bokföflaget Bonniers, 1965.

Wittmann, Reinhard. *Buchmarkt und Lektüre im 18. und 19. Jahrhundert: Beiträge zum literarischen Leben 1750–1880*. Tübingen: Niemeyer, 1982.

Wolf, Edwin II. *The Book Culture of a Colonial American City: Philadelphia Books, Bookmen, and Booksellers*. Oxford: Clarendon Press and New York: Oxford University Press, 1988.

Woodmansee, Martha. *The Author, Art, and the Market: Rereading the History of Aesthetics*. New York: Columbia University Press, 1994.

Wu, Duncan. *Wordworth's Reading, 1770–1799*. Cambridge and New York: Cambridge University Press, 1993.

Yerushalmi, Yosef Hayim. *From Spanish Court to Italian Ghetto: Isaac Cardoso: A Study in Seventeenth-Century Marranism and Jewish Apologetics*. New York: Columbia University Press, 1971; Seattle: University of Washington Press, 1981.

Zardin, Danilo. *Donna e religiosa di rara eccellenza: Prospera Corona Bascapè: I libri e la cultura nei monasteri milanesi del Cinque et Seicento*. Florence: Olschki, 1992.

Zur Geschichte von Buch und Leser im Frankreich des Ancien Régime: Beiträge zu einer empirischen Rezeptionsforschung. Edited by Günter Berger. Rheinfelden: Schäuble, 1986.

6. The Nineteenth Century

Allen, James Smith. *Popular French Romanticism: Authors, Readers, and Books in the Nineteenth Century*. Syracuse, NY: Syracuse University Press, 1981.

Allen, James Smith. *In the Public Eye: A History of Reading in Modern France, 1800–1940*. Princeton, NJ: Princeton University Press, 1991.

Altick, Richard D. *The English Common Reader: A Social History of the Mass Reading Public, 1800–1900*. Chicago: University of Chicago Press, 1957.

Bachmann, Martin. *Politik und Bildung: Die schweizerischen Lesegesellschaften des 19. Jahrhunderts unter besonderer Berücksichtigung des Kanton Zürich*. Frankfurt and Berne: Peter Lang, 1993.

Barbier, Frédéric. *L'Empire du livre: Le livre imprimé et la construction de l'Allemagne contemporaine (1815–1914)*. Paris: Cerf, 1995.

Bartine, David. *Reading, Criticism, and Culture: Theory and Teaching in the United States and England, 1820–1950*. Columbia: University of South Carolina Press, 1992.

Bednarska-Ruszajowa, Krystyna. *Bücher und ihre Leser in Wilna am Anfang des 19. Jahrhunderts*. Frankfurt and Berlin: Peter Lang, 1996.

Berengo, Marino. *Intellettuali e librai nella Milano della Restaurazione*. Turin: Einaudi, 1980.

Bertaux, Jean-Jacques. 'Lecture et musique en milieu populaire rural au XIXe siècle: Un example ornais'. *Recueil d'études offert en hommage au doyen Michel de Boüard*. Special issue of *Annales de Normandie*, 1 (1982): 37–58.

Bloch, R. Howard. *God's Plagiarist: Being an Account of the Fabulous Industry and Irregular Commerce of the Abbé Migne*. Chicago and London: University of Chicago Press, 1994.

The Book in Australia: Essays towards a Cultural and Social History. Edited by D. H. Borchardt and W. Kirsop. Melbourne: Australian Reference Publications, in association with the Center for Bibliographical and Textual Studies, Monash University, 1988.

Botrel, Jean-François. *Libros, prensa y lectura en la España del siglo XIX*. Madrid: Fundación Germán Sánchez Ruipérez, 1993.

Brodhead, Richard H. *Cultures of Letters: Scenes of Reading and Writing in Nineteenth-Century America.* Chicago: University of Chicago Press, 1993.

Brooks, Jeffrey. *When Russia Learned to Read: Literacy and Popular Literature, 1861–1917.* Princeton, NJ: Princeton University Press, 1985.

Carpenter, Kenneth E. *Readers and Libraries: Toward a History of Libraries and Culture in America.* Washington, D.C.: Library of Congress, 1996.

La Correspondance: Les usages de la lettre au XIXe siècle. Edited by Roger Chartier. Paris: Fayard, 1991.

Denning, Michael. *Mechanic Accents: Dime Novels and Working-Class Culture in America.* London and New York: Verso, 1987.

Erickson, Lee. *The Economy of Literary Form: English Literature and the Industrialization of Publishing, 1800–1850.* Baltimore and London: Johns Hopkins University Press, 1996.

Ericsson, Tom and Börje Harnesk. *Präster, predikare opch profeter: Läseriet i övre Norrland, 1800–1850.* Gideå: Vildros, 1994.

Finocchi, Anna. *Lettrici: Immagini della donna che legge nella pittura dell'Ottocento.* Nuoro: Ilisso, 1992.

Flint, Kate. *The Woman Reader, 1837–1914.* Oxford: Clarendon Press and New York: Oxford University Press, 1993.

Gilmore, William J. *Reading Becomes a Necessity of Life: Material and Cultural Life in Rural New England, 1780–1835.* Knoxville: University of Tennessee Press, 1989.

Hesse, Carla. *Publishing and Cultural Politics in Revolutionary Paris, 1789–1810.* Berkeley: University of California Press, 1991.

'Histoire de l'édition en France (XIXe–XXe siècle)'. *Bulletin de la Société d'histoire moderne et contemporaine,* 3–4 (1994): 35–72.

Howsam, Leslie. *Cheap Bibles: Nineteenth-Century Publishing and the British and Foreign Bible Society.* Cambridge and New York: Cambridge University Press, 1991.

L'Imprimé au Québec: Aspects historiques (XVIIIe–XXe siècle). Edited by Yvan Lamonde. Quebec: Institut Québécois de Recherche sur la Culture, 1983.

Jacobsson, Roger. *Boklig Kultur i Umeå före 1850: Om tryckeriverksamhet och bokförmedling.* Stockholm: Carlssons, 1995.

Jones, Aled. *Powers of the Press: Newspapers, Power and the Public in Nineteenth-Century England.* Hants and Brookfield, Vt.: Scolar Press, 1996.

Klancher, Jon P. *The Making of English Reading Audiences, 1790–1832.* Madison: University of Wisconsin Press, 1987.

Kuitert, Lisa. *Het ene boek in vele delen: De uitgave van literaire series in Nederland, 1850–1900.* Amsterdam: De Buitenkant, 1993.

Laplanche, François. *La Bible en France entre mythe et critique, XVIe–XIXe siècle.* Paris: Albin Michel, 1994.

Leer y escribir en España: Doscientos años de alfabetisación. Edited by Benito Escolano. Madrid: Fundación Germán Sánchez Ruipérez, 1992.

Levine, Lawrence W. *Highbrow/Lowbrow: The Emergence of Cultural Hierarchy in America.* Cambridge, Mass.: Harvard University Press, 1988.

Littérature populaire: Peuple et littérature. Colloque de l'université de Lausanne, 9 juin 1989, Études et mémoires de la section d'histoire de l'université de Lausanne, 1989.

'Le livre d'enfance et de jeunesse en France'. Edited by Jean Glénisson and Ségolène Le Men. Special issue of *Revue française du livre,* 82–3 (1994).

Livre et lecture au Québec (1800–1850). Edited by Claude Galarneau and Maurice Lemire. Quebec: Institut Québécois de Recherche sur la Culture, 1988.

'Le livre et ses lectures'. Special issue of *Romantisme*, 47 (1985).

Lyons, Martyn. *Le Triomphe du livre: Une histoire sociologique de la lecture dans la France du XIXe siècle*. Paris: Promodis-Cercle de la Librairie, 1987.

Lyons, Martyn. 'Fires of expiation: book-burnings and Catholic missions in Restoration France'. *French History*, 10/2 (June 1996): 240–66.

Lyons, Martyn. 'What did the peasants read? Written and printed culture in rural France, 1815–1914'. *European History Quarterly*, 27/2 (1997): 163–97.

Marchesini, Daniele. ' "Qualis pater . . . .?": La trasmissione dell'alfabetismo nell'-Italia otto–novecentesca'. *Annali di storia moderna e contemporanea*, 3 (1997): 435–47.

Martínez Martín, Jesús A. *Lectura y lectores en el Madrid del siglo XIX*. Madrid: Consejo Superior de Investigaciones Científicas, 1991.

Martino, Alberto. *Die deutsche Leihbibliotheke: Geschichte einer literarischen Institution (1756–1914)*. Wiesbaden: Harrassowitz, 1990.

Matlock, Jann. *Scenes of Seduction: Prostitution Hysteria and Reading Difference in Nineteenth-Century France*. New York: Columbia University Press, 1994.

Mesure(s) du livre. Colloque organisé par la Bibliothèque nationale et la Société des études romantiques, 25–6 mai 1989. Edited by Alain Vaillant. Paris: Bibliothèque nationale, 1992.

Meyer, Marlyse. *Folhetim: Uma história*. São Paulo: Companhia das Letras, 1996.

Myllyntaus, Timo. *The Growth and Structure of Finnish Print Production, 1840–1900*. Helsinki: Helsingin Yliopiston Talous-Ja Sociaalihistorian Laitoksen Tiedonantoja/Communications Institute of Economic and Social History, University of Helsinki, 1984.

Parent-Lardeur, Françoise. *Les Cabinets de lecture: La lecture publique sous la Restauration*. Paris: Payot, 1982.

Peterson, Carla L. *The Determined Reader: Gender and Culture in the Novel from Napoleon to Victoria*. New Brunswick, NJ: Rutgers University Press, 1986.

Pozzi, Gabriela. *Discurso y lector en la novela del siglo XIX (1834–1876)*. Amsterdam and Atlanta, Ga.: Rodopi, 1990.

Raffler, Marlies. *Bürgerliche Lesekultur im Vormärz: Der Leseverein am Joanneum in Graz (1819–1871)*. Frankfurt and New York: Peter Lang, 1993.

Ragone, Giovanni. 'La letteratura e il consumo: Un profilo dei generi e dei modelli nell'editoria italiana (1845–1925)'. In *Letteratura italiana*, gen. ed. Alberto Asor Rosa, (8 vols in 13 pts, Turin: Einaudi, 1982–91), vol. 2: *Produzione e consumo* (1983), pp. 687–772.

Readers in History: Nineteenth-Century American Literature and the Contexts of Response. Edited by James L. Machor. Baltimore: Johns Hopkins University Press, 1993.

Reading Books: Essays on the Material Text and Literature in America. Edited by Michele Moylan and Lane Stiles. Amherst: University of Massachusetts Press, 1996.

Richardson, Alan. *Literature, Education, and Romanticism: Reading as Social Practice, 1780–1832*. Cambridge and New York: Cambridge University Press, 1994.

Richer, Noë. *La Lecture et ses institutions, 1700–1918*. Le Mans: Plein Chant, 1987.

Savart, Claude. *Les Catholiques en France au XIXᵉ siècle: Le témoignage du livre religieux*. Paris: Beauchesne, 1985.

Scheidt, Gabriele. *Der Kolportagebuchhandel (1869–1905)*. Stuttgart: Metzler, 1994.

Schenda, Rudolf. *Volk ohne Buch: Studien zur Sozialgeschichte des populären Lesestoffe, 1770–1910*. Frankfurt: Klostermann, 1970.

Schenda, Rudolf. *Die Lesestoffe der kleinen Leute: Studien zur populären Literatur im 19. und 20. Jahrhundert*. Munich: Beck, 1977.

Schenda, Rudolf. *Folklore e letteratura popolare: Italia-Germania-Francia*. Rome: Istituto della Enciclopedia Italiana, 1986.

Schenda, Rudolf. *Von Mund zu Ohr: Bausteine zu einer Kulturgeschichte volkstümlichen Erzählens in Europa*. Göttingen: Vandenhoeck and Ruprecht, 1993.

Solari, Gabriella. 'Littérature à un sou, à deux sous, à trois sous: Permanences et transformations de l'impression populaire en Italie à la fin du XIXᵉ siècle'. In *Culture et société dans l'Europe moderne et contemporaine*, edited by Dominique Julia, Yearbook of the Department of History and Civilization/Annuaire du Département d'Histoire et Civilisation (Florence: European University Institute, 1992), pp. 59–88.

Stewart, Garrett. *Dear Reader: The Conscripted Audience in Nineteenth-Century British Fiction*. Baltimore and London: Johns Hopkins University Press, 1996.

Stora-Lamarre, Annie. *L'Enfer de la IIIᵉ République: Censeurs et pornographes (1881–1914)*. Preface by Michelle Perrot. Paris: Imago, 1990.

Tavoni, Maria Gioia. *Libri e lettura da un secolo all'altro*. Modena: Mucchi 1987.

Thiesse, Anne-Marie. 'Mutations et permanences de la culture populaire: La lecture à la Belle Époque'. *Annales ESC*, 39 (1984): 70–91.

Thiesse, Anne-Marie. *Le Roman du quotidien: Lecteurs et lectures populaires à la Belle Époque*. Paris: Le Chemin Vert, 1984.

Vicinus, Martha. *The Industrial Muse: A Study of Nineteenth-Century British Working-Class Literature*. New York: Harper and Row and London: Croom Helm, 1974.

Vincent, David. *Literacy and Popular Culture: England, 1750–1914*. Cambridge and New York: Cambridge University Press, 1989.

Webb, R. K. *The British Working-Class Reader, 1790–1848: Literacy and Social Tension*. London: Allen & Unwin, 1955.

Zavala, Iris M. *Lecturas y lectores del discurso narrativo dieciochesco*. Amsterdam: Rodopi, 1987.

7. The Twentieth Century

Bolter, Jay David. *The Writing Space: The Computer, Hypertext, and the History of Writing*. Hillsdale. NJ: Lawrence Erlbaum Associates, 1991.

Burgos, Martine, Christophe Evans and Esteban Buch. *Sociabilités du livre et communautés de lecteurs: Trois études sur la sociabilité du livre*. Paris: Bibliothèque publique d'information, Centre Georges Pompidou, 1996.

Certeau, Michel de. *L'Invention du quotidien*, vol. 1 of *Arts de faire*, Paris: UGE, 1980; new edn, ed. L. Giard. Paris: Gallimard, 1990. Translated into

English by Steven F. Rendall as *The Practice of Everyday Life*. Berkeley: University of California Press, 1984.

Chaintreau, Anne-Marie and Renée Lemaître. *Drôles de bibliothèques ... Le thème de la bibliothèque dans la littérature et le cinéma*. Preface by Roger Chartier. Paris: Cercle de la Librairie, 1990.

Chartier, Anne-Marie and Jean Hébrard. *Discours sur la lecture (1880–1980)*. Paris: Bibliothèque publique d'information, Centre Georges Pompidou, 1989.

The Culture of Consumption: Critical Essays in American History, 1880–1980. Edited by R. W. Fox and T. J. Jackson Lears. New York: Pantheon Books, 1983.

Debray, Régis. *Manifestes médiologiques*. Paris: Gallimard, 1994.

Écritures ordinaires. Edited by Daniel Fabre. Paris: Bibliothèque publique d'information, Centre Georges Pompidou, 1993.

Establet, Roger and Georges Felouzis. *Livre ou télévision: Concurrence ou interaction?* Paris: Presses Universitaires de France, 1992.

Fabiani, Jean-Louis. *Lire en prison: Une étude sociologique*. Paris: Bibliothèque publique d'information, Centre Georges Pompidou, 1995.

I giovani e la lettura. Introduction by Sergio Zavoli. Milan: Mondadori, 1995.

Gleize, Joëlle. *Le Double Miroir: Le livre dans les livres de Stendhal à Proust*. Paris: Hachette, 1992.

Hoggart, Richard. *The Uses of Literacy: Aspects of Working-Class Life with Special Reference to Publications and Entertainments*. London: Chatto & Windus, 1957.

Kaestle, Carl F. et al. *Literacy in the United States: Readers and Reading since 1880*. New Haven, Conn.: Yale University Press, 1991.

Kuhlmann, Marie, Nelly Kuntzmann and Hélène Bellour. *Censures et bibliothèques au XXe siècle*. Paris: Cercle de la Librairie, 1989.

Landow, George P. *Hypertext 2.0*. A revised, amplified edition of *Hypertext: The Convergence of Contemporary Critical Theory and Technology* (1991). Baltimore and London: Johns Hopkins University Press, 1997.

Language Machines: Technologies of Literary and Cultural Production. Edited by Jeffrey Masten, Peter Stallybrass and Nancy Vickers. London and New York: Routledge, 1997.

La Lecture littéraire. Actes du colloque tenu à Reims du 14 au 16 juin 1984. Edited by Michel Picard. Paris: Clancier-Guénaud, 1988.

Leenhardt, Jacques and Peter Jósza. *Lire la lecture: Essai de sociologie de la lecture*. Paris: Le Sycomore, 1982.

Lire en France aujourd'hui. Edited by Martine Poulain. Paris: Cercle de la Librairie, 1993.

Literacy On Line: The Promise (and Peril) of Reading and Writing with Computers. Edited by Myron C. Tuman. Pittsburgh: University of Pittsburgh Press, 1992.

Lyons, Martyn and Lucy Taska. *Australian Readers Remember: An Oral History of Reading, 1890–1930*. Melbourne and New York: Oxford University Press, 1992.

McAleer, Joseph. *Popular Reading and Publishing in Britain, 1914–1950*. Oxford: Clarendon Press and New York: Oxford University Press, 1992.

'Metamorphoses of the book'. Edited by Renée Riese Hubert. *Substance: A Review of Theory and Literary Criticism*, 82 (1997).

Nunberg, Geoffrey. 'The place of books in the age of electronic reproduction'. *Representations*, special issue, 'Future libraries'. 42 (1993): 13–37.

Ory, Pascal. *La Belle Illusion: Culture et politique sous le signe du Front populaire, 1935–1938*. Paris: Plon, 1994.

Page to Screen: Taking Literacy into the Electronic Era. Edited by Ilana Snyder. London and New York: Routledge, 1998.

Par écrit: Ethnologie des écritures quotidiennes. Edited by Daniel Fabre. Paris: La Maison des Sciences de l'Homme, 1997.

Peroni, Michel. *De l'écrit à l'écran*. Paris: Bibliothèque publique d'information, Centre Georges Pompidou, 1991.

Petrucci, Armando. *Scrivere e no: Politiche della scrittura e analfabetismo nel mondo d'oggi*. Rome: Editori Riuniti, 1987.

Picard, Michel. *La Lecture comme jeu: Essai sur la littérature*. Paris: Minuit, 1986.

Pour une sociologie de la lecture: Lecture et lecteurs dans la France contemporaine. Edited by Martine Poulain. Paris: Cercle de la Librairie, 1988.

Radway, Janice A. *Reading the Romance: Women, Patriarchy, and Popular Literature*. Chapel Hill and London: University of North Carolina Press, 1984.

Radway, Janice A. *A Feeling for Books: The Book-of-the-Month-Club, Literary Taste, and Middle-Class Desire*. Chapel Hill and London: University of North Carolina Press, 1997.

Regards européens: La lecture d'Est en Ouest. Paris: Bibliothèque publique d'information, Centre Georges Pompidou, 1993.

Richter, Noë. *La Lecture et ses institutions, 1919–1989*. Le Mans: Plein Chant, 1989.

Santonja, Gonzalo. *La República de los libros: El nuevo libro popular de la II República*. Barcelona: Anthropos, 1989.

Schön, Erich. *Zur aktuellen Situation des Lesers*. Munich: Oldenbourg, 1996.

Scotto di Luzio, Adolfo. *L'Appropriazione imperfetta: Editori, biblioteche e libri per ragazzi durante il Fascismo*. Bologna: Il Mulino, 1996.

Shavit, David. *Hunger for the Printed Word: Books and Libraries in the Jewish Ghettoes in Nazi-Occupied Europe*. Jefferson, NC: McFarland, 1997.

Texte et ordinateur: Les mutations du lire-écrire. Edited by Jacques Anis and Jean-Louis Lebrave. La Garenne Colombes: L'Espace européen, 1991.

Index